Managerial Behavior and Organization Demands

MANAGERIAL BEHAVIOR AND ORGANIZATION DEMANDS

MANAGEMENT AS A LINKING OF LEVELS OF INTERACTION

Second Edition

Edited by Robert T. Golembiewski • Frank Gibson • Gerald Miller
University of Georgia

F. E. PEACOCK PUBLISHERS, INC.
ITASCA, ILLINOIS 60143

Library of Congress
Catalog Card No. 77-95395
ISBN, 0-87581-233-3

Contents

III. Managing by Hundreds: Middle Management and Departmental Dynamics

IV. Managing by Thousands: Developing and Maintaining an Institution

Preface

This volume appears in a second reincarnation, as it were. It had been available to readers for a number of years and then went out of print when the original publisher discontinued the series of which it was a part. And now the title reappears, revised and under the auspices of a different publisher.

In its details, this volume is very different from its predecessor. Over 50 percent of the readings are new; and the introductory notes have been expanded and brought up to date.

In its basic thrust and design, however, no essential changes have been made. And that is for a very good reason: the need we saw a decade ago still remains, and we can do no better than to repeat what we wrote then.

This volume attempts to fill what we see as a real need and seeks to fill that need in a relatively novel way. The need is to bring to students and practitioners of administration a representative slice of the several managerially relevant literatures and to do so with a vehicle permitting flexibility of use in executive development programs as well as in regular course work. Our contribution lies not in perceiving this need, for we could hardly have more company. Rather, we stress our dual emphases. The several levels of managerial interaction and the different demands these levels make upon managers breathe a sense of reality into the volume which particularly distinguishes it. After all, life in organizations is in significant senses one of experiencing levels of phenomena, of coping with them, and of tying them together into cooperative effort. Thus any manager, at a minimum, must deal with people and with groups. "Level plus linkage" has received less attention than the "functions" (like accounting) or the "processes" (like leadership) of management, however.

Our hopes may be summarized. We hope to contribute to the dissemination of managerially relevant knowledge, and we also hope to augment the attention given to a significant perspective from which management may be viewed.

Like management, this effort is ineluctably cooperative. Thus we could hardly have given form to the volume had many researchers not labored long and well. Many other workers also contributed. We note particularly the typing and clerical skills of Sandra Daniel.

Athens, Georgia
June 1, 1977

Robert T. Golembiewski
Frank K. Gibson
Gerald J. Miller

Introduction

A. Major Target Audiences
B. Organizing This Volume
C. Orienting the Reader in Introductory Ways
"The Post-Industrial Organization," William Halal
"Administration as A Field of Study," C. L. Sharma
"The Contingency Theory of Management: A Path Out of the Jungle," Fred Luthans
"Organization Theory and Political Theory," Herbert Kaufman

This volume of readings has a straightforward rationale and an uncomplicated format. The immediate purposes are: to outline this rationale; to sketch and explain the format; and to establish some significant relations between the two.

As for rationale, we live on the knife-edge of an organizational revolution in both business and government. That revolution leaves few untouched, and it leaves almost everyone uncertain of our ability to stay on top of developments. Thus only a few observers see the contemporary burgeoning of organizations as thrusting us into an age of unparalleled good and plenty. The majority has no such benign view. Many see humankind being inexorably dragged toward a thoroughgoing manipulation beyond all previous experience, and still others see society reverting to a kind of modern dark ages filled with organizations which have grown so bloated that they suffocate in the offal of their own procedures and policies. Both groups of pessimistic observers share a common view of the dilemma of man. The organizational proliferation, which was once necessary to achieve more of the good things of life, now may be more bane than boon, they tell us. If we have not already passed the point,[1] they go on, we soon enough will reach the point of diminishing returns from adding to the size and complexity of our organizations.

For good or ill, there seems no stopping the organizational world because it is safer to get off. We must ride the tiger of our organization revolution because we rightly fear what it might do to us if we ever tried to get off. Consequently, the managers of our government and business organizations are increasingly hard pressed.

---

[1] For example, see Ralph P. Hummel, *The Bureaucratic Experience* (New York: St. Martin's Press, 1977).

A. MAJOR TARGET AUDIENCES

One of the major adaptations to our need to "hold on" to the contemporary developments in organizations is the increasing attention given to managerial training, both in schools and in executive development programs. In this sense, the rationale of this volume is patent. It is a small contribution to increasing our chances that the tiger of the contemporary organizational revolution will not become our master. The format and readings of this volume thus are chosen to transmit information necessary to facilitate managerial training.

We have two basic target audiences. Participants in the typical executive development program constitute one of these target audiences. Editorial selections from the managerially relevant literatures thus were guided by the experience of our considerable involvement in a wide variety of such programs for both business and government. The selections of readings also had to suit a target audience composed of students and faculty involved in the wide variety of courses which have a managerial focus and are given in our many schools of public and business administration. Such managerially oriented enrichment is particularly necessary in Public Administration which, for a variety of reasons, has moved but sluggishly toward exploring the relevant literatures.[2] The tragedy is that government administrators have a particularly intense need for such information.

B. ORGANIZING THIS VOLUME

Given this rationale, the basic strategy underlying the format of this volume leans heavily in spirit on the biblical advice given to Moses by Jethro during the great exodus. Relying on antiquity is no sign that we wish to flee to the safety of simpler days. Directly, Jethro's advice to Moses was reasonable under the circumstances. Moreover, almost all contemporary organizations in effect follow Jethro's advice. And that advice provides useful structure for the present volume.

What was Jethro's advice? Briefly, the exodus had been going poorly indeed for the Jews, and in large part because Moses had been forced into the role of a Universal Decision Maker. While Moses paused to make decisions both great and small, difficult and simple, the people he was leading out of bondage dawdled along the way. "You are not acting

[2] For multiple perspectives on why and how this condition came to be, see Robert T. Golembiewski, *Public Administration as a Developing Discipline,* Vol. I (New York: Marcel Dekker, 1977).

wisely," Jethro was emboldened by events to tell his son-in-law Moses, and Moses listened. The Bible notes that:

> Moses picked out able men from all Israel and put them in charge of the people *as officers over groups of thousands, of hundreds, of fifties, and of tens.* They rendered decisions for the people in all ordinary cases. The more difficult cases they rendered to Moses, but all the lesser cases they settled themselves.

The exodus then went far more quickly, and (we presume) Moses was a less frantic man. But Jethro—wise father-in-law that he was—did not press his luck. His advice having been given and accepted, Jethro "went off to his own country," perhaps to avoid giving further advice on the many problems that plague any structure for organizing work.

We, like Moses, shall organize incredible complexity in a simple way. Thus the bulk of this sampling of the vast managerially relevant literatures will be organized around these four themes:

I. Managing by Ones and Twos: Freeing-up Relations Between Individuals

II. Managing by Tens and Twenties: Supervising Immediate Work Units

III. Managing by Hundreds: Middle Management and Departmental Dynamics

IV. Managing by Thousands: Developing and Maintaining an Institution

Other guidelines for organizing this volume could have been used, and perhaps with an equally telling effect. However, we do make two major claims for the special usefulness of the four themes here, as well as for their focus on different levels of organization and their different demands. Although they are not magical boxes for sorting the total phenomena of management, the emphasis on the four levels does spotlight central tendencies in organizational demands that differ enough that we are ill-advised to neglect them. That is, as we view management, each of the four levels of organization detailed above imposes different demands upon the manager, and the manager must sink or swim in providing appropriate behaviors. These differences in the organizational demands at the several levels are marked enough to appear in public as well as in business organizations. These similar demands at similar levels appear even in organizations doing vastly different work, be it administrative or manufacturing. Hence the title of this volume: *Managerial Behavior and Organization Demands.*

Additionally, although students and practitioners alike recognize that different levels of organization *do* impose different demands on managers, most management texts neglect the point. Thus the focus of texts is likely to be on the major functional areas (such as production, engineering and accounting). Or the focus of texts may be upon general activities performed by all managers (such as leading, planning, and motivating). We shall not neglect either such functions or such activities, but we will treat them only as they appear concretely at some specific level of organization. This emphasis upon levels distinguishes this volume from most others, and this emphasis obviously (to make the point again) is reflected in the volume's title: *Managerial Behavior and Organization Demands.*

The differing demands of different levels of organization may be illustrated simply. For example, one set of organizational demands challenges the supervisor in the face-to-face management of his work-unit. Tersely, he manages people and their problems. Quite another set of behaviors must be supplied by the chief executive who, from a distance, attempts to guide an organization in the successful pursuit of its evolving concept of its mission and roles. In a crude but revealing sense, the top-level executive manages an institution and its problems.

Only a few managers can get off cheaply by serving the demands of one level of organization at the expense of others, however. Illustratively, the chief executive usually must be concerned with the face-to-face supervision of his immediate staff as well as with the management of the organization *qua* institution. This, in short, involves him in the management of tens as well as thousands. In addition, every chief executive—like the rest of humankind—can neglect his interpersonal relations only at great and possibly tragic cost. Chief executives are perforce involved in managing by ones and twos.

Exaggerations are sudden death for most arguments, but we need not carefully hedge our statement of the importance of levels in an organization. For much evidence supports the ubiquitous importance of levels in organizations. For example, our organization level may determine what we see, certainly a powerful effect. Sherman approached the point in these terms: "Rarely, if ever," he noted, "is an organizational problem one of 'good guys' vs. 'bad guys.' Rather, it is usually one between or among more or less decent people of different values and different self-interests, who see the problem from different perspectives."[3] And these different perspectives, in large part, have their roots in the particular job and in the particular level of that job in an organization. "Where one stands," Rufus Miles summarized, "depends on where he sits." Or, alternatively, "we see things not as they are, but as we are." As might be expected, then, the impact of where we sit on where we

---

[3] Harvey Sherman, *It All Depends: A Pragmatic Approach to Organization* (University, Alabama: University of Alabama Press, 1966), p. 62.

stand often is made starkly plain, as when a person changes jobs or rises in the hierarchy. Sherman tells of the staff man who had a ready explanation for every organizational difference. "If only people would talk to each other," he would lament, "there would be no problem." But the explanation seemed to lose its power when the individual accepted a high-level "line" job. Sherman described the change sharply: "Now he would say that there just wasn't time to talk to all the people who were involved with his operations, and he would bemoan the fact that it was so difficult to imbue the various staff departments with the same sense of urgency and priority that he felt for his operations."[4]

As for the mechanics of presentation, each section of this volume in turn will stress two types of materials. First, one or more pieces in each section will outline the kinds of demands typically imposed on managers at some one level of the organization. Second, other pieces in each section will have a multiple focus. They explore specific problems in depth; they trace the interrelations of problem areas; and they particularly highlight the kinds of behaviors and techniques which a manager can use to react successfully to the demands made upon him. Brief editorial comments will help identify the more salient aspects of each piece.

C. ORIENTING THE READER IN INTRODUCTORY WAYS

Let us illustrate the way we editors shall orient the reader to the materials below by dealing with the four readings that comprise this introductory section. In gross terms, this section is a microcosm of what follows. It seeks to orient the reader to our stage of organizational development, how we got there, and what we might do about it. More specifically, one article stresses the general demands that will be made on organizations as change occurs, and as we poke further and further into the future that soon becomes the immediate past. Three other articles within the area of significance established by the first piece indicate some specific difficulties in approaching change and its by-products. These three articles also sketch the progress that has been made on coming to grips with these demands upon organization members, on dealing with those demands in ways that permit some degree of conscious control over the conditions of our organizational experiences.

We may usefully provide more specific introductory substance. William Halal in "The Post-Industrial Organization" briefly describes the future problems that men in organizations may face as we move from an era of industrial development to the era of the "Information Society."

[4] *Ibid.*, p. 63.

Halal contrasts the bureaucratic model of organization, the dominant institutional form today, with the model which may be required in the future. He contends that the bureaucratic model will not be able to cope with the turbulence, novelty, and interdependence which we can expect in the future, and of which we even now have a good idea. Instead of the stability or even inflexibility associated with the bureaucratic model, the organization of the postindustrial society will be managed as an "open system," interacting more frequently with other organizations. Institutionally, moreover, organization life will be characterized by greater concern about employees as well as about the various publics and constituencies they affect. Halal believes that the basic outlines of the needed postindustrial technologies are evident even now.

The broad outlines of available perspectives and technologies are further discussed by both C. L. Sharma and Fred Luthans. Sharma's "Administration as a Field of Study" is a map of approaches to the development of a comprehensive theory of administration. The vantage point Sharma examines most closely is the "process school." This school of thought holds that administration or management is a composite of several processes such as planning, organizing, staffing, directing, and controlling. All these processes are interrelated and interdependent; and they are usually, but not necessarily, carried out at the same time. This view encourages one to see the breadth of simultaneous activities in organizations, as contrasted with an emphasis on techniques employed or on the personalities who fill administrative positions. The process approach to organizations, for Sharma, captures their dynamic qualities and unifies disparate approaches to viewing organization phenomena.

Fred Luthans' "Contingency Theory: A Path Out of the Jungle" is a blast at the process school which Sharma advocates. According to Luthans, no one approach to the unification of management theories is satisfactory. Each approach provides an inadequate path; no one leads us out of the jungle. Given more or less constant change, and given a diversity of environments and of structures required to meet the demands of those environments, no single method or approach will be satisfactory. Rather, Luthans believes that only a contingency approach—matching structure or approach with the specific situation at hand—can provide the unifying thread in organization theory. Although Luthans admits that no single contingency theory of management yet exists, he does outline the basic framework on which one might be based.

Whatever the eventual nature of a comprehensive model of administration, all is not at sixes-and-sevens. Administration raises basic issues which are much like those encountered in other areas of study, so multiple attention from several directions may eventually lead to an enlarging core of basic theory and methods. For example, some of the basic issues for inclusion in a satisfactory framework for organization theory are dealt with directly by Herbert Kaufman in "Organization Theory and Political Theory." Kaufman dwells on the actual "parallels between political theory, probably the oldest of the social sciences, and organization theory, perhaps the newest such discipline," and he finds these parallels "so totally unexpected." Kaufman's original expectations stand in stark opposition to his findings, these expectations emphasizing as they did the isolation and discontinuity of the two kinds of thought and analysis, one as old as reflective humanity and the other a johnny-come-lately, but both of massive significance. As he explains:[5]

> If there is any conscious agreement between the two fields, it is on their separateness from each other: political theorists and organization theorists alike seem to take for granted the impossibility of encompassing within a single theoretical framework propositions about states . . . and propositions about other forms of human association. In the literature of organization theory, one rarely finds references even to contemporary political theorists and almost never to those who wrote in the past. By the same token, political theorists rarely seem to find anything relevant to their interests in the work of students of organization.

Kaufman traces a uniform picture of similar problems similarly coped with, and he explains the similarities of both kinds in terms that imply an enormous scope for the problems of organization theory. Kaufman isolates three major parallelisms in organization theory and political theory: accounting for the obedience of man to man; explaining the coordination of human efforts; and reconciling individual needs and collective requirements. He accounts for the similar treatment of these theoretical problems in political theory and in organization theory in terms of three explanatory themes. First, similar treatment of similarly perceived problems could not be avoided because of the broad and overlapping areas covered by political theory and organization theory. "When all is said and done," Kaufman explains, "they both treat of phenomena that encompass vast areas, if not all, of human life."[6]

Second, parallelisms are products of this major datum. Both governments and businesses face similar problems of governance. Policy formation, succession, loyalty and revolution are among the major common components. Institutional differences notwithstanding, these significant common components encourage common approaches in the two areas of study.

---

[5] Herbert Kaufman, "Organization Theory and Political Theory," *American Political Science Review,* Vol. 58 (March 1964), p. 5.

[6] *Ibid.,* p. 10.

Third, Kaufman explains the parallelisms he observed by stressing common normative problems. That is, both political theory and organization theory face common questions. For what purposes should man be organized? What are the acceptable limits on enforcing compliance to some definition of the collective purpose? Since they drew on the common heritage of the western tradition in attempting to cope with such common questions, both political theory and organization theory generated a range of solutions that overlap closely.

We may boldly note one implicit conclusion from these four pieces. The stakes are high in our contemporary organizational revolution, and the game is as narrow as an individual's life history or as broad as man's total political and social existence.

THE POST-INDUSTRIAL ORGANIZATION*

William Halal

> I . . . believe—and hope—that politics and economics will cease to be as important in the future as they have been in the past; the time will come when most of our present controversies on these matters will seem as trivial, or as meaningless, as the theological debates in which the keenest minds of the Middle Ages dissipated their energies.
>
> —Arthur C. Clarke
> *Profiles of the Future*

Clarke's prediction captures the essence of the changes now sweeping through most industrialized nations. It seems rather clear that we are rapidly being thrust into what Daniel Bell has termed a "post-industrial society," in which economic progress, the use of political power, competition and conflict, and other similar concerns which have been essential to the development of industrial societies will gradually lose their importance. Post-industrial societies are expected to inevitably transcend these matters and focus on goals of human development and welfare, scientific exploration of the universe, and appreciating the spiritual basis of life. The magnitude of such changes and their abrupt discontinuities with the past appear to be so great that they can only be adequately described as a revolution; a revolution of such significance that only the most monumental transformations of history—the development of agricultural societies, the industrial revolution, and so forth—serve as useful comparisons.

The ultimate structural features and behavior of this evolving society are, as yet, uncertain and debatable. But the general properties of the emerging social order and its institutions seem quite unmistakable. In fact, some impacts of this revolution are already being experienced in most present social institutions. Government agencies, business corporations, universities, hospitals, military units, churches—all are experiencing symptoms of this impending reformation. With the completion of this process, as Warren Bennis pointed out some time ago, we shall inevitably witness the demise of bureaucracy as the dominant institutional form and the emergence of a new model of social organization.

---

* Reprinted with permission of author and publisher from *The Bureaucrat*, Vol. 3, No. 3 (October 1974), pp. 285–300.

BUREAUCRACY AND INDUSTRIALISM

Although there are great variations in existing organizations, they have mostly been managed along the lines of the bureaucratic model formulated by Max Weber, Frederick Taylor, Henri Fayol, James Mooney, and other proponents of "classical" organizational theory. This model is best exemplified by prominent organizations in government, industry and the military, where the principles of bureaucracy were first developed. Most such organizations embody an underlying philosophy based upon an extremely rational, mechanistic viewpoint emphasizing orderly technical and economic considerations reflecting the culture of industrial societies.

For instance, bureaucratic organizations characteristically focus on optimizing the performance of internal processes essential to their survival and success, which are usually stated as techno-economic goals. Government agencies tend to focus on the efficient processing of clients or provision of services in order to improve various indices such as benefit-cost ratios or cost-effectiveness; industrial corporations typically concentrate on improving their manufacturing and marketing operations for the purpose of profit maximization. This emphasis on techno-economic goals was, of course, perfectly justified in the industrial past, since these were crucial concerns.

The bureaucratic model is also orderly with regard to social structure. Typically, the structure of such organizations reflects high degrees of job specialization, coordinated by a hierarchical structure of authority relationships. The assembly line worker performing countless repetitions of some simple mechanical task offers the most notorious instance of job specialization, but numerous other examples are equally common in the clerical office work comprising the bulk of activities in government agencies and most other organizations of this type. Coordinated integration of this division of labor necessitates the pyramid-like chain of command which forms bureaucratic hierarchies. Such structures were a logical counterpart to the goals of most organizations, because they permitted increased efficiency and easily accommodated the relatively simple tasks organizations faced.

To ensure adequate control of this complex organizational apparatus, power usually tends to be concentrated at higher levels of the hierarchical structure. The discretion for major decisions is centralized in appointed officials and highly placed civil servants in government offices, chief executives and their staff in corporations, and commanding officers in the military. This form of control is augmented by formal rules, procedures, and policies which ensure that behavior is in accordance with formally prescribed, programmed patterns. To a great extent, this centralization of power seems inevitable in industrial societies, since most people have not yet obtained the education, sophistication, and resourcefulness necessary for self-direction. Moreover, the routine nature of industrial technology permits such control.

The bureaucratic model describes an organization which is constructed and operated along the principles of a machine, albeit a social machine. These elaborate social mechanisms offered a high degree of reliability, stability, and efficiency which were well suited to the demands of the industrial era. But these demands are changing.

SHIFTING ORGANIZATIONAL FOUNDATIONS

Although these dominant bureaucratic features (techno-economic goal emphasis, hierarchical structure, and centralization of power) may have been appropriate organizational modes in the industrial past, there are reasons to believe that they are beginning to outlive their usefulness and are increasingly inappropriate for the dramatically different conditions confronting our institutions today. Bureaucratic organizations seem too rigidly structured to cope with the immense problems now resulting from the development of more sophisticated values in employees, the difficulties of rationally coordinating increasingly complex technological reality, and the demands placed upon organizations by an increasingly turbulent social environment.

Individual Values and Employee Motivation

For a number of reasons, important changes in social values and behavior seem to occur during the transition from industrial to post-industrial conditions. Improved education and widespread access to information through media such as television causes people to become more knowledgeable. Increased material affluence results in a shift from materialistic values to more idealistic concerns for self-esteem, equitable treatment, and personal meaning. More permissive relations with parents and authority figures result in a greater sense of self-sufficiency and independence. These changes in social character seem to signal the passage from a society composed predominantly of "economic men" adhering to a "Protestant ethic" to more sophisticated forms of social character, which could be described by newer models such as "social man," "technological man," or "intellectual man."

Only such a subtle, but powerful, transformation of the modal human personality can reasonably account for the disruptive changes in behavior which have appeared in industrial nations throughout the world during the past decade. Student disorders have challenged the existing system not only of their universities but of the entire world. Women have announced their emancipation from the domination of men, workers have demanded rights which go beyond their financial welfare, racial minorities seek their self-esteem and equal treatment, and such diverse groups as the clergy, GIs, homosexuals, and prisoners of penal institutions have adamantly proclaimed more demanding attitudes. Based upon such observations and recent attitudinal studies, it is hard to avoid the conclusion that most persons today demand a great deal more from their social institutions than they did in the past. A critical question for today must be, "Are these demands beyond the capacity of the classical bureaucratic form to respond effectively?"

Organization and Post-Industrial Technologies

The forms of technology employed by organizations have also significantly changed in recent years. During early stages of industrialization, most work involved relatively simple forms of technology, best represented by the physical processes of mass production: repetitive operations which facilitate establishing routines, independent tasks which can be separated into specialized jobs, and processes which are easily understood and predictable. However, these are the very tasks which best lend themselves to automation and cybernation, and hence, they are rapidly being eliminated. This trend is easily observed in the declining proportion of jobs in manufacturing industries, which are now exceeded by the service industries. In time, it can be expected that the amount of labor devoted to such physical technologies will diminish to less than ten percent of the labor force, thus paralleling the similar dimunition of agricultural workers which occurred earlier this century.

As a result, it seems clear that the evolving post-industrial society will virtually eliminate most physical forms of labor and instead will concentrate on what Peter Drucker has called the "information" industries. The prevalent fields of employment by the close of this century will include research, computerization, services, communications, education, and the like. These technologies involve dramatically different features from those with which existing organizational forms have been designed to deal. The component tasks associated with the "info-comm" technologies are so unique that programmed routines are often inappropriate. Interaction between various parts of a problem make it difficult to separate into specialized jobs, and the uncertainty involved in such, as yet, poorly understood processes makes the prediction of outcomes far more problematical than it is for processes involving the repeated execution of similar tasks.

Socioeconomic Environment

Another significant development now affecting organizations involves the social environment in which they operate. The classical bureaucracy requires a stable, predictable environment. In terms of general systems theory, they are, by and large, perceived as "closed systems." Although such stable conditions may have generally existed in the past, they are no longer valid assumptions for the future. A number of features about the emerging post-industrial society suggest that an "open-system" model will be essential to organizational survival. Increasing functional specialization among organizations results in such great interdependence that random local events create perturbations throughout the social order. Also, cheaper, faster, more pervasive forms of communications and transportation result in more frequent interaction between the organization and its environment. Additionally, the rapid rate of social and economic change concomitant with the transition from industrial to post-industrial eras inevitably generates a continual series of hectic, unrelenting crises disrupting the organization. Future organizations will be unable to accommodate these frequent, turbulent interactions with their environment if they continue to rely principally upon rigid internal processes, as they have in the past.

As a result of the above developments, our traditional institutions have been increasingly suffering serious problems. Because bureaucracies typically offer work roles which are highly specialized, the resulting routine jobs offer insufficient interest and challenge to satisfy the more sophisticated workers of today. Also, the authoritarian, centralized form of leadership employed in bureaucracies is increasingly unacceptable and often results in a sense of oppression because employees are prevented from effectively influencing their working lives. As a result, problems of worker alienation are becoming more and more widely experienced among many groups, including most blue-collar workers, and even middle managers. As reported in a comprehensive task force study conducted by the Department of Health, Education and Welfare titled *Work in America,* this alienation appears to be the primary cause for the current high rates of personnel turnover, accidents, absenteeism, industrial sabotage, pilferage, low productivity, wildcat strikes, and other manifestations of worker dissatisfaction; in summary, an alienation which may ultimately become prohibitively costly to organizations and society at large.

This employee alienation would perhaps be tolerable if it were the necessary price for having more productive organizations, but increasingly serious failings have been observed in the effectiveness of our organizations as well. Because of the development of more complex technologies and the increased turbulence of the social environment, many salient societal problems are appearing because bureaucratic organizations are unable to effectively cope with these new challenges. The succession of crises which have buffeted industrial societies lately—political corruption, shortages of various critical resources, rampant inflation, environmental decay, urban congestion, and other problems forming the litany of modern societal ills—serve as a growing indictment of many of our institutions.

The Watergate scandals have recently highlighted the failure of almost all branches and levels of government to serve their legitimate purposes of serving the public. The ineffectiveness of corporations in some of our major industries—energy, autos, the railroads, and so on—reveals the inadequacy of most private firms today. The military failure in Vietnam demonstrated the ineffectiveness of present military organizations. Within universities, the student disorders of the sixties may have faded, but many of the troublesome issues which caused these disruptions have not been resolved and merely lie dormant. The failure of our present philosophy of organization is so great that it is hard to find an institution or organization which deserves recognition for truly effective performance.

Fortunately, a number of promising developments have also occurred during the past decade or so which suggest possible solutions to these difficulties. The Human Relations Movement and the notion of Participative Management which were advocated some time ago by such scholars as Elton Mayo, Douglas McGregor, Rensis Likert, and Chris Argyris challenged the existing norms of authoritarian, centralized leadership in organizations. Later, the work of Abraham Maslow, Frederick Herzberg, John Ford, Porter and Lawler, Victor Vroom, and others in the field of motivation suggested concepts like job "enlargement," "enrichment," and "rotation." This has begun to reverse the trend toward increased task specialization, in order to create more challenging, satisfying, and productive work roles. The Organization Development movement (OD) has provided the beginnings of interest and expertise in conducting planned organizational change for the purpose of creating more effective and humane organizations. More recently, the notion that organizations should be responsible for their impact on various constituencies whom they affect has gained wide appeal; this is an especially prominent issue among corporations who are being asked to adopt the concept of Corporate Social Responsibility and to measure such performance by a Social Audit of their contributions to employees, the local community, the general public and their customers, as well as their stockholders.

We have also seen the introduction of novel organizational structures such as project management and matrix organizations which suggest alternatives to the traditional hierarchy. Other forms of structure have also been proposed as alternatives to the hierarchical norm, the most prominent being Warren Bennis's concept of an "adaptive" organization which employs temporary, ad hoc project teams operating in an organic fashion. Most recently, the inviolable norm of the five-day, forty-hour work week has been breached by such practices as the four-day week, gliding-time, flex-time, and other variations providing increased flexibility for the benefit of employees, employers, and the public. We are also witnessing the first practical applications of sophisticated information and decision systems, offering a glimpse at the unprecedented potential capabilities of "quantum management" for eliminating clerical routine and improving managerial decisions.

All these concepts have been proposed as alternatives to the existing bureaucratic model and make up what may be called an evolutionary trend toward the creation of more varied, pragmatic, and more effective organizational models. The following paragraphs describe an idealized model of those new norms which seem likely to coalesce out of the emerging individual concepts into a coherent, workable philosophy of organization, appropriate to the post-industrial society.

THE POST-INDUSTRIAL ORGANIZATION

The "post-industrial organization" stands out in sharp contrast to the bureaucratic model. It can be illustrated by such present-day examples as research laboratories, think-tanks, university faculties, firms centered upon complex technologies, and therapeutic teams in hospitals. The previously cited report, *Work in America,* summarizes many experimental programs based upon these concepts which have been conducted in a variety of organizations. As suggested by these examples, the post-industrial organization reflects a philosophical foundation emphasizing scientific and humanistic values. It is based upon a concern for successfully challenging the complexity, uncertainty, and novelty which are inherently posed by problems in intellectual fields of endeavor.

For a number of important reasons, future organizations will have to shift their focus from internal operations to an emphasis on interactions with their environment. The difficulties posed by an interdependent world, increased social turbulence, and rapid change will necessitate a predominant concern for problems of organizational "boundary interaction." This trend will be facilitated by the development of automation, cybernation, and information technology, such that most internal operations will be fairly easily handled by a small number of technicians and service workers. The bulk of employees—who are expected to be highly educated professionals of various types—will be left free to address the more complex, important issues of developing viable objectives, maintaining effective relationships with various constituencies, coordinating joint operations with other organizations, and other such types of "boundary maintenance."

In addition, a continued shift of social values toward more symbiotic, rather than competitive, norms should result in a very different conception of the ultimate goals of organizations. We may witness the development of a society in which organizational performance and success is judged, not by the increase in resources of power which the organization can claim or control, but by the size and quality of its contributions to society. Even now, such a reorientation appears to be taking shape. Government agencies are placing an increased emphasis on effectively serving their clients, firms are beginning to seriously consider the use of the corporate social audit, and in the military—as the recruitment posters advertise—"The Army wants to join *you!*"

Additionally, the post-industrial organization may be expected to develop a more "organic" form of structure. Although the traditional hierarchy may remain, it will be relegated to a mere skeleton-like framework which will support rapidly changing project teams composed of skilled workers operating in an informal, egalitarian fashion. Such teams will be formed to address the many unique problems which cut across interdisciplinary lines, thus creating a need for persons of broad, multidisciplinary backgrounds who are able to think more in terms of a systems approach to problems rather than having skills in limited fields of specialization. Also, the nature of the relationship between individuals and the organization should change such that employees may work flexible schedules of their choosing and may act more as consultants or "free agents," rather than being employees of one particular organization. These more flexible working relationships should all be made possible by improved informational systems which allow effective control of the individual's performance through the monitoring of results, thus releasing employees from direct managerial supervision.

INFORMATION EQUALS POWER

Perhaps the most significant difference between the classic bureaucratic and post-industrial models of organizations relates to the manner in which power is employed. In the first place, the sources of power in the evolving model will be different from today's. In the classic bureaucracy, power derives primarily from hierarchical position and from access to and control of resources. While these traditional sources of power will continue to obtain in the future, they will be increasingly tempered and constrained by a third significant source of power: information or knowledge.

Of course, throughout history knowledge has been a source of political, economic, and military power, to one degree or another. The technological know-how for the creation of Greek-fire and tempered steel were long closely held as state secrets by those nations who possessed them. Sir Josiah Wedgwood built an economic empire upon a secret process for manufacturing dinner ware. During the full flowering of the industrial system in nineteenth-century Great Britain, numerous statistical formulae were jealously guarded secrets of manufacturers seeking to assure quality control and reduce production costs in such diverse fields as brewing and metallurgy. Between now and the year 2000, however, the role of information as a source of power will be extrapolated from the specifics of the past to a general rule for the post-industrial future. In fact, so pervasive will this transition be that the Japanese are already referring to the post-industrial period as the "Information Society."

Whether the era into which we are moving is called "Post-Industrial" or "Informational," it is clear that the basic ground rules will be the same. During the next 25 years, decisions will increasingly be based upon a much better grasp of the "facts" than in the past. This will be true both because of the capabilities offered by information technology and because of the imperatives forced upon us by the realities of articulate competition for limited resources. This "articulate competition" will be another prominent feature of the coming decades, since institutions will be operating within a social environment of mobilized interests with a historically unparalleled level of education.

In such a milieu, the possessors of information will assume growing importance. Even today, the proprietors of automated data bases sell their information for a wide variety of uses. Each year, increasing sums of money are spent, in both the public and private sectors, to acquire information. This emphasis on information pervades every part of our society. Public agencies increasingly restrict Madison Avenue to limit their advertising to factual material. "Truth-in-lending" and "truth-in-packaging" are both hallmarks of the information society; the little caveat on every cigarette package was, perhaps, the first harbinger of the information era.

There are numerous other signs of our arrival in the age of information. Certainly, a comparison of the typical legislative rhetoric of 50 years ago with today's will reveal startling differences in content. Yesterday's commonplace appeals to emotion and traditional values have largely given way to data-laden technical debates. The output of the press, too, has shifted significantly, in terms of both what is covered and how. Today's star reporters rely far more upon facts and less upon style than did their predecessors. Indeed, the media today find themselves at the center of a very basic political controversy largely because they have been one of the first major social institutions to move broadly into the information age, to the distress of those institutions, both public and private, which still cling to the old, closed models of organizations.

Within the bureaucracy itself, the impacts of burgeoning info-comm technology will be several, and, in some cases, conflicting. The increasing professionalization of all employees, and the broadening of their motivations to include loyalties to profession *as well as* to employer will generate increased potential for conflict between executive management and their professional cadres. With the continued expansion of low-cost mass communications, professional societies will become more active advocates in an arena of increasingly educated and demanding public concern. In this, the professionals will find willing allies in the mass media. Executive management in both the private and public sectors will fight a vigorous but losing battle against "information seepage." (To this degree, the White House "plumbers unit" represented another early manifestation of the rocky transition from a closed to an open society.)

The growing independence of an increasingly professionalized and "self-actualizing" work force, *just at the same time that info-comm technology begins to permit massive centralization of decision-making,* will also certainly generate serious conflicts within the bureaucracy. This will continue until there is some change in the basic self-perceptions of these two groups, in terms of their shifting roles. In general, the future role of professional middle management will be that of intelligence-gathering, and the analysis of alternative strategies and goals. Executive management will continue to make major policy, goals-setting, and research decisions. However, they will have to acquiesce to a greater independence of middle managers, not only as a professional demand and a cultural expectation, but also as a necessary check against the less objective (less *factual,* more value-based) decision-making of the executive level. In the foregoing context, the disparate yet symbiotic roles of executive management and middle management in the information age might be characterized as follows: middle management will be primarily concerned with factual analysis; executive management will be primarily concerned with decision-making based upon the assimilation of these facts with the less precise considerations such as social values and polity.

THE TRANSITION AHEAD

Realization of the foregoing concepts has thus far generated considerable controversy. Many management programs based upon "post-industrial" principles have been quite successful, but, on the whole, their effectiveness has been rather limited. Workers have often failed to respond with the predicted enthusiasm and have reflected a failure to understand or believe in these new arrangements. Unions, for instance, have characteristically opposed such innovations, claiming they are not in the interest of their members. Many members of management have also opposed such programs, fearing they would result in loss of managerial control and in threats to managerial sovereignty. Moreover, the history of experimental attempts to adopt such concepts is marked with episodes of organizational trauma and disruption, in addition to the wasted investment in money and time. As a result of such mixed outcomes, responsible critics argue that these ideas are merely passing fads, or the utopian ideals of academics and scholars holding ivory tower values which do not reflect those of the general public.

It appears more likely that these difficulties are the result of sociopsychological barriers which confront all forms of innovation. Most attempts to employ these concepts have suffered from the lack of strong, genuine perception of the need for change on the part of management and workers, from prejudice against such ideas which challenge fundamental beliefs, and from a lack of sophistication and knowledge in applying these rudimentary ideas. Most importantly, adoption of these concepts has usually been attempted in a piecemeal, fragmentary fashion, which is unlikely to be successful since the existing philosophy of bureaucracy subtly rejects such alien organizational features.

It has become increasingly clear from the growing literature and experience in planning organizational change that successful change of so fundamental a character must stem from the realistic needs and genuine support of management and employees, and must involve a fundamental change in the entire culture of the organization. Also, broad changes in attitudes concerning work, management, and organizational norms will be necessary before such concepts are socially acceptable.

It may be, therefore, that widespread modifications of the existing bureaucratic model are unlikely to occur until some precipitating factors cause a wholesale move toward these new concepts. There are many possible scenarios in which one could envision such a revolutionary change occurring: revolts by employees, the unionization of white-collar workers and possibly managers, widespread failures of major organizations (e.g., Penn Central, Lockheed), the emulation of organizations which have adopted such alternative forms with economic success, or a cultural revolution triggered by waves of new social values, ethics, and expectations.

The manner, timing, and details of this coming transition are uncertain and, of course, numerous developments such as the eruption of nuclear war, massive economic depression and political dictatorship would obviously disrupt this evolutionary trend. However, barring such disasters, it seems fairly certain that these changes are likely if organizations are to successfully cope with the conditions of a post-industrial world. When this occurs, we may expect our major institutions to become radically transformed into social systems which will be more complex, automated, and fragile; but they will also be more humane, flexible, and effective. Many persons will find these predictions utopian and perhaps naive. Of course, the skeptics may prove to be correct, but the past history of conservative opposition to revolutionary predictions seems to offer eloquent evidence that such doubts are often the result of limited vision or the natural human attraction to the serenity of old, tried values and institutions. Overwhelming opinions of the most knowledgeable "experts" once ridiculed the notion that the earth was round, that democracy would work, or that men could fly. To quote another appropriate passage from Arthur C. Clarke's predictions in *Profiles of the Future:*

> If this book seems completely reasonable and *all* my extrapolations convincing, I will not have succeeded in looking very far ahead; for the one fact about the future of which we can be certain is that it will be utterly fantastic.

ADMINISTRATION AS A FIELD OF STUDY*

C. L. Sharma

Administration is a way of conceptual thinking for attaining predetermined goals through group effort. As a concept, it is of universal application. It emerged with the human race and will continue to be employed as long as mankind survives. It is an indispensable ingredient of group effort and is characteristic of all types of undertakings in which people engage to achieve objectives collectively. It may vary in form with the nature of the enterprise but, in substance, it remains the same. Its rudiments are discernible even in the most primitive and simple society, but

---

* Reprinted with permission of C. L. Sharma and the International Institute of Administrative Sciences, Rue de la Charité 25, Brussels, Belgium, and originally published by the *International Review of Administrative Science,* Vol. 32, No. 4 (1966), pp. 287–300.

it becomes increasingly sophisticated in its structure and application as the society becomes more advanced and complex. This becomes readily evident as one compares the administration of the Greek city states with that of the large industrial complexes and continental governments of our time.

THE NATURE OF ADMINISTRATION

The following observations can be made about the nature of administration:

1. Administration is a process consisting of a number of subprocesses. Principally, the subprocesses are planning, organizing, staffing, directing, coordinating, and controlling. These subprocesses are interrelated and interdependent and are usually, but not necessarily, carried out simultaneously and continuously in an ongoing enterprise.
2. Administration presupposes a formally organized group of people working together as members of an enterprise. Without group activity, there is no opportunity for the operation of administration. The group may be composed of as few as two persons. The activities of an individual working by himself, which are not complementary to those of any other person, do not lend themselves to the application of administration. People work in groups to attain goals which ordinarily are beyond the possibility of individual accomplishment. It is inconceivable that the group effort would be productive without the assistance of administration, but it is also axiomatic that in the absence of the former the latter would simply be inoperative.
3. For administration to operate, the group of people must be working toward a specific objective or a set of objectives. A group which does not seek to attain an objective or a set of objectives is not the concern of administration. For example, administration is inapplicable to a crowd which has no group goals.
4. Usually, administration is provided with broad objectives, but it is the responsibility of administration to refine them, define them, and render them attainable.
5. Administration seeks to achieve the enterprise objectives by intelligently utilizing the efforts of a group of people, and its success is measured in terms of the accomplishment of predetermined objectives.
6. Administration implies getting the things done through subordinates. An efficient administrator is one who gets the work done through the efforts of his subordinates rather than doing it himself.

7. As administration implies the ability to get the work done through subordinates, it is a distinct skill, different from specialized technical expertness. An administrator may possess some technical skill, but it would be of no use to him in the discharge of his administrative responsibilities.
8. Administrative skill is not a technical skill in the sense of engineering skill or skill in medicine. Yet it is a specialized skill which would significantly determine the achievement of enterprise goals.
9. Administration has emerged as a distinct and identifiable discipline that can be studied, taught, learned, and practiced, and has universal application.
10. The discipline of administration has accumulated some principles concerning the administration of certain aspects of enterprise, and more are in the process of identification. These principles are reasonably well-established, generally accepted, and widely practiced. However, because of the preponderance of human element in administration, the principles are not absolute and infallible and need to be used as guides with great caution.
11. Administration is intangible and invisible. However, orderliness in work, achievement of objectives, and satisfaction of employees are indices of its efficient and continuous operation.
12. Provision of resources, human and material, falls within the purview of administration. It is the responsibility of administration to provide for them in quantity, quality, and variety necessary to attain the objectives of the enterprise.
13. Although administration is ultimately responsible for the provision of resources, both human and material, for the enterprise, primarily it is concerned with the efficient direction of human effort in the manipulation of non-human resources to accomplish the enterprise goals. People are the subject of administration, not land, capital, building, or raw materials.
14. Administration embraces the total enterprise and permeates all parts of it, with varied emphases on its subprocesses at different levels of the organizational structure.
15. Administration is employed at all levels of the organizational structure of an enterprise. At higher levels of the structure it is characterized by more policy formulation, and at lower levels, by more policy execution.
16. Since administration is an inseparable feature of organized activity, the principles of administration would apply to all types of enterprises irrespective of the nature of activities they may be engaged in. The pervasive character of administration can be judged from the

fact that no enterprise can be initiated and have a continued existence, without its operation, in any society at any time.

17. The universality of the principles of administration also makes them transferable. Administrative skill is different from technical skill in the sense that it is basically the same regardless of the nature of the enterprise to which it may be applied. Therefore, able executives can change enterprises, diverse in nature, without any loss in efficiency.
18. Administrative skill is conditioned by the cultural advancement of a society. Such factors as social discipline, scientific knowledge, technical know-how, communication system, industrial achievements, and legal provisions would set a limit on the competency of administrators.
19. Administration is chiefly a mental activity. It may, and usually it does, involve some manual work, but that is not sufficient enough to negate its dominant characteristic.
20. Administration is not an end in itself; it is only a means to accomplish the enterprise objectives.

THE PURPOSE OF ADMINISTRATION

Administration has emerged out of the necessity of man to cooperate. Man has learned the value of cooperation from the realization that through collective effort he can accomplish what he individually can not. Cooperation presupposes some kind of work division among the participating individuals. The division of work is necessitated by human limitations—the inability of the individual to be at two places at the same time, to do two things at the same time, to master more than a small fraction of the vast accumulation of knowledge and skill, and to perform all tasks equally well, as men differ in nature, capacity, and skill. The technological advance has accentuated the imperativeness of the division of work and has substantially reduced the significance of the individual in modern gigantic enterprises. The logical method of dividing work among members of a group is according to their differing abilities attributable to heredity and environment. This results in efficient utilization of individuals with diverse capabilities, and leads to specialization in skills.

Thus, group effort has come to be an irrefutable fact of our time and an indispensable instrument for satisfying most of the human needs. Now, the question arises: Who should guide the group effort? This challenge has been met by administration which provides for the acquisition and integration of human and material resources necessary to attain the predetermined objectives of the enterprise. . . . Therefore, it is administration which leads the group effort to fruition. Without administration, the enterprise would disintegrate and dissolve, if it ever originates.

Administration is a means and not an end in itself. Therefore, the ultimate goals of administration cannot be different from those of the enterprise. Administration comes into being to serve the enterprise and cannot justify its existence otherwise. However, in order to attain the goals of the enterprise, the administration must seek the fulfillment of numerous immediate and intermediate goals. These would include orderliness in activities performed, supply and intelligent utilization of human and material resources, elimination of waste and inefficiency, economy in operations, welfare of employees, satisfaction of clientele, anticipation and resolution of problems, provision of guidance, and others. Effectuation of these subordinate goals is requisite to the realization of enterprise goals, which administration alone can bring about.

No enterprise can succeed in attaining its objectives that does not employ effective administration to its service. To a large extent, the accomplishment of goals of economic, social, political, military, or religious enterprises depends upon the application of efficient administration. Group effort is responsible for the material advancement of a society, which, in turn, is buttressed by continuous and diligent administration. Satisfaction of varied and multiplying human needs will continue to require a greater degree of group effort, which will place unprecedented demand on administration. Efficient administration contributes significantly to the success of an enterprise, and, thereby, cumulatively leads to the prosperity of a society.

ADMINISTRATION—A SCIENCE OR AN ART?

The controversy concerning the classification of the discipline of administration—a science or an art—has not been settled. Admittedly, such a discussion is of academic interest only and does not serve any useful purpose. However, whether administration be classified as a science or an art will depend upon the definition of these terms.

If by science is meant a discipline in which principles can be established through experimentation, administration can not qualify to be called a science because the human element in administration would defy the conducting of rigorous scientific experiments. On the other hand, if by science is meant a systematically organized body of knowledge in a subject field in contrast with a mere collection of traditions, practices, or personal reminiscences, administration would be considered a science just as much as political science or military science. Administration has evolved into a discipline which is now taught in professional schools and which provides a field for fruitful research.

Art is a skill in the application of which the possessor brings to bear his distinctiveness and individuality. The term "art" is used in two senses: First, it may refer to a skill as that of a poet, playwright, or a creative painter. It is commonly understood that such a skill is a gift of nature and can not be acquired through training. Administration is not an art in this sense. Secondly, the term "art" may refer to a skill which can be acquired through training, e.g., the skill of a violinist or that of a teacher. Administration would be considered an art in this sense because administrative skill can be learned, and its use affords an opportunity for the application of individual judgment.

Thus, administration may be considered a science as well as an art because it partakes of the characteristics of both. It is a science because it has a well-organized and evolving body of subject matter. To be more exact, it is an applied science because it makes use of the basic sciences, both exact and inexact, drawing rather heavily on the latter. At the same time, it is an art because the administrator would use his skill in the application of his knowledge of administration, which would inevitably reflect his individuality.

THE PROFESSIONAL STATUS OF ADMINISTRATION

A profession is considered to be an occupational group that possesses the following characteristics: (a) Existence of an esoteric body of knowledge, (b) rigorous formal training, (c) formation of a representative association, (d) development of a code of ethics to guide the behavior of its members, (e) insistence on social service as the dominant motive, (f) considerable autonomy in its practice, and (g) establishment of criteria for admission into the profession.

When the professional status of administration is examined against these characteristics, it becomes obvious that it falls far short of the well-established professions of theology, law, or medicine, in all respects, but particularly with respect to the development and enforcement of a code of ethics governing the behavior of its members and the criteria for entry into the profession. Administration, at present, also varies in the degree of sophistication in its application to the various types of enterprises in different societies. Nevertheless, remarkable progress has been made toward professionalization during the last three decades, which is very encouraging in view of the fact that administration, as a discipline, is still in its infancy. Therefore, it would be appropriate to conclude that administration is in the process of acquiring the status of a profession, but it can not claim to have attained it yet.

THE SCHOOLS OF THOUGHT IN ADMINISTRATION

Administration has emerged as a phenomenon of unusual significance during the last three decades and has attracted the attention of scholars engaged in the various fields of study. These scholars have attempted to formulate a conceptual framework to explain the phenomenon of administration, but the diversity of their vantage points has impeded the formation of a consensus. Their explanation of it is analogous to the description of an elephant given by six blind persons. Each point of view contains some grain of truth, but does not encompass the phenomenon in its entirety. These intellectual exercises may, at best, be regarded as different approaches to develop a comprehensive and systematic theory of administration. Among the more significant ones are the following:

1. The administrative process school.
2. The empirical school.
3. The human behavior school.
4. The social system school.
5. The mathematics school.
6. The decision theory school.

The Administrative Process School

This school considers administration as a work process for achieving the objectives of an enterprise. This approach has evolved from the logical analysis of the mental activities essential in the utilization of human and material resources to attain the desired results. These activities have been identified, analyzed, refined, and organized, and constitute the subprocesses of the administrative process. This conceptual framework is of universal application discernible in every group activity, and can be employed for the achievement of objectives of an enterprise as a whole or any constituent part of it. Although there exist some differences among authorities with respect to the nomenclature and classification of the subprocesses, the basic ideas are very similar. The concept of administration, according to this school, involves the accomplishment of predetermined enterprise objectives through the intelligent use of human and material resources.

The approach used by this school may also be designated as "operational" because, essentially, it attempts to analyze the numerous activities of administrators in order to identify the basic functions of administration, and then to deduce the fundamental principles governing these basic functions. Practitioners and scholars in the field of business have been primarily responsible for developing and expounding the administrative process thought, and Henri Fayol, Oliver Sheldon, and Ralph C. Davis would be considered as original contributors to it. The proponents of this school, while cognizant of the value of other disciplines to their approach, refrain from drawing upon them liberally in the development of their theory lest this might make it intellectually cumbersome, and further because of their belief in the segmentation of knowledge as a prerequisite to progress in any field. They fervently hope that verification of the theory through research would bring about improvement in administrative practices.

The administrative process school lately has been criticized severely and parallel concepts have been offered as replacements. These concepts form the subject of discussion in the succeeding paragraphs in this section.

The Empirical School

This school seeks to develop a theory of administration by analyzing the past experiences of successful administrators. The assumption is that an insight into the successful administrative practices would equip the prospective administrator with the competency to administer effectively in comparable situations. This school employs the case study method and the comparative approach expounded by Ernest Dale. The proponents of this school, from the study of cases, have drawn certain generalizations which tend to substantiate the concepts of the administrative process school of thought. However, the experiences of the past should serve only as useful guides and should not be applied slavishly and indiscriminately, as the problems of the future are not likely to be similar to those of the past. This school is also known as the "experience" school because its advocates concentrate on the study of experiences to understand and explain the phenomenon of administration. From the procedures of this school, it can reasonably be inferred that, in the last analysis, there would be very little difference, if any, between the process and the empirical schools of thought, or between the operational and comparative approaches of investigation employed.

The Human Behavior School

This school believes that human beings are the prime movers in an organized activity and, therefore, a grasp of human behavior should constitute the nucleus of administration. The behavioral sciences, especially individual and social psychology, by lending their theories, methods, techniques, and orientation, have contributed to the development of this school. They have brought forth the understanding that maximum individual and group effort toward the realization of enterprise goals is possible only when psychological principles are applied to the administration of the enterprise. The proponents of this school vary in their position from advocating an understanding of human behavior as an essential element of administration to considering human behavior as identical with administration. Some recommend human relations as an art to be mastered by the administrator, others regard leadership and administration as synonymous, and still others view administration as coterminous with the field of social psychology.

This school, by giving prominence to the human aspect as an important element of administration in realizing enterprise goals, has made a significant contribution to our knowledge of administration. The concepts of human relations, motivation, and leadership have been firmly established in the theory of administration, and their importance can not be discounted in successful culmination of group activity. However, the assertion that human behavior is inclusive enough to be co-extensive with administration is tantamount to an exaggeration of one element beyond all proportions.

The Social System School

This school considers administration as a social system, that is, a system of cultural interrelationships. Utilizing the sociological concepts, this school seeks to identify the various social groups in the enterprise, discover their cultural relationships, and integrate them into a social system. This school believes that man and his environment suffer from a number of biological, physical, and social limitations which can be surmounted only through cooperation. A formal organization in which people can communicate with each other and are willing to contribute to the realization of enterprise goals offers the best opportunity for cooperation.

This school is often confused with the human behavior school. This may be because both of these schools draw inspiration from the research in behavioral sciences. Present research and publications in the area of organization theory or in the social systems stem from the conceptual framework of this school.

The significant contributions of this school include recognition of enterprise as a social organism, awareness of the institutional foundations of administrative authority, the role of informal organization in realizing enterprise goals, the knowledge of factors that sustain an organization, an understanding of group behavior in the social systems, and an insight into the social obligations of administration. Admittedly, sociological findings have contributed measurably to administrative effectiveness, but it would be a mistake to consider administration and sociology as one and the same thing.

The Mathematics School

This school believes that administration is a logical process and, therefore, can be expressed in terms of mathematical symbols and relationships. Its proponents consider the function of administration to establish mathematical models and processes that can be employed to predict the outcome in advance. The measurements of known variables can be substituted in the formulas and the information about the unknown can be obtained for the varied situations.

This school has made a significant contribution to the field of industrial administration, especially by way of operations research and linear programming. Its usefulness can further be assessed from its demand for an orderly thinking, its requirement of precisely defining the problem, its insistence on systematic use of logical methodology, its concern for measurability of results, its ability to handle complex problems with ease, and its partial success in reducing the element of subjectivity in administration.

Notwithstanding its great value in administration, mathematics would be regarded only as a tool of administration rather than a school of administration. Mathematics serves most by providing the skills and techniques to improve the administrative practices and its significance can not be disputed. However, despite its impressive sophistication, it can not encompass the total field of administration. It can, at the most, be applied to the physical aspects of administration, but the intangible, intricate, and often baffling human aspects would surely elude its grasp.

The Decision Theory School

This school considers decision-making as the real function of administration—decision being the rational method of choosing, from among possible alternatives, a course of action. Just what the decision theory is concerned with is not definite because some theorists concentrate their attention on the decision itself, others include in their consideration those who make the decision, and still others analyze the decision-making process as well. Further, some study the decision in terms of its economic rationale, others examine the forces operative within the enterprise that might affect the decision, and still others would evaluate even the factors external to the enterprise that might have a bearing on the decision.

The decision theory school has grown out of the area of economics and clearly exhibits the impact of economic theorists on its development when it employs such concepts as marginal utility and economic behavior under uncertainties. Similarly, the influence of the mathematics school is discernible in the use of models and equations in decision-making.

Initially, the decision theory school merely evaluated the alternatives in selecting a course of action. But lately it has begun to examine all the activities of the enterprise through the decision-making approach. This obviously has expanded the scope of the school which now encompasses the total enterprise.

Decision-making is characteristic of administration and is a vitally important function in an enterprise, but it is difficult to conceive of administration as only decision-making without some provision for implementation. No one would deny the contributions of decision theory to administrative thought, but, by itself, it can not explain all the aspects of administration.

Concluding Comments on the Schools of Thought in Administration

1. The schools of thought discussed above represent major approaches to the development of a theory of administration and are indicative of the keen interest shown in the discipline by scholars in the related disciplines.
2. Some schools of thought have conceived of administration in narrow terms whereas others have taken a broader view of it. The range of perspective is conditioned by the attitude of the theorists. Those who have a predilection for one aspect of administration over others or those who employ a particular technique for analyzing administration which tends to restrict their vision, fail to comprehend the phenomenon of administration in its totality.
3. By and large, the schools of thought are not contradictory but complementary to one another. The differences in their positions stem from the specialized backgrounds of their exponents.

THE ADMINISTRATIVE PROCESS

For the exposition of the field to administration in this paper, the approach recommended by the school of thought which considers administration as a process has been utilized with some modifications. However, before presenting the reasons for the choice, it is necessary to examine the process itself in detail.

The administrative process is not merely a theoretical concept, it is also a technique of administering enterprises, currently in use. As a technique of administration, it represents the third stage in the process of evolution, being preceded by two other stages—the "scientific management" stage and the "organization and system" stage. The evolution of these stages in administration has also been associated with the evolution of the predominant types of administrators. These stages have been characteristic of the business and industrial enterprises in the United States and owe their development to scholars and practitioners in business and industry.

Until the beginning of the twentieth century, there prevailed an economy that was simple and undeveloped. During this period there was little need for a theory of administration because the enterprises were small and almost all the administrative functions were performed by the owner. The owner operated the enterprise, made all decisions for it, possessed absolute authority over its destiny, and was accountable to none. During the last two decades of the nineteenth century, some of the owner-managers were very forceful and dynamic. They stimulated unprecedented progress in the economy of the country and established a firm industrial base. Being prompted by the concepts of Social Darwinism and the Protestant ethic, they employed all the means, ethical and otherwise, to further their own interests. By their spectacular successes, they augmented the position of the owner-manager in power, prestige, and influence. By 1905, they faded away because of death, retirement, public opinion, and the anti-trust action.

Early in the twentieth century the economy advanced and became more complex. The corporate form of business enterprises began to emerge with capital requirements often exceeding the resources of the individual entrepreneur and thereby rendering the public sale of stock inevitable. The increasing size and complexity of corporate enterprises necessitated the separation of ownership from administration. Thus, a new type of business administrators appeared who operated and controlled the enterprises which they did not own. While they were interested in the prosperity of the enterprises they administered, they were also keen in accumulating personal wealth by using the resources of the enterprises. They were unscrupulous about using others' capital and their sole objective was quick profit. They contributed to the pace of the economy, but their influence waned after 1930 as a result of loss of public confidence in them.

It was during this period that the "scientific management" movement started and exerted a forceful influence on industry. "Scientific management" was an intellectual approach to the practice of administration. It sought to eliminate waste and inefficiency in industry. "The conceptual framework of scientific management, based on Taylor's principles, was: (a) Science, not rule of thumb; (b) harmony, not discord; (c) cooperation, not individualism; (d) maximum output in place of restricted output; and (e) the development of each man to his greatest efficiency and prosperity." The "scientific management" represented the *first* stage in administrative thought. It advanced concepts that could be identified, taught, learned, and practiced, and dealt a severe blow to the position of craftsmanship.

During the 1930's, the *second* stage in administrative thought emerged which may be labeled as "organization and system" stage. An organization was established for the enterprise to serve as a mechanism, and a system of operating and control procedures was instituted to facilitate the workflow. "Scientific management" methods continued to be employed to eliminate waste and inefficiency in operations. Different connotations came to be attached to the terms "administration" and "management." "Administration" represented the ownership point of view and performed the functions of setting goals, formulating policies, establishing organization, and exercising general control for the enterprise. "Management," on the other hand, was responsible for the performance of work within the enterprise.

It was during this period that the professional or career administrators made their appearance; they have been dominant since. The professional administrators neither own the enterprises they operate, nor do they use their resources for their personal interests. They serve as trustees of other people's money, make efficient use of human and material resources for the enterprise, have a sense of responsibility to the investors, employees, consumers, and the public, and are paid for their services. The corporate form of enterprise with a team of administrators has almost replaced the one-man-management enterprise.

During the 1940's, the administrative thought passed into the *third* stage of its evolution, which is designated as "administrative process" stage and which is in vogue today. This approach considered administration as a process rather than an event or a set of procedures and techniques. Scholars endeavored to identify the administrative process, refine it, and analyze it into subprocesses. Further professionalization of administration led to the elimination of the distinction between the terms "administration" and "management," which are now interchangeable. It is interesting to note that the "administrative process" stage in administrative thought evolved in England, France, and the United States independently about the same time and under similar conditions.

Administrative process as a conceptual framework is a composite of a number of subprocesses which are interrelated and interdependent and are usually, but not necessarily, carried out simultaneously and continuously for the attainment of enterprise objectives. The subprocesses are: planning, organizing, staffing, directing, and controlling. In addition, there are two more subprocesses—decision-making and coordinating—which are different from the preceding ones in that they do not fall on the same continuum but are inherent in each one of them. Their pervasive character manifests itself in the fact that regardless of what the administrator does, he essentially makes decisions and seeks to establish and maintain coordination. Some authorities subsume them under other subprocesses, but their cruciality warrants a separate treatment of them on the basis of equality. Further, the administrator would not be able to carry out the subprocesses effectively unless he is assisted by the authority of his position and the communication system of the enterprise. Therefore, authority and communication may be considered as indispensable tools of administration and inalienable elements of the administrative process. Differences of opinion exist with respect to the classification and the nomenclature of the subprocesses, but the concept of administration as a process seems to have met general agreement.

Planning

Planning means determining what shall be done. It comprises a wide range of activities including investigating, forecasting, setting objectives, formulating policies, developing programs, and deciding procedures. These activities need to be carried on for the total enterprise as well as its various segments. Generally speaking, planning consumes more time of executives at the higher levels than it does at the lower levels of the organizational structure, and planning at the higher levels acts as a constraint to all the activities of the enterprise.

Organizing

Organizing means dividing the work of the enterprise into a number of activities, grouping them in a meaningful way, and determining their assignment to employees. In order to obtain coordinated effort, it involves tying them together vertically through delegation of authority and responsibility, and binding them together horizontally through certain administrative devices. This would result in an organizational structure indicating the arrangement of all the activities to be performed, and depicting the authority relationships within the enterprise.

Staffing

It is the responsibility of administration to see that the human and material resources are made available in quantity, quality, and variety appropriate for attaining the enterprise goals. It means procurement of personnel according to the organizational structure and the provision of material resources which they will need to work with in the discharge of their responsibilities. However, administration basically deals with people and seeks to achieve the enterprise goals through them. Thus, people are the subject of administration and not material resources. Therefore, administration's primary responsibility is to ensure continued supply of manpower, that is, staffing, which includes selection, training, evaluation, promotion, compensation, and separation of employees.

Directing

Directing means guiding the activities of the subordinates to predetermined goals. In directing, the administrator would use such devices as command, suggestion, request, instructions, coaching, reward, penalty, and others. Directing subsumes motivating and supervising of the subordinates as well.

Controlling

Controlling involves measuring performance against the plan, ascertaining if there exists any discrepancy, and adopting corrective measures to ensure the realization of predetermined objectives. Controlling also includes innovating which means devising ways to bring about improvement in the setting of goals and their attainment.

Decision-making

Decision-making means selecting a course of action from a number of alternatives. Decision-making pervades the entire administration because, essentially, the administrator makes a series of decisions in his application of the administrative process to the enterprise. Decision-making permeates all parts of the enterprise and deals with every possible subject. Some authorities treat decision-making under planning, which gives the impression that decision-making is part of planning only. However, decision-making can be perceived intertwined equally intimately with other subprocesses as well.

Coordinating

Coordinating implies synchronizing individual and group efforts for the harmonious operation of the enterprise. Coordinated activities are essential for the attainment of enterprise goals. Some authorities do not consider coordination as a separate subprocess of administration. They maintain that coordination is the essence of administration and that each of the administrative subprocesses is an exercise in coordination. However, although it may be difficult to conceive of coordination as a distinct subprocess, or it may appear highly plausible that coordination will accrue from the exercise of other administrative subprocesses, it is unrealistic to assume that it will obtain without assiduously striving for it. The fact that coordination inheres in all the administrative subprocesses is a vindication of its pervasiveness and a manifestation of its indispensability.

No administrator can succeed in the exercise of the administrative process necessary for materializing the goals of the enterprise unless he has the necessary authority vested in him and a system of communication available to him. Without authority and communication, organized activity can neither be initiated nor sustained, and the group would disintegrate into an aggregate. Thus, authority and communication may be viewed as tools the administrator needs to work with to accomplish his tasks.

Authority

Administrative authority is the power of the superordinate to require the subordinate to act in consonance with the achievement of the enterprise goals. Administrative authority entitles the superordinate to make decisions within the limits of his authority and to see that they are implemented. The concept of administrative authority includes compliance on the part of the subordinate. This compliance, however, can be secured in a number of ways: through request, suggestion, persuasion, command, coercion, or sanction. The present trend is toward increased use of request, suggestion, and persuasion, but they are always fortified with authority, should the subordinate find them unacceptable. Administrative authority also carries with it commensurate administrative responsibility as a corollary lest it might degenerate into a license.

Communication

Communication is a means through which the administrator conveys his requests, suggestions, instructions, or commands to his subordinates for their action, and receives suggestions, grievances, and complaints from them for his consideration and action. The channels of communication—upward, downward, or sideways—provide a network of communication connecting all the members of an enterprise, and constitute a system which is co-extensive with the size of the enterprise. The communication system, however, would not be deemed adequate unless it also links the enterprise with the external world. Efficient communication facilitates the dissemination of ideas, acceptance of policies, securing of cooperation, and the attaining of enterprise goals. Communication sustains the organizational structure of the enterprise and renders the operation of the administrative process feasible. The administrator has a wide variety of media and techniques to choose from to communicate with his subordinates.

The Contributions of the Administrative Process School of Thought

The administrative process school of thought has dominated the scene for almost three decades and its impact is discernible in the writings of the scholars and the administrative behavior of the practitioners. It has made significant contributions to the theory and practice of administration, some of which are as follows:

1. The process school of thought has provided the foundation for present day education in administration. Henri Fayol first presented his concepts in 1916 in France; Oliver Sheldon, in 1923 in England; and Ralph C. Davis, in 1935 in the United States. There is a striking similarity among the ideas of these scholars although they developed them independently, being unaware of the contributions of the others. The concepts of these scholars and their successors form the core of the administrative process school of thought and the nucleus of the discipline of administration.
2. The process school of thought considers administration as a process rather than an event or a cluster of techniques, and its concepts are being utilized by all types of enterprises, public or private, large or small, in their operation. Although some concepts from other schools

of thought have now been incorporated in the theory of administration, it can not be denied that the concepts from the process school of thought, by far, constitute the bulk and are difficult to replace. The successful operation of huge industrial complexes, continental governments, and intercontinental enterprises may, in a substantial measure, be attributed to the application of the concepts of the administrative process school of thought.

3. The process school of thought has furnished a conceptual framework for the administration of enterprises. It has contributed to the development of administration as a separate and distinct discipline that can be studied, taught, learned, and practiced. Thus, it has refuted the claim of charismatic leadership to indispensability for the administration of enterprises.
4. The process school of thought has led scholars to think of administration in terms of objectives, processes, and guiding principles instead of descriptions of procedures, techniques, and methods. Thus, it enables the administrator to change the varied types of enterprises without any loss in efficiency.
5. The process school of thought enables administration to be operative for the total enterprise or any functional part of it. Formerly, only certain activities of the enterprise were considered to fall within the purview of administration—for example, production and personnel in the case of business administration—but the administrative process approach encompasses all the activities of the enterprise.
6. The process school of thought has provided a conceptual framework of administration which is inclusive, understandable, and time-proven. The concepts of this school of thought are the outcome of mature judgment of scholars and practitioners. Some of them have been analyzed, modified, and improved upon by the later scholars. The process school is at present firmly established as the third stage in the evolution of the administrative thought.

The Weaknesses of the Administrative Process School of Thought

The administrative process school of thought has lately been subjected to severe criticism. Some critics have suggested drastic revision of it, while others have recommended its complete abandonment. The following are pointed out as its notable weaknesses:

1. One of the problems that constantly puzzle the administrators is how to secure maximum contribution of efforts from the employees toward the attainment of enterprise goals. The process school of thought recommends motivational methods based on the concept of economic

man. Research in organizational behavior has demonstrated the inadequacy of these measures as motivating devices because man does not always respond to economic stimuli. The social codes, conventions, and traditions prevalent within the enterprise tend to encourage conformity among members even at the cost of personal sacrifice. Factors like varied preference scales of values, taxation, job security, technological advance, and unionization of labor render the problem of employee motivation increasingly complex. Thus, the administrative process conceptual framework fails to furnish satisfactory answers to problems inherent in the proper ways and means to provide for necessary employee motivation.

2. The process school of thought requires the administrator to seek the attainment of enterprise goals with maximum efficiency and at minimum cost. Because of its preoccupation with efficiency and elimination of waste, the administration often forgets its real purpose of service and becomes an end in itself. In business enterprises, it particularly feels obligated to protect the interests of the investors only and has been oblivious of the interests of employees, consumers, and the general public. The conceptual framework of the process school of thought does not include such concepts as human relations, public relations, and employee satisfaction. This provides an opportune ground for the clashes of interests which sporadically explode into conflicts and strife in enterprises.
3. The process school of thought has treated labor as a commodity. This old commodity concept of labor is incompatible with the present or future values in our society. Labor can no longer be slighted as an inert, passive, and docile "commodity"; it is a vigorous, aggressive, and paralyzing force to be reckoned with. Labor will have to be viewed as an invaluable asset, the intelligent use of which is indispensable for the attainment of the enterprise goals. This changed concept of labor would necessitate modification in the conceptual framework of the process school of thought.
4. The process school of thought utilizes the concepts of the Protestant ethic and Social Darwinism which have stimulated the growth of the economy but which also have provided justification for the exploitation of the many in the interest of the few. However, the emergence of the egalitarian society with its concepts of equality, liberty, and justice has challenged the concepts of the old social order. Administration can not continue to operate in a world of its own creation, and, if it wants to be effective, it has no alternative but to readjust its conceptual framework to make it consistent with the realities of the changing society.
5. Being efficiency oriented, the process school of thought is meticulous

in planning, rigorous in execution, and exact in evaluation, all geared to the attainment of the predetermined enterprise goals. Such an administration is not likely to provide an opportunity for the exercise of initiative, creativity, and discretion on the part of the employees because they are required to coordinate their efforts according to the predetermined plan. Under the circumstances, the individual is reduced to the level of a mechanical gadget—passive, subservient, and dependent—and is debarred from making full contribution of his total potentialities. Further, since the administration is passionately devoted to the attainment of the enterprise goals, the satisfactions and needs of the employees are likely to go unheeded, which may result in the creation of a dissatisfied, disgruntled, and revengeful work force, and which may cause bitterness, suspicion, and distrust between them and the administration. The administrative process conceptual framework needs to be modified so that the individual worker is viewed as a human being with self-esteem, dignity, and pride, and not just a cog in the wheel.

PROSPECTS FOR THE FUTURE

Dissatisfaction with the weaknesses of the administrative process school of thought has impelled scholars to look for a theory of administration in other directions. The outcome of their intensive search has been the appearance of a number of parallel schools of thought, referred to earlier, each one of which claims to offer an acceptable and workable theory of administration. These schools of thought are the fruits of the labor of scholars engaged in diverse, but related, disciplines—psychology, sociology, anthropology, mathematics, and others. That these schools of thought, in themselves, possess the potentiality of dislodging or replacing the administrative process school of thought is beyond the range of probability, because they suffer from a number of serious limitations, too difficult to surmount. Therefore, some kind of synthesis in which the process school of thought would incorporate the needed and useful concepts from other schools of thought to eradicate its deficiencies and to expand its scope so as to make it inclusive portends the direction for the development of a new theory of administration. That a beginning has been made on these lines is evidenced by the inclusion of a number of concepts—e.g., employee satisfaction, public relations, decision-making—within the conceptual framework of the process school of thought. The eclectic approach, with the process school of thought as a core, capable of dealing with all the problems of an enterprise may very well mark the *fourth* stage in the process of evolution of the administrative thought.

THE CONTINGENCY THEORY OF MANAGEMENT: A PATH OUT OF THE JUNGLE*

Fred Luthans

Management theory has taken divergent paths in recent years. The author discusses each of these as well as the movement to unify existing schools of thought. The process approach, traditional and classical, has been supplanted by the quantitative, the behavioral, and the systems approaches. The author defines these and explains their role in management theory and their function in actual practice. Singly, none of these theories can be applied to every organization and management problem, and currently a theory is emerging that can be used to draw the disparate elements together. This new approach is the contingency theory of management, which can be applied situationally.

Over a decade ago Harold Koontz wrote about the existing management theory jungle in which he identified six different theoretical schools of thought.[1] Although Koontz wrote the article to defend the process approach, his efforts have turned out to be a losing battle. The traditional management process has failed to unify management theory.

Today a jungle of management theories still exists, but there are some clearly identifiable paths that seem to be leading out of the jungle. The purpose of this article is to identify the paths and trace them through the jungle and beyond. The figure accompanying this article can be used as a guide to the discussion; it shows that the path leading up to the current jungle was the process approach. Other names applied to this path were classical, traditional, universal, operational, and functional.

The starting point for this process approach can be traced to the work of Henri Fayol. In 1916, he identified the universal functions of management as planning, organizing, commanding, coordinating, and controlling. He also described some universal principles of management such as unity of command and equal authority and responsibility. Unfortunately, Fayol's work on the functions and principles of management did not become part of the mainstream of management theory in this country until the 1950s. Since that time, there have been many

---

* Reprinted with permission of author and publisher from *Business Horizons*, Vol. 16, No. 3 (June 1973), pp. 67–72. Copyright 1973 by the Foundation for the School of Business at Indiana University. Reprinted by permission.

other process theorists, but they have not added much to Fayol's original conception of management theory.[2]

Much of the terminology has been changed; for example, Fayol's commanding is now known as directing or leading. Also the meanings of Fayol's functions have become broader; for example, planning now incorporates decision making, and directing incorporates communication, motivation, and leadership. The principles have also changed in terminology and number. Yet, despite these changes, the universality assumption is still made, and the process approach as a theoretical base for management remains basically the same as that given by Fayol over fifty years ago.

The process approach has undoubtedly had some unjustifiable criticism over the years. However, it is also true that it was not strong enough to weather the storm of protest in recent years. This approach became overgrown and entangled by other theoretical approaches. By 1960 the process path had been completely overrun, and two separate paths emerged in opposite directions. These new paths became known as the quantitative and behavioral approaches to management.

THE NEW PATHS

Quantitative Approach

The quantitative approach has its roots in the scientific management movement that actually predates the process approach. However, as a major thrust in management theory, the quantitative approach really got under way about 1960. This new approach made a clean break from the traditional process orientation of management.

During the 1960s the quantitative approach was characterized by the techniques of operations research. Various mathematical models were developed to solve decisional problems. However, it soon became apparent that, although OR techniques were effective tools for management decision making, this approach fell short of providing a theoretical base for management as a whole.

Starting in about 1970, the quantitative approach turned away from emphasis on narrow operations research techniques toward a broader perspective of management science. The management science approach incorporates quantitative decision techniques and model building as in the OR approach, but it also incorporates computerized information systems and operations management. This latter emphasis in the quantitative approach marked the return toward a more broadly based management theory.

Behavioral Approach

At about the same time the quantitative approach broke off from the process base, the behavioral approach struck out on its own. At first the behavioral path was characterized by human relations. Simplistic assumptions were made about human beings, and equally simplistic solutions to behavioral problems were offered. The human relations movement in the 1960s searched for ways to improve morale, which was assumed would lead to increases in productivity. This approach certainly did no harm, but it also produced few, if any, results.

Around 1970, about the same time the quantitative approach moved from emphasis on narrow operations research to a broad management

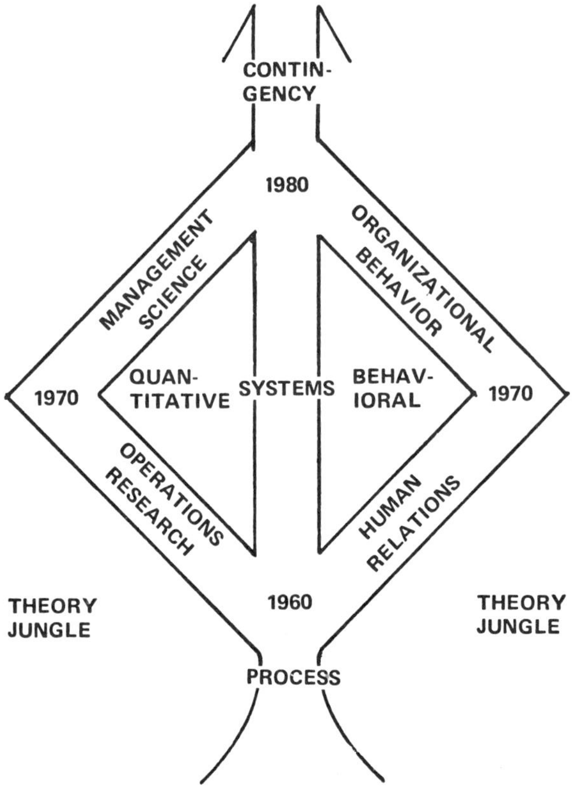

New Directions in Management Theory

science perspective, the behavioral approach had a parallel development. This path veered toward a more broadly based organizational behavior approach, and now relies heavily on the behavioral sciences and makes more complex assumptions. More direct attention is devoted to organization theory and organization development. Organizational behavior is the result of the interaction between the human being and the formal organization.

Systems Approach

While the quantitative and behavioral approaches were going their separate ways, a new trend appeared—the systems approach. During the 1960s to the present, it took up where the process approach left off in unifying management theory.

As a specific, theoretical approach, systems can be traced back to the natural and physical sciences nearly a quarter of a century ago. The application to management has been more recent. The systems approach —physical, biological, or managerial—stresses the interrelatedness and interdependency of the parts to the whole. Systems has served as a magnet to attract the quantitative and behavioral approaches to management.

At the present time, both the management science and organizational behavior detours are heading back toward the main path of systems. In management science, the new emphasis on computer applications and operations management techniques are systems based. The same holds true for organizational behavior. The formal organization is viewed as a system consisting of structure, processes, and technology, and the human being is conceived of as a system containing a biological-physiological structure, psychological processes, and a personality.[3]

Whether systems will actually unify the quantitative and behavioral approaches to management only time will tell. To date, the quantitative, behavioral, and systems approaches are clear but distinctly separate paths through the jungle. However, as indicated by the figure, both the behavioral and quantitative paths are headed toward the systems path. If the three approaches do come together in the next ten years, then the results may be something entirely different. This something that is different from the sum of the parts is referred to in the figure as the contingency theory of management.

CONTINGENCY THEORY

The beginning of a path called contingency or sometimes situational is just starting to emerge.[4] The figure indicates that by 1980 this path may be the one that leads management out of the existing jungle of theories. The pressure leading to a contingency theory has largely come from people who are actually practicing management.

For the past fifteen years, scholars, consultants, and practicing managers have attempted to apply either quantitative or behavioral approaches, depending on their orientation, to all situations. The performance results of this universalist assumption were generally disappointing. Certain quantitative approaches worked in some situations with some types of problems but not in others. The same was true for behavioral approaches. For example, job enrichment seemed to work well with skilled technicians but not unskilled machine operators.[5]

Two of the difficulties encountered in practice were that the quantitative people could not overcome behavioral problems and the behavioral people could not overcome operations problems adaptable to quantitative solutions. In the 1970s it is becoming more and more apparent that neither the quantitative nor behavioral approaches have all the answers for all situations.

Many of today's management theorists believe that a systems-based theory can solve the quantitative/behavioral dilemma. The December 1972 issue of the *Academy of Management Journal* was entirely devoted to general systems theory (GST) applied to management. The authors weighed the pros and cons of whether GST can unify management. The majority concluded that the systems approach is appealing and has a great deal of future potential, but is as yet incomplete. The open, as opposed to closed, systems view is able to cope better with the increased complexity and environmental influence facing today's managers. Systems concepts such as entropy (a system will become disorganized over time) and equifinality (a system can reach the same final state from different paths of development) are quite applicable to the present managerial situation.

Despite the advances made in general systems development and the trend for both the quantitative and behavioral approaches to move toward a systems base, a contingency path seems better suited to lead management out of the present theory jungle. Kast and Rosenzweig, who are closely associated with the systems approach, support this view, at least for the present. They call for a contingency approach, a midrange concept that falls somewhere between "simplistic, specific principles" and "complex, vague notions."

The contingency approach "recognizes the complexity involved in managing modern organizations but uses patterns of relationships and/or configurations of subsystems in order to facilitate improved practice."[6] Important breakthroughs in various subsystems of management (organization design, leadership, behavior change, and operations) have already demonstrated the value of the contingency approach.

CURRENT CONTINGENCY APPROACHES

Pigors and Myers have been associated with a situational approach to personnel management for the past twenty-five years. However, the work of Joan Woodward in the 1950s marks the beginning of a situational approach to organization and to management in general. She clearly showed in the British companies studied that organization structure and human relationships were largely a function of the existing technological situation. Armed with this and supporting follow-up evidence, some organizational theorists such as Lawrence and Lorsch began to call for contingency models of organizational structure.[7]

Organization Designs

The contingency approach to organization design starts with the premise that there is no single design that is the best for all situations. The classical approach was to say that a bureaucratic design would lead to maximum efficiency under any circumstances. The neoclassical theorists pushed decentralization for all conditions. It is inferred that even the modern free-form systems and matrix designs have universal applicability. In practice, the classical, neoclassical, or modern structural designs did not hold up under all situations.

For example, bureaucracy was not able to cope with a highly dynamic situation; decentralization did not work well in a highly cybernated situation; and the free-form, matrix designs were not adaptable to a situation demanding cutbacks and stability. Even Warren Bennis, who has been a leading advocate of discarding classical, bureaucratically organized structures and replacing them with modern free-form, behaviorally oriented structures, has recently retrenched. Ironically, because of his actual experience as a practitioner, he now admits that bureaucratic structures may be appropriate in certain situations.[8]

The contingency designs are conditional in nature. The bureaucracy may work best in a stable situation and the free form in a dynamic situation. Technology, economic and social conditions, and human resources are some of the variables that must be considered in a contingent organization design.

Model of Leadership

More has probably been written about leadership than any other single topic. Although all this attention has been devoted to it, for years research was not able to come up with any concrete results. Most often the leader and his traits were examined. Recently, the work of Fred

Fiedler, who emphasizes the importance that the situation has in leadership effectiveness, has produced a significant breakthrough. Based on years of empirical research, Fiedler was able to develop a contingency model of leadership effectiveness.

In simple terms, the model states that a task-directed leader is most effective in very favorable and very unfavorable situations, but that a human relations-oriented leader is most effective in moderately favorable and moderately unfavorable situations.[9] Of special interest, however, is his ability to classify situations according to the three dimensions of position power, acceptance by subordinates, and task definition. This type of classification is the necessary goal of any contingency approach.

Model of Behavioral Change

Although not generally recognized in a managerial context, the contingency approach has been widely applied to behavioral change in mental health and education. Based on the principles of operant conditioning, this approach assumes that behavior depends on its consequences. Therefore, to change a person's behavior, he must be able to perceive a contingent relationship between his behavior and the consequence of that behavior. This contingent relationship, once established, will affect the frequency of subsequent behavior.

The author is currently directing a major field research program that is using this contingency concept. The approach is called Organizational Behavior Modification (O.B. Mod.). It can be used to train industrial supervisors through a process method of instruction to be contingency managers of their workers. Preliminary results of this program are very encouraging.[10] The study has demonstrated that when first-line supervisors apply O.B. Mod. techniques to their subordinates, desirable job behaviors leading to improved performance can be accelerated through the use of reinforcement and undesirable behaviors can be decelerated through the use of punishment.

However, the key to the success of the approach depends upon the worker's ability to perceive the contingency that if he behaves a certain way, then his behavior will result in a certain consequence. The if-then contingency pattern used in O.B. Mod. is similar to the contingency approaches used in organizational design and leadership style.

Approaches in the Quantitative Area

Although the examples so far are primarily drawn from organizational behavior, the quantitative areas have also begun to use contingency approaches. Operations research itself is actually based on a situational premise. The starting point in developing any OR model is to account for the situational givens. However, as OR was applied through the years this premise was often abused. Questionable initial assumptions which were often totally divorced from reality were cranked into OR models. However, in recent years with the development of a broader management science approach, more attention is being given to situational factors. Recent books in the management science area have begun to use a situational framework. For example, Stanley Young states that:

> We must know under what conditions it is advisable to move from Linear Programming to rule of thumb and then back to Linear Programming. There is an over-concern with single decision rule, and we must learn how to use different combinations of rules under a variety of operating conditions.[11]

This article suggests that a contingency approach may be the path out of the existing theoretical jungle in management. The process path was split by the behavioral and quantitative paths. However, neither of these approaches by itself seems capable of leading management out of the jungle. Currently, the systems path seems to be drawing them together toward a unified theoretical development, but by the time the juncture is reached in the future, something may emerge which differs from the sum of the parts. This outcome is predicted to be the contingency theory of management.

The successful contingency approaches in the behavioral and quantitative areas which are beginning to surface are evidence of the potential that a contingency theory may have for leading management out of the theory jungle. The overall goal of a contingency theory of management would be to match quantitative, behavioral, and systems approaches with appropriate situational factors.

Although this goal would be difficult to reach, the contingency theory could serve as an effective framework for development. Fiedler's work proves that it is possible. His contingency model could serve as a prototype. The challenge for the future is to develop a contingency theory for management as a whole.

NOTES

1. The six schools identified by Koontz were the management process, empirical, human behavior, social system, decision theory, and mathematical schools. Harold Koontz, *Academy of Management Journal* (December 1961), pp. 174–88.
2. Probably the most widely recognized standard bearers of the process

approach in modern times are Harold Koontz and Cyril O'Donnell, authors of *Principles of Management* (New York: McGraw-Hill Book Company, 1972). The book, which came out in 1955, is in its fifth edition.

3. Fred Luthans, *Organizational Behavior* (New York: McGraw-Hill Book Company, 1973).
4. For example see Robert J. Mockler, "Situational Theory of Management," *Harvard Business Review* (May–June 1971), pp. 146–55, and Fremont E. Kast and James E. Rosenzweig, *Contingency Views of Organization and Management* (Chicago: Science Research Associates, Inc., 1973).
5. William E. Reif and Fred Luthans, "Does Job Enrichment Really Pay Off?" *California Management Review* (Fall 1972), pp. 30–37.
6. Fremont E. Kast and James E. Rosenzweig, "General Systems Theory: Applications for Organization and Management," *Academy of Management Journal* (December 1972), p. 463.
7. Joan Woodward, *Industrial Organization* (London: Oxford University Press, 1965). Follow-up evidence from William L. Zwerman, *New Perspectives on Organization Theory* (Westport, Conn.: Greenwood Publishing Corporation, 1970). For examples of support for contingency models see Paul R. Lawrence and Jay W. Lorsch, "Differentiation and Integration in Complex Organizations," *Administrative Science Quarterly* (June 1967), pp. 1–47, and, more recently, Y. K. Shetty and Howard M. Carlisle, "A Contingency Model of Organization Design," *California Management Review* (Fall 1972), pp. 38–45.
8. Warren Bennis, "Who Sank the Yellow Submarine?" *Psychology Today* (November 1972), pp. 112–20.
9. Fred Fiedler, *A Theory of Leadership Effectiveness* (New York: McGraw-Hill Book Company, 1967).
10. Fred Luthans, Robert Ottemann, and David Lyman are currently in the process of writing the study in monograph form. Published results may be available in late 1973 or 1974.
11. Stanley D. Young, "Organization as a Total System," in Fred Luthans, ed., *Contemporary Readings in Organizational Behavior* (New York: McGraw-Hill Book Company, 1972), p. 109. For other examples see David W. Miller and Martin K. Starr, *Executive Decisions and Operations Research* (Englewood Cliffs, N.J.: Prentice-Hall, 1970) and Thomas R. Prince, *Information Systems for Management Planning and Control* (Homewood, Ill.: Richard D. Irwin, Inc., 1970).

ORGANIZATION THEORY AND POLITICAL THEORY*

Herbert Kaufman

If two men of similar talents, identical training, shared values, and common interests were to study the same phenomena it would not be at all remarkable if they approached the phenomena in the same way, described them in the same terms, employed the same logic in analyzing them, drew the same conclusions from them, and formulated the same theories about their causes.

If, however, two men of similar talents but of rather divergent training, professing differing objectives, and displaying varied (perhaps even conflicting) concerns were to pursue studies of phenomena each believed to be quite distinct from the other's field of inquiry, it would be most astounding if their findings and inferences should turn out to be closely parallel in many important respects, particularly if there were little evidence of communication between them.

That is why the parallels between political theory, probably the oldest of the social sciences, and organization theory, perhaps the newest such discipline, are so totally unexpected. If there is any conscious agreement between the two fields, it is on their separateness from each other: political theorists and organization theorists alike seem to take for granted the impossibility of encompassing within a single theoretical framework propositions about states—that is, the relation of governments to subjects, and the relations of governments to each other—and propositions about other forms of human association. In the literature on organization theory, one rarely finds references even to contemporary political theorists and almost never to those who wrote in the past. By the same token, political theorists rarely seem to find anything relevant to their interests in the work of students of organization. Measured by the acknowledged exchange of information between the disciplines, the gulf between them is wide and seldom bridged.

Perhaps such a gulf is inescapable. Political theorists draw heavily upon history, philosophy, and personal experience for their ideas and evidence; organization theorists rely heavily upon sociology, social psy-

---

* A paper delivered at the Annual Meeting of the American Political Science Association, New York City, September, 1963. I should like to acknowledge the patient criticism and instruction given me by my colleague, Professor Roger Masters, who saved me from many errors, misinterpretations, and oversights, and tried vainly to save me from those that remain in the text. Reprinted with permission of author and publisher from *American Political Science Review,* Vol. 58 (March 1964), pp. 5–14.

chology, economics, and, when possible, on controlled experimentation. Political theorists are frankly normative; organization theorists generally believe their work is value-free. Political theorists deal willingly with the intangible aspects of human associations, for it is difficult to measure the outputs of governments and governmental agencies; organization theorists are more at home with organizations producing tangible products and measuring their performance ultimately in terms of profit. The fields do seem to have quite different traditions, methods, goals, and subject-matters.

But all this merely makes the similarities in the problems they investigate and in their findings more surprising and intriguing.

I

For example, both organization theorists and political theorists encountered the same enigma: In order that the human systems may come into being and continue, men often have to do, at the behest of others, tasks that are unpleasant or even hazardous (such as working on assembly lines or going to war), and must refrain from doing what they would greatly enjoy (such as helping themselves to the property of others or saying whatever they please wherever and whenever the spirit moves them). What accounts for obedience and docility entailing such self-sacrifice, self-restraint, self-denial, without which neither states nor other associations could long survive?

Political philosophers and organization theorists have offered essentially the same range of explanations: the rationality of men and the conditioning of men's minds.[1]

Because men are rational, they can calculate what they would lose if everyone were to follow his own impulses and preferences without restraint. They can also see that collective action will be taken against individuals who disobey. Out of fear of the consequences, they submit. They can calculate, too, the advantages they may gain from organized life and activity. They can see that the gains usually outweigh the costs. Out of hope for the benefits, then, as well as out of fear, rational men yield to the wills of others.[2]

At the same time, according to many political and organization theorists, men obey because obedience to certain commands from certain sources is a conditioned reflex. Even in infancy, every individual is introduced to the exercise of authority; maturation is in many ways a process of learning when to obey, whom to command, and under what circumstances to do either. That is, from his social environment generally, and also by virtue of the deliberate drill and indoctrination to which he is subject, every man is prepared for his social roles. He comes to yield to others because he learns it is right and proper to do so, and he may even come to cherish his submission. The will to obey is implanted in him; depending on the discipline one draws upon for appropriate language, he is educated, indoctrinated, trained, socialized, acculturated, programmed, or brainwashed.[3]

Interestingly enough, political theorists have from the very beginning made more strenuous efforts to incorporate the non-rational (*i.e.,* the conditioned) elements of men's behavior into their hypotheses than have the organization theorists. For men are born into political systems, and the possibilities of withdrawal are much more limited. It is not clear that joining or remaining in a political system is really a matter of rational choice at all, except in isolated instances. Organization theorists, on the other hand, deal more extensively with associations that men presumably choose to enter and may leave at any time. To explain membership and all it entails, students of organization lean toward a rather literal application of social-contract theory and utilitarianism; many eighteenth- and nineteenth-century political philosophers, who employed these concepts as metaphors to aid in understanding the rational component of behavior, would find little in most modern organization theory with which to quarrel. And some organization theorists would doubtless be surprised to discover how many political philosophers in ancient and medieval times were aware there were social norms and group loyalties that a ruler dared not violate without risking extensive disobedience.

At any rate, more or less independently of each other, drawing in different ways on different bodies of experience, political theorists and organization theorists have dealt in very similar fashion with the obedience of man to man.

II

They have also dealt similarly with organizational structures for the achievement of coordination. For purposes of this discussion, coordination means ordering the direction, volume, and timing of flows of activities, goods, and services so that the functioning of one element in a system at least does not prevent or negate or hamper the functioning of other elements, and at best facilitates and assists the functioning of other elements. Coordination is not always a goal of system designers; the separation of powers, for example, encourages some contradictions and deadlocks in order to protect other values. But it is often among the principal values, and practically never is a matter of total indifference. And when political theorists and organization theorists discuss methods of promoting coordination, they end up in much the same positions.

Fundamentally, coordination is accomplished by two processes: central direction, which means that the activities of the elements of a system respond chiefly to cues and signals from some common source, and reciprocal relations, which means that the elements respond to cues and signals from each other. Every system employs some blend of the two processes. Moreover, the systems are not mutually exclusive; an increase in reliance on one does not necessarily produce a decrease in the other. On the contrary, effective central direction often permits a higher degree of reciprocal cueing, as in a well-trained platoon, and *vice versa*. Whatever the blend of modes of coordination and whatever the general level of coordination in any system, these may be explained in terms of the relative weight assigned to each of the two underlying processes.

Political theorists who believe men are inclined to take advantage of one another tend to stress central direction as the best means of coordinating them. Without an overriding central figure, according to them, any system breaks down in disorder, confusion, and internal warfare. Hobbes, of course, presented this argument in its purest, most logical form.[4] On the other side, philosophers who assume the interests and tendencies of men are harmonious emphasize the possibility and desirability of coordination through reciprocity, and regard central direction as an exploitative or disturbing factor in what would otherwise be a highly coordinated system distributing maximum satisfaction to all its members. The anarchists, both Marxist and non-Marxist, pushed this reasoning to its logical extreme.[5] It matters little for this discussion whether the extremists on both sides meant their doctrines to be taken literally or as analogies for the sake of clarity and vigor of statement. They bracketed the range of possibilities. In the history of political thought, not only the extremes, but virtually all conceivable intermediate positions, have at some time or other been advanced or defended.

During most of the short history of organization theory, few theorists seriously questioned the premise that central direction (expressed structurally as a hierarchy of authority because of the need of leaders to delegate formal powers and because of the assumed inability of men to supervise directly more than a small number of colleagues) is the primary method of achieving coordination; indeed, hierarchy and organization were sometimes treated as almost synonymous.[6] Yet very early some questioning voices were heard, particularly after experimental studies in the sociology of industry drew attention to the responsiveness of workers to cues and signals emanating from sources other than (and sometimes hostile to) the designated managers of the firms examined. Mary Parker Follett, a political scientist of Pluralist persuasion, became well known to students of organization for her advocacy of "power with rather than power over" and for her criticism of "the illusion of final responsibility."[7] Later on, Argyris[8] and Thompson and others[9] would search explicitly for a pattern of organization that is non-hierarchical. An electronics firm on the West Coast recently reorganized itself on what are alleged to be non-hierarchical lines.[10] It would be grossly inaccurate to equate these organizational analysts with the anarchists, but there can be no question that organization theory has begun to display an awareness of a range of positions on the central-reciprocal scale that political philosophers have explored extensively for centuries.

I do not intend to imply that political philosophy is somehow superior to organization theory, or that organization theory is a mere branch of the history of political thought. My object in pointing out similarities between their treatments of coordination is simply to demonstrate that these seemingly unrelated disciplines confront common problems in common ways.

III

Another such problem is the reconciliation of individual or other narrow objectives with the objectives of the collectivity. Political theorists discuss it in terms of special interests as against the general or public interest. Organization theorists speak of personal or subgroup goals *vis-à-vis* organizational goals. But the issues are the same.

In both fields, the dominant opinion seems to be that every collectivity is in some sense goal-seeking, or purposive. That is, there is some general interest or organizational goal shared or at least acknowledged by nearly all the participants in the system, and although the overarching purpose is accomplished by the labor of individuals, it is distinct from the goals or interests of individuals; rather, it is viewed as an attribute of the system as a whole. There is little agreement on the specifics of the general interest, and even a given commentator may switch from one to another interpretation as conditions change. (Implicitly, however, one goal can be discerned in every interpretation: the survival of the system.) Yet, although students of states and of organizations may never arrive at a consensus on exactly what the shared interests of human associations are, many of them tend to take it for granted that one exists for every human association.[11]

A substantial number of political theorists, on the other hand, have taken the view that virtually every definition of the public interest is but a reflection of the personal interests of the definer, and consequently, the only realistic way to understand the performance of a system is to construe its output (or its policies) as nothing more than the resultant of the interplay of many special interests. The representatives of each interest may invoke the symbol of the public interest as an honorific, perhaps even with sincere conviction that the actions they espouse *are* better for the system and all the members of the system, but what is actually decided and done is the product of negotiations and understandings among specialized groups and individuals.[12]

Among organization theorists, the counterpart to this point of view is seldom advanced even tacitly, let alone explicitly; it is distinctly a minority position. Barnard, however, comes close to it. Although he discusses organizational purposes at length, and attributes great importance to them, they are not central to his analysis. He defines formal organizations without referring to goals, and he describes them largely in terms of individual motivations and objectives coordinated with each other through an "economy of incentives." The "absolute test" of efficiency is survival of the organization. An organization is thus portrayed as a kind of marketplace in which each man pursues his own goals by offering a contribution in return for those inducements (selected from the range of inducements provided, consciously or unwittingly, by the system) that appeal to him. The enterprise is an arena in which each participant offers his wares and services in exchange for what he can get. From the elaborate network of agreements, accommodations, and behaviors come products, wages, salaries, profits, prices, dividends, interest, taxes, working conditions, and all the other outputs of a complex system. Managers, workers, suppliers, customers, stockholders, creditors, competitors, government regulators, consultants, academics, and others may all see different transcendent purposes in the undertaking, so that its ends are in a sense the sum of all the special purposes.[13] To this extent, this view resembles in many respects the view of the state espoused by the political theorists mentioned above. What is sometimes referred to as a collective purpose is merely the resultant of a constantly shifting adjustment among individual and subgroup purposes.

Over the relationship of private interests to the general interest, organization theorists and political theorists have divided into similar camps. Again, the resemblances between the fields are impressive.

IV

The foregoing illustrations do not exhaust the parallels between organization theory and political theory.[14] But they are probably sufficient to establish the point of departure for this discussion, namely, that striking similarities have developed in two disciplines that seem to be quite different in their interests and methods.

Why should this occur? Why should two fields of study with such discrepant premises and perspectives converge?

Perhaps it is because the discrepancies are, after all, merely the distinctions between different species of the same genus. When all is said and done, they both treat of phenomena that encompass vast areas, if not all, of human life. We are all members of at least several organizations, and organizations give characteristic content and general form to our lives. Moreover, states, governments, the branches and agencies of governments, political parties, and interest groups are organizations like other organizations even though they have their unique attributes. What aspect of civilized existence then lies outside the scope of organization theory?

At the same time, every organization is sometimes construed as a political system, with all the problems of leadership, policy formation, succession, strategy, rivalry, resistance, revolution, and influence that this implies.[15] If organizations are an all-embracing subject of inquiry, politics is an equally comprehensive theme. To be sure, organization theorists tend to avoid political institutions in searching for data, and political philosophers tend to concentrate on those institutions immediately associated with public governments. But they may end with strong similarities because they are both addressed to phenomena permeating the whole of human affairs. Fields that take so much for their province must have far more overlap than is immediately obvious.

Furthermore, they both start from normative bases. Political theorists were historically engaged in a quest for the ideal political system; organization theorists began by seeking "the one best way"—*i.e.,* the most efficient way—to organize production and distribution. There are probably some in both disciplines who still believe such ideal arrangements, superior to all alternatives under any conditions and at any time, are attainable; most contemporary theorists, I believe, now adopt a relativist position, holding that the definition of the ideal changes as circumstances change, and perhaps even that a wide variety of organizational and political patterns may satisfy equally well the requirements of any particular definition. At any rate, men in both fields set out to discover the "laws" or "principles" governing social behavior so as to formulate proposals for improvement consonant with the constraints imposed by reality. Sometimes they try to sharpen their thinking by reasoning from admittedly over-simplified hypotheses, such as man in a state of nature or completely rational man. Eventually, however, they complicate their models by adding variables that render the hypotheses better approximations of the real world. (Such variables are more often discovered by non-normative research of an historical or experimental kind than by intuition.) Conceivably, the fields may come to resemble each other because they have parallel normative underpinnings.

But the explanation of the resemblances may not lie in the character of the disciplines at all; perhaps it is to be found rather in the nature of the world the disciplines purport to describe. The convergence *could* result from the existence of such pronounced and persistent regularities in large-scale human associations that no matter which such associations one examines and what approach one adopts, the sum of the findings of each set of observers will inevitably be much the same as those of any other set. When all the blind men compare their notes, they *do* end up with a description of an elephant, and the description by each team of blind men will not differ materially from the description produced by any other team, because, after all, it *is* an elephant they are studying. The consensus of two relatively insulated fields, when the whole range of their content is reviewed, lends corroboration to the impression that our ideas about organizations and politics have a substantial degree of validity.

V

Whatever the explanation of the similarities between organization theory and political theory, one obvious implication of the similarities is that the two fields can probably learn a great deal from each other. In the literature on organizations, political theorists will find reports on experiments and rigorous logical analyses bearing heavily on the concerns of political philosophy. In the history of political thought, which may be regarded as a collection of descriptive models of social behavior or a series of tentative propositions about the ways men act in organized groups, organization theorists will find a rich store of ideas they seem to be toiling to reproduce independently.

But my purpose in writing this piece is not merely to labor the obvious point that scholars in two disciplines stand to gain by sharing their materials more extensively in the future than they have in the past. More important are the indications that theory in both areas is to a large extent imprisoned by the premises and perspectives and reasoning of an earlier day, trapped into recapitulating and refining familiar concepts instead of developing new approaches and assumptions that might free theory from the cycling loop into which it has fallen. Although there are important exceptions, it appears that much modern writing in both fields tends to retrace established paths instead of finding new ones. Those who are not conversant with the history of thought often devote their energies to rediscovering triumphantly old and even ancient ideas, and to reviving traditional controversies. Those who have mastered the history of thought often apply themselves to proving there is nothing new under the sun. Each for his own reasons ends up operating within confines identified with prior generations: Each for his own reasons fetters his imagination.

To be sure, the exceptions are notable. Some strikingly original recent approaches to the study of human behavior, such as computer simulation of individual thought processes and social situations, may well have dramatic consequences for the viewpoints and findings of the social sciences. By and large, however, it is the *scarcity* of unconventional ideas rather than the problems of choosing among them that impresses the observer. Even sophisticated methods of research and analysis, bound by the outlooks and assumptions of earlier times, add only a little to our knowledge and insight.

This is hardly surprising; we are all products of our heritage, and it is not easy to conceive of altogether new ways of looking at things, however urgent may be the need for novel ideas. That is why it is important to try not only to invent new concepts, but also to seek them out in our current environment by borrowing from seemingly unrelated disciplines, and by picking up the threads of inquiry previously explored and prematurely dropped. One such concept seems to me to hold particularly great promise of putting organization behavior in a perspective quite unlike the one from which we seem unable to escape, and thus to provide stimuli and generate perceptions which apparently lie beyond the scope of our ordinary frame of reference. I refer to what in its broadest terms may be described as the treatment of human organizations as a form of life rather than as an artifact designed, created, and directed exclusively by the human intellect.

Such a biological analogy in political theory was drawn in classical antiquity and occasionally in later periods of Western history,[16] and it has even appeared in the writings of one or two contemporary organization theorists.[17] But the logic of it has never been rigorously followed out in the light of modern knowledge and, perhaps even more pertinently, in the light of the growth and evolution of organizational forms in recent times. Currently out of fashion in political science, and in the social sciences generally,[18] this now neglected tradition strikes me as more likely to improve our understanding of human associations than it ever could before. And it probably requires a discipline as boldly inclusive, as young and therefore as flexible and open-minded, and as vigorous as organization theory, to dare to reopen this approach and to employ it successfully.

VI

Seen from this angle, what would the world of organizations look like? Probably crowded, continually changing, difficult to analyze, viscous. For compared to an individual organism, organizations do not display a notably high level of integration most of the time; the responsiveness of their components to each other is relatively slow and uncertain. Their boundaries are often loosely defined, easily changed, and permeable. Most organizations contain, are contained by, and overlap other organizations; they are unusual among the forms of life in that they can share constituent elements with each other. They interact with their surroundings, usually exchanging something (either acquired or produced) from inside their boundaries for something beyond their boundaries. Generally, there are subsets of elements within them that exercise greater influence over the other elements with respect to certain processes than the other elements exercise over these subsets; and some subsets interact extensively with the environment beyond the boundaries as well as with elements within the boundaries. There are reasons to suspect that organizations have a high rate of mortality, and though one can point to many individual cases of long-lived organizations, the number that disappear every year is probably staggering.[19]

Yet the number of human organizations in the world at any given moment is also probably enormous. Virtually every individual is a member of at least several organizations, and while this does not mean there are necessarily more organizations in the world than there are people, it indicates that the ratio of organizations to people is quite substantial. Consequently, with so many organizational claims on the resources at the disposal of human beings, including time and obedience, some organizations lose out in the competition for these resources. (In part, the shortage results from a highly unbalanced distribution of claims and resources. But it is also plausible that the number of organizations making claims on resources increases more rapidly than the volume of available resources—by a kind of Malthusian law—so that the possible ways of allocating resources are likely always to exceed the reservoir of resources available.) That is, as is true with other forms of life, organizations make upon the resources essential to their survival demands that tend to press beyond the limit of supply, and the demands are kept more or less in check by the demise of organizations or declines in the rate at which new ones form. It should be noted, incidentally, that from this standpoint, an employer, a veterans association, a trade union, a political party, a neighborhood civic group, a bowling club, a church, and a government agency, and other groups, though superficially unconnected, may all be in competition with one another, for they may all be rivals for the resources (again including the time and obedience) of the same persons.[20]

Under these circumstances, what determines which organizations will survive? One possible determinant is the deliberate strategy of organizations to adapt to conditions; those making the appropriate choices will continue. Much of organization theory, economic theory, and political theory is devoted to the analysis of this sort of rationality.

But it is also conceivable that the biologist's approach could be useful here. When conditions prove fatal to some members of a population while other members survive and even flourish, biologists tend to ascribe the good fortune of the survivors to chance variations in their make-up that protect or even favor them under prevailing conditions. May we not also postulate that in the world population of organizations—those comparatively poorly integrated, sluggish, fragile entities—random variations occur which may make no difference under one set of circumstances, but which may favor or impede some organizations when circumstances change? Admittedly, the calculated strategies may in the end turn out to *be* the critical factor; the biological analogy does not preclude this possibility. But it directs attention also to other factors that may be important, factors easily neglected if we concentrate exclusively on rationality.

For example, size may be more important in survival than anything an organization *does* in response to a challenge; all organizations of a greater than given size may endure even though they all respond differently, while smaller organizations may disappear no matter what they do. (By the same token, of course, a change of conditions may wipe out the giants and multiply the pygmies.) Or a substantial measure of self-containment may characterize all the organizations that persist after a drastic modification of the environment (though another environmental shift may favor organizations highly dependent on outside sources). Or in one context, all surviving organizations may exhibit extreme centralization; in another, only the decentralized ones may remain. Sometimes highly specialized organizations may be the only ones to come through; at other times, only diversified ones may weather a new situation. Those attributes an organization happens to have when changes occur may be more significant than the course of action its leaders elect to pursue; indeed, the paths of action themselves may be determined as much by organizational characteristics as by human intellect.

Now, it is true that an organization can take steps to increase or decrease its size or its self-containment or its centralization or its specialization; these do not lie beyond the scope of manipulation. Thus, organizational *characteristics* as well as organizational *policies* are subject to rational adjustment. Nevertheless, at any given time, any population of organizations will include exceedingly diverse members. For there will be many different judgments as to what adjustments will be advantageous, what adjustments dysfunctional; all organizations will not estimate the future in the same way, and even those that do will differ about the appropriate preparations for that future. Moreover, fortuitous elements, such as personality, the unique history of an organization, tradition, acts of nature, and unplanned internal developments, will produce different consequences in different organizations. So even if all relevant organizational attributes could be rationally controlled, organizations would vary, and every environmental change would benefit some organizations and injure others. But there is no obvious reason to assume that all such attributes are rationally planned; many seem quite accidental, and the selective process is thus intensified.

But human organizations enjoy an advantage that their biological counterparts do not: they have the capacity, at least theoretically, to observe and imitate their more successful fellow-organizations. Logically, then, when conditions change, can they not wait to see the effects and follow the lead of the flourishing ones? In this way, it would seem, most could survive any challenge. In fact, however, organizations can rarely adjust very swiftly. To maintain flexibility for speedy transformation may require the sacrifice of other advantages. Furthermore, every organization contains equilibrium-maintaining mechanisms that resist and moderate change; stability cannot be thrown to the winds. Most organizations therefore cannot alter themselves instantaneously, and differences among them will remain even after the initial impact of environmental changes has indicated which forms are favored.

For these reasons, then, organizational forms may play no less a part in organizational survival than do organizational policies, and we may anticipate that environmental variations will always wipe out some organizations and improve the fortunes of others. A kind of "natural selection" is taking place, in other words, an evolutionary process going on continuously.

Even if this could be demonstrated, what difference would it make? What contribution could it make to the development of organization theory? Where does it lead?

Since we have hardly explored the process, it would be rash to venture a prediction. We can only hope it may prove as useful to the study of organizations as it did to the study of biology. And we can only speculate on what the nature of its utility might be. For example, it might stimulate comparisons of long-lived organizations that give us a better understanding of their longevity. It might facilitate evaluation of allegedly consistent and widespread trends toward specific patterns of organization, and explanation of those trends that do in fact occur.[21] It could encourage a more sophisticated typology of organizations than any we now have, and a better catalogue of relevant environmental conditions and their effects on each category. It might even improve our assessment of organizational survival strategies. But while no one can say exactly what will be uncovered by research based on a theory of organizational evolution, it is a line of inquiry, not well investigated up to now, that has a potential for illuminating regularities hitherto unperceived, or at least unarticulated, in the social sciences. And organization theorists are in the best position to conduct the inquiry because they do not limit themselves to any particular type or aspect of organization.

VII

I am not here proposing a simple return to Social Darwinism—which, in fact, is an egregious misnomer, since the doctrines thus alluded to have little to do with principles of natural selection described by Darwin and other biologists. Nor do I intend to suggest that organizations should be regarded as identical with organisms; on the contrary, it is their unique character as life-forms that I would emphasize. Nor, finally, do I consider this approach a substitute for others; if it has any value, it will be as an addition to our other instruments of analysis, not as a replacement for them. I am arguing only that the possibilities of employing this method rigorously have not been fully realized, and that it seems especially applicable to the study of organizational behavior.

The biological analogy is disturbing to many modern political theorists and organization theorists because it appears to many of them to downgrade human beings, to deny the importance of the gift of thought, to reduce persons to the level of social insects or of cells in a living system. Even if this were the case, it would not justify refusal to consider this frame of reference. When the people of the Western world were compelled by the findings of modern astronomers to abandon the belief that they were at the center of the universe (and thus to recognize what many of the ancients knew), when they were taught by modern biology that they are part of nature (which was also the ancient view), and when they were reminded by modern psychologists that they are something less than wholly rational creatures, the demotions were painful and met with resistance. Yet they added to man's intellectual stature by giving him a fuller and more accurate picture of the world in which he lives, and liberated him from flattering myths and misconceptions, in many ways more degrading than the truth. Men may conceivably become more godlike by accepting their own limitations than by refusing to envisage them at all. There can be excesses in individual-centered philosophies as well as in community-centered doctrines.

But the lesson from early political philosophy is that it is by no means necessary to deny the distinctively human qualities of mankind in order to treat human associations as natural phenomena. On the contrary, the classical opinion was that men fulfilled their potentialities as human beings *only* in the associations as natural to them as the air they breathe. For organization theorists to regard organizations as living forms, then, is not to equate human society with an anthill and people with ants. It may simply be a path to observations and to speculative and empirical inquiries to which our prevailing biases and preoccupations now blind us.

NOTES

1. A third explanation, offered initially by political philosophers of classical antiquity, was that some men are by nature followers and others are by nature rulers. The followers obey because it is their nature to do so, just as leaders command because that is *their* nature. This argument has few defenders among contemporary political theorists, and it is seldom articulated by organization theorists. But one may wonder whether the batteries of personality and aptitude and intelligence tests used for selecting executives do not rest ultimately on the assumption that there are "natural" leaders who should be identified, separated from the "naturally" subservient mass, and elevated to their "natural" managerial roles.
2. This reasoning underlies most social-contract philosophies of the origins of civil and political society. The emphasis was placed in some cases on escape from the risks and uncertainties of anarchy (as in Hobbes and Locke), in others on ascension to a higher, richer, distinctively human and civilized life (as in Rousseau, whose logic, in turn, parallels that of classical political theory). The hypothesized reasoning in men's decisions to form or join groups in which they must then submit to others is not far removed from the analysis by J. G. March and H. A. Simon, *Organizations* (New York, 1957), of individual calculations regarding "the decision to participate" in organizations (ch. 4). See also Simon's assertion that a distinctive feature of organization theory is its treatment of joining an organiza-

tion as an "all-or-none choice of participation or non-participation," in *Models of Man* (New York, 1957), p. 74 and chs. 10 and 11.

Organization theorists and most political philosophers exhibit little confidence in fear as a long-range mode of eliciting obedience. But for a few political theorists (Hobbes, for example), and for more than a few rulers and managers, it is the cornerstone of theory and practice.

3. Many political theorists recognized this. For example, according to H. V. Jaffa ["Aristotle," in L. Strauss and J. Cropsey, eds., *History of Political Philosophy* (Chicago, 1963), p. 75], Aristotle held that "Trained obedience, as distinct from brute direction, is the characteristic of being ruled politically or royally." Hume, says R. S. Hill ("David Hume," *ibid.,* pp. 511–12), considered that "The main support of the rule of the few over the many . . . is the opinion that those in authority have a right to that authority. This opinion is usually the fruit of time and habit. Custom is the great guide of human life; most men never think of inquiring into the reasons for the authority of the form of government to which they have become habituated." Rousseau (see A. Bloom, "Jean-Jacques Rousseau," *ibid.,* pp. 527, 531) believed "the manners of society are of as much or more concern than the institutions of government because manners underlie institutions and give them their force," and he saw an advantage in the ancient city "because it is small enough . . . for citizens to share a common heritage and a common way, because the particular wills can more easily be submerged in custom, and because the statesman can control the entirety." Burke (see F. Canavan, "Edmund Burke," *ibid.,* p. 603) also ascribed obedience to governments and laws to "opinion, habit, and acquired sentiment," and to the fact that "men think it right to submit to them," and Bentham (see H. M. Magid, "Jeremy Bentham," *ibid.,* p. 623) explained political society as arising from "the habit of obedience."

These interpretations may be compared with similar formulations by H. A. Simon, D. W. Smithburg, and V. A. Thompson in their *Public Administration* (New York, 1950), at pp. 188–201, attributing obedience in part to the authority of confidence (or expertise), of identification (or group loyalty), and of legitimacy (the feeling that one ought to obey). In like fashion, P. M. Blau and W. R. Scott, *Formal Organizations* (San Francisco: Chandler, 1962), at pp. 27–32, 140–45, stress "culturally defined role expectations" (p. 30) and internalization of social values (p. 144). R. V. Presthus, "Authority in Organizations," in S. Mailick and E. H. Van Ness, eds., *Concepts and Issues in Administrative Be-*

havior (Englewood Cliffs: Prentice-Hall, 1962), at p. 125, emphasizes socialization, or the acceptance of societal or group norms and values, as a key process producing acceptance of authority.

4. For a brief summary of his logic, see G. H. Sabine, *A History of Political Theory* (New York, 3d ed., 1961), pp. 167–69.
5. For an outline of recent anarchist thought (which is an updated version of anarchist philosophies of ancient times), see F. W. Coker, *Recent Political Thought* (New York, 1934), ch. VII. Also relevant are chs. VIII (on syndicalism), IX (on guild socialism), and XVIII (on pluralism).
6. *E.g.,* J. O. Mooney, *The Principles of Organization* (New York, 1947), pp. 14–15: "The scalar principle is the same form in organization that is sometimes called hierarchical. . . . The common impression regards this scale or chain merely as a 'type' of organization, characteristic only of the vaster institutions of government, army, church, and industry. This impression is erroneous. It is likewise misleading, for it seems to imply that the scalar chain in organization lacks universality. These great organizations differ from others only in that the chain is longer. The truth is that wherever we find an organization even of two people, related as superior and subordinate, we have the scalar principle. This chain constitutes the universal process of coordination, through which the supreme coordinating authority becomes effective throughout the entire structure." See also, M. G. Weiner, "Observations on the Growth of Information-Processing Centers," in A. H. Rubenstein and C. J. Haberstroh, eds., *Some Theories of Organization* (Homewood: Dorsey and Irwin, 1960), p. 150: "The transition from individuality to division of labor and the acceptance of hierarchy in the form of a leadership structure . . . represents the point at which an 'organization' can be said to exist."
7. H. C. Metcalf and L. Urwick, eds., *Dynamic Administration: The Collected Papers of Mary Parker Follett* (New York, 1941), especially pp. 101 ff. and ch. VII.
8. C. Argyris, *Personality and Organization* (New York, 1957).
9. V. A. Thompson, *Modern Organizations* (New York, 1961); G. G. Fisch, "Line-Staff is Obsolete," *Harvard Business Review,* Vol. 39, pp. 67–79 (1961); B. M. Bass, "Industrial Organization for the Space Age," unpublished manuscript, Graduate School of Business Administration, University of Pittsburgh, 1963. See also the query of W. M. Evan, "Indices of the Hierarchical Structure of Industrial Organizations," *Management Science,* Vol. 9, pp. 468–77 (1963), regarding the validity of the "iron law of hierarchy."

10. The firm is Non-Linear Systems, Inc., of Del Mar, California. Its structure and procedures are described by A. H. Kuriloff, "Management by Integration and Self-Control," *Proceedings of the Industrial Engineering Institute,* February, 1963.
11. Plato and Aristotle, for example, saw as the purpose of the city-state the promotion of the highest moral development of its citizens. For Hobbes, the end of government was the preservation of order. For Locke, it was the protection of "natural rights," such as the right to private property. For the Utilitarians, it was to produce the greatest good for the greatest number. For the early liberal economists, it was to furnish just enough service and regulation to permit the reciprocal processes of the market place to operate effectively. In all these instances, selected haphazardly from the broad array of goals postulated in political thought, the existence of a common purpose and interest is axiomatic.

    The same is true of most contemporary organization theory, although the specification of common interests is rarely articulated as explicitly as in political philosophy. Rather, it is assumed that every human association has *some* goals shared by all its members, and can be understood only in terms of those common purposes, *e.g.,* in H. A. Simon, D. W. Smithburg, and V. A. Thompson, *op. cit.,* at p. 3, purpose and cooperative action are described as the "two basic processes of what has come to be called administration. . . . Administration can be defined as the activities of groups cooperating to accomplish common goals." Similarly, P. M. Blau and W. R. Scott, *op. cit.,* at p. 1, declare that what organizations "all have in common is that a number of men have become organized into a social unit—an organization—that has been established for the explicit purpose of achieving certain goals." And C. Argyris, *Understanding Organizational Behavior* (Homewood: Dorsey, 1960) hypothesizes, at pp. 10–11, "that organizations are intricate human strategies designed to achieve certain objectives," and that the objectives of any organization include "achieving its goals (intended consequences)."
12. Bentham, for instance, defined the interest of any community as the sum of the interests of those who compose it (H. M. Magid, *op. cit.,* p. 622). A. F. Bentley, in *The Process of Government* (Bloomington: Principia, 1935), said (at p. 269), "All phenomena of government are phenomena of groups pressing one another, forming one another, and pushing out new groups and group representatives (the organs and agencies of government) to mediate the adjustments." D. B. Truman, using a similar framework of analysis in

The Governmental Process (New York, 1953), added (at p. 51), "In developing a group interpretation of politics, . . . we do not need to account for a totally inclusive interest, because one does not exist." See also, E. P. Herring, *The Politics of Democracy* (New York, 1940), ch. 30.

13. C. I. Barnard, *The Functions of the Executive* (Cambridge: Harvard University Press, 1938), pp. 73 ("a formal organization . . . [is] a system of consciously coordinated activities or forces of two or more persons"), 93, 137 ("The individual is always the basic strategic factor in organization."), ch. XI, and pp. 161–75. See also, H. A. Simon, *Administrative Behavior* (New York, 1947), pp. 103–107; Simon describes coordination in terms of adjustments among individuals' behaviors. But he does observe that the individuals must find one plan agreeable to all participants if they are to cooperate, thus introducing the equivalent of common purpose.
14. For an exploration of the political theory implicit in the writings of organization theorists, see D. Waldo, *The Administrative State* (New York, 1948).
15. *E.g.,* N. Long, "The Administrative Organization as a Political System," in S. Mailick and E. H. Van Ness, *op. cit.*
16. Plato, for instance, drew a parallel between the body and the city, and Hegel also turned to the metaphor of the organism. *Cf.* L. Strauss and J. Cropsey, *op. cit.,* pp. 16, 25, 630. And after Darwin, comparisons between social and biological evolution were commonly employed, though usually in a fashion that did violence to the biological theory.
17. See C. Barnard, *op. cit.,* p. 79: "Systems of cooperation which we call organizations I regard as social creatures, 'alive,' just as I regard an individual human being . . ." (His argument that an organization is more than the sum of its parts, as a person is more than the sum of his parts, is almost identical with that of Aristotle; *cf.* H. V. Jaffa, *op. cit.,* p. 66.) See also M. Haire, "Biological Models and Empirical Histories of the Growth of Organizations," in M. Haire, ed., *Modern Organization Theory* (New York, 1959), pp. 272–306; and P. Selznick, "Foundations of the Theory of Organization," *American Sociological Review,* Vol. 13, pp. 25–35 (1948), and *Leadership in Administration* (New York, 1957).
18. But see D. T. Campbell, "Evolutionary Theory in Social Science: A Reappraisal," unpublished paper, Northwestern University, 1961, and the references cited therein. See also R. Redfield, ed., *Levels of Integration in Biological and Social Systems* (Lancaster: Jacques Cattel Press, 1942).

19. The impression that large numbers of organizational fatalities occur is suggested in part by the frequency of business failures. Barnard, for example (*op. cit.,* p. 5), comments, "successful cooperation in or by formal organizations is the abnormal, not the normal, condition. What are observed from day to day are the successful survivors among innumerable failures. . . . Failure to cooperate, failure of cooperation, failure of organization, disorganization, disintegration, destruction of organization—and reorganization—are characteristic facts of human history."
20. In this connection see P. M. Blau and W. R. Scott, *op. cit.,* pp. 215–17.
21. For illustrations of the impression that there is a secular trend toward increasing centralization in modern life, see H. A. Simon, D. W. Smithburg, and V. A. Thompson, *op. cit.,* pp. 272 ff.; R. Redfield, *op. cit.;* R. Seidenberg, *Post-Historic Man* (Boston: Beacon, 1957).

Chapter 1

Managing by Ones and Twos: Freeing Up Relations Between Individuals

A. Introducing Some Complex Dynamics of A Talking to B

B. Tapping Human Needs and Motivation

"Basic Self-Actualization Trends of the Human Personality," Chris Argyris

"The New Look in Motivation Theory for Organizational Research," J. G. Hunt and J. W. Hill

"Improving Productivity and Job Satisfaction," Raymond A. Katzell and Daniel Yankelovich

C. Some Guides for Communicating/Motivating

"A Way of Analyzing Change: Force Field Analysis," based on National Training Laboratories, *Reading Book: Nineteenth Annual Summer Laboratories in Human Relations Training*

"Job Enrichment: How Important Is the Work Itself?", Theodore O. Prenting

"Beyond the Teaching Machine: Operant Conditioning in Management," Walter R. Nord

No manager is a social island. Whatever his level, therefore, every manager faces difficult problems of freeing up the relations between individuals in ways that permit effective and purposive interaction. We shall focus on three such problem areas: that of facilitating effective communication between the supervisor and another individual; that of the manager motivating other individuals or himself; and that of the manager helping to change his behavior or that of other individuals.

If these problem areas are boldly set forth, beyond them no simple statements are possible. Thus such supervisory efforts may be necessary going "up" the hierarchy to superiors, "across" the functional departments to peers, or "down" the chain of command to subordinates. Moreover, these efforts may involve individuals or groups. Such supervisory efforts to free up relations also must be "directionally" sensitive. For example, sometimes the need is simply for "more communication." Typically, however, the problem is qualitative as well as quantitative. Thus even an inept supervisor can increase the motivation of his employees to resist his authority, and easily. The typical managerial challenge is to control the direction as well as to increase the volume.

Our approach to the complexities of freeing up the relations between individuals in organizations explores three emphases. In turn, specific attention will focus on communicating, motivating, and changing behavior. The distinctions in foci should not be taken literally. Thus they comprise only avenues of approach to the same phenomena. The relevance of these foci is not restricted to managing by ones and twos, of course, but they do have their analytical uses, if their tentative status is recognized.

A. INTRODUCING SOME COMPLEX DYNAMICS OF A TALKING TO B

While freeing up relations between individuals in organizations has a high priority indeed, it should be recognized that this is no easy task. For example, compelling and widespread organizational demands distort or freeze communications between individuals. Their costs include motivational difficulties and behavioral rigidities.

In an early piece not reprinted here, Chris Argyris sees massive forces in organizational life that encourage nonauthentic communicating.[1] These forces have a perverse thrust, for nonauthentic communications induce significant problems of motivation and behavior. Argyris points out, for example, that a commonly held organizational value—one of several "pyramidal values" that generate the kind of organization structures with which we are most familiar—sanctions only expression that is "rational, logical and clearly communicated." Other expressive modes—emotional and interpersonal—are often treated in the breech. Thus "emotional" and "personal" references are heavily censored. Argyris sees such censoring and repression at the heart of many organizational problems.

Numerous significant difficulties derive from the fixation of the pyramidal values on rational and technical aspects. Let us trace one typical problem sequence. Individual A does not acknowledge his feelings about B, B experiences A as not "open," and consequently B will be "closed" and leery of taking risks in interacting with A. Hence A may have even greater difficulty acknowledging his feelings about B, so that the cycle spirals viciously to dangerous levels. The process, patently, has consequences as narrow as the relations of two individuals, and potentially as wide as the total organization of which they are individuals. At its worst, the process can degenerate into a personal and organizational

---

[1] Chris Argyris, "T-Groups for Organizational Effectiveness," *Harvard Business Review*, Vol. 42 (March 1964), pp. 64–70.

standstill compounded of an acute and unrealistic need to avoid "rocking the boat."

We can reinforce and deepen Argyris' approach by a brief reference to material concerning communications. In one of the better books on oral communication, Irving Lee analyzes the many potential obstacles that intervene between the sender and the receiver in oral communication.[2] The list of these obstacles is formidable. It includes semantic, psychological, and sociological elements. Given the potential obstacles, perhaps the major wonder is that communication breakdowns do not occur more often.

Any coping with the problems of oral communication must be based on an understanding of the stages or sequences in communication, and it must cope with such problems as Argyris manifestly proposes to do. We can rely on one of Wendell Johnson's contributions to supply some preliminary understanding of communication stages.[3]

In contrast to the broad strokes used by Argyris in describing communication difficulties, Johnson's focus is microscopic. He focuses on the several stages of the intrapersonal and interpersonal act of communicating between two individuals. This focus is dramatically spotlighted by the title of Johnson's piece, "The Fateful Process of Mr. A Talking to Mr. B." In contrast to Argyris, then, Johnson looks sharply and narrowly at the microprocesses of communication, marvels at their delicate complexity, and provides useful guidelines for making the best of a difficult set of conditions. More specifically, the flavor and considerable substance of Johnson's contribution is presented diagrammatically in Figure 1. Briefly, Johnson breaks down a communication sequence. That sequence is affected by the following.

1. Sensory limitations of both sender and receiver which are relevant to Stages 1 and 2 for the sender and which are relevant to Stages 1′ and 2′ for the receiver in Figure 1.
2. Preverbal stages of sender's nervous system or noiseless bodily states that are transformed into words, relevant to Stages 3 (for the sender) and 3′ (for the receiver).
3. Filters in both sender and receiver that pick and choose what is communicated overtly and what is heard and which intervene between Stages 3 and 4 as well as between Stages 3′ and 4′.
4. Symbolizations which select from an abundance of possible verbalizations in Stages 4 and 4′. Selections may be influenced by:
    a. for Freudians, the unconscious;

---

[2] Irving Lee, *How to Talk With People* (New York: Harper & Bros., 1962).

[3] Wendell Johnson, "The Fateful Process of Mr. A Talking to Mr. B," *Harvard Business Review,* Vol. 31 (January–February 1953), pp. 49–56.

b. for semanticists, the impositions of culture and usage;
c. for Pavlovians, the individual's learning experiences.

5. The "final draft" at Stage 5 and 5′ is the result of those limitations of symbolic forms imposed in Stages 4 and 4′.

Johnson, along with most writers in the field, stresses the intimate duality of both sending and receiving communications. That is, when *we tell something to somebody, we also tell him much about ourselves.* Similarly, what we "hear" tells us *about something* but it also tells us *about ourselves.* For example, Johnson's preverbal stages influence what we "tell" and what we "hear." And Johnson emphasizes the central role of the emotional component of man in communication. Neither individuals nor organizations, consequently, can safely avoid dealing with the full rational-emotional range.

B. TAPPING HUMAN NEEDS AND MOTIVATION

Three articles reprinted below take us more narrowly into the dynamics of relations between ones and twos while they also introduce us

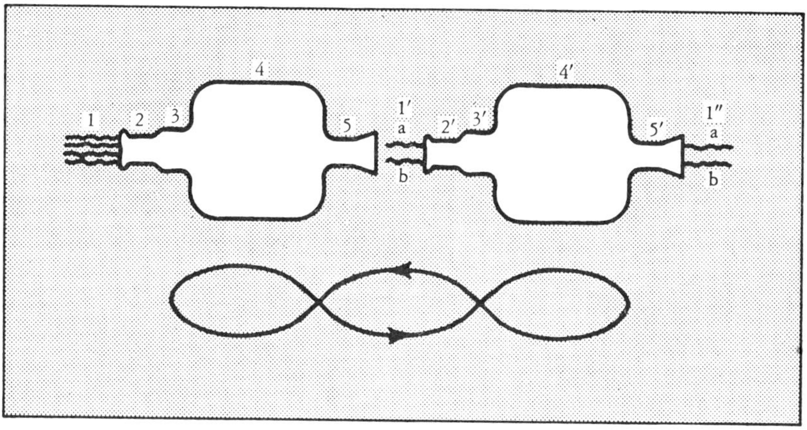

Key: Stage 1, event, or source of stimulation, external to the sensory end organs of the speaker; Stage 2, sensory stimulation; Stage 3, pre-verbal neurophysiological state; Stage 4, transformation of pre-verbal into symbolic forms; Stage 5, verbal formulations in "final draft" for overt expression; Stage 1′, transformation of verbal formulations into (a) air waves and (b) light waves, which serve as sources of stimulation for the listener (who may be either the speaker himself or another person); Stages 2′ through 1″ correspond, in the listener, to Stages 2 through 1′. The arrowed loops represent the functional interrelationships of the stages in the process as a whole. Source: Johnson, *op. cit.*, p. 50.

FIGURE 1
Stages in the Process of Communication

to factors that are as broad as life. Argyris' "Basic Self-Actualization Trends of the Human Personality" tentatively lists various dimensions along which individuals move toward personal maturity. This brief piece has profound implications for individuals and organizations. For example, individuals will be both more personally satisfied and more motivated toward outstanding performance as they are placed under structural arrangements and supervisory techniques that permit or encourage them "to grow." This brief notice suggests it all.

The revolutionary challenge in Argyris' formulation merely requires stating. Traditionally, the individual was chosen for employment as he fitted the organization. Thus the purpose of personality testing generally has been to cull rejects.[4] The concept of dimensions of personal growth oppositely implies that "the organization" also must be judged in terms of the degree to which it permits meeting the needs of its members. Altruism supplies only part of the explanation. For to the degree that organizations chronically fail the latter test, individuals can and will commit less of themselves to organizational purposes.

These suggested dimensions for personal growth should be applied as well as understood. Let us give an example of what we mean. An increasingly sophisticated research literature supports the broad conclusion that the management of men can consistently disregard man's need for personal growth only by despoiling man and usually only by reducing his effectiveness in organizations.[5] The reader consequently should find it profitable to continually apply the dimensions for personal growth as a standard against which to test what passes for managerial wisdom about how men must be managed. For example, consider the "pyramidal values" that prescribe what should be communicated in organizations. Does respect of these pyramidal values help the individual organization member "to grow," that is to move along the several dimensions of personal growth from the infant state toward mature, healthy adulthood? In this case, as in many others, conventional managerial wisdom does not measure up to the standard.

Argyris' dimensions for personal growth also imply significant questions about motivation, which questions demand explicit attention. J. B. Hunt and J. W. Hill's contribution, "The New Look in Motivation Theory for Organizational Research" provides just this attention in useful ways by examining the contributions of three well-known writers in the field—Maslow, Herzberg, and Vroom. Hunt and Hill do two

---

[4] See Robert T. Golembiewski, *Men, Management, and Morality* (New York: McGraw-Hill, 1965), esp. chapter 4.

[5] A number of supporting studies are reviewed in Chris Argyris, *Integrating the Individual and the Organization* (New York: Wiley, 1964), esp. pp. 35–112.

valuable jobs for us: they introduce several other models of human needs; and they provide useful critical analysis of them.

Maslow, of course, holds a preeminent position in the study of what motivates "man in organization," but Hunt and Hill properly point out the numerous problems encountered in trying to operationalize and then test Maslow's "hierarchy of needs." Maslow was sensitive to these difficulties and warned of them in the original work, but his warnings are often overlooked by those seeking answers to why men behave as they do.

There is a substantial overlap between the higher order needs in Maslow's hierarchy and Herzberg's motivators. Each suggests that once man's basic needs are satisfied he desires more intangible, more personal rewards if he is to produce at a satisfactory level. But it is in this statement that a most provocative kernel is hidden. In tracing the studies that have attempted to validate or invalidate Maslow and Herzberg, Hunt and Hill reach the same conclusion reached by others.[6] That is, hard data supporting relationships between motivation and production are strangely lacking.

Hunt and Hill consequently seek additional guidance on this crucial and unresolved matter. In this spirit, they introduce the Vroom model which they believe is more in line with the "thinking of contemporary psychologists and industrial sociologists" than are the treatments of Maslow and Herzberg.

Vroom's great strength lies in his construction of an operational model capable of testing a linkage described earlier by Brayfield and Crockett. They stated ". . . we might expect high satisfaction and high productivity to occur together when productivity is perceived as a path to certain goals and when these goals are achieved."[7] Vroom's model posits that "strong performance" (production) will occur only when the worker believes that such performance is *directly* linked to a goal he *strongly desires* (salary increase, promotion, etc.). Usefully, Vroom introduces the concept of first-level outcomes (organizational goals) and second-level outcomes, and he also suggests that the former (high performance) will occur only when the latter (promotion, salary increases) are seen as important and linked by the worker to his performance.

Katzell and Yankelovich approach the relationship between motivation (satisfaction) and productivity from a slightly different angle. As

---

[6] Frank K. Gibson and Clyde E. Teasley, "The Humanistic Model of Organization Motivation: A Review of Research Support," *Public Administration Review*, Vol. 33, No. 1 (January–February 1973), pp. 89–96.

[7] A. H. Brayfield and W. H. Crockett, "Employee Attitudes and Employee Performance," *Psychological Bulletin*, Vol. 52 (1955), p. 416.

industrial psychologists, these two writers are aware that a simple linkage between high worker satisfaction and high production does not exist. This is a sticky problem. If an organization is to invest in programs designed to improve employee satisfaction, it would be desirable that production remain at least unchanged or hopefully that it will increase.

C. SOME GUIDES FOR COMMUNICATING/MOTIVATING

Like Avis, we will all have to try harder to develop usable linkages between knowledge and action.

Communicating and motivating are complex and subtle matters, and especially because they commonly imply change to "new behaviors" rather than mere intensification of "old behaviors." Indeed, no little part of freeing up the relations between individuals is oriented toward creating the kind of climate in which defensiveness for its own sake is minimized, in which the "noisy feedback" of distorted cues is reduced, and in which necessary behavioral adaptations can be made more freely.

There are no simple guidelines for encouraging behavioral change in self or in others, but a number of straightforward techniques can play important roles in clarifying the involved dynamics. The summary statement, "A Way of Analyzing Change," sketches a technique termed "force-field analysis." The technique is rooted in sound theoretical notions that conceive any persisting behavior as a quasistationary equilibrium point, a balance of "driving forces" and "restraining forces." Useful guidelines for analyzing behavioral change are derived from this concept of behavior as a field of forces. Thus one can estimate the intensity of individual forces as well as determine their direction. The relative lengths of the "tails" of individual vectors of force then can indicate major targets for change. The ideal change strategy is to convert powerful restraining forces into driving forces. The effects of this change strategy on inducing movement to a new behavioral equilibrium point can be marked. Force-field analysis does not fail managers if they must settle for less than the ideal. For example, the technique suggests the particular usefulness of the strategy of removing restraining forces.

Ample evidence suggests that managerial action commonly neglects the change strategies suggested by force-field analysis. Thus, management generally resorts to adding driving forces in attempting to induce some desired change in behavior. Such driving forces—"artificial pressures," for example—commonly induce the emergence of new restraining forces, however. The result can be little or no behavioral change: the old equilibrium point can be maintained, more or less, because approximately equivalent but opposing forces have been induced. Paradoxically, this may be the best of this family of worlds. Thus some favored driving forces of management—e.g., "artificial pressure"—can induce significant defensive behaviors on the part of the employees. Such a reaction can overbalance the driving force added by management and, particularly in the long run, can result in less of the behavior that management hoped to increase. Certainly Argyris' piece suggests just such an unintended outcome.

If force-field analysis has its attractions, however, its limitations also are patent. We will stress two of these limitations. Analysis is but a prelude to action, and the problems of executing are formidable indeed. Few changes are minor, that is, and any change is likely to imply big risks for someone.

Force-field analysis stops short of describing specific ways in which the motivational force-fields of individuals can be influenced, of course. Fortunately, recent research does not shrink from the task. Indeed the bulk of the applicable literature is great and growing. We can only sample that literature here, but we feel we are sampling from a rich vein indeed. Two articles—Prenting's "Job Enrichment" and Nord's "Beyond the Teaching Machine: Operant Conditioning"—provide the specificity which force-field analysis lacks.

Job enrichment—a phrase deliberately chosen to separate the concept from job enlargement—means more, much more, than simply adding new activities to a person's job. To permit an assembly line worker to install the right rear door window of a Chevrolet in addition to installing the right front door window does little to "enrich" his task and raise his satisfaction level. Equally, however, giving the employee additional tasks beyond or below his competence level is not likely to make him a happier person. So true job enrichment requires insightful design. A flexible mind also helps, for there are doubtless many organizational tasks not amenable to enrichment, and certain employees do not desire any job change. What is needed obviously is the joining of task and employee needs. But this is not easy. To suggest, as others have done, that job enrichment should take place even if productivity is decreased is not likely to cause organizations to buy into the concept with enthusiasm. Prenting thus raises a warning flag as to unreasonable expectations while still recognizing the potential that exists in task enrichment.

Nord's essay on operant conditioning—"Beyond the Teaching Machine"—is on a different level indeed. Chiding McGregor, Maslow, and Herzberg for being unable to provide empirical "proof" for their theory of human motivation, Nord also takes job enrichment and other management techniques to task in applying the work of Skinner to the organizational scene. The basic issue is that critical old chestnut: is human behavior basically determined by nature, by inherent needs, or by specific reinforcers and socialization? Although McGregor and Herzberg are sensitive to environmental impacts on behavior, each appears to believe implicitly in certain assumptions about human "nature." McGregor's use of Maslow's hierarchy of needs strongly implies a series of "inborn" needs as the casual factors of behavior. In contrast, Skinner is an environmentalist to the nth degree. His focus is on stimulus → response, or S → R linkages.

Behavior modification or conditioned learning has been a part of the therapeutic literatures for some time,[8] and Skinner's work has been prominently distributed. Nord usefully places the S → R mechanism in a management setting, and examines various organizational rewards and punishments against this background. Whether his efforts are successful may well be determined by the willingness of management to use techniques often proved useful in therapy, as well as by the applicability in normal work settings of techniques whose basic applications have been helpful in "total institutions" like mental hospitals. Some recent studies in organizational settings, however, do imply the possibility of useful applications of the basic ideas of "behavior mod" or "behavior management" to some conventional worksites.[9]

---

[8] Joseph Wolpe, Andrew Salter, and L. J. Reyna (eds.), *The Conditioning Therapies: The Challenge in Psychotherapy* (New York: Rinehart & Wilson, 1964).

[9] For example, see Ed Pedalino and Victor U. Gamboa, "Behavior Modification and Absenteeism," *Journal of Applied Psychology,* Vol. 59, No. 6 (1974), pp. 694–98.

BASIC SELF-ACTUALIZATION TRENDS OF THE HUMAN PERSONALITY*

Chris Argyris

All organizations may be said to strive to achieve their objectives, maintain themselves internally, and adapt to their external environment. This multidimensional process may be called self-actualization. In order to make more precise predictions about the problems involved when human beings are considered for employment by the formal organization, it is necessary to be more explicit, if possible, about the demands the former will tend to make upon the latter. Since the human personality is a developing organism, one way to become more precise is to define the basic growth or development trends "inherent" in it (so long as it remains in the same culture). One can then logically assume that, at any given moment in time, the human personality will be predisposed to find expression for these developmental trends. Such an assumption implies another, namely, that there are basic development trends characteristic of a relatively large majority of the population being considered. This assumption might seem strained, especially to the psychologists inclined to stress individual differences. However, individual differences need not necessarily be ignored. As Kluckhohn and Murray point out,[1] people tend to have some similar basic psychological characteristics because of their biological inheritance and the socio-cultural matrix within which they develop. This does not preclude the possibility that each individual can express these basic characteristics in his own idiosyncratic manner. Thus the concept of individual differences is still held.

So much for the logic behind the developmental trends listed below. It is assumed that human beings in our culture:

1. Tend to develop from a state of passivity as infants to a state of increasing activity as adults. (This is what Erikson[2] has called self-initiative and Bronfenbrenner[3] has called self-determination.)

2. Tend to develop from a state of dependence upon others as infants to a state of relative independence as adults. Relative independence is the ability to "stand on one's own two feet" and simultaneously to acknowledge healthy dependencies.[4] It is characterized by the liberation

---

* From pp. 49–52 in PERSONALITY AND ORGANIZATION by Chris Argyris, Copyright © 1957 by Harper & Row, Publishers, Inc. By permission of the publisher. (Footnotes have been renumbered.)

of the individual from his childhood determiners of behavior (e.g., family) and developing his own set of behavioral determiners. This individual does not tend to react to others (e.g., the boss) in terms of patterns learned during childhood.[5]

3. Tend to develop from being capable of behaving only in a few ways as an infant to being capable of behaving in many different ways as an adult.[6]

4. Tend to develop from having erratic, casual, shallow, quickly-dropped interests as an infant to having deeper interests as an adult. The mature state is characterized by an endless series of challenges, where the reward comes from doing something for its own sake. The tendency is to analyze and study phenomena in their full-blown wholeness, complexity, and depth.[7]

5. Tend to develop from having a short time perspective (i.e., the present largely determines behavior) as an infant to a much longer time perspective as an adult (i.e., where the behavior is more affected by the past and the future).[8] Bakke cogently describes the importance of time perspective in the lives of workers and their families and the variety of foresight practices by means of which they seek to secure the future.[9]

6. Tend to develop from being in a subordinate position in the family and society as an infant to aspiring to occupy an equal and/or superordinate position relative to their peers.

7. Tend to develop from a lack of awareness of self as an infant to an awareness of and control over self as an adult. The adult who tends to experience adequate and successful control over his own behavior tends to develop a sense of integrity (Erikson) and feelings of self-worth.[10] Bakke,[11, 12] shows that one of the most important needs of workers is to enlarge those areas of their lives in which their own decisions determine the outcome of their efforts.

These dimensions are postulated as being descriptive of a basic multidimensional developmental process along which the growth of individuals in our culture may be measured. Presumably, every individual, at any given moment in time, can have his degree of development plotted along these dimensions. The exact location on each dimension will probably vary with each individual, and even within the same individual at different times. Self-actualization may now be defined more precisely as the individual's plotted scores (or profile) along the above dimensions.

It may be helpful to add a few words of explanation concerning these dimensions of personality development.

1. They comprise only one aspect of the total personality. All the properties of personality described previously must be used in trying to

understand the behavior of a particular individual. Much depends upon the individual's self-concept, his degrce of adaptation and adjustment, and the way in which he perceives his private world.

2. The dimensions are continua where the growth to be measured is assumed to be continuously changing in degree. An individual is presumed to develop continuously in degree, from the infant end to the adult end of each continuum.

3. The only characteristic assumed to hold for all individuals is that, barring unhealthy personality development, they will be predisposed toward moving from the infant end to the adult end of each continuum. This is a model (a construct) describing the basic growth trends. As such, it does not make any predictions about any specific individual. It *does,* however, presume to supply the researcher with basic developmental continua along which the growth of any individual in our culture may be described and measured.

4. So long as one develops in a particular culture one will never obtain maximum expression of these developmental trends. Clearly, all individuals cannot be maximally independent, active, and so forth all the time and still maintain an organized society. It is the function of culture (e.g., norms and mores) and society (e.g., family, friends, schools, churches, and laws) to inhibit maximum expression and to help an individual adjust and adapt by finding his optimum expression.

A second factor that prevents maximum expression and fosters optimum expression is the indivdual's own finite limits set by his personality. Some people fear the same amount of independence and activity that others desire. Also, it is common-place to find some people who do not have the necessary abilities to perform specific tasks. No given individual is known to have developed all known abilities to their full maturity.

Finally, defense mechanisms also are important factors operating to help an individual to deviate from the basic developmental trends.

5. The dimensions described above are constructed in terms of latent or genotypical characteristics. If one states that an individual needs to be dependent, this need will probably be ascertained by clinical inference because it is one that individuals are not usually aware of. Thus, if one observes an employee acting as though he were independent, it is possible that if one goes below the behavioral surface, the individual may be quite dependent. The obvious example is the employee who always seems to behave in a contrary manner to that desired by management. Although his behavior may give the appearance that he is independent, his contrariness may be due to his great need to be dependent upon management, which he dislikes to admit to himself and to others.

NOTES

1. Kluckhohn, Clyde, and Murray, H. A., "Personality Formation: The Determinants," in *Personality,* (ed) by above authors (New York: Knopf, 1949), pp. 35–37.
2. Erikson, E. H., *Childhood and Society* (New York: Norton, 1950). See also Kotinsky, R., *Personality in the Making* (New York: Harper, 1952), pp. 8–25.
3. Bronfenbrenner, Urie, "Toward an Integrated Theory of Personality," in *Perception,* by Robert R. Blake and Glen B. Ramsey (New York: Ronald Press, 1951), pp. 206–257.
4. This is similar to Erikson's "sense of autonomy" and Bronfenbrenner's "state of creative interdependence."
5. White, Robert W., *Lives in Progress* (New York: Dryden Press, 1952), pp. 339 ff.
6. Lewin and Kounin believe that, as the individual develops needs and abilities, the boundaries between them become more rigid. This explains why an adult is better able than a child to be frustrated in one activity and behave constructively in another. See Lewin, Kurt, *A Dynamic Theory of Personality* (New York: McGraw-Hill, 1935); and Kounin, Jacob S., "Intellectual Development and Rigidity," in *Child Behavior and Development* (ed.) Barker, R., Kounin, J., and Wright, H. R. (New York: McGraw-Hill, 1943), pp. 179–198.
7. White, Robert W., *op. cit.,* pp. 347 ff.
8. Lewin also cites the billions of dollars that are invested in insurance policies. Lewin, Kurt, "Time Perspective and Morale," in *Resolving Social Conflicts* (New York: Harper, 1948), p. 105.
9. Bakke, E. W., *The Unemployed Worker* (New Haven: Yale University Press, 1940), pp. 23–24.
10. Rogers, Carl R., *Client-Centered Therapy* (Boston: Houghton Mifflin, 1951).
11. Bakke, E. W., *op. cit.,* p. 247.
12. Bakke, E. W., *op. cit.,* p. 29.

THE NEW LOOK IN MOTIVATION THEORY FOR ORGANIZATIONAL RESEARCH*

J. G. Hunt
J. W. Hill

During the last few years the treatment of motivation with respect to industrial and other formal organizations has more often than not been in terms of models by Maslow or Herzberg.[1] Where theories are apparently so thoroughly accepted one naturally assumes a fairly substantial amount of data leading to empirical verification. However, as we shall show, there is relatively little empirical evidence concerning Maslow's theory; and while there are many studies bearing on Herzberg's theory, it remains controversial. After comparing these two approaches and reviewing their present status, we will describe a newer motivation theory developed by Vroom, which is similar to those developed by Atkinson et al. and Edwards in experimental psychology, and Peak, Rosenberg, and Fishbein in social psychology.[2] It is our contention, on both theoretical and empirical grounds, that Vroom's theory, more than Maslow's or Herzberg's, is in line with the thinking of contemporary psychologists and industrial sociologists and is the best yet developed for organizational use.

THE MASLOW MODEL

Maslow's theory hypothesizes five broad classes of needs arranged in hierarchical levels of prepotency so that when one need level is satisfied, the next level is activated. The levels are: (1) physiological needs; (2) security or safety needs; (3) social, belonging, or membership needs; (4) esteem needs further subdivided into esteem of others and self-esteem including autonomy; and (5) self-actualization or self-fulfillment needs.

The original papers present very little empirical evidence in support of the theory and no research at all that tests the model in its entirety. Indeed, Maslow argues that the theory is primarily a framework for future research. He also discusses at length some of the limitations of the model and readily admits that these needs may be unconscious rather than conscious. While Maslow discusses his model and its limitations in detail, a widely publicized paper by McGregor gives the impression

* Reprinted with permission of the Society for Applied Anthropology from *Human Organization,* Vol. 28, No. 2 (1969), pp. 100–109.

that the model can be accepted without question and also that it is fairly easy to apply.[3] In truth, the model is difficult to test, which is probably why there are so few empirical studies to either prove or refute the theory.

Porter provides the most empirical data concerning the model.[4] At the conscious level he measures all except the physiological needs. His samples are based only on managers, but they cover different managerial levels in a wide range of business organizations in the United States and thirteen other countries. Porter's studies have a number of interesting findings, but here we are primarily concerned with two: (1) in the United States and Britain (but not in the other twelve countries) there tends to be a hierarchical satisfaction of needs as Maslow hypothesizes; and (2) regardless of country or managerial level there is a tendency for those needs which managers feel are most important to be least satisfied.

A study by Beer of female clerks provides additional data concerning the model.[5] He examines the relationship between participative and considerate or human relations-oriented supervisory leadership styles and satisfaction of needs. He also goes one step further and argues that need satisfaction, as such, does not necessarily lead to motivation. Rather, motivation results only from need satisfaction which occurs in the process of task-oriented work. He reasons that a participative leadership style should meet this condition since it presumably allows for the satisfaction of the higher order needs (self-actualization, autonomy, and esteem). Beer found that workers forced to arrange needs in a hierarchy (as required by his ranking method) tend to arrange them as predicted by Maslow. He also found that self-actualization, autonomy, and social needs were most important while esteem and security needs were least important, although his method (unlike Porter's) did not allow a consideration of the relationship between importance and need satisfaction. Interestingly enough, there was no significant relationship between need satisfaction and Beer's measure of motivation nor between any of the leadership style dimensions and motivation. There were, however, significant relationships between leadership style dimensions and need satisfaction. Beer concludes that the model has questionable usefulness for a theory of industrial motivation although it may provide a fairly reliable measurement of the a priori needs of industrial workers.

We have found only three studies that systematically consider the Maslow theory in terms of performance.[6]

The first of these, by Clark, attempts to fit a number of empirical studies conducted for different purposes into a framework which provides for progressive activation and satisfaction of needs at each of the hierarchical levels. The findings are used to make predictions concerning productivity, absenteeism, and turnover as each need level is activated and then satisfied. While the article does not explicitly test the Maslow model, it is highly suggestive in terms of hypotheses for future research that might relate the theory to work group performance.

A second study, by Lawler and Porter, correlates satisfaction of managers' needs (except physiological) with rankings of their performance by superiors and peers. All correlations are significant but low, ranging from .16 to .30. Lawler and Porter conclude that satisfaction of higher order needs is more closely related to performance than satisfaction of lower order needs. However, the differences are not very great and they are not tested for significance. For example, correlations of superior ratings for the lower order security and social needs are .21 and .23 while for the higher order esteem, autonomy, and self-actualization needs they are .24, .18, and .30. Peer correlations are similar. Thus, unlike Lawler and Porter, we conclude that in this study the correlations for lower order needs are about the same as for higher order needs.

A more recent Porter and Lawler investigation seems to provide additional support for their earlier findings by showing that higher order needs accounted for more relationships significant at the .01 level than lower order needs. However, they do not report correlations between these needs and performance and so we cannot evaluate their conclusion as we did for their earlier study.

THE HERZBERG MODEL

A second frequently mentioned motivational model is that proposed by Herzberg and his associates in 1959.[7] They used a semistructured interview technique to get respondents to recall events experienced at work which resulted in a marked improvement or a marked reduction in their job satisfaction. Interviewees were also asked, among other things, how their feelings of satisfaction or dissatisfaction affected their work performance, personal relationships, and well-being. Content analysis of the interviews suggested that certain job characteristics led to job satisfaction, while *different* job characteristics led to job dissatisfaction. For instance, job achievement was related to satisfaction while working conditions were related to dissatisfaction. Poor conditions led to dissatisfaction, but good conditions did not necessarily lead to satisfaction. Thus, satisfaction and dissatisfaction are not simple opposites. Hence a two-factor theory of satisfaction is needed.

The job content characteristics which produced satisfaction were called "motivators" by Herzberg and his associates because they satisfied the individual's need for self-actualization at work. The job environment characteristics which led to dissatisfaction were called "hygienes" because they were work-supporting or contextual rather than task-determined and hence were analogous to the "preventative" or "environmental" factors recognized in medicine. According to this dichotomy, motivators include achievement, recognition, advancement, possibility of growth, responsibility, and work itself. Hygienes, on the other hand, include salary; interpersonal relations with superiors, subordinates, and peers; technical supervision; company policy and administration; personal life; working conditions; status; and job security.

There is considerable empirical evidence for this theory. Herzberg himself, in a summary of research through early 1966, includes 10 studies of 17 populations which used essentially the same method as his original study.[8] In addition, he reviews 20 more studies which used a variety of methodologies to test the two-factor theory. Of the studies included in his review, those using his critical incident method generally confirm the theory. Those using other methods give less clear results, which Herzberg acknowledges but attempts to dismiss for methodological reasons. At least nine other studies, most of which have appeared since Herzberg's 1966 review, raise even more doubts about the theory.[9]

While it is beyond the scope of the present article to consider these studies in detail, they raise serious questions as to whether the factors leading to satisfaction and dissatisfaction are really different from each other. A number of the studies show that certain job dimensions appear to be more important for *both* satisfaction and dissatisfaction. Dunnette, Campbell, and Hakel, for example, conclude from these and also from their own studies that Herzberg is shackled to his method and that achievement, recognition, and responsibility seem important for both satisfaction *and* dissatisfaction while such dimensions as security, salary, and working conditions are less important.[10] They also raise by implication an issue concerning Herzberg's methodology which deserves further comment. That is, if data are analyzed in terms of percentage differences between groups, one result is obtained; if they are analyzed in terms of ranks within groups, another result occurs. The first type of analysis is appropriate for identifying factors which account for differences between events (as Herzberg did in his original hypothesis). The second type of analysis is appropriate if we want to know the most important factors within the event categories (which is what Herzberg claims he was doing). Analyzing the findings of Dunnette and his colleagues by the first method, we confirm Herzberg's theory; but if we rank the findings within categories, as Dunnette et al. also did, we find no confirmation. If we want to know whether "achievement" is important in job satisfaction we must look at its relative rank among other factors mentioned in the events leading to satisfaction, not whether it is mentioned a greater percentage of the time in satisfying events than in dissatisfying events. This distinction in analytical methods was discussed several years ago by Viteles and even earlier by Kornhauser.[11]

We conclude that any meaningful discussion of Herzberg's theory must recognize recent negative evidence even though the model seems to make a great deal of intuitive sense. Much the same can be said of Maslow's theory.

Further Considerations in Using the Maslow and Herzberg Theories

Putting aside for the moment the empirical considerations presented by the two models, it is instructive to compare them at the conceptual

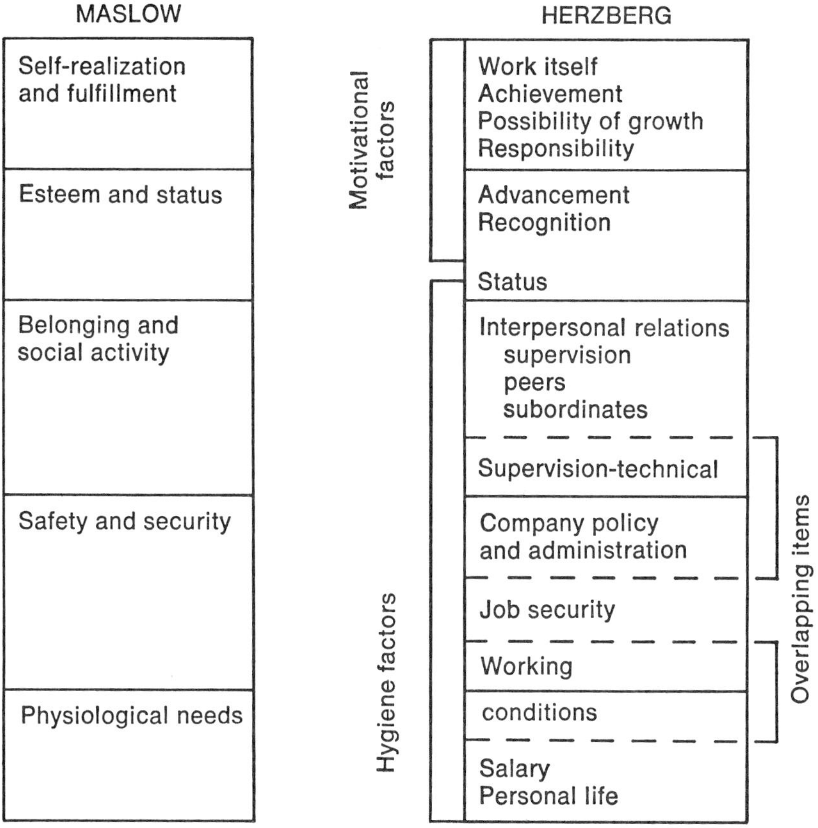

FIGURE 1
Maslow's need-priority model compared with Herzberg's motivation-hygiene model. (Adapted from K. Davis, *Human Relations at Work*, New York: McGraw-Hill, 1967, p. 37.)

level suggested in Figure 1. While the figure shows obvious similarities between the Maslow and Herzberg models, there are important differences as well. Where Maslow assumes that any need can be a motivator if it is relatively unsatisfied, Herzberg argues that only the higher order needs serve as motivators and that a worker can have unsatisfied needs in both the hygiene and motivator areas simultaneously. One might argue that the reason higher order needs are motivators is that lower order needs have essentially been satisfied. However, Herzberg presents some evidence that even in relatively low level blue-collar and service jobs, where presumably lower order needs are less well-satisfied, the higher order needs are still the only ones seen by the workers as motivators.[12]

Another important consideration is the relationship of these models to the accomplishment of organizational objectives. Even if there were unequivocal empirical support for the theories, there is need to translate the findings into usable incentives for promoting such objectives as superior performance, lower turnover, lower absenteeism, etc. If not, they are of little use to industrial organizations. As indicated earlier, there is relatively little evidence empirically relating Maslow's model to performance, or even to psychological well-being. Furthermore, the one Lawler and Porter study seems to show that satisfaction of higher and lower order needs are about equally related to performance, although their later investigation suggests that the former are more strongly related to performance than the latter. But we cannot tell for sure because correlations and differences between correlations are not reported.

Similarly, although Herzberg asked his respondents for effects of job events on their performance, he reports only two studies which attempt to measure performance independent of the respondent's estimate. These seem to show the performance is favorably influenced as more "motivators" are provided in the job.[13] However, insufficient data are presented to permit evaluation of the adequacy of the experimental design and performance measures. A study by Friedlander and Walton that considered employee turnover used a modification of Herzberg's technique and found that employees' reasons for staying on the job were different than their reasons for leaving.[14] The reasons for staying would be called "motivators" while those for leaving were "hygiene" factors.

We conclude that Herzberg's two-factor theory *may* be related to turnover and performance; but present studies are subject to serious criticisms. And we could find only two empirical investigations which related Maslow's model to any of these outputs.

In addition, it should be noted that neither model adequately handles the theoretical problem of some kind of linkage by which individual need satisfaction is related to the achievement of organizational objectives. Given the present formulation, it is entirely possible that there can be need satisfaction which is *not necessarily* directed toward the accomplishment of organizational goals. For example, an important organizational objective might be increased production, but workers might conceivably receive more need satisfaction from turning out a higher quality product at a sacrifice in quantity. They might also be meeting their social needs through identification with a work group with strong sanctions against "rate busting."

Finally, neither of these theories as they stand can really handle the problem of individual differences in motivation. Maslow, for example, explains that his model may not hold for persons with particular experiences. His theory is therefore nonpredictive because data that do not support it can be interpreted in terms of individual differences in previous need gratification leading to greater or lesser prepotency of a given need-category.[15] Herzberg, in similar fashion, describes seven types of people differentiated by the extent to which they are motivator or hygiene seekers, or some combination of the two, although he never relates these differences empirically to actual job performance. We turn then to a model which explicitly recognizes these issues and appears to offer great potential for understanding motivation in organizations.

THE VROOM MODEL

Brayfield and Crockett as long ago as 1955 suggested an explicit theoretical linkage between satisfaction, motivation and the organizational goal of productivity. They said:

> It makes sense to us to assume that individuals are motivated to achieve certain environmental goals and that the achievement of these goals results in satisfaction. Productivity is seldom a goal in itself but is more commonly a means to goal attainment. Therefore, . . . we might expect high satisfaction and high productivity to occur together when productivity is perceived as a path to certain important goals and when these goals are achieved.[16]

Georgopoulas, Mahoney, and Jones provide some early empirical support for this notion in their test of the "path-goal hypothesis."[17] Essentially, they argue that an individual's motivation to produce at a given level depends upon his particular needs as reflected in the goals toward which he is moving *and* his perception of the relative usefulness of productivity behavior as a path to attainment of these goals. They qualify this, however, by saying that the need must be sufficiently high, no other economical paths must be available to the individual, and there must be a lack of restraining practices.

More recently, Vroom has developed a motivational model which extends the above concepts and is also related to earlier work of experimental and social psychologists.[18] He defines motivation as a "process governing choices, made by persons or lower organisms, among alternative forms of voluntary activity."[19] The concept is incorporated in Figure 2, which depicts Vroom's model graphically. Here, the individual is shown as a role occupant faced with a set of alternative "first-level outcomes." His preference choice among these first-level outcomes is determined by their expected relationship to possible "second-level outcomes."

Two concepts are introduced to explain the precise method of determining preferences for these first-level outcomes. These concepts are *valence* and *instrumentality.* Valence refers to the strength of an individual's desire for a particular outcome. Instrumentality indicates an individual's perception of the relationship between a first-level outcome and a second-level outcome or, in other words, the extent to which a first-level outcome is seen as leading to the accomplishment of a second-level outcome.

Valence is measured by instructing workers to rank important individual goals in order of their desirability, or they may rate goals on Likert-type scales. Instrumentality can be measured by rating scales which involve perceived differences in the direction and strength of relationships between various first- and second-level outcomes. Important goals of industrial workers often cited in the empirical behavioral science literature are promotion, pay, pleasant working conditions, and job security. The goals can be ranked by individual workers in terms of their desirability. The resulting scores are measures of valence. In addition, each individual can be instructed to indicate on an appropriate scale the likelihood that a certain job behavior, e.g., high productivity, will lead to each of the four goals described. This score is the instrumental relationship between productivity and a specified goal. Obviously there are alternative methods of measurement available for the concepts; we will leave these for a more detailed discussion later.

Vroom expresses the valence of a first-level outcome to a person "as a monotonically increasing function of an algebraic sum of the products of the valences of all [second-level] outcomes and his conceptions of its instrumentality for the attainment of the [second-level] outcomes."[20]

For example, assume that an individual desires promotion and feels that superior performance is a very strong factor in achieving that goal. His first-level outcomes are then superior, average, or poor performance. His second-level outcome is promotion. The first-level outcome of high performance thus acquires a positive valence by virtue of its expected relationship to the preferred second-level outcome of promotion. Assum-

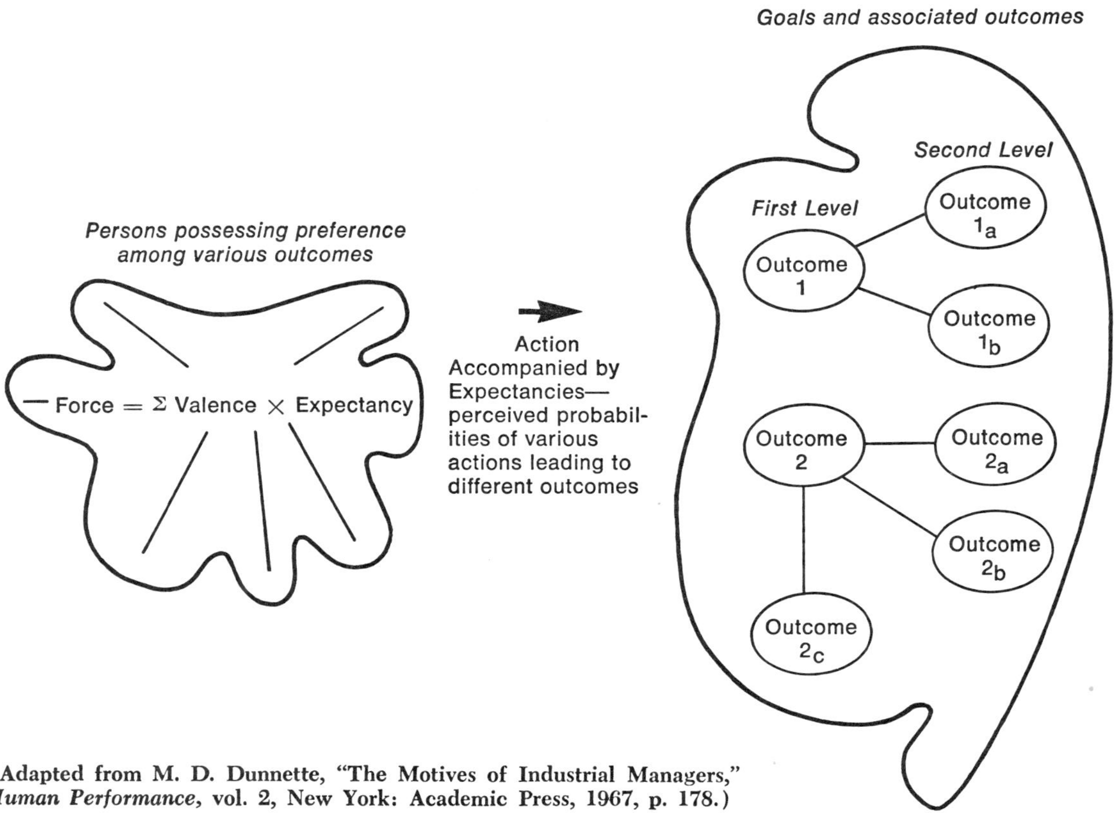

FIGURE 2
Vroom's motivational model. (Adapted from M. D. Dunnette, "The Motives of Industrial Managers," *Organizational Behavior and Human Performance*, vol. 2, New York: Academic Press, 1967, p. 178.)

ing no negative second-level outcomes associated with high performance and no other first-level outcomes that contribute to promotion, we expect motivation toward superior performance because promotion is important and superior performance is seen as instrumental in its accomplishment. Or, to put it in Vroom's terms, performance varies directly with the product of the valence of the reward (promotion) and the perceived instrumentality of performance for the attainment of the reward.

An additional concept in Vroom's theory is *expectancy.* This is a belief concerning the likelihood that a particular action or effort will be followed by a particular first-level outcome and can be expressed as a subjective probability ranging from 0 to 1. Expectancy differs from instrumentality in that it relates *efforts* to first-level outcomes where instrumentality relates first- and second-level outcomes to each other. Vroom ties this concept to his previous one by stating, "the force on a person to perform an [action] is a monotonically increasing function of the algebraic sum of the products of the valences of all [first-level] outcomes and the strength of his expectancies that the [action] will be followed by the attainment of these outcomes."[21] "Force" here is similar to our concept of motivation.

This motivational model, unlike those discussed earlier, emphasizes individual differences in motivation and makes possible the examination of very explicit relationships between motivation and the accomplishment of organizational goals, whatever these goals may be. Thus, instead of assuming that satisfaction of a specific need is likely to influence organizational objectives in a certain way, we can find out how important to the employees are the various second-level outcomes (worker goals), the instrumentality of various first-level outcomes (organizational objectives) for their attainment, and the expectancies that are held with respect to the employees' ability to influence the first-level outcomes.

Empirical Tests of Vroom's Model

Vroom has already shown how his model can integrate many of the empirical findings in the literature on motivation in organizations.[22] However, because it is a relatively recent development, empirical tests of the model itself are just beginning to appear. Here we shall consider four such investigations.

In the first study, Vroom is concerned with predicting the organizational choices of graduating college students on the basis of their instrumentality-goal index scores.[23] These scores reflect the extent to which membership in an organization was perceived by the student as being related to the acquisition of desired goals. According to the theory, the chosen organization should be the one with the highest instrumentality-goal index. Ratings were used to obtain preferences for 15 different goals and the extent to which these goals could be attained through membership in three different organizations. These two ratings were thus measures of the valences of second-level outcomes and the instrumentality of organizational membership for attainment of these outcomes, respectively. The instrumentality-goal index was the correlation between these two measures. But Vroom's theory also involves consideration of expectancy, i.e., how probable is it that the student can become a member of a particular organization. The choice is not his alone but depends upon whether he is acceptable to the organization. A rough measure of expectancy in this study was whether or not the student had received an offer by the organization. If he had received an offer, expectancy would be high; if not, it would be low. The results show that, considering only organizations from which offers of employment were actually received, 76 percent of the students chose the organization with the highest instrumentality-goal index score. The evidence thus strongly supports Vroom's theory.

The next study, by Galbraith and Cummings, utilizes the model to predict the productivity of operative workers.[24] Graphic rating scales were used to measure the instrumentality of performance for five goals —money, fringe benefits, promotion, supervisor's support, and group acceptance. Similar ratings were used for measuring the desirability of each of the goals for the worker. The authors anticipated that a worker's expectation that he could produce at a high level would have a probability of one because the jobs were independent and productivity was a function of the worker's own effort independent of other human or machine pacing. Figure 3 outlines the research design.

Multiple regression analysis showed that productivity was significantly related positively to the instrumentality-goal interactions for supervisor support and money, and there was an almost significant ($p \leqslant .10$) relationship with group acceptance. The other factors did not approach significance and the authors explain this lack of significance in terms of the situational context. That is, fringe benefits were dependent not so much on productivity as on a union/management contract, and promotion was based primarily on seniority. Thus the instrumentality of productivity for the attainment of these goals was low and the model would predict no relationship. The Galbraith and Cummings study thus supports Vroom's contention that motivation is related to productivity in those situations where the acquisition of desired goals is dependent upon the individual's production and not when desired outcomes are contingent on other factors.

A third study is that of Hill relating a model similar to Vroom's to behavior in a utility company.[25] Hill's model is based upon Edward's subjective expected utility maximization theory of decision making.[26] Here one given a choice between alternatives A and/or B will select that alternative which maximizes his subjective expected utility or expected value. If the outcomes associated with action A are more desirable than those associated with B, and their probability of occurrence is greater than or equal to those associated with B, then an individual will choose behavior A over behavior B. The basic concepts are subjective expectation and subjective utility or valence. Expectation and utility are multiplicatively related and can be measured by the same techniques used to test Vroom's theory. Where a relationship is found between Subjective Expected Utility (S.E.U.) and overt behavior, it can be interpreted as support for Vroom.

The behavior considered in Hill's study is that of job bidding. This behavior is encountered in organizations that post descriptions of job openings on employee bulletin boards and encourage qualified employees to "bid" (apply) for them. Here records were kept of the number of bids made over a three-year period by groups of semi-skilled electrical repairmen matched in learning ability, seniority in grade, and age. The men were asked about the consequences of bidding and not

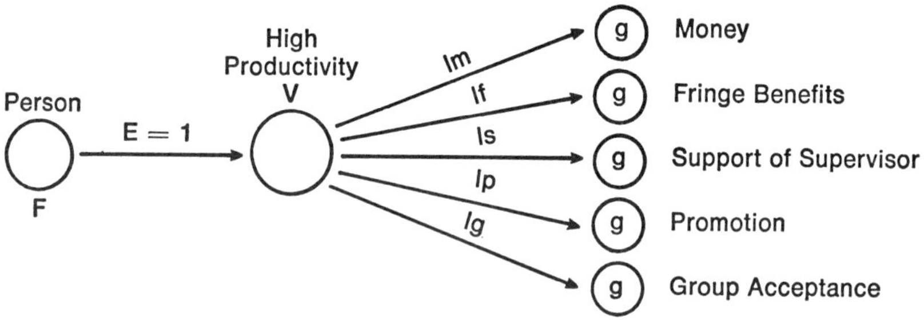

g = Desirability of a particular outcome (rating)
I = Instrumentality of production for particular outcomes (rating of relationship)
E = Expectancy (= 1 here because worker sets own pace and is assumed to be capable of high productivity)
V = (Valence) the sum of the cross products of instrumentality and g
F = (Force) expectancy times the valence of productivity
Productivity = Objective measures of amount of production in relation to the production standard.

FIGURE 3
Individual goals and productivity as measured by Vroom's model in one industrial plant. (Based on data from J. Galbraith and L. L. Cummings, "An Empirical Investigation . . . of Task Performance . . . ," *Organizational Behavior and Human Performance*, vol. 2, New York: Academic Press, 1967, p. 178.)

bidding on the next higher grade job, and rated the consequence on a seven-point scale of desirability and a similar scale of probability of occurrence. Bidders were those who had bid three or more times during that time.

Fourteen different S.E.U. indices were computed from interview data to determine the relative validity of each in predicting bidding behavior. Typical of these indices were: (1) the sums of the cross products of expectation and utility for the positive consequences of bidding ($\Sigma \overset{+}{S.E.U.}$); (2) the same score for the negative consequences of bidding ($\Sigma \overset{-}{S.E.U.}$); and (3) the cross products of the *mean* expectation and utility scores for positive and negative consequences ($\frac{\Sigma \overset{+}{S.E.U.}}{N}, \frac{\Sigma \overset{-}{S.E.U.}}{N}$). In addition to these S.E.U. indices, two traditional attitudinal and motivational measures were used. Semantic Differential scales measured each subject's respective evaluation of bidding and the next higher grade job and each subject's Need for Achievement was obtained.[27]

It was hypothesized that: (1) there would be a positive correlation between the S.E.U. indices and bidding; and (2) the S.E.U. indices would be more highly related to bidding behavior than the traditional measures.

We do not discuss relationships for all of the indices here but do consider results for one of the more comprehensive indices and those from multiple regression analysis. This index is the algebraic sum of the cross products of the positive and negative consequences of bidding minus the same score for not bidding for each individual. The correlation of this index with bidding was .26, $p \leqslant .05$ for a one-tailed test. The correlations between the two Semantic Differential scales and bidding were −.09 and −.25, respectively. Neither of these is significant for a one-tailed test predicting a positive correlation. The correlation between Need for Achievement and bidding was a nonsignificant .17. A multiple regression analysis determined the relative contribution of the S.E.U. indices to the prediction of bidding. A variable was selected for analysis on the basis of its relationship to the criterion and its intercorrelation with the other predictors. The multiple correlation for bidding and seven selected variables was .61, $p \leqslant .05$. This correlation included for S.E.U. indices, all of which had higher beta weights than the Semantic Differentials or Need for Achievement. Thus, these variables accounted for more variance in the criterion than did the traditional attitudinal and motivational measures. Both hypotheses were therefore confirmed. This study adds support to the usefulness of this type of model in the study of motivation.

Finally, Lawler and Porter report a study that attempts to relate managerial attitudes to job performance rankings by superiors and peers.[28] In it, 154 managers from five different organizations completed questionnaires concerning seven kinds of rewards, and their expectations that different kinds of behavior would lead to these rewards. The expectations and the ratings of the importance of instrumentality and valence, respectively, were combined multiplicatively to yield multiple correlations which were significantly related to supervisor and peer rankings of the manager's effort to perform his job well. The correlations were higher with effort to perform the job than with the rankings of job performance. Lawler and Porter predicted this result because they reasoned that job performance is influenced by variables other than motivation—e.g., by ability and role perceptions. Of course, Vroom's model is not a behavioral theory but one of motivation only. Motivation is not going to improve performance if ability is low or role perceptions are inaccurate. Vroom's model explains how goals influence effort and that is exactly the relationship found by Lawler and Porter.

CONCLUSION

Taken together, the four studies discussed in the previous section seem to show that Vroom's model holds great promise for predicting behavior in organizations. There still remain some unanswered questions. We do not know all of the goals that have positive valence in a work situation. We do not know how much of a difference in force is necessary before one kind of outcome is chosen over another. Nor do we know what combination of measures yields the best prediction in a given situation. The answers to these and other questions await further research.

One more point should perhaps be made concerning the four studies and their measurement of Vroom's concepts. While it is true that all of them used subjective measures, the model can in fact be tested with more objective devices. Instrumentality can be inferred from organization practices, expectations can be manipulated by instructions, and goals can be inferred from observed approach and avoidance behaviors. Of course, all of these techniques require assumptions concerning their relationship to the worker's subjective perceptions of the situation; but the model is certainly not bound to the methods of measurement used so far. Vroom specifies in considerable detail the different kinds of techniques that might be used to test his model.[29]

More work must be done before we can make any statements concerning the overall validity of Vroom's model. But the vigor of his formulation, the relative ease of making the concepts operational, and the model's emphasis on individual differences show considerable promise. We are also encouraged by the results of relatively sophisticated studies testing the theory. We believe it is time for those interested in organizational behavior to take a more thoroughly scientific look at this very complex subject of industrial motivation, and Vroom's model seems a big step in that direction.

REFERENCES

1. A. H. Maslow, *Motivation and Personality,* New York: Harper, 1954; "A Theory of Human Motivation," *Psychological Review,* vol. 50, 1943, pp. 370–396; *Eupsychian Management,* Homewood, Ill.: Irwin-Dorsey, 1965; F. Herzberg, B. Mausner, and B. B. Snyderman, *The Motivation to Work,* New York: Wiley, 1959; F. Herzberg, *Work and the Nature of Man,* Cleveland: World Publishing, 1966, pp. 130–131; V. H. Vroom, *Work and Motivation,* New York: Wiley, 1964.
2. J. W. Atkinson, J. R. Bastian, R. W. Earl, and G. H. Litwin, "The Achievement Motive, Goal Setting, and Probability Preferences," *Journal of Abnormal and Social Psychology,* vol. 60, 1960, pp. 27–36; W. Edwards, "Behavioral Decision Theory," *Annual Review of Psychology,* Palo Alto: Annual Reviews Inc., 1961, pp. 473–499; H. Peak, "Attitude and Motivation," *Nebraska Symposium on Motivation,* Lincoln: University of Nebraska, 1955, pp. 148–184; M. Rosenberg, "Cognitive Structure and Attitudinal Affect," *Journal of Abnormal and Social Psychology,* vol. 53, 1956, pp. 367–372; M. Fishbein, "An Operational Definition of Belief and Attitude," *Human Relations,* vol. 15, 1962, pp. 35–43.
3. D. McGregor, "Adventure in Thought and Action," *Proceedings of the Fifth Anniversary Convocation of the School of Industrial Management, Massachusetts Institute of Technology,* Cambridge, Mass.: M.I.T., 1957, pp. 23–30.
4. L. W. Porter, *Organizational Patterns of Managerial Job Attitudes,* New York: American Foundation for Management Research, 1964. See also M. Haire, E. Ghiselli, and L. W. Porter, *Managerial Thinking: An International Study,* New York: Wiley, 1966, especially Chaps. 4 and 5.
5. M. Beer, *Leadership, Employee Needs, and Motivation,* Columbus: Bureau of Business Research, Ohio State, 1966.
6. J. V. Clark, "Motivation in Work Groups: A Tentative View," *Human Organization,* vol. 19, 1960, pp. 199–208; E. E. Lawler and L. W. Porter, "The Effect of Performance on Job Satisfaction," *In-*

dustrial Relations, vol. 7, no. 1, 1967, pp. 20–28; L. W. Porter and E. E. Lawler, *Managerial Attitudes and Performance,* Homewood, Ill.: Irwin-Dorsey, 1968, pp. 148, 150.

7. Herzberg, Mausner, and Snyderman, op. cit.
8. Herzberg, op. cit., Chaps. 7 and 8. See also K. Davis, *Human Relations at Work,* 3d ed., New York: McGraw-Hill, 1967, pp. 32–36; R. J. Burke, "Are Herzberg's Motivators and Hygienes Unidimensional?" *Journal of Applied Psychology,* vol. 50, 1966, pp. 317–321.
9. For a review of six of these studies as well as a report on their own similar findings, see M. D. Dunnette, J. P. Campbell, and M. D. Hakel, "Factors Contributing to Job Satisfaction and Job Dissatisfaction in Six Occupational Groups," *Organizational Behavior and Human Performance,* vol. 2, 1967, pp. 143–174. See also C. L. Hulin and P. A. Smith, "An Empirical Investigation of Two Implications of the Two-Factor Theory of Job Satisfaction," *Journal of Applied Psychology,* vol. 51, 1967, pp. 396–402; C. A. Lindsay, E. Marks, and L. Gorlow, "The Herzberg Theory: A Critique and Reformulation," *Journal of Applied Psychology,* vol. 51, 1967, pp. 330–339. This latter study and one by J. R. Hinrichs and L. A. Mischkind, "Empirical and Theoretical Limitations of the Two-Factor Hypothesis of Job Satisfaction," *Journal of Applied Psychology,* vol. 51, 1967, pp. 191–200, are especially useful for suggesting possible reformulations and extensions of the theory which may help overcome some of the objections voiced in the studies mentioned above.
10. Dunnette, Campbell, and Hakel, op. cit., pp. 169–173.
11. M. S. Viteles, *Motivation and Morale in Industry,* New York: Norton, 1953, Chap. 14; A. Kornhauser, "Psychological Studies of Employee Attitudes," *Journal of Consulting Psychology,* vol. 8, 1944, pp. 127–143.
12. Herzberg, op. cit., Chaps. 7–9.
13. Herzberg, op. cit., Chap. 8.
14. F. Friedlander and E. Walton, "Positive and Negative Motivations Toward Work," *Administrative Science Quarterly,* vol. 9, 1964, pp. 194–207.
15. It should be noted that the Porter and Lawler research reported above extends the Maslow model by providing an explicit linkage between need satisfaction and performance and also implicitly recognizes individual motivational differences. To do these things, their research makes use of the Vroomian concepts discussed in the next section.
16. A. H. Brayfield and W. H. Crockett, "Employee Attitudes and Employee Performance," *Psychological Bulletin,* vol. 52, 1955, p. 416.

17. B. S. Georgopoulas, G. M. Mahoney, and N. W. Jones, "A Path-Goal Approach to Productivity," *Journal of Applied Psychology,* vol. 41, 1957, pp. 345–353.
18. This section is based especially on discussions in Vroom, op. cit., Chaps. 2 and 7. See also J. Galbraith and L. L. Cummings, "An Empirical Investigation of the Motivational Determinants of Task Performance: Interactive Effects between Instrumentality—Valence and Motivation—Ability," *Organizational Behavior and Human Performance,* vol. 2, 1967, pp. 237–257.
19. Vroom, op. cit., p. 6.
20. Vroom, op. cit., p. 17.
21. Vroom, op. cit., p. 18.
22. Vroom, op. cit.
23. V. H. Vroom, "Organizational Choice: A Study of Pre- and Post-decision Processes," *Organizational Behavior and Human Performance,* vol. 1, 1966, pp. 212–225.
24. Galbraith and Cummings, op. cit., pp. 237–257.
25. J. W. Hill, "An Application of Decision Theory to Complex Industrial Behavior," unpublished dissertation, Detroit: Wayne State University, 1965.
26. Edwards, op. cit., pp. 473–499.
27. For discussions of these measures, see C. Osgood, G. Suci, and P. Tannenbaum, *The Measurement of Meaning,* Urbana: University of Illinois, 1957; A. L. Edwards, *Personal Preference Schedule Manual,* New York: Psychological Corporation, 1959.
28. E. E. Lawler and L. W. Porter, "Antecedent Attitudes of Effective Managerial Performance," *Organizational Behavior and Human Performance,* vol. 2, 1967, pp. 122–142.
29. Vroom, *Work and Motivation,* op. cit., Chap. 2.

IMPROVING PRODUCTIVITY AND JOB SATISFACTION*

Raymond A. Katzell
Daniel Yankelovich
with Mitchell Fein,
Oscar A. Ornati, and
Abraham Nash

Methods for improving labor productivity have been known at least since the time of the Industrial Revolution. They exist at various levels and in various spheres of knowledge, including macroeconomics (shifting national investment priorities from consumption to production), microeconomics (increasing rate of machinery replacement), production engineering (more effective work methods), and personnel management (better training of workers).

Although not as well tested, various strategies for improving employee job satisfaction also have been developed. They include paying people better wages, furnishing job security, providing competent and considerate supervision, and giving employees work commensurate with their abilities and interests.

Why a resurgence of concern with productivity and quality of work life? Experience and studies have taught us how to improve *either* productivity or job satisfaction. What is not clear is how we can enhance *both* simultaneously. Some people even have argued that our best developed techniques for increasing one do so at the expense of the other. For example, work rationalization has often been accused of dehumanizing work, while industrial democracy has been criticized by some as the province of humanitarians who don't have to meet a payroll.

Our review, therefore, has focused on illuminating this area of obscurity: How can productivity and job satisfaction be increased together? In other words: How can we improve the economic performance of an organization and at the same time increase satisfaction of its workers?

We have limited our inquiry to certain topics that have been exten-

---

* Reprinted with permission of author and publisher from *Organizational Dynamics,* Vol. 4, No. 1 (Summer 1975), pp. 69–80. AMACOM, a division of American Management Associations.

 The book reports a study prepared with the support of Research Applied to National Needs Division of the National Science Foundation; the views expressed are those of the authors and should not be ascribed as views of the National Science Foundation.

sively studied and have shown considerable promise for meeting the objectives of our study. These topics deal with key structural relationships among organizational members and groups, especially the ways in which they are related in terms of responsibilities, control, and compensation. Also considered in our study were experiments that involved such extensive changes in the above factors that the end result amounted to a revision of the whole sociotechnical system.

Another important emphasis of our study was on trustworthy information. This meant restricting ourselves to objective and empirical facts generated by studies that were methodologically valid. We quickly discovered that our chosen topics have been the subject of endless opinions and advice, much of it inconsistent or ambiguous. Often the "facts" assembled to buttress opinions turned out to be imprecise or attributed to causes of questionable authenticity. In other words, we decided that we could learn more from a smaller number of studies of higher quality than from a larger number of more equivocal impressions.

In spite of this sharp focus, we discovered that research findings were not entirely unambiguous or consistent. However, there was enough agreement to suggest certain directions for policy, and it is on these implications that our article will focus. The reader should bear in mind that even these conclusions are not unequivocal and that some might choose to interpret the picture somewhat differently than we do.

THE POLICY MAKER'S DILEMMA

The most general conclusion to be drawn from the research findings is that policy makers must face up to a serious dilemma and find some way to resolve it. The dilemma is that policy makers would like to achieve two objectives in any work organization—one being to enhance productivity and performance, the other to improve the quality of employees' working life and job satisfaction. Many policy makers assume that the two goals are causally linked so that any improvement in job satisfaction will automatically produce a parallel improvement in productivity. But if any one fact clearly stands out from the massive accumulation of data—the hundreds of studies encompassed in this report—it is that worker job satisfaction and productivity do not follow parallel paths.

This does not mean that the two objectives are incompatible; in fact, there is evidence that they can be achieved together. Nor does it mean that the two goals are totally independent of one another. Under certain conditions, improving productivity will enhance worker satisfaction, and improvements in job satisfaction will contribute to productivity. What it does mean is that there is no certain relationship between the two. Indeed, the two objectives are so loosely coupled, there are so many intervening links between them, and the relationship is so indirect that efforts primarily aimed at improving worker satisfaction that are based on the assumption that productivity will thereby increase are more likely than not to leave productivity unchanged or at best improve it marginally. They may even cause productivity to decline. Indeed, a careful analysis of the findings shows that from a humanist point of view, the most popular, highly publicized, and appealing techniques currently being proposed to policy makers as means for accomplishing both ends simultaneously will most likely, by themselves, have only minimal impact. These include procedures such as job enrichment, management by objectives (MBO), autonomous work groups, participative management, and so forth.

In other words, a wide array of methods for improving workers' job attitudes or performance exists, but each of them characteristically tackles only a partial aspect of the workers' relationships to their jobs—their financial incentives, control over their work, working conditions, social relationships, or labor-management relations. No one of these, we have learned, ordinarily is enough to affect both productivity and satisfaction significantly, although in some instances, improvements in one or the other objective may be realized. For reasons that will be discussed later in this article, simultaneous large-scale and enduring improvements in performance as well as job satisfaction appear to depend on developing a combination of methods that relate human to economic concerns. Thus there may be ways to improve both productivity and job satisfaction even though as goals they are functionally independent. But there is no single-target program or standard formula that can be applied uniformly to any and all situations.

Our central conclusion, therefore, sounds both a negative note of warning about expecting too much from some of the currently fashionable but overly narrow approaches as well as a positive note of hope that marked and enduring improvements can be achieved that will promote both objectives.

Barriers to Progress

Further progress in improving both productivity and job satisfaction is complicated by two large obstacles—inadequate knowledge and "political" resistance to change. The knowledge obstacle derives from the need cited previously for using a variety of methods rather than any single approach and adapting them patiently and skillfully to each work setting. The multiple sources of resistance to change constitute a political obstacle in the broad sense of that term. Among the political barriers are the real or perceived adversary relations between management and workers. Managers may think that efforts to improve the quality of working life will compete with programs to improve economic performance; rank-and-file workers may see efforts to improve productivity as exploitative or inimical to their job security.

Thus the difficulty for the policy maker is that to effect large-scale improvements in the productive and human use of human resources, he must make numerous and far-reaching changes before the desired effects become visible. At the same time, political resistances require him to introduce changes cautiously, moving one step at a time.

STRATEGIES FOR IMPROVING JOB SATISFACTION AND PRODUCTIVITY

While it would be hard to exaggerate the difficulties of the task, they can be overcome by means of adequate knowledge and sufficient statesmanship on the part of both management and labor. In fact, a survey[1] that we conducted of the opinions held by managers and union officials regarding this subject suggests that there is much agreement between them, even though it is by no means complete. By and large, both groups say they would like to achieve the dual objectives of improving satisfaction *and* productivity. They also claim that they are ready to cooperate on specific programs, although cautiously and with some mistrust. What appears to be lacking is the specific agreement and knowledge, both theoretical and practical, of how to achieve the desired goals. The costs of changing—in terms of time, effort, and money—are also undoubtedly an implicit barrier.

1. The "Critical Mass" Principle

Perhaps the best way to think about the requirements for improving productivity together with job satisfaction is by rough analogy with the physicist's notion of "critical mass." The organizational changes required to achieve the critical mass must be sufficiently deep and far reaching: Superficial or narrow efforts tend to be transitory in their effects and as frequently mentioned in the research literature, hardly even noticed by workers. This does not mean that necessary changes must be made all at once; it does suggest that marked improvements in both satisfaction and performance will generally not show up until at least several major steps are taken that in combination create a qualitatively new and better sociotechnical system.

2. The "Motivation" Principle

Of course, programs will not achieve the dual objective—enhancing both productivity and job satisfaction—only by being comprehensive; the elements must be integrated around some general principle. We can best understand that integrating principle by reference to the basic distinction between work satisfaction and work motivation. Many people are satisfied with their jobs because their work is undemanding and requires only minimal effort on their part. Others are dissatisfied because they are highly motivated to do a good job but frustrated by obstacles in the work situation that prevent them from doing so. Thus we find that workers fall into any of four possible categories:

- Satisfied and highly motivated.
- Satisfied and weakly motivated.
- Dissatisfied and highly motivated.
- Dissatisfied and weakly motivated.

Forging the link between work satisfaction and productivity critically depends on increasing the size of the first of the four groups—people who are both satisfied and highly motivated. The other three groups fail to contribute to achieving one or both of the objectives.

Of all the factors that help create highly motivated and highly satisfied workers, the principal one appears to be that effective performance be recognized and rewarded—in whatever terms are meaningful to the individual, be it financial, psychological, or both. In order to enhance both productivity and job satisfaction, programs must function so that workers find effective performance to be rewarding and that doing what one finds rewarding results in effective performance. Conversely, performing ineffectively should not result in rewards, nor should doing rewarding things result in poor performance. Needless to add, we use the term "reward" to refer to any one of a number of gratifying consequences, including recognition, financial gain, and the satisfaction that comes from the successful use of the individual's full capabilities.

This principle adds up to the simple, but nonetheless valid, precept that the key to having workers who are both satisfied and productive is *motivation,* that is, arousing and maintaining the desire and will to work effectively—having workers who are productive not because they are coerced but because they are committed.

3. Shared Benefits

An extension of the previous principle is that workers at all levels must see that the program will be beneficial to them in terms that are important to them. For example, a productivity improvement program involving job changes in a mass production plant with a large number of unskilled and semiskilled workers would probably have little interest to these workers if they do not receive additional pay for increased productivity. Not that pay alone will positively affect their attitudes. Successful programs, in other words, will be characterized by a wide sharing of financial and other benefits throughout the organization.

4. Job Design

We can exemplify the preceding points by the research literature on job enrichment and redesign, one of the major strategies currently proposed for enhancing worker motivation. But before we summarize that research, it is important to avoid a common misunderstanding arising from ambiguity in the use of the terms "job enlargement," "job enrichment," and "job redesign." Sometimes these terms are used in an all-encompassing sense to cover not only the refashioning of the job itself but also greater work autonomy, more democracy in the work place, and even productivity-sharing incentive plans. At other times, the terms are used in a more specific sense and confined to modification in the character of the task itself—the activities and responsibilities that together constitute the "job." It is in this latter sense that we use these terms.

Our analysis of the literature on this topic indicates that job redesign programs are by no means a sure-fire road to improving both job satisfaction and productivity. We found examples in which job redesign improved workers' attitudes but not productivity, both attitudes and productivity, and neither attitudes nor productivity.

There are too few well-controlled studies to permit us to explain these inconsistencies with certainty, but it would seem that job redesign clearly had beneficial effects on both job attitudes and productivity only when the principles of critical mass, rewarding performance, and shared benefits were implemented.

More specifically, the critical mass principle operates here in two ways. Job redesign is likely to improve both attitudes and performance only when:

1. Changes in job content are sufficiently nontrivial to be perceptible to workers, typically in terms of greater self-regulation, diversity, meaningfulness, challenge, and social responsibility. (However, as will be noted below, what is not trivial to some workers may be quite trivial to others.)

2. Changes in job content are part of a more pervasive program of improved working policies and practices that also has as elements adequate pay and job security, proper resources and working conditions,

increased mutual influence by people at all levels, and constructive labor-management relations.

Not all workers are seeking greater challenge or responsibility, and hence not all will find enriched jobs to be more rewarding. Furthermore, to some workers, working may be more of a means to other ends such as increased income or socializing, and such workers would be less affected by changes in job content alone.

In short, rewards must be tailored to the person being rewarded. Expanding the content of jobs is more likely to be rewarding to workers whose "bread-and-butter" needs have been reasonably satisfied and who are now seeking opportunities for self-expression and growth, that is, particularly better-educated, younger workers and those in higher-level, white collar jobs.

The principle of shared benefits is not as manifest in the controlled experiments as it is in case studies and the experience of practitioners. Job changes that threaten job security, disrupt wage scales accepted as fair, or result in inequities in the distribution of resulting financial benefits seem likely to fail in their intent. This is prone to occur whenever workers believe that increased responsibility will not be matched by increased earnings or whenever managers anticipate that costs will exceed benefits. Job redesign is likely to work best when everyone involved stands to share equitably in the resulting financial benefits.

In addition, the studies reveal other obstacles or problems to overcome in implementing programs of job redesign. Some work systems are less amenable to the efficient restructuring of jobs than others. This especially is the case when jobs are closely interdependent on one another and/or tied to a complex machine technology.

Enlargement of the jobs of some workers may entail reduction of the jobs of others; for example, expanding the self-regulation of workers may diminish the number and scope of supervisory jobs. Inadequate absorption of supervisors somewhere in the revised organizational set-up can generate a destructive force.

Spelling out the conditions on which the effects of job design depend emphasizes several points:

- Failure to meet one or more of the necessary conditions may account for why some programs of job redesign may have negligible results.
- Where those conditions can be accommodated successfully, programs involving job redesign can serve as a useful way of helping improve job satisfaction and productivity.
- The conditions are sufficiently numerous and restrictive as to require considerable commitment to pervasive change on the part of the long-established organization. Programs should not be undertaken casually if they are to succeed.

• Because the preconditions are so numerous and basic, a critical mass of integrated changes is more likely to deal with them successfully than is a single-target program, such as job enlargement alone.

5. Patterns of Control

The redistribution of influence and control in organizations has been proposed as a road to improving worker motivation for an even longer time than has job redesign. Programs for redistributing control have ranged from a focus on greater self-regulation by the worker over his own job to greater autonomy for work groups, increased mutual influence throughout organizations via participative management, and formal modes of labor-management cooperation such as through codetermination or collective bargaining. All of these approaches may give workers a feeling of greater influence.

We have already seen that increased self-regulation is an element in job enrichment, the effects of which partly depend on whether the workers in question have needs for greater responsibility and autonomy. The same consideration also plays a part in the effects of programs for increasing control by workers. Some workers appreciate having greater influence; others resent it. The undoubted personal and cultural influences on the appropriateness of different patterns of control cannot be reduced to any single factor; therefore they have to be assessed in each situation.

On the other hand, it is possible to discern some general trends from the impact of various programs for shaping control patterns. We will discuss these first in general terms and then in terms of three foci of control: the individual job, the work group, and the organization as a whole.

Workers who see themselves as having more influence over what goes on in their jobs, their work groups, and their organizations generally have more favorable attitudes about their jobs than do those who believe they are less influential. Workers having more influence also are less prone to leave their jobs. The effects of control patterns on productivity are not as clear or as strong. However, we offer the following tentative conclusions: First, equalization of control among hierarchical levels does not appear in itself to affect productivity very much. Second, greater overall influence among members of an organization or group does seem to be conducive to better productivity. Third, a greater voice in defining work goals, methods, and compensation at both individual and group levels may be particularly effective in improving productivity.

In the individual job. As already noted, increased autonomy or self-regulation on the job is an element in job enrichment that may, given the right workers and the appropriate conditions, help enhance job satisfaction and productivity.

Management by objectives (MBO) programs, which feature an increased role for the worker in setting goals for his or her own job, represent one approach to increasing self-control relative to control by others. On the basis of a small number of studies using managerial and exempt employees, our review suggests that MBO programs serve to increase these employees' motivation to attain the goals set for their work and also improve their job satisfaction. Effects on actual job performance are not clear, but there are indications that they too may be positive. With rank-and-file workers, the utility of this approach has yet to be proved.

In the work group. Giving workers more "say" over what goes on in their groups usually has favorable effects on job satisfaction, work motivation, and turnover. Effects on productivity are more clearly favorable when the scope of influence includes goal setting, work methods, and compensation methods. Last, the programs are more likely to succeed if workers' personalities match the values of the program—that is, if employees tend to be independent and nonauthoritarian in their outlook.

In the organization as a whole. Organizations in which members at all levels exercise greater control over what goes on in the organization are typically more productive and have more highly motivated, better satisfied personnel than those where the total amount of control is relatively low. What is not clear, however, is whether high organizational control is the cause or the effect of having high motivation.

Those organizations where control is more equally shared by various echelons of the workforce usually have better-satisfied workers but are not consistently more productive. This may be due to the difficulty of equalizing control throughout large or complex organizations and/or to the importance of situational factors such as the personalities of members, task requirements, and amount of commitment to organizational goals.

What about the effects on job performance and satisfaction of formal mechanisms of participation such as labor-management committees and collective bargaining with unions? They have received little attention in the literature of behavioral science. From scattered available data, they appear to constitute useful ways of increasing worker participation and possibly also work motivation, but such positive results depend on a host of preconditions, chief among them being mutual trust between management and labor.

6. Patterns of Compensation

Workers who are more highly paid generally like their pay and their jobs better and are less likely to quit or be absent. Workers in a given job who are paid more than other workers with a comparable job are also likely to have higher motivation and productivity but only if their pay level is linked to their performance.

Workers whose compensation is out of line with their own standards of equity are less satisfied with their pay and jobs than those who believe that they are paid equitably. A related point is that satisfaction with pay is greater when it is clearly tied to performance than when it is not. Another important point: The potentially favorable results of improved compensation patterns are cancelled out if they have an adverse impact on other worker rewards such as job security and social relations.

7. Systemwide Changes

We have summarized our conclusions regarding the effects of three widely discussed structural programs for increasing employees' motivation and therefore their job satisfaction and performance: job redesign, increased participation by employees, and reward-for-performance. No one program, considered separately, has yielded unequivocal results in terms of both job satisfaction and productivity. Moreover, when the results were positive, they often tended to be disappointingly small. Positive results were likely to happen only when the programs "fit" other conditions in the situation.

These conclusions suggest that more positive effects might result from more extensive changes that create what amounts to new work systems. A dozen reasonably well-documented experiments of this sort suggested to us the following conclusions:

- Changes of the nature and magnitude of those represented in these systemwide studies can have major effects in raising the productivity and improving the economic performance of manufacturing plants. (They generally have not been tested in service organizations.)
- These changes also appear to have some favorable effect on the overall job satisfaction of the workers, although this finding is not as well documented nor does its magnitude seem to be as great as are the effects on productivity and other aspects of performance.
- There is evidence that people do work harder and that their job involvement and commitment may be increased, although again this impression is not solidly documented. The weight of the evidence suggests that the beneficial effects of these systems on employee productivity probably owe more to improvements in work methods and production capability than they do to increased worker motivation.

Critical Ingredients of Effective Systems

The totality of the findings reviewed above may be summarized by the following list of critical ingredients of systems that may attain the desired dual objectives of higher productivity and job satisfaction. Such systems, we believe, have potential to be *efficient*—in Barnard's use of the term—that is, not only productively effective but also serving to satisfy the needs and desires of their members. It is probably not essential that every system contain all of the ingredients in order to be efficient. Indeed, some may be inappropriate where the nature of the technology or the needs of the workforce call for different treatments. But it seems unlikely that much progress can be made if most are absent.

1. The pay of workers must be linked to their performance and to productivity gains.
2. Workers and work must be matched so as to create a work situation that workers will see as capable of meeting their needs and expectations and where they will have the capabilities and resources to be successful.
3. For workers who desire it, their work should provide opportunity for full use of their abilities, making a meaningful contribution, having challenging and diversified duties, and being responsible for others.
4. Workers at all levels must have inputs to plans and decisions affecting their jobs and working lives.
5. Appropriate resources, including work methods and equipment, must be provided to facilitate workers' performance and minimize obstacles to carrying out their jobs.
6. Adequate "hygiene" conditions must exist, including competent and considerate supervision, fair pay and fringe benefits, job security, good working conditions, and sound employee relations.

Our six-point list is not necessarily complete. There are other elements that theory and practice suggest as being of possible importance but that suffer from insufficient attention in the research literature. As a consequence, their role in improving both job satisfaction and performance has not yet been sufficiently well established to include them. One example of these possible elements is career structures that afford favorable future prospects for promotion, personal growth, and greater rewards. Another is revised use of time for work and leisure—the four-day week, sabbatical leave, educational leave, split schedules for couples, and early and partial retirement plans.

TOWARD IMPLEMENTATION

We hope that we have made clear that the principles and conclusions discussed above are by no means unambiguous. As we have noted, the research on which they are based is not always sufficiently convincing, in terms of either quality or quantity, to permit firm conclusions.

There is no doubt that joint productivity/quality-of-working-life programs face formidable obstacles. At the same time, it is also clear that for certain organizations, the rewards are well worth the effort to overcome them. It is therefore necessary for each organization to determine for itself whether the rewards are sufficiently great to merit such an undertaking.

How can this be done? We propose that each organization interested in determining whether or not it is ready to make a major commitment to overhauling its human resources management along the lines outlined in this report undertake a special study to answer the following eight questions. These can serve as an effective checklist to enable each organization to determine whether this type of approach is right for them in light of the conditions noted previously as prerequisites to its success. If any one of the eight questions cannot be answered positively, at least in part, then the likelihood of success is greatly reduced. If all can be answered positively, then the likelihood of success of such programs is great, and the organization can be confident about making a commitment that will pay off both in terms of enhanced economic performance and a dynamic, vigorous, and highly motivated workforce.

The eight-question checklist is as follows:

1. *Does the organization's performance depend substantially on the efforts of its employees?* We are using performance here in its broad sense, including intangible and qualitative aspects such as customer service and quality of workmanship as well as efficiency of production. Those organizations in which worker care and effort play a major part in performance and management places high priority on such factors are more open to change programs. Service organizations are particularly dependent on their workers' performance.

2. *Is the organization's background of employee and labor relations such that an expression of desire to enter upon cooperative ventures will be viewed by employees with some credibility?* Success depends on the existence of at least a moderate amount of good will and trust among employees and management, enough that the various parties are willing to give a new approach a try instead of undermining it in advance through cynicism and mistrust.

3. *Does the organization stand fairly high on "hygiene" factors?* If there is fear of job insecurity throughout the organization, if working conditions are substandard and a source of widespread complaint, or if pay levels are felt to be unjustly low, then the climate for launching new cooperative programs may not be right.

4. *Does the technology with which the organization is identified leave room for flexibility and change in the organization of work?* There are variations among organizations in the extent to which their established production system is amenable to the kinds of changes that may be needed to implement these programs. In some instances, experimentation may be more costly—in terms of investment and risk of failure—than in

others. Some high-technology, highly structured industries that might seem the least likely candidates (for example, a petroleum refinery) may turn out on closer inspection to have a surprisingly great potential for enhancing both productivity and worker quality of life.

5. *Is there a genuine interest at the policy-making levels of the organization in giving equal emphasis to the dual objectives?* Some organizations are not serious about improving their economic performance; others are intensely interested in productivity but have little concern for employees beyond serving as a means to this end.

6. *Is there willingness at the policy-maker level to share with workers at all levels the economic benefits of improved productivity?* If not, employees will soon lose interest. The program might even backfire if it becomes understood as only another device for generating greater profits for management with no benefit to workers.

7. *Is there willingness at the policy-maker level to let go of some power and authority in the interest of enhancing and enlarging the overall authority and power of the organization?* Beyond a doubt, a cooperative venture will mean sharing decision making among a larger group of people. If the key policy makers in the organization are unwilling to face such a prospect, the program is likely to bog down in the early stages.

8. *Is the workforce predominantly young, fairly well educated and does it possess actual or potential high-level technical skills that are needed in the organization?* A well-educated, young workforce—high school graduates and above—has different needs and responds to different motivations than one that is old, set in its ways, and lacking in potential for learning. There is an almost universal desire among young people today to make full use of their potential skills. Better educated, higher-skill workers are also generally more interested in seeing changes along the lines proposed here than are those at lower educational and job levels.

These eight questions are not easy to answer, but they all are answerable. We strongly urge any organization considering a program of the type described here to make the effort to answer them as thoroughly and formally as possible before making a major commitment.

At this point the policy maker may ask, "Why bother? Why go through so much trouble, effort, and expense to link together two objectives that have been pursued in the past separately? In the past, productivity was enhanced through intelligent applications of technology and capital, while worker satisfaction was achieved by improving the employee's standard of living. Why should we now abandon these successful and proven methods in favor of new approaches that are relatively unproven, difficult to apply, and obviously fraught with hazards?"

If this were 20 years ago, or even ten, such questions would be difficult to counter. But our interpretation of current social trends suggests that an increasing number of organizations, if they are to be viable in the future, must find a fresh approach to bring together productivity and job satisfaction rather than to let them go their separate ways.

NOTE

1. The findings of that survey are summarized in the book cited previously. A detailed report on the management sample is given in M. E. Katzell, *Productivity: The Measure and the Myth,* AMA Survey Report, AMACOM, New York, 1975.

A WAY OF ANALYZING CHANGE: FORCE-FIELD ANALYSIS*

No individual or organization has ever been exempt from change, but it is unlikely that either individuals or organizations have ever been challenged more by the need to change than they are today. The management of change is a major part of the responsibility of managers everywhere, whether the organization is concerned with health, education, or the production of goods or services.

This article is a modest contribution to successful coping with the ubiquitous problems of change. Let us sketch the personal and organizational challenges of change while we also outline our strategy for helping meet the challenge. Increasingly, managers in today's organizations must analyze change as it takes place, they must attempt to predict what changes will occur and what these changes imply, and they must plan to take deliberate action to induce desired changes. There is no magical way of doing the total job, and this is an awesome datum.

There is a second way of viewing the challenges of change. That is, any help in doing the job must be welcome. The present approach to providing such help is to introduce a simple but useful conceptual way for considering change. This aids in filling a critical need, for the diversity of behaviors involved in any process of change requires some conceptual tool to permit the ordering of complex reality. Without such conceptual "handles" reality too easily slips out of our grasp.

The conceptual tool introduced here—force-field analysis—derives from the pioneering work of the psychologist Kurt Lewin. He conceived of man in terms consistent with those of modern science. The behavior

* Based on National Training Laboratories, *Reading Book* (1965).

of man derives not from his "nature," for example, as it exists independently. Rather, man exists within a total field of forces, and his behavioral position at any point in time reflects the resultant balance of the forces acting upon him at that moment. Until that balance of forces is changed, the behavior persists. This condition is called "quasi-stationary equilibrium." More traditional approaches would despair of changing behavior unless man's "nature" were changed first.

Consider a typical profile of the production record of a work unit in some organization, to illustrate the general sense of Lewin's concept. Let us assume that production varies only within a narrow range, approximating a so-called "straight-line production norm." Why does this profile of productivity persist? An explanation consistent with Lewin's concept of behavior as a resultant of opposing forces within an individual's life-space takes this form:[1]

> [The pattern persists] because the forces that tend to raise the level of production are equal to the forces that tend to depress it. Among the forces tending to raise the level of production might be: (a) the pressures of supervisors on the work team to produce more; (b) the desire of at least some team members to attract favorable attention from supervisors in order to get ahead individually; (c) the desire of team members to earn more under the incentive plan of the plant. Such forces Lewin called "driving forces." Among the forces tending to lower the level of production might be: (a′) a group standard in the production team against "rate busting" or "eager beavering" by individual workers; (b′) resistance of team members to accepting training and supervision from management; (c′) feelings by workers that the product they are producing is not important. Granted the goal of increased productivity, these forces are "restraining forces." The balance between the two sets of forces, which defines the established level of production, Lewin called a "quasi-stationary equilibrium."

The verbal illustration of the notion of a field of forces also may be presented graphically. That is, we can depict the driving and restraining forces that peg our hypothetical straight-line production profile as in Figure 1. Essentially, the graphical representation facilitates description. Thus it enables us to "see" the pushes and pulls of the forces in opposition, holding productivity at a stable level. The figure also includes a further visual advantage. Thus both the driving and the restraining forces in Figure 1 are distinguished in terms of their (hypothetical) relative strengths. The force a′ is a more powerful restraining force than b′, for example, as is represented by the longer vector arrow for a′. Judgments about such relative strengths cannot always be accurately made in practice, of course, but we often have a strong intuitive idea about which forces in a particular situation are "stronger," and we do act on these

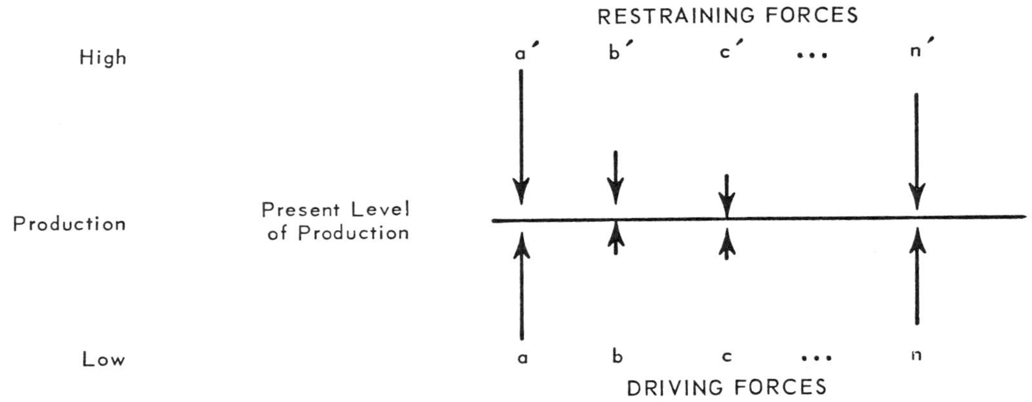

LEGEND:

(a) = supervisory pressure to raise output
(b) = employee desire to get ahead
(c) = employee desire to get incentive rates
(n) = other driving forces

(a′) = group norm restricting output
(b′) = employee resistance to training and supervision
(c′) = employee feeling of product insignificance
(n′) = other restraining forces

FIGURE 1
Illustrative analysis of the field of forces freezing a stable level of output

ideas. Force-field analysis requires that we recognize and consciously manipulate these intuitive estimates. The results of the exercise are often surprising. Thus a force we originally thought to be significant may become less so as the detailed forces are set down and compared with one another, that once potent force may have to be decomposed into several component forces which in turn derive from an entirely unexpected source. At the very least, the use of the force-field notion helps clarify the relevant aspects of a program of planned change even if serendipitous benefits do not result.

The approach to change via force-field analysis aids action as well as facilitates description. For example, the very notion of a field of forces implies three basic strategies for planned change. These strategies are:

1. the number and/or strength of driving factors could be increased;
2. the number and/or strength of restraining factors could be decreased; and
3. previously restraining forces could be changed into driving forces.

These three strategies for change may be illustrated briefly. First, the number or strength of driving forces could be increased variously, as by adding a new supervisor who gains the trust and respect of work-unit members. A derivative new desire to make the well-liked supervisor "look good," for example, might be a substantial driving force toward increased output.

Second, the number or strength of restraining forces could be decreased. For example, attempts could be made to demonstrate the importance of the contribution of the work unit to the commendable purposes of the parent organization or to the satisfaction of consumers provided by the product of the work unit.

Third, previously restraining forces could be converted into driving forces. The norm of low output, for example, suggests a particular target for this strategy. If that norm could be changed to sanction higher output, patently, a new driving force of considerable magnitude would replace a previously restraining force of some magnitude. As this description implies, this third strategy has high payoffs. Variations of the third strategy are correspondingly difficult to bring off, but despair is not in order. [Several contributions in the present volume demonstrate that the effort is not beyond our present capabilities. These include: Likert, "The Nature of Highly Effective Groups"; Sayles, "Work Group Behavior and the Larger Organization"; and several others.]

Because of its simplicity—and despite it—force-field analysis can be enormously useful for the administrative analyst. Of particular note, for example, is the fact that the technique permits and encourages several successive levels of analysis. Thus, in the case of the productivity of our hypothetical work unit, a second level of force-field analysis could be done on any one of the forces isolated at the first level of analysis. That is, to illustrate, the group norm restricting output might be described in terms of its specific driving and restraining forces. The products of force-field analysis at more than one level are various. Patently, increasingly fine and detailed analysis is possible. Moreover, force-field analysis at the second level and beyond may suggest ways of unfreezing attitudes that were not clear at the first level. Or, successive applications of force-field analysis may require reformulating what was thought to be the original change-problem.

Of course, a technique is only a technique. Together with the following useful guidelines for instituting planned change, however, force-field analysis acquits itself well. Useful guidelines include the following:[2]

1. to change any sub-system, relevant aspects of the total environment also must be changed;
2. to change behavior at any one level of a hierarchical organization often requires complementary and reinforcing change at levels above and below the target level;
3. to begin change, the target should usually be a point at which stresses exist, for these stresses can help motivate change in the system;
4. to work toward thoroughgoing changes in a hierarchical structure often implies starting at the policy-making level;
5. to plan any process of change, both the formal and informal organizations must be considered; and
6. to encourage the effectiveness and smoothness of change, individuals at many levels of an organization should participate in fact-finding, in diagnosing needed changes, in formulating goals and programs for change, and in reality-testing those goals and programs.

NOTES

1. "Change Does Not Have to be Haphazard," p. 58, from National Training Laboratories, *Reading Book, Nineteenth Annual Summer Laboratories In Human Relations Training, 1965* (mimeographed).
2. *Ibid.*, pp. 60–64.

JOB ENRICHMENT: HOW IMPORTANT IS THE WORK ITSELF?*

Theodore O. Prenting

With the publicity given theories of motivation and management's desire for greater productivity, it is perhaps inevitable we should reach the point where it is suggested that all factory jobs be redesigned and enriched and where, indeed, at least one European company has built an entirely new plant for just this purpose.[1] But before more companies take a similar approach, it is appropriate to look more carefully at job enrichment and at what may be less expensive, more direct responses to the "problem" of worker discontent.

Concern about the lot of industrial workers is certainly nothing new. With the advent of modern industry, however, the division of labor, most visible in assembly line work, has come under periodic attack for its real or supposed social and psychological consequences. Handicraft movements, such as that led by John Ruskin in England in the late nineteenth century, argued for the integration of tasks and the return of "craft pleasures" to work. Social philosophers have described the subdivision of industrial work as an abnormal form of the social division of labor, alienating man from his work and leading to antagonism between labor and capital. These earlier critics have their modern heirs in spokesmen for job enlargement and job enrichment who wish to restore to industrial work some of the skill, responsibility and variety eliminated by the subdivision of work. Yet, many recent studies show that subdivision of work, *by itself,* is not at the root of worker unhappiness as it may exist, and that reversing the process will not, necessarily, ease it.

A TASK FORCE VIEW OF WORK IN AMERICA—SOME CONTRADICTIONS

A well-publicized study, "Work in America: Report of a Special Task Force to the Secretary of Health, Education, and Welfare" (1973), essentially claims that workers are so dissatisfied with their work that the only solution is to redesign and enrich all factory jobs, *even if productivity is reduced.* Less publicized are the many scholarly papers written since that report which raise serious questions about its validity.

---

* Reprinted by permission from the January 1976 issue of the *University of Michigan Business Review,* Vol. 28, No. 1, pp. 26–30, published by the Graduate School of Business Administration, The University of Michigan.

For example, the model of worker attitudes and behavior used in the study, a model based on the Maslow-Herzberg concepts of a hierarchy of worker needs, has been questioned. The task force report argues that their educational and economic status places many workers in a position where having an interesting job is now as important as having a job that pays well. But as one author has pointed out, there is a weakness in the inherent static premises of the Maslow-Herzberg model itself. Even though individual earnings and family incomes may be higher today than they were, most American workers do not consider themselves affluent and they continue to seek higher pay to avail themselves of the new "necessities" our society can provide.[2]

Tangible evidence to support the task force study is also inconclusive with respect to increases in labor turnover rates, absenteeism, strikes, productivity or labor force participation. The report also fails to give equal attention to job enrichment plans that did not work. For example, GM's Truck and Coach Division shifted back from team assembly of motor homes to line assembly due to the complexity of the jobs and the inability of workers to meet production standards.[3]

Studies of workers in such activities as assembly do not bear out the sweeping task force views. In a study covering 3,800 factory workers involved in assembly in five different industries in five states, only about 20 percent expressed dissatisfaction with their jobs.[4] Depending upon the industry, from 79 percent to 88 percent of the assembly line workers, whose comments were obtained first hand, *liked* assembly work. They *did not want* added responsibilities, quality requirements or any significant changes in job content.

Nevertheless, the greatest discontent was found among auto assembly workers. Why should that be the case and why is it that the auto industry is practically the only one discussed in the popular literature on worker discontent?

The auto companies and their plants are big and impersonal. There is limited opportunity for advancement since, among other reasons, assembly plants are often physically separated from the machining plants where there might be more lucrative jobs. There is also little difference in pay rates among assemblers. Most importantly, many observers believe management has simply not achieved the rapport with its workers that other industries and firms have developed.

Studies on job enrichment schemes to date suggest that greater job satisfaction, improved quality and increased production flexibility *may be possible* at the expense of higher wages (due to greater operator skill required), larger and more costly space requirements, and significantly higher operator learning and facilities costs (the latter due to necessary duplication of facilities).[5] But a much-publicized new Swedish automobile plant designed literally from the ground up to allow for enriched jobs through a team approach to assembly may prove to be an expensive experiment, too expensive to be repeated without careful study.

The potential advantages might seem worth the costs, but studies show benefits are frequently only achieved for a short time period—until the newness wears off. Herzberg cautions that "job enrichment will not be a one-time proposition, but a continuous management function . . . perhaps the job will have to be enriched again."[6]

Business management publications have generally not given the shortcomings of the Herzberg model much publicity. But many studies appearing primarily in psychology journals have raised questions about the causal relationship in Herzberg's theory. As one critical analysis concludes:

> It is noteworthy that the two-factor theory has fared poorly in all of these investigations regardless of the methodology used. It seems that the evidence is now sufficient to lay the two-factor theory to rest. . . . We believe it is important that this be done so that researchers will address themselves to studying the full complexities of human motivation, rather than continuing to allow the direction of motivational research or actual administrative decisions to be dictated by the seductive simplicity of the two-factor theory.[7]

CONTROVERSY OVER THE HERZBERG MODEL

A common criticism of Herzberg's theory is that it is an oversimplification of the true complexity of human motivation. While Herzberg does not deemphasize the importance of his hygiene or maintenance factors (dissatisfiers) e.g., salary, supervision and working conditions, the danger is that his emphasis on the motivator factors (satisfiers) e.g., recognition, responsibility and work, itself, as well as his very use of the words motivator, satisfier and dissatisfier, may mislead management in its personnel policies and practices.

There is a question of whether the dichotomy between hygiene (dissatisfier) and motivator (satisfier) factors can be supported[8] and, if it cannot be, then it is impossible to test which set of factors contributes most of work motivation.[9]

Significantly, in Herzberg's own figures, reproduced in Exhibit I, certain "hygiene" factors as opposed to "motivator" factors are apparently not well distinguished in the workers' minds.[10] From a sample of 1,685 employees, salary, for example, was a factor 8 percent of the time characterizing 1,844 events on the job that led to extreme *dissatisfaction,* while 6 percent of the time it was a factor characterizing 1,753 events on the job that led to extreme *satisfaction.* Similar results are found with

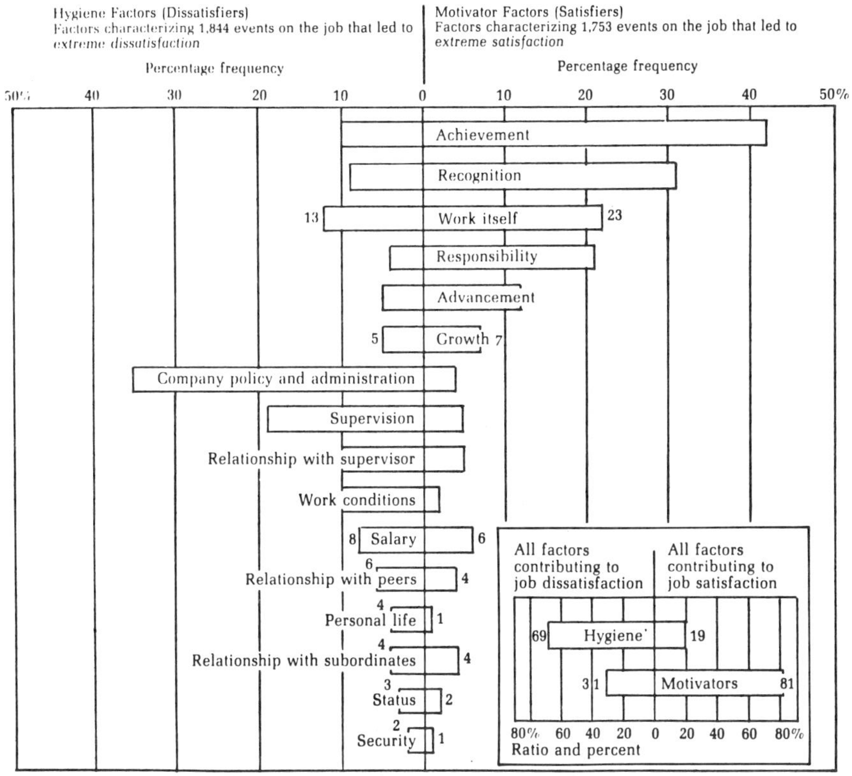

From: Frederick Herzberg, "One More Time: How Do You Motivate Employees?" *Harvard Business Review*, January-February 1968, p. 57.

EXHIBIT I
Factors Affecting Job Attitudes, as Reported in Twelve Investigations

the factor "relationship with peers," and there is no difference for "relationship with subordinates." Similarly, a major factor behind job enrichment, "work, itself," is a third-ranked "motivator," behind achievement and recognition. But it is also the "motivator" factor appearing most often in the "hygiene" column.

The economic limitations of unrestrained job redesign have received little attention in the literature, yet improved productivity through job enrichment programs is not at all assured. A review of ten studies shows an increase in production in only four cases.[11] But since the number of detailed studies is quite limited, one can merely warn that cost savings should not be anticipated.

The technical division of labor did not come about as a whim of management. As was the social division of labor that preceded it, technical division is simply a more economic way of producing goods and services. And, as Adam Smith pointed out, one of the great advantages of the division of labor lies in the ability of the machine designer to see more easily how a machine could do the more simplified tasks of the human worker.

Thus, for society to rush headlong into job enrichment is to retrogress technologically. What we should do is mechanize out of existence those jobs which are truly distasteful to the worker. Until then, however, the obvious economic answer is that we will simply have to pay workers what they believe compensates for the distaste, within the confines of what society is willing to pay for the end product. In addition, we should pay more attention to the selection of workers for particular types of work.[12] As Herzberg put it, "If you can't fully utilize an employee on the job, get rid of him, either via automation or by selecting someone with lesser ability."[13]

One might well ask, if workers are so unhappy with their work, why aren't they seeking redress through the collective bargaining process. An American labor union leader says, "If you want to enrich the job, enrich the paycheck . . . begin to decrease the number of hours a worker has to labor in order to earn a decent standard of living . . . give working people a greater sense of control over their working conditions."[14] Note that nothing is said about job content, in fact, it is denied by inference as a factor.

SOME ECONOMIC LIMITS ON JOB ENRICHMENT

The lesson for management from the job enrichment controversy is that not all people react in the same way to changes in job design and enrichment. Herzberg's contribution calls attention to work, itself, as a job factor, but individuals react as differently to expansion of their work as they do to other factors affecting their jobs.

In determining personnel policy, the needs and aspirations of diverse groups and individuals must be considered. Contrary to what some may have thought, good management and supervision; pride in oneself, the immediate work group and the company; a competitive environment; good working conditions and money are not any less important in formulating such policy.

Not all workers react favorably to enlarged or enriched jobs, nor are all jobs amenable to such enlargement. Herzberg admits that not all jobs can be enriched, and this holds true for much assembly and other repetitive work. Given the technology of the product being produced, the degree of operator control over the work pace and worker responsibility for methods and quality can only be relative, never absolute. One assembly task is not much different from the next and no amount of juggling will change them substantially.

In the new "job-enriched" Swedish auto plant, the operator time per unit could range from 3.6 to 54.8 minutes, depending upon whether the team chooses serial assembly or one-person-build for each unit. From the author's industrial experience, the lower end of the range is likely to be more common considering the learning and component/tool handling time involved and the rhythm of work so important to assembly operators. Assemblers seem to develop reflex patterns in their work cycle at times of about one-half to two minutes per unit, which is typical of most automotive assembly work. At times much greater than this, they must rethink each step possibly leading to forgetfulness and fatigue. Having to rethink five minutes worth of tasks ninety-six times in an eight-hour shift is likely to be far more fatiguing for the typical assembler than repeating a one-minute task 480 times in a reflex fashion.[15]

The high initial expenses (reportedly 10 percent higher) of the Swedish firm may make its plant more conducive to worker-freedom but such expense may not be necessary. Studies show that job rotation can be successful on existing assembly lines, and that operators can participate effectively in determining tooling to be used, work methods, speed of the line and quality of their output. Incentive wage payment systems seem to reduce the perceived repetitiveness of a job,[16] and the encouragement, rather than discouragement, of socializing on the line is now more widely recognized. As Friedman comments, "a social life emerges and enlivens the hours of work on the conveyor which appear so 'monotonous' to the external observer."[17] The auto companies and others can also do much to personalize the work place, even in existing plants, and they can work out avenues for employee growth and advancement if they choose to do so.

MANAGEMENT OPPORTUNITIES

Many researchers familiar with the industrial scene today are convinced the answers to worker unhappiness as it exists do not lie in more theories about its causes or in the expenditure of millions of dollars on new plants and equipment. Rather, the answers lie in genuinely involving the worker in more of the day-to-day management decisions affecting his working life. Consultative management has been preached for too long; it is high time it is practiced.

Inge Janerus, ombudsman of the Confederation of Trades Unions in Sweden, says he is not overly enthusiastic about the new Swedish plant. He believes the firm has gone to great lengths technologically for what ultimately will be seen as a relatively small improvement in workers' lives and conditions. He thinks other firms will get better results with fewer technological innnovations and more effort to provide greater worker self-government and to "press decision-making lower in the system."[18]

Much of management's ready acceptance of Herzberg's theory or, more specifically, of job enrichment can be traced to its tangible simplicity: Enrich the job and most personnel problems will be solved. Management shows a natural penchant for a unidirectional program, as past involvement with human relations and sensitivity training, the emphasis on communications, formalized job participation plans and others have demonstrated.

But management responses to workers dissatisfaction cannot be simplistic or small in number. Nor can management's answers be readily categorized under convenient labels of organization theory, industrial engineering or behavioral science. The answers lie in the contributions made by each of these fields and others, because only in concert do they make up the full dimension of a worker's job life.

CONCLUSIONS

Assuming recognition of the individual and individual differences as the keystone, a firm might start by asking itself how policy needlessly militates against the individual. From the contributions made by organization theory, one could question whether there are a reasonable number of different types of jobs available at each work site to satisfy the diverse needs and aspirations of workers. The auto companies, for example, might consider greater integration of their facilities, e.g. machining and assembly, or assembly and distribution, to allow more opportunity for worker movement, growth and advancement. Certainly, almost all companies should be exerting greater effort in the areas of selection and placement. In the field of industrial engineering, involvement by the worker should be sought wherever possible in considering alternative methods and tooling. Operators in many organizations could realistically exercise a voice in determining their work hours and even their work pace over different periods of the work day. Management should encourage experimentation in innovative wage incentive plans that will better recognize a worker's contributions to the firm. Better lighting, noise reduction and the like may be necessary in the workplace, but worker-suggested improvements to personalize it may be more effective.

Examples might be drapes on otherwise drab factory windows and the addition of green plants as seen in a number of European factories.

Behavioral science has much to offer, but many managers and supervisors do not need to learn new things as much as they need to put into practice what they already know. For a variety of reasons often carried over from the past, the attitudes of managers toward workers in some industries continue to be poor. A critique of these industrial "traditions" might reveal some obvious explanations of worker discontent.

Higher investment and operating costs may not be necessary or desirable for the company or the worker. Nor is there a need to subordinate productivity, so desperately needed in our economy today, to achieve human needs. The two goals can, and should be, reasonably compatible given management's desire to recognize the potential of the worker as an individual. This recognition of the individual is really at the heart of much of what Herzberg and other proponents of job enrichment are saying.

REFERENCES

1. Tom Wicker, "A Plant Built for Workers," *The New York Times,* May 21, 1974.
2. Harold Wool, "What's Wrong with Work in America?—A Review Essay," *Monthly Labor Review,* March, 1973, p. 42.
3. S. H. Fuller, "GM Zeros in on Employee Discontent," *Business Week,* May 12, 1973, p. 140.
4. A. A. Imberman, "The Blue Collar Blues—Today's Academic Hit Tune,"*Assembly Engineering,* July, 1973, p. 26.
5. T. O. Prenting, N. T. Thomopoulos, *Humanism and Technology in Assembly Line Systems* (Rochelle Park, New Jersey: Hayden Book Company, 1974), p. 47.
6. Frederick Herzberg, "One More Time: How Do You Motivate Employees?" *Harvard Business Review,* January-February, 1968, p. 62.
7. M. D. Dunnette, J. P. Campbell, M. D. Hakel, "Factors Contributing to Job Satisfaction and Job Dissatisfaction in Six Occupational Groups," *Organizational Behavior and Human Performance,* May, 1967, p. 173. (An original study, plus reports on ten others.)
8. M. D. Dunnette *et al., op. cit.,* p. 174.
9. A. C. Filley, R. J. House, *Managerial Process and Organizational Behavior* (Glenview, Illinois: Scott, Foresman and Company, 1969), pp. 385–386.

10. Frederick Herzberg, *op. cit.*, p. 57.
11. E. E. Lawler III, "Job Design and Employee Motivation," *Personnel Psychology,* Winter, 1969, p. 433.
12. T. O. Prenting, "Better Selection for Repetitive Work," *Personnel,* September-October, 1964, pp. 26–31.
13. Frederick Herzberg, *op. cit.*, p. 62.
14. William W. Winpisinger, "Job Enrichment: A Union View," *Monthly Labor Review,* April, 1973, pp. 54–55.
15. T. O. Prenting, N. T. Thomopoulos, *op. cit.*, p. 123.
16. N. R. F. Maier, *Psychology in Industry,* Second Edition (Boston: Houghton Mifflin Company, 1955), p. 476 and G. Friedmann, *Industrial Society* (Glencoe, Ill.: The Free Press, 1955), pp. 145–146.
17. G. Friedmann, "What Is Happening to Man's Work?" (Excerpts), *Human Organization,* Winter, 1955, p. 31.
18. Tom Wicker, "People Versus Production," *The New York Times,* May 24, 1974.

BEYOND THE TEACHING MACHINE: THE NEGLECTED AREA OF OPERANT CONDITIONING IN THE THEORY AND PRACTICE OF MANAGEMENT*

Walter R. Nord†

This paper maintains that the work of B. F. Skinner has not been recognized in the administrative and management literature to the extent that it deserves. The work of Skinner is highly consistent with that of many widely accepted students of management, except that Skinner's work deals specifically with scheduling reinforcements, does not require acceptance of the metaphysics of many of the "humanistic" psychologists, and is based on considerable empirical evidence. The power of positive reinforcement, the unanticipated consequences of punishment, and the value of partial reinforcement are stressed. Finally, the operant view is applied to some managerial problems. It seems clear that the conditioning approach can meaningfully integrate

* Reprinted with permission of author and publisher from *Organizational Behavior and Human Performance,* Vol. 4, No. 4 (November 1969), pp. 375–401.
† The author wishes to acknowledge the helpful comments of Dr. Ann Nord, Dr. Raymond Hilgert, and Mr. Timothy Parker.

much of the behavioral science literature and serve organizations in the areas of personnel development, job design, compensation and alternative rewards, and organizational design.

The work of B. F. Skinner and the operant conditioners has been neglected in management and organizational literature. The present paper is an attempt to eliminate this lacuna. When most students of management and personnel think of Skinner's work, they begin and end with programmed instruction. Skinner's ideas, however, have far greater implications for the design and operation of social systems and organizations than just the teaching machine. These additional ideas could be of great practical value.

While neglecting conditioning, writers in the administrative, management, and personnel literature have given extensive attention to the work of other behavioral scientists. McGregor and Maslow are perhaps the behavioral scientists best known to practitioners and students in the area of business and management. Since the major concern of managers of human resources is the prediction and control of the behavior of organizational participants, it is curious to find that people with such a need are extremely conversant with McGregor and Maslow and totally ignorant of Skinner. This condition is not surprising since leading scholars in the field of what might be termed the applied behavioral sciences have turned out book after book, article after article, and anthology after anthology with scarcely a mention of Skinner's contributions to the design of social systems. While many writers who deal with the social psychology of organizations are guilty of the omission, this paper will focus primarily on the popular positions of Douglas McGregor, Abraham Maslow, and Frederick Herzberg to aid in exposition.

Almost every book in the field devotes considerable attention to Maslow and McGregor. These men have certainly contributed ideas which are easily understood and "make sense" to practitioners. Also, many practitioners have implemented some of these ideas successfully. However, the belief in the Maslow-McGregor creed is not based on a great deal of evidence. This conclusion is not mine alone, but in fact closely parallels Maslow's (1965) own thoughts. He wrote:

> After all, if we take the whole thing from McGregor's point of view of a contrast between a Theory *X* view of human nature, a good deal of the evidence upon which he bases his conclusions comes from my researches and my papers on motivations, self-actualization, et cetera. But I of all people should know just how shaky this foundation is as a final foundation. My work on motivations came from the clinic, from a study of neurotic people. The carry-over of this theory to the indus-

> trial situation has some support from industrial studies, but certainly I would like to see a lot more studies of this kind before feeling finally convinced that this carry-over from the study of neurosis to the study of labor in factories is legitimate. The same thing is true of my studies of self-actualizing people—there is only this one study of mine available. There were many things wrong with the sampling, so many in fact that it must be considered to be, in the classical sense anyway, a bad or poor or inadequate experiment. I am quite willing to concede this—as a matter of fact, I am eager to concede it—because I'm a little worried about this stuff which I consider to be tentative being swallowed whole by all sorts of enthusiastic people, who really should be a little more tentative in the way that I am (pp. 55–56).

By contrast, the work of Skinner (1953) and his followers has been supported by millions of observations made on animals at all levels of the phylogenetic scale, including man. Over a wide variety of situations, behavior has been reliably predicted and controlled by operant and classical conditioning techniques.

Why then have the applied behavioral sciences followed the McGregor–Maslow approach and ignored Skinner? Several reasons can be suggested. First is the metaphysical issue. Modern Americans, especially of the managerial class, prefer to think of themselves and others as being self-actualizing creatures operating near the top of Maslow's need-hierarchy, rather than as animals being controlled and even "manipulated" by their environment. McGregor (1960) developed his argument in terms of Maslow's hierarchy. Skinner's position is unattractive in the same way the Copernican theory was unattractive. Second, Skinner's work and stimulus–response psychology in general appear too limited to allow application to complex social situations. Certainly, this point has much merit. The application of *S–R* theory poses a terribly complex engineering problem, perhaps an insoluble one in some areas. Nevertheless, the designs of some experimental social systems, which will be discussed later in this paper, demonstrate the feasibility of the practical application of Skinnerian psychology to systems design. A third possible reason for the acceptance of the McGregor and Maslow school and rejection of Skinner may stem from the fact that the two approaches have considerable, although generally unrecognized overlap. As will be shown below, McGregor gave primary importance to the environment as the determinant of individual behavior. Similarly, although not as directly, so does Maslow's hierarchy of needs. The major issue between Skinner and McGregor–Maslow has to do with their models of man. Skinner focuses on man being totally shaped by his environment. Maslow–McGregor see man as having an essence or intrinsic nature which is only congruent with certain environments. The evidence for any one set of metaphysical assumptions is no better than for almost any other set. Empirically, little has been found which helps in choosing between Skinner's and McGregor's assumptions. Further, since most managers are concerned mainly with behavior, the sets of assumptions are of limited importance. It should be noted, however, that if McGregor's writings were stripped of Maslow's model of man, his conclusions on the descriptive and prescriptive levels would remain unchanged. Such a revision would also make McGregor's ideas almost identical with Skinner's. With more attention to contingencies of reinforcement and a broader view of the possibilities of administering reinforcement, the two sets of ideas as they apply to prediction and control of action would be virtually indistinguishable.

The remainder of this paper will be devoted to three areas. First, the similarities and differences between McGregor and Skinner will be discussed. Then, a summary of the Skinnerian position will be presented. Finally, the potential of the Skinnerian approach for modern organizations will be presented with supporting evidence from social systems in which it has already been applied.

McGREGOR AND SKINNER COMPARED

The importance of environmental factors in determining behavior is the crucial and dominant similarity between Skinner and McGregor. As will be shown below, environmental determination of behavior is central to both men.

McGregor (1960) gave central importance to environmental factors in determining how a person behaves. For example, he saw employee behavior as a consequence of organizational factors which are influenced by managerial strategy. In a sense, Theory *X* management leads to people behaving in a way which confirms Theory *X* assumptions, almost as a self-fulfilling prophecy. In addition, McGregor's statement of Theory *Y* assumptions places stress on "proper conditions," rewards and punishments, and other environmental factors. Further, he recognized the importance of immediate feedback in changing behavior. Also, he noted that failure to achieve results is often due to inappropriate methods of control. These are the very terms a behaviorist such as Skinner uses in discussing human actions. Finally, McGregor (1966) noted stimulus-response psychology as a possible model for considering organizational behavior. However, he discarded the reinforcement approach because it did not permit intrinsic rewards to be dealt with. Such a view not only led him to discard a model which describes, by his own admission, important behaviors, but is based on an incomplete view of reinforcement.

McGregor's basic arguments could have been based on Skinner rather than Maslow. The major difference would be the assumption of fewer givens about human nature. In view of this similarity one need not choose either Skinner or McGregor. Rather, there is considerable overlap in that both focus on changing the environmental conditions to produce changes in behavior. Further, both writers place substantial emphasis on the goals of prediction and control. Both are quite explicit in suggesting that we often get undesired results because we use inappropriate methods of control. In fact, the emphasis that McGregor's (1960) first chapter gives to the role of environment in controlling behavior seems to place him clearly in the behavioral camp.

Certainly there are important differences between Skinner and McGregor as well as the marked similarities noted above. For example, McGregor's (1960) use of Maslow's hierarchy of needs implies a series of inborn needs as a focus of the causal factors of behavior whereas Skinner (1953) views environmental factors as the causes of behavior. This difference does not, however, suggest an unresolvable conflict on the applied level. Skinner too allows for satiation on certain reinforcers which will be subject to species' and individual differences. Proceeding from this premise, Skinner focuses on the environmental control of behavior in a more rigorous and specific fashion than did McGregor. For example, McGregor (1960) advocated a cultural approach to development which emphasizes the provision of the conditions for behavioral change as a management responsibility. He noted in a general way that features of the organization, such as a boss, will influence behavioral change. He added that the change would not be permanent unless the organizational environment reinforced the desired behavior pattern. Such a general approach is an assumed basis for Skinner, who proceeds to focus on the types of reinforcement, the details of the administration of reinforcement, and the outcomes which can be expected from the administration of various types of reinforcement. Thus, changes in behavior which are predicted and achieved by Skinnerian methods can be viewed as empirical support for the work of McGregor.

There are other commonalities in the thinking of the two men. Both assume that there are a wide number of desirable responses available to a person which he does not make, because the responses are not rewarded in the environment. Both suggest that many undesired responses are repeated because they are rewarded. Both are clearly advocating a search for alternatives to controlling behavior which will be more effective in developing desired responses.

At this same level of analysis, there seems to be one major difference which revolves around the issue of self-control. However, this difference may be more apparent than real. Skinner (1953) wrote "It appears, therefore, that society is responsible for the larger part of the behavior of self-control. If this is correct, little ultimate control remains with the individual (p. 240)." Continuing on self-control, Skinner adds: "But it is also behavior; and we account for it in terms of other variables in the environment and history of the individual. It is these variables which provide the ultimate control (p. 240)."

In apparent contrast, McGregor (1960) stated: "Theory *Y* assumes that people will exercise self-direction and self-control in the achievement of organizational objectives *to the degree that they are committed to those objectives* (p. 56)." Seemingly this statement contradicts Skinner in placing the locus of control inside the individual. However, this conflict is reduced a few sentences later when McGregor (1960) added, "Managerial policies and practices materially affect this degree of commitment (p. 56)." Thus, both writers, Skinner far more unequivocally than McGregor, see the external environment as the primary factor in self-control. While McGregor polemicized against control by authority, he was not arguing that man is "free." Perhaps the more humanistic tone of McGregor's writing or his specific attention to managerial problems faced in business is responsible for his high esteem among students of management relative to that accorded Skinner. While metaphorically there is great difference, substantively there is little. It would seem, however, that metaphors have led practitioners and students of applied behavioral science to overlook some valuable data and some creative management possibilities.

One major substantive difference between the two approaches exists: it involves intrinsic rewards. McGregor (1966) saw a dichotomy in the effects of intrinsic and extrinsic rewards, noting research which has shown intrinsic ones to be more effective. He concludes the "mechanical" view (reinforcement theory) is inadequate, because it does not explain the superior outcomes of the use of "intrinsic" over "extrinsic" rewards. Here, as will be discussed in more detail later in connection with Herzberg, the problem is McGregor's failure to consider scheduling of reinforcement. "Intrinsic" rewards in existing organizations may be more effective because they occur on a more appropriate schedule for sustaining behavior than do "extrinsic" rewards. Intrinsic rewards are given by the environment for task completion or a similar achievement, and often occur on a ratio schedule. The implications of this crucial fact will be discussed shortly in considering Skinner's emphasis on the scheduling of rewards. For the present, it is suggested that McGregor gave little attention to reinforcement schedules and made a qualitative distinction between external and internal rewards. He seems to agree with Skinner that achievement, task completion, and control of the environment are reinforcers in themselves. Skinner's work suggests, however, that these rewards have the same consequences as "extrinsic" rewards, if they are given on the same schedule.

By way of summary to this point, it appears that more humanistic social scientists have been preferred by managers to behaviorists such as Skinner in their efforts to improve the management of human resources. Perhaps the oversight has been due to the congruence between their values and the metaphysics of people such as McGregor and Maslow. The differences between McGregor and Skinner do not appear to involve open conflict.

To the extent the two approaches agree, the major criterion in employing them would seem to be the degree to which they aid in predicting and controlling behavior toward organizational goals. The work of Skinner and his followers has much to offer in terms of the above criterion. In particular, McGregor's followers might find Skinner's work an asset in implementing Theory *Y*. The remainder of this paper will develop some of the major points of the Skinnerian approach and seek to explore their potential for industrial use.

CONDITIONING—A SYNTHESIS FOR ORGANIZATIONAL BEHAVIOR

The behavioral psychology of Skinner assumes, like Theory *Y*, that rate of behavior is dependent on the external conditions in which the behavior takes place. Like Theory *X*, it stresses the importance of the administration of rewards and punishments. Unlike Theory *X*, Skinnerian psychology places emphasis on rewards. Like Theory *Y* it emphasizes the role of interdependence between people in a social relationship and thus views the administration of rewards and punishments as an exchange. For those who are unfamiliar with the work of Skinner and his followers, a brief summary follows. Like any summary of an extensive body of work, this review omits a lot of important material. A more detailed, yet simple, introduction to conditioning can be found in Bijou and Baer (1961) and Skinner (1953). Extensions of this work by social exchange theorists such as Homans (1961) suggest that the conditioning model can be extended to a systems approach, contrary to McGregor's (1966) belief.

Generally, conditioned responses can be divided into two classes. Each class is acquired in a different fashion. The first class, generally known as respondent or classically conditioned behavior, describes the responses which are controlled by prior stimulation. These responses, generally thought of as being involuntary or reflexive, are usually made by the "smooth muscles." Common ones are salivation and emotional responses.

Initially, the presentation of an unconditioned stimulus will elicit a specific response. For example, food placed on one's tongue will generally cause salivation. If a bell is sounded and then food is placed on the tongue, and this process is repeated several times, the sound of the bell by itself will elicit salivation. By this process, stimuli which previously did not control behavior such as the bell, can become a source of behavior control. Many of our likes and dislikes, our anxieties, our feelings of patriotism, and other emotions can be thought of as such involuntary responses. The implications of emotional responses are of major importance to the management of human resources and more will be said about them later. However, the second class of responses, the operants, are of even greater importance.

The rate of operant responses is influenced by events which follow them. These events are considered to be the consequences of behavior. The responses, generally thought to be voluntary, are usually made by striped muscles. All that is necessary for the development of an operant response is that the desired response has a probability of occurring which is greater than zero for the individual involved. Most rapid conditioning results when the desired response is "reinforced" immediately (preferably about one-half second after the response). In other words, the desired response is followed directly by some consequence. In simple terms, if the outcome is pleasing to the individual, the probability of his repeating the response is apt to be increased. If the consequence is displeasing to the individual, the probability of his repeating the response is apt to be decreased. The process of inducing such change (usually an increase) in the response rate is called operant conditioning. In general, the frequency of a behavior is said to be a function of its consequences.

The above description of operant conditioning is greatly simplified. The additional considerations which follow will only partially rectify this state. One crucial factor has to do with the frequency with which a given consequence follows a response. There are several possible patterns. Most obviously, the consequence can be continuous (for example, it follows the response every time the response is made). Alternatively a consequence might follow only some of the responses. There are two basic ways in which such partial reinforcement can be administered. First, the consequence can be made contingent on a certain number of responses. Two sub-patterns are possible. Every nth response may be reinforced or an average of 1/n of the responses may be reinforced in a random pattern. These two related patterns are called ratio schedules. The former is known as a fixed ratio and the latter is known as a variable ratio. Ratio schedules tend to generate a high rate of response, with the variable ratio schedule leading to a more durable response than both the fixed-ratio and continuous patterns. A second technique of partial reinforcement can be designed where the consequence follows the response only after a certain amount of time has elapsed. The first response made after a specified interval is then reinforced, but all other responses produce neutral stimulus outcomes. This pattern can also be either fixed or variable. Generally, interval schedules develop responses which are quite long lasting when reinforcement is no longer given, but do not yield as rapid a response rate as ratio schedules do. Obviously, mixed patterns of ratio and interval schedules can also be designed.

A second consideration about operant conditioning which deserves brief mention is the concept of a response hierarchy. All the responses which an individual could make under a given set of conditions can be placed in order according to probability that they will be made. In this view, there are two basic strategies for getting an individual to make the desired response. First, one could attempt to reduce the probability of all the more probable responses. Second, one could attempt to increase the probability of the desired response. Of course, some combination of these two approaches may often be used.

Strategies for changing the probability of a response can be implemented by punishment, extinction, and positive reinforcement. Generally punishment and extinction are used to decrease the occurrence of a response whereas positive reinforcement is used to increase its probability. An understanding of these three operations in behavior control is important, not only for knowing how to use them, but chiefly because of their unanticipated consequences or their side-effects.

Punishment is the most widely used technique in our society for behavior control. Perhaps, as Reese (1966) said, the widespread use of punishment is due to the immediate effects it has in stopping or preventing the undesired response. In this sense, the punisher is reinforced for punishing. Also, many of us seem to be influenced by some notion of what Homans (1961) called distributive justice. In order to reestablish what we believe to be equity, we may often be led to punish another person. This ancient assumption of ". . . an eye for an eye . . ." has been widely practiced in man's quest for equity and behavior control.

Whatever the reason for punishing, it can be done in two ways, both of which have unfortunate side-effects. First, punishment can be administered in the form of some aversive stimulus such as physical pain or social disapproval. Secondly, it can be administered by withdrawing a desired stimulus. The immediate effect is often the rapid drop in frequency of the punished response. The full effects, unfortunately, are often not clearly recognized. Many of these consequences are crucial for managers of organizations.

Punishment may be an inefficient technique for controlling behavior for a number of reasons. First, the probability of the response may be reduced only when the threat of punishment is perceived to exist. Thus, when the punishing agent is away, the undesired response may occur at its initial rate. Secondly, punishment only serves to reduce the probability of the one response. This outcome does not necessarily produce the desired response, unless that response is the next most probable one in the response hierarchy. Really, what punishment does is to get the individual to do something other than what he has been punished for. A third effect is that the punishment may interfere with the response being made under desired circumstances. For example, if an organizational member attempts an innovation which is met with punishment by his superiors because they did not feel he had the authority to take the step, it is quite possible that his creative behavior will be reduced even in those areas where his superiors expect him to innovate.

In addition to these effects there are some other important by-products of punishment. Punishment may result in a person making responses which are incompatible with the punished response. Psychological tension, often manifested in emotional behavior such as fear or anxiety, is often the result. Secondly, punishment may lead to avoidance and dislike of the punishing agent. This effect can be especially important to managers who are attempting to build open, helping relationships with subordinates. The roles of punishing agent and helper are often incompatible. Many line-staff conflicts in organizations undoubtedly can be explained in these terms. Finally, punishment may generate counter-aggression. Either through a modeling effect or a justice effect, the punished person may respond with aggressive responses towards the punishing agent or towards some other stimulus.

The second technique for behavior change, commonly called extinction, also focuses primarily on reducing the probability of a response. Extinction arises from repeated trials where the response is followed by a neutral stimulus. This technique generates fewer by-products than punishment. However, like punishment, it does not lead to the desired response being developed. Furthermore, to the extent that one has built up an expectation of a reward for a certain response, a neutral consequence may be perceived as punishing. Thus, extinction may have some advantages over punishment, but has many of the same limitations.

Positive reinforcement is the final technique for changing behavior. Under conditions of positive reinforcement, the response produces a consequence that results in an increase in the frequency of the response. It is commonly stated that such a consequence is rewarding, pleasing, or drive reducing for the individual. The operant conditioners, however, avoid such inferences and define positive reinforcers, as stimuli which increase the probability of a preceding response. Positive reinforcement is efficient for several reasons. First, it increases the probable occurrence of the desired response. The process involves rewarding approximations to the direct response itself immediately after it is made. The desired behavior is being directly developed as opposed to successive suppression of undesired acts. Secondly, the adverse emotional responses associated with punishment and extinction are apt to be reduced and in fact favorable emotions may be developed. Since people tend to develop positive affect to others who reward them, the "trainer" is apt to become positively valenced in the eyes of the "learner."

By way of summary, Skinner's (1953) approach suggested that the control of behavior change involves a reduction in the probability of the most prepotent response and/or an increase in the probability of some desired response. Punishment and extinction may be used. These means can only reduce the probability of the unwanted response being made. Also, they may have undesired side-effects. The third technique, positive reinforcement, has the important advantage of developing the desired response rather than merely reducing the chances of an undesired one. Also, positive reinforcement is apt to produce favorable rather than unfavorable "side-effects" on organizational relationships.

This approach seems to suggest that both or neither Theory *X* and Theory *Y* assumptions are useful. This section suggested that conditioning may be both Theory *X* and Theory *Y*. Perhaps since the operant view does not make either set of assumptions, it is neither Theory *X* nor Theory *Y*. Operant conditioning is consistent with Theory *Y* in suggesting that the limits on human beings are a function of the organizational setting, but like Theory *X*, implies something about human nature; namely that deprivation or threat of some sort of deprivation is a precondition for behavior to be controlled. From the managerial perspective, however, the nomological question is of little significance. The important thing to managers is behavior and the major point of this approach is that behavior is a function of its consequences. Good management is that which leads to the desired behavior by organizational members. Management must see to it that the consequences of behavior are such as to increase the frequency of desired behavior and decrease the frequency of undesired behaviors. The question becomes, how can managers develop a social system which provides the appropriate consequences? In many ways the answer to this question is similar to what Theory *Y* advocates have suggested. However, there are some new possibilities.

APPLICATIONS OF CONDITIONING IN ORGANIZATIONS

The potential uses of the Skinnerian framework for social systems are increasing rapidly. The approach has far more applicability to complex social systems than has often been recognized. McGregor's rejection of the stimulus-response or the reward-punishment approach as inadequate for management because it does not allow for a systems approach is quite inconsistent with this general trend and his own environmentally based approach. Recent work in the field of behavioral control has begun to refute McGregor's position. The Skinnerian view can be and has been used to redesign social systems.

The most complete redesign was envisioned by Skinner (1948) in his novel, *Walden Two.* In this book, Skinner developed a society based on the use of positive reinforcement and experimental ethics geared to the goal of competition of a coordinated social unit with its environment. In other words, the system is designed to reward behaviors which are functional for the whole society. Social change is introduced on the basis of empirical data. As a result of the success of this system, man is enabled to pursue those activities which are rewarding in themselves. Although the book is a novel, it can be a valuable stimulus for thought about the design of social organization.

In addition, Skinner (1954) has taken a fresh look at teaching and learning in conventional educational systems. He noted that the school system depends heavily on aversive control or punishment. The use of low marks and ridicule have merely been substituted for the "stick." The teacher, in Skinner's view, is an out of date reinforcing mechanism. He suggested the need to examine the reinforcers which are available in the system and to apply them in a manner which is consistent with what is known about learning. For example, control over the environment itself may be rewarding. Perhaps grades reinforce the wrong behavior and are administered on a rather poor schedule. It would seem that a search for new reinforcers and better reinforcement schedules is appropriate for all modern organizations.

These speculations suggest the potential for great advances. *Walden Two* is in many ways an ideal society but has been a source of horror to many readers. The thoughts about changes in teaching methods are also a subject of controversy. However, the environment can be designed to aid in the attainment of desired ends. People resist the idea that they can be controlled by their environment. This resistance does not change the fact that they are under such control. Recently, evidence has begun to accumulate that the Skinnerian approach can be employed to design social systems.

Much of this evidence was collected in settings far removed from modern work organizations. The reader's initial response is apt to be, "What relevance do these studies have to my organization?" Obviously, the relationship is not direct. However, if, as the operant approach maintains, the conditioning process describes the acquisition and maintenance of behavior, the same principles can be applied to any social organization. The problem of application becomes merely that of engineering. The gains may well be limited only by an administrator's ingenuity and resources.

Much of the evidence comes from studies of hospitalized mental patients and autistic children, although some has been based on normal lower class children. A few examples from these studies will serve to document the great potential of the conditioning methods for social systems. Ayllon and Azrin (1965) observed mental patients' behavior to determine what activities they engaged in when they had a chance. They then made tokens contingent on certain responses such as work on hospital tasks. These tokens could be exchanged for the activities the patients preferred to engage in. The results of this approach were amazing. In one experiment five schizophrenics and three mental defectives served as *S*s. They did jobs regularly and adequately when tokens were given for the job. Such performance was reported to be in sharp contrast to the erratic and inconsistent behavior characteristic of such patients. When the tokens were no longer contingent on the work, the performance dropped almost to zero. In a second experiment, a whole ward of 44 patients served as *S*s. A similar procedure was followed and 11 classes of tasks observed. When tokens were contingent upon the desired responses, the group spent an average of 45 hours on the tasks daily. When tokens were not contingent on responses, almost no time was spent on the tasks. The implications seem rather clear. When desired behavior is rewarded, it will be emitted, when it is not rewarded, it will not be emitted.

A great deal of related work has been reported. Ayllon (1966) and Wolf, Risley, and Mees (1966) have shown how a reinforcement procedure can be effective in controlling the behavior of a psychotic patient and of an autistic child respectively. These are but a few of the many studies in a growing body of evidence.

More important for present purposes are the applications of this approach in more complex social situations. The work of Hamblin *et al.* (1967) shows some of the interesting possibilities of the conditioning approach for school classes and aggressive children. A token system was used to shape desired behavior. Through the application of the conditioning approach to the school system, gains may be made in educating children from deprived backgrounds. Two examples will illustrate these possibilities.

The first example comes from a recent newspaper story. A record shop owner in a Negro area of Chicago reported seeing the report card of a Negro boy. The owner thought the boy was bright, but the report card showed mostly unsatisfactory performance. He told the boy he would give him $5 worth of free records if he got all "excellents" on the next report card. Ten weeks later the boy returned with such a card to collect his reward. The owner reported that similar offers to other children had a remarkable effect in getting them to study and do their homework. The anecdote demonstrates what everyone knows anyway: people will work for rewards. It also suggests the converse: people will not work if rewards do not exist. The problems of education in the ghetto and motivation to work in general, may be overcome by appropriate reinforcement. Further support for this statement comes from the work of Montrose Wolf.

Wolf (1966) ran a school for children, most of whom were sixth graders, in a lower class Negro area of Kansas City. The children attended this school for several hours after school each day and on Saturday. Rewards were given in the form of tickets which could be saved and turned in for different kinds of things like toys, food, movies, shopping trips, and other activities. Tickets were made contingent on academic performance within the remedial school itself, and on performance in the regular school system. The results were remarkable. The average regular school grade of the students was raised to C from D. The results on standard achievement tests showed the remedial group progressed over twice as much in one year as they had done the previous year. They showed twice as much progress as a control group. Other gains were also noted. Wolf reported that a severe punishment was not to let the children attend school. They expressed strong discontent when school was not held because of a holiday. He further noted that when reading was no longer rewarded with tickets, the students still continued to read more than before the training. Arithmetic and English did not maintain these increments. Thus, to some extent, reading appeared to be intrinsically rewarding.

A final point concerns the transferability of skills learned in such a school to society at large. Will the tasks that are not rewarding in themselves be continued? The answer is probably not, unless other rewards are provided. The task then becomes to develop skills and behavior which society itself will reward. If this method is applied to develop behavior which is rewarded by society, the behavior is apt to be maintained. The same argument holds for organizational behavior. It will be fruitless to develop behavior which is not rewarded in the organization.

In summary, evidence has been presented to show the relevance of the Skinnerian approach to complex social systems. Certainly the evidence is only suggestive of future possibilities. The rest of this paper attempts to suggest some of these implications for organizational management.

MANAGEMENT THROUGH POSITIVE REINFORCEMENT

The implications of the systematic use of positive reinforcement for management range over many traditional areas. Some of the more important areas include training and personnel development, compensation and alternative rewards, supervision and leadership, job design, organizational design, and organizational change.

Training and Personnel Development

The area of training has been the first to benefit from the application of conditioning principles with the use of programmed learning and the teaching machine. An example of future potential comes from the Northern Systems Company Training Method for assembly line work. In this system, the program objectives are broken down into subobjectives. The training employs a lattice which provides objective relationships between functions and objectives, indicates critical evaluation points, and presents a visual display of go-no-go functions. Progress through various steps is reinforced by rewards. To quote from a statement of the training method ". . . the trainee gains satisfaction only by demonstrated performance at the tool stations. Second, he quickly perceives that correct behaviors obtain for him the satisfaction of his needs, and that incorrect behaviors do not (p. 20)." Correct performance includes not only job skills, but also the performance of social interaction which is necessary in a factory setting. The skills taught are designed to allow for high mobility in the industrial world. The Northern System's method develops behavior which the economic and social system will normally reinforce and has been successful in training people in a wide variety of skills. Its potential in training such groups as the "hard-core" unemployed seems to be limited only by the resources and creativity of program designers.

The Skinnerian approach seems to have potential for all areas of personnel development, not only for highly programmed tasks. Reinforcement theory may be useful in the development of such behaviors as creativity. The work of Maltzman, Simon, Raskin, and Licht (1960) demonstrated this possibility. After a series of experiments employing a standard experimental training procedure with free association materials, these investigators concluded that a highly reliable increase in uncommon responses could be produced through the use of reinforcement. The similarity of their results to those of operant experiments with respect to the persistence of the responses and the effect of repetitions, led them to conclude that originality is a form of operant behavior. Positive reinforcement increased the rate at which original responses were emitted.

Support is also available for the efficacy of operant conditioning to more conventional personnel and leadership development. Three such contributions are discussed below. The first concerns the organizational environment as a shaper of behavior of which Fleishman's (1967) study is a case in point. He found that human relations training programs were only effective in producing on-the-job changes if the organizational climate was supportive of the content of the program. More generally it would appear that industrial behavior is a function of its consequences. Those responses which are rewarded will persist: those responses which are not rewarded or are punished will decrease in frequency. If the organizational environment does not reward responses developed in a training program, the program will be, at best, a total waste of time and money. As Sykes (1962) has shown, at worst, such a program may be highly disruptive. A second implication of operant conditioning concerns the content of personnel development programs in the area of human relations. If, as Homans (1961) and others have suggested, social interaction is also influenced by the same operant principles, then people in interaction are constantly "shaping" or conditioning each other. The behavior of a subordinate is to some degree developed by his boss and vice-versa. What more sensible, practical point could be taught to organizational members than that they are teaching their fellow participants to behave in a certain manner? What more practical, sensible set of principles could be taught than that, due to latent dysfunctions generated, punishment and extinction procedures are less efficient ways to influence behavior than positive reinforcement? Clearly, the behavioral scientists who have contributed so greatly to organizational practice and personnel development have not put enough emphasis on these simple principles. The third implication for personnel development is added recognition that annual merit interviews and salary increments are very inefficient development techniques. The rewards or punishments are so delayed that they can be expected to have little feedback value for the employees involved. More frequent appraisals and distribution of rewards are apt to be far more effective, especially to the degree that they are related to specific tasks or units of work.

Job Design

Recently, behavioral scientists have emphasized the social-psychological factors which need to be attended to in job design. McGregor and others have suggested job enlargement. Herzberg (1968) has argued that job enlargement just allows an individual to do a greater variety of boring jobs and suggests that "job enrichment" is needed. For present purposes, job enlargement and job enrichment will be lumped together. Both of these approaches are consistent with the conditioning view if two differences can be resolved. First, the definitions of motivation must be translated into common terms. Second, reinforcers operating in the newly designed jobs must be delineated and tested to see if the reinforcers postulated in the newly designed jobs are really responsible for behavioral changes or if there are other reinforcers operating.

With respect to the definitions of motivation, the two approaches are really similar in viewing the rate of behavior as the crucial factor. The major differences exist on the conceptual level. Both job enlargement and job enrichment are attempts to increase motivation. Conceptually, McGregor and Herzberg tend to view motivation as some internal state. The conditioning approach does not postulate internal states but rather deals with the manipulation of environmental factors which influence the rate of behavior. Actually, some combination of the two approaches may be most useful theoretically as Vinacke (1962) has suggested. However, if both approaches are viewed only at the operational level, it is quite probable that rates of behavior could be agreed on as an acceptable criterion. Certainly from the practitioner's viewpoint, behavior is the crucial variable. When a manager talks about a motivated worker, he often means one who frequently makes desired responses at a high rate without external prompting from the boss. The traditional view of motivation as an inner-drive is of limited practical and theoretical value.

If both approaches could agree on the behavioral criterion, at least on an operational level, the operant approach could be employed to help resolve some practical and theoretical problems suggested by the work of McGregor and Herzberg. Since, generally speaking, the external conditions are most easily manipulated in an organization, attention can be focused on designing an environment which increases the frequency of the wanted responses. As a result, practitioners and students of organization could deal with motivation without searching for man's essence. We can avoid the metaphysical assumptions of Maslow and McGregor until they are better documented. The issue of a two-factor theory of motivation proposed by Herzberg which recently has been severely challenged by Lindsay, Marks, and Gorlow (1967) and Hulin and Smith (1967) among others can also be avoided. Attention can be confined to developing systems which produce high rates of desired behavior. Thus the conceptual differences about motivation do not cause unresolvable conflict at the present time.

The second area of difference between McGregor–Herzberg and the operant explanation of the effects of job enrichment stems from the failure of Herzberg and McGregor to recognize the great variety of possible rewards available in job design. The Skinnerian approach leads to the development of a more comprehensive discussion of the rewards from enriched or enlarged jobs. In terms of the operant approach, both job enrichment and job enlargement are apt to lead to what would generally be called greater motivation or what we will call higher rates of desired behavior. McGregor and Herzberg suggest feelings of achievement and responsibility explain these results. The reinforcement approach leads to a search for specific rewards in these newly designed jobs.

Job enlargement can be viewed simply as increasing the variety of tasks a person does. Recent research on self-stimulation and sensory deprivation has suggested that stimulation itself is reinforcing, especially when one has been deprived of it. The increased variety of tasks due to job enlargement may thus be intrinsically rewarding due to a host of reinforcers in the work itself rather than to any greater feeling of responsibility or achievement. These feelings may be a cause of greater productivity or merely correlates of the receipt of these intrinsic rewards from stimulation. The evidence is not clear, but the effects of job enlargement can at least be partially explained in operant terms.

Some additional support for this idea comes from Schultz's (1964) work on spontaneous alternation of behavior. Schultz suggested that spontaneous alternation of human behavior is facilitated 1) when responses are not reinforced and/or are not subjected to knowledge of correctness, 2) by the amount of prior exercise of one response alternative, and 3) by a short intertrial interval. Low feedback and reinforcement, short intervals between responses, and the frequent repetition of one response are all characteristic of many jobs which need enlargement. Merely making different responses may be rewarding to a worker, thereby explaining some of the benefits noted from job enlargement. It has also been noted that people create variation for themselves in performing monotonous tasks. For example, ritualized social interaction in the form of social "games" is a form of such alternation workers developed noted by Roy (1964).

By way of summary, much of the current work on job enlargement and enrichment has attributed the effects to feelings of achievement or responsibility, without taking into account numerous other possible reinforcers which may be more basic. Further research to determine the efficacy of these various possibilities is needed before definite conclusions can be drawn. Do the feelings of achievement or responsibility operate as reinforcers in an operant manner? Do these feelings come from other more basic rewards such as task variety? Present data does not permit answers to these questions.

With respect to the benefits noted from job enrichment, an operant model may provide further insights. Herzberg (1968) maintained that some jobs can not be "enriched" or made more motivating in themselves. It is the contention of this paper that it is not the tasks which are the problem, but it is the reinforcement schedules. For example, what could be more boring, have less potential for achievement and realization of Herzberg's satisfiers, than the game of bingo? Yet people will sit for hours at bingo, often under punishing conditions (since the house takes in more than it pays out) and place tokens on numbers. Similar behavior is exhibited at slot-machines and other gambling devices. Most operational definitions of motivation would agree that these players are highly motivated. The reason is clear from the operant viewpoint. The reinforcement schedule employed in games of chance, the variable ratio schedule, is a very powerful device for maintaining a rapid rate of response. With respect to job design, the important requirement is that rewards follow performance on an effective schedule.

The type of rewards Herzberg (1968) called satisfiers may be important motivators because they are distributed on a variable ratio schedule. Herzberg's data do not rule out this explanation. Take achievement, for example. If a person is doing a job from which it is possible to get a feeling of achievement, there must be a reasonably large probability that a person will not succeed on the task. Often times, this condition means that some noncontinuous schedule of reinforcement is operating. An individual will succeed only on some variable ratio schedule. In addition, successful completion of the task is often the most important reward. The reward is, of course, immediate. A similar statement could be made about tasks which are said to yield intrinsic satisfaction, such as crossword puzzles or enriched jobs. Thus the factors Herzberg called motivators may derive their potency from the manner in which the rewards are administered. The task is immediately and positively reinforced by the environment on a variable ratio schedule. Often the schedule is one which rewards a very small fraction of a large number of responses. Since behavior is a function of its consequences, if jobs can be designed to reinforce desired behavior in the appropriate manner, "motivated" workers are apt to result. Some of Herzberg's results may be explained without resort to a two-factor theory more parsimoniously in terms of schedules of reinforcement. Herzberg's (1966) finding that recognition is only a motivator if it is contingent on performance further documents the operant argument.

Another suggestion for job design from the operant tradition was suggested by Homans. He explored the relationship of the frequency of an activity and satisfaction to the amount of a reward. He concluded that satisfaction is generally positively related to the amount of reward whereas frequency of an activity is negatively related to the amount of reward the individual has received in the recent past. In order to have both high satisfaction and high activity, Homans (1961) suggested that tasks need to be designed in a manner such that repeated activities lead up to the accomplishment of some final result and get rewarded at a very low frequency until just before the final result is achieved. Then the reinforcement comes often. For example, consider the job of producing bottled soda. An optimal design would have the reward immediate on the completion of putting the caps on the bottles, but the task would be designed such that all the operations prior to capping were completed before any capping was done. Near the end of a work day, all the capping could be done. High output and satisfaction might then exist simultaneously. In general then, the operant approach suggests some interesting possibilities for designing jobs in ways which would maximize the power of reinforcers in the job itself.

A similar argument can be applied to some problems faced in administration and management. For example, it is commonly recognized that programmed tasks tend to be attended to before unprogrammed ones. It is quite obvious that programmed functions produce a product which is often tangible. The product itself is a reinforcer. An unprogrammed task often requires behavior which has not been reinforced in the past and will not produce a reward in the near future. It may be beneficial to provide rewards relatively early for behavior on unprogrammed tasks. This suggestion will be difficult to put into practice because of the very nature of unprogrammed tasks. Perhaps the best that can be done is to reward the working on such tasks.

Compensation and Alternative Rewards

Although whether money is a true "generalized reinforcer" as Skinner suggests has not been demonstrated conclusively, for years operant principles have been applied in the form of monetary incentive systems. Opsahl and Dunnette (1966) concluded that such programs generally do increase output. However, the restriction of output and other unanticipated consequences are associated with these programs. Many writers have attributed these consequences to social forces, such as the desire for approval from one's peers. Gewirtz and Baer (1958), for example, have shown that social approval has the same effects as other reinforcers in an operant situation. Dalton's (1948) famous study on rate-busters may be interpreted to show that people who are more "group-oriented" may place a higher value on social approval and hence are more apt to abide by group production norms than are less "group-oriented" people. Thus, it is not that money in piece-rate systems is not a potential reinforcer, but rather other reinforcers are more effective, at least after a certain level of monetary reward.

The successful use of the Scanlon Plan demonstrates the value of combining both economic and social rewards. This plan rewards improved work with several types of reinforcers, and often more immediately and directly than many incentive systems. The Scanlon Plan combines economic rewards, often given monthly, with social rewards. The latter are given soon after an employee's idea has been submitted or used.

Related arguments can be made for other group incentive programs. Often jobs are interdependent. The appropriate reinforcement for such tasks should be contingent upon interdependent responses, not individual ones. Even if the jobs are independent, the workers are social-psychologically interdependent. Social rewards are often obtainable by restricting output. It is hardly surprising that individual incentive programs have produced the unanticipated consequences so often noted. Further, since rewards and punishments from the informal group are apt to be administered immediately and frequently they are apt to be very powerful in controlling behavior.

In general then, money and other rewards must be made contingent on the desired responses. Further, the importance of alternative rewards to money must be recognized and incorporated into the design of the work environment. The widely known path-goal to productivity model expresses a similar point.

Another problem of compensation in organizations is also apparent in an operant context. Often, means of compensation, especially fringe benefits, have the unanticipated consequence of reinforcing the wrong responses. Current programs of sick pay, recreation programs, employee lounges, work breaks, and numerous other personnel programs all have one point in common. They all reward the employee for not working or for staying away from the job. These programs are not "bad," since often they may act to reduce problems such as turnover. However, an employer who relies on them should realize what behavior he is developing by establishing these costly programs. Alternative expenditures must be considered. If some of the money that was allocated for these programs was used to redesign jobs so as to be more reinforcing in themselves, more productive effort could be obtained. This idea is certainly not new. A host of behavioral scientists have suggested that resources devoted to making performance of the job itself more attractive will pay social and/or economic dividends.

Another interesting application of conditioning principles has to do with the schedule on which pay is distributed. The conventional pay schedule is a fixed interval one. Further, pay often is not really contingent on one's performance. The response needed to be rewarded is often attending work on pay day. Not only is pay often not contingent upon performance, but the fixed interval schedule is not given to generating a high response rate. In a creative article, Aldis (1966) suggested an interesting compensation program employing a variable ratio schedule. Instead of an annual Christmas bonus or other types of such expected salary supplements, he suggested a lottery system. If an employee produced above an agreed upon standard, his name would be placed in a hat. A drawing would be held. The name(s) drawn would receive an amount of money proportionate to the number of units produced during that period of time. This system would approximate the desired variable ratio schedule.

In addition to the prosperity of the owners of gambling establishments, there is some direct evidence that variable ratio schedules will be of use to those charged with predicting and controlling human behavior. A leading St. Louis hardware company,* although apparently unaware of the work of the operant conditioners, has applied an approximate variable ratio schedule of reinforcement to reduce absenteeism and tardiness. Although the complete data is not available, the personnel department has reported surprising success. A brief description of the system will be presented below and a more detailed study will be written in the near future.

Under the lottery system, if a person is on time (that is, not so much as ½ minute late) for work at the start of his day and after his breaks, he is eligible for a drawing at the end of the month. Prizes worth approximately $20 to $25 are awarded to the winners. One prize is available for each 25 eligible employees. At the end of six months, people who have had perfect attendance for the entire period are eligible for a drawing for a color television set. The names of all the winners and of those eligible are also printed in the company paper, such that social reinforcement may also be a factor. The plan was introduced because tardiness and absenteeism had become a very serious problem. In the words of the personnel manager, absenteeism and tardiness ". . . were lousy before." Since the program was begun 16 months ago, conditions have improved greatly. Sick leave costs have been reduced about 62%. After the first month, 151 of approximately 530 employees were eligible for the drawing. This number has grown larger, although not at a steady

---

* The author wishes to thank Mr. C. for making this information available and one of his students, Richard Weis, for informing him about this program.

rate to 219 for the most recent month. Although the comparable figures for the period before the program were unfortunately not available, management has noted great improvements. It would appear that desired behavior by organization participants in terms of tardiness and absenteeism can be readily and inexpensively developed by a variable ratio schedule of positive reinforcement. The possibilities for other areas are limited largely by the creativity of management.

The operant approach also has some additional implications for the use of money as a reward. First, many recent studies have shown money is not as important as other job factors in worker satisfaction. Herzberg (1968), among others, has said explicitly that money will not promote worker satisfaction. Undoubtedly, in many situations, Herzberg is correct. However, crucial factors of reward contingencies and schedules have not been controlled in these studies. Again, it appears that the important distinction that can be made between Herzberg's motivators and hygiene factors is that the former set of rewards are contingent on an individual's responses and the latter are not. If a work situation were designed so that money was directly contingent on performance, the results might be different. A second point has to do with the perception of money as a reward. Opsahl and Dunnette (1966) have recently questioned pay secrecy policies. They maintained that pay secrecy leads to misperception of the amount of money that a promotion might mean. The value of the reinforcers is underestimated by the participants suggesting that they are less effective than they might otherwise be. Certainly, alternative rewards are likely to be "over chosen." By following policies of pay secrecy, organizations seem to be failing to utilize fully their available monetary rewards.

In addition to underutilization of money rewards, organizations seem to be almost totally unaware of alternative reinforcers, and in fact see punishment as the only viable method of control when existing reinforcers fail. What are some alternatives to a punishment centered bureaucracy? Some, such as job design, improved scheduling of reinforcement, and a search for new reinforcers, have already been suggested. There are other possible reinforcers, a few of which are discussed below.

The important thing about reinforcers is that they be made immediately contingent on desired performance to the greatest degree possible. The potential reinforcers discussed here also require such a contingent relationship, although developing such relationships may be a severe test of an administrator's creativity. One of the more promising reinforcers is leisure. It would seem possible in many jobs to establish an agreed upon standard output for a day's work. This level could be higher than the current average. Once this amount is reached, the group or individual could be allowed the alternative of going home. The result of experiments in this direction would be interesting to all concerned. Quite possibly, this method might lead to a fuller utilization of our labor force. The individual may be able to hold two four-hour jobs, doubling his current contribution. Such a tremendous increase in output is quite possible as Stagner and Rosen (1966) have noted, when the situation possesses appropriate contingencies. Certainly, the problems of industrial discipline, absenteeism, and grievances which result in lower productivity might be ameliorated. Another possible reinforcer is information. Guetzkow (1965) noted that people have a strong desire to receive communication. Rewarding desired performance with communication or feedback may be a relatively inexpensive reinforcer. Graphs, charts, or even tokens which show immediate and cumulative results may serve this function. Some of the widely accepted benefits from participative management may be due to the reinforcing effect of communication. Certainly the "Hawthorne effect" can be described in these terms. In addition, social approval and status may be powerful reinforcers. Blau's classic study described by Homans (1961) on the exchange of approval and status for help is but one example. People will work for approval and status. If these are made contingent on a desired set of responses, the response rate can be increased. At present, often social approval is given by one's peers, but is contingent on behavior which is in conflict with organizational goals.

In addition to these reinforcers, there are certain social exchange concepts such as justice, equity, reciprocity, and indebtedness which deserve attention. Recent research has demonstrated that an unbalanced social exchange, such as one which is inequitable or leaves one person indebted to someone else, may be tension producing in such a way that individuals work to avoid them. In other words, unbalanced exchanges are a source of punishment. Relationships, such as those involving dependency, which result in such social imbalance can be expected to have the same latent consequences as punishment. Techniques which employ social imbalance to predict and control behavior can be expected to be less efficient in most respects than ones based on positive reinforcement.

The crucial variable in distributing any reward is contingency. Managers have been quick to point out that the problem with a "welfare-state" is that rewards do not depend on desired behavior. This point is well taken. It is surprising that the same point has not been recognized in current management practices.

Organizational Climate and Design

Important aspects of human behavior can be attributed to the immediate environment in which people function. The potential then exists to structure and restructure formal organizations in a manner to promote the desired behavior. Once this point is recognized and accepted by managers, progress can begin. This reaction of managers to this approach is often, "You mean my organization should reward people for what they ought to do anyway?" The answer is that people's behavior is largely determined by its outcomes. It is an empirical fact rather than a moral question. If you want a certain response and it does not occur, you had better change the reinforcement contingencies to increase its probable occurrence.

The first step in the direction of designing organizations on this basis involves defining explicitly the desired behaviors and the available reinforcers. The next step is to then make these rewards dependent on the emission of the desired responses. What are some of the implications of such reasoning for organizational design?

Already the importance of organizational climate has been discussed in connection with human development. Some additional implications merit brief consideration. A major one concerns conformity. Often today the degree to which people conform to a wide variety of norms is lamentably acknowledged and the question is asked, "Why do people do it?" The reasons in the operant view are quite clear: conformity is rewarded, deviance is punished. People conform in organizations because conformity is profitable in terms of the outcomes the individual achieves. In fact, Nord (in press) and Walker and Heyns (1962) presented considerable evidence that conformity has the same properties as other operant responses. If managers are really worried about the costs of comformity in terms of creativity and innovation, they must look for ways to reward deviance, to avoid punishing nonconformity, and to avoid rewarding conformity. Furthermore, the way in which rewards are administered is important. Generally, if rewards are given by a person or group of people, a dependency relationship is created, with hostility, fear, anxiety, and other emotional outcomes being probable. Dependence itself may be a discomforting condition. It is therefore desirable to make the rewards come from the environment. Rewards which have previously been established for reaching certain agreed upon goals are one such means. Meaningful jobs, in which achievement in itself is rewarding are another way. In general, to the degree that competition is with the environment or forces outside the organization, and rewards come from achievement itself, the more effective the reinforcers are apt to be in achieving desired responses.

A final point concerns the actual operation of organizations. Increasingly it is recognized that a formal organization, which aims at the coordination of the efforts of its participants, is dependent on informal relationships for its operation. As Gross (1968) noted,

> In administration, also, "the play's the thing" and not the script. Many aspects of even the simplest operation can never be expressed in writing. They must be sensed and felt . . . Daily action is the key channel of operational definition. In supplying cues and suggestions, in voicing praise and blame, in issuing verbal instructions, administrators define or clarify operational goals in real life (p. 406).

More generally, what makes an organization "tick" is the exchange of reinforcers within it and between it and its environment. The nature of these exchanges involves both economic and social reinforcers. Many of these are given and received without explicit recognition or even awareness on the part of the participants. The operant approach focuses attention on these exchange processes. As a result, it may prove to be an invaluable asset to both administrators and students of administration and organization.

A final advantage of the operant approach for current organizational theory and analysis may be the attention it focuses on planned and rational administration. Gouldner (1966) noted "Modern organizational analysis by sociologists is overpreoccupied with the spontaneous and unplanned responses which organizations make to stress, and too little concerned with patterns of planned and rational administration (p. 397)." The Skinnerian approach leads to rational planning in order to control outcomes previously viewed as spontaneous consequences. This approach could expand the area of planning and rational action in administration.

REFERENCES

ALDIS, O. Of pigeons and men. *In* R. Ulrich, T. Stachnik and T. Mabry (Eds.), *Control of Human Behavior.* Glenview, Ill.: Scott, Foresman, 1966, 218–221.

AYLLON, T. Intensive treatment of psychotic behavior by stimulus satiation and food reinforcement. *In* R. Ulrich, T. Stachnik and T. Mabry (Eds.), *Control of Human Behavior.* Glenview, Ill.: Scott, Foresman, 1966, 170–176.

AYLLON, T., AND AZRIN, N. H. The measurement and reinforcement of behavior of psychotics. *Journal of the Experimental Analysis of Behavior,* 1965, **8,** 357–383.

BIJOU, S. W., AND BAER, D. M. *Child Development.* Vol. 1. New York: Appleton-Century-Crofts, 1961.

DALTON, M. The industrial 'rate-buster': a characterization. *Applied Anthropology,* 1948, **7,** 5–18.

FLEISHMAN, E. A. Leadership climate, human relations training, and supervisory behavior. *In* Fleishman, E. A. (Ed.), *Studies in Personnel and Industrial Psychology.* Homewood, Ill.: Dorsey, 1967, 250–263.

Free records given for E's, pupils' report cards improve. *St. Louis Post Dispatch,* December 3, 1967.

GEWIRTZ, J. L., AND BAER, D. M. Deprivation and satiation of social reinforcers as drive conditions. *Journal of Abnormal and Social Psychology,* 1958, **57,** 165–172.

GOULDNER, A. W. Organizational analysis. *In* Bennis, W. G., Benne, K. D., and Chin, R. (Eds.), *The Planning of Change.* New York: Holt, Rinehart, and Winston, 1966, 393–399.

GROSS, B. M. *Organizations and Their Managing.* New York: Free Press, 1968.

GUETZKOW, H. Communications in Organizations. *In* March, J. G. (Ed.), *Handbook of Organizations.* Chicago: Rand McNally, 1965, 534–573.

HAMBLIN, R. L., BUSHELL, O. B., BUCKHOLDT, D., ELLIS, D., FERRITOR, D., MERRITT, G., PFEIFFER, C., SHEA, D., AND STODDARD, D. Learning, problem children and a social exchange system. Annual Report of the Social Exchange Laboratories, Washington University, and Student Behavior Laboratory, Webster College, St. Louis, Mo. August, 1967.

HERZBERG, F. One more time: How do you motivate employees? *Harvard Business Review,* January–February, 1968, 53–62.

HERZBERG, F. *Work and the Nature of Man.* Cleveland: World, 1966.

HOMANS, G. C. *Social Behavior: Its Elementary Forms.* New York: Harcourt, Brace and World, 1961.

HULIN, C. L., AND SMITH, P. A. An empirical investigation of two implications of the two-factor theory of job satisfaction. *Journal of Applied Psychology,* 1967, **51,** 396–402.

LINDSAY, C. A., MARKS, E., AND GORLOW, L. The Herzberg theory: a critique and reformulation. *Journal of Applied Psychology,* 1967, **51,** 330–339.

MALTZMAN, I., SIMON, S., RASKIN, D., AND LIGHT, L. Experimental studies in the training of originality. *Psychological Monographs: General and Applied,* 1960, **74** (6, Whole No. 493).

MASLOW, A. *Eupsychian Management.* Homewood, Ill.: Dorsey, 1965.

MCGREGOR, D. *The Human Side of Enterprise.* New York: McGraw-Hill, 1960.

MCGREGOR, D. *Leadership and Motivation.* Cambridge, Mass.: M. I. T. Press, 1966.

NORD, W. R. Social exchange theory: an integrative approach to social conformity. *Psychological Bulletin,* (in press).

Northern Systems Company, A proposal to the department of labor for development of a prototype project for the new industries program. Part one.

OPSAHL, R. L., AND DUNNETTE, M. D. The role of financial compensation in industrial motivation. *Psychological Bulletin,* 1966, **66,** 94–118.

REESE, E. P. *The Analysis of Human Operant Behavior.* Dubuque, Ia.: William C. Brown, 1966.

ROY, D. F. "Banana time"—job satisfaction and informal interaction. *In* Bennis, W. G., Schein, E. H., Berlew, D. E., and Steele, F. I. (Eds.), *Interpersonal Dynamics.* Homewood, Ill.: Dorsey, 1964, 583–600.

SCHULTZ, D. P. Spontaneous alteration behavior in humans, implications for psychological research. *Psychological Bulletin,* 1964, **62,** 394–400.

SKINNER, B. F. *Science and Human Behavior.* New York: Macmillan, 1953.

SKINNER, B. F. The science of learning and the art of teaching. *Harvard Educational Review,* 1954, **24,** 86–97.

SKINNER, B. F. *Walden Two.* New York: Macmillan, 1948.

STAGNER, R., AND ROSEN, H. *Psychology of Union-Management Relations.* Belmont, Cal.: Wadsworth, 1966.

SYKES, A. J. M. The effect of a supervisory training course in changing supervisors' perceptions and expectations of the role of management. *Human Relations,* 1962, **15,** 227–243.

VINACKE, E. W. Motivation as a complex problem. *Nebraska Symposium on Motivation,* 1962, **10,** 1–45.

WALKER, E. L., AND HEYNS, R. W. *An Anatomy of Conformity.* Englewood Cliffs, N. J.: Prentice-Hall, 1962.

WOLF, M. M. Paper read at Sociology Colloquium, Washington University, December 5, 1966.

WOLF, M. M., RISLEY, T., AND MEES, H. Application of operant conditioning procedures to the behavior problems of an autistic child. *In* R. Ulrich, T. Stachnik and T. Mabry (Eds.), *Control of Human Behavior.* Glenview, Ill.: Scott, Foresman, 1966, 187–193.

Chapter 2

Managing by Tens and Twenties: Supervising Immediate Work Units

A. Adapting to "Being in the Middle"
   "Strategic Leniency and Authority," Peter M. Blau
   "Three Supervisory Adaptations to 'Artificial Pressure'," Chris Argyris
B. Understanding and Dealing with Groups
   "The Nature of Highly Effective Groups," Rensis Likert
   "Work Group Behavior and the Larger Organization," Leonard R. Sayles
   "Autonomous Work Groups Continuing at the Rushton Mine," Gerald I. Susman
C. Deciding on a Managerial or Leadership Style
   "Three Styles of Leadership and Their Uses," Robert T. Golembiewski
   "In Defense of Theory Y," Edgar H. Schein

Most managers in organizations are pulled in two directions, whether they are first-level supervisors or middle managers or high-level executives. That is, managers as superiors often directly monitor the activities of relatively few people immediately "below" them. These managers at the same time respond as subordinates to one or a few individuals immediately "above" them in the hierarchy.

This duality has a simple consequence: most managers have big troubles in their immediate supervision of small work units. For under the glare of face-to-face conditions and without the protection of greatly superior formal status, matters of consequence must be worked out in the heat of action rather than in cool logic. Policies and procedures must be shaped with people rather than with paper. Any failure in working things out implies a breakdown in the crucial process of linking the efforts of one level of organization with those levels near it. Consequently, managers must be sensitive to the desires of "their people."[1]

[1] The general point is perhaps made most sharply by the degree to which the jailors in a maximum-security prison are dependent upon the goodwill of the prisoners. See Gresham Sykes, *The Society of Captives* (Princeton, N. J.: Princeton University Press, 1958).

At the same time, there are those higher in the hierarchy who monitor action attentively with a particular eye for any supervisor who too ardently serves the needs of subordinates. Suspended in this dynamic web of often conflicting interests, the immediate manager struggles with his direct supervision of tens and twenties.

A. ADAPTING TO "BEING IN THE MIDDLE"

The stresses placed on immediate supervisory relations in organizations are significant, and they often are crucial. Indeed, the simultaneous pressures from "immediately below" and from "on high" have long been cited as especial sources of difficulty in organizations, and particularly so at the first level of supervision. The image of the "man in the middle" is consequently now a familiar one in the management literature. Many men in organizations at all levels know the feeling personally.

Peter Blau outlines one of these double-edged adaptations to the conflicting demands imposed on immediate supervisors in his "Strategic Leniency and Authority." Blau describes immediate supervisors as typically bargaining their discrete neglect of violations of organizational policies to increase their influence with their immediate subordinates. In this variation, then, only cheaters prosper. More seriously, the resort to such surreptitious supervisory greasing-of-the-ways starkly reflects the ill-resolved managerial problems that organizations thrust into the unwilling hands of immediate supervisors. These ill-resolved problems force jerry-built supervisory adaptations that raise significant organizational issues related to authority and discipline. These issues also may have moral implications for the individual.

Argyris' "Three Supervisory Adaptations to 'Artificial Pressure' " sketches yet another set of common supervisory reactions to the pressure of being "in the middle," and they have more narrowly personal implications. Briefly, Argyris develops a picture of top-level management's keeping supervisors at lower levels "on their toes" by "putting on the pressure" through the use of "staff" personnel handling budget matters. In the largest part, this managerial strategy seems a counsel of despair. The strategy is compounded of top management's knowledge of the difficulty of controlling work at a distance in their concept of "organization" and of management's fear that if it were not for "artificial pressure" supervisors would indulge in an orgy of serving the selfish interests of their own work-units and consequently would sacrifice production. Even granting that the strategy of top management achieved its ends—and that is doubtful—Argyris demonstrates that supervisors in the plants he studied adopted behaviors that over the long run could hardly serve their needs or those of their organization. Supervisors "handled" managerial pressure in one or more of these ways:

1. "passing on" the pressure in the form of heightened conflict between departments;
2. acting out the conflict in line-staff conflicts; and
3. internalizing the pressure by being overcontrolled or overcontrolling.

The mixed consequences of such managerial pressure can be suggested variously. For example, as Argyris notes, "artificial pressure" often encourages the development of groups among employees who use their social power for self-protection. Consequently, a supervisor often will be placed in an uncomfortable position by managerial action designed to reduce the power of informal groups. He can join informal groups of employees protecting themselves from perceived arbitrary managerial action; or he can oppose such groups, thereby risking further loss of already weakened supervisory influence.

Managerial "pressure" seems ill-advised, whatever the outcome. Whether the supervisor fights or joins the informal group, the organization stands to lose. In either case, also, the supervisor's position must be an uncomfortable one. This double bind illustrates those unfortunate products of management's awkward handling of informal organizations among its employees.

References like that above to the requirement that management treat groups in useful ways need not remain at a general level. Indeed, three contributions reprinted in this volume permit a considerable specificity about ways informal organizations among employees can be managed to serve the needs of group members as well as the interests of the formal organizations in which the groups exist. The range over which greater specificity is possible may be outlined. The three pieces respectively deal with: (1) the description of types of groups encountered in organizations, the description of which emphasizes the forces that underlie group development; (2) an introduction to some dimensions for specifically characterizing small groups in ways that have managerial relevance; and (3) a survey of the leadership dynamics necessary to take advantage of what is presently known about small groups in organizations.

B. UNDERSTANDING AND DEALING WITH GROUPS

Because of the importance that we attach to groups in organizations, we have included three major pieces on this subject. Rensis Likert in "The Nature of Highly Effective Groups" develops the concept of the group at work, pointing out both the dangers and potential values in their existence. In his effort to develop an "ideal model," Likert sketches the properties and characteristics of groups and discusses at length the respective roles of the leaders and members of groups.

Despite the attraction of an ideal type, the fact remains that groups come in such various forms that, patently, a "group" is not a "group." Some groups are managerially useful; others generate Excedrin-sized headaches and sometimes heartaches.

The task of describing some important types of groups is accomplished by Leonard R. Sayles in "Work Group Behavior and the Larger Organization." Sayles focuses on three types of groups—friendship cliques, task groups, and interest groups—which may or may not overlap in organizations. Each of these types of groups is shown to have an important impact on performance and satisfaction, particularly as they tie individuals to organizational purposes or as they bind individuals together in resistance to formal authorities. Reciprocally, the organization of work is shown to help determine the kinds of groups that will develop. The two generalizations preoccupy Sayles. Throughout, consequently, he searches for ways of integrating the demands of work and of social relations to serve both individual and organizational needs.

Since knowledge is in important senses an infinite regression, we must press toward even more specific group differentiation. That is, it is patently important to isolate (for example) friendship cliques. But it is then necessary to specify differentiating characteristics of the subspecies "friendship cliques," and the scientific cycle is thereby triggered to repeat itself. This recycling has a serious purpose. For only to the degree that we can increasingly specify group properties will it become increasingly possible to integrate the demands of work and the demands of man's social relations. Only thus will it become increasingly possible to serve both individual and organizational interests.

In any discussion of management techniques, the bottom line is: Did the technique work? Was production affected? Is absenteeism down? Are wastage and turnover high or low? Susman's "Autonomous Work Groups Continuing at the Rushton Mine" briefly and critically assesses an experiment that addresses just such bottom-line issues. The results, good and bad, serve as a useful guide to the pitfalls and benefits of permitting workers to participate in production decisions.

C. DECIDING ON A MANAGERIAL OR LEADERSHIP STYLE

Knowledge of group properties is not the end of the line. For example, some of our knowledge about group properties can be extended conveniently to that most popular of managerial topics, leadership. "Three

Styles of Leadership" by Robert T. Golembiewski illustrates the possible. The article's strategy is plain. Differences in group norms and in member personality characteristics in one work unit, for example, are shown to be important conditions that will influence the choice of an appropriate style of leadership for the supervisor of that unit. Three styles of leadership are considered, and the available research literature is sampled to illustrate how one style or another is more or less appropriate as conditions vary. "Appropriate" here refers to the increased probability of high production and high satisfaction.

Several possible stumbling blocks in the article require brief notice. First, a supervisor's style of leadership is usually a matter of more or less rather than of either/or. Their styles, in short, are defined in terms of the relative incidence of various behaviors. For example, most individuals are complex enough that they normally perform some behaviors that can be considered "group-centered" even though their style is basically "leader-centered." The three gross leadership styles in the article are not up to the task of providing the specificity required for the full range of such differences in degree as they exist in nature. The general distinctions are useful for our analytical purposes, however, as they do highlight important consequences of differences in supervisory styles.

Second, and also related to man's complexity, most supervisors at least in the short run have wide enough response repertoires to honestly supply behaviors appropriate to most individual and group conditions. Over the long run, however, the performance of low-preference behaviors has many undesirable consequences for all concerned. The long-run implication of the present argument recommends the placement of individuals in conditions demanding behaviors from them which are high-preference behaviors in their response repertoires. Some research has in fact gone a considerable distance down this particular road.[2] In any case, the argument of the article certainly is not for dishonest role-playing by individuals who are "not really that way."

The charge of personal phoniness by supervisors for organization purposes could not be wider of the present mark. Indeed, the long-run implication of the last two previewed articles is for increasingly genuine relations as both supervisor and employees are assigned to work units in such ways that they can employ high-preference behaviors while they serve organizational purposes. Individuals scoring high on "authoritarianism," for example, might be assigned to the same work unit, and their

---

[2] William C. Schultz, *FIRO-B* (New York: Rinehart, 1958); and Raymond E. Hill, "Interpersonal Compatibility and Workgroup Performance," *Journal of Applied Behavioral Science*, Vol. 11 (April 1975), pp. 210–19.

supervisor also might be chosen for his tendency to provide behaviors which members of his specific work unit are predisposed to accept. Present random methods of assignment encourage more cat-and-mousing. That is, both supervisor and supervised attempt to play nonauthentic games in providing behaviors that at once seem culturally correct but which often are inappropriate because they require individuals to supply behaviors which they consider relatively undesirable. The general prescription of an authoritarian style of supervision, and its general failure to provide superior results, adequately illustrates the present casual approach to assignment as well as one of its common products.

Third, it seems a truism that managerial styles must be situationally appropriate or they will be ineffective. The contemporary way of expressing the point refers to "contingency theory," "contingent" in the sense that effective style depends on a broad range of situational and personality features that may vary significantly from organization to organization and from time to time. Two general developments of the contingency view appear in this volume—in the Introduction and in Chapter 3—and several contingency-based treatments of leadership are conveniently available elsewhere.[3]

In this volume as in most that emphasize people in organizations, McGregor's works are prominently mentioned. And when that mention is made, one finds little in the way of middle ground. McGregor is either strongly attacked or passionately defended. Edgar Schein assumes the latter posture in his "In Defense of Theory Y." But in defending McGregor, Schein adds constructively to the original work. Theory Y is difficult to classify. Is it a theory of participative management, of worker needs and drives, or of organizational constructs? From a management point of view, Schein is probably correct when he holds that Theory Y is "a description of how *effective* managers viewed human behavior." Equally, however, the thrust of Theory Y provides a guide to selecting management material from the ranks. The latter point is a definite contribution.

There are, of course, blind spots in all management techniques or perspectives. And Theory Y is no exception. Typically, attempts at utilizing Theory Y practices run afoul of Theory X climates, workers, or executives. Such conditions can be overcome, and awareness is the first stage of effective managerial coping. It is that awareness which this chapter and its several selections seek to heighten.

---

[3] Kirk Downey, Don Hellreigel, and John Slocum, editors, *Readings in Organizational Behavior: Contingency Views* (St. Paul, Minn.: West Publishing Co., 1977).

STRATEGIC LENIENCY AND AUTHORITY*

Peter M. Blau

The hierarchy of authority in a bureaucracy, essential for coordination, often produces among its lower echelons profound feelings of inequality and apathy that impede identification with the organization's objectives. The initiation of needed adjustments by the operating members of the organization presupposes, in addition to the five conditions already discussed, a method of hierarchical coordination that minimizes these harmful consequences for work motivation. After analyzing the ways in which bureaucratic authority is exercised, we shall return to this problem at the end of this chapter.

To start with, let us consider another paradox between official requirements and actual practice. In theory, bureaucratic superiors are expected to exert strict and impersonal control over subordinates. But in fact, immediate supervisors and foremen frequently "play ball" with their subordinates and let them "get away with" infractions of many rules. What accounts for this leniency?

STRATEGIC LENIENCY AND AUTHORITY

A psychological explanation of the failure to enforce strict discipline among subordinates might attribute it to poor leadership. Some supervisors are overly lenient, it could be held, because inborn or acquired personality traits prevent them from asserting their authority over others and maintaining effective leadership. Note that this explanation assumes as a matter of course that the bureaucratic superior who appears lenient merely indulges his subordinates and is less effective than the disciplinarian in discharging his supervisory responsibilities. Empirical evidence however, indicates that the very opposite is the case.

A study of twenty-four clerical sections in an insurance company analyzed the relationship between method of supervision and productive efficiency.[1] In closely supervised sections, whose heads gave clerks detailed instructions and frequently checked up on them, productivity was usually lower than in sections where employees were given more freedom to do the work in their own way. Moreover, supervisors who were primarily concerned with maintaining a high level of production,

---

interestingly enough, were less successful in meeting this goal than those supervisors who were more interested in the welfare of their subordinates than in sheer production; in the latter case, productivity was generally higher. Finally, groups who worked under more authoritarian supervisors were, on the whole, less productive than those supervised in a relatively democratic fashion. Other studies have also found that disciplinarian supervisors are less effective than more liberal ones.[2]

Such findings are often misinterpreted as signifying that democratic ways are superior to authoritarian ones. But this is a rather loose use of the term "democratic," the exact meaning of which is worth preserving. Since "democracy" denotes rule from below (literally, "people's rule") and not from above, one person's supervision of others can, by definition, not be democratic. This is not the place for a discussion of the relation between democracy and bureaucracy; the final chapter is reserved for this purpose. But here it should be noted that tolerant supervisory practices, in contrast to disciplinarian ones, are neither democratic nor an indication that controlling power over subordinates has been surrendered. On the contrary, leniency in supervision is a potent strategy, consciously or unconsciously employed, for establishing authority over subordinates, and this is why the liberal supervisor is particularly effective.

Let us clarify the concept of authority. First, it refers to a relationship between persons and not to an attribute of one individual. Second, authority involves exercise of social control which rests on the *willing* compliance of subordinates with certain directives of the superior. He need not coerce or persuade subordinates in order to influence them, because they have accepted as legitimate the principle that some of their actions should be governed by his decisions. Third, authority is an observable pattern of interaction and not an official definition of a social relationship. If a mutinous crew refuses to obey the captain's orders, he does not in fact have authority over his men. Whatever the superior's official rights to command obedience and the subordinates' official duties to obey him, his authority over them extends only to conduct that they voluntarily permit to be governed by his directives. Actual authority, consequently, is not granted by the formal organizational chart, but must be established in the course of social interaction, although the official bureaucratic structure, as we shall see presently, facilitates its establishment.

What are some of the practices of a lenient foreman or supervisor? Above all, he allows subordinates to violate minor rules, to smoke or talk, for example, despite the fact that it is prohibited by management. This permissiveness often increases his power over them by furnishing him with legitimate sanctions that he can use as he sees fit. If an action of his subordinates displeases him, the supervisor can punish them by commanding: "Cut out the smoking! Can't you read the sign?" Had he always enforced the rule, this penalty would not have been available to him. Indeed, so crude a use of sanctions is rarely necessary. The mere knowledge that the rule exists and, possibly, that it is enforced elsewhere, instills a sense of obligation to liberal superiors and induces subordinates more readily to comply with their requests.

Whereas the disciplinarian supervisor generally asserts his official prerogatives, the lenient and relaxed one does not. The latter attempts to take the wishes of his subordinates into account in arranging their work schedule, although he has the right to assign their work at his own discretion. Sometimes he goes to special trouble to accommodate a subordinate. Instead of issuing curt commands, he usually explains the reasons for his directives. He calls his subordinates by their first names and encourages their use of his first name (especially in democratically minded American organizations). When one of his subordinates gets into difficulties with management, he is apt to speak up for him and to defend him. These different actions have two things in common: the superior is not required to do them, and his subordinates greatly welcome his doing them. Such conduct therefore creates social obligations. To repay the supervisor for past favors, and not risk the cessation of similar favors in the future, subordinates voluntarily comply with many of his requests, including some they are not officially required to obey. By refraining from exercising his power of control whenever it is legitimate to do so, the bureaucratic superior establishes effective authority over subordinates, which enables him to control them much more effectively than otherwise would be possible.

Complementary role expectations arise in the course of interaction between superior and subordinates and become crystallized in the course of interaction among subordinates. As the superior permits subordinates to violate some rules and to make certain decisions themselves, and as they grow accustomed to conform with many of his directives, they learn to expect to exercise discretion in some areas and to follow supervisory directives in others, and he learns to expect this pattern of conduct from them. The members of the work group, by watching one another at work and talking among themselves about the manner in which they perform their duties, develop social consensus about these role expectations and thereby reinforce them. The newcomer to the group, who must be taught "how things are done around here" as distinguished from "what's in the book," provides an opportunity for further affirming this consensus by making it explicit.

The resulting common role expectations are often so fully internalized that employees are hardly aware of being governed by them. The members of one department might find it natural for their supervisor to interrupt their work and tell them to start on a new task. The members of another department in the same organization might consider such a supervisory order as gross interference with their work, since they had become accustomed to using their discretion about the sequence of their tasks, yet readily comply with other directives of the supervision. These role expectations of independence from the supervisor in some areas and unquestioning obedience in others define the limits of his authority over subordinates.

NOTES

1. Daniel Katz, Nathan MacCoby, and Nancy C. Morse, *Productivity, Supervision and Morale in an Office Situation,* Ann Arbor: Institute for Social Research, University of Michigan, 1950, especially pp. 17, 21, 29.
2. See, for instance, F. J. Roethlisberger and William J. Dickson, *Management and the Worker,* Cambridge: Harvard University Press, 1946, pp. 452–53.

THREE SUPERVISORY ADAPTATIONS TO "ARTIFICIAL PRESSURE"*

Chris Argyris

One of the most common of the factory supervisors' attitudes about budgets was that budgets were used as a pressure device to increase production efficiency. Many cases were cited to support this point. Finance people also admitted that budgets helped "keep people on the ball" by raising their goals and increasing their motivation. The problem of the effects of pressure applied through budgets seems to be the core of the budget problem.

THE CAUSES OF PRESSURE

Employees and front-line supervisors believe that the cause for pressure from the top is due to top management's belief that most employees are basically or inherently lazy. Employees and front-line supervisors

---

* Reprinted with permission of author and publisher from *What Budgets Mean to People* (New York: Controllership Foundation, 1952).

also feel that top management believes that employees do not have enough motivation of their own to do the best possible job.

The interviews with top management officials revealed that the employees' beliefs were not totally unfounded, as a few quotations from some of the top management (both line and finance) make clear:

> I'll tell you my honest opinion. Five per cent of the people work, ten per cent of the people think they work. And the other eighty-five per cent would rather die than work.
>
> I think there is a need for more pressure. People need to be needled a bit. I think man is inherently lazy and if we could only increase the pressure, I think the budget system would be more effective.

Such feelings, even if they are never overtly expressed toward employees, filter through to the employees in very subtle ways. Budgets represent one of the more subtle ways. Once the employees sense these feelings exist in top management, they may become very resentful.

THE EFFECTS OF PRESSURE

How do people react to pressure? In three of the plants studied factory supervisors felt they were working under pressure and that the budget was the principal instrument of pressure. Management exerts pressure on the work force in many ways, of which budgets is but one. Budgets, being concrete, seem to serve as a medium through which the total effects of management pressure are best expressed. As such they become an excellent point of focus for studying the effect of pressure on people in a working organization.

THE CREATION OF GROUPS

An increase in tension, resentment, suspicion, fear and mistrust may not be the only result of ever stronger management pressures transmitted to supervisors, and in turn, to employees. We know, from psychological research, that people can stand a certain amount of pressure After this point is passed, it becomes intolerable to an individual. We also know that one method people have to reduce the effect of the pressure (assuming that the employees cannot reduce the pressure itself) is to join groups. These groups then help absorb much of the pressure and the individual is personally relieved.

The process of individuals joining groups to relieve themselves of pressure is not an easy one. It does not occur overnight. The development of a group on such a basis seems to have the following general stages of growth.

> First, the individuals "feel" the pressure. They are not certain, but they sense an increase in pressure.
>
> Second, they begin to see definite evidences of the pressure. They not only feel it, they can point to it.
>
> Since they feel this pressure is on them personally, they begin to experience tension and general uneasiness.
>
> Next, the people usually "feel out" their fellow workers to see if they sense the pressure.
>
> Finding out that others have noted the pressure, the people begin to feel more at ease. It helps to be able to say, "I'm not the only one."
>
> Finally, they realize that they can acquire emotional support from each other by becoming a group. Furthermore, they can "blow their top" about this pressure in front of their group. Gradually therefore, the individuals become a group because in becoming a group they are able to satisfy these needs:
>
> 1. A need to reduce the pressure on each individual
> 2. A need to get rid of tension
> 3. A need to feel more secure by belonging to a group which can counteract the pressure.

In short, a new, cohesive group has developed to combat management pressure. In a sense, the people have learned that they can be happier if they combine against this management pressure.

Suppose now that top management, aware of the tensions which have been generated and the groups which have been formed, seeks to reduce the pressure. The emphasis on budgets is relaxed. Perhaps even the standards are "loosened." Does this then destroy the group? After all, its primary reason for existence was to combat the pressure. Now, the pressure is gone. The group should eventually disintegrate.

The answer seems to be that the group continues to exist!

The evidence for this is not as conclusive as it should be. Therefore, the following explanation should be considered primarily in the realm of inference and conjecture rather than scientific fact.

These factors seem to operate to keep the group in existence:

1. There is a "time lag" between the moment management announced the new policy and the time the workers put it into effect.
2. The individuals have made a new and satisfactory adjustment with each other. They have helped to satisfy each other's needs. They are, as the social scientist would say, "in equilibrium" with each other. Any attempt to destroy this balance will tend to be resisted even if

the attempt represents an elimination of a "bad" or unhealthy set of conditions. People have created a stable pattern of life and they will resist a change in this pattern.

3. The individuals fear pressure will come again in the future. Because of this feeling, they will tend to create unreal conditions or to exaggerate existing conditions so that they can rationalize to themselves that pressure still exists and, therefore, the need for the group also exists.

PRESSURE ON FRONT-LINE SUPERVISORS

But what about the foreman? Strong pressures converge upon him. How does he protect himself from these pressures?

He cannot join a group against management, as his work force does. For one reason, he probably has at least partially identified himself with management. For another reason, he may be trying to advance in the hierarchy. Naturally, he would not help his chances for advancement if he joined a group against management.

The evidence of the previous chapters seems to indicate that the line supervisor cannot pass all the pressure he receives to his employees. Time and time again the factory supervisors stated that passing the pressure down would only create conflict and trouble which would lead to a decrease in production.

The question arises, where does the pressure go? How do the supervisors relieve themselves of at least some of the pressure? There is evidence to suggest at least three ways in which pressure is handled by the supervisors:

1. Interdepartmental strife. The foremen release some of the pressure by continuously trying to blame fellow foremen for the troubles that exist. "They are," as one foreman expressed it, "trying to throw the dead cat in each other's backyard."

   In three plants observed, much time was spent by certain factory supervisors in trying to lay the blame for errors and problems on some other department.
2. Staff versus factory strife. The foremen released much of the pressure by blaming the budget people, production control people and salesmen for their problems. The data already presented concerning factory supervisors' attitudes toward budget people substantiate this point.
3. "Internalizing" pressure. Many supervisors who do not express their feelings about the pressure have in reality "internalized" it and, in a sense, made it a part of themselves. Such damming up of pressure seemed to be expressed in the following ways:

(i) Supervisor A is quiet, relatively nonemotional, seldom expresses his negative feelings to anyone, but at the same time he works excessively. Supervisor A can be found working at his desk long after the others have gone home. As one supervisor expressed it, "That guy works himself to death."

(ii) Supervisor B is nervous, always running around "checking up" on all his employees. He usually talks fast, gives one the impression that he is "selling" himself and his job when interviewed. He is forever picking up the phone, barking commands and requesting prompt action.

Both of these types (or a combination of these types) are expressions of much tension and pent up emotions that have been internalized. People working under such conditions finally are forced to "take it easy," or they find themselves with ulcers or a nervous breakdown.

But that is not the end of the problem. Constant tension leads to frustration. A frustrated person no longer operates as effectively as he was accustomed. He finds that he tends to forget things he used to remember. Work that he used to do with pleasure, he now delegates to someone else. He is no longer able to make decisions as fast as he did months ago. Now he finds he has to take a walk or get a cup of coffee—anything to get "away from it all."

THE NATURE OF HIGHLY EFFECTIVE GROUPS*

Rensis Likert

. . . the form of organization which will make the greatest use of human capacity consists of highly effective work groups linked together in an overlapping pattern by other similarly effective groups. The highly effective work group is, consequently, an important component of the newer theory of management. It will be important to understand both its nature and its performance characteristics. We shall examine these in this chapter, but first a few words about groups in general.

Although we have stressed the great potential power of the group for building effective organizations, it is important to emphasize that this does *not* say that all groups and all committees are highly effective or

---

* Reprinted with permission of author and publisher from *New Patterns of Management* (New York: McGraw-Hill, 1961), pp. 139–154, © 1961, McGraw-Hill. Used with permission of McGraw-Hill Book Company.

are committed to desirable goals. Groups as groups can vary from poor to excellent. They can have desirable values and goals, or their objectives can be most destructive. They can accomplish much that is good, or they can do great harm. There is nothing *implicitly* good or bad, weak or strong, about a group.

The nature of the group determines the character of its impact upon the development of its members. The values of the group, the stability of these values, the group atmosphere, and the nature of the conformity demanded by the group determine whether a group is likely to have a positive or negative impact upon the growth and behavior of its members. If the values of the group are seen by the society as having merit, if the group is stable in its adherence to these values, and if the atmosphere of the group is warm, supportive, and full of understanding, the group's influence on the development of its members will be positive. A hostile atmosphere and socially undesirable or unstable values produce a negative impact upon the members' growth and behavior.

Loyalty to a group produces pressures toward conformity. A group may demand conformity to the idea of supporting, encouraging, and giving recognition for individual creativity, or it may value rigidity of behavior, with seriously narrowing and dwarfing consequences. This latter kind of pressure for conformity keeps the members from growing and robs the group of original ideas. Many writers have pointed to these deleterious effects of conformity. They often overlook the capacity of groups to stimulate individual creativeness by placing a high value on imaginative and original contributions by their members. As Pelz's findings demonstrate, groups can contribute significantly to creativity by providing the stimulation of diverse points of view within a supportive atmosphere which encourages each individual member to pursue new and unorthodox concepts.

Some business executives are highly critical of groups—or committees—and the inability of committees to accomplish a great deal. Their criticisms are often well warranted. In many instances, committees are wasteful of time and unable to reach decisions. Sometimes the decisions, when reached, are mediocre. Moreover, some members of management at various hierarchical levels use committees as escape mechanisms—as a way to avoid the responsibility for a decision.

The surprising thing about committees is not that many or most are ineffective, but that they accomplish as much as they do when, relatively speaking, we know so little about how to use them. There has been a lack of systematic study of ways to make committees effective. Far more is known about time-and-motion study, cost accounting and similar aspects of management than is known about groups and group processes. Moreover, in spite of the demonstrated potentiality of groups, far less research is being devoted to learning the role of groups and group processes and how to make the most effective use of them in an organization than to most management practices. We know appreciably less about how to make groups and committees effective than we know about most matters of managing.

We do know that groups can be powerful. The newer theory takes this into account and tries to make constructive use of the group's potential strength for developing and mobilizing human resources.

In this and other chapters the use of the term "group" may give the impression that groups have the capacity to behave in ways other than through the behavior of their members. Thus, such expressions appear as the "group's goals," "the group decides," or the "group motivates." In many instances, these expressions are used to avoid endless repetition of the words, "the members of the group." In other instances, something more is meant. Thus, in speaking of "group values," the intent is to refer to those values which have been established by the group through a group-decision process involving consensus. Once a decision has been reached by consensus, there are strong motivational forces, developed within each individual as a result of his membership in the group and his relationship to the other members, to be guided by that decision. In this sense, the group has goals and values and makes decisions. It has properties which may not be present, as such, in any one individual. A group may be divided in opinion, for example, although this may not be true of any one member. Dorwin Cartwright puts it this way: "The relation between the individual members and the group is analogous to the distinction made in mathematics between the properties of a set of elements and the properties of the elements within a set. Every set is composed of elements, but sets have properties which are not identical with the properties of the elements of the set."

THE HIGHLY EFFECTIVE WORK GROUP

Much of the discussion of groups will be in terms of an ideal organizational model which the work groups in an organization can approach as they develop skill in group processes. This model group, of course, is always part of a large organization. The description of its nature and performance characteristics is based on evidence from a variety of sources. Particularly important are the observational and experimental studies of small groups such as those conducted by the Research Center for Group Dynamics (Cartwright & Zander, 1960; Hare et al., 1955; Institute for Social Research, 1956; Institute for Social Research, 1960; Thibaut & Kelly, 1959). Extensive use is made of data from studies of large-scale organizations. Another important source is the material from the National Training Laboratories (Foundation for Research on Human Behavior, 1960d; National Training Laboratories, 1953; National Training Laboratories, 1960; Stock & Thelen, 1958). The NTL has focused on training in sensitivity to the reactions of others and in skills to perform the leadership and membership roles in groups.

In addition to drawing upon the above sources, the description of the ideal model is derived from theory. Some of the statements about the model for which there is little or limited experimental or observational data have been derived directly from the basic drive to achieve and maintain a sense of importance and personal worth. At several points the author has gone appreciably beyond available specific research findings. The author feels, however, that the generalizations which are emerging based on research in organizations and on small groups, youth, and family life, personality development, consumer behavior, human motivation, and related fields lend strong support to the general theory and the derivations contained in this book.

It has been necessary to go beyond the data in order to spell out at this time in some detail the general pattern of the more complex but more effective form of organization being created by the higher-producing managers. The author hopes that the theory and model proposed will stimulate a substantial increase in basic and developmental research and that they will be tested and sharpened by that research.

The body of knowledge about small groups, while sufficiently large to make possible this description of the ideal model, is still relatively limited. Without question, as the importance of the work group as the basic building block of organizations becomes recognized, there will be a great increase in the research on groups and our knowledge about them. The over-all pattern of the model described here will be improved and clarified by such research. Our understanding of how to develop and use groups effectively will also be greatly advanced.

The following description of the ideal model defines what we mean by *a highly effective group*. The definition involves reference to several different variables. Each of them can be thought of as a continuum, i.e., as a characteristic which can vary from low to high, from unfavorable to favorable. For example, a group can vary from one in which there is hostility among the members to one in which the attitudes are warm and friendly. The ideal model is at the favorable end of each variable.

THE NATURE OF HIGHLY EFFECTIVE WORK GROUPS

The highly effective group, as we shall define it, is always conceived as being a part of a larger organization. A substantial proportion of persons in a company are members of more than one work group, especially when both line and staff are considered. As a consequence, in such groups there are always linking functions to be performed and relationships to other groups to be maintained. Our highly effective group is not an isolated entity.

All the persons in a company also belong to groups and organizations outside of the company. For most persons, membership in several groups both within and outside the company is the rule rather than the exception. This means, of course, that no single group, even the highly effective work group, dominates the like of any member. Each member of the organization feels pressures from membership in several different groups and is not influenced solely by loyalty to any one group.

Since the different groups to which a person belongs are apt to have somewhat different and often inconsistent goals and values, corresponding conflicts and pressures are created within him. To minimize these conflicts and tensions, the individual seeks to influence the values and goals of each of the different groups to which he belongs and which are important to him so as to minimize the inconsistencies and conflicts in values and goals. In striving for this reconciliation, he is likely to press for the acceptance of those values most important to him.

The properties and performance characteristics of the ideal highly effective group are as follows:

1. The members are skilled in all the various leadership and membership roles and functions required for interaction between leaders and members and between members and other members.

2. The group has been in existence sufficiently long to have developed a well-established, relaxed working relationship among all its members.

3. The members of the group are attracted to it and are loyal to its members, including the leader.

4. The members and leaders have a high degree of confidence and trust in each other.

5. The values and goals of the group are a satisfactory integration and expression of the relevant values and needs of its members. They have helped shape these values and goals and are satisfied with them.

6. In so far as members of the group are performing linking functions, they endeavor to have the values and goals of the groups which they link in harmony, one with the other.

7. The more important a value seems to the group, the greater the likelihood that the individual member will accept it.

8. The members of the group are highly motivated to abide by the major values and to achieve the important goals of the group. Each member will do all that he reasonably can—and at times all in his power—to help the group achieve its central objectives. He expects every other

member to do the same. This high motivation springs, in part, from the basic motive to achieve and maintain a sense of personal worth and importance. Being valued by a group whose values he shares, and deriving a sense of significance and importance from this relationship, leads each member to do his best. He is eager not to let the other members down. He strives hard to do what he believes is expected of him.

9. All the interaction, problem-solving, decision-making activities of the group occur in a supportive atmosphere. Suggestions, comments, ideas, information, criticisms are all offered with a helpful orientation. Similarly, these contributions are received in the same spirit. Respect is shown for the point of view of others both in the way contributions are made and in the way they are received.

There are real and important differences of opinion, but the focus is on arriving at sound solutions and not on exacerbating and aggravating the conflict. Ego forces deriving from the desire to achieve and maintain a sense of personal worth and importance are channeled into constructive efforts. Care is taken not to let these ego forces disrupt important group tasks, such as problem-solving. Thus, for example, a statement of the problem, a condition which any solution must meet, a suggested solution, or an item of relevant fact are all treated as from the group as a whole. Care is taken so that one statement of the problem is not John's and another Bill's. A suggested solution is not referred to as Tom's and another as Dick's. All the material contributed is treated as *ours:* "One of our proposed solutions is *A*, another is *B*." In all situations involving actual or potential differences or conflict among the members of the group, procedures are used to separate the ego of each member from his contribution. In this way, ego forces do not stimulate conflict between members. Instead, they are channeled into supporting the activities and efforts of the group.

The group atmosphere is sufficiently supportive for the members to be able to accept readily any criticism which is offered and to make the most constructive use of it. The criticisms may deal with any relevant topic such as operational problems, decisions, supervisory problems, interpersonal relationships, or group processes, but whatever their content, the member feels sufficiently secure in the supportive atmosphere of the group to be able to accept, test, examine, and benefit from the criticism offered. Also, he is able to be frank and candid, irrespective of the content of the discussion: technical, managerial, factual, cognitive, or emotional. The supportive atmosphere of the group, with the feeling of security it provides, contributes to a cooperative relationship between the members. And this cooperation itself contributes to and reinforces the supportive atmosphere.

10. The superior of each work group exerts a major influence in establishing the tone and atmosphere of that work group by his leader-

ship principles and practices. In the highly effective group, consequently, the leader adheres to those principles of leadership which create a supportive atmosphere in the group and a cooperative rather than a competitive relationship among the members. For example, he shares information fully with the group and creates an atmosphere where the members are stimulated to behave similarly.

11. The group is eager to help each member develop to his full potential. It sees, for example, that relevant technical knowledge and training in interpersonal and group skills are made available to each member.

12. Each member accepts willingly and without resentment the goals and expectations that he and his group establish for themselves. The anxieties, fears, and emotional stresses produced by direct pressure for high performance from a boss in a hierarchical situation is not present. Groups seem capable of setting high performance goals for the group as a whole and for each member. These goals are high enough to stimulate each member to do his best, but not so high as to create anxieties or fear of failure. In an effective group, each person can exert sufficient influence on the decisions of the group to prevent the group from setting unattainable goals for any member while setting high goals for all. The goals are adapted to the member's capacity to perform.

13. The leader and the members believe that each group member can accomplish "the impossible." These expectations stretch each member to the maximum and accelerate his growth. When necessary, the group tempers the expectation level so that the member is not broken by a feeling of failure or rejection.

14. When necessary or advisable, other members of the group will give a member the help he needs to accomplish successfully the goals set for him. Mutual help is a characteristic of highly effective groups.

15. The supportive atmosphere of the highly effective group stimulates creativity. The group does not demand narrow conformity as do the work groups under authoritarian leaders. No one has to "yes the boss," nor is he rewarded for such an attempt. The group attaches high value to new, creative approaches and solutions to its problems and to the problems of the organization of which it is a part. The motivation to be creative is high when one's work group prizes creativity.

16. The group knows the value of "constructive" conformity and knows when to use it and for what purposes. Although it does not permit conformity to affect adversely the creative efforts of its members, it does expect conformity on mechanical and administrative matters to save the time of members and to facilitate the group's activities. The group agrees, for example, on administrative forms and procedures, and once they have been established, it expects its members to abide by them until there is good reason to change them.

17. There is strong motivation on the part of each member to com-

municate fully and frankly to the group all the information which is relevant and of value to the group's activity. This stems directly from the member's desire to be valued by the group and to get the job done. The more important to the group a member feels an item of information to be, the greater is his motivation to communicate it.

18. There is high motivation in the group to use the communication process so that it best serves the interests and goals of the group. Every item which a member feels is important, but which for some reason is being ignored, will be repeated until it receives the attention that it deserves. Members strive also to avoid communicating unimportant information so as not to waste the group's time.

19. Just as there is high motivation to communicate, there is correspondingly strong motivation to receive communications. Each member is genuinely interested in any information on any relevant matter that any member of the group can provide. This information is welcomed and trusted as being honestly and sincerely given. Members do not look "behind" the information item and attempt to interpret it in ways opposite to its purported intent. This interest of group members in information items and the treatment of such items as valid reinforces the motivation to communicate.

20. In the highly effective group, there are strong motivations to try to influence other members as well as to be receptive to influence by them. This applies to all the group's activities: technical matters, methods, organizational problems, interpersonal relationships, and group processes.

21. The group processes of the highly effective group enable the members to exert more influence on the leader and to communicate far more information to him, including suggestions as to what needs to be done and how he could do his job better, than is possible in a man-to-man relationship. By "tossing the ball" back and forth among its members, a group can communicate information to the leader which no single person on a man-to-man basis dare do. As a consequence, the boss receives all the information that the group possesses to help him perform his job effectively.

22. The ability of the members of a group to influence each other contributes to the flexibility and adaptability of the group. Ideas, goals, and attitudes do not become frozen if members are able to influence each other continuously.

Although the group is eager to examine any new ideas and methods which will help it do its job better and is willing to be influenced by its members, it is not easily shifted or swayed. Any change is undertaken only after rigorous examination of the evidence. This stability in the group's activities is due to the steadying influence of the common goals and values held by the group members.

23. In the highly effective group, individual members feel secure in making decisions which seem appropriate to them because the goals and philosophy of operation are clearly understood by each member and provide him with a solid base for his decisions. This unleashes initiative and pushes decisions down while still maintaining a coordinated and directed effort.

24. The leader of a highly effective group is selected carefully. His leadership ability is so evident that he would probably emerge as a leader in any unstructured situation. To increase the likelihood that persons of high leadership competence are selected, the organization is likely to use peer nominations and related methods in selecting group leaders.

An important aspect of the highly effective group is its extensive use of the principle of supportive relationships. An examination of the above material reveals that virtually every statement involves an application of this principle.

LEADERSHIP FUNCTIONS

Several different characteristics of highly effective groups have been briefly examined. The role of the leader in these groups is, as we have suggested, particularly important. Certain leadership functions can be shared with group members; others can be performed only by the designated leader. In an organization, for example, the leader of a unit is the person who has primary responsibility for linking his work group to the rest of the organization. Other members of the group may help perform the linking function by serving as linking pins in overlapping groups other than that provided by the line organization, but the major linking is necessarily through the line organization. The leader has full responsibility for the group's performance and for seeing that his group meets the demands and expectations placed upon it by the rest of the organization of which it is a part. Other members of the group may share this responsibility at times, but the leader can never avoid full responsibility for the adequate performance of his group.

Although the leader has full responsibility, he does not try to make all the decisions. He develops his group into a unit which, with his participation, makes better decisions than he can make alone. He helps the group develop efficient communication and influence processes which provide it with better information, more technical knowledge, more facts, and more experience for decision-making purposes than the leader alone can marshal.

Through group decision-making each member feels fully identified with each decision and highly motivated to execute it fully. The over-all performance of the group, as a consequence, is even better than the excellent quality of the decisions.

The leader knows that at times decisions must be made rapidly and cannot wait for group processes. He anticipates these emergencies and establishes procedures with his group for handling them so that action can be taken rapidly with group support.

The leader feels primarily responsible for establishing and maintaining at all times a thoroughly supportive atmosphere in the group. He encourages other members to share this responsibility, but never loses sight of the fact that as the leader of a work group which is part of a larger organization his behavior is likely to set the tone.

Although the leader accepts the responsibility associated with his role of leader of a group which is part of a larger organization, he seeks to minimize the influence of his hierarchical position. He is aware that trying to get results by "pulling rank" affects adversely the effectiveness of his group and his relationship to it. Thus, he endeavors to deemphasize status. He does this in a variety of ways that fit his personality and methods of leading, as for example by:

- Listening well and patiently
- Not being impatient with the progress being made by the group, particularly on difficult problems
- Accepting more blame than may be warranted for any failure or mistake
- Giving the group members ample opportunity to express their thoughts without being constrained by the leader pressing his own views
- Being careful never to impose a decision upon the group
- Putting his contributions often in the form of questions or stating them speculatively
- Arranging for others to help perform leadership functions which enhance their status

The leader strengthens the group and group processes by seeing that all problems *which involve the group* are dealt with by the group. He never handles such problems outside of the group nor with individual members of the group. While the leader is careful to see that all matters which involve and affect the whole group are handled by the whole group, he is equally alert not to undertake in a group-meeting agenda items or tasks which do not concern the group. Matters concerning one individual member and only that member are, of course, handled individually. Matters involving only a subgroup are handled by that subgroup. The total group is kept informed, however, of any subgroup action.

The leader fully reflects and effectively represents the views, goals, values, and decisions of his group in those other groups where he is performing the function of linking his group to the rest of the organization. He brings to the group of which he is the leader the views, goals, and decisions of those other groups. In this way, he provides a linkage whereby communication and the exercise of influence can be performed in both directions.

The leader has adequate competence to handle the technical problems faced by his group, or he sees that access to this technical knowledge is fully provided. This may involve bringing in, as needed, technical or resource persons. Or he may arrange to have technical training given to one or more members of his group so that the group can have available the necessary technical know-how when the group discusses a problem and arrives at a decision.

The leader is what might be called "group-centered," in a sense comparable with the "employee-centered" supervisor described in Chapter 2. He endeavors to build and maintain in his group a keen sense of responsibility for achieving its own goals and meeting its obligations to the larger organization.

The leader helps to provide the group with the stimulation arising from a restless dissatisfaction. He discourages complacency and passive acceptance of the present. He helps the members to become aware of new possibilities, more important values, and more significant goals.

The leader is an important source of enthusiasm for the significance of the mission and goals of the group. He sees that the tasks of the group are important and significant and difficult enough to be challenging.

As an over-all guide to his leadership behavior, the leader understands and uses with sensitivity and skill the principle of supportive relationships.

Many of these leadership functions, such as the linking function, can be performed only by the designated leader. This makes clear the great importance of selecting competent persons for leadership positions.

Roles of Membership and Leadership

In the highly effective group, many functions are performed either by the leader or by the members, depending upon the situation or the requirements of the moment. The leader and members, as part of their roles in the group, establish and maintain an atmosphere and relationships which enable the communication, influence, decision-making, and similar processes of the group to be performed effectively. This means not only creating positive conditions, such as a supportive atmosphere, but also eliminating any negative or blocking factors. Thus, for example, groups sometimes have to deal with members who are insensitive, who are hostile, who talk too much, or who otherwise behave in ways adversely affecting the capacity of the group to function. In handling such a problem, the group makes the member aware of his deficiency, but does this in a sensitive and considerate manner and in a way to assist the member to function more effectively in the group. The members of most ordinary groups stop listening to a member who expresses himself in a fuzzy or confused manner. In a highly effective group, the members feed back their reaction to the person involved with suggestions and assistance on how to make his contributions clear, important, and of the kind to which all will want to listen. Friendly assistance and coaching can help a member overcome excessive talking or help him to learn to think and express himself more clearly.

Benne and Sheats (1948) have prepared a description of the different roles played in well-functioning groups. These roles may at times be performed by one or more group members, at other times by the leader. The list, while prepared on the basis of roles in discussion and problem-solving groups, is useful in considering the functions to be performed in any work group which is part of a larger organization.

The following material is taken from the Benne and Sheats article (pp. 42–45) with slight modifications. Group roles are classified into two broad categories:

1. *Group task roles.* These roles are related to the task which the group is deciding to undertake or has undertaken. They are directly concerned with the group effort in the selection and definition of a common problem and in the solution of that problem.
2. *Group building and maintenance roles.* These roles concern the functioning of the group as a group. They deal with the group's efforts to strengthen, regulate, and perpetuate the group as a group.

Group Task Roles

The following analysis assumes that the task of the group is to select, define, and solve common problems. The roles are identified in relation to functions of facilitation and coordination of group problem-solving activities. Each member may, of course, enact more than one role in any given unit of participation and a wide range of roles in successive participations. Any or all of these roles may be performed, at times, by the group "leader" as well as by various members.

A. Initiating-contributing: suggesting or proposing to the group new ideas or a changed way of regarding the group problem or goal. The novelty proposed may take the form of suggestions of a new group goal or a new definition of the problem. It may take the form of a suggested solution or some way of handling a difficulty that the group has encountered. Or it may take the form of a proposed new procedure for the group, a new way of organizing the group for the task ahead.

B. Information seeking: asking for clarification of suggestions made in terms of their factual adequacy, for authoritative information and facts pertinent to the problems being discussed.

C. Opinion seeking: seeking information not primarily on the facts of the case, but for a clarification of the values pertinent to what the group is undertaking or of values involved in a suggestion made or in alternative suggestions.

D. Information giving: offering facts or generalizations which are "authoritative" or involve presenting an experience pertinent to the group problem.

E. Opinion giving: stating beliefs or opinions pertinent to a suggestion made or to alternative suggestions. The emphasis is on the proposal of what should become the group's view of pertinent values, not primarily upon relevant facts or information.

F. Elaborating: spelling out suggestions in terms of examples or developed meanings, offering a rationale for suggestions previously made, and trying to deduce how an idea or suggestion would work out if adopted by the group.

G. Coordinating: showing or clarifying the relationships among various ideas and suggestions, trying to pull ideas and suggestions together or trying to coordinate the activities of various members or sub-groups.

H. Orienting: defining the position of the group with respect to its goal by summarizing what has occurred; departures from agreed upon directions or goals are pointed to, or questions are raised about the direction the group discussion is taking.

I. Evaluating: subjecting the accomplishment of the group to some standard or set of standards of group functioning in the context of the group task. Thus, it may involve evaluating or questioning the "practicality," the "logic," or the "procedure" of a suggestion or of some unit of group discussion.

J. Energizing: prodding the group to action or decision, attempting to stimulate or arouse the group to "greater" activity or to activity of a "higher quality."

K. Assisting on procedure: expediting group movement by doing things for the group—performing routine tasks, e.g., distributing materials, or manipulating objects for the group, e.g., rearranging the seating or running the recording machine, etc.

L. Recording: writing down suggestions, making a record of group decisions, or writing down the product of discussion. The recorder role is the "group memory."

Group Building and Maintenance Roles

Here the analysis of member-functions is oriented to those activities which build group loyalty and increase the motivation and capacity of the group for candid and effective interaction and problem-solving. One or more members or the leader may perform each of these roles.

A. Encouraging: praising, showing interest in, agreeing with, and accepting the contributions of others; indicating warmth and solidarity in one's attitudes toward other group members, listening attentively and seriously to the contributions of group members, giving these contributions full and adequate consideration even though one may not fully agree with them; conveying to the others a feeling that—"that which you are about to say is of importance to me."

B. Harmonizing: mediating the differences between other members, attempting to reconcile disagreements, relieving tension in conflict situations through jesting or pouring oil on troubled waters, etc.

C. Compromising: operating from within a conflict in which one's ideas or position is involved. In this role one may offer a compromise by yielding status, admitting error, by disciplining oneself to maintain group harmony, or by "coming half-way" in moving along with the group.

D. Gate-keeping and expediting: attempting to keep communication channels open by encouraging or facilitating the participation of others or by proposing regulation of the flow of communication.

E. Setting standards or ideals: expressing standards for the group or applying standards in evaluating the quality of group processes.

F. Observing: keeping records of various aspects of group process and feeding such data with proposed interpretations into the group's evaluation of its own procedures. The contribution of the person performing this role is usually best received or most fittingly received by the group when this particular role has been performed by this person at the request of the group and when the report to the group avoids expressing value judgments, approval, or disapproval.

G. Following: going along with the group, more or less passively accepting the ideas of others, serving as an audience in group discussion and decision.

The *group task roles* all deal with the intellectual aspects of the group's work. These roles are performed by members of the group during the problem-solving process, which usually involves such steps as:

1. Defining the problem
2. Listing the conditions or criteria which any satisfactory solution to the problem should meet
3. Listing possible alternative solutions
4. Obtaining the facts which bear on each possible solution
5. Evaluating the suggested solutions in terms of the conditions which a satisfactory solution should meet

6. Eliminating undesirable solutions and selecting the most desirable solution

The *group building and maintenance roles* are, as the label suggests, concerned with the emotional life of the group. These roles deal with the group's attractiveness to its members, its warmth and supportiveness, its motivation and capacity to handle intellectual problems without bias and emotion, and its capacity to function as a "mature" group.

The membership roles proposed by Benne and Sheats, while they are not definitive or complete, nevertheless point to the many complex functions performed in groups and dealt with by leader and members. The members of a highly effective group handle these roles with sensitivity and skill, and they see that the emotional life of the group contributes to the performance of the group's tasks rather than interfering with them.[1]

The highly effective group does not hesitate, for example, to look at and deal with friction between its members. By openly putting such problems on the table and sincerely examining them, they can be dealt with constructively. An effective group does not have values which frown upon criticism or which prevent bringing friction between members into the open. As a consequence, it does not put the lid on these emotional pressures, causing them to simmer below the surface and be a constant source of disruption to the performance of group tasks. The intellectual functions of any group can be performed without bias and disruption only when the internal emotional tensions and conflicts have been removed from the life of the group. Differences in ideas are stimulating and contribute to creativity, but emotional conflict immobilizes a group.

Group building and maintenance functions and group task functions are interdependent processes. In order to tackle difficult problems, to solve them creatively, and to achieve high performance, a group must be at a high level of group maintenance. Success in task processes, fortunately, also contributes to the maintenance of the group and to its emotional life, including its attraction to members and its supportive atmosphere.

In the midst of struggling with a very difficult task, a group occasionally may be faced with group maintenance problems. At such times, it may be necessary for the group to stop its intellectual activity and in one way or another to look at and deal with the disruptive emotional stresses. After this has been done, the group can then go forward with greater unity and will be more likely to solve its group task constructively.

The leader and the members in the highly effective group know that the building and maintenance of the group as well as the carrying out of tasks need to be done well. They are highly skilled in performing each of the different membership and leadership roles required. Each member feels responsible for assuming whatever role is necessary to keep the group operating in an efficient manner. In performing these required roles, the member may carry them out by himself or in cooperation with other group members. Each exercises initiative as called for by the situation. The group has a high capacity to mobilize fully all the skills and abilities of its members and focus these resources efficiently on the jobs to be done.

The larger the work group, the greater the difficulty in building it into a highly effective group. Seashore (1954) found that group cohesiveness, i.e., attraction of the members to the group, decreased steadily as work groups increased in size. This finding is supported also by other data (Indik, 1961; Revans, 1957).

To facilitate building work groups to high levels of effectiveness it will be desirable, consequently, to keep the groups as small as possible. This requirement, however, must be balanced against other demands on the organization, such as keeping the number of organizational levels to a minimum. This suggests the desirability of running tests and computing the relative efficiencies and costs of different-sized work groups. It is probable also that the optimum size for a group will vary with the kind of work the group is doing.

The highly effective group as described in this chapter, it will be recalled, is an "ideal model." It may sound completely unattainable. This does not appear to be the case. There is impressive evidence supporting the view that this ideal can be approximated, if not fully reached, in actual operations in any organization. This evidence is provided by the highest-producing managers and supervisors in American industry and government. If the measurements of their work groups and the reports of their work-group members are at all accurate, some of these managers have built and are operating work groups strikingly similar to our ideal model.

This chapter started by observing that groups can have constructive or destructive goals and can achieve these goals fully or partially, that there is nothing inherently good or bad about groups. If we reflect on the nature and functional characteristics of the highly effective group, however, some qualification of our initial comments may be warranted. In the highly effective group, the members can and do exercise substantial amounts of influence on the group's values and goals. As a consequence, these goals reflect the long-range as well as the short-range needs, desires, and values of its members. If we assume that the long-range desires and values will reflect, on the average, some of the more important long-range values and goals of the total society, we can draw some inferences about the highly effective group. These groups will, in terms of probability, reflect the constructive values and goals of their society. They are likely to be strong groups seeking "good" goals.

NOTES

1. Although the Benne and Sheats list does not define each category unambiguously, it is useful in helping a group analyze and improve its processes. Another list has been prepared by Bales (1950) which has relatively precise definitions. The Bales list will be of interest to those who wish to do research on group processes or who wish to observe and analyze them systematically.

BIBLIOGRAPHY

Bales, R. F.
1950 "Interaction Process Analysis: A Method for the Study of Small Groups." Reading, Massachusetts: Addison-Wesley.

Benne, K. D. and Sheats, P.
1948 "Functional Roles of Group Members." Journal of Social Issues, 4 (2): 42–45.

Cartwright, D. and Zander, A.
1960 "Group Dynamics: Research and Theory," Second Edition. Evanston, Illinois: Row, Peterson.

Foundation for Research on Human Behavior
1960 "An Action Research Program for Organization Improvement." Ann Arbor, Michigan: Author.

Hare, P., Borgatta, E. F. and Bales, R. F.
1955 "Small Groups." New York: Knopf.

Indik, B. P.
1961 "Organization Size and Member Participation." Unpublished Doctoral Dissertation. The University of Michigan.

Institute for Social Research
1956 "Publications: 1946–1956." Ann Arbor, Michigan: Author.

Institute for Social Research
1960 "Publications: September 1956–January 1960." Ann Arbor, Michigan: Author.

National Training Laboratories
1953 "Explorations in Human Relations Training." Washington: National Education Association.

National Training Laboratories
1960 "An Annotated Bibliography of Research, 1947–1960." Washington: National Education Association.

Revans, R. W.
1957 "The Analysis of Industrial Behavior. Automatic Production Change and Control." London: Institution of Production Engineering.

Seashore, S. E.
1954 "Group Cohesiveness in the Industrial Work Group." Ann Arbor, Michigan: Institute for Social Research.
Stock, Dorothy and Thelen, H. A.
1958 "Emotional Dynamics and Group Culture." Washington: National Training Laboratories (NEA).
Thibaut, J. W. and Kelley, H. H.
1959 "The Social Psychology of Groups." New York: Wiley.

WORK GROUP BEHAVIOR AND THE LARGER ORGANIZATION*

Leonard R. Sayles

The individual's most immediate and meaningful experiences of work are obtained in the context of the work group and his work associates. The larger organization is experienced by indirection, but membership in the small group contributes directly to the shaping of attitudes and behavior toward the entire world of work. For this reason of potency, therefore, the contribution of the small group to the total organization has been a subject of substantial research by those interested in human relations in industry.

CONCEPTIONS OF THE WORK GROUP

As Whyte observes, the individual is *not* a member of a single group within a larger structure.[1] Rather, he typically interacts in a variety of settings within the organization. It is the task of the researcher to identify those interaction patterns which are focused and concentrated so that it is reasonable to speak of a "group."

If we follow all the members of the organization through their hours on the job, or find some "high" vantage point and observe the total of

---

* Reprinted with permission of author and publisher from *Research in Industrial Relations* (New York: Harper and Bros., 1957), pp. 131–145. Copyright © 1957 by Harper & Brothers.

A substantial portion of the material included is from a study by the author sponsored by the Bureau of Industrial Relations of the University of Michigan on the relationship of work group behavior to technological and organizational factors. Our major emphasis is on industrial work groups, although examples will be drawn from other work settings.

all interactions, we are likely to be impressed with this proliferation of memberships. Most apparent is membership, except for that unique individual, the president, in some *command group;* that is, the employee shares a common supervisor with a number of colleagues. Distinguishable from this group, but closely related, is a *functional* or *task group*—those employees who must collaborate in some fashion if the work task defined by the organization is to be accomplished. In fact, both of these groups are rather well defined by the larger organization, and the group typically retains those boundaries.

However, there are two other kinds of clusterings that tend to overlap and penetrate the organization in unexpected ways. They are not defined by the formal organization and are often included under the general term, informal organization. One has received much attention from researchers: the *friendship clique.* The other is less well studied, but equally important. That is the *interest group.* This is comprised of those employees who share a common economic interest and seek to gain some objective relating to the larger organization.

Memberships in these groups are not exclusive; often they will overlap considerably. However, the motivations of the members, and, more important, their behavior, are distinctive; and we have no reason to believe that the boundaries will be perfectly coincident.

The Command Group. Perhaps the most obvious kind of small group in the large organization is composed of the supervisor and his immediate subordinates. As Jacques observes, the entire organization is composed of interconnected *command groups,* the subordinates in one group being superiors in their own command group, with the exception of the first level.[2] While we might expect that research would have emphasized this unit of the organization, if we exclude the manifold studies of leadership styles dealt with elsewhere in this volume, there are relatively few systematic explorations of the relationship between the leader and his subordinates as a group, as individuals, and among the subordinates themselves. Jacques' volume is a notable exception.[3] His examination of the command group has a strong psychiatric flavor. He stresses the leader's ambivalence: his *authority* over his subordinates and *dependence* upon them, his sense of isolation, the problem of integrating pair relationships (leader and individual subordinates) with cohesiveness among subordinates, and the mixed feelings of the subordinates as a group who find the leader both expendable and indispensable (one to be protected or exposed?).

The Friendship Clique. This has been conceived as the elementary building block of human organization. As Mayo writes, "Man's desire to be continuously associated with his fellows is a strong, if not the strongest human characteristic."[4]

At the workplace we find a multitude of friendship groups representing the diverse interests of the workers placed there by the organization. The boundaries of these clusterings appear to reflect the employees' off-the-job interests and associations or previous work experience. Age, ethnic background, outside activities, sex, marital status, and so on, comprise the mortar that binds the clique together.

The friendship group has emerged as the agency which welds the individual to the organization. Loyalty, even attachment, to the total organization with its impersonality, extended hierarchy, and social distance becomes ambiguous. However, attachment to the immediate and easily perceived face-to-face group is the predominant reality of organization experience. For the individual it provides a source of personal security in an impersonal environment.

Where cliques are largely nonexistent, as in the rapidly expanding aircraft plants of California, turnover can be enormous. The presumption is that stable social groups take time to crystallize; during the period of formation many potential members will leave voluntarily because they do not find an established unit with which they can affiliate. This in turn inhibits the formation of permanent groups; the process is self-defeating.

Thus Lombard and Mayo conclude that the naive administrator who seeks to break up these cliques because of the inefficiency and wasted motion of the purely social activities involved is actually doing a disservice to the organization.[5] In fact, they find that it takes skillful leadership to encourage their formation, at least in organizations undergoing rapid expansion. A recent well-received text[6] in the field of public administration comes out strongly on the side of encouraging on-the-job social life, concluding that production increased when social conversation was allowed. However, a study employing methods of precise interaction observation is unique in casting some doubts as to the positive correlation between social interaction and productivity.[7]

More serious criticism of the universal efficacy of friendship cliques, however, involves considerations of personality and work structure differences. A study of "rate busters" disclosed a significant majority who were indifferent to, if not hostile to, the social groupings they found on the job.[8]

A recent examination of British longshoremen finds that approximately half of the longshoremen on the docks studied have consciously avoided social entanglements of work group membership. Given an opportunity to join semipermanent gangs, they prefer random work assignments that leave them free to come and go at will, with no group responsibility.[9]

Formation of social groups also appears to be a function of the structure of the work situation itself. Argyris, in his Bank study, finds that incidence of informal social groupings among tellers is less than for bank employees who have less interaction with customers.[10] This conclusion would confirm a basic hypothesis of Chapple, that individuals seek some equilibrium in their rate and range of interaction.[11]

From this theoretical approach, we would expect that the whole range of group activities, not just social life, would be influenced by the interaction pattern fostered by the job. The previously cited study by the University of Liverpool researchers, for example, notes that dockworkers who were members of semipermanent crews were rarely found among the informal leaders of the longshoremen or among the active participants in the union.[12] Moving in the other direction, Lipset concludes that because some jobs handicap workers in maintaining adequate off-the-job relations with other friends (e.g., unusual working hours as among printers, actors, and policemen), they tend to form more closely knit "fellow worker" groups, as evidenced by their record of high participation in local union activities.[13]

Similarly, George Strauss has observed an unusually high degree of membership participation in certain occupational groups involving relative isolation from fellow workers, like insurance salesmen, utility meter readers and substation operators.[14]

Such studies add to the trend toward considering the *need for social relations* as a variable worth studying in itself. It would be interesting to know, for example, whether industrial occupations in which there is high inter-worker dependence in the work process, such that almost constant interaction is required, show less social life than groups characterized by relatively independent operations.

The Task Group. Perhaps one of the most important aspects of small group behavior in large organizations is their relation to the work process itself. The formally designated task builds a group structure, just as do individual social needs and the organizational authority structure.

More specifically, the work process stimulates group controls of (1) work method, (2) output standards of productivity, and (3) relative compensation and prestige relationships.

1. Impact on Work Method.

The experience of working in close proximity on a day-to-day basis induces methods that may depart from the organization's original conception of the job, or at least "fills in" the specific details of the operation not specified in the formal work plan. Thus, employees may exchange repetitive jobs, although such trading is illegal; one worker may do two jobs while a colleague rests; or, as Whyte[15] found, they may change the sequence of the operations to reduce tensions and provide short cuts. Roy observed similar "adjustments" in relations among tool room clerks, job sellers, and machinists where the objective was maximizing piece rate earnings.[16]

Some of these informal, or unplanned for, work methods may decrease worker output. For example, workers' machinations in Roy's machine shop tended to overstate make-ready time during job changes. However, other worker innovations, such as those described by Whyte, undoubtedly increase the total product. Gross found that radar teams, through communication circuits set up during off-the-job social periods, were compensating for deficiencies in the information provided by the formal organization.[17]

Similarly researchers have analyzed the initiative exhibited by a group of department store salesmen in evolving a new work pattern that solved a serious internal morale problem created by a new incentive system.[18]

However, the work structure can be designed so that elaborations of the informal group necessarily work in opposition to the major objectives of the organization. Recent studies of changes in the method of mining coal, conducted by the Tavistock Institute in Great Britain, illustrate such organization.[19] The change from jobs completed by small groups of miners in one shift to successive operations carried out by three shifts resulted in reduction of interaction and communication and a consequent decrease in the miners' recognition of their total responsibility for the operation.[20]

Thus the Tavistock studies suggest that the goal of the engineer in designing the technological organization is to provide the work group with a relatively autonomous task so that responsible *internal* leadership can develop. This kind of organizational structure is, in fact, the very essence of decentralization:

> A primary work organization of this type has the advantage of placing responsibility for the complete . . . task squarely on the shoulders of a single, small, face-to-face group which experiences the entire cycle of operations within the compass of its membership. For each participant the task has total significance and dynamic closure.[21]

The development of mutually convenient methods of conducting the work process can extend to the "job" of collective bargaining. We have ample evidence that union-management relationships at the work group level often depart radically from established practices and attitudes prevailing at higher levels, and may in fact contradict these other, more "formal" relationships.[22]

Aside from evolving methods which seem most convenient to work group members, the pattern of doing the job is fitted to the status system of the group. Those members with most prestige, if at all possible, receive the best jobs. Where possible, working location and equipment are similarly "assigned." And where these are not under group control, helping and trading can be adjusted to the status system. The exchange-of-favors system readily responds to the prestige hierarchy. Of course, the evaluation placed on jobs is itself a product of group interaction.

The methods evolved within the group for task completion become firmly established. Where outside forces (e.g., technological change) threaten to induce changes, the ranks close and resistance is applied. In part, of course, this may be the natural reaction of the culprit fearing punishment for rule infractions. A more reasonable explanation of the informal group's resistance to change, however, is the intimate relationship between the task group as an entity and the work methods they have evolved. A threat to one is a real threat to the other.

2. Impact on Output Standards.

Probably more attention has been given to this aspect of task group behavior than to any other. Starting with the work of Mathewson, and extending through the Western Electric studies, a long and distinguished line of studies indicate that work groups often formulate quite specific output standards and obtain close conformity from their members in *maintaining* these standards. Productivity itself is increasingly conceived of as a group phenomenon.

Several reasons have been advanced as to why output control occupies a place of such importance in the life of the group. Work standards are one of the most important aspects of the job, which can in some fashion be influenced by worker action. The energy expenditure required by the job is largely determined by the number of units required, rather than by the nature of the job itself. Presumably without group control management would be able to utilize individual differences, and competition for promotion and greater earnings, to obtain higher and higher standards. This would penalize particularly the slower worker and the older employee. It might, however, penalize all workers by cutting piece rates, where such exist, and/or reducing the number of employees required by the operation. "Run away" output might have internal ramifications. We have observed situations where group controls were weak, and younger, low-prestige employees exceeded the production and earnings records of their "betters." The results were calamitous for the status hierarchy of the department and ultimately for the effectiveness of the formal organization.

Output control is a basic objective of group action as well as an essential element in maintaining group stability. Not only the relationship of the members to one another, but the durability of the worker relationship to his job depends on the efficacy of this process. Again we need to note that the resultant is not always unfavorable to management. We have many instances on record where the group has sanctioned increasingly high productivity,[23] rejected fellow workers who could not maintain high output, and resisted threats to existing high quality standards.

Evidently a great deal of the interest in "informal group relations" is the result of this presumed relationship between output standards evolving within the group and actual worker productivity. Wilensky in an earlier chapter [of *Research in Industrial Human Relations*] reviews some of the efforts to find the magic formula to convert group norms from "low" to "high."

Some of the earliest research on productivity was based on the assumption that internal harmony in the work group would produce higher performance records. Increasingly researchers have become disillusioned with the relationship between social satisfaction and worker effort. Perhaps one of the most telling blows to the impetus to devote substantial energies to building work groups that are "sociometrically sound" is the provocative study of Good and Fowler in a low morale plant. They found "the informal relationships which developed were such as to maintain pressures toward high production in the face of considerable *animosity* toward the owners and *among the workers themselves*."[24] While their findings are severely limited by the somewhat unique environment they chose, it has become recognized that the relationship between friendship and output is a complex one.

More recently, Seashore finds in a study in a large "heavy equipment manufacturing company" that highly "cohesive" work groups are more likely to have output records that diverge *in either direction* from plant averages.[25] By implication, then, tightly knit work groups are almost as likely to have notably *poor* production records as outstandingly *good* ones.

The present author is inclined to believe that these inconsistencies in research results are due to an overemphasis on output as a part of informal group equilibrium. Control over output is also a major weapon in the arsenal of the group engaging in conflict with management, other work groups, and even the local union. We need to know more about the *total situation* facing a given work group, including these external factors, before predicting its work performance.

The evolution of the method of *group decision* for gaining acceptance for changes in production methods and output standards is recognition of the potency of group standards. The theory presumes that leadership methods that involve the entire work group in the change process have two major advantages:

(*a*) They can eliminate the major barrier of existing group standards which militate against any change, per se.

(*b*) More positively, they commit the individual to new efforts in the context of his group membership. In a sense, the individual "promises" his fellows to accomplish some change in his behavior. Valuing the opinions of his associates, he feels bound to maintain his agreement.

Ideally the "decision" itself becomes the new standard or norm of conduct for the task group. Similarly efforts to develop plant-wide incentive systems are premised on the assumption that output and effort are dependent on the relation of the work group to the total social system of the plant.[26]

3. Impact on Relative Compensation and Prestige Relationships.

The fact that jobs take on a significant social meaning can be seen in the importance attached to wage differentials within the group itself. For example, we have many instances on record when management assigned an equal value to each job and the group found significant distinguishing characteristics. Jobs ranked by employees as *more important or desirable* are expected to have higher earnings than jobs ranked below. The established hierarchy is reinforced over time by the gradual perfection of the correlation between esteem accorded particular workers and prestige accorded to their jobs. The "more important" workers have moved to the "more important" jobs. (The importance attached to the job is not only a function of the earning capacity but also the quality of the surroundings, equipment, the tempo of the work required, etc.) Problems occur only when changes are introduced which violate the established hierarchy.

A persistent problem has been that jobs which the group evaluates as relatively undesirable may need to be compensated at a higher rate than the "desirable" jobs, in order to attract adequate personnel. However, this differential may be contrary to the status system of the work group. Similarly, jobs evaluated (by the group) as desirable may lack characteristics which would bring them a high rating under the organization's formal ranking plan. These contradictions between the group and the organization's ranking system become more important during periods of relative labor shortage, when new recruits are difficult to obtain and when the group undergoes aging.

While these several concepts of the "informal group" are not identical, and in some cases not even complementary in their basic dimensions, they do have one common feature. All stress equilibrium, the development of a system of interpersonal relations which stabilizes the work situation (among subordinates and between superior and subordinates), an interconnected series of friendship linkages, work flow relationships, output levels, and status-income relations. The objectives are the maintenance of individual and group stability by insuring a predictability of day-to-day events and effecting a *modus vivendi* as between individual on-the-job needs and the requirements of the formal organization.

As such, the *informal group* in any and all of its meanings is serving well-recognized and accepted human needs. Its existence and continued preservation are hardly matters for surprise. The building up of routines, of established methods of accomplishing tasks, of predictable social relationships, of group roles—these are all elements of structuring which social scientists have found typical of the human group. In fact, the elements define the group.

Particularly through the setting and maintenance of group standards, informal groups have protected their memberships from possible indiscretions that might reflect adversely on them all; also they have provided support for the individual, by acting as a buffer to outside organizations and by sustaining him through the provision of *known and acceptable* routines of behaving within the face-to-face work group.

Thus the informal group, as perceived in such studies, *reacts to* the initiations of other organizations, particularly management. Being defined in equilibrium terms, the reaction is always an attempt to *regain* the previous undisturbed state—to protect work methods, social relationships, and output levels incorporated in the norms of the group.

Concerted Interest as the Focus. Workers also band together into *interest groups.* These are formed not only to protect their members but also to exploit *opportunities* to improve their relative position. Improvements can take the form of "looser standards," a preferred seniority position, more overtime, more sympathetic supervision, correction of "inequities," better equipment, and countless other less tangible goals that make the job a better one and that often serve to substitute for the more traditional kinds of promotions and mobility.

Distribution of these benefits may be much influenced by pressures of united and determined informal groups. What management feels is "equitable," just as what the union determines is in the "members' interest," is determined to a large extent by attitudes expressed by those individuals who can support their demands by group reinforcements. Those work groups which for one reason or another are unable to exercize similar power in the market place of the plant are penalized.

This is not the traditional concept of the informal group seeking conformity with established norms of conduct. These are much more "free enterprise" units, interacting in a struggle for maximization of utility. All are not equally aggressive in the struggle for self-improvement or equally well equipped with the wherewithal to do battle via the grievance procedure and the more direct pressure tactics on union and management. Some lack the spirit of combat, others the means, while only a restricted few are endowed with the characteristics associated with sustained "activity" and progress toward the goals they seek.

Much of what we say implies a degree of dual or even treble *disloyalty.* Other groups, management, the union, and fellow workers, are perceived as either barriers or sources of assistance. From the point of view of the interest group, it is not high identification or loyalty that counts, but rather the right tactics in using or ignoring these other aggregations.

Thus, management is neither "good" nor "bad," liked or disliked as such. In fact, this approach suggests that it may not always be fruitful to think in pro-management and pro-union terms. It may well be that a group which is satisfied with *itself,* with its ability to protect and improve its own interests, is more favorable to *both* union and management.[27]

The results for the larger plant may not be a system tending toward equilibrium at all. We might expect that certain combinations of pressure groups actually involve the organization in increasing instability—a trend toward disequilibrium. We have observed plants where the interaction of these groups involves increasingly greater discontent, turmoil, and nonadaptive behavior. That is, their behavior tends to reinforce the very problems it was designed to solve.

Similarly, the internal structure of these groups is much more responsive to changes in its external environment than is often implied in the concept of the informal work group as a relatively durable, impervious entity. Literally overnight, technical changes introduced by management can convert a cohesive task force into a disunited, apathetic "rabble," squabbling over internal differences. Similarly, we have observed a group of weakly-united employees become a force of some magnitude in the social system of the plant within a brief period, with no changes in personnel.

The existence of these *interest group* types suggests that greater attention should be given to matching supervisory "types" with group "types." We have tended to think of effective supervision as being the product of a relationship between a good leader and his group, on the assumption that the group of subordinates was a constant. In fact, variations in the effectiveness of supervision may be as much due to inherent differences in the group itself as to the leadership practices exhibited by the supervisor.

THE INTERNAL DYNAMICS OF THE WORK GROUP

We have concentrated primarily on the relationship of the small group to the larger organization, the functions served, the "compatibilities" and "incompatibilities." Therefore, we have failed to explore much of the research that stresses the intriguing inner processes of these groups, as semiautonomous organizations. This means neglecting the processes of self-selection and exclusion developed in the work of Moreno and his colleagues in the field of sociometry. We have also omitted the prolific findings of the "group dynamics school" with its emphasis on leadership patterns and role differentiation, factors contributing to cohesiveness, and the impact of the group itself on membership perceptions and attitudes. Bales and his associates at Harvard have probed deeply into the "ebb and flow" of the problem-solving process within the group. The sequential member roles have been analyzed effectively.

For our purposes it would seem appropriate at least to make specific reference to the work of George Homans. His work places substantial emphasis on the relationship of the internal life of the group to the outside environment (primarily the attitudes, organizational structure, and work method induced by management).[28] "Elaborations" of behavior and sentiment induced in the small group in turn modify the larger organization. While we believe an overemphasis on the concept of *equilibrium* may be misleading, Homans' theorizing does provide a framework within which to relate the small group to the larger organization of which it is a part.

CONCLUSION

Clusterings of workers-on-the-job all have these characteristics: They stem from the uniqueness of individual personality, which refuses to combine into larger "wholes" without changing those entities. The sum of a group of individuals is something more than the total of the constituents; it is a new organization, because most of the members (there are significant exceptions as we have noted) obtain satisfaction in gaining acceptance as a part of the group, and the group itself wields an influence over its members. Put in another way, there are pressures toward *conformity* within the group. These pressures result in the establishment of accepted ways of living together. The way of life of the group includes a complex system of customs and rules, vested interests, and interaction patterns which govern the relationship of members of the group to one another and to the larger environment of which it is a part.

This observance of group-sanctioned behavior and attitudes "fills out" the rationally conceived organization. What is on paper an organization becomes a "living, breathing" social organism, with all the intricacies, emotions, and contradictions we associate with human relations. While no organization would long persist which did not provide its members with this opportunity for spontaneous "human relations," a major problem of the larger organization becomes one of successfully incorporating the small group.

NOTES

1. William F. Whyte, "Small Groups in Large Organizations," in *Social Psychology at the Crossroads,* John Rohrer and Muzafer Sherif, eds. (New York: Harper, 1951), pp. 303–304.
2. Elliot Jacques, *The Changing Culture of a Factory* (New York: Dryden Press, 1952), pp. 273–297.
3. There are two other noteworthy recent exceptions. Argyris devotes a small volume to the relationship between a plant manager in a medium-sized factory and his immediate subordinates. (Chris Argyris, *Executive Leadership* [New York: Harper, 1954]). Two researchers at the Harvard Business School provide us with a very revealing study of the day-to-day changes in the relationship between a first-line supervisor and assembly-line girls during a period of technological changes—Harriet Ronken and Paul Lawrence, *Administering Changes* (Boston: Graduate School of Business Administration, Harvard University, 1952).
4. Elton Mayo, *Social Problems of an Industrial Civilization* (Boston: Graduate School of Business Administration, Harvard University, 1945), p. 111.
5. Elton Mayo and George F. Lombard, *Teamwork and Labor Turnover in the Aircraft Industry of Southern California* (Boston: Graduate School of Business Administration, Harvard University, 1940).
6. Herbert Simon, Donald Smithburg, and Victor Thompson, *Public Administration* (New York: Knopf, 1950), pp. 113–114.
7. A. B. Horsfall and Conrad Arensberg, "Teamwork and Productivity in a Shoe Factory," *Human Organization,* VIII (Winter 1949), pp. 21 ff.
8. These men tended to have a rural background emphasizing individualism. Orvis Collins and Donald Roy, "Restriction of Output and Social Cleavage in Industry," *Applied Anthropology,* V (Summer 1946), pp. 1–14.
9. University of Liverpool, *The Dock Worker* (Liverpool: University Press of Liverpool, 1954), pp. 61 ff.

10. Chris Argyris, *Organization of a Bank* (New Haven: Labor and Management Center, Yale University, 1954), p. 129.
11. Eliot D. Chapple, "Applied Anthropology in Industry," in *Anthropology Today,* A. L. Kroeber, ed. (Chicago: University of Chicago Press, 1953), pp. 819–831. Many of the observations in this section are based on the theoretical work of Chapple.
12. University of Liverpool, *op. cit.,* p. 72.
13. Seymour M. Lipset, "The Political Process in Trade Unions: A Theoretical Statement," in *Freedom and Control in Modern Society,* Monroe Berger, Theodore Abel, and Charles Page, eds. (New York: Van Nostrand, 1954), pp. 101–102.
14. Personal correspondence, Professor Strauss, University of Buffalo.
15. William F. Whyte, "The Social Structure of the Restaurant," *The American Journal of Sociology,* LIV (January 1949), pp. 306–307.
16. Donald Roy, "Quota Restriction and Goldbricking in a Machine Shop," *The American Journal of Sociology,* LVII (March 1952), pp. 427–442.
17. Edward Gross, "Some Functional Consequences of Primary Controls in Formal Work Organizations," *American Sociological Review,* XVIII (August 1953), pp. 370–371.
18. Nicholas Babchuck and William Goode, "Work Incentives in a Self-Determined Group," *American Sociological Review,* XVI (October 1951), p. 686.
19. E. Trist and K. Bamforth, "Some Social and Psychological Consequences of the Longwall Method of Coal-Getting," *Human Relations,* IV, No. 1 (1951).
20. The same problem can arise even though the employees are not separated into different time shifts. A study of a textile mill provides us with an example of the impact of worker-machine allocations. Cf. A. K. Rice, "Productivity and Social Organization in an Indian Weaving Shed," *Human Relations,* VI, No. 4 (1953).
21. Trist and Bamforth, *op. cit.,* p. 6.
22. Cf. Melville Dalton, "Unofficial Union-Management Relations," *American Sociological Review,* XV (October 1950), pp. 611–619.
23. Cf. George Strauss, "Group Dynamics and Intergroup Relations," in William F. Whyte and others, *Money and Motivation* (New York: Harper, 1955), pp. 90–96.
24. William Goode and Irving Fowler, "Incentive Factors in a Low Morale Plant," *American Sociological Review,* XIV (October 1949), p. 624; italics added by author.
25. Stanley Seashore, *Group Cohesiveness in the Industrial Work Group* (Ann Arbor: Institute for Social Research, University of Michigan, 1954), p. 98.
26. Cf. William F. Whyte and others, *Money and Motivation, op. cit.,* p. 225.

27. These areas . . . [are] further elaborated in the author's . . . study, *Technology and Work Group Behavior* (Ann Arbor: Bureau of Industrial Relations, University of Michigan, 1956).
28. George Homans, *The Human Group* (New York: Harcourt Brace, 1950).

AUTONOMOUS WORK GROUPS CONTINUING AT THE RUSHTON MINE*

Gerald I. Susman

A well-known experimental effort to improve mine productivity, efficiency, and safety by using autonomous work groups has been continued at the Rushton Mining Company in Osceola Mills, Pennsylvania.

Almost a year ago, in August 1975, the local union voted 79 to 75 not to extend work autonomy to other areas of the mine. The vote followed a year-long project, ending in February 1975, in which one section of the mine had applied the autonomous work concept to three crews, consisting of nine members and one foreman each. The union members had previously decided that after the experimental year the mine should either become completely autonomous or not at all.

NEGATIVE INFLUENCES

Among the factors influencing the negative vote were perceived inequities in the privileges enjoyed by autonomous section members, who all received top pay rates; fears that the program might harm the union, despite endorsement by the United Mine Workers of America; and changes in the national contract, which narrowed the differentials between pay grades and led some miners to feel that they had little to gain by an affirmative vote.

EACH CREW DECIDES

Four months later, in December 1975, the union members authorized their officers to develop a new work plan for the entire mine. It was decided that, rather than writing a formal plan, the miners would let each section evolve its own degree of autonomy, and at present nine

---

* Reprinted with permission of author and publisher from *World of Work Report,* (August 1976) p. 3.

of the 12 crews have done so. The manner of evolution depends upon the personalities and skills of the men and the mining conditions they face at any particular time. Some of the crews are now as autonomous as was the original experimental section. By and large, the most experienced crews with a higher level of training have chosen the greatest degree of autonomy.

THE ORIGINAL EXPERIMENT

The Rushton project took shape because of the growing concern of UMWA leaders and mining company managers with questions of productivity, absenteeism, turnover, safety, and wildcat strikes. The top UMWA leadership and the President of Rushton Mining Company, Warren Hinks, Jr., decided that safety and productivity goals need not be conflicting, and could be better achieved if miners could share in the decisions affecting their work.

In summer 1973, a Rushton labor-management committee decided that one of the three sections would apply the autonomous work concept to its three crews. The miners would make most of their own production decisions, leaving the foremen to monitor Federal and state mine safety laws. This meant that foremen would no longer face the conflict of being responsible for both production and safety. Foremen were also expected to handle training, scheduling, and coordination with mine departments.

EVALUATING THE PROJECT

A research team—consisting of Professor Eric Trist of the University of Pennsylvania and Professor Gerald Susman and Grant Brown of Pennsylvania State University—followed the Rushton effort and helped create a number of procedures for handling grievances and problems. . . .

APPARENT ACHIEVEMENTS

During the year-long experiment, it was found that the autonomous section's achievements, as compared to those of a control group, included: substantially fewer safety violations, the lowest accident rate, a tie with another section for the lowest rate of absenteeism, and allowing for inflation, a favorable trend in reducing supply costs. At the same time, there was no decrease in production: in fact, it rose slightly; then midway through the year the experimental section became the highest producer in the mine for 10 months, mining 25 percent more coal than the control group.

CONTINUING TRENDS

The experimental section's safety record continues to surpass records of other groups, as does its absenteeism rate—5 percent, compared to an industry range of approximately 12 to 20 percent. Based on costs noted during the initiation of the experiment, and taking inflation into account, relative controllable costs seem to be continuing a downward trend. In addition, the accident rate is decreasing from the level recorded at the outset of the experiment.

THE PRESENT STATUS

Most of the mine crews are presently developing their own autonomous work relationships. A steering committee composed of all the union officers and seven supervisors and managers meets quarterly to plan further training and development. A gain-sharing system is also being devised—a modified Scanlon plan, based on labor efficiency and reduced costs—which will assess labor efficiency and share the gains three ways, among the company, the managers, and the miners.

THREE STYLES OF LEADERSHIP AND THEIR USES*

Robert T. Golembiewski

Managers who have tried to keep track of research and thinking on the subject of leadership may well sympathize with the centipede that was asked how it managed its legs, for this innocent question, the limerick tells us, reduced the unfortunate creature to lying "distracted in a ditch considering how to run."

The question asked in the leadership literature—"How does one lead men?"—is every bit as disconcerting as the one put to the centipede.

---

* Reprinted by permission of the publisher from PERSONNEL, 38 (July–August 1961), pp. 34–45, © 1961 by American Management Association, Inc.

Nevertheless, the parallel between them is not quite exact. The centipede, until he had to think about it, was only doing what came naturally and doing it well. Leadership in the work situation, however, does not belong to the order of instinctive behavior. Doing what comes naturally in striving for leadership often leaves too much to be desired.

Though management has tended to be all too receptive to endorsements for this, that, or the other leadership approach, its interest has sound foundations. In the first place, a considerable body of evidence shows that the productivity of a work unit is affected by the kind of leadership the unit receives. In the second, decisions about what style of leadership to adopt must to some extent be made for the company as a whole rather than being left to the intuitions of individual managers. Still, management's interest has not been satisfied, for the evidence supporting any one leadership style can always be countered, and frequently is, by evidence supporting its precise opposite. The bewildered organization that has tried and abandoned one style after another may well be pardoned for asking, "Where do we go from here?"

Fortunately, it is beginning to look as if a theory based on empirical findings is at last in the making. No one yet knows exactly what its ultimate content will be, but its outlines can now be perceived and—even more important—can be put to use to improve managerial practice.

At this point, it may be useful, therefore, to review the research findings that form the skeleton of this theory and to examine their practical implications. But before doing so, it is necessary to define the term "leadership"—though this in itself is a question that has stirred up endless controversy. For the purposes of this article, however, "leadership" will be taken to mean the consistent ability to influence people in desired ways.

On the classification of leadership styles, fortunately, there is more agreement. Most authorities recognize three basic types: "leader-centered," or "autocratic"; "group-centered," or "democratic"; and "individual-centered," or "free-rein."[1] The supposedly modern view, of course, is that the group-centered style is the most conducive to productivity. By contrast, the traditional view admits only the leader-centered style, regards the group-centered style as a plaything of psychologists, and dismisses the free-rein style as constituting not leadership, but rather its surrender.

EACH IN ITS PLACE

Supporters of any all-or-nothing view have one thing in common: they will often be surprised to find that the research literature does not consistently support any one leadership style. The reason for this lies not in any failing of the research itself but in the simple fact that there is no "best" style. Indeed, the question "Which kind of leadership should we use?" prevents any useful answer. The question should be, rather, "Which kind of leadership *when?*"

This "when," it is worth pointing out, constitutes an integral part of the question, for every scientific formulation must at some point specify the conditions it covers. Even the well-tested law explaining what happens when objects are dropped holds true only for objects that are heavier than air. If the objects are dropped at certain points in space, moreover, they will "fall up," or float.

This approach provides a partial explanation of the apparent chaos of the research literature. Many studies that seem to contradict each other are simply accounts of leadership phenomena under different conditions. Studies based upon observation of similar conditions, on the other hand, have yielded a pattern of consistent results.

Fortunately, leadership study has now taken on a "situational" approach. The main point of this approach has been well expressed in popular terms by Auren Uris, who advises the would-be leader as follows: "The skill with which you apply the three basic tools of leadership—autocratic, democratic, and free-rein techniques—determines your personal success as a leader."[2]

What, then, are the conditions that should be taken into account in the choice of a leadership style? There are many. Four among them, however—personality, task characteristics, task roles, and group characteristics—are particularly important and have been explored in a number of research studies. A separate examination of each of these conditions should provide some guidelines for translating such advice as Uris' into action.

Personality

As the advocates of group-centered leadership often fail to realize, not all people can function well under the same kind of leadership. There are, for example, many people whose personalities make them unfitted for a group- or individual-centered style.[3] Such a person was Administrator H, described in Harold Lasswell's *Psychopathology and Politics.*[4] A childhood marked by unfortunate sexual experiences and domination by an overbearing, prudish father had left him sharply, though unconsciously, ambivalent toward authority. Consequently, he worked well under supervision but invariably became careless when he was given substantial freedom on the job.

Needless to say, giving free rein to a subordinate like H would bring nothing but trouble, though over the long run his personality might possibly change enough to permit a looser kind of supervision. Studies of "authoritarianism" confirm these common-sense conclusions about how to deal with men like Administrator H. Authoritarians behave in ways that reveal compulsive conformity based upon a view of the world as menacing and unfriendly. Though they are not necessarily people of low intelligence, they think in relatively few channels, from which they cannot be moved. In addition, they seek security through the exercise of authority or, better still, through surrender to some powerful authority figure.

Studying authoritarianism in military groups, Medalia formulated and tested the following two hypotheses:[5]

1. People with strong authoritarian tendencies will be more likely to accept formal military leaders with the conventional traits of the "good officer" than will people with weak authoritarian tendencies.

2. People with strong authoritarian tendencies will be more likely to re-enlist than will people with weak authoritarian tendencies.

The data that emerged from his study are shown in Table 1. Not only do these findings support both hypotheses but, when one takes into account certain technical factors in the study that tended to obscure any relations, they suggest a very strong relation between personality and leadership style.

The practical advantages of adapting leadership style to personality characteristics seem clear from this study. In the groups analyzed, it could mean a 23 per cent increase in the acceptance of the formal leader by his subordinates and a 14 per cent increase in the intent to reenlist. These figures indicate the need for developing a valid diagnostic indicator of the leadership style to which an individual will respond best. Comparable changes in a business organization would certainly prove well worth the cost of meshing leadership style and personality factors.

TABLE 1
Relation of Authoritarianism in Members of a Military Group to Acceptance of Formal Heads and Intent to Re-enlist

		Authoritarianism			*Difference Between High and Low*
		High	*Medium*	*Low*	
Leader Acceptance					
Above Median		59%	52%	36%	+23
Below Median		41	48	64	−23
	Total	100%	100%	100%	
Intent to Re-enlist					
Yes or Undecided		38%	34%	24%	+14
No		62	66	76	−14
	Total	100%	100%	100%	

A word of qualification must, however, be inserted here. Most people have wide "response repertoires." That is, they are able to perform the wide range of behaviors required by the various styles of leadership despite their personal preference for a particular style.

This adaptability was demonstrated by Berkowitz in an experiment with a communication network that channeled a great deal of information to some positions and very little to others.[6] Half the subjects were assigned to communication positions in which they would have to act in ways that were not congruent with their personalities: submissive people were placed in central positions, dominant people in peripheral positions. The other half were assigned to the positions appropriate to their personalities. Though the two kinds of subjects at first performed quite differently, Berkowitz found, the "misplaced" subjects generally managed to adjust to the demands of their positions by the last of the three trials in the experiment.

Berkowitz' experiment, however, was brief. The findings of other research projects indicate that if it had continued, the subjects in the first group would ultimately have displayed reactions ranging from dissatisfaction to attempts at sabotaging the work process. Just when it is that such reactions begin to appear will be determined by circumstances and personalities. But when they do hit, they hit hard.

A manager, then, may vary his style of leadership, but he cannot force people to act forever in ways that are uncongenial to their personalities. This imposes a difficult task upon the manager and the organization—ascertaining the behavior preferences of the individual subordinates and then arranging the work so as to allow them to carry out their tasks in the manner they prefer. Unless this is done, the formal head will remain just that, rather than being accepted by his men as their leader.

Task Characteristics

The second major condition affecting the usefulness of any given leadership style is the nature of the task to be performed. Though little work has so far been done in classifying tasks, it should be adequate here to note that tasks may be distinguished in terms of (1) the obviousness of the solution to the problem or of the work itself and (2) the amount of cooperation the task requires.

Unfortunately, research to date has for the most part assumed that all tasks are quite complex and require a great deal of interpersonal cooperation. Because socioemotional factors affect performance most strongly when the task is of this kind, the leader-centered style, which tends to generate emotional flareups, usually shows up poorly under these circumstances, while the group-centered style shows up well.

Many tasks, however, do not have these assumed characteristics. One of Deutsch's experiments illustrates the value of distinguishing between kinds of tasks.[7] The prediction to be tested was that internally cooperative groups would be more effective than internally competitive groups. When groups of both kinds attempted to solve human relations and puzzle problems, it was found, the "cooperative" groups did indeed perform better on a number of measures of effectiveness, including quantitative and qualitative output, member satisfaction with group functioning and output, and amount of aggressive behavior. But on several measures the differences between the two kinds of groups were more marked for the human relations problem than for the puzzle problem. It seems as if the objectively demonstrable nature of the puzzle solution made it difficult for members of the "competitive" groups to block each other in subtle ways. (Certainly, the nature of the task would have made direct blocking seem ridiculous.) The open-endedness of the human relations problem, on the other hand, gave them ample opportunity to run each other ragged.

In terms of leadership style, these data suggest that the leader-centered style is particularly inappropriate to tasks that have more than one possible solution and that require a considerable amount of interpersonal cooperation. More important still, the data seem to leave little room for the leader-centered style even on tasks with just the opposite characteristics, for, as has already been noted, the group-centered style generally proved the more effective not only for the human relations problem but for the puzzle problem as well. In actual business and industrial situations, it should also be pointed out, emotional tensions can affect performance adversely at any number of points in the operation—at far more points than in Deutsch's experimental situation. Moreover, the marked preference most people show for the group-centered style furthers its claim to being the more useful of the two.

This does not mean, however, that the leader-centered style should be rejected out of hand. A situation in which most of the operators are strongly authoritarian and the task is a simple one requiring little cooperation is obviously tailor-made for authoritarian leadership.

THE ROLE OF INTELLIGENCE

Calling a task "simple" of course implies some relation between the task itself and the intelligence of the people who are to perform it. The importance of taking this relation into account in deciding upon a leadership style has been demonstrated by a simple experiment with a game based on "Twenty Questions."[8] As Table 2 indicates, though all the subjects worked on essentially the same task, the "Brights" did their best under a group-centered style, and the "Dulls" under a leader-centered style. The relation was especially marked for the "Dulls," whose problem-solving efficiency was only half as high under group-centered leadership as under authoritarian leadership.

TABLE 2

Effects of Leadership Style and Members' Intelligence Upon Group Performance in "Twenty Questions" Game

Members' Intelligence and Leadership Style		*Measures of Performance*	
		Median No. of Questions Asked Per Problem	*Per Cent of Problems Solved*
Bright	Group-centered	15.5	100.0
	Leader-centered	18.5	87.5
Dull	Group-centered	31.0	37.5
	Leader-centered	24.5	75.0

Regulating work assignments by task and personality characteristics may seem like a great deal of bother, but the 100 per cent performance difference for the "Dulls" suggests that the extra bother will more than pay its own way. Indeed, business would most likely find it profitable to subsidize the research necessary for the development of even more precise ways of differentiating people than those now available. The "Brights" in this experiment—to give just one illustration of the value of this greater precision—probably included some authoritarian subjects. (Though low intelligence is frequently accompanied by high authoritarianism, high intelligence is not so frequently accompanied by low authoritarianism.) Excluding the authoritarians from the "Bright" sample would probably have had two effects: the performance of the remaining "Brights" under group-centered conditions would have improved, and that of the "Brights" under leader-centered conditions would have deteriorated. In the industrial situation, both the individual and management could profit from a more comfortable "fit" of employees to their tasks.

Task Roles

Still another question to be considered in choosing a leadership style is "Who does what?"—that is, "What are the roles of the leaders and followers?" Though the very notion of leadership implies a set of roles different from those of followership, just what functions are covered by each set cannot be rigidly prescribed. Indeed, the distribution of functions is often the product of social consensus, and may vary even among work teams performing the same operation in the same organization.

Roles do, however, fall into three broad categories: roles peculiar to the superior, roles peculiar to the subordinate, and "mixed" roles, whose functions are performed by either or both. The general argument here, by way of preview, is that each of these three classes implies a different leadership style.

Evidence indicates that supervisors who are successful in influencing their subordinates' behavior in the desired directions—that is, supervisors who are leaders—work at sharpening these differences in roles. In a study by Kahn and Katz, supervisors of section gangs on a railroad and supervisors of clerical sections in an insurance company were asked how much of their time was usually spent in supervisory matters, and how much in other matters.[9] Their answers, shown in Table 3, revealed that the supervisors with low-producing sections were two or three times more likely to perform the same duties as their men, or to perform the paperwork aspects of their jobs, than the supervisors with high-producing sections.

These findings can be explained by a little common-sense reasoning: The behavior of the low-producing supervisors reflects either a lack of consensus about roles in their work groups or their own failure to respect an existing consensus. Whatever the case, conflict is likely, and must inevitably result in productivity losses.

Not only should the superior differentiate his functions from those of his subordinates, but he should, of course, perform certain *specific* functions. The amount of planning he does, for example, is directly related to the productivity of his section. Some interesting data on this score were obtained by asking foremen in a tractor factory whether they were able to plan their work ahead as much as they liked.[10] Though their answers, given in Table 4, suggest that the high-producing foremen actually did more planning than the low-producing foremen, it

TABLE 3

Time Spent in Supervising in Relation to Section Productivity

Section Productivity	*50% or More of Time Spent in Supervising %*	*Less Than 50% of Time Spent in Supervising %*	*Not Ascertained %*	*Total %*
Insurance company				
High	75	17	8	100
Low	33	59	8	100
Railroad				
High	55	31	14	100
Low	25	61	14	100

TABLE 4

Foremen's Perception of Opportunity for Planning in Relation to Section Productivity

	Foremen's Responses			
*Section Productivity** %	*Can Plan Ahead As Much as Needed* %	*Sometimes Have Trouble Planning Far Enough Ahead* %	*Can Seldom or Never Plan Ahead* %	*Total* %
97–101	37	42	21	100
91–96	51	32	17	100
86–90	29	41	30	100
80–85	29	46	25	100
50–79	14	40	46	100

* Productivity is expressed as per cent of standard.

should be noted that the foremen were talking about the fulfillment of their planning expectations, not about how much planning they actually did or how much they thought necessary. It seems reasonable to assume that high-producing foremen were more aware of the importance of planning than the others. Thus their less-than-complete satisfaction may reflect high hopes rather than low accomplishment. If this is so, then they must have been even more active in planning their work than the table suggests.

Tables 3 and 4 deal with but two of the three categories of roles outlined above: roles peculiar to the subordinate and roles peculiar to the superior. There is, however, substantial evidence of the harm that superiors do in failing to respect the third category of roles: those whose performance is "mixed." The conflict generated by supervisory insensitivity to this third category is, of course, the subject of much of the human relations literature.

But what leadership styles do these three categories demand? As the provisional model in Table 5 shows, it seems likely that the superior's roles are best handled with a leader-centered style, "mixed" roles with a group-centered style, and the subordinate's roles with a free-rein style. This does not, however, mean that the superior should surrender all his power over certain functions. On the contrary, every role assumes a set of guidelines for behavior, and the three leadership styles are merely different techniques for developing and enforcing them. When the guidelines are violated—whatever the leadership style under which they were developed—the supervisor is put into a decisive position.

If, for example, a worker insisted on tightening bolts with his teeth, his fellow workers and his supervisor would undoubtedly be scandalized and would agree that the worker's freedom in deciding how to perform

TABLE 5

A Provisional Model of Roles and Appropriate Leadership Styles

Category of Roles	*Typical Function*	*Generally Appropriate Leadership Style*
1. Roles peculiar to the superior	Setting general goals	Leader-centered
2. "Mixed" roles	Relocating machines on which individuals have worked for many years	Group-centered
3. Roles peculiar to the subordinate	Deciding how to use a tool	Free-rein

this operation did not extend quite so far as all that. Group pressure—especially in a work unit operating under group-centered leadership—might encourage him to change his ways. But the supervisor would still be on the spot, formally and socially. He would have to supplement this pressure and perhaps take formal action. When violations of the behavioral guidelines are winked at, the supervisor invariably comes off a loser.

The supervisor who would be a leader, then, must have a deft touch. A useful criterion for determining when to step in can be found in the concept of "relevance," that is, in how the issue ranks in terms of its importance to, say, the employees, the organization as a whole, or the boss.

The more relevant an issue is to the group, experimental evidence shows, the more willing the group is to accept a relatively authoritarian way of dealing with it. Thus a leader who is strongly supported by his group may depend primarily on free-rein and group-centered styles, which encourage member involvement. When a relevant issue arises, however, he will exercise substantial influence, and, in fact, the group will expect him to do so. (The leader-centered superior with a work unit of authoritarians will, of course, hold a tight rein on most matters and therefore need not have such a delicate touch. But such situations are rare.)

An issue may, of course, be relevant to the formal organization but not to the group. If, for example, the work unit neglects its responsibilities to the company on the question of the level of production, the superior may have to use a leader-centered style despite the group's reluctance to have him do so. On less relevant matters, however, he would do well to balance it with a group-centered or free-rein style, which would reduce any tension generated by the leader-centered style. The "relevance" concept, in other words, supplements the model in Table 5, for an unanticipated relevant item may appear in any one of the three categories. The handling of such items will in the long run determine whether the formal head continues to function as a leader or loses his control over the group.

Group Characteristics

Discussing the relevance of an issue for a work group implies that the group has developed certain common standards *of* its own and *on* its own. This characteristic of groups—the tendency to develop group norms and group goals—may be accompanied by fairly powerful mechanisms for imposing the group's will upon its members and upon the outside world. The group therefore plays a large part in determining the success of the various leadership styles. Group properties have, of course, been examined at length in the social science literature, and this author has sketched their broad implications for organization performance elsewhere.[11]

One aspect worth considering here is the degree to which the group *as a group* accepts its formal head. If the group feels that its supervisor is not fulfilling its needs, it may find itself a more satisfactory leader from within its own ranks. This should not be a matter of indifference to industrial managers, for the emergence of an informal leader who acts as spokesman for a work unit is often associated with low productivity. In the Kahn and Katz study, workers in railroad section gangs were asked, "Is there some one man in the section who speaks up for the men when they want something?" Fewer than one in six respondents in the high-producing sections answered *yes,* while over half the respondents in the low-producing sections did so.[12]

MUST THE LEADER BE LIKED?

Such data as these, however, should not be taken as an endorsement of group-centered leadership. All three styles are equal to the task of winning informal acceptance for the formal head, though under different conditions. Moreover, the supervisor is not always well advised to try to raise his informal status to the level of his formal status. He must consider, among other things, the nature of his group's norms, which he will have to respect if he is to gain informal acceptance. If, as is by no means uncommon, the norms favor low output, his attempt to gain high informal status may force him to compromise his formal position.

The dangers of such an attempt are illustrated in a study of aerial bombardment crews by Adams.[13] Each member of each crew was ranked on several measures of status within the crew—formal rank, popularity, reputed flying ability, and so on. When the formal ranks of the members of any crew were quite similar to their ranks on the other measures, Adams found, the crew as a whole did well on "social performance" (harmony, intimacy, and the like). The crews that showed up best in these two respects, however, were not the best in "technical performance" (e.g., bombing accuracy). These findings seem reasonable. The popularity of the formal leaders of these crews was probably based in part upon their respect of a norm opposed to outstanding technical performance. Obviously, it did not make them particularly effective in their formal position. On the contrary, their closeness with their men helped the crews resist the demands of the "outside" organization.

A supervisor inheriting a work unit with a low-output norm faces a difficult task in choosing a style of leadership. If he employs a free-rein style, he will most likely succeed only in supporting the group norm. At the other extreme, the use of a leader-centered style may well harden the group's resistance to the formal organization. Even if the supervisor succeeds in breaking the group norm, he will most likely arouse antagonisms bound to affect the work process sooner or later.[14] (One major exception must be noted here: Groups of authoritarians, as has already been pointed out, will generally respond well to a leader-centered style. But this offers little practical consolation, given the apparent rarity of such groups.) Finally, it is the group-centered style, paradoxical though it may seem, that offers the best chance of success in changing a low-output norm, and group-centered leadership has actually proved useful in a number of instances. The reason for this seems to be that low output is a means by which the members of a work unit protect themselves against some perceived threat. A group-centered style often acts to make the group members feel less threatened and thus reduces their need for the low-output norm. But this is not inevitable.

In sum, every leadership style stands liable to failure in the attempt to develop and enforce a more acceptable output norm. If none of them works, the supervisor has no choice but to stop being a practicing psychologist and recommend that the unit be broken up.

CONCLUDING NOTES

The difficulties of choosing a leadership style, then, are great even if only a single condition is considered. From the two preceding paragraphs alone it should be clear that the question of how to lead any given work group is far more complex than is recognized by any existing generalizations, all of which call for a single leadership style. To compound this complexity, however, the four sets of conditions discussed in this article always appear in combination, so that some elements in a situation may favor one style while some elements favor another.

In fact, our increasing knowledge of the complexity of the question has outmoded the traditional designations of leadership styles. These designations, which suggest exclusive categories, ought to be modified so as to express the ways in which leadership styles continuously change in response to changing situations. The suggestions presented above outline the nature of the necessary changes. Needless to say, though these suggestions are consistent with the available research findings, they will need further verification before they can be considered rules for action.

Finally, it must be noted that the foregoing discussion has centered on the question, "What are the conditions under which various leadership styles are most useful?" and has, in effect, neglected the question "What *should be* the dominant leadership style?" This neglect should not be taken as indicating that the question of value is unimportant. Rather, it recognizes that in practice the choice of a leadership style implies, and is preceded by, a value choice. In the field of leadership, as in every other, the use of empirical regularities must always be guided by considerations of what ought to be.

NOTES

1. For a typical treatment, see A. Uris, *How to Be a Successful Leader.* McGraw-Hill Book Company, Inc., New York, 1953, pp. 32–39.
2. *Ibid.,* p. 31.
3. Many personnel men are aware of these personality effects and therefore recruit only from those groups of people whose general social training seems likely to produce the personality characteristics appropriate to the organization's leadership style. Thus some companies seek out rural workers because of their alleged amenability to formal discipline.
4. *The Political Writings of Harold D. Lasswell.* The Free Press, Glencoe, Ill., 1951, pp. 127–35.
5. N. Z. Medalia, "Authoritarianism, Leader Acceptance, and Group Cohesion," *Journal of Abnormal and Social Psychology,* LI, No. 2 (1955), pp. 207–13.
6. L. Berkowitz, "Personality and Group Position," *Sociometry,* XIX, No. 4 (1956), pp. 210–22.
7. M. Deutsch, "The Effects of Cooperation and Competition upon Group Process," in *Group Dynamics: Research and Theory,* ed.

D. Cartwright and A. Zander. Row, Peterson and Company, Evanston, Ill., 1953, pp. 319–53. See especially tables 23.5, 23.7, 23.9, and 23.11.
8. A. D. Calvin *et al.,* "The Effect of Intelligence and Social Atmosphere on Group Problem-Solving Behavior," *Journal of Social Psychology,* XLV, First Half (1957), pp. 61–74.
9. R. L. Kahn and D. Katz, "Leadership Practices in Relation to Productivity and Morale," in Cartwright and Zander, *op. cit.,* p. 615.
10. *Ibid.,* p. 619.
11. R. T. Golembiewski, "The Small Group and Public Administration," *Public Administration Review,* XIX, No. 3 (1959), pp. 149–56.
12. Kahn and Katz, *op. cit.,* p. 616.
13. S. Adams, "Status Congruency as a Variable in Small Group Performance," *Social Forces,* XXXII, No. 1 (1953), pp. 16–22.
14. Such a situation is analyzed in R. T. Golembiewski, "O & M and the Small Group," *Public Administration Review,* XX, No. 4 (1960), pp. 205–12.

IN DEFENSE OF THEORY Y*

Edgar H. Schein

Many authors have interpreted the group behavior of workers as evidence against McGregor's Theory Y. To be specific, they have argued that because workers are often alienated from work and/or are often fundamentally in conflict with the organization that employs them, it is not possible to apply participative theories in many kinds of situations. Therefore, by implication, Theory Y is inadequate or wrong. Furthermore, they have alleged that union or other group membership limits the degree of participation possible and makes workers unresponsive to certain kinds of management incentives. The smart manager is advised to learn something about the resolution of intergroup conflicts, collective bargaining, and other power/political strategies if he is to solve his productivity problems.

---

* Reprinted by permission of the publisher and author from ORGANIZATIONAL DYNAMICS, Vol. 4, No. 1 (Summer 1975), © 1975 by AMACOM, a division of American Management Associations. This paper is based on a presentation made at the Western Electric Conference, Chicago, Ill., November 11, 1974. The whole proceedings will be published as a book, *Man and Work in Society,* by Van Nostrand Rheinhold Company.

In this article I will reexamine these various arguments and will attempt to show that not only is Theory Y valid and sufficient for what it tries to do, but that most of the evidence from worker group behavior does in fact support Theory Y. There are four keys to this argument: First, Theory Y is a theory of human motivation, *not* a theory of how to manage or run an organization; second, Theory Y does *not* argue that human needs and organizational goals are always congruent and integratable, but that such integration is possible if management chooses to make it possible; third, Theory Y does *not* imply participative management or any kind of management—it is only a statement about what people are fundamentally like and what kind of organizational behavior they are capable of if the conditions within the organization are appropriate; and fourth, most of the research on group behavior, including the research on reference groups, union-management conflict, and conflict resolution supports Theory Y assumptions as to human behavior.

Moreover, I will argue that where management practices have failed to elicit a high degree of motivation and involvement from workers, it was because of inconsistencies and conflicts within the managerial practices themselves, not because of the resistance of workers or the interests of unions. If management wants to reduce union-management conflict, increase productivity and worker involvement, and elicit high levels of commitment from workers, it is often within their power to do so, but not without major cultural changes in the philosophies that govern most organizations and that put a higher premium on values other than productivity and worker involvement.

I would like to reiterate what Douglas McGregor said many years ago: When workers fail to exhibit behavior consistent with Theory Y assumptions at their place of work, it is likely that past management practices, organizational traditions, and control systems have conditioned them to seek their involvement elsewhere, possibly in their peer groups and/or unions, possibly in their family and/or leisure time. But this does not constitute evidence for anything other than the fact that management has been unwilling to pay the price necessary to unlock worker motivation or has found it unnecessary to do so because they could obtain adequate levels of productivity and quality without high levels of worker commitment.

Why is it so important to justify Theory Y? My basic belief, based on more than 15 years of working with all kinds of organizations, is that we need more Theory Y managers at all levels of organizations, but especially at the higher levels. As organizations and technology become more complex in response to more turbulent environments, it becomes progressively more important for managers to hold the set of assumptions about human behavior that McGregor attempted to capture in his Theory Y notion. In saying this, I do not mean that we need more of any given type of managerial style or system. I am not arguing for participative management, delegation, or power equalization. I am arguing for the capacity on the part of the manager to view human behavior objectively and realistically and to match his managerial tactics to the requirements of the task. As I will try to show, Theory Y gives us this flexibility because it is based on an accurate appraisal of human behavior. By contrast, Theory X is a distortion based on a basic misconception of human nature that, in addition, restricts the manager's freedom of choice because of the limiting assumptions it makes. I see no inconsistency between contingency theories of organization and Theory Y. As originally conceived by McGregor, Theory Y is a contingency theory.

WHAT DID THE HAWTHORNE GROUP STUDIES SHOW?

Let us begin reviewing the now classic bank wiring room studies that led to the "discovery" that worker peer groups and cliques substantially influenced the productivity level, the quality level, the relationship to supervision, and the implementation (or lack of it) of company policies. Let me summarize what I consider to be the major significant findings from the bank wiring room study:

- Workers in the room developed a group structure that not only operated on the informal level but also influenced in various ways the formal routine of the group. For example, workers traded jobs in specific violation of a company policy, which had been developed on the basis of industrial engineering studies that argued that once job requirements were matched with worker skill levels, any job trading would reduce quality. Workers undermined the policy by putting pressure on the supervisor, that is, by making him look bad by building difficult-to-find flaws into the equipment unless he cooperated with the job-trading practices.
- Workers undermined or sabotaged the management control system by developing their own norms of "a fair day's work for a fair day's pay" and by creating a system of sending work out of the room, making it appear as if the group had achieved the desired "straight line output" when it actually resulted from storing up extra products from days when workers felt energetic and feeding them into the system on days when they had underproduced. This artificial creation of a straight-line output was condoned by supervision, and the obvious restriction of output involved in the concept of a fair day's work also was tolerated by management. Indeed, *Management and the Worker* by Roethlisberger and Dickson contends that management was, on the whole, satisfied with the

productivity of the work group even though it was clearly below their physiological or fatigue limits.

• Workers did not respond logically to management's incentive system. Indeed, the productivity of individual workers had more to do with group membership and the internal conflicts that developed between two cliques within the room than with individual motivation, talent, or managerial incentives. Workers spent a lot of time pressuring each other to live within the production norms of the group, and they ostracized only the high producers in the group. Workers spent a great deal of energy and creativity on essentially nonproductive activities; in fact, they expended a lot of time and energy on defeating some of the goals and policies of management.

These findings, the first of their kind, have been replicated repeatedly in other studies of employee behavior. The studies of William F. Whyte and Chris Argyris in particular have documented the degree to which workers direct their energies into antimanagement, nonproductive kinds of activities. Melvin Dalton's classic study of management-worker interrelations, *Men Who Manage,* shows how informal relations among members of the organization are actually necessary to get tasks accomplished. Data such as these, as well as studies of union-management conflict, have been cited as evidence that Theory Y is an erroneous concept of workers' motivation and that there is little hope of integrating worker needs with organizational goals. But before we leap to that conclusion, let us reexamine what Theory Y actually says.

WHAT DOES THEORY Y STATE?

Theory Y states, in essence, that a man is capable of integrating his own needs and goals with those of the organization; that he is not inherently lazy and indolent; that he is by nature capable of exercising self-control and self-direction, and that he is capable of directing his efforts toward organizational goals. Theory Y is what McGregor called a "cosmology," a world view, a set of assumptions about what human nature is really like, that a person carries inside his head. Every one of us has his own theory of what motivates people, what makes them tick, what constitutes their human nature. The actual behavior that we exhibit toward people tends to be a reflection of those deep-down inner assumptions that we make. McGregor articulated a set of assumptions that most nearly fits what we know about adult human behavior.

Let me repeat, Theory Y is a set of assumptions about human nature that a given person holds, consciously or subconsciously. It is not a managerial philosophy; it is not a management style; it is not a property of an organization or a management system; it is not a set of external managerial behaviors or strategies.

To use McGregor's own words:

> Theory X and Theory Y are *not* managerial strategies: They are underlying beliefs about the nature of man that influence managers to adopt one strategy rather than another. In fact, depending upon other characteristics of the manager's view of reality and upon the particular situation in which he finds himself, a manager who holds the beliefs that I called Theory X could adopt a considerable array of strategies, some of which would be typically called "hard," and some of which would be called "soft." The same is true with respect to Theory Y.

McGregor went on to acknowledge that insofar as Theory X and Theory Y are views of human nature that adhere to each individual, it is possible to discover among managers *other* sets of assumptions about human behavior. What McGregor argued, however, was that Theory Y was the set of assumptions most consistent with what we know about human behavior. I am, in turn, arguing that this position is *still* correct. If we want to identify the set of assumptions that comes closest to what we know about human behavior, Theory Y has to be our choice. Furthermore, McGregor did not believe that he had invented Theory X and Theory Y but that he merely was describing the basic concepts about people of effective and ineffective managers whom he had encountered in his consulting. He pointed out over and over again in his teaching that Theory Y was a description of how effective managers viewed human behavior.

When I attempt to get this point across in a classroom, I find myself relying on a simple tactic. I ask students to fill out two questionnaires. One questionnaire contains a set of assumptions about human nature, derived from McGregor's writing. The respondent is asked to indicate to what extent he agrees with statements such as:

- It is only human nature for people to do as little work as they can get away with.
- When people avoid work, it is usually because work has been deprived of its meaning.
- People tend to raise their standards if they are accountable for their own behavior and for correcting their own mistakes.

Next, students fill out a second questionnaire that tests their own managerial behavior in a series of hypothetical situations—how participative they are, how much they delegate, how much they attempt to elicit from subordinates, their degree of self-control, and so forth. We then score each questionnaire separately so that each student now has two different scores on himself. The first one, his Theory X-Theory Y score, reflects his statements about his agreement or disagreement with certain assumptions about human behavior; the second score records his tendency to use participative types of managerial strategies and tactics. What becomes apparent immediately to the students is that the correspondence between the two sets of scores is far from perfect. They tend to correlate at about the .6 level, suggesting that if we believe in Theory Y assumptions, we also tend to believe in participation, but there is no necessary or automatic connection between the two sets of concepts.

We then explore managerial situations in which Theory Y managers may decide to use autocratic methods or tight control systems because (1) the nature of the task demands it, (2) there are time pressures, or (3) subordinates have lived for so long in an organization climate in which autocratic methods are the rule that they are unable to respond constructively to participative methods, and so forth—they "goof off" and generally take advantage of the situation. We also explore the idea that the Theory Y manager diagnoses carefully the organizational situation he finds himself in, including the culture and climate of the organization, its past history of management practice, the nature of the workforce, the kind of technology it has, the degree of unionization, and its labor relations history. The Theory Y manager typically is predisposed toward involving people, but there is nothing in the theory that dictates that he must do so. Nor is there any implication in the theory that participative methods will work under all circumstances.

Sources of Confusion

I believe that McGregor himself muddied the conceptual waters when he linked to his analysis of managerial assumptions about human behavior a value position that it was management's obligation to create opportunities for self-actualization. This point comes out most clearly if we quote McGregor's original statement from his paper "The Human Side of Enterprise":

> (1) Management is responsible for organizing the elements of productive enterprise—money, materials, equipment, people—in the interest of economic ends.
> (2) People are *not* by nature passive or resistant to organizational needs. They have become so as a result of experience in organizations.
> (3) The motivation, the potential for development, the capacity for assuming responsibility, the readiness to direct behavior toward organizational goals are all present in people. Management does not put

them there. It is a responsibility of management to make it possible for people to recognize and develop these human characteristics for themselves.

(4) The essential task of management is to arrange organizational conditions and methods of operation so that people can achieve their own goals best by directing their own efforts toward organizational objectives.

In point one McGregor clearly links management to the economic goals of organizations. Point two is the essential statement of human nature that is claimed here as being correct in terms of the available data. Point three mixes an assumption about human nature, with which I agree, with a value position that is articulated in the last sentence of point three, with which I do *not* agree. Point four is clearly a value position, which should be argued as a separate issue, and should be clearly differentiated from McGregor's assumptions about human nature.

The evidence from industrial relations research clearly contradicts the adoption of point four as a viable philosophy of management. It is often neither possible nor desirable for management to create conditions for the integration of individual and organizational objectives. Given McGregor's own philosophy and his utopian vision of what organizations could be, it is easy to see why he added the value position to the theoretical position. But his confusing the issue should not blind us to recognizing that he was probably much more right about his scientific position (that it is possible for people to achieve their own goals best through directing their efforts toward organizational objectives) than he was about his value position (that it is management's task to make this integration possible across a wide variety of technologies and organizational situations).

Situational Approach to Theory Y

My own value position is that the manager must be a good situation diagnostician and be flexible in his behavior. He must be logical and think rationally. If he is to perceive clearly what his behavioral options are, he must also see clearly the relationship between his assumptions about human nature and those behavioral options. If he holds Theory X assumptions, he is not being logical or responsive to data and consequently will be limited in his choices of managerial style. If he holds Theory Y assumptions, he is more likely to examine the full range of alternatives available to him and choose wisely among them, taking into account the technological, economic, and group realities that face him. Clearly, one of his options is to facilitate conditions that make it possible for his employees to meet their needs best by linking themselves to organizational goals. If he chooses that option after a thorough diagnosis of the factors that will aid and hinder such integration, he must also face the problem of initiating a major change effort that will build the support systems necessary to make that option work. All too often the manager expects instant success and if he does not get it, he assumes that his basic theory of human nature was wrong rather than questioning his own strategy and tactics of implementation.

For example, many companies have launched programs of management by objectives or performance appraisal systems based on mutual target setting between boss and subordinate only to find after a few years that the paperwork was dutifully being carried out but organizational effectiveness had not increased. The problem in most such cases is that a management system that requires Theory Y managers is installed in an organization with too many Theory X managers and too many autocratic or paternalistic traditions. Such systems can only work if we start with Theory Y managers and change the climate of the organization.

Given these considerations, I think we can favor the selection and/or training of Theory Y managers without in any way committing ourselves to a participative, power equalization, or human relations philosophy of management under any and all conditions. I believe that organizations need Theory Y managers, especially as the environmental pressures on organizations become more complex. It is then up to those managers to decide what kind of management strategy will work best in their situation. The social scientist should assist their efforts by continuing to give them data about what happens under varying conditions, but I certainly would argue against prescribing the participative or job-enrichment or self-actualization-through-work kind of philosophy as a cure-all for whatever ails the organization. Here I align myself squarely with the industrial relationists in arguing for contingency theories and for caution in generalizing across tasks, industries, and so forth.

DOES RESEARCH REFUTE THEORY *Y*?

Now we come to a crucial logical point. If workers behave in a demonstrably antiorganizational, antimanagerial manner (as they did in the bank wiring room or as they do in a highly unionized, conflict-ridden industry such as the automobile industry), does this mean that Theory Y assumptions are incorrect? If workers feel more linked to external reference groups in the community, or if they are alienated from their work, or if they put family concerns ahead of work concerns, does this constitute negative evidence for Theory Y? Clearly, my answer is no. Such data do constitute negative evidence for participative management, but they do not constitute negative evidence for Theory Y because in all of the situations described above, workers are energetic and involved, although usually in antimanagement activities. It is not inconsistent with Theory Y when workers expend effort in resisting, sabotaging, undermining, or taking advantage of management efforts if these same workers feel linked to antiorganizational peer groups or external reference groups or are alienated from the work itself because of technological or economic factors.

To put it positively, workers who expend great quantities of energy defeating management's control systems, or workers who loaf on their jobs while expending great energy on their hobbies at home, or workers who are hard at work becoming leaders in their militant union, are all behaving consistently with Theory Y. However, the organization or group that has captured their involvement happens not to be the organization that employs them.

WHAT SHOULD MANAGEMENT BE AND DO?

I can best summarize my previous argument with the aid of Figure 1. My basic contention is that we must learn to separate conceptually the manager's assumptions about human nature, whether he is basically Theory X or Theory Y, from his action tendencies or style and his actual managerial behavior.

I believe that a Theory X manager will tend to constrict and limit employee behavior with control systems, industrial engineering standards, and his own stereotypes of what is good and bad management. I believe he will be conceptually limited, inflexible, and therefore have a predisposition to develop autocratic or paternalistic solutions to management problems.

In contrast, I believe that a Theory Y manager, by virtue of his more realistic appraisal of human nature, will tend toward involving employees as much as the task and total situation warrant. He will be more diagnostic in his orientation and more realistic in his appaisal of tasks, time pressures, organization climates, and bargaining strategies.

Will a Theory Y person automatically be a good manager? We might assume from much of the above that holding Theory Y assumptions about people will make someone a good manager and holding Theory X assumptions about people will make someone a bad manager. My conclusion is different. I claim that the Theory Y person will have greater potential for being a good manager, especially at higher and more complex managerial jobs, but he must have appropriate training and experience for this potential to be realized. The other side of the coin is that

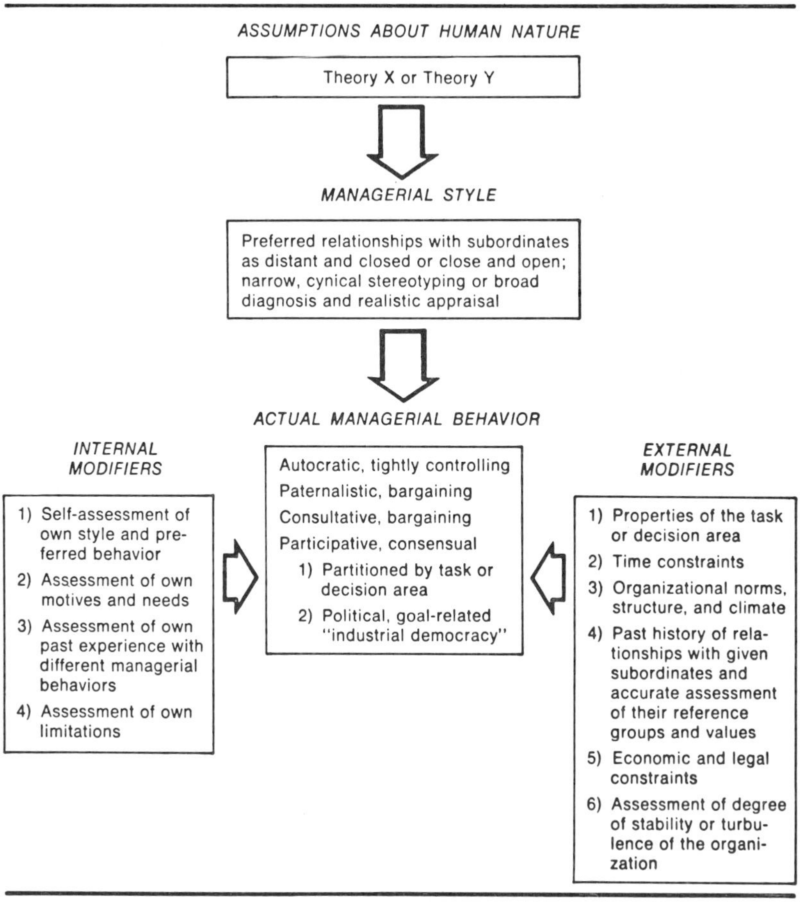

FIGURE 1
How Theory Y Relates to Managerial Style and Behavior

the Theory X person who receives excellent management training can probably be effective in many kinds of managerial situations, but his potential will be limited by the inflexibility of his style. Let us be very clear that *both* types need training and experience in being a manager before they can become effective at any level. As we will see, however, certain kinds of developmental training such as training in group dynamics and the management of complex, matrix situations will be more successful with the Theory Y individual because the concepts are more congruent with his initial assumptions.

Is it possible for a Theory X person to become a Theory Y person? My answer is yes, but only through fairly significant growth or development experiences over a period of time. Initial assumptions about human behavior are probably learned fairly early in life and are taken for granted by the individual. Only when he encounters some strong disconfirming experiences will he begin to question his initial assumptions and begin to reassess the nature of the reality around him. Such initial disconfirmation happens often in sensitivity training in which the individual learns that his fellow participants can be trusted more than he had assumed. Once he begins to reexamine his work relationships and cautiously experiments with higher levels of trust, he may find confirmation for a new point of view and move gradually toward more of a Theory Y orientation. But such growth experiences are neither easy nor automatic. All I am willing to assert on the basis of my own experience is that such growth is possible.

Some Concrete Applications

In order to illustrate the above conclusions, let us examine how a Theory Y manager would deal with certain situations, especially those that are alleged to show that Theory Y is not valid. For example, Quinn Mills points out that when several units of a company or several companies deal with a single national union that is applying a coordinated strategy, they may require employees at a plant to continue on strike even though the labor-management relations at that plant might not warrant it. There is little that the management of that plant can then do to improve relations since the employees are constrained by their dual loyalties to the company as well as the union. Faced with this situation, I believe that a Theory X manager would probably become angry, feel that the continued strike was proof of his cynical view of human nature, and set about tightening management controls in order to weaken the union. The Theory Y manager, facing the same situation, would understand the dilemma of dual loyalty and his employees' decision to strike. He would understand that they had, in effect, no choice, and he would not become angry or cynical but would set about working out a realistic plan with his own employees that would minimize the long-range negative impact of the strike on his own plant. He would reassure his employees that he understood their position and would focus his energies on dealing with the national union (the outside group) rather than on trying to undermine or weaken his own employees' union commitments.

Plant managers who are strongly Theory Y in their personal beliefs and who want to stimulate a climate of greater trust have been able to do so over a period of time, even in the face of strong and initially cynical unions. The result is not that the union goes away or is weakened but that the time needed to reach an agreement through collective bargaining is dramatically shortened. Once there is a degree of mutual trust, the union is still there but the dealings with the union take on more of a problem-solving character instead of hostile bargaining between enemies. Once the problem-solving climate has been established, it is possible for the union and management to look for integrative solutions. In this context, the Theory Y manager seeks to strengthen the union since he recognizes the need for it and welcomes the problem-solving process that collective bargaining makes possible. Once the employee learns that both management and his union are attempting to do what is best for everyone concerned, there is less need for the kind of self-protection that the workers in the bank wiring room exhibited. Is this utopian? Possibly, but I know of enough examples from my own consulting experience to believe that we can hope to improve the industrial relations climate markedly if we find Theory Y managers to run plants and to negotiate with workers.

Mills's assumption that the worker "is likely to limit his 'participation' to what he thinks his supervisor would like to hear" is probably correct in the kind of climate that Theory X managers typically establish, but it is not inherent in the labor-management context. I would agree with him that "in general, the process of participative management is more difficult and complex than has been recognized," partly because of the danger that management, in its efforts to reward participation, will give in too much on issues of efficiency. But there is nothing in Theory Y that says the manager has to give in. Rather, the Theory Y manager would assert that a worker is capable of understanding and accepting the economic constraints that operate in a business and that force management to seek a high degree of efficiency. The manager must not only have the faith that the worker can understand and accept such constraints, but he must also make the effort to think it through clearly and communicate his logic clearly and explicitly to the worker. All too often, the manager is not clear in his mind why he will not go along with a particular union demand, or he will not explain to the union why the company cannot afford a particular benefits package or pay raises. Part of the reason that management has not seen fit to educate the workers in the economic realities of their company may be because they operate too much on Theory X assumptions. The Theory Y manager would lay the groundwork by educating workers in the economics of the industry and would find it easier to argue against unrealistic demands from unions because the criteria of what is realistic would be shared jointly between labor and management. The degree to which the manager chooses to be participative it itself a choice, varying from permitting employees to be involved only in decisions that affect their immediate tasks or work setting to various versions of "industrial democracy" in which employees are given a formal voice in setting company policy through worker councils or membership on boards of directors.

Participative management can be a fraud and fraught with dangers for the workers, but only when participation is practiced by Theory X managers looking for a way to defraud their workers. The Theory Y manager would not undertake a participative program in the first place unless he could see overall gains for both the company and the workers. So it does little good to argue about the merits or demerits of participation per se. What I am arguing is that whether or not it works and whether or not it is safe for the worker to participate has much more to do with the nature of the industry and the task and has much more to do with the manager's assumptions about human nature—whether he is a Theory X or Theory Y kind of manager.

What if a company is operating in an industrial relations climate in which strong trade unions consistently undermine productivity by limiting what the employee can work on? If such a company has Theory Y managers at the top, it can change the total climate by working with the trade unions at a national level. One large industrial conglomerate that decided its survival depended upon changing its basic relationship with its unions, nationwide, launched a 20 year change program that involved simultaneous programs at the national level aimed at changing relations with the national offices of the union, massive efforts to find more Theory Y managers for the major plants, large-scale change programs to examine the pros and cons of more participation at the shop-floor level on a plant basis, education programs for all levels of plant management, a new incentive scheme more consistent with the changing goals of the company, trial sites and research evaluations of pilot aspects of the program, and many other separate activities. Clearly, if a company decides it is important enough, there is much that it can do to overcome an unfavorable industrial relations climate.

If such programs fail, it is often because the tasks workers are asked to perform are technologically meaningless and/or frustrating, leading to alienation and the organization of defensive counterorganizational groups. But only a Theory X manager would think of giving workers a "sense" of participation in inherently meaningless work.

The Theory Y manager, in that type of situation, would not use participative methods because he would recognize that in the long run phony participation would boomerang. Instead, he would acknowledge that the situation was inherently noninvolving, and he would undertake to assess the costs and benefits of a change in the technology. If the economic realities preclude changing the technology (as may be the case in the auto industry), the Theory Y manager would "level" with his employees and would accept their demands for higher pay or fringe benefits to compensate them for the inherently meaningless work. He would consult them about how to make the plant more human, but he would acknowledge frankly the economic facts that make a change in technology of the work impossible.

Theory Y and Group Dynamics

Many critics of the human relations movement, participative management, and by implication Theory Y argue that intergroup conflict within the organization (for example union-management conflict, interdepartmental conflict, and so forth) is not only inevitable but can be a productive force both for employees and management. Out of the inherently different interests of different groups can arise new ideas and new solutions to problems.

George Strauss put it this way:

> There is general agreement that, on occasion, conflict can be very useful to organizations both as a means of bringing issues to top management's attention which might otherwise be ignored and as a form of competition within the firm which serves as a substitute for that of the market place. The trick is how to handle such conflict so that it remains productive.

The main problem with the analysis of lateral conflicts as inevitable and as something that can be made productive for the organization is that it fails to distinguish task- or work-related conflict (which implies highly involved employees competing to implement their view of what is best for the total organization) from intergroup or interindividual conflict based on personal power needs, representing the interest of outside groups or needs for self-protection from higher levels of management.

A Theory Y manager is prepared to deal with task-related conflict and to seek integrative solutions if the organization is prepared to adjust work flows, organization structure, and so forth to permit the solution to be implemented. The Theory X manager assumes that conflict is always politically and selfishly motivated; therefore, he seeks to bargain or "bull" his way through it by win-lose strategies rather than to even consider integrative solutions. In other words, the tactics of conflict resolution the manager uses will be related to his assumptions about people, as Robert Blake has shown in analyzing the conflict resolution styles of his different "grid" types. The production-oriented 9,1 manager tends to suppress conflict or make a unilateral decision. The abdicating 1,1 or compromising 5,5 manager tends to compromise by mutual bargaining or to avoid recognizing the conflict in the first place. The 1,9 manager yields to worker pressure. Only the 9,9 manager, the one who would be (in McGregor's terminology) a Theory Y person, attempts to find integrative solutions because he believes that each party of the conflict is acting in good faith.

The above points imply a degree of diagnostic skill in handling groups and conflict situations. I have argued that the Theory Y manager is more likely to be able to learn these skills than the Theory X manager. It has been my observation that most managers, whether X or Y, lack group-dynamics skills to a significant degree. This lack of skill shows up in mismanaged staff meetings, underproductive committees, conflict-ridden task forces and project teams, and mismanaged intergroup relations. Clearly, having Theory Y assumptions does not make one an expert in handling group situations, but the individual needs Theory Y assumptions in order to believe in groups in the first place. The Theory Y manager is more likely to recognize that groups are a fact of life to be dealt with and managed. As the examples above have tried to show, he will accept the reality of dual loyalties in his employees and will accept the realities of interfunctional or interdivisional conflict within his organization. He will analyze the costs and benefits of such conflict, and he will need group skills to either manage the conflict productively or to create a reward system that reduces the conflict in the first place. He will recognize that conflict is not inevitable but rather the consequence of how groups and individuals are managed. He will know when conflict is productive (in task areas) and when it is destructive (in interpersonal areas). Theory X managers who learn group-dynamics skills typically come across as stilted, phony, and manipulative and eventually lose the support of their group.

We have enough examples (the Scanlon Plan, wartime economies, Alfred Marrow's two companies—Weldon and Harwood, some of the plants in Procter and Gamble and General Foods, recent experiments within Western Electric, team production experiences in the aircraft industry and more recently at Volvo, and parts of Corning Glass) to know that it is possible for groups to work with and for the organization that employs them. But it takes Theory Y managers to use them productively, and it takes tasks and organizational conditions that make such group involvement possible and productive. Let us, once and for all, recognize that contingency theories and industrial relations theories are consistent with and complementary to Theory Y and put behind us the conceptual confusion that has muddied this field for so long.

SELECTED BIBLIOGRAPHY

Theory Y was first promulgated by Douglas McGregor in 1960 in his now classic *The Human Side of Enterprise* (McGraw-Hill, 1960) and was updated in his posthumously published *The Professional Manager* (McGraw-Hill, 1967).

The Hawthorne studies were reported in full detail by Fritz Roethlisberger and W. J. Dickson in *Management and the Worker* (Harvard University Press, 1939) and subsequently analyzed and put into a broader group theory by George Homans in *The Human Group* (Harcourt, Brace & World, 1950). Other group data dealing with how the informal organization interacts with formal procedures are well documented by Chris Argyris in *Personality and Organization* (Harper, 1957) and Melville Dalton in his classic study, *Men Who Manage* (Wiley, 1959). The response of workers to economic incentives was thoroughly analyzed by William F. Whyte in *Money and Motivation* (Harper, 1955).

The best-stated critique of participative management theories is D. Quinn Mill's article "Industrial Relations and the Theory of Human Resource Management" (*Sloan Management Review,* 1970, 12) and his recent article in *Organizational Dynamics* (Spring 1975), "Managing Human Relationships Among Organizations: Theory and Practice." In the same vein, George Strauss has published a critique in his article "Organizational Behavior and Personnel Relations" (*A Review of Industrial Relations Research,* 1970, 1).

For a few examples of participative management studies, the reader is referred to Robert Blake and Jane S. Mouton's *The Managerial Grid* (Gulf, 1964), Alfred J. Marrow's *Management by Participation* (Harper, 1967), and F. Lesieur's *The Scanlon Plan* (Wiley, 1958). The author's own views on the analysis of organizations and an eclectic view of how to stimulate greater organizational health are set forth in Edgar H. Schein's *Organizational Psychology* (Prentice-Hall, 1970) and *Process Consultation* (Addison-Wesley, 1969).

Chapter 3

Managing by Hundreds: Middle Management and Departmental Dynamics

The management of hundreds may be circumscribed as a specific area of concern, but only roughly. Thus we may boldly designate the management of hundreds as within the province of the middle manager, but only if we do not press too hard for the meaning of "middle manager." Without pretending to cope with the designational issues involved, we settle here for describing a "middle manager" as one of a large and variegated class of managers whose field of activity lies between that of the first-line supervisor and those realms presided over by managers who can truly be labeled "executives."

In sum, middle managers supervise managers and are conduits through which executive policies begin to be put into action. In contrast, first-line supervisors manage workers.

However tentative, this rough circumscription of the province of the middle manager permits several rough but useful distinctions. Executives formulate and monitor policy; middle management provides advice on which policy is based and develops the procedures and personnel capable of making that policy "go"; and the first-level supervisors oversee the actual performance of work. In the federal service, more specifically, middle managers head organizational cadres of hundreds, although larger and smaller exceptions abound.

Middle managers may be either "line" or "staff," but the demands on them are similar: insistence from above to follow "policy"; and pleas from below to "be realistic." These two herniating sets of forces make the role of middle management difficult and often uninviting.

Some of the difficult and uninviting demands made upon the middle manager may be boldly set down. Consider the linking of policy and procedure. The middle manager does not make policy, but is often cast in the role of an advisor concerning policy, and almost always is responsible for implementing policy. Being an "organizational engineer" has its advantages, no doubt, but the role has many difficult aspects. For example, middle managers must tailor procedures and work flow to policies decided upon by others. These policies often are expressed in archaic terms, reflect subtle compromises and imply interests often indifferent about or opposed to the immediate interests of the middle manager. Yet he must take much of the "heat" from both above and below if the policies, when they are put into practice, sit poorly with operating personnel.

Other difficult and uninviting demands made of middle managers abound. For example, the middle manager does not usually directly supervise larger numbers of employees, yet he is responsible in diverse ways for the oversight of hundreds of employees subdivided into immediate work units of tens or twenties under first-line supervisors. The middle manager thus must learn to select capable people, and to trust them or be run ragged trying to be everywhere at once. To a similar point, although the middle manager typically is not involved in collective bargaining with employee representatives, he frequently is the target of employee ire when grievances occur or are imagined.

Problems also derive from the middle manager's commonly having risen to his level by demonstrating unusual competence in a narrow specialty. Unfortunately, the criterion of choice often is beside the point of the challenges facing the middle manager. The point cannot be done justice here, but we can outline a case. That is, the middle manager constantly faces problems that require a sophisticated knowledge about many fields, problems that require a particular ability to integrate knowledge in action. In other terms, it is middle management's common challenge to integrate diverse "staff" contributions into the "line" effort.

The task of integrating line and staff contributions is a mammoth one, whatever a middle manager's qualifications. Thus two seasoned observers conclude that: "There is probably no other single area of management which in practice causes more difficulties, more friction, and more loss of time and effectiveness."[1] Their judgment is comparatively mild, in fact. In any case, their summary judgment seems appropriate. Consider only that "staff" typically is "not in the chain of command" and consequently may not be directly "responsible for performance." In addition, the "line" often views "staff" as "interfering outsiders" with little knowledge of and less sympathy for the "real go-go-go" of an organization. These few observations indicate the kinds of dross out of which the middle manager must make organizational gold.

A summary may be hazarded. At his best, the middle manager can be a crucial and creative link between high levels and low. He can compress the data bubbling up to him in forms useful for upper-level decision making, and he can give practical life to executive philosophy and policies as they are applied "downward." At his worst, the middle manager can be a kind of well-paid cattle prod for top management, attempting to shock first-level supervisors into a frenzy of activity. As one middle manager complained: "We sit here all day pushing papers from top to bottom and back again. All the while we are left out of the actual operations at the bottom, and we don't take part in decisions at the top. We just push."[2]

Nor do these conflicting demands reflect all, or even the major stresses, in the middle manager's role. The threat of imminent obsolescence also contributes to the great and probably growing discomfiture of the middle manager. At worst, the prophets of gloom maintain, electronic data processing (EDP) means the disappearance of vast numbers of middle management jobs. At best, others argue, the manager's power and status will be reduced drastically in our increasingly automated world. Neither alternative inspires the confidence of middle managers.[3]

This chapter, consequently, has three emphases. It focuses on the organizational demands that will increasingly challenge the "new" middle manager; it reflects the demands long felt by the "old" middle manager; and it also highlights some basic changes in organizational design required for the complex coordination required in today's and especially tomorrow's organizations but which make greater demands on the "new" middle manager.

---

[1] Harold Koontz and Cyril O'Donnell, *Principles of Management* (New York: McGraw-Hill, 1959), p. 135. For some of the subtle reinforcers/effects of problems in this area, see Philip Browne and Robert T. Golembiewski, "Line-Staff Concept Revisited: An Empirical Study of Organizational Images," *Academy of Management Journal*, Vol. 17 (September 1974), pp. 406–417.

[2] Keith Davis, *Human Relations at Work* (New York: McGraw-Hill, 1962), p. 195.

[3] Herbert A. Simon, *The New Science of Management* (New York: Harper & Bros., 1960), for example, reflects both emphases.

A. OVERALL PERSPECTIVE ON MIDDLE MANAGERS OF TODAY AND TOMORROW

Let us begin with a broad conclusion, which some may question but which seems reasonable enough to us. Not long ago, to make the point by contrast, some observers foresaw a withering away of middle management due to electronic data processing and automation. Our contrasting view implies a new significance for middle management in an automated society. Shaul some time ago expressed the essential position here.[4] He forecast important changes in the middle manager's participation in control. Aside from that, he sees new demands being made on the middle manager while the old demands refuse to wither away. In contrast to being a threat, Shaul sees EDP as raising the status of the middle manager. New problems certainly will be created, and the middle manager's job will be more complex, but he will have a greatly increased volume of information to analyze, evaluate, and apply. Moreover—since time-consuming clerical work and "guesstimates" that once were the hallmark of middle management can be made faster and better by machines—the middle manager will be increasingly free to concentrate on the nonroutine. The nonroutine substance that can receive attention may be suggested by this list: motivating, leading, training, coordinating, and advising. The middle manager may assume many of the functions commonly considered to be in the province of executives.

The upgrading of the middle manager role seems motivated by multiple sources. In a technical sense, as organizations grow larger and if they remain essentially centralized, the level of effective decision-making tends to rise further and further above the level at which action or immediate work takes place. Diseconomies can quickly occur under such circumstances. Reducing the flow of information up and down increasingly complex hierarchies, for example, often motivates some degree of decentralization, which in turn requires upgrading the jobs of supervisors at middle and low levels. Especially in government, the growing clamorous demand for effective and swift delivery of services in client-centered organizations also supports a similar organizational trend. The various calls for decentralization and client participation, for example, clearly imply new stresses and opportunities for the public manager, and especially at middle levels. Broadly political considerations, in sum, seem to be operating in ways that often impact on the middle-management role. Supporting systems of ideation also have recently developed to provide

[4] Donald R. Shaul, "What's Ahead for Middle Management?" *Personnel,* Vol. 41 (November 1964), pp. 8–16.

ready rationales for public policies that reinforce often-felt technical needs for additional decentralization.[5]

To be sure, the traffic is far from unidirectional, and the basic position is still in the complex process of resolution. For example, affirmative action considerations increasingly create unparalleled centralization of personnel choices and decisions at the same time that strong pressures are felt to be more responsive to clients and local interests. This is a classic double bind, clearly, and its resolution is far from certain or clear.

Consequently, no one can credibly argue for the present conclusion without reservations. Indeed, the most popular expressions[6] of the impact of automation on management challenge our position at some significant points. And little hard research exists, in any case. What direct research has been accumulated,[7] however, strongly suggests that the present summary statement is a close approximation of managerial reality under the impact of automation.

Major perspective on the anticipated new significance of the middle manager inheres in E. R. Uyterhoeven's "General Managers in the Middle." Many business and public organizations have moved away from the standard model which departmentizes in terms of functions at the level immediately below the top, as when specialized heads of operations, personnel, finance, and so on, report to some chief executive. In the functional model, that is, departmentation by specialist functions reaches far up in the organization, typically just below the topmost level of organization, which is intended to integrate the several specializations. In various other organizing modes, however—as in project teams, autonomous work teams, independent profit centers, matrix organizations,[8] and so on—the trend of the last decade or so, especially, has been to locate integrative managers at lower and lower levels of organization. The derivative impacts on middle managers are profound. For example:

- Many middle managers have more extensive authority than they would have in a functional organization.
- The issues facing middle managers have a more distinctly "political"

[5] For a detailed look at one influential variety of such thought, see Robert T. Golembiewski, "A Critique of Democratic Administration and Its Supporting Ideation," *American Political Science Review,* Vol. 71 (December 1977), pp. 1488–1507.

[6] Harold J. Leavitt and Thomas L. Whisler, "Management In the 1980's, *Harvard Business Review,* Vol. 36 (November–December 1958), pp. 13–27, provides the classical expression of the most common position.

[7] Dominic G. Parisi, "The Impact of a Change in Information Technology on Management Organization Structure . . . ." (Unpublished Ph.D. Dissertation, Northwestern University, June 1966.)

[8] Jay R. Galbraith, "Matrix Organization Designs: How to Combine Functional and Project Forms," *Business Horizons,* Vol. 14 (February 1971), pp. 29–40.

flavor than previously, with hierarchy being less important and other modes growing more important—bargaining, trading, compromising, negotiating, and so on.

- The middle manager often is required to perform or encourage various "change-agent" roles, to be as much or more of a teacher or helper as a hierarchical figure.

Uyterhoeven's selection provides multiple evidence concerning the main themes developed above. The evolving middle management job reflects all the signs of growing subtlety and significance, especially given the diminished value of command/obey linkages in the kinds of organizations about which Uyterhoeven writes. His middle manager increasingly seeks to motivate, to inspire innovation, and to induce facile or even growthful change. Those outcomes can seldom be commanded; they must be nourished.

If anything, John F. Mee's argument in "The Manager of the Future" goes even further than Uyterhoeven in attributing subtlety and significance to the managerial role, and especially that of the middle manager. Basically, Mee sees a definite if gradual evolution of today's "professional manager" into a "public manager," by which he means an "institutional leader who will manage enterprise for the best balanced interests of the state and the nation to preserve and maintain our private enterprise system."

Mee's scenario is admittedly futuristic, and he acknowledges that various traumas might impede or even preclude its development. But Mee marshals an imposing array of forces that encourage a basically new concept for the middle manager; and it seems unlikely that these forces can be finessed. The very probable outcome, then, is additional challenge and opportunity for middle managers, greater freedom and greater responsibility.

The arguments of Uyterhoeven and Mee require a new intensity and seriousness in approaching an old question: What type of person is required to fill positions in middle management? The required profile seems clear enough. The new middle manager must be well versed in modern computational and behavioral techniques; he must be able to utilize machines to help solve problems related to people, as well as to use people to solve problems related to technology; and he must be able to converse meaningfully with many specialists in their own special and often exotic languages. The new middle manager, therefore, must be a "professional generalist." That is, he must be an expert in the integration of many fields and in the considerable substance of each. The new middle manager is sharply distinguished in the latter sense from the "amateur generalist" of broad classical training patterned on the British model. Fritz Morstein-Marx's warning of many years ago about the narrow specialist consequently has a contemporary immediacy. "But it is in the nature of the expert to cherish what he knows," Morstein-Marx noted, "to worship at the altar of his own knowledge, and to smite both ignorance and heresy with inspired zeal."[9]

A wide range of evidence implies that modern technology permits less and less room for the "narrow specialist." For example, most evidence suggests that the massive adoptions of the computer imply either greater decentralization or at least no significant reversal of the trend toward decentralization. The available evidence deals with the opinions of managers about what the computer implies for management, as well as with actual longish experiences with computer installations. Directly, the overall trend to decentralization implies that more and more decisions will be made at lower levels of organization, thereby robbing the "narrow specialist" of places to hide. Lipstreu sees the computer as having such an impact on the supervisor's job, for example. He concludes that: "The supervisor will surely regain some of his lost discretionary authority. Automaticity of work requires that he make decisions at the work level quickly, decisions which formerly were made at higher levels in the hierarchy. His work will increasingly resemble that of present middle management. . . ."[10] And compelling evidence suggests that the computer will require *better* middle managers and may also create a need for *more of* them.[11]

The prospects for providing the "new" middle managers are not uniformly dismal, of course. The burgeoning graduate schools of administration and management on the business side reflect an aggressive effort to meet the growing demand for "professional middle managers." And the increasing resort to a wide variety of executive development experiences also reflects a general desire to impart appropriate skills and attitudes to those already in business and government organizations. However, it is still a matter of running fast enough to stand still.[12]

---

[9] Fritz Morstein-Marx, "The Mind of the Career Man," *Public Administration Review,* Vol. 21 (Winter 1961), pp. 8–15.

More recent attacks on technocracy are even more exuberant. Illustratively, see David Schuman, *Bureaucracies, Organizations, and Administration* (New York: Macmillan, 1976), esp. pp. 13–37.

[10] Otis Lipstreu, "Organizational Implications of Automation," *Journal of the Academy of Management,* Vol. 3 (August 1960), p. 123. See also Otis Lipstreu and Kenneth A. Reed, "A New Look at the Organizational Implications of Automation," *Journal of the Academy of Management,* Vol. 8 (March 1965), pp. 24–31.

[11] John F. Burlingame, "Information Technology and Decentralization," *Harvard Business Review,* Vol. 38 (November–December 1961), pp. 121–26.

[12] For broad perspective, consult Mary Green Miner and John B. Miner, *Policy Issues in Contemporary Personnel and Industrial Relations* (New York: Macmillan, 1977).

B. SOME SPECIAL PRESSURES ON MIDDLE MANAGERS

In very definite senses, Uyterhoeven and Mee are fanning an already-roaring fire, for middle managers have long faced a range of pressures which these two observers report will only get much worse. And the impact will be especially great on the functional "specialist," the role-incumbent who is often remote from the actual work, and who lacks sufficient involvement in the complex lateral negotiations concerning goods and services that characterize the environment of today's middle manager.

One particular disadvantage of the specialist is his narrow preoccupation with "vertical" or hierarchical relations. Here organizational history decidedly walks—if indeed it is not running—away from the specialist. The new middle manager must be sensitive to vertical relations, but lateral or horizontal relations are increasingly relevant for him. In modern organizations the manager rarely controls all of the resources necessary to carry out his organizational activities. He must, therefore, engage in a constantly changing set of relations with superiors and subordinates, staff personnel, and his own peers in order to get the goods and services he needs.

Leonard R. Sayles's "Lateral Relations in Work" provides insight into the horizontal dimensions of the managerial job and their implications for managerial behavior. Sayles's contribution is particularly useful because it emphasizes line-staff relations, which increasingly constitute a major tension point for middle managers.

Sayles's argument may be illustrated briefly. Thus he distinguishes seven types of lateral relations, in all. We briefly here illustrate only three of those types. "Trading relations" comprise those processes by which the terms of future relations are established. Here the manager is a vendor or a customer in a selling situation with another manager, and each side bargains for gain. "Work-flow relations" involve activities that must be performed by different individuals or groups in a relatively fixed sequence. Failure to meet deadlines in such relations can cause a total breakdown. "Service relations" often are significant in determining whether deadlines are met, referring as they do to various supporting activities that from time to time are crucial to work-flow relations. Service relations consequently imply the maximum potential for intra-organizational conflict. Service relations imply these and other sources of conflict: they lack the regularity of work-flow relations; they are more likely to carry incompatible demands; and they encourage temporary alliances between organizational units based on reciprocity.

Sayles's contribution implies the great and growing importance of line-staff integration in lateral relations. All of Sayles's types of lateral relations intimately (if differentially) involve staff activities, thus underscoring their importance for the middle manager. Unfortunately, the traditional notion of "staff" is rooted in a concern with vertical relations only. That is, "staff" is defined residually in the traditional concept as "outside the line of command," "advisory only," or "as thinking rather than acting." By implication, in the traditional view, vertical relations are sufficient to define the role of staff. As Sayles shows, the orthodox view is myopic. For example, staff officials will be deeply involved in service relations which (as Sayles shows) have very significant lateral components that escape the vertical chain of command.

The social structures we call "cliques" exacerbate the pressures on middle managers that derive from lateral flows of work, but also provide major opportunities for creative management. Consider that the internal interest groups or cliques in an organization "represent sources of energy. . . [that may] lend life and strength to an organization."[13] But such informal groups—while they can facilitate the process of infusing with value a technical structure—also can subvert the goals of an organization. That is, groups can have norms that sanction high levels of output, but they can also serve to restrict output.

Real dilemmas inhere in the management of cliques, then, and there are no real ways to finesse the issues they raise.

The middle manager's unavoidable task includes these major components: to recognize the existence of cliques, to use them when they contribute to the goals of the organization, and to restrict them when they begin to subvert these goals. Melville Dalton helps in this complex task in his "Power Struggles In the Line." He identifies five different types of internal interest groups, or "cliques." They are: vertical symbiotic; vertical parasitic; horizontal defensive; horizontal aggressive; and random cliques. Of the five, the first two normally occur within a single department, but the remaining three cut across agency lines. Vertical cliques are the most troublesome in organizations and, unfortunately, they also are the most frequent.

The dilemmas of managing internal interest groups can be illuminated by a knowledge of interpersonal and group dynamics, and structural innovations also may "slip between the horns" of those dilemmas. This is no small service, for internal interest groups are both ubiquitous and potent.

What is the character of this illumination and help? For example, Golembiewski's "Civil Service and Managing Work"—to be introduced below—implies ways of structuring work to take advantage of the social power of vertical cliques encompassing entire units of organization de-

---

[13] Philip Selznick, *Leadership in Administration* (New York: Harper & Row, 1957), pp. 93–94.

partmentalized in terms of product or in terms of total flow of work. Where function or process guides departmentation, vertical cliques can cause significant integrative problems to the degree that the functionally specialized formal units of organization also are effective social units. Therefore, the intent on limiting the arbitrary power of vertical cliques in a traditional structure often can do so only by attempting to destroy the internal interest groups that give "life and strength to an organization." Unorthodox structural arrangements help the manager avoid this cruel dilemma, and it is to such arrangements we now turn.

C. STRUCTURAL VARIATIONS IMPACTING ON MIDDLE MANAGERS

Given great and growing stresses on middle management, glimmers of hope suggest that structural rearrangements can be of substantial help. Three selections below variously provide such glimmers as they commonly deal with alternative models for organizing work. The three pieces come from the same mold, in that they all deal with alternative models for organizing work. One selection deals with two generalized comparative models; the second reports on the results of one experiment about the differential effects of alternative structural forms; and the third selection reports on a common way of seeking to reconcile some common findings in opposition, which are reflected in available research. Despite their various foci, the three pieces imply a similar conclusion. In sum: traditional notions about organizing work are poorly adapted to the challenge of usefully managing lateral relations in organizations.

The three concluding selections of this chapter help in managing lateral relations as well as in understanding why they exist and why they can be significant. Directly, they reflect a common rationale. Thus mere critical carping provides no answer to the difficulties of managing lateral relations in organizations. Structural redesign alone can accomplish the job. And structural redesign, in turn, depends upon subtle but significant changes in the attitudes and concepts about organizing held by both managers and the managed in public and business organizations. The three selections aim at just such attitudinal and conceptual changes.

Let us introduce the general alternative models first. Directly, orthodox theory about organizing provides an ill-equipped ballpark for playing out the complex dynamics of lateral relations. Similarly, that theory is ill-suited for the training of generalists. Innovation in ways of thinking about organization is necessary to improve matters and this is the dominant theme of Robert T. Golembiewski in his "Civil Service and Managing Work," which emphasizes lower and middle levels of management.

In sum, the original goals of our public personnel systems have worked themselves out to inhibit effective management. No significant modifications are necessary to apply the argument to business and industry. Particular difficulties derive from the fact that most public agencies, like business organizations, are organized in terms of functions or processes. Departmentation around functions or processes is prescribed by scientific management dogma, but so much the worse for the dogma. Such departmentation invariably results in a limited span of control, an unwieldy "managerial entity," and diminished managerial control over the work environment. Golembiewski sketches the senses in which product-oriented structure removes many blocks to "effective management," roughly defined as high productivity and high participant satisfaction. The article also details structural arrangements and managerial techniques necessary to develop generalists at relatively low levels of organizations, and thus it directly helps meet the new demands facing the middle manager.

The logic of the two models—reinforced by central tendencies in the literature—imply that they generally will generate opposed patterns of consequences. Golembiewski's paper seeks to be tentatively certain about those two patterns of consequences, which are also outlined in several of the following paragraphs.

A significant note precedes this outline of contrasting consequences of the two structural models, however. The unorthodox model for organizing developed in Golembiewski's paper does more than facilitate the management of hundreds, be it noted. The senses in which that model eases the problems of managing tens and twenties, for example, may be sketched briefly. Top management must shoulder the responsibility for overloading the inherently difficult relations of direct supervision without adding to the stature of the supervisory position. This reflects the grip of the orthodox theory of organization, which implies that top management's control can be increased only by despoiling the supervisory job. The supervisor's job is increasingly narrowed, for example, as management respects the "principle of specialization" and spins off more and more activities to "staff" units which dilute the supervisor's control over the work environment. Thus the first-level supervisor usually is "responsible for production." But significant aspects of hiring, firing, rewarding, and punishing typically are influenced if not directly controlled by such staff units as Personnel. The unorthodox model provides one avenue of escape from such dreary consequences of the traditional pattern for organizing work. The discussion of enhanced supervisory "power" under the unorthodox model, for example, illustrates the values of such escape.

Similarly, the unorthodox model for organizing also facilitates the management of ones and twos in complex ways. For example, "job enlargement" and "job rotation" are more simply administered under that model. The full argument cannot be detailed here, but economical illustration should suggest the advantages of the unorthodox model in moderating difficulties involved in trying to meet the needs of individuals at work. Thus employees in an "unorthodox" organization need not experience the psychological and sociological problems of switching their immediate unit of organization to participate in a program of job rotation. For that unit of organization contains multiple specialties. In contrast, the traditional theory of organization departmentizes around processes at lower levels. A program of job rotation thus is likely to require movement between immediate units of organization.

The advantages of the unorthodox model for organizing work seem substantial, in general, although the research literature certainly contains conflicting evidence as well. Illustratively, independent research demonstrates the common attractive payoffs in productivity and satisfaction of such techniques as job rotation and job enlargement. Some of the readings above provide us with the theory capable of explaining why individuals in organizations tend to respond positively to such techniques. For example, as jobs are enlarged most individuals will experience an enhanced opportunity to move toward greater personal growth along the dimensions suggested by Argyris. Obviously, to illustrate the point, the individual can utilize a wider range of his capabilities on an enlarged job than on a routine job. The positive effects of such growth possibilities appear even when the job enlargement seems minor. This suggests the enormous latent energies that can be unleashed when individuals are allowed the opportunity to move along the dimensions of personal growth.[14] For example, such positive effects were striking even in comparisons of the behaviors of operators performing ten simple mechanical operations with the behaviors of operators performing five. This does not seem to be much of a difference, but in this case it provided enough of a difference, at least for a while.

These details of the complex mutual advantages of the unorthodox model at the several levels of organization might be elaborated into very long descriptive chains, but our goal is more to outline than detail. Specifically, we seek to suggest the variegated analysis that is possible and we seek to motivate the reader to accept the full challenge. And what we have done thus far should economically serve to meet our

---

[14] Impressive substantiation of the positive effects of even minor enlargement of jobs is presented by Robert N. Ford, *Motivation Through the Work Itself* (New York: American Management Association, 1969).

The approach also may be very tricky to apply, as has been amply established by Linda L. Frank and J. Richard Hackman, "A Failure of Job Enrichment: The Case of the Change That Wasn't," *Journal of Applied Behavioral Science*, Vol. 11 (October 1974), pp. 413–36.

interests. Hence we leave the further details of developing such interrelations—as well as the joy of the necessary discoveries—to the reader.

Let us not exaggerate our case in the name of brevity, however. Of course, job enlargement does not always have positive consequences. Indeed, we now know quite a bit about the conditions under which job enlargement will "work" and those under which it has not,[15] but our argument here is more gross. If managers do bet—and they must—the probabilities are that job enlargement will prove useful.

Again our argument turns into itself. Job enlargement will require new managerial attention to training and development, and this necessity suggests one important component of what the new job of the middle manager may become.

An important caution is in order here. The immediately preceding discussion takes a global approach, which is at once its strength and its weakness. It seeks comprehensiveness and pays a cost in providing only a gross level of resolution. What is needed, pretty clearly, is a more precise treatment of the generalizations attempted above. It is well and good that, on balance, the literature seems to indicate the value of job enlargement. But what conditions, specifically, are more conducive to successful applications? And what conditions imply less optimistic results?

A second selection below—"Effects of Flat and Tall Organization Structure" by Rocco Carzo, Jr., and John N. Yanouzas—exemplifies one significant effort toward the kind of greater specificity required, and it also illustrates one useful approach to gaining that specificity. Carzo and Yanouzas utilize experimental organizations to test some effects of the alternative structures detailed above.

The experimentation by Carzo and Yanouzas presents a diverse set of stimuli. First, without question, the investigators artfully illustrate that the key issues of organizational analysis can be subjects of the kind of controlled experimentation that has been so powerful in other areas of inquiry. Second, their results are variously consistent/inconsistent with the patterns of structural consequences sketched by Golembiewski. Third, it is far from clear how this variable consistency/inconsistency is to be interpreted. Perhaps the most reasonable posture for the reader is to adopt a questioning one concerning any claims as to "the one-best way" to organize.

Don Hellriegel and John W. Slocum, Jr., introduce us to the most common way of explaining such consistencies/inconsistencies about the

---

[15] See Robert T. Golembiewski, *Approaches to Planned Change* (New York: Marcel Dekker, 1978), esp. chap. 8.

effects of alternative structures. Which structure is the best? Well, it all depends, Hellriegel and Slocum in effect respond in their "Organizational Design: A Contingency Approach."

On what does the choice of a structural model depend, more specifically? The contingency approach focuses on the degree of "differentiation" of an organization, which is largely a function of the nature of the environment within which an organization operates, of what is its business and what technology it uses. Specifically, "differentiation is defined as the differences in cognitive and emotional orientations among managers in different functional departments, and the differences in formal structure among these departments."[16] When differentiation is low, the contingency theory advises, the traditional or functional model may be more appropriate, or even necessary. When differentiation is high, the unorthodox model becomes increasingly appropriate and failure to acknowledge that crucial point may have enormous costs.

The selection by Hellriegel and Slocum must be consulted for details and examples, but a couple of points should be clear even here. Thus the contingency theorist would argue that comparisons of "flat" versus "tall" organizations—such as that attempted by Carzo and Yanouzas —would yield different patterns of consequences, depending upon the specific environments and technologies of the organizations being compared. Relatedly, the contingency theory would argue that the attractive consequences Golembiewski attributes to the unorthodox model would be most likely to occur in organizations with a high degree of differentiation. Conditions of low differentiation might favor the traditional model somewhat more in terms of efficiency or productivity.

---

[16] Jay W. Lorsch, "Introduction to the Structural Study of Organizations," pp. 2–3, in Gene W. Dalton, Paul R. Lawrence, and Jay W. Lorsch, *Organizational Structure and Design* (Homewood, Ill.: Irwin, 1970).

GENERAL MANAGERS IN THE MIDDLE*

Hugo E. R. Uyterhoeven

Traditionally, the job of general manager has been equated with that of a company's chief executive. General manager and boss have been thought of synonymously. Yet, increasingly, corporate organizations are providing for general management positions at levels below the chief executive; and, as a result, the number of general managers at the middle level is rising.

The middle-level general manager phenomenon (i.e., a general manager who is responsible for a particular business unit at the intermediate level of the corporate hierarchy) is a direct outgrowth of the movement toward a divisional form of organization. For example, while the *functional* organization requires only one general manager, the *divisional* organization provides for a variety of business units, each requiring a general manager. Often the process of divisionalization extends several levels down into the organization (i.e., group, division, department), further increasing the need for general managers at lower levels.

The shift from functional to divisional organization occurred in the United States largely during the last two decades and is currently taking place in Europe. It is a worldwide phenomenon necessitated by the greater product-line diversity as well as the growing international operations of a vast majority of the larger corporations.

Although the divisional organization is now a familiar phenomenon, little attention has been directed at obtaining a clear understanding of the middle-level general management position. Of course, one approach would be to refer to what is known about the top-level general manager, but this knowledge is not really applicable–the two positions are significantly different. Furthermore, general management at the middle organizational level is, in a number of respects, more difficult.

In this article, I shall attempt to (a) define the characteristics and responsibilities of the middle-level general manager's job and (b) draw the implications for the individual assigned to it (hereafter referred to as "middle manager") as well as for the company that employs him.

MANAGING RELATIONSHIPS

The middle manager, like most managers, accomplishes his goals largely by managing relationships. There are few things which a man-

* Hugo E. Uyterhoeven, "General Managers in the Middle," *Harvard Business Review,* Vol. 50, No. 2 (March–April 1972), pp. 75–85.

SUPERIORS
PEERS
SUBORDINATES

ager can do alone; he must usually rely on the support, cooperation, or approval of a large number of people. As the textbooks say, he "gets things done through others."

Managing relationships at his level in the organization, however, is a threefold task, requiring the middle manager to act as subordinate, equal, and superior:

- Upward, he relates to his boss as a subordinate; he takes orders.
- Downward, he relates to his team as a superior; he gives orders.
- Laterally, he often relates to peers in the organization as an equal; for example, he may have to secure cooperation from a pooled sales force or solicit assistance from corporate staff services.

Thus the middle manager wears three hats in fulfilling his general management role. In contrast, the top-level general manager acts primarily as a superior—this alone is a significant difference between the two positions.

Managing the triple set of relationships is most demanding; it is analogous to a baseball player having to excel simultaneously in hitting, fielding, and pitching. The middle manager must be able not only to manage all three relationships, but also to shift quickly and frequently from one to another.

In view of these conflicting and changing demands, it is often difficult for the middle manager to arrive at a consistent pattern of behavior. Moreover, in the process of satisfying the requirements of one set of relationships he may reduce his effectiveness in managing another. For instance, a middle manager who follows orders from headquarters to the letter may thereby, in the eyes of subordinates, either weaken his authority or appear unreasonable and unresponsive. Consider this illustration from an internationally divisionalized company:

Headquarters restricted the freedom of one division manager to purchase from the outside, an order which threatened to undermine his authority as a general manager. He was torn between the dilemma of (a) asserting his authority with his subordinates by ignoring or fighting headquarters' orders, or (b) weakening his image as a superior by following headquarters' orders. Being a good subordinate would have weakened him as a superior; yet, by being a strong superior, he would have been a disloyal subordinate. As it turned out, the general manager held prolonged negotiations with a peer in the pooled sales force to arrive at a mutually satisfactory solution, but this made the general manager appear inconclusive and indecisive to his subordinates.

In order to successfully manage such multiple relationships, and their often conflicting and changing demands, the middle manager should recognize the full scope of his job. For instance, he should:

1. Make the network of relationships explicit. To whom does he have to relate? What are the key relationships?

2. Identify, in his specific situation, the triple set of requirements. What is expected of him as a good subordinate? What is required to be an effective colleague and equal? And what does it take to provide leadership as a superior? This analysis should force the middle manager to focus not only on his own goals and abilities but also on those of his "opposite numbers" at all three levels.

3. Recognize the difficulty of achieving consistent behavior in view of conflicting demands and be willing to wear three hats at the same time. Success will involve the balancing of all three roles. Sometimes it requires trade-offs. Under such complex circumstances, it helps to proceed explicitly.

4. Communicate his understanding of the job to others in the organization with whom he must relate. (These others should bear in mind that, singly, they are part of but one of the multiple relationship sets that he has to manage; their expectations and responses should take this into account.)

A Playing Coach

In some respects, the middle manager is the leader of his unit who delegates, guides, and plans; in other respects, however, he has specific operating responsibilities and must "roll up his sleeves" to achieve output and to meet his targets. Therefore, he is both a delegator and a doer, both a strategist and an operator, or, to use another sports analogy, both a coach and a player. In contrast, his superiors are usually coaches and his subordinates are normally players.

Continuing the analogy, sports experience indicates that it is easier to excel either as a coach or as a player and that the playing-coach job is clearly the most difficult—the skills of a successful player are different from those of a successful coach, but the playing coach must possess the skills of both. Likewise, the dual role of a middle manager combines different skills and actions. On the one hand, he needs a broad overview, detachment, and a long-run perspective. On the other hand, he needs detailed knowledge and experience, the ability to involve himself directly and deeply, and a sense of urgency.

Acting both as player and as coach, the middle manager must constantly balance the two roles and sometimes make trade-offs. Is he going to be too much of a player, too involved in operating details and in doing things himself? Or is he becoming too much of a coach by staying aloof, by delegating too much, by not getting sufficiently involved? It is easy to misperceive one's role, especially in regard to the latter.

For example:

Top management in a large divisionalized corporation assigned a promising middle manager to a recent acquisition. Charged with enthusiasm for his new position, the manager saw himself as primarily a delegator, an organization builder whose job was to oversee the installation of parent company procedures and guide the acquisition's integration with staff services of the parent. He had not considered becoming directly involved in operating details or concentrating attention on increasing sales, both of which his immediate superior, the former owner/manager, saw as primary responsibilities of the middle-management position.

This question of balance—of asking oneself, "To what extent do I get involved in actual operations and to what extent do I delegate?"—is most delicate. And the balancing of the two roles is, of course, also influenced by the demands, expectations, and abilities of the middle manager's superiors and subordinates. The choice is not entirely free.

THE BILINGUAL MANAGER

In keeping with his dual role, the middle manager usually receives abstract guidance from his superiors in the form of goals that he must translate into concrete action.

If, for example, a company's chief executive sets the goal of a certain percentage increase in earnings per share (and mentions it to financial analysts, thereby making it an even stronger commitment), how does he go about achieving this goal? He will communicate it to his group vice president, who will salute and pass it on to his divisional general manager, who, in turn, will salute and pass it on to the middle manager. The latter will salute, turn around, and find nobody to pass the goal on to. To use Harry Truman's famous dictum, this is where the buck stops.

The buck stops at the middle manager, who must assume the bilingual role of translating the strategic language of his superiors into the operational language of his subordinates in order to get results. He must turn the abstract guidance of, say, more earnings per share or meeting the budget into the concrete action required to achieve the results.

Often the middle manager is presented these abstract goals carrying the label, "difficult but achievable." While such labels may have a motivating purpose, they are basically a euphemism for the following proposition: top management knows the results it wants to see, has no idea how to achieve them, and assigns the middle manager the twofold duty of figuring out how to perform the task and then getting it done (i.e., the boss tells what he wants, not how he wants it accomplished).

Strategy Considerations

There are several reasons for the foregoing results-oriented procedure. One explanation is that the middle manager is closest to the action; therefore he has most of the data, and hence is in the best position to make the decisions relevant to translating goals into action. A second explanation states that it is superior's privilege to push decision making down and let his subordinates sweat it out. Why should he stick his neck out when he has a subordinate to do it for him?

The implications of top management's approach, however, are more important than the explanations. First of all, the middle-level general manager is provided with a much broader *de facto* responsibility than is usually codified in job descriptions or organization charts. Consequently, he must often be more of a strategist than he realizes. It is important, therefore, that he go beyond the formal definition of his job, functioning broadly enough so that he deals explicitly with the full scope of his real responsibilities. A narrow understanding of his role, by contrast, may cause him to ignore critical tasks; he cannot assume a responsibility he does not recognize.

But with responsibility goes risk, particularly where the goals are abstract and the charter is unclear. The risk is further compounded by the many constraints, external as well as organizational, within which the middle manager operates. However, along with risk goes opportunity. As Harry Truman put it, "If you can't stand the heat, get out of the kitchen." To be a strategist rather than just an order taker is exciting, even without the job's ceremonial attributes.

Formulating strategy for translating abstract goals into concrete action requires the ability to develop plans. In doing so, the middle manager must take into account external factors of an economic, political, marketing, technological, or competitive nature. Moreover, in line with his dual role, he must achieve congruence between the goals of subordinates (whose commitment is essential) and the goals imposed by superiors (whose approval he seeks).

This strategic task is both intellectual and administrative in nature, and the communication of plans is as critical as their development. Often, communication is most effectively accomplished not through proclamation but, rather, through "teaching" the general management point of view during day-to-day activities.

Summing up, to translate goals into action the middle-level general manager must:

- Define his job realistically and broadly.

- Assume full responsibility for translating the abstract goals into concrete action through strategic decision making and planning, taking into account both external and organizational factors.
- Effectively communicate his decisions and plans to both his superiors and subordinates.

From Action to Measurement

The middle manager must be able to translate not only from abstract guidance into concrete action but also from concrete action into abstract measurement. His superior measures success in terms of results and is less interested in *how* it has been accomplished. Consequently, the middle manager's performance is most often appraised by matching the abstract results of his actions with the abstract guidance that he has been given.

This fact of organizational life sometimes leads to misunderstanding. In one company, for example, a middle manager was unable to meet his goals, and invoked his actions to show why. Top management, however, perceived the explanations as excuses. Concrete action was not part of its measurement system.

In terms of the total equation, there can be real problems when the signals from abstract measurement contradict those from abstract guidance. Where this occurs, the translation process frequently gets reversed. Instead of starting with the abstract guidance (goals) to develop specific action, the middle manager starts with the abstract measurement (required results) and translates backward to his plan of action. Here are two illustrations:

☐ In one company, top management emphasized the need for its divisions to have ample productive capacity. In the measurement of performance, however, excess capacity was looked on unfavorably. As a result, division managers added capacity very cautiously, achieving high plant-utilization ratios at the expense of lost sales (which did not show up in the measurement system).

☐ And in another company, top management stressed the need for new product and market development; yet the middle managers were measured on the basis of short-term profitability. With R&D and marketing expenses reducing short-term profitability, pressures to achieve the latter created an obvious reluctance to incur the former.

Translating action into measurement involves the same skills as translating goals into action. One language is operational and involves a variety of dimensions, whereas the other is abstract and is often in terms of a single dimension. The required ability is to relate these two different languages. And when measurement and goals are contradictory, the middle manager must be able to tread a thin line between the two, sometimes making trade-offs.

Furthermore, he must cope with an additional problem: the language of corporate measurement is sometimes inadequate for measuring and guiding the activities of his subordinates. While top management typically measures the middle manager on the basis of profit and loss, the middle manager has to evaluate his subordinates in terms of different quantitative measures (such as costs, production and sales volume, number of rejects, and so on) as well as qualitative judgments (such as adequacy of the plant layout, effectiveness of the R&D effort, comprehensiveness of the marketing activities). These measures not only are different in kind and more numerous, but also require greater expertise and more intimate knowledge of specifics.

RESPONSIBILITY/AUTHORITY

The middle manager typically assumes full responsibility for his unit and is evaluated on the results of the total operation. There is no way to shift the blame as might be done in a functionally organized setup, where marketing could claim that production did not deliver on time or production could point the finger at marketing for not bringing in enough orders.

Like the chief executive, the middle manager has to account for the performance of others. Unlike the chief executive, however, he has only limited authority in the pursuit of his goals. He often needs cooperation from equals, say, in a centeralized R&D department; and he receives solicited, or unsolicited, guidance from superiors. Thus responsibility and authority do not overlap. The former exceeds the latter.

While textbooks state categorically that such an imbalance is wrong and that responsibility should be backed up with the necessary authority, the responsibility/authority discrepancy is an inevitable fact of life where divisionalization penetrates the organization. To function effectively in this imperfect world, the middle manager must meet two requirements:

1. In spite of the limited authority, he must be willing to accept full responsibility and take action accordingly. At the same time, he should recognize that he cannot do everything himself, that he must cooperate and coordinate with others. The ability to manage multiple relationships is critical here.

2. While he always has the opportunity to "go to court," to appeal to his superiors when cooperation from equals is not forthcoming, he should rely on this route only as a last resort or when the issue is clear-cut—preventive settlements, even if they involve compromises, may

be preferable. By going to court, he is asking somebody higher up to stick his neck out. The fact that this "somebody" has attained a higher position probably means that he is good at *not* sticking his neck out and is unlikely to be receptive unless a middle manager picks his fights wisely, carefully, and infrequently.

Inevitable Politics

Discrepancies between responsibility and authority, coupled with all of the previously discussed factors—multiple relationships, the playing-coach role, translation from goals to action and back to results—necessarily result in a structure that requires managers to coexist in a political atmosphere. There are different interests and interest groups, conflicting goals and ambitions, and positions of power and weakness.

Moreover, this coexistence is not necessarily peaceful. Career objectives and prestige, as well as positions of influence, are at stake, and the general manager in the middle is an easy and accessible target—malcontent soldiers do not pick on the general directly; they go for his officers.

The position of the middle manager is further exposed by a measurement system requiring direct and frequent responses. To meet his goals, he needs cooperation and assistance and is therefore vulnerable to sabotage. In a political sense, he is up for reelection continuously. Thus he must possess a political sensitivity as well as the constitution to stomach pressures and conflicts. He has to be aware of the configuration of the power structure and the direction of political winds. Unfortunately, in this potentially volatile atmosphere, managers often fail to ask an obvious but key question: "Who are my friends and who are my enemies?"

A MAJOR TRANSITION

The middle manager's job is usually an individual's first try at general management. Typically, he has been selected on the basis of outstanding achievement as a functional specialist; hence his previous experience is not transferable to this new terrain. His new position represents a major transition. Fred Borch, General Electric's chairman of the board and chief executive officer, considers the step from functional to general management to be the greatest challenge of a manager's entire career.

Indeed, the skills and activities which led to success in a manager's functional career—whether marketing, manufacturing, engineering, R&D, control, or finance—are usually those of specialization, of deep involvement in a narrow area. The specialist knows more and more about less and less.

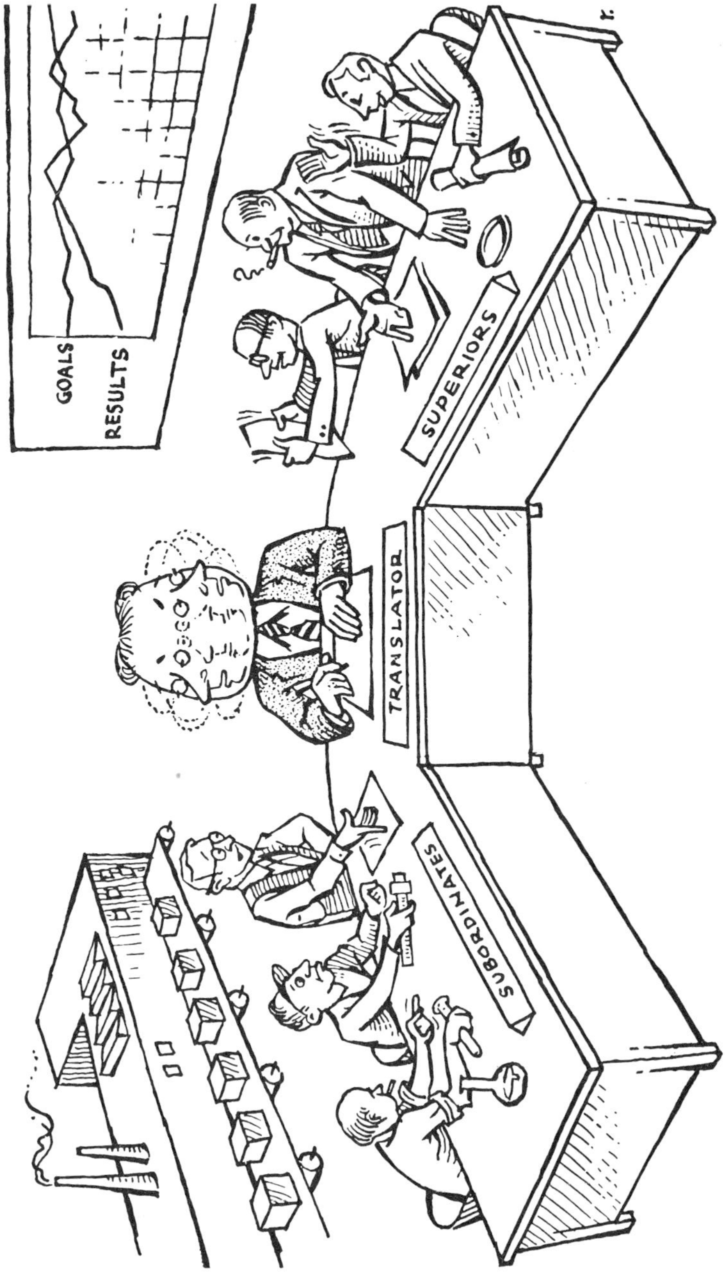
GOALS
RESULTS
SUPERIORS
TRANSLATOR
SUBORDINATES

In the medical and legal professions, specialization is the usual route to excellence and eminence. The manager, too, during the early phases of his career, follows this pattern; he establishes a track record by excelling in a particular specialty. But unlike the doctor and the lawyer, his career progression pattern is brutally shifted.

Having earned his spurs as a specialist, the manager is given a new and drastically different challenge, that of excelling as a generalist. Instead of knowing more and more about less and less, he now shifts to knowing less and less about more and more.

This transition, in turn, represents a major risk. Previously, each step up the functional specialization ladder led to familiar challenges which required proven skills. Now, the challenges are new and the skills unproven. Not all managers will be able to make this transition; not all will possess the required general management skills; and in spite of earlier successes, not all will successfully meet the new challenge.

Overcoming Resentment

In making his major and risky transition, the middle manager, as noted earlier, does not always face a friendly working environment; rather, he may find that his promotion has caused resentment. Some may consider themselves better qualified, because of age or seniority; they may view the new middle manager's capabilities and background as insufficient for the job. Others may resent the promoted individual because he represents an "educated elite."

Yet the new middle manager needs the support of those very people who may resent his appointment. Their cooperation is essential, and he will face constant obstacles until he has it. In overcoming this possible handicap of resentment, administrative skills and experience are of utmost importance. Unfortunately, however, these skills are typically the new middle manager's short suit; he is more often long on technical abilities and experience, which are obviously less relevant to the task.

Acclimating to New Terrain

Since promotions do not always occur within the same department, the middle manager often comes from another segment of the organization. As a newcomer, he will probably be unfamiliar with his unit's history, opportunities, and problems. And obtaining facts or information to accurately diagnose the situation will not be easy, for the following reasons:

- While superiors have assessed the unit's performance in terms of its abstract results, the middle manager has to evaluate it in terms of concrete action. The latter is much harder to determine than the former.
- The middle manager will have to acquaint himself not only with the "formal" organization of his unit, but with its "informal" structure as well. While the formal structure can be found in manuals and organization charts, the informal one has to be discovered through daily activities and interpersonal relationships.
- Politics may color the facts given. Certain information may be deliberately withheld, while other aspects may be overemphasized.

In summary, the newcomer's fact-finding mission is difficult and hazardous, and he will be required to sift through information that is often contradictory, tough to evaluate, and not always obvious.

Furthermore, he will be dealing with a new set of people, and thus will have to establish new relationships. This is a particularly difficult challenge to the manager who not only is undertaking his first general management job but also is possibly resented as a newcomer. Since relationships cannot be ordered from above, the middle manager will have to earn his own way. He will have to gain the confidence and respect of his counterparts not by virtue of the uniform he wears, but instead by the quality of his daily activities.

Managerial Acrobatics. Without essential facts and established relationships, it is difficult for a middle manager to get off to a fast start. Yet he often walks into a situation that requires quick and decisive action. In this event, he will have to walk a tightrope between (a) an early commitment based on inadequate facts and nonexisting relationships and (b) indecision while he establishes his facts and relationships.

The first course of action is often preferred, since it establishes a manager's authority and image. He may also be responding to pressures that are pushing him in this direction. The risks, however, are great. Before he proceeds on such a path, it is worthwhile for him to pause and consider the long-run implications of action that precedes the establishment of facts and relationships. What, for example, are the chances of making major mistakes? While it is often argued that the wrong action is preferable to no action at all, it is important for the middle manager to get off to a good start, not just a fast one. Things that start badly usually get worse.

Experimental Leadership

In making his transition, a middle manager often functions as an agent of change. He may have received his assignment from top management in order to bring about changes in his new unit, or his own ambition may push him to develop new approaches. This implies experimentation and a process of learning through trial and error. Experimentation, however, means vulnerability. The middle manager's unit, for instance, may have been chosen as the experimental laboratory for the entire organization; and, since an experiment is easier to defeat than a long-established policy, the forces of resistance mentioned earlier may be encouraged to mount opposition, or even sabotage. Where the agent of change is an inexperienced newcomer, it is particularly easy to shift blame to his shoulders.

Experimental leadership rarely permits one to move ahead at great speed in a single direction. It involves slow testing and occasional back-tracking that may be viewed by subordinates as indecision and defeat. Thus, they may interpret experimental leadership as lack of leadership, withholding their support and blaming their leader for inexperience or ignorance.

Under this handicap, success may be difficult to achieve. Top executives, in such circumstances, may not always come to the rescue. They may be watching rather than supporting the experiment. This is their privilege. From their vantage point, why should they stake their reputations, possibly their careers, on the uncertain outcome of an experiment?

Thus it is unrealistic to expect rescue from above. More importantly, to judge the soundness and results of an experimental change, whether initiated from above or by the middle manager himself, an objective and neutral superior is needed. He can also act as a mutually acceptable arbiter where conflicts arise, as in situations of limited authority.

The middle manager may be better served in the long run by having such a neutral arbiter above him rather than a prejudiced ally. In the former instance, cooperation and support can be obtained through candid and open negotiation; the availability of an objective judge encourages reasonable attitudes from all parties concerned. In the latter instance, resistance from others will go "underground," which obviously makes the task of obtaining cooperation and support more difficult. A case from one large company illustrates this point:

One of the divisions had to rely heavily on a centralized R&D department for its custom-made product innovations. Conflicts arose between the market-oriented division and the technology-oriented R&D department, so the division manager took his case to superiors. A new, marketing-oriented group vice president overwhelmingly ruled in favor of the division. Subsequently, the R&D department's contributions declined because of alleged "technical difficulties" and "conflicting demands from other divisions."

CHALLENGE & OPPORTUNITY

The preceding description of the characteristics of the middle-management position portrays it as a major challenge, as indeed it is. Why would anyone want to accept such an ill-defined, open-ended, risky assignment? Yet, as I pointed out earlier, with risk goes opportunity; and with open-endedness goes a job of considerably broader scope than what is stated in the formal job description.

Why is it not possible, then, to design this job by including all the positive elements and eliminating all the drawbacks? The answer is that the drawbacks are inherent in a divisional organizational structure—they can be excluded only by eliminating the structure itself.

A divisional structure, however, is essential to the conduct of large-scale operations for a diverse range of products in a variety of countries. It also permits a large number of managers to assume general management responsibilities early in their careers, sometimes in their early or middle thirties after less than 10 years of business experience. In contrast, the functional organization usually offers an individual manager his first attempt at general management only during his middle fifties, after some 25 to 30 years of business experience.

The choice, then, is between having a broad opportunity to assume an imperfect general management job at an early age and having a very limited opportunity to hold a "perfect" general management job late in one's career. To put it in the context of Churchill's famous statement: early in a man's career, the middle-management job is the worst assignment except for all the others. Moreover, the advantages and opportunities are many, both for the company and for the aspiring executives:

☐ The chance to run one's own show at a young age, rather than having to wait for a quarter of a century, should increase the probability of advancement, as well as make a business career more exciting.

☐ The shift from specialist to generalist early in one's career is less perilous, and failure is less painful, than if the shift occurs later. If a manager has spent some 25 years as a specialist, he is apt to be firmly set in his ways and will find it difficult to make a major change. A younger manager, on the other hand, should still be flexible and able to adapt more easily to a different set of job requirements. Failure is also easier to take—and to overcome—early in one's career than it is later on. (Putting a 25-year track record on the line is a major risk and one that might well destroy a man's entire career.)

☐ The early shift from specialist to generalist is also less risky from the company's viewpoint. When a manager who has been a specialist for a quarter of a century is selected for the president's job, the total conduct of the company is entrusted to someone with no record in general

MULTIPLE RELATIONSHIPS
FROM GOALS TO ACTION
FULL RESPONSIBILITY
LIMITED AUTHORITY
SPECIALIST/ GENERALIST
FROM ACTION TO MEASUREMENT
POLITICAL ENVIRONMENT
PLAYING COACH
r. ring
PEERS
SUPERIORS
SUBORDINATES

management. It is not at all certain that a successful engineering, marketing, manufacturing, or finance vice president will turn into a first-rate general manager. In the divisional organization, however, the middle manager typically manages one of several profit centers. Thus risk is greatly reduced by entrusting to an unproven general manager only a small segment of the total enterprise.

□ A large number of general management slots in an organization enables a corporation to attract and retain many capable managers and avoids an elimination contest for a company's single general management position. This large reservoir of general managers can be transferred and promoted as new opportunities arise. Since the scarcest resource of a company is usually competent management, overcoming this hurdle may eventually constitute a major competitive advantage.

□ The middle-management phenomenon is conducive to management development and training. A manager can start in a small profit center, establish a track record there, transfer to a larger unit, and so on. Thus both the breadth and the challenge of the general management job can be increased as he moves up in the ranks. His confidence and versatility will also be enhanced, fostering personal career development as well as strengthening corporate competence.

□ Middle managers are close to the action. Leadership and coordination, therefore, take place on the battlefield rather than from distant headquarters. Decisions are made more quickly by better informed people, who can more closely monitor an action's impact and ensure its proper implementation.

CONCLUSION

There are some important implications that can be drawn from the characteristics of the middle-level general management job; and they affect not only the man who holds it but his superiors as well.

One common pitfall is that superiors tend to judge middle managers in terms of their own jobs. They believe that middle managers have the same opportunities, prerogatives, and power that they do and therefore should shoulder similar responsibility. This same belief is frequently shared by the middle managers themselves.

As I have attempted to show, however, the middle manager's job is quite different from that of the top-level general manager. The job itself is demanding enough. It should not be made more difficult by an incorrect understanding of its scope and characteristics.

Top management often fails to recognize that imperfection is a fact of life in the middle-managment job. Furthermore, formal job descriptions frequently reflect sacred dogmas like overlapping authority and responsibility. Such ostrich-like attitudes create unrealistic expectations among all parties involved. Unrealistic expectations inevitably produce disenchantments and failures. Reality, even though it may not correspond to the demands of theoretical elegance, must be faced. If reality imposes imperfection, as it does, then imperfection must be recognized and accepted, rather than swept under the rug.

Need for Ratification

Given his job's characteristics, the middle manager can govern effectively only with the consent of those being governed. While he is formally promoted or demoted by his superior, the jury usually consists of his subordinates and peers. By giving or withholding their support, they greatly influence the middle manager's career.

This need for ratification is easily overlooked or underestimated by the middle manager. He may approach his job with supreme confidence in his own abilities, viewing his new appointment as evidence of his importance and talents. Where change is required, he may see himself as the new leader destined to bring order out of chaos and turn failure into success.

At the same time, he may see his subordinates as old-timers who have failed in the past to meet the challenge. Hence he may doubt their abilities and downgrade their importance. A middle manager who approaches his job by overestimating his own importance and underestimating that of his subordinates is erecting a self-imposed barrier to ratification. He is creating the conditions for a self-fulfilling prophecy—with himself as the ultimate victim.

Accommodation & Compromise

Another important implication for the middle manager is the necessity of finding his way in a maze of accommodation and compromise. He cannot always make quick decisions, take a straightforward course of action, or follow completely rational and logical solutions. He must bring what he judges as necessary within the realm of what is possible.

Often it is difficult to adjust to such a complex challenge. While he may have made his mark as a technical expert whose previous successes were based on purely rational solutions to technical problems, optimization may not be the most successful approach in his new role. Rarely do perfect solutions exist for the middle manager. There are *viable* solutions, however, and they require constant accommodation and compromise.

Job Strategy

Given the difficulty and challenge of general management at middle organizational levels, the job should be approached as explicitly as possible. The middle manager must attempt to define the following:

- The scope of his multiple relationships within the organizational structure as well as the specific people to whom he must relate.
- The "playing coach" role.
- The "bilingual" task of translating goals to action and action to measurement.
- The implications of having full responsibility while holding limited authority.
- The "political" environment in which he has to survive from a position of limited power and great vulnerability.

Just as companies formulate corporate strategy by matching their resources to their environment, so can the middle manager formulate his job strategy—he can identify his total organizational environment and match this with his strengths and weaknesses as well as his personal values.

Looking at his job in strategic terms should help him face varied daily challenges, overcome frustrations, and develop a consistent pattern of behavior. Obviously, a job strategy should be not a ceremonial proclamation but, instead, a plan of action which the middle manager "carries in his back pocket" to guide him in his daily actions.

A managerial record, like a judicial one, is established through the cumulative impact of a series of decisions, many of which set precedents. If these decisions can be related not only to the specific demands of each separate issue but also to an overall philosophy and master plan, their internal consistency and cumulative impact will establish a strong and cohesive organizational fabric. This is the landmark of an effective and successful manager.

THE MANAGER OF THE FUTURE*

John F. Mee

Coming events cast their shadows before—if we study those shadows, we can observe the forces and factors that are shaping the manager of the future.

There will be managers in the future. The pathologists can predict with certainty that bleeding will always stop; managers can predict with certainty that the future will eventually involve them. Their concern is whether or not they are prepared for the changing social, economic, technological, and political environments that emerge as the future unfolds.

MANAGERS OF THE PAST

Managers of the past can be described and classified in relation to the environments in which they operated. The antecedents of the managers in our English-influenced culture can be recognized in sixteenth century Tudor England. They were the office-holders in the royal household, in the major departments of state, and in the army and the navy. They were men to whom administration and management was a professional life commitment, and their function was to administer the affairs of the state and the economy within the rules of the social order.

After the separation of the United States from England, our constitution provided that individuals might own private property. Our government, founded on the concept of government by law rather than government by men, established an environment of opportunity for the owner-manager in a private enterprise economy. For over a century, the owner-managers of small enterprises flourished, managing by right of ownership rather than by birthright in a predominantly agricultural society.

Some of those owner-managers thrived with the changing environment at the turn of the century, and, using their authority of ownership, developed our basic industries and promoted our industrial society. Facing death from the impact of the Sherman Act they resorted to corporate forms of business organizations to perpetuate their firms. The

* Reprinted with permission from author and publisher from *Business Horizons*, Vol. 16, No. 3 (June 1973), pp. 5–14.

growth of large and complex organizations with the capability of generating a trillion dollar gross national product originated with these "captains of industry."

They were followed by a new breed of managers who are now classified as corporate speculators and exploiters. These managers, who had financial or legal backgrounds, gained control of the business organizations that they managed for corporate share owners. The era of the speculators and exploiters was rather short. They met with an ignominious end in the decade of the 1930s because they were unable to manage business organizations for the benefit of society through the intelligent use of human and capital resources.

During that decade the federal government set about helping managers with legislative guidelines and regulations. The health of the economy was deemed too important to trust to capricious managers with improper human values and undesirable social ethics. The flow of legislation regulating business activities and the pressures for social responsibilities and objectives of business were initiated by the failures of these managers.

Following the debacle of the thirties, a class of managers known as professional managers appeared; most operating managers of business enterprise today are in this category. The term professional managers is used because these men manage for pay and do not own any significant share of the enterprises they manage. They profess to have the knowledge, the skills, and the value systems suitable for setting objectives and then attaining them through the utilization of other people's money, talents, and physical facilities. Some of them acquire professional manager citations from their professional associations to reinforce their image.

Evaluated by their records of economic progress and the creation of material wealth, our American managers have the best performance records in the history of the world. U.S. resources include 6 percent of the world's population and 7 percent of the land area of the world; with these, our managers have generated over half of the wealth of the world and about 35 percent of the world's annual income. They have achieved the world's first trillion dollar gross national product. The combined efforts of Russia, Japan, West Germany, and the United Kingdom —with double the population of the United States—would be required to equal that figure.

That is a formidable record of managerial achievement; why, then, are managers experiencing so much dissatisfaction with their performance? Why are today's professional managers, working on the objectives established for the decade of the sizzling sixties, absorbing attacks for matters that previously have not been considered germane to operating businesses? Despite the most outstanding performance of managers in all history, they are criticized and attacked by:

Consumer groups and regulatory agencies

Aroused antipollutionists who often press for hasty, costly, or sometimes unavailable solutions

Ecologists who are more concerned with preserving the wilderness than creating employment opportunities

Civil rights activists who demand more jobs for minority groups from top to bottom ranks

Naive and well-meaning activists who clamor for democracy on boards of directors

Employees who want relief from boring and monotonous work assignments.

Recognizing merit in some of the criticism, perhaps too many well-meaning people are finding themselves influenced by the extremists and activists who can proclaim without responsibility. James Roche of General Motors Corporation has tried to bring the extremist view into perspective: "Profits are the incentives, the driving force behind economic expansion and rising employment. It takes about $25,000 investment to create one new job opportunity. Just to keep pace with the rising labor force each year requires an opening of about 1.75 million new jobs."

Obviously, the managers of the future must be mindful of several worthwhile corporate objectives, but they had better not lose sight of the primary objective of a business, that of staying in business. No profits, no business. Survival is the first priority of managing.

Managers in the future will be expected to create wealth, generate profits, and provide employment for the fulfillment of the public policy outlined in the Employment Act of 1946. Furthermore, they will be expected to utilize the human resources of the nation in accordance with the spirit of equal economic opportunity, civil rights, equal employment opportunity, and, at the same time, adhere to the clear air and clean water guidelines of the Environmental Protection Agency within the Occupational Health and Safety Act standards. Managers will be challenged to create almost 2 million new employment opportunities a year with people working fewer hours per week. The four-day work week is on the horizon with "gliding work time" a probability. A 28-hour work week has been predicted for the turn of the century, compared with 37.3 hours in 1970, 49 hours in 1930, 57 hours in 1900, 70 hours in 1850, and 84 hours in 1800.

Future managers will be expected to create more goods and services with more profits and more employment, and to deal with employees' demands for more leisure, more services, and more conveniences in a technological economy in a scientific society. The role of future managers will be complicated further by energy and power shortages and pressure to guard the environment from damage.

Some of the most obvious and pressing factors and forces in the changing economic, social, and political situation have been cited to illustrate that managers of the future will be operating in an environment different from that in which managers of the past operated. The question of managerial concern is now posed. What knowledge, skills, and values will be required for the future manager's survival and success?

MANAGERS OF THE FUTURE

According to the time schedule, a new type of manager should now be emerging to cope with the complexity of factors and forces in a society that is struggling to adapt to changing human values and rapid technological advances. It is probable that the manager of the future will be classified as a "public manager" or a "public oriented executive." Harlan Cleveland, in his recent book *The Future Executive,* predicts the role of the future public executive and gives reasons for his or her emergence.

Today's professional manager will modify his style and begin the transition towards the era of the public manager; the potential managers among the some 8 million students in the universities today will complete the transition during the last portion of the century. The manager will develop from a hired man for private corporation shareholders into a business institutional leader who will manage enterprise for the best balanced interests of the state and the nation to preserve and maintain our private enterprise system. This development could be changed, of course, in the event of war, epidemic, depression, or some other unforeseen catastrophe.

The environmental factors and forces at work, such as changing human values along with the growing size and complexity of organizational patterns, are blurring the traditional lines between what is private and what is public. The future managers of private enterprise—profit or nonprofit—will gravitate toward the concept that they are responsible for people in general and reluctantly accept the government as a monitor of business affairs. Concurrently, the government will contract to the private sector of the economy a growing proportion of public business because public managers will be better qualified to achieve the results desired by the body politic.

The National Aeronautics and Space Administration is a prime example of this method of operation. No large business organization, whatever its formal ownership, will be able to escape social and public responsibility. Public managers will be faced with the major responsibility for merging human values with the potential from technological advances to conserve human energy in the creation and distribution of goods and services for improved life styles.

For the managers of the future, policies for the conduct of their firms will be formulated mostly by their sense of direction as modified by negotiation with their colleagues and peers. Private enterprise will prevail, but managers will be sensitive to the need to satisfy multiple claimants for the benefits flowing from national and multinational corporations.

Actually, it is the success of past managers that has developed this trend toward the concept of the public manager. The managers of our corporate enterprises have succeeded in creating most of the wealth of the nation; they also have attracted most of the nation's competent personnel into the work force of the corporations. Corporations, therefore, have the greatest capability of achieving state and national goals for economic and social progress. If the managers of private enterprise do not adopt the public manager concept, the alternative would not be acceptable to the advocates of the private enterprise system that has been the foundation of the American dream.

Future Managerial Situation

The first priority for managers of the future will be the survival of the companies that they manage and their own survival as managers. If present professional managers could send a scout into the future, receive reports, and ensure their survival by being prepared, such reports probably would include subject areas that already are discernible. The public manager in the future will perform functions with resources that may have names the same as or similar to present ones, but they will change in concept and nature in response to changing human values and environmental conditions.

The manager of the future will deal with highly complex organizations. The organizational vehicle will not be the hierarchical pyramid in which decisions are centralized and most of the planning and control are done at the top. The future manager's organizational mechanism will be in the nature of systems that will have interlaced webs of tension with loose control; power will be diffused among plural centers of decision. Decision making will become an increasingly intricate process of multilateral brokerage both inside and outside the organization.

As organizations become more horizontal and less vertical in structure, the style by which they will be governed will be more consensual, collegial, and consultive. The more challenging the objective and the more formidable the problems to be resolved, the more authority and power will be diffused so that a larger number of capable people can work toward achievement and problem solving. Collective leadership is not for the expression of democratic feelings; it is an imperative of size and complexity. The manager of the future must manage more complexity for survival.

Evidence of the increasing complexity of organizations is easily observable in the growth and influence of multinational firms, bank holding companies, and conglomerate corporations. Multinational firms already dominate much of the production of the world, and they are growing at a rate double the purely domestic companies. Some of them exert great influence on the world's financial affairs and have grown in economic size beyond all but the wealthiest nations. They are creating an economic and social movement that rivals the impact of the industrial revolution. Bank holding companies, as of mid-1972, held nearly 40 percent of all commercial banks in the nation with 58 percent of all deposits and 60 percent of all U.S. assets. The responsibilities of the managers of these complex organizations are greater than those faced by previous managers; the consequences of error and mismanagement could have serious negative impacts on the world economy.

Managers of these organizations have the opportunity to influence the peace of the world and the living standards and life styles of the peoples of less developed nations because the influence of their operations can transcend national boundaries more readily than that of governments or religious orders. However, they can only achieve their potential by managing with the concept and style of a public oriented manager. J. J. Servan-Schreiber, in his book *The American Challenge,* paid tribute to the genius and viability of American managers: "American industry spills out across the world primarily because of the energy released by the American system—by the opportunity for individual initiative, by the innovative knack of teams, by the flexibility of business structure and by the decentralization of business decision."

The manager of the future will encounter an accelerating growth in the size and complexity of organizational systems that seem destined to move away from formal, authoritarian, and hierarchical managing. The trend is toward more informal, fluid ways of bargaining, brokerage, advice, and consent. Management will be practiced less as a system of authority and more as a resource in an organizational system to achieve desired results.

The view of William Blackie, the past chairman of Caterpillar Tractor Company, reflects the changing concept: "Insofar as authority has meant the power to order or command, its definition will be modified by the addition of some such qualification as 'but expect or deserve to be obeyed or followed only if you can satisfy those being ordered or led'." Accord-to Blackie, the boss-man relationship will prevail and embrace both a superior and a subordinate. The gap will be narrowed, however, because of the rapidity with which the well-educated subordinate is acquiring skill and experience. The essential requirement is that both parties understand and appreciate the basic nature of their respective responsibilities.

The manager of the future will realize that employees will be more inclined to take authority from agreed-upon objectives and the nature of the work than from the dictation of an authoritarian boss. More than one mode of thinking can be utilized. The future manager will be a multiplier of the work of others; in the more complex organizations of the future, he will find it necessary to utilize the knowledge and skills that others possess. He will be responsible for results and for "getting it all together," rather than for preoccupying himself with individual processes.

Authority as used by the future manager will be modified by the changing values and motivations of university students as they populate the organizations of business. By 1985, college graduates will outnumber those without a high school education in the U.S. work force, and managers will have as a resource the most highly educated personnel in the history of the world. Employees will regard themselves as partners in management and expect to have their talents utilized for self-esteem and self-realization. The better educated young people today, especially those in the so-called new culture or counter culture, tend to demand their rights, resist authority and regimentation that try to put them into an organizational harness too tight for comfort, and search for their own identity instead of allowing themselves to be "housebroken" by endless procedures and processes.

Before anyone makes a quick decision that universities are subversive places and our young people have revolutionary ideas, it might be enlightening to read *The Unanimous Declaration of the Thirteen United States of America.* In this document, popularly known as the Declaration of Independence, one will find written:

> We hold these truths to be self-evident, that all men are created equal, that they are endowed by their Creator with certain unalienable Rights, that among these are Life, Liberty, and the pursuit of Happiness—That to secure these rights, governments are instituted among Men, deriving their just powers from the consent of the governed—That whenever any form of government becomes destructive of these ends, it is the Right of the People to alter or to abolish it, and to institute new government, laying its foundation on such principles, and

> organizing its powers in such form, as to them shall seem most likely to effect their Safety and Happiness.

If a substitution of the words "management" for "government" and "employees" for "people" is made in the reading of that document, one can better understand why there is a trend in the concept of management by the consent of those managed. Of course, there is no reference to women. The proposed 27th amendment to the constitution might remedy this original writing. Some thirty states have ratified the amendment with thirty-eight required to provide equal rights for women by the enactment of an Equal Rights Act. Depending upon one's point of view, an equal rights act may be necessary to enlarge opportunities for women. With few exceptions, most professions and trades employed about the same percentage of women in 1970 as in 1950, twenty years previously.

Henry B. Schacht, commenting on the changing trend in organizational design and the use of human resources, has stated that managers must learn to handle both the underprivileged and the bright young people, especially those who are calling for a change [*Business Horizons,* August, 1970, pp. 29–34]. He adds:

> What this means is shorter, flatter organizations; it means responsive management; it means a true willingness to allow people to participate in setting their own destiny; it means that the militaristically-oriented hierarchy that has characterized societies and most business enterprises is a thing of the past, and the quicker we recognize it the better. . . . all organizations will have to think of their key assets in terms of people and knowledge. People can be the most flexible of all assets; knowledge is the one thing that will give us insight into change and the consequences of change. Many companies say that people are its most important resource, but few believe it. Many people say that they live or die with their people but then spend all of their time analyzing balance sheets and income statements.

Current professional managers who make the transition to public oriented managers will master the methods required to achieve objectives in organizations with more complex and decentralized relationships; they will develop the skills to use a modified concept of authority that will enable personnel to exercise self-commitment and self-control for the achievement of agreed upon results instead of emphasizing processes.

For the realization of high motivation and performance of personnel in more complex organizational relationships, authority must be applied with the consent and cooperation of those managed. Future managers will cope with the challenge of generating purposeful action while more and more employees demand the satisfaction of getting into the act.

Future External Forces on Managers

All organizations exist and operate in an environment of some kind. External forces and factors in the environment will complicate the work of future managers. Before the end of the present decade, for example, managers of all organizations in the United States will be faced with the problem of adapting their operations to the metric system of weights and measurements. (The meter unit of measurement was determined by measuring the distance from the North Pole to the equator and then dividing by 10 million. The meter is 3.3 feet or 1.1 yards in the English system.) At present, the United States and Burma are the only major nations still using the English system. Because of the world trend, Congress asked in 1968 for a sweeping investigation of the question. This investigation involved public hearings and surveys on almost every activity in our society—from education, manufacturing, and the consumer to international trade and national security. The recommendation of the Secretary of Commerce was that the United States should adopt the metric through a nationally coordinated program.

This conversion will affect all managers of business enterprise, especially the manufacturers. Temperature will be measured by Celsius instead of Fahrenheit; length will be computed by centimeters and kilometers rather than by inches and miles; mass weight will change from ounces and pounds to grams and kilograms; area will be determined by square meters and square kilometers instead of by square feet and square miles; hectares will replace acres; and volume will be measured by milliliters and liters.

Present managers are planning for the costs of conversion, which will be relatively greater in the manufacturing industry. The greatest burden of costs will be in production and industrial educational programs, particularly in the machine tool and automotive industries. The conversion will entail considerable costs for manufacturers during a time when costs will be increasing for pollution and environmental damage control.

The material wealth of the nation, measured by either the metric system or the passing English system, stems from the managerial use of the basic factors of production, land, labor, and capital. The manager of the future will be more restricted in his use of land than his predecessors. Managers of the past have enjoyed freedom of decision in the use of private land, regardless of whether or not it was devoted to its highest and best use. The market system prevailed. The future manager, however, will be confined to operating within federal and state land-use policy. A bill now in Congress (S. 268) will give grants to states for the development of plans for private land use.

J. Irwin Miller, a prominent Indiana industrialist, in a recent issue of *U.S. News and World Report,* expressed his views concerning corporate survival by serving effectively and well some real current need of society. He wrote:

> We have a fixed amount of land in the continental United States. Contained in that fixed amount of land is a fixed amount of natural resources. On the fixed amount of land, then, with a finite quantity of resources, there exists a growing population of human beings. By the end of the century there will be somewhere between 50 and 100 million more people in this country. . . . Growing demand for a shrinking supply of land and materials can prudently be expected only to accelerate the rise in cost of capital construction despite the miracles that need performing in labor costs, regulations and design.

Land-use policy for the guidelines of the future manager stems from the growing population that requires more land for living, domestic and foreign consumption, recreation, and energy sources. Future managers will be expected to create the equivalent of a new city for a million people about every four months during the remainder of the century. They will also be expected to produce for a per capita consumption of some 700 British thermal units of energy by the year 2000, in comparison with 377 in 1970, and at the same time protect the environment from water and air pollution and trash.

Proposed legislation in Congress (S.1283) will create a new federal agency with authority to relieve the fuel shortage. The legislation will create five "government-industry" corporations to develop technology to turn coal into gas, extract oil from shale rock, and harness geothermal energy. Soon legislation may be passed for the control of trash pollution in addition to water and air pollution. Currently we are producing enough trash annually to fill the Panama Canal four times over with a disposal cost of some $5 billion a year. This cost is exceeded only by that for schools and roads in the public services. Our trash volume will triple in the next decade to harass the future manager as increased demands will be made for the discharge of his social responsibilities.

Although the land resource is considered fixed for the future manager, he will have an increasing supply of labor flowing from the enlarging population. However, this labor resource will be different from that of the past and will require a different style of managing. This style must recognize the consent of the managed with an orientation around results rather than activities in more viable organizations. The members of the labor force of the future will be the best educated in history with knowledge and skills that many managers will need but will not possess. Furthermore, employees' expectations and value systems will be different.

Over 80 percent will be high school and college graduates who will expect managers to utilize their talents and abilities in interesting and challenging work opportunities with a minimum of boredom and monotony. Their work styles and life styles may be as important to them as their pay scales. They will resist being used as impersonal "inputs" in complex organizations under authoritarian supervisors. They will be products of the new knowledge industry that may account for half of the GNP by the end of the century, and they will expect managers to fulfill their responsibilities for both economic and social objectives.

In the future labor force, some will be specialists, others technologists, and many humanists. Some will have broad preparation, such as the proposed "poly-socio-econo-politico-technologist" background that has been conceived by Simon Ramo, vice-chairman of TRW, Inc. The manager of the future will be expected to utilize intelligently this highly competent labor force and avoid underemploying or wasting human resources. The wealth of the state and the nation will be measured more by the productivity of the labor force than by gold bullion, and future managers may be evaluated more on their abilities to skillfully utilize a growing labor force than to use capital equipment. The human asset will appear on the balance sheet of the future. Advancing technology will aid the future manager in his use of resources, but he will need to arrange a satisfactory combination of ethical human values with the flow of science and technology.

The capital resources available to managers in the future should be adequate if inflation can be controlled. National personal income in the United States has passed the lofty mark of a trillion dollars per annum for another historical first. No other nation has come close to this annual flow of personal income from wages, salaries (with fringe benefits), interest, rent, dividends, and social welfare, and the income to business proprietors and professional personnel. Reasonable savings and investment of a portion of this personal income can provide adequate capital resources for future managers to combine with land and labor resources for the maintenance of a healthy economy.

The public managers of the future will differ more in their values and attitudes than in their knowledge and skills. One can already discern in the United States that the line between public and private is narrowing because all private enterprise has some degree of public responsibility. The larger and more complex the enterprise, the more public responsibility it is expected to carry. Regardless of their personal values, more managers in private enterprise are serving more and more as public managers or executives.

If the manager of the future makes the transition from the firm-oriented professional manager of today to the public oriented manager, the business foundation of democracy and private enterprise can be maintained with managerial freedom to set objectives and policies for the best balanced interests of the economy. Furthermore, the future public manager can be recognized for making contributions to society as beneficial as those made by doctors, lawyers, ministers, engineers, educators, and scientists.

The public manager of the future can lessen the credibility gap in management that has widened since 1965. It is ironic today that our citizens want business to become more active in public leadership, yet believe that business is doing less than before, according to a recent Louis Harris survey. The future public manager will perform the essential managerial functions in society in a manner that will enhance his credibility. Alec Mackenzie, in his recent book *The Credibility Gap in Management,* states that "credibility is that quality, state, or condition that produces believability or trustworthiness." He comments that credibility depends more upon relationships with people than upon systems. Somehow, the public is inclined to believe that business is out of phase with current expectations and demands. It is not the capability and competence of business managers that are being questioned, it is their sense of priorities and good faith.

At a time when the public is crying for a new leadership style, some managers are retreating into fixed behavior patterns. They are charged with proclaiming a modern managerial theory but continuing to execute in antiquated managerial practices. Unless the manager of the future assumes a role similar to the public manager concept, there looms the possibility of the establishment of a public management commission because of the importance of managers in our economy and to prevent serious management failures in essential corporations that affect the public interest.

If governmental commissions are considered essential for the proper utilization of the resources of land, labor, and capital, it is not inconceivable that public pressures could develop for monitoring the application of the management resource in our society. Without the resource of management to utilize other resources, little is accomplished. Managers who learn to manage with a public orientation will obviate any need for a public management commission. Their value systems will embrace the service of multiple claimants in society by the setting and the achievement of both the economic and the social objectives of their firms.

The public manager of the future has the opportunity to achieve the prestige and the recognition that managers have earned but not received on the basis of contributions to society. Congress or a state legislature can recognize the importance of the future public managers by establishing a national or a state Management Day. For the contributions that managers make to economic and social progress, it would be suitable to have two holidays in one week, Labor Day on Monday and Management Day on Tuesday. This would focus attention on the relationship of both segments of our private enterprise society. Together they have produced the biggest national output, the highest personal income, and the highest standard of living in the world.

LATERAL RELATIONS IN WORK*

Based on Leonard R. Sayles

The literature of organizational behavior places major emphasis on superior-subordinate relationships. This generalization applies not only to the classical school represented by Weberian scholars. It applies equally to the newer schools represented by such people as Simon, Presthus, Blau and Etzioni. Much of the research and writing on supervisory techniques, leadership styles, motivation and human relations also focuses narrowly on the authority-responsibility issues characteristic of vertical relations.

Emphasis or no, however, much of the interaction that takes place in an organization occurs "horizontally." These horizontal relations associate individuals who are not immediately tied together by the vertical chain of command. Rather these individuals are, in one way or another, dependent on each other in meeting suborganizational goals. Leonard Sayles has noted seven categories of such relationships. The seven categories that Sayles uses are:

1. trading relations
2. work-flow relations
3. service relations
4. advisory relations
5. auditing relations
6. stabilizing relations
7. innovating relations.

---

* From *Managerial Behavior* by Leonard R. Sayles, pp. 58–82. Copyright © 1964, McGraw-Hill. Used with permission of McGraw-Hill Book Company.

The inappropriateness of a fixation on vertical relations will be illustrated diversely. The demonstration may be previewed briefly. For example, the distinction between "line" and "staff" in organization reflects a vertical emphasis. The "unity of command" is reserved theoretically to the "line" by making the "staff" advisory and service only. Practice is another matter, however. As will be shown, the lateral relations of line and staff are manifold, significant and in essential senses beyond the scope of vertical authoritative relations. Sayles's last five types of lateral relations reflect a particularly high potential for line-staff conflict, although that potential is high enough in the first two types.

We may briefly describe Sayles's seven categories of lateral relations, with particular emphasis on the inability of vertical relations to account for or to contain the required dynamic lateral interactions of line and staff. According to Sayles, "trading" refers to the processes by which the terms of some future relationships are established. Trading relations have a high priority. Consider only a skeletal rationale based on the datum that many organizational units must meet specified goals in modern organizations, and usually under conditions of a high level of interdependence among units. Thus it becomes vital for each line manager to contact those in the organization who can "help" him in meeting the goals of his unit. Since help is seldom given without a concomitant responsibility or obligation—whether the help is provided by line or staff—it becomes necessary to work out formal or informal terms of a reciprocal relationship. As organizations become increasingly dependent on external groups in meeting goals, the trades that are crucial to successful management involve not only relations "internal" to the organization but also those with "external" suppliers or customers. This is particularly true, for example, when business firms work on a government defense contract.

The "flow of work" also requires ubiquitous lateral relations. Practically all work in a complex organization must be performed in an orderly sequence. That is, A must perform a function before B can perform his. B thus becomes dependent on A as, in turn, C is intimately dependent on B. Sayles calls such mutual dependencies among A, B, and C work-flow relations. Work-flow relations grow increasingly significant as an organization's skill-mix and product-mix become more complex, as when automation or computerization takes place.[1] Given that automation or computerization will become more and more intensive and extensive in tomorrow's organizations, work-flow relations will become increasingly critical.

"Service" relations are subtly distinguished from the lateral contacts required by the work flow. In the former, "multiple feeds" or inputs come to a service unit; outputs *in some order* go out to multiple customers. In either case, basically lateral relationships must exist among organizational peers. The strains and conflicts in these situations cannot be solved by the mere issuance of an order or by overhead impositions or priorities about who gets what and when.[2] Exceptions and flexibility often require less formal but workable relations. Thus conflicts often must be worked out by individuals of similar rank on a give-and-take basis. The successful manager in service relations is one who understands the "rules" that govern the game of compromise and who can negotiate successful trade of scarce resources. A preoccupation with organizational dogma—e.g., that the "line" is formally superior to "staff"—is not particularly useful in such negotiations. Indeed, just such an insistence may be a major source of friction in lateral relations.[3]

The literature on "line-staff" is replete with examples of the delicateness of what Sayles terms "advisory relationships," although no more so than with service relations. The source of the difficulty is patent. In the traditional concept, staff personnel have no authority over line officials. Indeed, staff and line commonly report up separate hierarchies. Consequently, staff must depend on "selling" its ideas. This makes tense the process of developing advisory relations, for most students and managers recognize that only a fine line separates "advice" from "orders." Hence comes the usual counsel that staff personnel be circumspect in their dealings with line units, lest staff violate their formal role. No one-way street exists, however, for line personnel can hardly neglect the often valuable aid that staff can provide, even if it has an "order" quality. Such resistance may only encourage staff to act as an informer to gain top management's support of staff programs. Hence the high potential for conflict in advisory relations develops.

Auditing, stabilizing and innovating relationships—like service and advisory relations—also involve delicate contacts between line and staff personnel. A quality-control unit which makes checks of output, or an accounting unit that performs a post-audit, exemplifies staff units involved in auditing relationships. Many line managers feel the relationship is one-sided, i.e., that power lies with the auditor. This makes the line manager's life difficult, for the successful "line" manager should use contacts with the auditor to improve the performance of his own unit and, perhaps, to dilute the severity of any criticism going "up the line." In the same breath, however, the line manager must recognize that his "helper" can be a "hurter" and an "orderer." Also, the line manager may have a limited ability to rectify the balance.[4] The conflict of reality with prescription can prove a great source of line-staff tension.

Stabilizing relations operate on a pre-audit or pre-clearance basis. This contrasts with the *post hoc* nature of the auditing relationship. Staff units created to examine and approve production plans, personnel changes or structural rearrangements are involved in stabilizing relations. Conflict in these relations results almost inevitably in delays in clearance, minute inspection of all submitted plans and a general hostile reaction to requests for timely decisions. Here staff service becomes control over the line. Favorable relations not only can speed requests for prior clearance but can result in advice and aid from the stabilization personnel.

Finally, staff units in modern organizations exist whose sole function is to innovate, to plan, to create, to research. Such groups usually try to stay aloof from other units in the organization in order to retain that independence and autonomy usually considered necessary for their work. Often, however, the research unit requires support in the form of data, personnel or other resources from other units. This dependence consequently also requires a reciprocal relationship in which staff and line must cooperate. That reciprocity is more intermittent than in service relations, for example, but it may be crucial.

The examples above establish the incidence and significance of reciprocal and lateral relations. Without denying the importance of vertical relationships, one can argue that the success or failure of a particular organizational unit depends as much on effective lateral relations with other line and staff units as it does on vertical command relations. At the very least, we know that lateral relations take up much of the time of managers at all levels.[5]

NOTES

1. See, particularly, George P. Shultz and Thomas L. Whisler, editors, *Management Organization and the Computer* (Glencoe, Ill.: Free Press, 1960).
2. For a case study of some of the difficulties of overhead control, see Robert H. Guest, *Organizational Change* (Homewood, Ill.: Irwin-Dorsey, 1962).
3. The point is illustrated neatly by George Strauss and Leonard R. Sayles, *Personnel: The Human Problems of Management* (Englewood Cliffs, N. J.: Prentice-Hall, 1960), p. 365.
4. The "Corelli Case" presents a classic case of the lower-level line manager's disadvantage in a conflict with a staff unit. In John D. Glover and Ralph M. Hower, editors, *The Administrator* (Homewood, Ill.: Irwin, 1957), pp. 681–685.

5. Robert Dubin, "Business Behavior Behaviorally Viewed," esp. pp. 14–25, in George B. Strother, editor, *Social Science Approaches to Business Behavior* (Homewood, Ill.: Irwin-Dorsey, 1962).

POWER STRUGGLES IN THE LINE*

Melville Dalton

Although the term "clique" *denotes* a small exclusive group of persons with a common interest, it too often *connotes* a group concerned with questionable activity. Without these moral overtones, the term can aptly apply to the initiating nucleus of many group activities in and out of industry. Certainly the negative feeling associated with the term is carried too far, for cliques and secrets are inseparable and essential for group life. We would question, for example, whether parents covertly checking on their children's activities in school and community are "conspirators"; whether the indirect attempts all of us make to learn more of our acquaintances than they voluntarily tell us is "immoral"; and whether the widespread "manipulations" by both leaders and followers in all areas of life in competitive societies to win ends is "villainy." Villainy may develop in all these cases, but not necessarily. Cliques may work for moral as well as immoral ends. Whether or not we are able to preach what we practice, the organization will fall apart without sustaining action by some clique. All organizations must have "privy councils" similar in some sense to the meaning of that phrase in feudal times. One may well ask, what organization is without secrets held by some members, usually the more responsible, from other members with the intent and eventual result of helping all *loyal* members? Too often uncertainty hallows and hides the developing defects of official doctrine for changing situations. Responsible members must nevertheless try to fit the department, or firm, to inescapable conditions. And in doing this they necessarily "socialize" and "discuss problems," which is easily seen by opponents as "clique" activity "undermining" the organization.

More of this later, but for now let us think of a clique as the informal association of two or more persons to realize some end. The end is usually a calculated one, but it may be multiple and differ for some

---

* Reprinted from *Men Who Manage* by Melville Dalton, pp. 52–67. Copyright © 1959, John Wiley & Sons, Inc. Reprinted by permission of John Wiley & Sons, Inc.

members. Typical ends in an industrial plant are: to increase the status and reward of one or all members; to get more support in job activities; to find social satisfactions; to hide facts or conditions that would be frowned on by superiors; to escape unpleasant situations or annoyances; to get more privileges, especially those peculiar to higherups; and to share the limelight with superiors.

Many factors contribute to the rise of cliques. A few that are intrinsic or recur and that can be summarized quickly include: (1) division of labor, (2) variations in identification with the firm, (3) changes in the industrial community, and (4) compulsions of growth.

Division of Labor

Formal division of labor and assignment of responsibility encourages cliques, especially in a society stressing equal opportunity. Isolation of personnel in this way provokes a given group to magnify the importance of its function in the system and to ignore and minimize that of others. This leads to challenges and defenses. Work groups and their supervisors compare and rank contributions to the organization. This is particularly true of newer departments, and is of course not confined to industry. In the FWD, for example, there were numerous tiffs among material men, expediters, estimators, and job analysts, with each very status-conscious, defending his contribution as *the vital one*. The condition is probably commoner where education is higher and contribution is less tangible, for the repetition and intensity of defenses seem greater in staff than line. In both, however, departmental boasting extends to accomplishments and competence of the department head.[1] In Milo's chemical department—and in at least two of the chemical firms in Mobile Acres—there were disputes between chemists on the one hand, and samplers and vat operators on the other, about whose function "is most important" and who "actually produces." This job identity forces personnel into defensive action to get their share of credit and honors. Leaders call on subordinates for help to protect departmental interests and to expose the errors of others. Though seen as a distinct unit, the department is compared with others in performance of assignments, original contributions, etc., all of which encourages clique effort to conceal shortcomings and preserve appearances.

Clique action usually accompanies reorganization and the new divisions of labor that come wtih expansion. Departmental resistance to the new system is often apprehension that new procedures will limit old personal arrangements and "rights." Some supervisors are thrown into panicky opposition by talk of formalizing loose practices. They mouth platitudes about the threat to "democratic" relations, when they really fear the change and the unpleasant lag before they can build a new reservoir of unofficial advantages and in some measure again control the deference of subordinates. They argue that "formalizing things" will force them to "work for" instead of "working with" the company.

Differences in Feeling for the Firm[2]

Variations in the emotional ties of personnel with their firm are unavoidable. Differences in age, ability, expectations, and personal and community responsibilities lead to a *differential identification.* Given human agents in close association, with similar standards of what is desirable, and obviously they will clash over available rewards. Whatever the goals of the organization, there will be rivalry for higher posts, a voice in policy, and recognition from leaders. Without benefit of formal rules, and even forbidden, rivalries find expression in cliques.[3] Moreover, the individual's identification with the firm will vary with success or failure. The gap between his expectations and reality can never close, because our society almost demands that he never be satisfied. With this fluctuating identification a given employee is willing to engage in action at one time that he would not at another. We may say, overneatly, that his view of the firm changes with his success in advancing and protecting himself through participation in the inescapable aggressive and defensive cliques.

Other factors influence the degree of organizational attachment. Some members are in a department by chance and are looking elsewhere. Some entered by choice but are disillusioned and remain to please their families, or because they feel "too old to make a change," or "could not get the same money" elsewhere, or "have too much seniority." Some are indifferent or resigned and say, "All jobs are alike when you have to work for somebody else." Others are embittered and glad to see superiors embarrassed with problems. In other words, some officers are devoted career members, some are lukewarm toward the firm, while some hardly identify at all.

Changes in the Industrial Community

A changing market and technology, with plant expansion and turnover of personnel, promotes and requires cliques. New personnel and methods may make the organization more desirable for some but less so for others, so that one finds a range of commitments to the organization, as well as the department. This of course means that responsible officers cannot count equally on all members. Having to depend on some more than others their "interaction rate" is consequently much greater with some than with others. Hence despite formal equality, prescribed relations, and assumed objectivity, they draw close emotionally to some and share community as well as job experiences with them. During work crises these persons turn to each other spontaneously. They share knowledge of developing events and judiciously withhold information from the untried, and especially from those who have "talked out of turn" or are likely to. Their ties are, of course, seen and variously interpreted. Some of the other members may be alienated and, intentionally or not, aggravate differences in the department. But in any case department affairs will be dominated by the necessarily small closed corps of officers who become the center of influence and attention, or a clique in our sense of the word.

Rapid turnover of personnel even in an otherwise relatively stable firm naturally weakens group unity. One finds "old-timers" drawing together into cliques because they "have been through things together" and "can count on each other." Irregular transfers of individuals in and out of departments, or the sometimes required systematic shifting of personnel around a circuit in the firm, gives a certain vagrant character to the movers and creates social instability and demand by some for closer relations. As a threat to existing informal arrangements these "floaters" are seen as strangers of a kind.

Under these several conditions demands for "loyalty" force departmental and subgroup identifications. But for some, or even many, this allows only tenuous concern with the organization as a whole, and limited or distorted awareness of departmental affairs. Alert and driving cliques then become the generators of action.

Compulsions of Growth

Organizations have an expansive force and they act to preserve themselves.[4] Milo's action toward its Office was a case in point, and we shall see in the next chapter that this also holds for departments. Often disparagingly termed "empire building," these strains of growth are typical and may be quite lawful, but they jar the organization and induct various clique actions. Two practices always present in organizations, decision making based on limited information and avoidance of decision when possible, increase with the firm's rate of expansion.

Repeatedly middle level executives must act on limited knowledge. Some pressures forbid delay: the placating of powerful associates or influential union officers; the creation of a suitable post for an able but impatient subordinate; the handling of covert internal practices long ignored but now suddenly big with threat to the firm. Here any action may seem like a gamble. These problems become more acute when carried to a superior who refuses to act, but directly or indirectly penalizes the subordinate officer for failure to act successfully on his own. As head of the department the latter turns to his subordinates for loyal support. At each level this is really a request (*a*) for closer ties to conceal current departmental actions and alternatives from outsiders; (*b*) for the keeping of secrets from emotionally marginal members who may be both ambitious and incompetent enough to exploit debatable points of policy; and (*c*) for obedience to understood orders. In effect it calls forth an action clique from the mixture of fit, half-fit and unfit subordinates.

Avoidance of decision may fall into several types, but two are noteworthy and stimulate clique action. In one of these, *sympathetic avoidance,* supervisory subordinates know that their chief is upset by decisions calling for ingenuity or marked departure from formal routine. Yet they see that official procedures are inadequate for meeting his demands. So to prevent the complications that might follow from forcing a decision on him, they develop clique action to protect him as well as to evade him. Their practices require that they keep key persons among interlocking departments informed of changes in unofficial methods, and that, at the proper time, they teach new members the distinctions between their practices and *official misleading instructions.*[5]

In the other escape from decision, *avoidance by misdirection,* the department chief or similar high officer wishes to elude a subordinate, or colleague in another department, who seeks to force a decision on him. To escape, the chief calls his closest associates to aid him by telling pursuers and telephone callers that he is where he is not—in some part of the plant or in the community "looking after company business." The chief's motivation frequently is fear of making changes in response to pressures from one quarter that will only bring pressures from another. Hence he engages in clique action to avoid action. Sometimes, too, he works on the theory that his pursuers will "cool off" and find a solution "if they are given a little time and *have* to." . . .

P. F. Drucker[6] praises skill in avoiding action and holds that in some cases any action would be equivalent to a "surgical operation." Also instructive are the comments from a roundtable of executives.[7] One executive says:

> Life in a large corporation is pretty much like politics. A fellow gets along pretty much on what kind of an organization he has been able to gather around him. . . . As far as I am concerned the lone wolf with no friends will get nowhere, either in business or politics.

TYPES OF CLIQUES

Though cliques arise from dynamic situations and engage in many actions, they can be classified roughly. Typing may be in terms of their recurrence, what they do, the situations they spring from, or their effects. Probably the simplest relevant scheme, however, is to label cliques chiefly on the basis of their relation to the formal chart and the services they give to members. Such a scheme is, of course, not exhaustive or exclusive.

Approached in this way, cliques fall into three general groups: *vertical, horizontal,* and *random.* Vertical cliques can be broken down to vertical *symbiotic*[8] and vertical *parasitic;* and horizontal to horizontal *aggressive* and horizontal *defensive* cliques. Vertical cliques usually occur in a single department. The tie is between the top officer and some of his subordinates. It is vertical in the sense that it is an up-and-down alliance between formal unequals. It could be represented as a rectangle with the altitude greater than the base, e.g., ▯. Horizontal cliques, on the other hand, cut across more than one department and embrace formal equals for the most part. The horizontal clique can be symbolized as a rectangle with a base greater than its altitude, e.g., ▭.

Vertical Symbiotic Clique

In this relation, the top officer is concerned to aid and protect his subordinates. He does this by concealing or minimizing their errors, occasional lapses, etc. He does what favors he can to meet their immediate needs and to solidify their future in the firm. He interprets their behavior favorably to critical members of the department and to his own superiors. He humanizes the painful impersonal situations and the demands he must make.

The subordinates fully advise him of real or rumored threats to his position. They tell him of current work situations, confer on ways of dealing with "troublemakers" outside the clique, and discuss interdepartmental maneuvers. When urgency demands action and the chief is unavailable or there is no time for consultation, lower members confer and make moves with the chief's welfare in mind, and in terms of his known attitudes. Thus for all levels involved, there is a satisfying exchange of services. This is the most common and enduring clique in large structures. It is more than "team work" because only a nucleus of departmental personnel is involved. As it sweeps other members along they may follow gratefully, indifferently, or with some hostility. It is most effective when lower members are relatively indifferent about promotion or reasonably patient in waiting.

Vertical symbiotic cliques formed the real power centers in Milo, and they occurred at the divisional as well as the departmental level. Though not quite ideal because of Taylor's resentment, the Blanke-Dicke-Peters clique was an example extending into the divisional level, and the Hardy-Springer-Ames clique was another. However, several things make the clique less important at divisional levels. Personal ambitions and opportunities to move to other plants, for example, make the clique less stable there than at departmental levels. More subject to direct claims from the top, too, division heads usually want no official knowledge or part in taboo activities below them that they are sure department heads can contain. The latter understand that they are to serve as screening stations for conversion of unavoidable irregularities into reports befitting divisional dignity. Despite the weakness of a symbiotic vertical tie extending into the divisional level, these heads are caught in unofficial actions. . . .

Vertical Parasitic Clique

This is *the clique* of popular thought, the one that writers of supervisory manuals have in mind when they make such statements as, "No person may work under the direct or indirect supervision of an officer to whom he is related by blood or marriage."

This is a negative approach which assumes that collusive behavior is inevitable among persons with kinship ties who are in certain job relations. Apparently the implied dangers are thought to be confined to such persons and situations. This is not the case, and the approach explains nothing about how the clique works, or of its relation to other unmentioned cliques that may preserve it in some form. If this kind of clique is regarded as organizationally harmful, it deserves more study.

The term "parasitic" is used because the exchange of services between lower and higher clique members is unequal. The lower ranked person or persons receive more than they give and may greatly damage the higher officer. This clique need not be a family affair. It may be based on a friendship developed earlier in the plant or elsewhere, when the current higher and lower ranking officers were on the same job level. The subordinate person owes his position to one of his superiors. He reports to this person what he regards as pertinent facts in his work area. His information may be of use to the superior, but often its importance is exaggerated. It is useful where it is accurate and the higher officer has real need of it—but in such cases the clique relation moves toward the symbiotic type. The problem arises when the lower member is thought to "carry tales" to the higher, whether he does or not. In this event his rejection by the group leads him to resentful distortion and overstatement.

Since management theoretically places members on merit only, the belief that special aid is given the lower member of the clique obviously inspires fear in associates that he has advantages they lack and will win still more by informing on them. Where this feeling is widespread, the group resists the chief and misinterprets his best efforts. He may exchange aid with the lower member, but group alertness to hide things from the lower member cuts the volume of favors he can send up as compared with that coming down to him. Much of the harm of this clique to the firm stems from its interference with operation of the symbiotic type. Given the values of personnel, the fringe identification of some members, and the incentives applied by higher management, *a symbiotic clique is essential for a given department to compete on a par with other departments* for favors from higherups and to set up workable arrangements with other departments.

The uneven exchange holds when the clique includes members of the work groups. In at least two cases in Milo, workmen informed to general foremen with whom they had been intimate before the foremen entered management. The foremen granted favors that eluded vigilance of the union and were repaid with information and cooperation on rush jobs. But the exchange showed a more tangible balance in favor of the workmen.

Formal regulations against the action we ascribe to this clique are evaded in various ways to allow the soliciting member to receive special aid and favors. An arrangement used at Milo, similar to what is described below as an aggressive horizontal clique, worked in effect to establish the parasitic clique in at least six situations. That is, two or more higher officers on comparable levels agreed to aid each other's relatives or friends on an exchange basis. One officer made a place in his department for the solicitee of the other, or promoted the person ahead of others, or gave him more desirable work or more freedom from regulations in exchange for like aid for *his* protégé from a colleague. This cooperation, of course, promotes other understandings and joint action across departments.

HORIZONTAL CLIQUES

Horizontal Defensive Clique

Cutting across departments and including officers, as we noted, of nearly the same rank, this clique is usually brought on by what its members regard as crises. Threatened reorganization, introduction of disliked methods or a control such as that of the FWD or the Office, efforts by

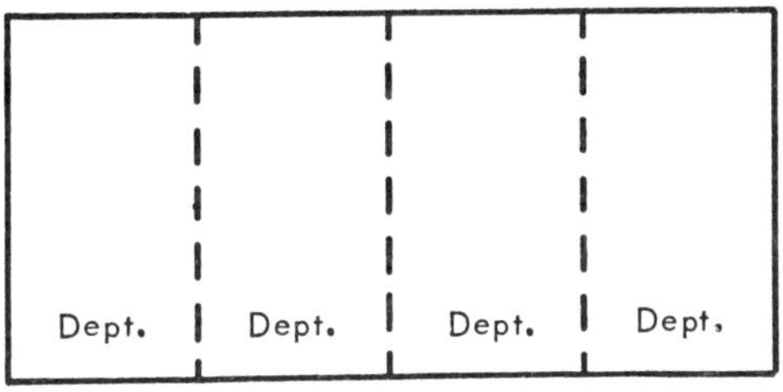

FIGURE 1
Horizontal clique.

lower and middle management to shift responsibility to each other for problems that have developed, or opposition among the same groups as reassignment of duties is made after a reorganization, are all conditions that bring on crises. This clique may also arise across departments when day and night supervision hold each other responsible as the source of illegal strikes, serious accidents, rejection of the product by a customer, etc.

Usually this clique is strong for only the limited time necessary to defeat or adjust to a threat. Since nothing is served by its persisting longer, it lapses to dormancy until another crisis, but when active it forces the symbiotic cliques into quiescence. However, it is inherently weak because of the vertical breaks likely to occur from action by resurgent symbiotic cliques. That is, as a horizontal structure the clique is made up of departmental segments, each restrained temporarily by the chief's preoccupation with interdepartmental action.

Horizontal Aggressive Clique

This type is distinguished from the defensive clique chiefly by its goals and the direction of its action. Its members are the same, and they are likely to have some ties based on past cooperative victories in getting favors and outwitting others. Their action is a cross-departmental drive to effect changes rather than resist them, to redefine responsibility, or even directly shift it. As with defensive action, interdepartmental friction subsides as the clique becomes a mutual aid bloc. Its goals may be to get increased operating allowances; to bring on advantageous reorganization or to win favored consideration over other units of the corporation; to obtain an advantage in forthcoming union-management negotiations; to check the expansion of some staff group; or to advance some member to a higher post so he can help the clique. And of course any executive level, top management, division chiefs, department heads, spontaneously forms this clique when it sets out to correct extreme action by other cliques at lower levels.

When advancement of some member is successful his placement graphically distorts the clique toward the vertical form, but this does not of course necessarily destroy old horizontal ties. For in his new post, the promoted officer frequently finds that his present assistants do not measure up to his earlier ones.[9] He may then contrive to bring one of his former associates closer to him formally. Obviously the continuation of old ties and understandings hinders adjustment to a new circle. Where the promoted officer does work to draw advantages from earlier associations, he and its members behave remarkably like campaigning politicians. They introduce praise and blame into the stream of plant gossip where it will bring highest returns. If conditions allow, the upgraded officer criticizes the state of the product as it enters his department. He attributes defects to laxity under the responsibility of the person to be discredited. He cooperates with his favorite chiefs to decrease their costs at the expense of others. He talks and exchanges favors with intimates among the superiors of those he wishes to aid, as in the cases above where rules against nepotism were reinterpreted. To aid his own candidates he may omit the subtleties of faint praise and positively damn the chances of others by attacks on their personal untidiness, excessive drinking, extramarital activities; or their disgraceful family squabbles, unmanageable children, impossible personality, and the like. Or, if the condition is known to exist, he may stress the person's stomach ulcers as proof of his shortcomings.

Blanke, Geiger, Meier, and Boesel were an aggressive horizontal clique. At one time they were all in the same division. As we noted, Blanke was then departmental chief with Geiger as his assistant. Meier and Boesel were assistant heads in other departments. When Blanke moved to head another division, Geiger succeeded him. Then with two other officers eligible in service and experience, Boesel became the next department head. Conversations with Geiger and others indicated that Blanke and Geiger greatly aided Boesel and that the three of them worked for Meier who came last to full superintendency. As superintendents, Meier, Boesel, and Geiger then cooperated closely to win favors from Revere. Through strong support from Boesel and Meier, Geiger had as much influence in the division as Revere. Although Blanke was in a different division and all faced new distractions, the old ties were revived on occasion to surmount official barriers.

The Random Clique

This clique is called *random* because its members usually cannot be classified in terms of formal rank, duties, or departmental origin, though they associate intimately enough to exchange confidences. Typically they have no consciously shared formal goal in the plant or point of company policy they are working to change, but the attraction is clearly friendship and social satisfaction. This can of course also exist in the other cliques, but friendship is not their end and may be hardly present. As compared with the more functional cliques this one is random in the sense that its members may come from any part of the personnel, managers and managed, and that they do not anticipate important consequences of their association.

As a rule, members of the random clique are not solidly in any of the more functional cliques. And usually they have never been in them, or if so, they are rejectees for indiscreet talk and failure in action. They are most often apathetic persons who are not sure why they are in the department. But being there they are given things to do, including the less desirable tasks, and they mechanically follow the routines. Consequently they resent, and do not fit into, the changing informal arrangements around them. They would like to escape the confusion to find simpler and more permanent recreational relations. As a result they get away from their jobs when possible to indulge in unguarded talk about people and events.

Their friends are like themselves. From the cafeteria to the showers they meet and gossip about their home departments and their dissatisfactions. Though only on the rim of events they do interact superficially with members of the other cliques. As would be expected, they learn few if any important secrets because of the barriers between themselves and these pivotal groups. And they may miss the meaning for larger issues of what they do learn. Nevertheless this relatively aimless association is important in plant affairs. As small unattached gossip groups moving freely around the firm, these cliques are both a point of leaks from the functional groups as well as a source of information for them. As such, the random clique intensifies informal activities in the plant.[10] The incomplete bits of information members exchange may mean little out of their larger context to an apathetic person, but much to an alert member of some functional clique. Discrete items supplied by a random clique on, for example, cost manipulation, or "gentlemen's agreements" at some level of union-management trading, may fit so well into the puzzle of an interested action clique that its members will clinch or change their pending action.

Instances from Milo show the circuitous routes of information leaks and the effects on others. The assistant chief chemist, Miller, received a confidential monthly salary "adjustment" of a hundred and twenty-five dollars. He wished to hide this from his subordinates, who were also pressing for salary increases to maintain the gap between themselves and the surging unionized stillmen and samplers. However, Miller did tell his wife, who belonged to a woman's club in the community. She told members of the club, one of whom was the wife of Sand, a line foreman from a third department. Sand was intimate in the plant with Wheeler, one of the samplers. Wheeler played golf with Sand and spent considerable time in Sand's office. Sand eventually passed the secret from his wife to Wheeler. Apparently seeing it as a joke on the chemists, Wheeler told them. Angered at Miller's "unfairness," some of the chemists wanted to face him with their knowledge and use it as a lever. Others overruled this, but "to get even" all cooperated with the samplers to conceal line errors and deviations from Miller, and to reduce the number of their own analyses.

In another case, superintendent Smith learned from his neighbor, Haller, a Milo employee whose loquacity was guarded against in his own department and encouraged elsewhere, that Boesel had arranged with his grievance committeeman to promote a workman contrary to the seniority record. Smith sought a similar deal with his own grievance man but was refused.[11] Smith's anger struck fear in Boesel and his union ally that Hardy and the president of the union local might be called in. They returned the promoted workman to his old position temporarily, though later both Boesel and Revere made deals with the union adverse to seniority principle. This incident made enemies of Smith and Boesel, and Boesel never learned the source of the leak.

CONTROL OF CLIQUES

Given the nature of personnel, and the official frameworks they create, even the cliques essential for intertwining official and informal actions occasionally get out of hand and must be curbed. These are the vertical symbiotic and the two horizontal forms. They normally function (*a*) to build working harmony from the differing skills and abilities, private feuds, and shifting identifications of employees in endless turnover; and (*b*) to adapt the personnel and changing technology to each other. But when this function fails, or other factors give one department a force in events unwarranted by its contributions, eventual action by a high level horizontal aggressive clique corrects the distortion.

Clique correctives are perforce applied expediently. Conflicting reports on the clique, questions of who the members are and their degree of involvement, and the indispensability of constructive clique skills, work to order the steps taken and to grade the rigor of correctives.

Restrictive action is typically initiated by (1) guarded attacks on the effects of the clique's expanding influence, and followed by a hint, from the presiding officer at a formal meeting, that not all sins are pardonable.

If this is ineffective, and conditions permit it, (2) efforts are made to hold the structure as it is and to contain the clique. Greatly influenced by impersonal factors as well as the rank, quality, and extra-clique ties of members, this is a first step in some firms, a last resort in others. Failure to contain the clique may lead to (3) transfer or promotion of the clique leader, and, as in the case of Nevers in Chapter 7, he may receive surprising aid from the firm when he moves to another unit or another company. (4) If pretext and expediency interlock well, clique members may be dispersed about the firm. (5) Sometimes an offensive clique is nullified by neatly justified withdrawal and rotation of members about the firm. In other cases, (6) conditions and matching ingenuities may dictate direct or indirect change of structure or method in adjacent work areas to disrupt clique routines and thus weaken it. Instead of changes, circumstances may call for (7) informal punishments adapted to known sensibilities of key members. (8) Where the corrective clique agrees that certain members of the disruptive clique are expendable, demotions are made, with and without pretext, and members may abide by the change or quit the firm.

Since human ingenuity seems inexhaustible, and managerial structures and industrial technologies are so varied, these corrective steps obviously represent only some of the actions that are taken. Some of these points require further comment.

For example take the first point—complaints against an injurious clique in the hierarchy. Direct communication to top officers is taboo, as everybody knows, because intermediate levels may be involved. Formal "open door" policy may welcome detoured grievances, but subordinates fear leaks of their message and hidden reprisal from those they by-pass. The theory that each supervisor must know all that goes up through his level is sound but incomplete: it has not been news for at least two thousand years that the intermediate levels of various hierarchies wish to interpret and color reports on the way up to protect themselves and to please higherups.[12] Hence initial opposition to a hurtful clique usually resorts to anonymous communication by a letter typed on an outside machine and handled entirely by a non-employee. If the letter shows enough knowledge of irregular behavior, action of some kind is sure to be taken. Even though the behavior reported has been ordered or tacitly acquiesced to by the addressee, some changes must be made to preserve organizational decorum.

Containment is sometimes accomplished by setting up problem committees that include one or more clique members,[13] who share assignments, meet deadlines, prepare progress reports, and otherwise work with the group, which weakens the clique and promotes organizational consciousness.

Transfer or promotion of the clique's key member is sometimes possible and effective. New abilities are suddenly discovered in him that fit him for another post, usually staff, where it is hoped that neither the function nor new associates will channel his genuine abilities into aberrant action. The post may entail standard duties or be only a sinecure. As we saw with Blanke, who was not promoted to break up a clique, this may not entirely check old horizontal aggressive clique actions, but the new preoccupations are a powerful restraint. Sometimes intercompany relations allow cooperative transfers of gifted incorrigibles, as was done between Milo and Fruhling.

Where all members of a deviant clique are considered indispensable and above the humiliation of what cannot be concealed as obvious disciplinary action, all may be dispersed to different parts of the firm, or incorporated into some kind of rotating system to limit expression of excessive clique skills or to use them where they are needed. The potential tumult of dispersal may be more disruptive than the clique. But decisions usually favor the risk, for one finds the expanding firm expediently creating new posts for this purpose, and the more static company maintaining a reserve of active and dormant sinecures as a safety valve for this and other pressures.

Rotation as a remedy also has its pros and cons. It does hasten the breakup of undesirable cliques, hinders the formation of others and offers new promise to frustrated officers. But used injudiciously, it disturbs essential personal ties. The common pretext for its employment, "Everybody is more valuable to the organization because they know more about plant operations," is often suspected as a "trick" or resisted as "pushing people around," as any change is likely to be seen. In theory the rotated persons "get a fresh outlook." By the time they return, if they do, both they and the earlier situations have changed. Rotation is of course not always a mask, but is also used for broadening individual perspectives.

When personnel shuffles are inadequate or impossible, changes are made in methods and duties to balance pressures, reduce inequities, or to bring less troublesome realignments. Sometimes the problem area is seemingly ignored while the personnel and methods in an interlocking department are reorganized as needed to break routines of the troublesome clique and refocus its interests.

Where clique members are not regarded as indispensable, but their rank is such that a blunt release would raise questions about the original appointing officer's judgment, some one of the group may be singled out as a link to be broken, and as an example. Such a person habitually will not receive the information or aid he requires to function, or new "temporary" and logically sound but impossible assignments will be given to him. With calculated aid from others he will involve himself in trouble, grow weary of the job, become suspicious of clique members, and ask for a transfer or quit.

As implied earlier, almost never would an able executive be discharged for clique activity. Higher managers value these skills as necessary for cutting a way through or around chaotic situations. Public relations and the equalitarian ideology may require denial, but top managers are more disposed to pardon than punish occasional excesses of the social skill required for organizational coherence and action.

NOTES

1. There is of course nothing "unnatural" about such behavior, but it is contrary to expectations. On the other hand, loyalty to the system rather than to the unifying leader, or department head, may handicap him severely. See M. E. Dimock, *The Executive in Action,* Harper and Brothers, New York, 1945, p. 249.
2. For general remarks on "identification," see [C. I.] Barnard, [*Functions of the Executive,* Harvard University Press, Cambridge, 1938] pp. 83–86; H. A. Simon, [*Administrative Behavior,* The Macmillan Company, New York, 1948,] pp. 110–112, 204–214; C. L. Shartle, *Executive Performance and Leadership,* Prentice-Hall, Englewood Cliffs, N.J., 1956, pp. 156–161. And though expressed in different terms, see L. Reissman, "A Study of Role Conceptions in Bureaucracy," *Social Forces,* 27:305–310, March, 1949.
3. C. I. Barnard notes the potential for covert action in democratic organizations. See his *Organization and Management,* Harvard University Press, Cambridge, 1948, pp. 39–47.
4. [M. E.] Dimock, [*The Executive in Action,* Harper and Brothers, New York, 1945], pp. 53–68; Herbert Blumer, "Group Tensions and Interest Organizations" in Milton Derber, ed., *Proceedings of the Second Annual Meeting, Industrial Relations Research Association,* 1949, pp. 150–159.
5. Quite apart from decision making, this coaching in the finesse of workable illegalities may be given in any organization. For example, embarrassing disturbances often result when new conductors come on the job and disrupt established practices between older conductors and daily commuting passengers on the interurban railway systems in metropolitan areas. Usually the commuter from the suburb to downtown on such trains carries a fifty- or sixty-ride monthly commutation book of tickets. Because the tickets are sold at reduced rates, the company declares tickets void that are pre-

sented separately from the book. That is, officially the conductor is to take the book from the passenger, tear out the ticket, and return the book. However, because trains at rush hours are usually full to standing room only, passengers, with the blessing of the conductor, speed up collection by tearing out the ticket and having it ready for him. Ignorant of this arrangement, the new conductor follows official precept and rejects tickets removed from the book. Passengers and conductor are of course outraged with each other. Fellow conductors in adjacent cars allow this to continue for some time, apparently as part of a hazing ordeal required of the newcomer, and to insure that he is sound before they acquaint him with their "illegal" but effective technique.

6. Peter F. Drucker, *The Practice of Management,* Harper and Brothers, New York, 1954, p. 361.
7. Eli Ginzberg, ed., *What Makes an Executive?* Columbia University Press, New York, 1955, p. 148.
8. The term *symbiotic* is adapted from the biological term *symbiosis* (*syn,* together, and *bios,* life) which refers to a mutually beneficial *internal* partnership between two different kinds of organisms. This is related to the term *commensalism* (*com,* together, and *mensa,* table) which is reserved by some students for *external* associations between two quite different kinds of animals, who live together in effect as messmates or fellow boarders. Examples of commensalism are the tie between the Dor beetle and its blind mite partner, the hermit crab (some) and sea anemones, the Nile crocodile and one of the plovers, and the "tuatara" lizard and the petrel. Symbiotic relations include those between heather and its fungus partner, and termites and their flagellates. Our aim is not to force rigid parallels or to precisely follow biological usage. See R. W. Hegner, *College Zoology,* The Macmillan Company, New York, 1942, 5th edition, pp. 155, 702–703, and use of the term by sociologists: R. E. Park, "Symbiosis and Socialization: A Frame of Reference for the Study of Society," *American Journal of Sociology,* 45: 1–25, July, 1939; E. Gross, "Symbiosis and Consensus as Integrative Factors in Small Groups," *American Sociological Review,* 21: 174–179, April, 1956.
9. Frequently there is reluctance to break old emotional ties and to face the problems of developing new ones. His feeling is understandable if there are strong differences in attitude between his earlier and present associates on the issue of literal or loose interpretation of official doctrine. He may also be committed to aid one or more of his earlier associates. This last is related to a kind of spoils system and has been observed by numerous executives. See H. Frederick Willkie, *A Rebel Yells,* D. Van Nostrand Company, New

York, 1946, pp. 186–88, and Eli Ginzberg, ed., *What Makes an Executive?* Columbia University Press, New York, 1955, p. 156, where it is noted that changes in top leadership often mean that the "new man promoted his own associates" to the detriment of other well-qualified individuals. Sometimes correction of this evil creates others.

10. The random clique is not, of course, the only source of leaks. Under stress, members of the functional cliques may tell things they would not normally, and for calculated purposes they may deliberately pass a secret to a known "two-way funnel."
11. It is common (. . .) for grievance officers and managers to pair off in cliques and to oppose like cliques as all pursue peaceful informal adjustments with small concern for their official roles under the contract.
12. See the actions of Sejanus in Tacitus, *Historical Works,* E. P. Dutton & Co. (Everyman's Library), New York, no date, especially Vol. 1, book iv, sections 1, 2, 3, 8, 39–59, book v, sections 6–9; and Frederick the Great's countermeasures in W. S. Dorn, "Prussian Bureaucracy in the 18th Century," *Political Science Quarterly,* 46: 403–423 (1931), 47: 75–94, 259–273 (1932); B. B. Gardner and D. G. Moore, *Human Relations in Industry,* R. D. Irwin, Homewood, Ill., 1955, 3rd edition, pp. 95–101.
13. C. L. Shartle, *Executive Performance and Leadership,* Prentice-Hall, Englewood Cliffs, N. J., 1956, p. 60.

CIVIL SERVICE AND MANAGING WORK: SOME UNINTENDED CONSEQUENCES*

Robert T. Golembiewski

Nature seldom allows us to get what we wish without paying her price. This truism is commonly illustrated by the delicate balance in animal life which often cannot be disturbed to satisfy man's wants (*e.g.,* for fox hunting) without demanding of man in return (*e.g.,* by increases in the rabbit population and in crop damage).

The several civil service systems in this country also illustrate this bittersweet combination of intended and unintended consequences. The argument here will not go to the extreme of one observer, in whose

* Reprinted with permission of author and publisher from *American Political Science Review,* LVI (December 1962), pp. 961–973.

judgment the United States Civil Service Commission was the single greatest obstacle to the successful waging of World War II.[1] Rather, the focus here will be upon several characteristics of our civil service systems that have as presumably unintended consequences an increase in the burdens of managing work. For the most part, the analysis of management problems will derive from the research literature dealing with behavior in organizations, a field of study presently seething with activity.

I. THE GOAL-MATRIX OF OUR CIVIL SERVICE MOVEMENT

The nature of these unintended consequences is suggested by the matrix of goals, or purposes, underlying our civil service movement. The primary goal, of course, was the separation of the management of public work from party patronage. Within this overriding goal, Sayre has noted three early subsidiary purposes of our public personnel systems:[2]

1. the guarantee of equal treatment of all employees and all applicants for employment;
2. the application of the logic (or theory) and methods of "scientific management"; and
3. the development of a public career service.

These goals define the field of my present effort. Detailed analysis later will demonstrate the significance for the management of work of the unintended consequences which derive from the ways adopted to achieve these purposes. I take this opportunity to suggest the general nature of these consequences.

Consider first the general tethers on the management of work implicit in the historical pursuit of the three purposes listed. The guarantee of equal treatment, to begin with, has never quite made peace with the managerially convenient notion that unequal contributions demand unequal reward. To take a recent and characteristic example, the teachers' union in Illinois has lately expressed violent opposition to a proposal for merit pay increases based upon performance. This opposition goes deeper than the convenience of seniority or of hours of graduate study as objective criteria for pay increases and far deeper than the blatant protectionism of hacks. However lofty the motives, their effect is clear. In practice, the struggle toward the "equal treatment" goal virtually forced public personnel systems into a monumental preoccupation with technique and mechanics. As Sayre concluded,[3]

> Its main effect has been to move personnel administration, in the words of Gordon Clapp, "into the cold objective atmosphere of tests, scores, weighted indices, and split-digit rankings" so completely that "these technical trappings have become symbols of the merit system."

The management of work pays a stiff price for such technical elegance. Work is notoriously insensitive to such easy capture, and the most subtly contrived managerial rewards and punishments might be frustrated by an awkward distribution of test scores. Moreover, these technical trappings put powerful weapons into the hands of "staff" people. That more than one "line" manager has been stymied by one of these "split-digit rankings" without accepting the results as divinely ordained, moreover, does nothing to lessen the often intense jurisdictional tugs-of-war encouraged by the traditional "line-staff" distinction. These tensions are apt to be increased by the time lag inherent in centralized administrative systems, and public personnel systems are usually operated centrally.

The logic and methods of "scientific management," second, tended to condemn managers to a treadmill even as it aided them. Scientific management was imported from the "practical" world of business where its impact was enormous.[4] But the impact was not one-way. Thus there is no denying the useful revolution in viewing work that the methods of scientific management sparked. However, as recent research particularly demonstrates,[5] the assumptions in the logic (or theory) of scientific management concerning man and his work were mechanistic caricatures. Consequently, the manager tended to be less effective in direct relation to the degree that he patterned his behavior on the logic of the approach. That is, the reasonable methods of scientific management often were guided by an inadequate theory. Consequently, the usefulness of engineering a task with the methods of scientific management must be differentiated sharply from the usefulness of organizing a task's component sequential steps in terms of the theory of scientific management.[6]

The establishment of a public career service, third, also tended to have unintended and unfavorable consequences which counterbalanced the favorable and intended consequences. As Sayre put it,[7]

> Stated in its most positive terms, this objective represents an effort to provide the conditions of work which will attract and hold a public service of optimum talents. In its negative aspects, the goal has been translated into an elaborate system of protectionism. In the area of methodology the negative connotations have slowly but surely won the dominant position. . . .

Such protectionism, of course, often would bind the manager severely even as it safeguarded him (and his subordinates) from arbitrary removal.

In sum, then, striving toward the purposes of the civil service movement had its general costs. Three more specific sets of restrictions that burden the management of work in our civil service systems will concern us presently.

These costs of our civil service systems, however, must be kept in perspective. Today we can profit from hindsight and a sophisticated research literature. The efforts to achieve the separation of the civil service from patronage, in contrast, came before enough was known about the conceptual and operational problems of the description of organization, personality, or "position" to preclude an uncomplicated Tinker Toy approach to all three of these elements of personnel administration. That is, simple assumptions took the place of an understanding of empirical phenomena which were at least more complex and often essentially different from the assumptions.

Consequently, the early approach to public personnel administration is understandable, if inadequate. The compulsions of life could not wait on the scientific explanation of the universe. However, necessity should not be suffered to be a virtue, lest the original simplistic assumptions become too deeply buried under a specialized literature. Students of public personnel administration, fortunately, have done considerable self-critical work of late. The determined, if preliminary, efforts since World War II to outgrow its early biases are a leading feature of the reorientation currently underway in public administration.[8]

II. SUPERVISORY POWER AND CIVIL SERVICE

Perhaps the most rewarding clue to supervisory effectiveness in recent research exploits the "power" concept. "Power" refers, in general, to the ability to control the job environment. Getting recommendations for promotion accepted, for example, indicates that a supervisor has relatively high power. "Power" thus conceptually complements "authority," which refers to the degree to which the formal organization legitimates a supervisor's control of the job environment. Typically, all supervisors at the same level monitoring similar operations have similar authority; and typically, these supervisors will differ in their power.

Power seems to be related to effective supervisory performance, whether it is exercised upwards, as influence with superiors, or downwards, as control of the specific job site. Pelz, for example, studied some fifty measures of supervisory practices and attitudes without finding any marked correlations with employee morale and attitudes. When the influence of a supervisor with his superior was specified, however, rather sharp differences were observed. High supervisory power was associated with effective performance.[9] Consequently, as Likert concluded, a supervisor must be an effective subordinate as well as an effective superior.[10] Otherwise, reasonably, a supervisor cannot be expected to influence his subordinates consistently.

Similarly, power expressed as control of the job site is associated with effective performance. Likert provides much supporting data. A comparison between the top third and the bottom third of departments. (ranked in terms of productivity) is particularly relevant here. Personnel in the "top" departments, in contrast with the "bottom" departments, uniformly attributed greater influence over "what goes on in your department" to these four sources: higher management; plant management; department manager; and the workers themselves. Moreover, the "top" departments also desired that greater influence be exercised by all four sources than did the "bottom" departments. Significantly, the greatest differences between the "top" and "bottom" departments are in the power attributed to department managers (their primary supervisors) and in the power the men desired that department managers exercise.[11] These are reasonable results. A low-power supervisor has little leverage for motivating his men *via* his control over the job site. That is, the men have little reason to take him seriously.

If the reasons for the importance of supervisory power to effective performance seem clear enough, our civil service systems do little to ease the burdens of managing work *via* increases in supervisory power. This is particularly lamentable because much evidence suggests that the "power" variable may be influenced substantially by the design of the job, by the organization structure (of which more later), and by training. The supervisor's personality, in short, does not appear to be the crucial (or major) factor in determining power.

Although only empirical research can establish the point definitely, there seems ample evidence of this failure of civil service systems to respond to the need to facilitate the management of work by increasing supervisory power. On the broadest level, the first and third primary goals of the civil service movement certainly do not encourage supervisory power; and (as will be demonstrated) the application of the logic and methods of scientific management has the same effect.

To become more specific, these limitations on supervisory power have many practical impacts. For example, first-line supervisors seem to have less control over hiring and firing than their counterparts in business. The difficulty in business organizations of firing or reductions-in-force need not be underplayed, but the elaborate review procedures and the novel "bumping" arrangements[12] often found in our civil service systems probably admit of less flexibility in public agencies even on the part of officials at relatively high organizational levels. Raw turnover ratios seem to support this position.[13] Similarly, the emphasis upon seniority in promotions and pay increases in the public service plus the failures of supervisory rating of employee performance[14]—both common in our civil service systems—suggest that the environment in public agencies has not been conducive to the general heightening of supervisory power.

Some counterforces are at work, although they do not promise imminent change in the present condition of limited encouragement of supervisory power. Thus the federal program for rewarding superior performance permits a modest increase in supervisory power. Even in this case, however, apparently many agencies have preferred to ride very close herd over the recommendations of lower-level supervisors or (in at least one case of which I have personal knowledge) to neglect the immediate supervisor altogether. Thus this program not only died aborning as an opportunity to increase supervisory power, but its administration may even further reduce that power.

All this, be it noted, is not by way of an argument for arbitrary managerial or supervisory action. Just such abuses, of course, supplied motivation for the restraints emphasized above. The stress here, rather, is upon ways of reinforcing formal authority so as to permit greater effectiveness consistent with the policies of an agency. Just as in the case of any delegation, that is, attempts to increase supervisory power imply training and the development of suitable overhead controls. Moreover, "power" in the relevant research does not imply heavy-handed coercive techniques, which most subjects interpret as lack of control of the environment. Evidence such as that reviewed below in the context surrounding footnotes 48–51 supports this point.

The task of inducing high supervisory power, then, is more delicate than a mere reversal of gears toward the "spoils system" or advocacy of an administrative law of the jungle.

III. JOB DESIGN AND CIVIL SERVICE

Similarly, our civil service systems tend to limit the potential for increasing managerial effectiveness implicit in job design. The second primary goal noted above is the chief culprit, with strong support from the goal of "equal treatment." Their interaction in increasing managerial burdens can be illustrated in two ways, by considering specific job content, and by considering the place of the job in the broad organization structure.

In its doctrine about simplifying job content, particularly, the logic of scientific management makes difficulties for managing work effectively. As in industry, at low organization levels, the process of routinization often has been carried too far in the public service. The effects of "job enlargement" on employee performance, at least in business concerns,[15] suggest the contribution to effective management that may be gained by adding content to a worker's responsibilities. This may be accomplished by increasing the scope of jobs or by rotating individuals through several jobs.[16] The crucial factor does not seem to be the number of task-elements given to an individual or the complexity of these elements. Patently, a job could become too complex. Rather, the significant point seems to be that various techniques of job enlargement, when they work, work because they increase the worker's control over his job environment.[17] Hence the success of plans for increasing the employee's control over factors which are not in his flow of work, such as that often called "bottom-up management."[18]

The effects of "job enlargement" may be explained in terms of the earlier analysis. In Likert's study, as already noted, employees in high-producing units felt that they themselves exercised and desired more power over their work than did individuals in low-producing units. This is consistent with the favorable effects on output commonly reported in the "job enlargement" literature, while it suggests an apparent paradox. Note that Hi-Pro units ranked themselves *and* three levels of supervisors as higher on "power" than did Lo-Pro units. This might seem curious, but only if one assumes that there is only so much "power" to be had, so that what superiors gain subordinates must lose. The fact seems to be, on the contrary, that a high-power supervisor can afford to (and usually does) allow his subordinates to exercise greater power also.[19] A low-power supervisor is in such an insecure position that he can seldom bring himself to be so generous. The real paradox, then, is that the apparently most straightforward way of adding to one's power is often the most direct way of reducing it. The common mechanical conceptions of organized activity implicit in scientific management discourage such thinking.

The often marked consequences of job enlargement may be illustrated briefly. Machine operations in an industrial concern, for example, had been plagued by an array of difficulties: productivity and quality were falling; and tension between operators and inspectors was growing. The crucial factor was that the tool in this particular operation, when dulled to a certain point, would suddenly begin producing pieces which did not meet specifications. Inspectors were not always able to spot such sudden deteriorations in the product quickly, and operators (inspection not being *their* job) did not always cease work even when the quality was obviously unacceptable. Inspection reports helped little when they did come, the operators marking them down as "ancient history." The solution was easy. Simple gauges were given to operators to make periodic checks on their production, and the operators were allowed to decide when it was necessary to resharpen their cutting tools. The consequences: runs of defective products became shorter and less frequent; the nagging tension between inspectors and operators was reduced; and output zoomed.

Examples need not be confined to industrial operations. In a paperwork operation, similarly, a rather simple change increased output by 30 percent and reduced employee turnover by 70 percent.[20]

Although the design of the job could be an important means of reducing the problems of managing work, however, our civil service systems do not encourage the exploitation of such techniques as job enlargement. Consider only one feature which has an inhibiting effect, the very detailed job descriptions common in the public service. That these are an important part of the mechanisms for guaranteeing equal treatment of employees and for developing a career service does little to encourage flexibility in job design. Employee unions and the civil service commission staff can make much of these job descriptions, even in cases in which employees solidly favor changes of a job-enlargement sort. The difficulty is not necessarily avoided by job descriptions which conclude: "or other duties the supervisor may designate." Custom, employee unions, and an overprotective civil service commission can void such open-end descriptions.

Perhaps, however, this leans too heavily on personal (and limited) experience. Some administrators no doubt pay little attention to detailed job descriptions, except for such purposes as convincing the civil service commission that an individual deserves a multi-step promotion. And it may be argued that the significant point is not whether detailed job descriptions exist, but whether strong employee unions exist. Even in such cases, however, the detailed job description is part of the institutional framework within which management and union must function.

In determining the place of the job in the broad organization pattern, our civil service systems also increase the problems of managing work. Consider two characteristics which tend to dominate patterns of organization in the public service, a limited span of control and organization by function or (at lower levels) by process. These characteristics largely derive from the impact of scientific management upon public personnel administration. Analysis of these two characteristics is particularly useful because it demonstrates, among other features, their tendency to reduce supervisory power.

The analysis of these two characteristics is facilitated by some simplified graphics.[21] Figure 1A presents the orthodox organization of functions (or processes) A, B, C—which may be taken to be any components whose integration is required to perform some administrative task

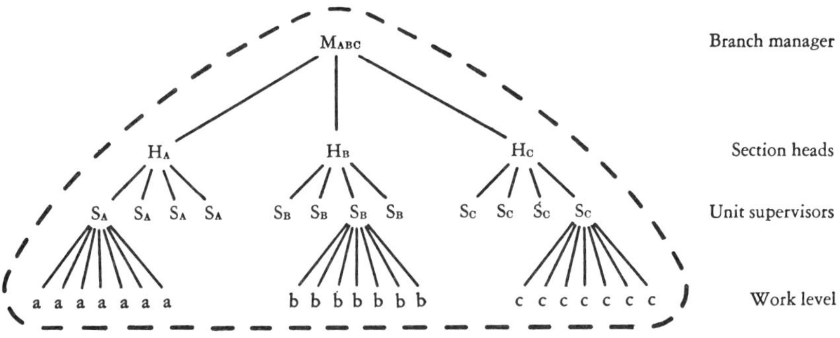

FIGURE 1A
Functional (Process) Organization with Narrow Span of Control

—under the condition of a limited span of control. Figure 1B presents the more unorthodox organization by product (or discrete subassembly), which permits a far broader span of control.

The functional model, with modest reservations, can be considered *the* pattern for government organizing. This does not do full justice to the diversity of actual organizational arrangements, admittedly. Various factors—size, pressure of work, geography, and the like—have encouraged significant deviations from the functional model. Thus the Justice Department long ago surrendered the fancy of having every government lawyer in the department. The functional model, however, is commonly encountered in practice and it is certainly the most commonly prescribed model in the literature, as in the Hoover Commission's *Report on the General Management of the Executive Branch.*

The following contrast of the functional model with the product model, then, requires that two points be kept in mind. First, the func-

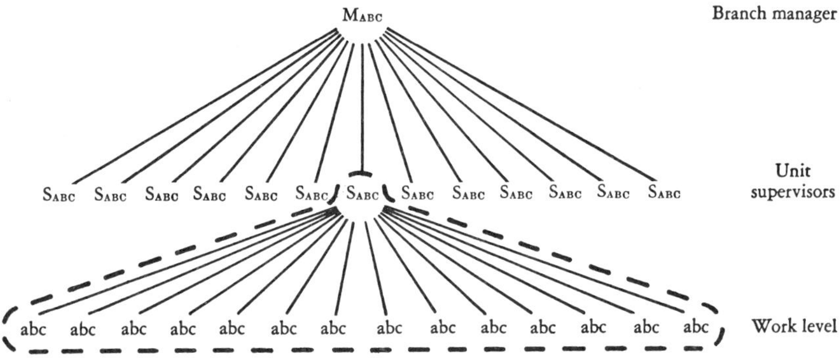

FIGURE 1B
Product (Discrete Sub-Assembly) Organization with Broad Span of Control

tional model does not guide all public organizing, but it is nonetheless influential. Second, the product model will not always be a feasible alternative, although it often will be. The contrast, that is, has much to recommend it, although hardly everything. Thus, although the analysis may have an either-or flavor, many other factors would serve to soften the contrast in practice and would guide the choice in specific cases of the functional model, the product model, or combinations of the two.

These simple variations in the organization of jobs in larger structures can have profound consequences for the management of work. In general, the type of structure common in most public agencies (see Figure 1A) incurs substantial costs avoided by the less familiar structure in Figure 1B. These costs derive from three features associated with these two patterns of structure: job enlargement; the size of the "managerial entity"; and supervisory power.

First, to point up the obvious, Figure 1B is based upon job enlargement at all levels. Each employee at the work-level in Figure 1B performs all three components of the task, and each supervisor's responsibilities encompass all three. Figure 1A's emphasis upon routinization limits the scope, and perhaps thereby the effectiveness of the management of work. Of course, there are some limits on the functions or processes (A, B, C, . . .) that may be strung together. In general, however, the limits seem to be very broad indeed.[22]

Second, the "managerial entity" is vastly larger in Figure 1A than in Figure 1B. The size of the managerial entity can have profound consequences. It may appear, for instance, that the structure in Figure 1B puts too much strain on the capacities of management, because of the apparently greater demands it imposes upon the supervisors. In reality, however, structures such as that in Figure 1A often imply greater (and different) demands upon management talent. Figure 1B structures reduce in significant ways the management burden carried by M_{ABC} and the supervisors as well. The difficulties faced by M_{ABC} in structures like that in Figure 1A cause considerable problems for supervisors, for example, by tending to reduce their supervisory power. Many of the problems associated with sizeable organizations, more generally, derive not from the aggregate size of the organization, but from the size of its component managerial entities. Thus the manager in our hypothetical organization in Figure 1A directs the work of 99 employees and encounters the difficulties to be enumerated below; the manager in Figure 1B oversees the work of 195 employees, yet significant problems facing the management of work are reduced.

The "managerial entity" concept warrants further analysis. Worthy defines it in these terms:[23]

> The administrative unit can be no smaller than that portion of the organization falling within the jurisdiction of an individual who controls enough elements of the total process to make effective decisions regarding the total process.

A high-level managerial entity might be organized around some total product, for example, water resource development in the Kings River Valley. The processing by each of several competing teams of all categories of mail received by the Government Printing Office, with each team handling all correspondence from writers whose names begin with designated letters of the alphabet, illustrates the kind of discrete subassembly around which a low-level managerial entity might be organized.

At whatever level of organization, then, a "managerial entity" contains that parcel of process-components necessary for the performance of some discrete task. The areas enclosed by the heavy dotted lines in the two figures above symbolize "managerial entities." Interpretively, any S_{ABC} in Figure 1B can "get all the way around" our hypothetical administrative task. In Figure 1A, in contrast, only M_{ABC} can do this job. M_{ABC} in Figure 1A has a managerial entity which contains 100 individuals; that of S_{ABC} contains only 15.

Many of the problems in sizeable organizations derive from the failure to restrict the size of the organization's managerial entities. Haire's analogy seems apt in this connection. He suggested the mushrooming problems caused by the growth in the size of organizations *via* the "square-cube law" applied to the story of Jack and the Beanstalk:[24]

> . . . Jack had nothing to fear from the Giant. If he were, as he is pictured, ten times as large as a man and proportioned like one, Jack was perfectly safe. The Giant's mass would be 10^3 or a thousand times a man's, because he was ten times as big in every dimension. However, the cross section of his leg bones would have increased in only two dimensions, and they would be 10^2 or a hundred times as big as a man's. A human bone simply will not support ten times its normal load, and the Giant, in walking, would break his legs and be helpless.

In a similar way, arithmetic increases in the size of the managerial entity seem to generate exponential increases in the problems of the management of work. Meeting these increases in size within the framework of the type of organization structure in Figure 1A does nothing to reduce these difficulties.

This general position can be elaborated. The size of the managerial entity, in sum, is likely to affect such significant features of administration as: the time lag between the perception of a problem and action on it, which influences supervisory power; the style of supervision; the measurement and the motivation of performance; and the training of subordinates.

Patently, first, decisions will tend to be pushed upward in an organization such as that in Figure 1A; for only M_{ABC} oversees all of the components which require integration. As a result, delegation to supervisors is all but restricted to routine matters, that is, those which involve the single component supervised by any supervisor and only that component.

The separation of decision-making from the action level often has significant costs. Overloading upper levels may make time-pressure a very serious factor, the more so if the stakes are high. A shutdown in any of the sections in Figure 1A might cause output to drop as low as zero. The manager, then, is under great pressure to assure that A, B, and C are integrated, and he is likely to exert that pressure downward. This does not encourage upward communication, in turn, which is difficult enough in the "tall" organization described in Figure 1A. (Notice that Figure 1B, with 69 per cent more people, has one less organization level than Figure 1A.) The efforts of the manager to fight the daily battle of integration of the components of his operation and to get the information required for his job, finally, will tend to undercut any efforts by the supervisors to gain high power. The common development of large "staff" units complements this tendency.

In contrast, decisions in Figure 1B organizations would strongly tend to be forced down to the action level, and certainly at least to the level of S_{ABC}. Indeed, M_{ABC} may have no other reasonable alternative, given his broad span of control. Upward communication and supervisory power often will be affected favorably. M_{ABC}, consequently, should be freed from the unremitting pressure of integration implicit in a Figure 1A structure. Downtime at any work station, for example, will not cause difficulty throughout the managerial entity. Output would fall at most by 1/N. The manager therefore could devote himself to motivating superior performance, to training and counseling, and the like, rather than attempting to eliminate the possibility of error.

These comments on decision-making, second, suggest that the two types of structures encourage different styles of supervision. The structure in Figure 1A encourages "close supervision," *i.e.,* detailed instructions, persistent attempts to direct and observe performance, and the like. The limited span of control, of course, permits this, and the pressure for the integration of the task components may force it. The structure in Figure 1B encourages "general supervision," *i.e.,* monitoring performance in terms of results with considerable freedom for the employee so long as he is performing up to standard. Close supervision of janitors, for example, would require such directions as: "You will sweep from left to right, forty strokes per minute," and correspondingly close checks on performance. General supervision, in contrast, would assume competence and give such instructions as: "Sweep the floors in such time that you are able to get your other work done and so that the floor will reflect *x* units of light from a refractometer." The refractometer provides the check on performance. Acknowledgedly, this goes a little far. All of the components of general supervision are there, however, especially the measure of performance.

Structures of the type in Figure 1A pay a heavy cost to the degree that they in fact do encourage close supervision. In one study, for example, less than 30 percent of the work teams whose first- or second-level supervisors practiced close supervision had high output. Nearly 70 percent of the work units receiving only general supervision had high output.[25]

The reader may suppose, third, that the manager and supervisors in a Figure 1B organization would face an impossible task in motivating and measuring performance. For general supervision must be based upon performance standards, and what will keep standards high if the supervisor "gets off their backs?" But the several units headed by an S_{ABC}, each performing the same task, obviously set the stage for a relative measure of performance. They are in competition with each other, which tends to keep performance high. This would complement the added contributions to be expected because of the job enlargement practiced in 1B-type structures. At the same time, reduced "line-staff" conflict seems implied by this potential for motivation and measurement, "staff" development being in large part due to top-level management's difficulties in motivating and, especially, measuring performance.

Figure 1A organizations do not offer the same possibilities. One might try to encourage competition within, for example, some S_A unit, or between the S_A units and the S_B units. But competition of that sort, as experimental studies suggest, is not likely to aid performance on most tasks,[26] since the tasks themselves are not comparable, and may indeed be incommensurable. The point may be driven home by considering this proposition: Assembling all As (or Bs or Cs) in organizationally separate units encourages the restriction of output and invites substantial jurisdictional conflict when the responsibility for an error must be assigned. Much evidence supports this proposition.[27] Responsibility is far more difficult to assign in a 1A-type structure, for at least three inspections would be required to permit accurate assignment of praise or blame, one after each of the component operations. Figure 1B organizations would require only one such inspection. Such considerations, and there are many others, attest to the difficulties of motivating and measuring performance in Figure 1A organizations.

These features of Figure 1B organizations suggest a way out of the objection that public agencies are not guided by "profit" and that therefore performance measurement is difficult. In Figure 1A organizations, in business, the measurement of macroscopic profit does little to determine the often crucial measurement of the effectiveness of constituent units. Hence many business enterprises have approached the type of organization sketched in Figure 1B by establishing "individual profit centers" within (for example) a plant. Their services are then "sold" internally, sometimes with the useful provision that outside purchase is possible if price or quality are not considered appropriate by the "buyer."[28] This encourages self-discipline of both "buyer" and "seller." Comptroller W. J. McNeil worked for years to install arrangements of this sort in the Department of Defense, for the provision of common procurement of goods and services, as a means of economy and of strengthening the Secretary's hand.

In any case, fourth, Figure 1B organizations seem to have a definite advantage in the training of subordinates. Patently, S_{ABC} faces training challenges not available to S_A (or S_B or S_C) in the normal course of events. Reasonably, then, organization structures such as that in Figure 1B should tend toward the early elimination of those without management ability, while it would attract the more able. Reasonably, also, high satisfaction and output should characterize Figure 1B organizations. These expectations, indeed, are supported by some research in the Sears, Roebuck chain[29] and elsewhere.[30]

Despite these (and other) advantages of 1B structures, our public personnel systems do not provide a congenial home for them. The dominant emphasis in these systems—and it is no doubt often a necessary emphasis—is negative rather than positive. As one observer with high-level experience in both government and industry noted:[31]

> . . . no matter how well briefed on federal service peculiarities the private business executive may be, one of the first things he notices in public administration is this emphasis on procedure and routine. This emphasis is admittedly necessary and desirable provided it does not make method an end in itself. When it does, over-organized bewilderment results. The newcomer to top management positions in the federal service frequently feels that the organization and methods set up with the laudable idea of keeping him from doing wrong actually result in making it excessively difficult to do right.

This emphasis, despite its legitimacy, seems to have been overdone at all levels. Overdone or not, it is something to know what it costs to preserve the emphasis in Figure 1A structures.

Generations of organization theorists have labored hard to preserve the fiction of the unity of command in our public affairs, this being the very slender thread by which we demonstrate that the electorate really does control the administration through its election of the president. One may judge the impact of this theory upon supervisory practices from the longevity of the logically consistent but unrealistic notion that "politics" and "administration" are somehow separate. This notion, of course, is the keystone of our civil service systems. Their failure to respect the realities of delegation hardly augurs for better treatment of this matter at lower organization levels. Comfortable as the fiction of unity of command may be to many, multi-line relations exist. We may choose to neglect this datum for various reasons, as the Hoover Commission did in arguing for a structure such as that in Figure 1A.[32] But this neglect may prove embarrassing,[33] and it is very likely that our theoretical simplicism has a high cost. Gaus long ago put the argument for a multi-line view in these convincing terms:[34]

> Such a theory . . . is the only one which fits the facts of contemporary delegation of wide discretionary power by electorates, constitutions, and legislatures to the administrators [who] must, of necessity, determine some part of the purpose and a large part of the means whereby it will be achieved in the modern state.

Finally, the accepted pattern of organization in public agencies (as well as in business concerns) is functional. This reflects the historic strength of the model sketched in Figure 1A and suggests the barriers which will restrain attempts to approach the Figure 1B model in organizing.

IV. JOB DESCRIPTION AND CIVIL SERVICE

It says worlds, while it avoids an enormous complexity, to note that our civil service systems typically are based upon a duties classification, as opposed to a rank classification. Public personnel specialists have gone in for a duties classification with a sometimes uncritical zeal. As Nigro explains:[35]

> In a duties classification, the beginning point is a detailed analysis of the tasks required in the individual position. In fact, the tendency in the United States has been to make fairly minute investigations of job content.

The emphasis need not be exaggerated, for the specialists have providently refrained from stressing the content of all jobs. The handling of secretarial positions—whose importance is usually measured by secretaries and bosses in terms of what the boss does rather than what the secretary does—is perhaps the most striking illustration of what has been called the "realistic" approach to classification.[36] But the bias of job description in this country has not moved very far from the classic expression it was given, for example, in the 1932 classification plan for Philadelphia. Nigro called this "one of the best books of specifications on record." It listed twenty individual classes of clerks, for each of which specifications had been developed. Specifications also were stated for thirty additional classes of principal and chief clerks in the various city departments.[37]

The inspirations for this emphasis on job description in our public personnel systems seem clear enough. The logic and methods of scientific management—which encouraged the view of organization as a "delicate mechanism" of gear-like "positions" whose driveshaft was the line of command—clearly had their influence. Moreover, position classification provides the bases for equal treatment, general formal policies and procedures regarding recruitment, salary, promotions, and the like. Finally, position classification encourages the attempt to group similar jobs into a reasonable number of classes, sub-classes, and so on. This provided a ladder-like framework upon which a permanent career service could be built.

Despite its contribution to achieving the goals of our civil service movement, the American approach to job description has its unintended costs. Some obvious costs will be considered immediately; subsequent analysis will consider one less obvious set of costs in some detail.

Since one product of position classification was to be a manageable number of classes, first, this required a procrustean neglect of distinguishing job characteristics. The position approach, second, became the victim of its own imprecise terms. Consider the common observation that the "position" is the "universal building block of all organizations."[38] The observation has a certain validity, since all organizations contain positions. It tended to mislead the unwary, however, into supposing that "organization" is only a set of positions. The temptation to think of organization as some massive mechanical structure of positions linked by lines of authority was strong, since it apparently served to simplify the problems of personnel work.

The emphasis upon a duties classification, third, implies a substantial rigidity. Consider the difficulties of dealing with the many positions which have a kind of life cycle, with stages that impose varying demands on the incumbent. Developing an administrative role may be a very delicate task, while playing the role thereafter may be child's play. This phenomenon is difficult to accommodate within the framework of most of our public personnel systems. Some adaptations may be made quickly enough. But often it is necessary to waste a "big" man on a job too small for him or to give a "small" man a job too big for him. Similarly, the emphasis upon a duties classification makes it difficult to utilize positions for training purposes without the stretching of a point or two by the position analyst. The traditional question—What does the incumbent do?—is not appropriate for such positions, for he may, in fact, contribute little toward immediate task performance.

The abortive struggles toward a Senior Civil Service, and then a Career Executive Program, for the federal government, reflect the tenacity of the grip of these two types of inflexibilities.[39] For it was intended that the highly mobile and select corps of administrators in such programs would be used in both of the ways alluded to above, that is, as experienced "firefighters" and as trainees getting the "big picture." The rank-in-job bias in our civil service systems played not a little part in the lack of action.

Fourth and finally, the approach *via* a duties classification taken in this country is not the only available one. Indeed, in public administration, it appears that only Canada and Brazil follow our example closely. Many personnel systems—public and business—emphasize broad and general classes rather than narrow and detailed ones. Some of the spirit claimed for the British civil service, for example, is suggested by this open-end description of the few grades of "scientific officer" in Her Majesty's service:[40]

> It is not possible to define with precision the duties of the various grades but, broadly speaking, the duties of the grades above principal scientific officer include responsibility for the administration and direction of scientific work while the principal scientific officer and lower grades concentrate on the scientific work itself. . . .
>
> But the posts of senior principal scientific officer and above may, with Treasury authority, be created for outstanding individual research workers.

Not infrequently, on the business side, executives will take the more extreme ground that they will not tolerate even an organization chart at their level, lest it force them into patterns of action which may become inappropriate, just as these patterns develop a vested interest in protecting personnel.

This general approach to job description has its virtues. For example, by all accounts, the British achieve great flexibility, avoid the sometimes gross artificialities of more "precise" efforts, and (one supposes) increase the power of the supervisors whose discretion is obviously emphasized. Their approach also seems to avoid that situation which haunts position analysts and outside observers alike: that an Einstein would have the same grade as any other physicist doing "similar work."

These problems of the American approach are known well enough, although they do not prove the inferiority of a detailed approach to job description in the lower classifications. These problems may have profound consequences for the management of work. At its worst, taking the mechanical aspects of job description too seriously can disrupt the flow of work. Moderation on the part of both "line" and "staff" seems indicated. The decentralization of much personnel work in the federal service suggests that just such a mature moderation has set in.

Other factors encourage a diluted devotion to the methods and theory implicit in the duties classification in this country. Here let us consider only this feature: it is not obvious that the common attempts at precision are precise about all (or most) of the elements of work which are important. This should encourage a healthy skepticism in developing and administering duties classifications. For, first, the technology of duties classification cannot support great precision now, nor is it likely to do so in the immediate future. Second, if a duties classification purports to describe the behaviors required for the effective performance of an organization's work, existing efforts commonly miss many significant possibilities. If it merely codifies existing practices it may not be worthy of vigorous support, for duties classifications are at least implicitly prescriptive.

The specific dimensions which characterize tasks are but imprecisely known. The usual guidelines for classification—level in the hierarchy, formal authority and responsibility, funds administered, and the like—are not sufficient for doing the job tidily. For example, they do not take into account whether Supervisor X is the informal as well as formal leader of his work unit. It is impractical and unjust to treat Supervisor X's job as the same whatever the answer to this question. Moreover, if a job description is prescriptive, a supervisor's socioemotional performance cannot be overlooked. We may fairly ask of an approach which preaches and seeks precision: Precision about what?

The question remains, what is significant in describing a task? It is a disarming question. Existing research does not suggest that it has an obvious or an uncomplicated answer. Factor analysis, a sophisticated mathematical technique, perhaps offers the most hope of developing a set of dimensions which will permit us to describe jobs precisely. A technical discussion of factor analysis hardly can be attempted here. In general, however, the technique permits an initial judgment as to the number of independent dimensions necessary to account for the variation in some batch of scores (*e.g.*, in rankings by several analysts of jobs in terms of the discretion they require incumbents to exercise). The technique has been utilized, for example, to isolate the various kinds of intellectual abilities measured by intelligence tests. There is no way to solve such problems *a priori*. Factor analysis, in sum, might well complement and direct the enormous amount of observation that normally goes into developing a duties classification and into keeping it current.

Applications of factor analysis to job description suggest the problems which must be met. The technique, for example, has been applied to the ratings of a very large number of characteristics of various jobs. Existing results do not suggest that a synthesis is imminent. A simple manual task, for example, required only a few factors to describe it in one study.[41] Another factor analysis of more complex tasks isolated twenty-three factors.[42] Yet only seven factors were considered necessary to describe the 4,000 jobs listed by the U.S. Employment Service.[43] Thus existing work does not suggest a clear pattern. To further complicate matters, there seem to be "families" of tasks for which individual sets of factor dimensions probably must be developed.[44]

Despite the inconclusiveness of such factor analytical work, two points seem clear. First, the dimensions isolated thus far do not closely resemble the guidelines implicit in much classification work. In fact, the factors need not have any obvious connection with "commonsense" notions.[45] Second, the isolation of such factors is only the initial step. Factor analysis provides a rough map of those things which are important descriptively. Successful prediction, however, is the crucial test. Such validatory work might take such a form: If the task has dimensions *a* and *d,* individuals with such-and-such training, proficiency, attitudes, and personality will prove to be high producers.

Even this preliminary factorial work has clear implications for our public personnel systems. Duties classification will have limited usefulness to the degree that task dimensions are not developed and the validatory work referred to above is not undertaken. The interim question of whether the pursuit of precision about characteristics—which may or may not be functionally important in describing the task—is worthwhile probably must remain open. The answer is not obviously in the affirmative. A fundamental reevaluation of the common approach to job description in this country seems required, while we await the scientific explanation which will permit great precision. It would seem useful to attempt to test whether general classification provides savings beyond the reach of the detailed classification.

If detail there must be in job description, many factors could fruitfully be included in the usual duties classification. One such is the style of supervision.

Different jobs seem compatible with different styles of supervision. On the available evidence, general statements under this head must be tentative, largely because we know so little about the dimensions along which tasks differ. An example, however, may be hazarded. Provisionally, jobs may be conceived as differing in the degrees to which their performance is programmed and to which their successful performance requires interpersonal cooperation. When a task is unprogrammed and requires high interpersonal cooperation, a permissive supervisory style has seemed most appropriate for those subjects tested. An authoritarian supervisory style will cause the least socioemotional dislocation on tasks which are highly programmed and require little interpersonal cooperation.[46] These are general relations, indeed, and require much specification of intervening conditions. Similarly, individuals with differing personality characteristics tend to perform most effectively under different supervisory styles.[47] Meeting the needs of employees *via* an appropriate supervisory style probably would serve to increase the power of supervisors, or at least to provide supervisors with a favorable environment in which to seek high power.[48]

The specification of such factors as the supervisory style congenial to a job is particularly important because the logic of scientific management encourages the choice of a generally inappropriate style. Thus close supervision—which is consistent with this theory—seems to be associated with high output in only a minority of cases, as already noted. If one had to make a choice between the two types of supervision, then, it is not crystal clear that one would be well advised to obey the logic of scientific management.

This analysis can be extended. Close supervision, patently, is encouraged by a structure such as that in Figure 1A. Supervisory pressure would seem to be most directly applicable in this model, which in turn might suggest high supervisory power. Things, however, do not seem to happen this way often. Likert reports that the more "unreasonable pressure" reportedly exerted by a supervisor, the less the power attributed to that supervisor.[49] Moreover, evidence suggests that greater supervisory pressure serves to isolate the supervisor from his men by increasing the danger of communication.[50] In addition, pressure seems inversely related to output. For example, ten of eleven departments in Likert's study which reported little outside pressure to control the pace of work were above-average producers. Nine of ten departments reporting great pressure were below-average producers.[51] Reasonably, then, job descriptions might well profit from the specifications of such job-relevant factors as the style of supervision.

This discussion of two approaches to job description—through those factors normally included, and through those factors which are often neglected—permits of simple summary. There seem to be very substantial costs of commission and omission in the job descriptions common in our civil service systems. These costs complicate the management of work, however nicely the systems fit the three core goals underlying the American approach to public personnel administration.

V. SUMMARY

Our federal Civil Service Commission has been accustomed to serve more than one master. As one commentator noted:[52]

> "For whom does the Civil Service Commission work?" We used to reply, "Well, we think it works first for its congressional committees, second for the status employees, third for the American Legion in support of veterans' preference laws, fourth for civil service employees' unions, and possibly fifth for the President." Since the end of World War II, the President has moved up in this list but it is difficult to tell just how far.

The analysis above, in essence, argues that yet another master requires service, the development of a work environment within which a professional manager can do his most effective job. Substantial revisions in traditional thinking and technique about our civil service systems will be required to that end.

NOTES

1. John Fisher, "Let's Go Back to the Spoils System," reproduced in part in Dwight Waldo, ed., *Ideas and Issues in Public Administration* (New York, 1953), pp. 200–1.
2. Wallace Sayre, "The Triumph of Technique Over Purpose," *Public Administration Review,* Vol. 8 (Spring, 1948), pp. 134–35.
3. *Ibid.,* p. 134.
4. Dwight Waldo, *The Administrative State* (New York, 1948), pp. 47–64.
5. See my *Behavior and Organization* (Chicago: Rand McNally, 1962), esp. chs. 1–4.
6. See my "Organizing Work: Techniques and Theories," *Advanced Management—Office Executive,* Vol. 1 (June, 1962), pp. 26–31.
7. Sayre, *op. cit.,* pp. 134–35.
8. The outlines of this reorientation are drawn sharply in O. Glenn Stahl, *Public Personnel Administration* (New York, 1956), pp. 577–82.
9. Donald C. Pelz, "Interaction and Attitudes Between Scientists and Auxiliary Staff," *Administrative Science Quarterly,* Vol. 4 (De-

cember, 1959), pp. 321–36, and Vol. 4 (March, 1960), pp. 410–25.
10. Rensis Likert, *New Patterns of Management* (New York, 1961), p. 114.
11. *Ibid.,* pp. 56–57.
12. James E. Drury, *The Displaced Career Executive Program* (Inter-University Case Program, University of Alabama Press, 1952).
13. Stahl, *op. cit.,* p. 473.
14. Felix Nigro, *Public Personnel Administration* (New York, 1959), p. 295.
15. Chris Argyris, *Personality and Organization* (New York, 1957), pp. 177–87, summarizes many relevant studies.
16. *Ibid.,* p. 177.
17. *Ibid.,* p. 180.
18. William Givin, *Bottom-Up Management* (New York, 1949).
19. The point has been amply demonstrated in experimental situations. See James G. March, "Influence Measurement in Experimental and Semi-Experimental Groups," *Sociometry,* Vol. 19 (March, 1956), pp. 26–71.
20. Peter F. Drucker, *The Practice of Management* (New York, 1954), pp. 291–92.
21. The parent of this analysis may be found in James C. Worthy, *Big Business and Free Men* (New York, 1959), pp. 90–99.
22. The point is supported by the example in Drucker, *op. cit.,* p. 291. See also Argyris, *op. cit.,* pp. 177–87.
23. Worthy, *op. cit.,* pp. 92–93.
24. Mason Haire, ed., *Modern Organization Theory* (New York: Wiley, 1959), pp. 273–74.
25. Dorwin Cartwright and Alvin Zander, eds., *Group Dynamics* (Evanston, 1953), esp. pp. 617–19.
26. Robert T. Golembiewski, *The Small Group: An Analysis of Research Concepts and Operations* (University of Chicago Press, 1962), pp. 202–4.
27. Eliot D. Chapple and Leonard R. Sayles, *The Measure of Management* (New York, 1961), pp. 18–45.
28. W. H. Mylander, "Management by Executive Committee," *Harvard Business Review,* Vol. 33 (May, 1950), pp. 51–58.
29. See William F. Whyte, *Man and Organization* (Homewood, Ill.: Irwin, 1959), pp. 11–16.
30. Ernest Dale, "Centralization versus Decentralization," *Advanced Management,* Vol. 21 (June, 1956), p. 15.
31. Marver Bernstein, *The Job of the Federal Executive* (Washington, D.C.: Brookings Institution, 1958), pp. 34–35.

32. Hoover Commission, *Report on the General Management of the Executive Branch* (Washington, D.C., 1949), pp. 1, 3–4.
33. As, *e.g.*, in *Morgan vs. United States,* 298 U.S. 468, where the Secretary of Agriculture was rebuked for deciding a case he had not heard in person.
34. In Gaus, Leonard D. White, and Marshall E. Dimock, *The Frontiers of Public Administration* (University of Chicago Press, 1940), p. 91.
35. Nigro, *op. cit.,* p. 85.
36. Julius E. Eitington, "Injecting Realism into Classification," *Public Personnel Administration,* Vol. 15 (March, 1952), pp. 31–35.
37. Nigro, *op. cit.,* pp. 98–99.
38. Leonard D. White, *Introduction to the Study of Public Administration* (New York, 1948), p. 28.
39. Paul P. Van Riper, "The Senior Civil Service and the Career System," *Public Administration Review,* Vol. 18 (Summer, 1958), pp. 189–200.
40. Royal Commission on the Civil Service, *Introductory Factual Memorandum on the Civil Service* (London: Her Majesty's Stationery Office, 1953), p. 54.
41. A. W. Melton, *Apparatus Tests,* AAF Aviation Psychological Program, Research Report No. 4 (Washington, D.C.: Government Printing Office, 1947).
42. L. L. McQuitty, C. Wrigley, and E. L. Gaier, "An Approach to Isolating Dimensions of Job Success," *Journal of Applied Psychology,* Vol. 38 (1954), pp. 227–32.
43. E. J. McCormick, R. H. Finn, and C. D. Scherps, "Patterns of Job Requirements," *Journal of Applied Psychology,* Vol. 41 (1957), pp. 358–64.
44. Launer F. Carter, William Haythorn, and Margaret Howell, "A Further Investigation of the Criteria of Leadership," *Journal of Abnormal and Social Psychology,* Vol. 45 (1950), pp. 350–58.
45. The naming of factors is not always an easy task, for any factor normally has "loadings" of several variables. Hence the sometimes exotic designations of factorial structures.
46. Robert T. Golembiewski, "Three Styles of Leadership and Their Uses," *Personnel,* Vol. 38 (July–August, 1961), pp. 38–39.
47. Allen D. Calvin, Frederick K. Hoffman, and Edgar L. Harden, "The Effect of Intelligence and Social Atmosphere on Group Problem-Solving Behavior," *Journal of Social Psychology,* Vol. 45 (February, 1957), pp. 61–74.
48. Likert, *op. cit.,* pp. 93–94.
49. Likert, *op. cit.,* pp. 56–57.

50. *Ibid.*, p. 45.
51. *Ibid.*, p. 20.
52. Bernstein, *op. cit.*, p. 76.

EFFECTS OF FLAT AND TALL ORGANIZATION STRUCTURE*

Rocco Carzo, Jr.
John N. Yanouzas

In a laboratory experiment, tall and flat organization structures were tested for their effects on group performance. Comparisons of performance on the time taken to complete decisions showed no significant difference between tall and flat organization structures. Although it took longer to process decisions through the several levels of a tall structure, groups with flat organization took more time to resolve conflicts and to coordinate efforts. Tall organization structures were superior on two other measures of performance: profits and rate of return on revenues. Apparently the greater number of levels in the tall structure provided for more frequent evaluation of decisions and better performance on these two variables.

Empirical studies on the effects of organization structure have been mostly in field research. The purpose of this study[1] was to test the effects of organization structure in a laboratory experiment, specifically, tall and flat structures and their effects on organizational performance. A secondary purpose was to analyze the learning-curve patterns in the performance of organized groups.

THEORETICAL CONSIDERATIONS

Worthy's study (1950) of Sears Roebuck and Company was one of the first extensive and a widely accepted empirical study on the effects of flat and tall organization structure. Worthy argued that small organizations had better employee morale and productivity than large organizations. He stated that the advantages of small organizations could be incorporated into large organizations by using fewer levels of administra-

---

* Reprinted with permission of author and publisher from *Administrative Science Quarterly*, Vol. 14, No. 2 (June 1969), pp. 178–191.

tion; that is, a flat organizational structure with a wide span of supervision rather than a tall or multilevel organization with a very narrow span of supervision.

At Sears, according to Worthy, the merchandising vice president had 44 senior executives reporting directly to him. The typical retail store at Sears had "forty-odd department managers reporting to a single store manager" (1959: 109). With this organization, the manager of a Sears department store did not have time to solve all the problems and was therefore forced to delegate decision-making authority to subordinates. When managers of departments were forced to manage, they learned to manage: "They cannot be running constantly to superiors for approval of their actions; they have to make their own decisions and stand or fall by the results. In the process, they make mistakes, but that, too, contributes to their growth and maturity" (Worthy, 1959: 110). The broad, flat type of organizational structure, according to Worthy, made it possible to do a better job and allowed individuals to develop and grow in ways that were not possible under the traditional tall organizational structure.[2]

While Worthy's views have gained wide acceptance, there has been empirical evidence that raises reasonable doubts about their validity. Meltzer and Salter (1960), for example, after studying completed questionnaires from 75 percent of all physiological scientists working in organizations in the United States, had serious doubts about the negative relationship between the number of organizational levels and productivity as stated by Worthy. A questionnaire study by Porter and Lawler (1964), on managerial attitudes, seemed to indicate that a tall structure was better in producing security and satisfaction of social needs, while a flat structure was better for self-actualization. Both studies concluded that there is no simple relationship between structure and performance and that a flat organization structure was not unequivocally superior to a tall organization structure. While these questionnaire studies do not settle the issues, they raise enough questions about the relation of structure and productivity to indicate a need for further research.

The need for further research is also indicated by the controversy that persists over the so-called principle of "span of supervision" or "span of control." Fayol (1949), Hamilton (1921) and Urwick (1956), to name only a few, have argued that man's available energy, knowledge, time and abilities are confined to narrow limits, he is unable to supervise the work of more than a few subordinates successfully. Graicunas (1937) hypothesized that the number of possible relationships that a supervisor might be required to manage increased exponentially with an arithmetic increase in the number of subordinates assigned directly to him. The conclusion, in traditional theory, is that supervisors should have a narrow span of supervision. Some writers are very specific about this prescription, as for example, "No supervisor can supervise directly the work of more than five or, at the most, six subordinates *whose work interlocks*" Urwick, (1956: 41).

The critics of the span-of-supervision principle emphasize that other, and perhaps more difficult, problems are created when the number of subordinates assigned to an executive is limited to a very few. For example, as an organization reduces the number of subordinates reporting to supervisors, it creates a tall organization by increasing the number of supervisory levels and supervisors. Corresponding administrative expenses for executive salaries, office space, and secretarial assistance also increase. Also, an increase in supervisory levels is said to cause communication problems. Communications in an organization are subject to different interpretation at each level. The more levels there are in an organization, the greater is the likelihood of distortion, so that the final recipient of a communication may get the wrong message or wrong emphasis. In addition, it takes longer to process information through the many levels of a tall structure. Many levels of supervision in an organization also dilute the influence of the most senior executive. The resulting administrative distance between top and lower-line officials may have a demoralizing effect on the latter. The critics essentially say that the decision and communication processes of a tall organization take longer and are of poorer quality than the processes of a flat organization.

Some of the hypothesized distortions in communications can be explained by the status differences of formal organization. The supervisor has two responsibilities, which conflict with each other. His decision-making responsibility requires that he be given adequate information by subordinates. However, his responsibility for evaluating the performance of subordinates means that he likely gets information that is not adequate or correct (Read, 1962). According to Hoslett, "The subordinate tends to tell his supervisor what the latter is interested in, not to disclose what he doesn't want to hear, and to cover up problems and mistakes which may reflect adversely on the subordinate. He tends to tell the boss those things which will enhance his position and indicate his success in meeting the problems of the day" (1951: 109). In addition to this distortion in the upward flow of communication, Hoslett points out that this status relationship creates a distortion in the downward flow of communication. In his efforts to maintain the status difference, the supervisor is not candid in his relationships with subordinates. He does not wish to admit mistakes or reveal conditions which would reflect adversely on his ability and judgment: "To do so would undermine his position as a superior being in the formal organization" (Hoslett, 1951: 109).

As a solution to the problems caused by the tall organization with its narrow spans and many levels of supervision, critics such as Worthy offer the flat organization with relatively wide spans and few levels of supervision. However, there has been little research evidence to support the cases for either the flat or tall organization.

The field studies cited indicate that different organization structures produce significant differences in performance. Most of the literature on the theory of formal organization postulates that different structural arrangements produce significant differences in performance. However, several laboratory experiments on the effects of communication networks seem to indicate that the differences in performance on at least one variable, "time to complete an assigned task," are not significant.

One of the first to indicate nonsignificant differences in performance was the study by Guetzkow and Simon (1955). This research effort was a refinement of the empirical work of Leavitt (1951), who found that groups working in a wheel network took less time to complete tests than groups in a circle network. Guetzkow and Simon made a distinction between: "(a) the effects of communication restrictions upon performance of the operating tasks; and (b) the effects of the restrictions upon a group's ability to organize itself for such performance" (1955: 233). The results supported their hypothesis that communication restrictions would only indirectly affect the efficiency with which the task was performed by "influencing the ability of the members to organize themselves for optimum performance in their line operation" (Guetzkow and Simon, 1955: 238). Although different network groups had varying degrees of difficulty in achieving efficient organizational arrangements, there was no significant difference in time taken to complete the task after they reached an optimum organization.

If, as Guetzkow and Simon concluded, differences in performance were really a reflection of differences in the groups' ability to organize, then it should be possible to impose an organization structure, that is, eliminate the necessity for organizing, and produce nonsignificant performance results under different communication structures.

This possibility was realized in experiments by Carzo (1963), Yanouzas (1963) and Cain (1964). The purpose of these studies was to determine the effects of communication restrictions on group performance when an organization was imposed on the group. A seven-man group had a definite hierarchy of three levels. Each position in the organization had a specialized task and a title that was descriptive of the task. The central position, located at the top of the hierarchy, was occupied by a member responsible for coordinating all other tasks in the organization and making final decisions on the assigned problem from an overall analysis. Subordinate managers were responsible for decision making in their particular area of specialization.

Two different communication structures were tested. There was a highly restricted communication net called a "tight" structure in which subjects were allowed to communicate only through a chain of command. Communication under a less restricted loose structure was total; that is, each subject was allowed to communicate with every other member of the group.

During the early periods, it was found that the loosely structured groups were the fastest in time taken to make decisions, while the tightly structured groups showed a faster learning rate. During the second half of the experiment, there was no significant difference between the groups for the time required to make decisions. Therefore, even when organizing efforts were made unnecessary, groups still displayed the kind of behavior found by Guetzkow and Simon.

The present study is a modification of the studies just reported. In the previous experiments, the hierarchical relationships were held constant, while different communication networks were tested. In this study the communication network was the same for all groups, while two different hierarchies were tested, a flat structure and a tall structure, with each member of a group allowed to communicate with every other member.

RESEARCH DESIGN

Each organization had 15 members, the group size being arbitrarily determined by the researchers. The tall structure had four levels and a span of supervision of two. The subjects were seated spatially in a manner that approximated the relationships shown in the chart (Figure 1a). The flat structure had two levels, with all positions connected directly to the president's position, that is, the president had a span of supervision of 14 (Figure 1b). The subordinate subjects were seated in a semi-circle, each one approximately equidistant from the president.

Every position in each organization had a specialized task and a title that was descriptive of and commensurate with the task. There was a definite hierarchy in each organization with the president's office as the central position at the top of the hierarchy. The president was responsible for coordinating all tasks and for making final decisions on the assigned problem from an overall analysis. All subordinates to the president were responsible for decision making in particular market areas. The role of each subject was prescribed, but was different in the two organizations because the flat structure had no intermediate levels of supervision, although the overall size and task assigned were the same as in the tall structure.

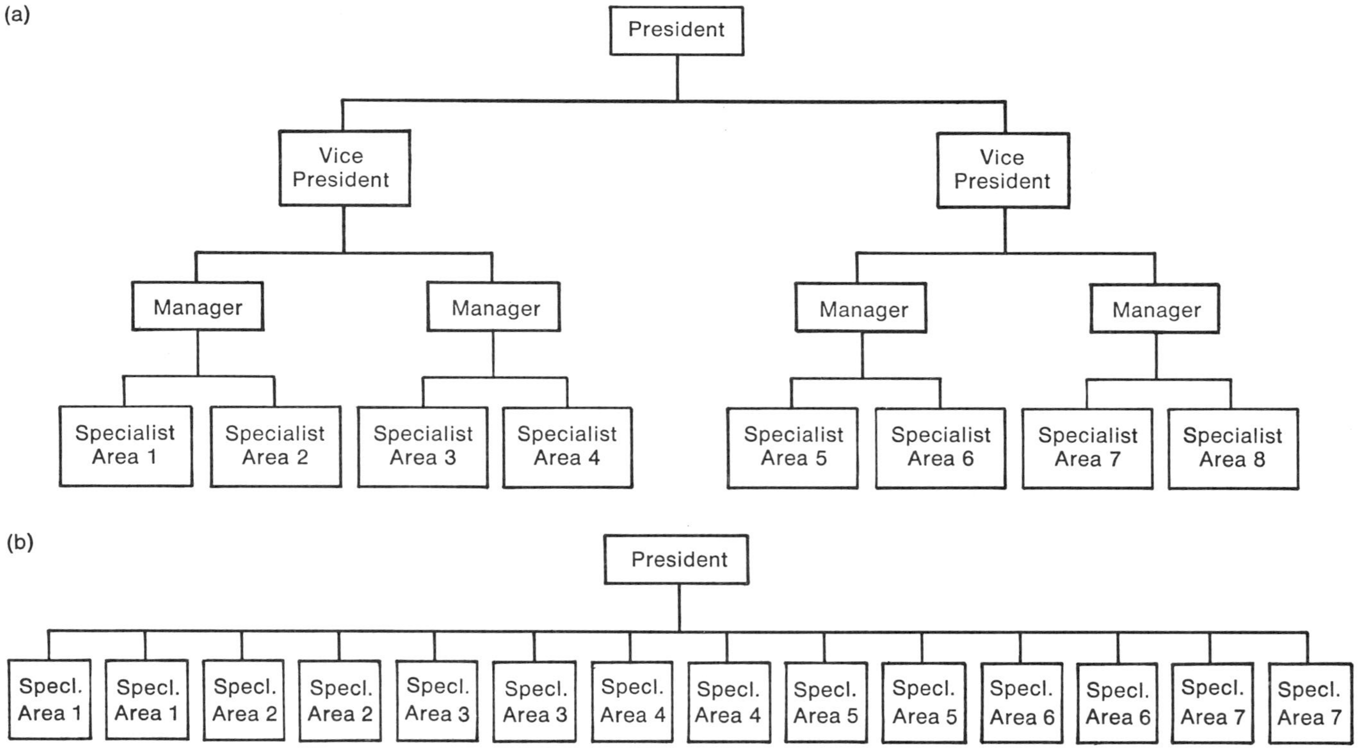

FIGURE 1
Organization Chart of (A) Tall Organization and (B) Flat Organization

Experimental Task

The task of the experiment required that organization produce ordering decisions in limited time periods. The organization sold one product in several market areas. Individual tasks were assigned, so that each market area received specialized attention. The subjects assigned to a market area were instructed to make a decision or recommendation on how much to order for that area. After this decision was made, it was passed up to the next higher level in the organization. The president was responsible for making a final decision for each area. He could accept the recommended decisions made at the lower levels or adjust the recommendations according to what he thought was best for the organization as a whole.

Subjects were asked to think of the organization as a business firm trying to produce decisions on a quantity of goods to order from its suppliers. Before making a decision on what to order, organization members first had to estimate demand. In practice, then, the task had two phases; the first phase involved a demand decision, and the second phase involved an ordering decision.

At the beginning of the experiment, each member of the organization was given a record of demand. The record contained a number of demand quantities, each with a probability of occurrence. For example, a hypothetical distribution for a specific market area might appear as shown in Table 1. The probability distribution was applicable in each decision period; that is, demand was a random variable with a given probability distribution.

At higher levels, organization members had more inclusive probability distributions than at lower levels. Given this information, higher-level members were able to evaluate and adjust decisions made at lower levels. The president, for example, had a probability distribution that covered all the possible demand quantities for all market areas; so that he had the necessary data to make overall evaluations and decisions.

After estimating demand, subjects made the ordering decision. In making the ordering decision, they were asked to consider the following: (1) an estimate of demand, (2) inventories left from the previous period, (3) back orders from the previous period, and (4) a capacity restriction on the amount that could be ordered from suppliers. The capacity restriction applied only to the amount ordered by the president.

TABLE 1
Example of Record of Demand for a Market Area

Demand Quantity	7	8	9	10	11	12
Probability of occurrence	0.10	0.15	0.25	0.20	0.15	0.15

Organization members at lower levels could order any amount they thought appropriate for their respective areas. The president then had to adjust the amounts recommended for the areas, so that the total amount ordered by the organization was less than or equal to the capacity of suppliers.

The time simulated in the experiment was three years, each year consisting of 20 periods. The organization had to produce one decision per period. The decision time for each period could not exceed 20 minutes. This limitation applied to the whole organization; that is, the president had to indicate the ordering decision within 20 minutes after the completion of the previous decision. If a decision had not been completed within the 20 minutes maximum, the decision made by the president in the previous period was used. If a decision was made in less than 20 minutes, the organization proceeded to the next decision.

Payoffs to Subjects

Subjects were guaranteed an hourly wage of $1.50. They could earn more than this minimum wage, however, based upon their performance in the experiment. A bonus was given according to how effectively the organization as a whole performed, and was equally distributed to all members of the organization. It was possible for the organization to receive negative points for poor performance, but in no event could any member earn less than $1.50 per hour.

The organization was evaluated on the basis of performance over the entire year or 20-decision period. Revenues and costs were accumulated for the 20-decision periods, and the difference was the profit for the year. There was a single measure of performance (as far as subjects were concerned), the rate of return on sales revenue; for example:

Revenue for the year (20 periods)	$50.00
Costs for the year (20 periods)	40.00
Profit for the year	$10.00

Rate of return on sales revenue was ($10/$50) × 100 = 20 per cent.

Bonuses were paid on the basis of $0.70 per member for each percentage point earned on sales revenue. Thus, in the above example, each member of the organization would receive 20 percentage points times $0.70, or $14.00. The maximum that would be paid for any year was set at $15.00 per person. The minimum, as previously indicated, was the guaranteed $1.50 per hour rate. Subjects received the largest of the two amounts, that is, between the bonus and guaranteed rate. In the example, if the 20 decision periods had lasted four hours, each subject would receive $14.00 instead of the guaranteed amount of $6.00.

There was also a bonus to the organization for taking less than the allotted 20 minutes to submit a decision. Revenues were increased by \$0.10 for each minute less than the 20 minutes allowed. This bonus was added to the revenue that resulted from each decision and, therefore, contributed to the total revenue for the entire 20 decision periods.

Communication and Decision Process

Although each member of the organizations could communicate with any other member, there were certain procedures, specified by the researchers, which had to be followed to complete the experimental task.

One form, called the "memory form" was used by subjects to evaluate alternatives, to transmit recommended order quantities, and to record the results of the final decision made by the president. The form had 20 rows, one for each decision period of the simulated year. The columns of the form permitted entries for: demand, amount ordered, backorders, and inventories, all stated in physical units. From this record, subjects could make other entries under the column headings of: revenue, cost of goods sold, inventory cost, and backorder cost. There was also a column for entries of bonuses earned on decisions that took less than 20 minutes. This bonus, plus revenues, minus all costs made up the entries under the column heading, profit. Thus, during the experiment, this form gave subjects a visual display of past performance; it provided a means of evaluating alternative order quantities; and it was used as a device for transmitting information.

The only other form possessed by subjects was the probability distribution of demand quantities illustrated in Table 1. Every decision began with this form as subjects attempted to estimate demand for a period.

Flat structure. As illustrated in Figure 2, the decision and communication process in the flat structure began with an estimate of demand. At the same time that subordinates 2 through 15 were estimating demand for their respective areas, the president was making an over-all demand estimate. The demand estimate and inventory and back order considerations served as a basis for evaluating alternatives and making decisions on the quantity to order. Subordinates recorded their decisions on the memory form and transmitted them to the president. After receiving these recommendations, the president compared their total with his own decision and the capacity restriction, and reconciled the differences by conferring with subordinates. His final decision was recorded and transmitted to the researcher, who then revealed actual demand, computed back orders, inventories, and units sold in each area, and the revenue, costs, and profits for the total organization on a blackboard visible to all members. From this information, organization members computed revenues, costs and profits for their respective market areas

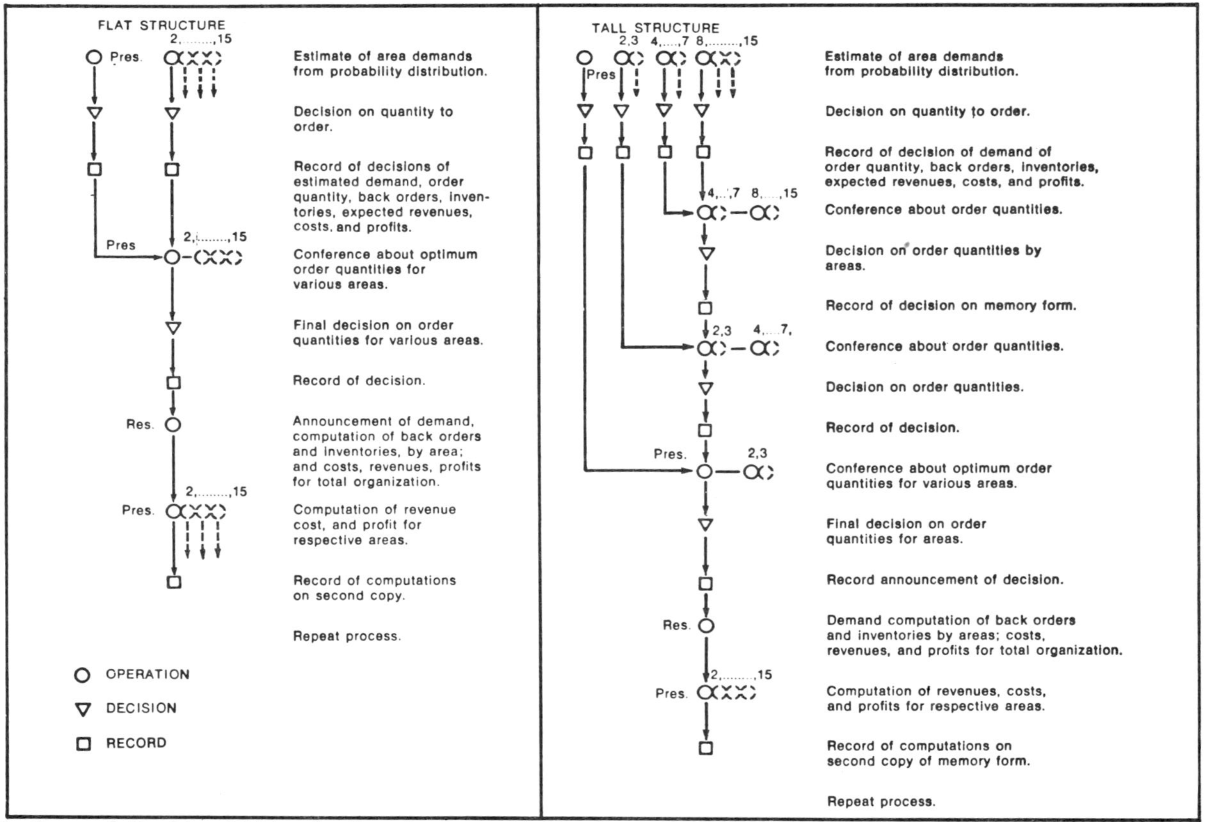

FIGURE 2
Procedure for Communication and Decision Making in Organizations with Flat Structure and Tall Structure

on another copy of the memory form. The process was then repeated for the next decision period.

Tall structure. Figure 2 also shows that the communication and decision process in the tall structure was more complex than that in the flat structure. At the same time that subordinates 8 through 15 were estimating demand for their respective areas, intermediate supervisors 4 through 7, and 2 and 3, and the president were making more comprehensive demand estimates. The initial decision on the quantity to order for market areas was successively evaluated at each level of the organization until the president, in consultation with intermediate supervisors 2 and 3, made the final decision. Thereafter, the process was identical to the process of the flat structure, until it began again for the next decision period.

Experimental Design

The experimental design for this project was a factorial treatment with two independent variables, one of these being organizational structure. The two levels on this variable were the tall structure and the flat structure.

It was assumed that performance would change as subjects gained experience with the experimental task, therefore, organizational experience was considered the other independent variable. Furthermore, it was expected that experience would be a factor in the outcome of each decision period. Thus, each of the 60 decision periods or trials was considered as a level of the independent variable, organizational experience.

Hypotheses

Three measures of the dependent variable were used for this experiment. Decision time, the time taken by the group to make decisions, was considered as an indicator of the output of the system. The other two measures, profits and rate of return on sales revenue, were considered as indicators of the quality of the decision output of the system.

Industrial practice, as well as scientific research, has established that individuals and organized groups improve their performance after repeated exposure to a given task. Experiments with small groups such as those reported by Guetzkow and Simon (1955), Carzo (1963), Yanouzas (1963), Cain (1964), and Jones (1966) show a learning curve similar to that found in several industries (especially the aircraft industry: Andress, (1954), that is, an exponential decay function on the time taken to make decisions. This leads to the first hypothesis:

Hypothesis 1. As subjects gain experience with the experimental task, their performance, as measured by the time taken to make decisions, displays a pattern of improvement; i.e., a learning curve.

In addition, these same small-group experiments, seem to indicate that the way groups are organized has no significant effect upon the pattern of improvement in time required to make decisions; therefore:

Hypothesis 2. There is no significant difference in the patterns of improvement or learning curves, in decision time for different structures.

With respect to performance over all trials, past experience (e.g., Leavitt and Shaw) seems to indicate that different communication nets do produce significant differences in the time required to make decisions. On simple problems, Leavitt (1951) found that groups in a wheel pattern with one person in a central position completed tasks faster than groups in a circle pattern where all subjects were in equal positions. On complex problems, Shaw (1954) found that groups in the circle arrangement took less time to solve problems than groups in the wheel arrangement. Since the communication nets of this experiment were the same for all groups; that is, all groups used an "all channel" net, and assuming that structure has no effect on the time variable,[3] there should be no significant difference in the time required to make decisions; therefore:

Hypothesis 3. There is no difference in overall performance as measured by time taken to make decisions for the different structures.

The intermediate levels of a tall structure provide for repeated evaluation of decisions and, therefore, for more analysis than in a flat structure; consequently, the decisions should be better than decisions in flat structures. Specifically for this experiment, then, one can hypothesize as follows:

Hypothesis 4. Groups operating under a tall structure display better overall performance, as measured by profits and rate of return on sales revenue, than groups performing under a flat structure.

The quality of performance should also show a "learning-curve" effect, since there would be a pattern of improvement as subjects gained greater experience with the task; therefore:

Hypothesis 5. As subjects gain experience with the experimental task, their performance, as measured by profits and rate of return on sales, shows a pattern of improvement; that is a learning curve.

Since the elements of the learning situation, that is, stimulus and reinforcement were not a function of structure but of the experimental task, and since the experimental task was the same for all groups, structure should not have a significant effect on the pattern of improvement; therefore:

Hypothesis 6. There is no difference in the pattern of improvement (learning curve) of profits and rate of return on sales for the different structures.

Test of Design

Subjects were selected randomly from the male, junior and senior class enrollments of the College of Business Administration at The Pennsylvania State University. The flat and tall structures were assigned to the groups on a random basis. Four different groups of 15 subjects were selected, with two groups performing under each structure. Subjects were then assigned to each of the fifteen positions in the experimental organization on the basis of grade-point averages. Subjects with the highest grades were assigned to the president's position, the next highest to positions at the second level, the next highest to positions at the third level, and so on, until all positions were filled. It was easier to make assignments in the flat structure, since there were only two levels of organization.

Each group was tested on three successive evenings. For example, if a group was tested on a Monday evening, it would be tested on Tuesday and Wednesday evenings of the same week. Each group made twenty decisions in each evening. The problems for the second and third evenings were exactly the same as those faced by the group in the first evening.

Use of the same problems on successive evenings served as a basis for establishing the reliability of the testing instrument. An analysis of variance was used to estimate reliability, and gave the following coefficients of reliability on each of the performance variables: decision time, 0.954; profits, 0.837; rate of return on sales revenue, 0.831. An analysis of variance was also used to estimate validity. The performance of the groups operating under each structure was compared to determine whether the effect of structure was uniform. The results showed that the experiment was valid and that variations in performance of groups under their respective structures could reasonably be ascribed to chance.

RESULTS

For the variable, organizational structure, the focus was on whether it affected performance over all trials; for the variable, organizational experience, however, the focus was on the effect over successive trials. It was assumed that differences in performance found between trials were a result of difference in the amount of practice.[4] This learning effect is examined below in terms of variance, trend of means, degree of curva-

TABLE 2
Summary of Analysis of Variance for Time, Profits, and Rate of Return

VARIABLES	*SS*	*d.f.*	*Mean Square*	*Ratio F*
Time				
Structures	0.88	1	0.88	0.12
Error (a)	15.05	2	7.53	—
Trials	992.64	59	16.82	5.32*
Structures × Trials	205.19	59	3.48	1.10
Error (b)	372.57	118	3.16	—
Profits				
Structures	477.43	1	477.43	8.11†
Error (a)	117.74	2	58.87	—
Trials	4809.54	59	81.52	7.89*
Structures × Trials	2677.48	59	45.38	4.39*
Error (b)	1218.81	118	10.33	—
Rate of Return				
Structures	2000.46	1	2000.46	7.47‡
Errors (a)	535.64	2	267.82	—
Trials	23633.98	59	400.58	7.92*
Structures × Trials	13448.25	59	227.94	4.45*
Error (b)	6045.24	118	51.23	—

* Significant at 0.01 level
† Significant at 0.12 level
‡ Significant at 0.14 level
Error (a) is variation due to Trials × groups within structures
Error (b) is variation due to Trials × groups within structures

ture, and cumulative average performance. The results of the analysis of variance for the performance variables are summarized in Table 2.

Decision Time

Decision time was defined as the amount of time required by a group to complete a communication and decision process. A decision period started when the researchers revealed the actual demand and the results of a previous ordering decision; that is, revenue, costs, and profits, and the inventory and back orders that resulted from the previous decision. The decision period ended when the president indicated the amount ordered by the organization.

The analysis of variance summarized in Table 2 indicates that the F ratio for the structure effect on decision time is not significant. Thus, when decision time is analyzed over all the trials (decision periods), there is no significant difference for the different structures. This finding supports Hypothesis 3.

The F ratio for the effect of trials (decision periods) on decision time is significant; that is, when performance is analyzed over the two struc-

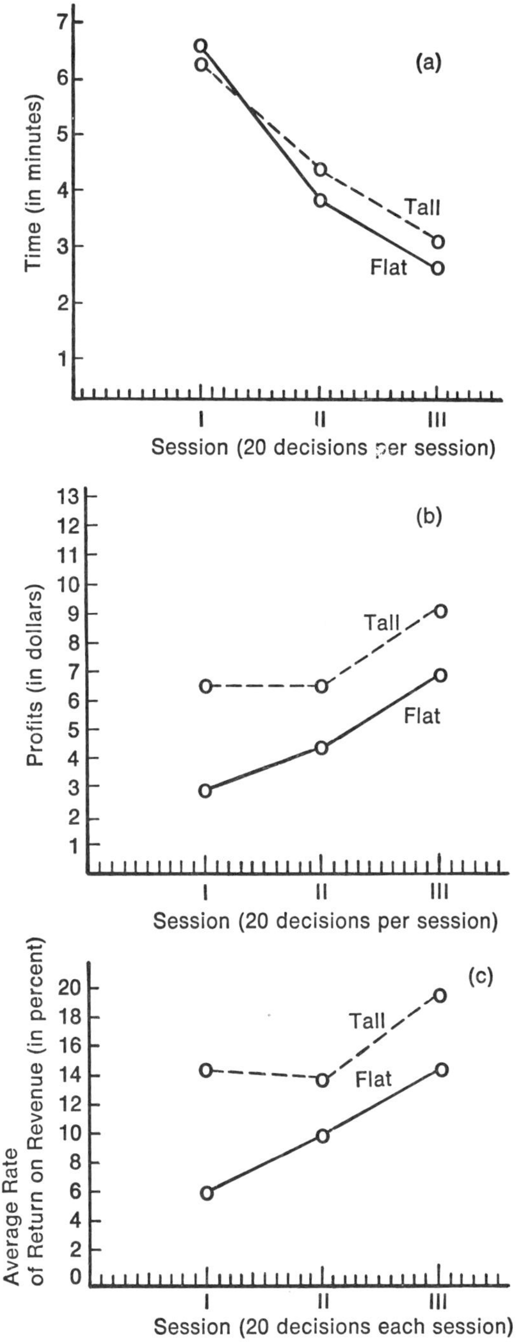

FIGURE 3
For Each Session; (A) Average Decision Time; (B) Average Profits; (C) Average Rate of Return

TABLE 3
Analysis of Variance for Linear and Quadratic Components on Decision Time, Profits, and Rate of Return

TRIALS	*SS*	*d.f.*	*Mean Square*	*F Ratio*
Time				
Linear Component	533.61	1	533.61	168.86*
Structures × Trials	9.15	1	9.15	2.90
Quadratic Component	136.87	1	136.87	43.31*
Structure × Trials	1.18	1	1.18	0.37
Higher-Order	322.16	57		
Structure × Trials	195.92	57		
Error (b)	372.57	118	3.16	—
Profits				
Linear Component	490.96	1	490.96	47.53*
Structures × Trials	7.98	1	7.98	0.77
Quadratic Component	352.77	1	325.77	34.15*
Structures × Trials	108.41	1	108.41	10.50*
Higher-Order	3965.81	57		
Structures × Trials	2561.09	57		
Error (b)	1218.81	118	10.33	
Rate of Return				
Linear Component	2587.0	1	2587.0	50.50*
Structures × Trials	75.53	1	75.53	1.48
Quadratic Component	1331.17	1	1331.17	25.98*
Structures × Trials	795.77	1	795.77	15.53*
Higher Order	19715.81	57		
Structures × Trials	12576.95	57		
Error (b)	6045.24	118	51.23	

* Significant at 0.01 level
Error (b) is variation due to Trials × groups within structures.

tures, there is a significant difference for the different trials. This finding indicates that performance changed as the result of practice or experience with the experimental task. When the decision times were averaged for each session (20 decisions for each session) and plotted, as shown in Figure 3a, the trend is downward and both curves appear to have a quadratic component. An analysis of variance of the trends, summarized in Table 3, indicates significant linear and quadratic components. The findings of a downward trend and a quadratic component support Hypothesis 1.

Next, it is possible to determine if the trend of means of the trials for the two structures is of the same form. The interaction effect, as shown in Table 2, is not significant; that is, the mean square, structure × trials, indicates that the learning curves for the flat and tall structures are of the same form. This finding supports Hypothesis 2.

The conformity of the learning curves is supported by the nonsignificant interaction effect, shown in Table 3, for the linear component and for the quadratic component of the trends for the two structures. The similarity of the learning curves is illustrated even more vividly when decision times are averaged cumulatively and plotted as shown in Figure 4a.

Profits

Profit was defined as the difference between total revenues and total costs. Table 2, indicates that when profits are analyzed over all the trials, there is a significant difference for the different structures. This result supports Hypothesis 4. Furthermore, when profits are analyzed over the two structures, there is a significant difference for the different trials. This finding indicates that there was also a significant change in profits as a result of experience with the experimental task. When profits were averaged for each session (20 decisions for each session) and plotted, as shown in Figure 3b, the trend is upward, and both curves seem to have a quadratic component. The analysis of variance of the trends (Table 3), indicates significant linear and quadratic components. The finding of an upward trend and a quadratic component supports Hypothesis 5. The interaction effect (Table 2), is significant, indicating that the trend of means for trials for the two structures is of a different form. This result does not support Hypothesis 6. The value of F in Table 3 indicates that the quadratic components of the trends for the two structures differ significantly. The curves for cumulative average profits are plotted in Figure 4b.

Rate of Return

Rate of return on sales revenue was defined as the ratio of profits to sales revenue. The results for this were almost identical to the results found on profits; and since rate of return is a relative measure, it is considered as the more important indicator of over-all group performance.

The analysis of variance (Table 2), indicates a significant structure effect. This result supports Hypothesis 4. Table 2, also indicates that there is a significant trials effect. Thus, as group gained greater experience with the experimental task, they improved their performance significantly on the rate of return. When the results for the rate of return are averaged for each session and plotted (Figure 3c), the trend is upward and both curves seem to have a quadratic component. The analysis of variance for the rate of return (Table 3), indicates both a significant linear component and a significant quadratic component. This result supports Hypothesis 5. The form of the two curves are significantly different as indicated by the significant interaction effect in Table 2. This

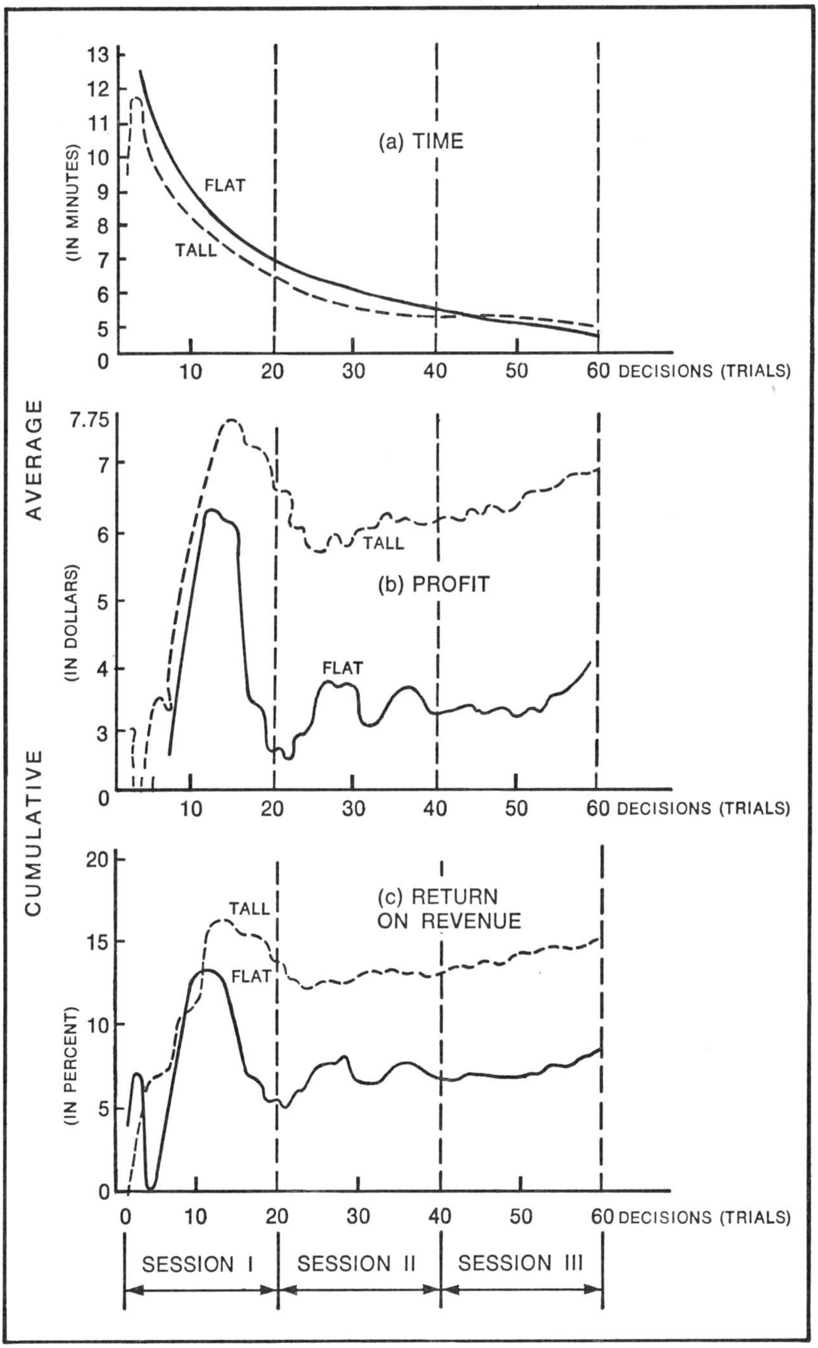

FIGURE 4

Trials (decision periods) 1–60: (A) Cumulative Average Decision Times, (B) Cumulative Average Profits; (C) Cumulative Average Rate of Return on Revenues result does not support Hypothesis 6. The F value in Table 3 indicates that the quadratic component of the trends for the two structures differ significantly. The cumulative average curves are shown in Figure 4c.

DISCUSSION

As expected from the results of past experiments and industrial practice with organized groups, subjects performing under the organizational structures of this experiment displayed a "learning-curve" behavior. Analysis of the data for this experiment indicates that this change in behavior was a result of practice with the experimental task. As subjects gained experience with the task, they improved their performance.

Decision Time

Although experience affected behavior on the time variable, organizational structure had no significant effect on the time taken to make decisions or on the pattern of improvement. The absence of a structure effect on decision time does not seem to agree with the arguments presented earlier, that the decision and communication processes of the tall organization take longer than the processes of the flat organization. The arguments and their applicability to this experiment are summarized below.

First, the greater number of levels between the top and bottom echelons in a tall structure interrupts the flow of information more frequently than in a flat structure in which there is a direct connection between top and bottom echelons. The delays caused by these interruptions in the tall structure supposedly extend the time required for decision making beyond that which is required by the flat structure. This argument was not supported by the results of this experiment.

Apparently, the disadvantages of a wide span of supervision in the flat structure offset the advantages of direct links between top and bottom echelons. The difficulties of a flat structure seemed to be most evident when the president rejected or altered the recommendations of subordinates and attempted to make a final decision on how to allocate orders among the seven market areas. After receiving recommendations from his 14 subordinates on how much to order in each market area, the president had to reconcile the total of recommended orders with the capacity restriction. Since total recommendations always exceeded capacity, the president was forced to scale down the requests of subordinates. Invariably, this led to much discussion with area specialists and debate among them.

In the tall structure there was the same problem of reconciling total recommendations with the capacity restriction; but the discussions were much more orderly and resolution was faster because the president and intermediate supervisors had to deal with only two subordinates. Also, many of the problems of allocation were resolved for the president as the recommendations filtered through the levels of the tall structure. The absence of a difference on the time variable, then, may be explained partly by the fact that the greater time required for decisions to pass through several levels of a tall structure is offset by the time required to resolve differences and coordinate the efforts of many subordinates in a flat structure.

Another reason given for impediments in the flow of information is the status differences among participants at different levels in the organization. It was argued that he has difficulty in obtaining information, because subordinates, realizing that he evaluates their performance, tend to report only information favorable to them. Such inadequate information flows tend to delay decision processes. For example, when problems at lower levels are not reported to higher-level officials, the decisions required to solve the problems will not be made. If information is inadequate, the decision maker must spend more time gathering the required information; if it is inaccurate, then decisions may be inappropriate.

The problem of status difference is more prevalent in tall structures, since there are more levels. Decision and communication processes should, therefore, require more time in a tall structure than a flat structure. However, in this experiment, there were practically no status differences between the levels of the organizations. Although the president and intermediate supervisors were placed in a higher position with regard to the importance of their jobs, they were not required to evaluate the performance of subordinates. Also, rewards were not distributed to members on the basis of the positions they occupied in the organization; rewards for organizational performance were distributed equally to each member of the organization.

The difficulties of processing information freely, where there are a number of levels and status differences, apply to downward communications as well as to upward communications. Again, the tall structure is supposed to be at a disadvantage. However, in the experiment this disadvantage was removed by providing instant feedback of results to all levels simultaneously. As soon as the president reported his decision, the researchers presented the results of this decision on a blackboard visible to all subjects; therefore, there was little need for downward communications in the experiment.

On the basis that status differences of the tall structure would be unimportant and that the advantage of a direct link between top and bottom echelons would be counteracted by the variety of activity in the flat structure, the researchers hypothesized, as stated in Hypothesis 3, that structure would not have a differential effect on average performance as measured by time required to make decisions. As noted, this hypothesis as well as Hypothesis 2 which stated that the learning curves would have the same form, were supported by the results.

Profits and Rate of Return

On the two performance variables that were considered to be indicators of the quality of decisions, the groups displayed different patterns on each trial. As illustrated in Figures 4b and c, performance of the groups under each structure on the first 20 trials (Session I), was quite erratic. It appears as though they were going through a trial-and-error process in familiarizing themselves with the problem. From trials 21 through 40 (Session II), they appear to have learned and to have stabilized their performance. Thereafter, in trials 41 through 60, performance steadily improved. Considering their performance on Sessions I and II, and the fact that there was a limit on profits (cost of goods sold was fixed at 60 percent of each sales dollar), it is reasonable to assume that if the groups had continued for more than 60 decisions, their performance would have stabilized again or at least approach the limit.

On these two variables, there was a significant difference between the performance of the groups operating under the flat structure and those operating under the tall structure. The superior performance of the groups under the tall structure may be explained by the fact that their decisions were subjected to more analysis than the decisions of the groups under the flat structure. The intermediate supervisory levels apparently were an advantage to groups with the tall structure. They provided the means for repeated evaluation of decisions, and the output was of much better quality than the output of groups in the flat structure.

In addition, the narrow span of supervision in the tall structure permitted a much more orderly decision and communication process. Freed from the burdens that arise from having many subordinates, decision makers appeared to be able to develop a better understanding of the problem. Although the performance of groups with a tall structure was significantly better than with a flat structure, the design of the experiment did not include structural characteristics that seem to cause problems in communication, such as, status differences.

SUMMARY

In this study, four different groups of 15 subjects were organized—two under a flat structure and two under a tall structure. The flat organization structure had two levels, with 14 subordinates reporting directly to the president. The tall structure had four levels, with each supervisor limited to two subordinates. Each position had an assigned task which required decisions on a market-order problem. The president was responsible for making an over-all decision for the organization, which he made after receiving recommendations from subordinates on the amounts to order. His main task was to reconcile differences among recommended orders, a capacity restriction, and his own estimates of optimum order quantities. Group performance was measured on three variables: time taken to complete decisions, profits, and rate of return on sales revenue.

On all three performance variables, groups under each structure showed patterns of improvement as they gained experience with the experimental task. On the time variable, the pattern of improvement was not significantly different for the two structures; the patterns for decision time appeared to follow a function similar to learning curves found in industrial settings. For each structure, patterns for profits and rate of return on sales revenue was erratic on the first 20 decisions, and transient (that is, steadily improving on the stable pattern) on the third 20 decisions.

Structure had no significant effect on the decision time. This result was attributed to counteracting forces in the flat structure and to the elimination of some of the barriers to communication in the tall structure.

Structure did have a significant effect on performance as measured by profits and rate of return on sales revenue. Groups under the tall structure showed significantly better performance than groups under the flat structure. This result was explained by the fact that the tall structure, with a greater number of levels, allowed group members to evaluate decisions more frequently, and that the narrow span of supervision provided for a more orderly decision process.

NOTES

1. This research was supported by research grants from the Ford Foundation and two units of The Pennsylvania State University; the Central Fund for Research and the Center for Research of the College of Business Administration. The authors wish to acknowledge their indebtedness to Mr. Harsha B. Desai of The Pennsylvania State University, who collaborated on the formulation, implementation, and analysis of this study.
2. Support for Worthy's conclusions was found in a small-group study by Jones (1966).

3. The basis for this assumption is explained in the "Discussion" section.
4. We use "trend analysis" as discussed by Edwards (1960: 244–250).

REFERENCES

Andress, Frank J.
1954 "The learning curve as a production tool." Harvard Business Review, 32: 88.

Cain, Geraldine S.
1964 "Some effects of organization structure on problem solving." Unpublished Doctoral Dissertation, The Pennsylvania State University.

Carzo, Rocco, Jr.
1963 "Some effects of organization structure on group effectiveness." Administrative Science Quarterly, 7: 393–424.

Edwards, Allen L.
1960 Experimental Design in Psychological Research. New York: Holt, Rinehart and Winston.

Fayol, Henri
1949 General and Industrial Management. London: Sir Issac Pitman.

Graicunas, V. A.
1937 "Relationship in organization." Pp. 52–57 in Luther Gulick and Lyndall F. Urwick (eds.), Papers on the Science of Administration. New York: Institute of Public Administration.

Guetzkow, Harold, and Herbert A. Simon
1955 "The impact of certain communication nets upon organization and performance in task-oriented groups." Management Science, 1: 233–250.

Hamilton, Sir Ian
1921 The Soul and Body of an Army. New York: George H. Doran.

Hoslett, Schuyler Dean
1951 "Barriers to communication." Personnel. 28: 109.

Jones, Halsey R.
1966 "The effects of the number of organization levels upon selected aspects of organization performance." Unpublished Doctoral Dissertation, The Pennsylvania State University.

Leavitt, Harold J.
1951 "Some effects of certain communication patterns on group performance." Journal of Abnormal and Social Psychology, 46: 38–50.

Meltzer, Leo and James Salter
1960 "Organizational structure, and the performance and job satisfactions of physiologists." American Sociological Review, 27: 351–362.
Porter, L. W., and E. E. Lawler, III
1964 "The effects of 'tall' versus 'flat' organization structures on managerial satisfaction." Personnel Psychology, 17: 135–148.
Read, William H.
1962 "Upward communication in industrial hierarchies." Human Relations, 15: 3–15.
Shaw, Marvin E.
1954 "Some effects of problem complexity upon problem solution efficiency in different communication nets." Journal of Experimental Psychology. 48: 211–217.
Urwick, Lyndall F.
1956 "The manager's span of control." Harvard Business Review, 34: 39–47.
Worthy, James C.
1950 "Organizational structure and employee morale." American Sociological Review, 15: 169–179.
1959 Big Business and Free Man. New York: Harper.
Yanouzas, John N.
1963 "The relationship of some organization variables to the performance of decision groups." Unpublished Doctoral Dissertation, The Pennsylvania State University.

ORGANIZATIONAL DESIGN: A CONTINGENCY APPROACH*

Don Hellriegel
John W. Slocum, Jr.

For those firms that operate in a stable environment—an unchanging technology and a certain market—a mechanistic management system is efficient. A great many corporations, however, must have a flexible organizational structure, which can adapt to constant changes in technology and fluctuations in the market. These firms are often characterized by their organic approach to management design. In this article,

* Reprinted with permission of author and publisher from *Business Horizons*, Vol. 16, No. 2 (April 1973), pp. 59–68. Copyright, 1973, by the Foundation for the School of Business at Indiana University. Reprinted by permission.

the authors develop a model for organizational design based on the variables of internal needs and external conditions and illustrate their model with nationally known firms as examples. The model's quadrants are: high uncertainty/low integration; high uncertainty/high integration; high certainty/low integration; and high certainty/high integration.

During the past several years, many approaches incorporating open systems concepts have been advanced in organizational design. Underlying these new approaches is the idea that the internal functioning of an organization must be consistent with the demands of the organization's tasks, market environment, and technological capabilities and with the needs of its members if the organization is to be effective. Rather than searching for the one best way to organize, these approaches seem to be leading to the development of a situational theory of organizational design. Different environmental conditions external to the firm necessitate different organizational relationships within it.

This approach raises several questions. Is the organizational structure necessary to operate successfully in the automobile industry different from that needed in the fast-food-service industry? Is there one best way to structure and administer organizations by which the major economic criteria (return on investment, profit or loss, and net worth) can be reasonably satisfied? Given the task of organizing a functional unit—such as a research and development laboratory—how can we motivate its personnel to work effectively? What system of management should be adopted?

The need for answering these questions is imperative if an effective understanding of complex organizations is to be achieved. One of management's major concerns is that the market environments facing their organizations are becoming more diverse and are constantly changing. Also, the technology of production is becoming more complex. Organizations are increasingly multinational, operating over wider geographical areas and under more diverse economic and cultural conditions.

ORGANIZATION-ENVIRONMENT MODEL

This article cannot address itself to all the issues raised in the preceding paragraphs. It will, however, present a model relating types of management systems and structures to particular market and technological conditions. The model will offer a way of understanding the complexities of any organization and provide a basis for managerial decisions about matters of organizational design.

Organizations cope with their external environment by creating organizational units or functions specifically to handle uncertainty arising from two sources. The first source of uncertainty is the number of changes in product lines and the length of production runs. For example, a job shop usually handles numerous jobs which require different machine feeds and speeds, realignment of men, and reorganization of other resources. However, in an oil refinery, once the operation has been established and is functioning, the number of product line changes is substantially less than those in a job shop. Uncertainty arises because the exact nature of the relationships between men and machine has not been worked through and because production standards have not been finalized.

The second source of uncertainty is the structure of the marketplace. The number of competitive products, manufacturers, and price ranges can lead to market uncertainty. Volkswagen, for example, operated in a market with few competitors until recently. Practices adopted in the 1950s and early 1960s are no longer effective in keeping Volkswagen a leader in its market. The quality and quantity of its competition have created market uncertainty and have reduced Volkswagen's foremost position in the marketplace.

To deal with these variations in the external environment, an organization becomes segmented into different units. Accordingly, each unit has as its major concern the problem of dealing with the uncertainty in its specific market environment. For example, the vice-president of broadcasting, learning and leisure at Westinghouse faces different problems and sources of market uncertainty than the vice-president in charge of power generation. The units must be linked together for the successful accomplishment of the organization's goals. This need for a division of labor and the simultaneous need for unified effort have led to studies of two fundamental activities of organizations—differentiation of activities and their integration.

DIFFERENTIATION AND INTEGRATION

Complex organizations are often characterized by a high degree of task specialization. For example, NASA headquarters is organized so that particular departments are responsible for the performance of specialized activities. The Office of Manned Space Flight is concerned with the Apollo program, while the Office of Space Science and Applications is concerned with propulsion and bioscience activities. Each of these departments is internally divided to meet its various demands.

As organizations specialize in order to cope more effectively with their environment, they become more differentiated or segmented: "Differentiation is defined as the state of segmentation of the organizational system into subsystems, each of which tends to develop particular attributes in relation to the requirements posed by the relevant external environment."[1] Organizations and their subunits are categorized as more or less differentiated according to their emphases on certain concepts. Four of the specific dimensions which comprise the differentiation concept are illustrated in Figure 1. One can map out the differentiation of the organization and any of its subunits along this continuum.

One might propose, for example, that the corporate structure of Westinghouse Electric Corporation matches several of these dimensions quite well and should be placed toward the differentiated end of the continuum. That is, it is concerned with long-range planning, consumer products, and relationships among its employees, and it has many departments. On the other hand, the power generation product division of Westinghouse might be placed far on the right side, as it has relatively little need for differentiation because of the relatively homogeneous structure of the market environment, the few changes in technology, and its limited product lines.

Thus, each subsystem of the entire organization may be placed at any one point along this continuum. In successful firms, the formal organizational structure and these dimensions tend to be consistent with the demands from the corresponding parts of their environment. Since it is beyond the scope of this article to describe complex organizations on all these dimensions in detail, we will use the corporate level to show how organizations can be categorized using the concept of differentiation.

The second important consideration in the design of organization structures is integration. "Integration is defined as the process of achiev-

1. Time orientation: long- or short-range planning
2. Goal orientation: market or scientifically oriented
3. Interpersonal orientation: concern for getting work done or concern for relationships with others
4. Formal hierarchical structure: many parts or few parts

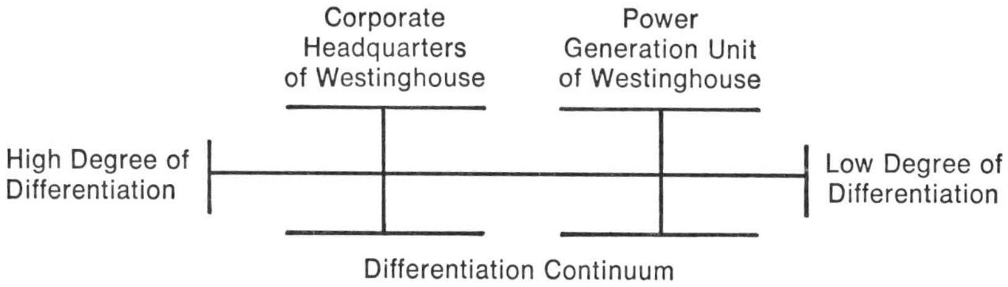

FIGURE 1
Dimensions of Differentiation

ing unity of effort among the various subsystems in the accomplishment of the organization's task."[2] Differentiation specifies that the activities required for organizational performance be separated. However, in most organizations, activities must also be coordinated or brought together again so that the organization acts as a consistent whole.

Organizations such as NASA, which require a high state of differentiation and a high degree of integration to operate in their unstable environments, have a different structure than organizations not requiring a high degree of integration. For example, large department store chains, such as the May Company or Sears, have different structures and simpler means for achieving integration. The meshing of diverse activities may be accomplished by executive committees, task teams, project managers, and project offices.

The problems of integration for organizations operating in relatively stable environments, characterized by a constant technology and a homogeneous market structure, are substantially different from those problems of organizations operating with changing technologies in heterogeneous markets. The organization operating in a stable environment can rely upon the hierarchical structure and established procedures to

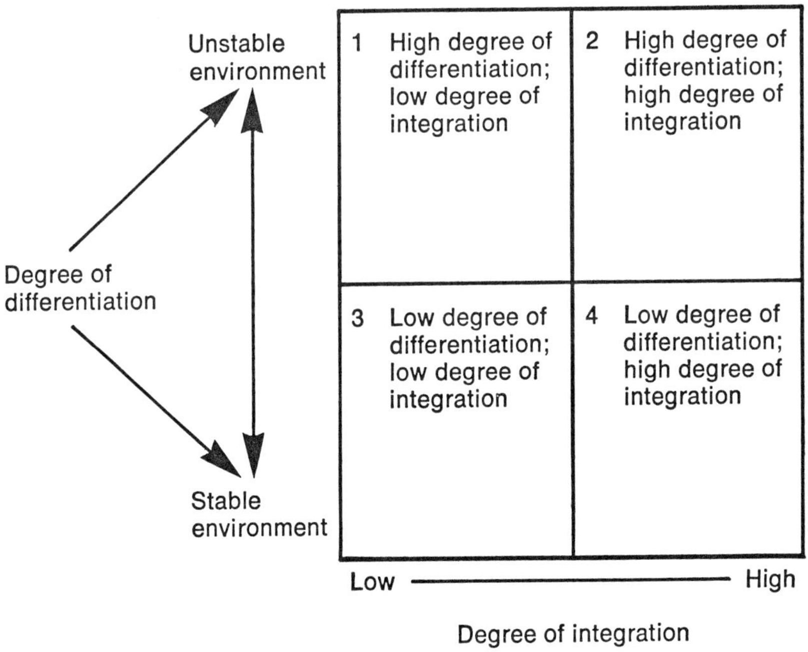

FIGURE 2
Differentiation–Integration Grid

ensure coordination, whereas elaborate integrating mechanisms may be needed for those firms in an unstable environment.

The varying degree of uncertainty, differentiation, and integration across organizations has been incorporated in Figure 2. This figure suggests a contingency approach to organizational design, emphasizing the relationship between the internal mechanisms of an organization and its external environment. Each unit must fit the demands of the environment. For example, in highly heterogeneous markets and changing technologies, successful organizations tend to become more differentiated than organizations in more homogeneous and stable technological environments.

Problems of integrating diverse activities in complex organizations can also vary from high to low, depending upon the degree of coordination needed to achieve the organization's objectives. By dichotomizing and cross-classifying differentiation and examining the possible modes of integration required by the organization's environment, we can see the possible ways in which organizations can vary in terms of these two variables. To better understand the relationship between differentiation and integration, we shall explore each of the quadrants in terms of these two dimensions.

THE FOUR QUADRANTS

High Uncertainty/Low Integration

Successful firms operating under these conditions tend to be highly differentiated into units or functions. The uncertainty of the environment necessitates that the firm be adaptive and flexible. Firms operating in this quadrant have been described along the following dimensions: wide span of control, few levels of authority; low number of rules and regulations; advisory and informational communications content; knowledge-based authority; high ratio of administrative personnel to production personnel; and decentralized decisionmaking.

At the corporate level, General Motors is an example of a large corporation with a high degree of differentiation and low need for integration. GM is decentralized along product lines; this structure permits quick and effective response to changes in each product's environment. Each of GM's product departments—Pontiac, Oldsmobile, and so on—is a profit center responsible for its own sales, marketing research, and manufacturing processes. Since each of the product lines is a profit center, and thus semiautonomous from other product lines, a low degree of integration is needed at the corporate level.

Within each product line, however, the degree of integration will vary depending upon the demands of the environment. For example, the Vega plant in Lordstown, Ohio, within the Chevrolet division, requires a high degree of integration because of the requirements of assembly-line technology.

The integration of these diverse product lines is accomplished at GM through top management committees, which provide policy guidelines for decisions that are made by executives of each product line. The policy-making responsibilities of top management are divided into two areas: financial and administrative. The financial committee provides guidelines for capital expenditures, methods of accounting to be followed by the product line managers, rate of return on investment, and other financial matters. The administrative committee is concerned with issues like long-range planning activities, production and sales policies, and purchase commitments.

Thus, the day-to-day operating decisions are handled at the product manager level, while long-term decisions requiring coordination among the various product lines are the concern of top management committees. The multidivisional structure of General Motors provides for adaptability to unstable market conditions. With its increasing trend toward differentiation and its lessening need for integration, this firm has fostered a managerial and structural system which can respond effectively to changes in its environment.

In a study of some twenty industrial firms in the United Kingdom, researchers have found that an "organic" management system is appropriate for firms that operate in changing market environments, while mechanistic systems are more appropriate for firms operating in a relatively stable environment.[3] The accompanying table summarizes the characteristics of the organic and the mechanistic systems.

In general, the organic system provides for more frequent changes of positions and roles, less hierarchical structure, and more dynamic interplay among the various functions of an organization. Continual readjustment and redefinition of individual tasks are necessary when the firm is adjusting to a changing market situation. The unstructured and dynamic marketplace often creates demands upon the organization that can best be handled through technical expertise and influence rather than bureaucratic rules.

Obviously, all firms cannot be classified as either totally organic or totally mechanistic. In many firms, it will be necessary to operate such functions as research and development with a more organic approach and other sections, such as an assembly line, with a more mechanistic system. The major finding of the British study was that, for firms operating in a changing environment, those with a characteristically organic management system were more successful than firms with a mechanistic one. Instead of providing for permanent, highly structured relations among functions, the organic system has less structure, and relies more on the ability of the different functions to cope with the uncertainties of their particular environments. Integration is achieved through the hierarchical structure and through committees.

High Uncertainty/High Integration

Effective means for dealing with problems of uncertainty in complex organizations can also be accomplished with a high degree of integration (quadrant 2, Figure 2). The greater the differentiation between any two highly interdependent units, the more difficult it becomes to achieve a high degree of integration. For example, Hughes Aircraft Company is organized into seven product lines—space and communications, systems, aerospace, industrial electronics, Hughes International, Santa Barbara Research Center, and research laboratories. When Hughes Aircraft is awarded a contract, the work is subcontracted to the appropriate divisions. If the contract is awarded to the systems division, the manager of that division determines the extent to which other divisions will be utilized in completing the contract.

The horizontal communication requirements in this kind of organization are more complex compared to those of Westinghouse, General Motors, or other organizations with less need for integration. The impact of a newly awarded contract requires that a large number of people in various divisions work closely together to successfully complete the contract. The continuous influx of new contracts, with their subsequent allocation of products or tasks to other divisions, places constant burdens on the organization. This procedure not only requires changes in the number and orientation of people, but also in the mix of managerial, professional, and technical personnel required to complete any project.

The pressures from new technologies and short lead times have made it necessary to establish some formalized managerial agency to provide overall coordination of these activities. One of the most frequently used management integrative mechanisms is that of project management.

Project management provides a means of integrating diverse functions of an organization and controlling all related activities involved in the project from start to finish. This approach requires organizational modification, emphasizing the development of horizontal communications, diagonal information-decisions networks, and authority systems not found in more conventional forms of organizations.

The project form of management is illustrated in Figure 3. The functional managers—manufacturing, engineering, and marketing—are re-

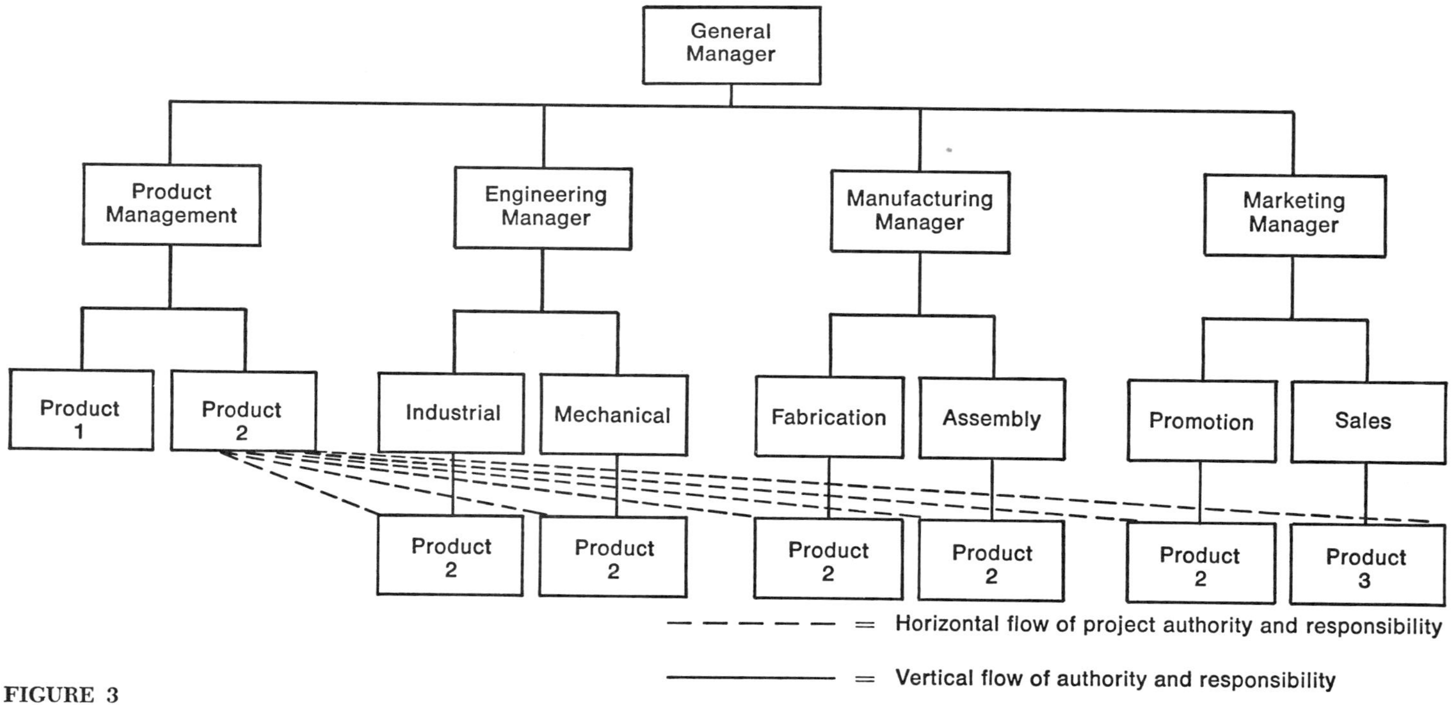

FIGURE 3
Functional Organization with Project Management

SOURCE: Adapted from David I. Cleland and William R. King, *Systems Analysis and Project Management* (New York: McGraw-Hill, 1968), p. 177, and Jay Galbraith, "Matrix Organization Design: How to Combine Functional and Project Forms," *Business Horizons,* XIV (February 1971), p. 36.

sponsible to the general manager for their special activities. The project manager reports to the general manager. He has personnel from the other divisions (for example, manufacturing, engineering, and marketing) assigned to him as required on a temporary basis until the project has been completed. Thus, there are two flows of authority in this kind of organization—the vertical flow of functional authority from the various functional managers and the horizontal flow of project authority of the project manager.

Problems associated with dual authority relationships have been discussed at length by many researchers.[4] The project manager's authority and influence flow in different directions than those described by some classical management theorists. A project manager's authority flows horizontally across the superior-subordinate relationships existing within the functional activities of an organization. Throughout the life span of a given project, personnel at various levels and with varying skills must contribute their efforts to allow for the sequential development of the project. For each new project awarded to the firm, new lateral information and decision-making networks must be worked out, which might differ significantly from those followed in the functional scheme.

In essence, the project manager has no clear-cut communication channels; he is faced with a web of communications that frequently crosses vertical lines of authority and involves outside subcontractors. His authority is *de facto* and stems from his charge from top management to get the project done within time and cost constraints. In practice, the project manager must rely heavily upon the alliances he builds with his peers through negotiations, knowledge, and resolution of conflict. These relationships replace the lack of formal authority over all the resources needed to complete the project.

Thus, a project manager's success will partly depend upon his ability to influence other organizational members through information and communication inputs rather than just upon his formal authority in the organization.[5] Authority cannot be dictated in advance because of the changing nature of project work and the dynamics of the many competing projects which vie for the firm's scarce resources.

The emphasis upon flexibility rather than permanency of job assignments strongly affects the employees who work for organizations using project management. Subordinates in project organizations have been reported to be significantly more insecure concerning possible employment, career retardation, and personal development than subordinates in a functional organization.[6]

As a consequence, project employees may feel less loyal to the organization and are more likely to report that they are frustrated on the job. As the project begins to phase out, members attempt to latch on to new projects for fear of being laid off upon completion of their project. However, the organization cannot always absorb these employees in other projects, either because of the cycle stage of the project or because of the lack of contract awards. This fear of possible unemployment is confirmed in project organizations by such examples as the layoff of aerospace engineers in the Boeing Corporation in 1971 when the SST contract was not funded.

High Certainty/Low Integration

Firms operating in quadrant 1 were in unstable environments because of continually emerging scientific knowledge, the impact on markets of this new scientific and technological knowledge, and the uncertainty that the firm will be able to maintain its competitive advantage in the marketplace. In a stable environment, is the same organization structure and management system effective? The model suggests that firms operating in relatively stable market structures (homogeneous) with little need for integration are more effective if they adopt a different organization structure and management system.

Continental Can Corporation might be one example of a firm operating in quadrant 3 (see Figure 2). The container industry's technology and market are relatively stable, emphasizing delivery and quality control. The remarks of one marketing executive in the container industry illustrate this point:

> We and our competitors all use the same machines produced by the same company. The product has got to be virtually the same as your competitor's unless your process is off, as you produce to the same specifications. Nor is there any process competition in this industry. So all we have to know is: How many cases does the customer want, and when.[7]

The most important part of this statement is the relative certainty of the container market. This certainty has led several researchers to suggest that, in industries such as this, effective firms would not be as differentiated as they would be in uncertain environments.[8]

In the container industry, it has been found that the most effective firms had the lowest need for integration.[9] Integration in the high-performing firms was accomplished through the managerial hierarchy. No special departments, teams, or roles (other than the scheduling clerk) had been established to facilitate the integrative function. Decision-making prerogatives were maintained at the top of the organization within the hands of managers who had the requisite knowledge to make decisions. This was especially true for technical and quality-control problems.

Characteristics of Organic and Mechanistic Management Systems

	Type of Organization System	
Organizational Characteristic Index	*Organic*	*Mechanistic*
Number of hierarchical levels	Few	Many
Degree of centralization of decision making	Low	High
Quantity of formal rules	Low	High
Specificity of goals	Low	High
Span of control	Wide	Narrow
Content and direction of communications	Advice and information; lateral	Instructions and decisions; vertical
Role relations	Consultation; interdependence	Rules and regulations; independence
Specificity of required activities	Low	High
Knowledge-based authority	High	Low
Position-based authority	Low	High

SOURCE: Adapted from Ralph M. Hower and Jay Lorsch, "Organizational Inputs," in John Seiler, *Systems Analysis in Organizational Behavior* (Homewood, Ill.: Dorsey Press, 1967), p. 168.

In less effective firms operating in this quadrant, efforts to decentralize decision making did not fit the environmental demands; moreover, lower-level managers were not able to resolve interdepartmental conflict because they did not possess the knowledge and influence to do so. This might suggest that, in a stable environment, high-performing organizations more closely fit the classical closed-system organizational model.

High Certainty/High Integration

The major characteristics of the managerial system of this quadrant have been summarized in the table. Successful firms in a stable industry tend to adopt a management system referred to as "mechanistic." There is more reliance on prescriptive rules, operating regulations, and formal procedures. Decisions are reached at higher levels of the organization and communicated down the scalar chain of authority. The spans of supervision tend to be narrow.

A typical franchise arrangement, such as McDonald's, Kentucky Fried Chicken, Pancake House, and Dunkin' Donuts, are examples of firms operating in this quadrant. The market environment is homogeneous. Promotional strategies and production technology are similar among competitors. The managers of the franchise have market-oriented goals and short-time horizons in terms of service and future markets; they have been described as more likely to be preoccupied with getting the job done (high production-oriented) than with maintaining good interpersonal relations (low people-oriented).

The integrative mechanisms employed by McDonald's, for example, not only include a detailed organizational structure but also continual service, through bookkeeping systems, company troubleshooters, and advertising, to ensure that the franchise manager conforms to McDonald's rules and regulations. The company's operations manual consists of 385 pages of details covering the most minute facet of operating an outlet. It spells out, for example, what equipment (such as cigarette, gum, candy, and pinball machines) is not permitted on store premises.

The franchise manager is visited monthly by one of thirty field service managers. The franchise sends weekly financial reports to the company, and the manager must attend a three-week intensive training at the so-called "Hamburger U." in Elk Grove, Illinois. While attending Hamburger U., the new manager is exposed to such techniques as how to regulate production in order to meet the service standard of "No customer has to wait for more than 50 seconds." He also learns how to organize the grill man, "shake" man, and countermen into an effective team.

These managers also learn the strict standards for personal grooming, the few variations allowed in types of food because of regional tastes, and how to deal with college students as customers and employees. The company also provides the franchise manager with a different maintenance reminder for each day of the year, such as, "Lubricate and adjust potato-peeler belt" or "Contact snow removal company." Because each member of the McDonald's organization has a specified role, it is not difficult to get integrated programs of action.

The quality of collaboration that exists among departments at headquarters to achieve unity in the franchise is great. The design department at the parent organization, for example, works closely with the site and location department to ensure that the franchise meets the standards set by the organization and blends with the general architectural style of the community. Once these departments have reached an agreement, the franchise operator must erect the structure according to the plans set for that location. Fred Turner, McDonald's president since 1968, says: "In an age when so many Americans are on the move, one of our main assets is our consistency and uniformity. It's very important that a man who's used to eating at a McDonald's in Hempstead, Long Island, knows he can get the same food and service when he walks into one in Albuquerque or Omaha."[10]

The companies we have used to analyze how organizations vary in their internal structure to handle different environmental circumstances (market and technology) and needed levels of integration were only illustrative. The environment is a major determinant of an organization's internal structure.

In the differentiation-integration model we saw that, as each part of the organization strives to cope with a different part of its external environment, it demands a different mode of integration. Effective organizations operating in unstable environments develop organic management systems, while effective organizations in stable environments tended to have mechanistic management systems.

NOTES

1. Paul Lawrence and Jay Lorsch, *Studies in Organizational Design* (Homewood, Ill.: Richard D. Irwin, Inc., 1970), p. 6, and also "Differentiation and Integration in Complex Organizations," *Administrative Science Quarterly,* XII (June 1967), p. 3.
2. Lawrence and Lorsch, "Differentiation and Integration," p. 4.
3. L. Burns and G. M. Stalker, *The Management of Innovation* (London: Tavistock Publications, 1964).
4. George A. Steiner and William G. Ryan, *Industrial Project Management* (New York: Macmillan Co., 1968); Jay R. Galbraith, "Matrix Organizational Design: How to Combine Functional and Project Forms," *Business Horizons,* XIV (February, 1971), pp. 29–40; Arlyn Melcher and Thomas Kayser, "Leadership Without Formal Authority: The Project Department," *California Management Review,* XIII (Winter 1970), pp. 57–64; and David Wilemon and John Cicero, "The Project Manager—Anomalies and Ambiguities," *Academy of Management Journal,* XIII (September 1970), pp. 269–82.
5. Gary Gemmill and David Wilemon, "The Project Manager as an Influence Agent," *Journal of Marketing,* XXXVI (January 1972), pp. 26–31; John M. Stewart, "Making Project Management Work," *Business Horizons,* VIII (Fall 1965), pp. 54–71; and Richard D. Hodgetts, "Leadership Techniques in the Project Organization," *Academy of Management Journal,* XI (June 1968), pp. 211–19.
6. Clayton Resser, "Some Potential Human Problems of the Project Form of Organization," *Academy of Management Journal,* XII (December 1969), pp. 459–67.
7. Paul Lawrence and Jay Lorsch, *Organization and Environment* (Homewood, Ill.: Richard D. Irwin, Inc., 1969), p. 92.
8. Lawrence and Lorsch, *Organization and Environment,* p. 103. See also Burns and Stalker, *Management of Innovation,* and Charles Perrow, *Organizational Analysis: A Sociological View* (Belmont, Calif.: Wadsworth Publishing Co., 1970).
9. Lawrence and Lorsch, *Organization and Environment,* p. 103.
10. Anthony Lukas, "As American as McDonald's Hamburger on the Fourth of July," *New York Times Magazine,* July 4, 1971, pp. 5–29.

Chapter 4

Managing by Thousands: Developing and Maintaining an Institution

A. Value-Setting Processes in Organizations
  - *Leadership in Administration,* Philip Selznick
  - "The CEO's Behavior," Chris Argyris
  - "Understanding Your Organization's Character," Roger Harrison

B. Encouraging Innovation in Organizations
  - "The Diffusion of New Work Structures," Richard E. Walton
  - "The Politics of Implementing MBO," George S. Odiorne

C. Providing a Systemic Perspective in Organizations
  - "Progress and Problems in Systems Analysis," Edward S. Quade

Many demands of organized life that can be sloughed off at lower levels, plus many demands far beyond the perspective or competence of lower levels, constitute the executive workload. "Executive" here refers to the chief officers of firms as well as of major departments of government and includes officers of the larger subdivisions of both. At the lower boundary, for example, the plant manager of a multiunit decentralized firm is certainly in the business of managing thousands in the sense intended here, and some of his major department heads also might be carrying responsibilities greater than those of middle management.

Managing by thousands covers much organizational ground, then, and most of it is crucial ground indeed. Our approach to extensiveness and significance will be straightforward and undoubtedly too simple for the complexity of the relevant phenomena. However, we can hardly avoid some attempt to provide some structure that will aid in exploring the variegated executive realms. Our attempt will have three components:

- Some characteristics of the top-management role will be outlined.
- Some major demands imposed on executives will be sketched.
- Some major problems inhering in top-management jobs will be detailed.

Characteristics and demands and problems, then, are seen as three aspects of that seamless cloth of reality we refer to as the management of thousands.

Caution is the order of the day when considering the characteristics of the job of the top-level manager. We shall be cautious while we attempt to say something relatively specific. Three characteristics of the executive job strike us as being particularly relevant. First, the activities of top-level managers influence thousands, although they may directly supervise small departments or even only a handful of individuals. Second, top-level management is preoccupied with developing and maintaining a social institution that gives organic meaning and continuity to technical procedures, formal policies, and paper procedures. Third, top management deals with matters of scope that often have broad and significant ethical implications. In this sense, the executive role sharply contrasts with the "organization engineering" orientation of middle management.

These three characteristics of the job of the executive imply harsh organizational demands. In sum, the management of thousands imposes such multifaceted and onerous demands on executives that their actions will have significant consequences on many people, whether for good or ill. The consequences are variously practical, social, and ethical; and they are uniformly profound. A summary consequence has a magisterial stature. Increasingly, man's freedom must be found in organizations if it is to be found anywhere. Top-level managers will help satisfy or will contribute to frustrating the quest for freedom of Organizational Everyman. Patently, there is no denying the crucial integrative role of the top-level executive.

The derivative organizational demands on the top-level executive have no end, but two of these demands seem significant enough to set down. To an unusually high degree, to emphasize a first demand, the top-level executive has no place to hide from the problems that percolate up to his level. "The buck stops here," stated President Truman in expressing the major demand of his august office. To be sure, some executives follow Calvin Coolidge's opposed advice. When ten problems could be perceived as building up in intensity, Coolidge observed, the wise executive had only to wait and nine of them would somehow be resolved before they reached him. Nevertheless, that tenth problem can raise merry hell, and when it does the executive cannot escape its consequences.

Relatedly, but independently, the top-level executive must experience unique organizational demands because no one else sits exactly where he does.[1] It is he who can best attempt to balance the conflicting demands of the component activities of his organization simply because he

---

[1] Richard E. Neustadt insightfully applies this notion to the office of the presidency. See his *Presidential Power* (New York: Wiley, 1960). Peter F. Drucker develops a similar analysis for the business executive in *The Effective Executive* (New York: Harper and Row, 1966).

is above direct identification with any one of those activities. This summarizes both opportunity and difficulty. In any case, and make no mistake about it, the "view from the top" is different. The view from the top, because only the top man sits there, must be general and comprehensive. And pity the organization whose chief executive comes at his work with a narrower bias. In contrast, even very high-level officials heading large functional units in centralized organizations may adopt—or may be forced by their subordinates to adopt—parochial and partial perspectives because of where *they* sit.

Sometimes, indeed, a single individual has the unusual opportunity to experience the varying demands made on "ultimate generalists" and "high-level specialists." Simon recounts the story of one Nelson Eckart of the San Francisco Utilities Department who wore three organizational hats: he was head of the Water Department; he served in the place of the recently deceased head of the Hetch Hetchy Power development; and he was acting Utilities Manager during the month-long absence of the department head Cahill, who was in charge of a wide range of local utilities including water and power development. The experience was unnerving. On Cahill's return, Eckart quit. It was some time before the complex reasons for the move became clear to Cahill. As Simon summarized Cahill's search-and-discovery pattern of why Eckart left:[2]

> [Cahill] discovered in fact a letter Waterman Eckart had written asking for more water-works, another letter Hetch Hetchy Eckart had written asking for more HH dough, and a final letter Acting Utilities Manager Eckart had written denying both of his own requests. Naturally, Cahill asked what the devil. "From up here," Eckart explained, "things don't look the same as they do from down there."

The characteristics and demands of top-management jobs imply rather narrow boundaries within which the executive can operate effectively. Let us illustrate these boundaries in terms of two continua, the extremes of each of which the executive must labor to avoid. One of these continua may be labeled "stability/change." Patently, any organization has short-run objectives. These objectives cover a broad range: answering letters; building bridges; or providing information. Thus the executive must create an organization that has some characteristics of the proverbial well-oiled machine. "Stability" thus becomes an executive guideline, but fixation on that objective must be avoided. Every organization also has longer-run goals such as adapting to a newer technology or to a developing organizational mission and role. Preparing

---

[2] Herbert A. Simon, *Administrative Behavior* (New York: Macmillan, 1957), p. 214n.

the way for regular "change" then is an executive responsibility whose demands must be delicately traded off against the demands of steady-state operations. Extremism on this continua definitely will get its comeuppance, in the short run or the long.

The executive cannot console himself that he has but few such continua with which to contend. For example, a second continuum requiring executive tightrope walking may be called "chaos/conformism." That is, every functioning organization is infused with value. The same job may be done differently in two "similar" organizations, for example, and these differences reflect various sets of norms and values. These norms may have roots in the personalities of organizational members, in idiosyncratic common experiences, or perhaps even in minor variations in technology or architecture, but differences there will be.[3]

Consequently, executive carelessness about the value aspects of an organization can be serious. At the very least, the executive will have missed the opportunity to consciously put his personal mark on his technical organization. At the worst, values may develop and persist which are in direct and major conflict with the organization's public objectives. Informally enforced restrictions on output, for example, typify the normative "chaos" that can result from an executive's shrinking from the task of infusing an organization with values he considers appropriate. On the other hand, rigid preoccupation with punctilious adherence to any organization's normative minutiae may result in an enervating "conformism" in which organizational members cooperatively trudge into mindless oblivion. Again, the executive must conceive and execute delicate tradeoffs to avoid the costs of paying too much attention to one boundary condition or the other.

The problem is not merely hypothetical, if we are to believe the many critical voices raised concerning our organizational revolution. Thus William H. Whyte's *The Organization Man* drew a very definite portrait of organizations tending toward one extreme of the chaos/conformism continuum, and he developed a convincing sketch of the attendant danger both within the organization and outside.[4] Some have noted the lack of caution in Whyte's argument,[5] but he has his many followers. For example, Seidenberg not only argues that Whyte depicts what organizations are becoming; in addition, Seidenberg argues that matters can-

---

[3] Many demonstrations of the point exist. Illustratively, see Roger Harrison, "Understanding Your Organization's Character," *Harvard Business Review*, Vol. 50 (May 1972), pp. 119–29, which is reprinted below.

[4] William H. Whyte Jr., *The Organization Man* (Garden City, N.Y.: Doubleday Anchor Books, 1957).

[5] Robert T. Golembiewski, *Men, Management, and Morality* (New York: McGraw-Hill, 1965), esp. pp. 38–53.

not be otherwise.[6] Our organizational revolution is spiraling inward on itself, as it were, and this devolution into ever decreasing circles of flexibility will end only as organizations almost literally suffocate on their own immensity and rigidity.

The characteristics, demands, and problems of top-management jobs all point to their creative and crucial potential. This is the case whether we see the possibility of successfully coping with the contemporary organizational revolution, or whether at best we only hope that we can play for time within narrow limits. The exquisite dilemmas confronting chief executives can only be hinted at here, but that hint is suggestive. Consider the matter of emotional support. If a chief executive often must help create the conditions under which emotional support is provided members of the organization, his getting emotional support usually is problematic. One executive tersely put his view of the matter: "The top man in an organization has to have the capacity to love those he works with in an organization, and get his love elsewhere," he explained. There was no avoiding this central executive dilemma, as he saw it. He simply could not get that love from others in the organization. "There has got to be somebody to hate if things go wrong," he described his own major liability, "and he's it. So he has got to get his love from somewhere else."[7] Other chief executives may stress needs other than love, of course. But similarly—because of where the chief executive sits—satisfying those needs often poses dilemmas. We have in mind a portly dean who cherishes his few moments of exercise on a bicycle. But because of his feelings about the dignity required by his office, the dean takes his precious exercise only late at night. Consequently, the little exercise he does get is gained only by sacrificing safety.

What the executive must do, how he must do it, and who he is, consequently, are issues of great moment, and we direct ourselves to these issues.

We approach these issues crabwise. We reject the traditional approach to executive selection and competence. This approach stresses the listing of traits that identify the successful executive or would-be executive. The interested reader can find these various listings in the literature. The number of necessary traits, for example, cover a substantial range. Stryker presents fourteen traits of successful executives;[8] Greenleaf and

---

[6] Roderick Seidenberg, *Post-historic Man* (Boston: Beacon Press, 1957).

[7] Richard D. Hodgson, Daniel J. Levinson, and Abraham Zaleznik, *The Executive Role Constellation* (Boston: Division of Research, Harvard Graduate School of Business Administration, 1965), p. 376.

[8] Perrin Stryker, "On the Meaning of Executive Qualities," *Fortune*, Vol. 46 (June 1958), pp. 116–19 and 136–39.

Mapel settle for only three.[9] The content of the traits also varies widely. Thus two students settled for these global traits: the courage to dream, the ability to organize and the strength to execute.[10] Other observers are content only with categories complex enough to deter a Philadelphia lawyer, such as those categories deriving from the involved interpretation of depth-analytic techniques like the Rorschach.

Despite their variety, attempts to isolate traits for executive selection have common limiting biases. These attempts focus on the executive rather than on what he is executing. Moreover, the usual approach to traits admits only a few variables, and they narrowly focus on the executive. Finally, the trait notion is static. If an executive has the appropriate traits he will be successful, by implication, whatever the conditions.

We are more comfortable with an approach that is oriented around both the executive and his institution, that acknowledges multiple variables, and that is dynamic. Basically, the executive operates in a value-laden environment, which he helps create for good or ill, and to which he responds whether consciously or not. Because this is the case, we can question whether a set of "executive traits" exists. Grossly, different organizations reflect different values at different points in time; and the same organization can change its operational values by an act or will, or change may be precipitated by external forces. Whether any one set of traits would serve such various value sets may be doubted.

We can focus on the interaction of organizational properties and individual characteristics to develop three related themes that reveal the multidimensional complexity and subtlety of the executive role. In turn, the discussion below focuses on the executive role in

- Value-setting processes in organizations;
- Encouraging innovation in organizations; and
- Providing a systemic perspective in organizations.

A. VALUE-SETTING PROCESSES IN ORGANIZATIONS

One of the principal executive activities—perhaps *the* central one—involves establishing and maintaining as well as changing a rank order of objectives for an organization. Without such a hierarchy of values, an organization wastes time on countless decisions which need not have

---

[9] R. T. Greenleaf and E. B. Mapel, "The Trained Executive: A Profile," in M. Joseph Dooher and Vivienne Marquis, editors, *The Development of Executive Talent* (New York: American Management Association, 1952), pp. 21–25.

[10] *Ibid.*

been made, or which could have been made better if a hierarchy of objectives existed.

Philip Selznick's *Leadership in Administration* (parts of which are reprinted here) brings complementary attention to the full range of value-setting processes in organizations that define the executive's major focus for Selznick. His standards are high. Those in a position to articulate goals must do so, even if this means conflict within the organization and attack from outside. Nor can executives settle for superficial acceptance of the goals defining their institution. Although every executive must achieve minimum conditions for an organization's continued existence, Selznick argues, any executive fails if he does not recognize that he is primarily "an expert in the promotion and protection of values." The executive's primary value-oriented activities are:

- Defining the institutional mission and role;
- Developing an institutional embodiment of purpose;
- Defending the institutional purpose; and
- Managing internal conflict.

As the executive forfeits these tasks, and especially the first three, so also does that executive become an "organizational engineer." That is, by forfeiture, he acts like a middle manager rather than an executive.

Let us sharpen one sense in which an executive's serving as "an expert in the promotion and protection of values" requires promoting and protecting new values. Here lies perhaps *the* distinctly executive task. Consider, by way of illustration, the propositions that organizations generally must grow in order to prosper and that different ways of growing require different ways of organizing. Orderly growth, therefore, is a function of the appropriateness of an organization's structure for its growth strategy, which Chandler defines as "the determination of the basic long-term goals and objectives of an enterprise and the adoption of courses of action and allocation of resources necessary for carrying out these goals."[11] If growth strategies are consciously or unconsciously changed without appropriate changes in structure, organizational chaos is the major by-product.

The character and the significance of Chandler's strategies for growth may be detailed briefly. The strategies—roughly, in order of application and sophistication—include:

- Expanding production of a good or service at one site;
- Opening field units;
- Adding functions; and
- Diversifying into many product and service lines.

---

[11] Alfred D. Chandler, Jr., *Strategy and Structure* (Cambridge, Mass: M.I.T. Press, 1962), esp. pp. 13–16.

Strategy significantly influences the appropriateness of alternative structures. For example, the orthodox theory of organization is relatively appropriate where the basic strategy of growth is increased volume of a limited product line. Here, also, the narrow specialist has advantages that far outweigh his disadvantages. When the basic strategy of growth becomes the diversification of products or services, both the orthodox theory and its specialist-oriented human products have relatively greater costs than the unorthodox model and its generalist human products. Details supporting the summaries proposed by the preceding sentences may be found in Golembiewski, "Civil Service and Managing Work," reprinted in the previous chapter.

Executives managing thousands, that is to say, are enmeshed in the complex practical problems of developing appropriate strategic values to maintain their organizations in the several tomorrows as well as in the compelling today. Their failures are written in terms of outmoded organizations and obsolescing human skills and attitudes. Let us illustrate the practical and value issues involved in moving to sophisticated strategies for growth. Practically, the derivative demands on the executive in managing thousands are multiple in this regard: to anticipate and to avoid the intolerable elements in the future when managing today's work; to build toward suitable change while steady-state operations continue; and to do so far enough in advance to avoid organizational turmoil but not so far as to invite rejection. Integrating diversity thus well characterizes the executive job.

Normatively, the issues facing executives also are momentous. If decentralization is appropriate for advanced strategies of organizational growth—and particularly for diversification—that strategy also implies major changes in the values and attitudes of many organizational members. Decentralization—like centralization—must rest on a bedrock of appropriate attitudes and values. Decentralization—also like centralization—is not merely a technical matter. Decentralization reflects a life-style; it is infused with value. The point cannot be made fully. However, consider only this attempt to describe decentralization. Two scholars observe that the social climate associated with decentralization defies easy cataloguing. "Such a social climate," they explain, "is full of contradictions and enigmas." Indeed, it mixes apparently diverse values. "On the one hand it would seem to be welfare-centered, with a certain flavor of devotion to human uplift," they explain. "On the other it retains the production drive and competitive atmosphere so characteristic of the industrial scene in the past."[12] Therefore, the executive must face the task of combining the diverse in infusing a decentralized organization with value.

---

[12] John M. Pfiffner and Frank P. Sherwood, *Administrative Organization* (Englewood Cliffs, N.J.: Prentice-Hall, 1960), p. 201.

Cases in point abound concerning the executive's key role in value setting and the enormous stakes involved. Chris Argyris provides ample documentation of both points, and far more besides, in his "The CEO's Behavior: Key to Organizational Development." Argyris draws a tragic picture of the CEO, or the chief executive officer. The very qualities that characterize prime candidates for a CEO role, in sum, may imply serious problems for the systems over which they preside, as well as for the people in those systems. Basically, the professed attitudes of the CEO often do not square with his behavior, and this creates serious ethical and practical dilemmas for the executive, for his subordinates, and for their common organizational system.

Argyris is a sympathetic observer, but a pessimistic or at least a cautious one. He reviews four kinds of programs often relied on to "involve every level of management in a confrontation with the issue of leadership style" and finds them all variously lacking. Argyris directs attention to *the* critical need in such cases. The CEO may say he wants such a confrontation over leadership style but, in countless subtle ways, he often will signal that he really prefers submission and dependence from his subordinates. Argyris consequently concludes that the common need is to work with the CEO so as to make attitudes and behaviors more congruent, a central task for which there are no magic answers.

Roger Harrison provides useful counterpoint to Argyris' theme of individual/organizational interfaces. Basically, "Understanding Your Organization's Character" presumes that all organizations will be value-loaded, that they all will have an "ideological orientation." Usefully, Harrison describes four different kinds of value or ideological orientations:

- Power
- Role
- Task
- Person

Moreover, Harrison also describes four interests of people which correspond to the four ideological orientations above.

The derivative 4×4 classification supports much useful analysis. Thus Harrison's approach helps show why and how conflict can develop between an organization and its specific numbers as when, for example, an individual is person-oriented but his organization ideology values a power-orientation. Relatedly Harrison shows how the several organizational orientations can be variously troublesome, given different kinds of missions and roles. For example, a role-orientation can be appropriate for an organization with a stable technology and product line, especially if both are relatively simple. However, a role orientation could be very troublesome in a high-technology environment.

B. ENCOURAGING INNOVATION IN ORGANIZATIONS

Implicit in much of this discussion is another major executive role—that of facilitating appropriate innovation. One way to put the point is that an executive who helps an organization build norms and values supportive of timely change has really done his job. One could even credibly argue that a steady-state organization needs only managers, not executives.

Richard E. Walton directs effective attention to this central feature of the executive role in his "Diffusion of New Work Structures: Explaining Why Success Didn't Take." Essentially, Walton tracks eight work experiments that seem highly promising, he estimates the extent of their successful diffusion throughout the host organization, and he speculates as to why that diffusion was relatively puny.

Let us approach Walton's excellent analysis from a slightly different direction than he did, without in any way redoing the work he has done so well. In a negative way, that is, Walton's analysis implies why the executive role can be so profound in successful innovation. Overall, the forces against innovation are so great that very skillful and willful executive interventions are virtually required. Consider only one example of the barriers to innovation. Walton explains innovations that:

> Even if they offer relative advantages over existing work structures, their character and results are not highly communicable; they are not congruent with existing norms and values; their potential effect in a given work situation is pervasive rather than fractional; they are not readily reversed without incurring social costs; and too many affected parties serve as gatekeepers for the effective implementation of the innovations.

The need for executive intervention, patently, is writ large in even this brief catalog of barriers to change. And, clearly, only a skillful and determined executive intervention is likely to suffice. Innovation can seldom be commended, in short.

Much the same conclusion about the centrality of the executive role emerges from George S. Odiorne's "The Politics of Implementing MBO," in addition to the useful perspective he provides on a management innovation as an example of who gets what, when, and how. Much more than Walton, Odiorne focuses on the forces that get involved, one way or another, in the political skirmishes that determine whether or not an innovation gets effectively implemented. Thus Odiorne draws attention to "unit loyalty," among many other forces, as a major factor in the diffusion of innovations. In sum, innovations are often urged for the "good of the system," or as "necessary to preserve the organization." In contrast, the operational loyalties for many organization members are likely to reside more basically in much smaller units, such as "the gang I work with." The water cooler in the corner may be *the* center of local loyalties, in short, and the critical executive role often will involve variously enlarging the perspective of organization members. For example, the executive may seek to:

- Show how the cosmopolitan loyalty is consistent with the local loyalty;
- Encourage people to rise above their local loyalties for the "larger good," which much be carefully defined and acceptable to the mass of organization members;
- Carefully bargain about variances in applications of innovations so as to gain the support of local units without compromising the integrity of the innovation; and
- Etc., etc.

Clearly, these activities imply great skill and subtlety.

C. PROVIDING A SYSTEMIC PERSPECTIVE IN ORGANIZATIONS

And now these introductory notes again double-back on themselves. This chapter began by highlighting the uniqueness of the executive role: because of where executives sit, their perspectives and views are most likely to be global, comprehensive, and systemic. And it is to this theme that these last few words return. Indeed, the whole of this volume argues for a "systems approach" to organizational phenomena. The piece by Edward S. Quade—"Progress and Problems in Systems Analysis"—reinforces this intention by reviewing the mechanics and some of the splendid gains made lately in "systems analysis." As Quade notes, much of the progress has been made via the use of mathematical tools. It is equally correct, as Quade also observes, that systems analysis admits of the full range of approaches to organizational phenomena. It is to this end that the selections of this volume contribute.

LEADERSHIP IN ADMINISTRATION*

Philip Selznick

Leadership is not a familiar, everyday idea, as readily available to common sense as to social science. It is a slippery phenomenon that eludes them both. What leaders do is hardly self-evident. And it is likely that much failure of leadership results from an inadequate understanding of its true nature and tasks. Most of this essay will be devoted to identifying and analyzing the chief functions of institutional leadership. By way of introduction, however, it may be helpful to state a few simple guiding ideas here.

1. *Leadership is a kind of work done to meet the needs of a social situation.* Possibly there are some individuals more likely to be leaders than others, possessed of distinguishing personal traits or capacities.[1] Whether or not this is so, we shall here be concerned with leadership as a specialized form of activity, a kind of work or function. Identifying what leaders do certainly bears on (and is perhaps indispensable to) the discovery of requisite personal attributes; but the questions are of a different kind and may be treated separately.

To know the nature of the work done by leaders, we must know something about the social situations they are called upon to handle. This immediately suggests that there must be a very wide variety of activities associated with leadership.[2] However, it does not follow that the *nature* of leadership varies with each social situation. If that were so, there would be nothing determinate about it; its study would be a scientific blind alley. In fact, of course, we must assume that significant leadership patterns are relatively few; and that these patterns are related to *types* of social situations. This means that certain very general activities of leaders—e.g., facilitating communication within the group—reflect equally general characteristics of all human groups; and that the functions of leadership will be understood only as we develop a better understanding of the main types of groups and the recurrent problems they face. In other words, a theory of leadership is dependent on a theory of social organization.

We shall not be concerned here with all leadership, but with leadership in large-scale organizations. This will require some consideration of the nature of such enterprises, including the characteristic problems

---

* Abridged from pp. 22–28, 33–43, 62–64, 149–154 in *Leadership in Administration* by Philip Selznick. Copyright © 1957 by Harper & Row, Publishers, Incorporated. Reprinted by permission of the publisher. (Footnotes have been renumbered.)

that arise within them. It will be necessary to understand the institutional aspects of large-scale organizations, for the central argument will stress the close connection between these aspects and the key functions of leadership. Although institutional leadership must share the general characteristics of all leadership, we shall not deal with the latter problem directly.

2. *Leadership is not equivalent to office-holding or high prestige or authority or decision-making.* It is not helpful to identify leadership with whatever is done by people in high places. The activity we have in mind may or may not be engaged in by those who are formally in positions of authority. This is inescapable if we are to develop a theory that will be useful in diagnosing cases of inadequate leadership on the part of persons in authority. If this view is correct, it means that only some (and sometimes none) of the activities of decision-makers are leadership activities. Here again, understanding leadership requires understanding of a broader social process. If some types of decisions are more closely related to leadership activities than others, we should learn what they are. To this end in this analysis let us make a distinction between "routine" and "critical" decision-making.

3. *Leadership is dispensable.* The word "leadership" has its own halo, easily inviting the tacit assumption that, being a good thing, it is always in order. It may indeed be that all human groups require at all times *some* leadership activities. But if leadership is anything determinate, we should know how to distinguish its presence from its absence; similarly, if there are some social situations that especially require leadership, we should know how to tell them apart from other social situations. The idea is developed in this essay that leadership is not equally necessary in all large-scale organizations, or in any one at all times, and that it becomes dispensable as the natural processes of institutionalization become eliminated or controlled. This will provide some clues to the general conditions that call for leadership decisions.

These premises emphasize the futility of attempting to understand leadership apart from the broader organizational experience of which it is a phase. A theory of leadership will necessarily reflect the level of sophistication we have reached in the study of organization. We are dealing with an activity, with a function, with work done; we can make no more sense of it than is allowed by our understanding of the field within which that activity takes place.

THE DEFAULT OF LEADERSHIP

When institutional leadership fails, it is perhaps more often by default than by positive error or sin. Leadership is lacking when it is needed;

and the institution drifts, exposed to vagrant pressures, readily influenced by short-run opportunistic trends. This default is partly a failure of nerve, partly a failure of understanding. It takes nerve to hold a course; it takes understanding to recognize and deal with the basic sources of institutional vulnerability.

One type of default is the failure to set goals. Once an organization becomes a "going concern," with many forces working to keep it alive, the people who run it can readily escape the task of defining its purposes. This evasion stems partly from the hard intellectual labor involved, a labor that often seems but to increase the burden of already onerous daily operations. In part, also, there is the wish to avoid conflicts with those in and out of the organization who would be threatened by a sharp definition of purpose, with its attendant claims and responsibilities. Even business firms find it easy to fall back on conventional phrases, such as that "our goal is to make profit," phrases which offer little guidance in the formulation of policy.

A critique of leadership, we shall argue, must include this emphasis on the leader's responsibility to define the mission of the enterprise. This view is not new. It is important because so much of administrative analysis takes the goal of the organization as given, whereas in many crucial instances this is precisely what is problematic. We shall also suggest that the analysis of goals is itself dependent on an understanding of the organization's social structure. In other words, the purposes we have or can have depend on what we are or what we can be. In statesmanship no less than in the search for personal wisdom, the Socratic dictum—know thyself—provides the ultimate guide.

Another type of default occurs when goals, however neatly formulated, enjoy only a superficial acceptance and do not genuinely influence the total structure of the enterprise. Truly accepted values must infuse the organization at many levels, affecting the perspectives and attitudes of personnel, the relative importance of staff activities, the distribution of authority, relations with outside groups, and many other matters. Thus if a large corporation asserts a wish to change its role in the community from a narrow emphasis on profit-making to a larger social responsibility (even though the ultimate goal remains some combination of survival and profit-making ability), it must explore the implications of such a change for decision-making in a wide variety of organizational activities. We shall stress that the task of building special values and a distinctive competence into the organization is a prime function of leadership.

In this sense, the leader is an agent of institutionalization, offering a guiding hand to a process that would otherwise occur more haphazardly, more readily subject to the accidents of circumstance and history. This is not to say that the leader is free to do as he wishes, to mold the organization according to his heart's desire, restrained only by the quality of his imagination and the strength of his will. Self-knowledge means knowledge of limits as well as of potentialities.

The default of leadership shows itself in an acute form when *organizational* achievement or survival is confounded with *institutional* success. To be sure, no institutional leader can avoid concern for the minimum conditions of continued organizational existence. But he fails if he permits sheer organizational achievement, in resources, stability, or reputation, to become the criterion of his success. A university led by administrators without a clear sense of values to be achieved may fail dismally while steadily growing larger and more secure.

Finally, the role of the institutional leader should be clearly distinguished from that of the "interpersonal" leader. The latter's task is to smooth the path of human interaction, ease communication, evoke personal devotion, and allay anxiety. His expertness has relatively little to do with content; he is more concerned with persons than with policies. His main contribution is to the efficiency of the enterprise. The institutional leader, on the other hand, *is primarily an expert in the promotion and protection of values.* The interpretation that follows takes this idea as a starting point, exploring its meaning and implications. . . .

Drawing on general psychoanalytic theory, Erich Fromm distinguishes "static" and "dynamic" adaptation:

> By static adaptation we mean such an adaptation to patterns as leaves the whole character structure unchanged and implies only the adoption of a new habit. An example of this kind of adaptation is the change from the Chinese habit of eating to the Western habit of using fork and knife. A Chinese coming to America will adapt himself to this new pattern, but this adaptation in itself will have little effect on his personality; it does not arouse new drives or character traits.[3]

This may be compared with the idea of routine psychological processes suggested above. Static adaptation is not static, strictly speaking: it is, one might say, "everyday" dynamics. It is routine learning, and the study of it centers on such factors as motivation, practice, etc. It is ordinary, responsive behavior, subject to such normal tendencies as stimulus generalization. Most human responses are of this routine sort. It is natural that, wherever the training and control of large numbers is involved, as in industrial or military life, the students of these processes will have the major role.

Yet certain critical areas of experience belong to a different realm:

> By dynamic adaptation we refer to the kind of adaptation that occurs, for example, when a boy submits to the commands of his strict and

> threatening father—being too much afraid of him to do otherwise—and becomes a "good" boy. While hc adapts himself to the necessities of the situation, something happens in him. He may develop an intense hostility against his father, which he represses, since it would be too dangerous to express it or even to be aware of it. This repressed hostility, however, though not manifest, is a dynamic factor in his character structure. It may create new anxiety and thus lead to still deeper submission; it may set up a vague defiance, directed against no one in particular but rather toward life in general. While here, too, as in the first case, an individual adapts himself to certain external circumstances, this kind of adaptation creates something new in him, arouses new drives and new anxieties. Every neurosis is an example of this dynamic adaptation.[4]

"Dynamic" here connotes more than simple activity, change, or growth. It suggests certain impelling forces that have a quite different origin and role from the routine tissue tensions of hunger, toothache, and sex. In dynamic adaptation, there is no simple one-to-one relation between an isolated stimulus and its response, a particular drive and its satisfaction, even if one accepts the idea that to some degree the total organism is implicated in all responsive behavior. The point is not the degree of involvement, but the reconstruction of need, the change in posture and strategy, the commitment to new types of satisfaction.

The relevance of these remarks for organizational theory is not far to seek. "Static adaptation" occurs in organizations as well as in personalities. The day-to-day functioning of the organization requires the continuous solution of problems. For the most part, the existing structure—both the informal human relations and the more formal patterns of communication and control—is competent to meet issues as they arise *without internal crisis.* As the daily work proceeds, changes occur, but normally these do not significantly affect the nature of the enterprise or its leadership. Even changes to top personnel may not be significant, if succession is orderly and fundamental policy is firmly established. The corporation grinds out sales and products; the union continues its ceaseless round of negotiations; the government agency extends approved services to assigned publics. Within broad limits, we sometimes say, these large organizations "run themselves"; yet we understand that this holds only for routine activity. In organizational life, just as in individual behavior, this routine functioning and adaptation is quantitatively preponderant. And the proper tooling of everyday activity is a legitimate and necessary preoccupation of management.

Yet in organizations, too, it is plainly necessary to focus attention on dynamics, to study less routine kinds of adaptation. There is a vital sector of organizational experience that cannot be understood as simple problem-solving in which the organization remains essentially intact. Rather, in this sector we find such adaptations of leadership to the interplay of internal and external forces as result in basic institutional changes. This is the area of "character-defining" commitments, which affect the organization's capacity to control its own future behavior. The range of discretion becomes limited, often in unanticipated ways; or it may be significantly broadened. For example, a government agency may adapt itself to a potentially hostile clientele by appointing representatives of the clientele to the agency staff. This has far-reaching consequences for policy, and is not understandable as simple "economic" personnel procurement.

In organizations, "dynamic adaptation" takes place in the shadowy area where administration and policy meet. We must take this, not in the obvious sense that administrative devices execute and form policy, but rather in the sense that organizational processes profoundly influence the kinds of policy that can be made, and policy in turn shapes the machinery of organization in ways that cannot be accounted for on the premises of efficient functioning. At the same time, this is precisely the area of "critical experience" upon which we wish to focus.

When we discuss the bearing of military unification on strategy, the social composition of administrative staffs, the restrictive consequences of administrative alliances, the abandonment of old agencies for new ones, the relation of autonomy to the defense of a program, the unorthodox administrative practices of Franklin Roosevelt, and similar matters, we find ourselves outside the area where administration can be made routine. We are squarely in the field where leadership counts and where managerial *expertise* is of secondary importance.

The term "leadership" connotes critical experience rather than routine practice. This is suggested in the following comment by Barnard:

> The overvaluation of the apparatus of communication and administration is opposed to leadership and the development of leaders. It opposes leadership whose function is to promote appropriate adjustment of ends and means to new environmental conditions, because it opposes change either of status in general or of established procedures and habitual routine. The overvaluation also discourages the development of leaders by retarding the progress of the abler men and by putting an excessive premium on routine qualities.[5]

However, it is easy to overemphasize the *personal* element. While personal qualities are important, and reflect differences in self-conception, too much attention to them may obscure the essential distinction. Even the person free of "routine qualities" may in fact be performing a routine function if he devotes his main energy to greasing the wheels of organization, albeit in human terms. In thinking of leadership, we too often have in mind the personal relation of leader and follower, especially as it involves such psychological mechanisms as identification. This emphasis leads us away from the role of leadership in the making of critical decisions.

It is in the realm of policy—including the areas where policy-formation and organization-building meet—that the distinctive quality of institutional leadership is found. Ultimately, this is the quality of statesmanship which deals with current issues, not for themselves alone but according to their long-run implications for the role and meaning of the group. Group leadership is far more than the capacity to mobilize personal support; it is more than the maintenance of equilibrium through the routine solution of everyday problems; it is the function of the leader-statesman—whether of a nation or a private association—to define the ends of group existence, to design an enterprise distinctively adapted to these ends, and to see that that design becomes a living reality. These tasks are not routine; they call for continuous self-appraisal on the part of the leaders; and they may require only a few critical decisions over a long period of time. "Mere speed, frequency, and vigor in coming to decisions may have little relevance at the top executive level, where a man's basic contribution to the enterprise may turn on his making two or three significant decisions a year."[6] This basic contribution is not always aided by the traits often associated with psychological leadership, such as aggressive self-confidence, intuitive sureness, ability to inspire.

THE CONCEPT OF ORGANIZATION CHARACTER

Our general perspective may be clarified further if we continue the psychological analogy. In particular, the process of "character-formation" seems worth exploring for the insights it may yield to students of institutionalization and critical decision-making. When we have seen the connection between these two phenomena we shall be in a better position to analyze the nature and tasks of institutional leadership.

The idea of "character" as used by personality analysts is not altogether clear, but its usefulness is scarcely in doubt. There seems to be general agreement on four attributes.

First, character is a *historical* product. "The character as a whole," writes Fenichel, "reflects the individual's historical development."[7] Character is the "ego's habitual ways of reacting." In this sense every individual has a unique character.

Second, character is in some sense an *integrated* product, as is suggested by the term "character-structure." There is a discoverable pattern in the way the ego is organized; and the existence of such a pattern is the basis of character analysis.

Third, character is *functional,* in the sense that it is no mere accidental accretion of responsive patterns. Character development fulfills a task set by the requirements of personality organization: the defense of the individual against inner and outer demands which threaten him. "Biologically speaking, character formation is an autoplastic function. In the conflict between instinct and frustrating outer world, and motivated by the anxiety arising from this conflict, the organism erects a protection mechanism between itself and the outer world."[8] Whatever the special content of varying theories of character-formation, they share an emphasis on the *reconstruction of the self* as a way of solving anxiety-laden problems.

Fourth, character is *dynamic* in that it generates new strivings, new needs and problems. It is largely through the identification of these needs that diagnosis proceeds, as when the discovery of excessive dependency or aggressiveness suggests that the patient has a particular type of character-structure.

Now let us compare these attributes of character with the discussion above of how organizations become institutions. The following points were emphasized there:

1. The technical, rational, impersonal, task-oriented formal system (the "organization") is conditioned by the responsive interaction of persons and groups.

2. In the course of time, this responsive interaction is patterned. A social structure is created. This patterning is *historical,* in that it reflects the specific experiences of the particular organization; it is *functional* in that it aids the organization to adapt itself to its internal and external social environment; and it is *dynamic,* in that it generates new and active forces, especially internal interest-groups made up of men committed to particular jobs or policies.

3. Organizations become institutions as they are *infused with value,* that is, prized not as tools alone but as sources of direct personal gratification and vehicles of group integrity. This infusion produces a distinct identity for the organization. Where institutionalization is well advanced, distinctive outlooks, habits, and other commitments are unified, coloring all aspects of organizational life and lending it a *social integration* that goes well beyond formal co-ordination and command.

The study of organizational character-formation is, then, a phase of institutional analysis. Here the emphasis is on the embodiment of values in an organizational structure through the elaboration of commitments —ways of acting and responding that can be changed, if at all, only at the risk of severe internal crisis. As in the case of individuals, the emergence of organizational character reflects the irreversible element in experience and choice. A great deal of management practice, as in the hiring of personnel, may be viewed as an effort to hold down the number of irreversible decisions that must be made. On the other hand, a wise management will readily limit its own freedom, accepting irreversible commitments, when the basic values of the organization and its direction are at stake. The acceptance of irreversible commitments is the process by which the character of an organization is set.

We have suggested that "critical" experience is closely related to organizational self-definition and self-reconstruction. This experience reflects the "open-endedness" of organizational life—the existence of alternative ways of responding and changing. Critical experience calls for leadership. Experience is less critical, and leadership is more dispensable, when the range of alternatives is limited by rigid technical criteria. The more limited and defined the task, the more readily can technical criteria prevail in decision-making. That is one reason why critical experience increases as we ascend the echelons of administration, where decisions based on broader interests must be made. But when the organization is not so limited, when it has the leeway to respond in alternative ways, there is room for character-formation, which enters to give structure to precisely this area of freedom.[9] Hence leadership, character, and critical decision-making are linked as aspects of the same basic phenomenon: the institutionalization of organizational life.

Perhaps the most obvious indicator of organizational character as a palpable reality is the abandonment of old organizations and the creation of new ones when changes in general orientation seem required. A new program does not always call for a new organization, but where a new point of view is to be embodied, there is often recourse to a fresh start. The fear is that the character of the old organization will create resistances to the full development of the new program. In practical terms, this usually means that the new program, even if accepted in good faith, may be threatened by personnel or budgetary procedures, and by many other operating routines that are uncongenial to it. An organization requiring considerable flexibility in personnel practice may find itself seriously hampered as part of a larger enterprise that must, considering the interests of the whole, enforce more rigid standards. Or, where long-established habits of work prevail, a new program may find itself quickly redefined into terms that sustain the received patterns. Issues of this sort were involved when the Roosevelt administration set up many new agencies, as in agriculture, instead of channeling new programs through existing organizations.

CHARACTER AS DISTINCTIVE COMPETENCE

In studying character we are interested in the *distinctive competence or inadequacy* that an organization has acquired. In doing so, we look beyond the formal aspects to examine the commitments that have been accepted in the course of adaptation to internal and external pressures.

For purposes of illustration, let us examine briefly two rather different organizational experiences which have been previously investigated and reported, and in which the phenomenon considered here was studied. We may then consider some further applications and theoretical implications.

1. *Policy and character in the TVA experience.* In a study of the Tennessee Valley Authority,[10] the policy of channeling a federal program through local agencies was examined. In particular, the agricultural activities of the Authority were carried out in co-operation with the Extension Services of the land-grant colleges in the seven Valley states. This co-operation was extensive; in effect, the Extension Service organizations became the operating arm of the TVA in the agricultural field. In assessing the consequences of this arrangement, it was necessary to inquire into such commitments of the Extension Services as (1) might affect the way in which the TVA agricultural program was administered, and (2) might have a broader influence on policy-making in the TVA as a whole.

The "character" of the Extension Service was reflected in the following set of related commitments: (1) The involvement of the county agricultural agent in "courthouse" politics; (2) the intimate relation between the Extension Service and the American Farm Bureau Federation; (3) a tendency of the extension agents to deal with the relatively more prosperous elements of the local farm population and to reflect certain dominant attitudes, such as those toward farm tenancy; (4) a shift in the role of the Extension Service from a primarily educational emphasis to the acceptance of responsibility for "action" programs. These and related commitments, it was found, significantly affected the ability of the TVA to achieve an agricultural program that would be free of restrictive pressures. In addition, the TVA's commitment to the Extension Service involved it in the national struggle for control of the U.S. agricultural programs, drawing it into the Farm Bureau camp.

Further, the commitment created a group *inside* TVA that defended general Extension Service attitudes and objectives and successfully exerted pressure on other TVA programs. . . .

[TVA gained considerable advantages from such concessions as reserving a strip of land around reservoirs for public access, recreation, and conservation. These advantages included the support of important local interests and of a powerful national lobby. Such are the fruits of developing a distinctive organizational competence that make it a key responsibility of executive leadership.]

The relation of leadership to organizational character may be more closely explored if we examine some of the key tasks leaders are called on to perform:

1. *The definition of institutional mission and role.* The setting of goals is a creative task. It entails a self-assessment to discover the true commitments of the organization, as set by effective internal and external demands. The failure to set aims in the light of these commitments is a major source of irresponsibility in leadership.

2. *The institutional embodiment of purpose.* The task of leadership is not only to make policy but to build it into the organization's social structure. This, too, is a creative task. It means shaping the "character" of the organization, sensitizing it to ways of thinking and responding, so that increased reliability in the execution and elaboration of policy will be achieved according to its spirit as well as its letter.

3. *The defense of institutional integrity.* The leadership of any polity fails when it concentrates on sheer survival: institutional survival, properly understood, is a matter of maintaining values and distinctive identity. This is at once one of the most important and least understood functions of leadership. This area (like that of defining institutional mission) is a place where the intuitively knowledgeable leader and the administrative analyst often part company, because the latter has no tools to deal with it. The fallacy of combining agencies on the basis of "logical" association of functions is a characteristic result of the failure to take account of institutional integrity.

4. *The ordering of internal conflict.* Internal interest-groups form naturally in large-scale organizations, since the total enterprise is in one sense a polity composed of a number of sub-organizations. The struggle among competing interests always has a high claim on the attention of leadership. This is so because the direction of the enterprise as a whole may be seriously influenced by changes in the internal balance of power. In exercising control, leadership has a dual task. It must win the consent of constituent units, in order to maximize voluntary co-operation, and therefore must permit emergent interest blocs a wide degree of

representation. At the same time, in order to hold the helm, it must see that a balance of power appropriate to the fulfillment of key commitments will be maintained. . . .

CREATIVE LEADERSHIP

To the essentially conservative posture of the responsible leader we must add a concern for change and reconstruction. This creative role has two aspects. First, there is what we have called the "institutional embodiment of purpose." Second, creativity is exercised by strategic and tactical planning, that is, analyzing the environment to determine how best to use the existing resources and capabilities of the organization. This essay has not treated the problem of externally oriented strategies. On the other hand, what can be done to establish policy internally depends upon the changing relation between the organization and its environment.

The inbuilding of purpose is a challenge to creativity because it involves transforming men and groups from neutral, technical units into participants who have a peculiar stamp, sensitivity, and commitment. This is ultimately an educational process. It has been well said that the effective leader must know the meaning and master the techniques of the educator. As in the larger community, education is more than narrow technical training; though it does not shrink from indoctrination, it also teaches men to think for themselves. The leader as educator requires an ability to interpret the role and character of the enterprise, to perceive and develop models for thought and behavior, and to find modes of communication that will inculcate general rather than merely partial perspectives.

The main practical import of this effort is that *policy will gain spontaneous and reasoned support*. Desired ends and means are sustained and furthered, not through continuous command, but as a free expression of truly accepted principles. This presumes that at least the core participants combine loyalty to the enterprise with a sensitive awareness of the principles by which it is guided. Loyalty by itself is not enough, just as blind patriotism is insufficient. There must also be an ability to sense when a course of action threatens institutional integrity.

To be sure, this ideal of rational, free-willed consent is virtually impossible to achieve in organizations that have narrow, practical aims and whose main problem is the disciplined harnessing of human energy to achieve those aims. But such organizations, just because of this narrowness, are but meagerly institutionalized and have correspondingly little need for executive statesmanship. The creativity we speak of here is particularly necessary—and peculiarly possible—where, as discussed earlier, the transition from organization to institution is in process or has occurred.

To create an institution we rely on many techniques for infusing day-to-day behavior with long-run meaning and purpose. One of the most important of these techniques is the elaboration of socially integrating myths. These are efforts to state, in the language of uplift and idealism, what is distinctive about the aims and methods of the enterprise. Successful institutions are usually able to fill in the formula, "What we are proud of around here is. . . ." Sometimes, a fairly explicit institutional philosophy is worked out; more often, a sense of mission is communicated in more indirect but no less significant ways. The assignment of high prestige to certain activities will itself help to create a myth, especially if buttressed by occasional explicit statements. The specific ways of projecting a myth are as various as communication itself. For creative leadership, it is not the communication of a myth that counts; rather, creativity depends on having the will and the insight to see the necessity of the myth, to discover a successful formulation, and above all to create the organizational conditions that will sustain the ideals expressed.

Successful myths are never merely cynical or manipulative, even though they may be put forward self-consciously to further the chances of stability or survival. If a state university develops a concept of "service to the community" as its central ideal, as against more remote academic aspirations, this may have its origins in a sense of insecurity, but it will not be innocent in application. To be effective, the projected myth cannot be restricted to holiday speeches or to testimony before legislative committees. It will inevitably color many aspects of university policy, affecting standards of admission, orientations of research, and the scope of the curriculum. The compulsion to embody the myth in practice has a dual source, reflecting inner needs and outer demands. Externally, those who can enforce demands upon the institution will not be content with empty verbal statements. They will expect conformity and the myth itself will provide a powerful lever to that end.

The executive acts out the myth for reasons of self-expression, but also for quite practical administrative reasons. He requires *some* integrating aid to the making of many diverse day-to-day decisions, and the myth helps to fulfill that need. Sharp discrepancies between theory and practice threaten his own authority in the eyes of subordinates; conformity to the myth will lessen "trouble" with outside groups. Not least important, he can hope that the myth will contribute to a unified sense of mission and thereby to the harmony of the whole. If the administrator is primarily dedicated to maintaining a smooth-running machine, and only weakly committed to substantive aims, these advantages will seem particularly appealing.

In the end, however, whatever their source, myths are institution builders. Making the myth effective willy-nilly entrenches particular objectives and capabilities, although these may not be the ones that initially inspired the sponsors of the enterprise. Myth-making may have roots in a sensed need to improve efficiency and morale; but its main office is to help create an integrated social organism.

The art of the creative leader is the art of institution-building, the reworking of human and technological materials to fashion an organism that embodies new and enduring values. The opportunity to do this depends on a considerable sensitivity to the politics of internal change. This is more than a struggle for power among contending groups and leaders. It is equally a matter of avoiding recalcitrance and releasing energies. Thus winning consent to new directions depends on how secure the participants feel. When many routine problems of technical and human organization remain to be solved, when the minimum conditions for holding the organization together are only precariously met, it is difficult to expend energy on long-range planning and even harder to risk experimental programs. When the organization is in good shape from an engineering standpoint it is easier to put ideals into practice. Old activities can be abandoned without excessive strain if, for example, the costs of relatively inefficient but morale-saving transfer and termination can be absorbed. Security is bartered for consent. Since this bargain is seldom sensed as truly urgent, a default of leadership is the more common experience.

On the same theme, security can be granted, thereby releasing energies for creative change, by examining established procedures to distinguish those important to a sense of security from those essential to the aims of the enterprise. Change should focus on the latter; stability can be assured to practices that do not really matter so far as objectives are concerned but which do satisfy the need to be free from threatening change. Many useless industrial conflicts have been fought to protect prerogative and deny security, with but little effect on the ultimate competence of the firm.

If one of the great functions of administration is the exertion of cohesive force in the direction of institutional security, another great function is the creation of conditions that will make possible in the future what is excluded in the present. This requires a strategy of change that looks to the attainment of new capabilities more nearly fulfilling the truly felt needs and aspirations of the institution. The executive becomes a statesman as he makes the transition from administrative management to institutional leadership.

NOTES

1. This problem has received considerable attention, with largely negative but still inconclusive results. See Ralph M. Stogdill, "Personal Factors Associated with Leadership: A Survey of the Literature," *J. Psychology,* 1948, 25: 35–71; also William O. Jenkins, "A Review of Leadership Studies with Particular Reference to Military Problems," *Psychological Bulletin,* 1947, 44: 54–77.
2. Indeed, the current literature on this subject, in part as a reaction against the "trait" approach, in part due to the influence of "situational" or "field" theory in social psychology, has made this a central conclusion. Thus Jenkins, *op. cit.,* p. 75, finds: "Leadership is specific to the particular situation under investigation. Who becomes the leader of a given group engaging in a particular activity and what the leadership characteristics are in the given case are a function of the specific situation, including the measuring instruments employed. There is a wide variation in the characteristics of individuals who became leaders in similar situations, and even greater divergence in leadership in different situations." But note the following by Stogdill, *op. cit.,* p. 65: "The evidence suggests that leadership is a relation that exists between persons in a social situation, and that persons who are leaders in one situation may not necessarily be leaders in other situations. Must it then be assumed that leadership is entirely incidental, haphazard, and unpredictable? Not at all. The very studies which provide the strongest arguments for the situational nature of leadership also supply the strongest evidence indicating that leadership patterns as well as non-leadership patterns of behavior are persistent and relatively stable."
3. Erich Fromm, *Escape from Freedom* (New York: Rinehart, 1941), p. 15.
4. *Ibid.,* pp. 15–16.
5. C. I. Barnard, *Organization and Management* (Cambridge: Harvard University Press, 1948), pp. 204 f.
6. E. P. Learned, D. N. Ulrich, and D. R. Booz, *Executive Action,* Harvard University Graduate School of Business Administration, Boston, 1951, p. 57.
7. Otto Fenichel, *The Psychoanalytic Theory of Neurosis* (New York: Norton, 1945), p. 470.

8. Wilhelm Reich, *Character-Analysis,* New York, 1949, p. 159.
9. Cf. Karl W. Deutsch, "Communication in Self-Governing Organizations," in *Freedom and Authority in Our Time* (New York: Harper, 1953): "The importance of memory is the greater, and the effects of its loss the more severe, because a functioning memory implies the probability of eventual *individuation.* Two organizations might set out with exactly the same structure, and yet the different experiences from the outside world would eventually produce different stocks of memories in each, and eventually different kinds of behavior even in the presence of identical stimuli. Then such organizations might function in some respects similarly to individuals with pecularities of personality; and as their memory-guided behavior might influence their intake of subsequent memories, such organizations might be capable of considerable internal evolution" (p. 275).
10. Philip Selznick, *TVA and the Grass Roots* (Berkeley and Los Angeles: University of California Press, 1949).

THE CEO'S BEHAVIOR*

Chris Argyris

Contrary to popular opinion, business leads all other segments of society in recognizing "the human side of enterprise." Most of the innovative techniques that relate interpersonal behavior to organizational effectiveness originated, not in schools, hospitals, religious institutions, or government agencies, where they are frequently used, but in modern business organizations.

Today, one can find executives in all parts of the globe who have heard of Theory Y and who are genuinely interested in moving beyond pious rhetoric to implement it. In this country, more and more executives are examining their own behavior to determine whether or not they actively encourage their subordinates to be frank, trusting, and willing to take risks—three qualities they profess to value.

There is increasing evidence, however, that a chief executive's concern about the quality of his relationships with his subordinates may not

* Chris Argyris, "The CEO's Behavior: Key to Organizational Development," *Harvard Business Review,* Vol. 51, No. 2 (March–April 1973), pp. 55–64, Copyright © 1973 by the President and Fellows of Harvard College; all rights reserved.

perceptibly affect his behavior. A company president may be genuinely committed to Theory Y, but either unwilling or unable to pattern his own behavior accordingly. This problem must be carefully analyzed and eliminated before the gap between theory and behavior undermines the real progress that has been made.

In most businesses, the person responsible for this credibility gap is the chief executive officer. Therefore, in this article I shall discuss the management programs which CEOs profess to support, and also analyze the discrepancies between management theory and executive behavior.

LEADERSHIP PHENOMENA

For the past decade I have recorded, observed, and analyzed top management decision making in some 50 private and public organizations. I have had access to more than 50,000 samples of management behavior, culled from more than 200 meetings. An analysis of these combined experiences reveals five related leadership phenomena:

1. Most chief executives have three characteristics in common—they are articulate, competitive, and persuasive. They compete vigorously for "air time," excel in one-upmanship, and stimulate win-lose competition.
2. CEOs differ significantly from all other executives in my sample. They are more competitive, and (unconsciously) encourage conformity among their subordinates and discourage others from taking risks.
3. The win-lose style of competition that dominates top management groups is an outgrowth of the chief executive's own leadership style. At the same time, CEOs claim to value vice presidents who, like themselves, are articulate, persuasive, competitive, and speak their minds. They believe that this "fit" between their own and their subordinates' leadership styles creates a self-reinforcing system.
4. Interviews with vice presidents suggest, however, that the system is self-reinforcing in ways not understood by most chief executives. Although most of the vice presidents in the sample are articulate and competitive, they report that they do not always speak their minds. The stronger the win-lose dynamics within the top executive group, the more carefully they measure and plan their statements. Yet they try to disguise their caution because success within their organizations depends on a show of forcefulness.
5. In all but two cases, the CEOs whose vice presidents feel the need to exercise caution claim to put a high premium on candor in their relationships with their subordinates. They support management programs which emphasize personal growth, risk taking, and trust.[1]

Subordinates' Reactions

Let me say that I am convinced the typical chief executive whom I interviewed and observed is sincerely motivated. He is genuinely committed to human development for its own sake, as well as for the sake of his company's well-being and future effectiveness. He sincerely wants to create an environment within his company which will stimulate organizational development and simultaneously encourage human development.

Most of the executives in my sample are highly intelligent. Those in their late 30's, 40's, and early 50's are especially adept at conceptualizing problems and issues. It is my belief that the primary reason for the CEO's inability to follow through on his good intentions is a lack of training. Nothing in his educational background—either in college or in executive training programs—prepared him to develop behavior consistent with his values.

In addition, the CEO does not get feedback from his subordinates. Although his vice presidents are aware of his commitment to the idea of human development, they know from painful personal experience that there is a wide gap between theory and behavior.

What is more important, these vice presidents realize that their chief executive either is not aware of his inconsistencies or does not wish to discuss them. Given this situation, subordinates choose to play it safe, to act as if discrepancies do not exist.

In one multibillion-dollar business, for example, the chief executive liked to tell his divisional presidents that he approved of "wild ducks." In private, they would retort, "Yes, all flying in the same direction!"

If the CEO values frankness, why do his vice presidents choose to be so cautious? The most frequent reason given is to protect the *boss:* "Hell, if he really knew his impact, he would be upset." Second in frequency is the desire to protect the *organization:* "Maybe organizations need men with compulsion and drive." Third, vice presidents want to protect *themselves.* In one organization, for example, a chief executive frequently repeated that he valued any vice president who had "guts." Aside to his associates, one of his vice presidents said: "We have guts; we just don't want them spilled all over the place."

The CEO experiences an uneasy ambivalence when confronted with reactions to his behavior. He is proud of being perceived as dynamic, intense, and aggressive, yet disturbed by reports that his vice presidents consider him "overpowering" and "difficult to deal with." He is particularly disturbed because he believes that he has chosen subordinates who are not easily intimidated.

It is true that a few vice presidents do feel free to take risks, but even they believe that the chief executive would be "upset" if he knew how his behavior affected others. For this reason, they do not usually level with their chiefs.

Self-Perceived Attributes

To understand the interaction between chief executives and their subordinates, it is useful to know how these top men describe themselves. During our discussions, they identified four characteristics basic to their leadership styles:

1. They set difficult goals for themselves.
2. They are single-mindedly, almost slavishly, committed to achieving their goals.
3. They need continuous feedback. Consequently, they set goals that will provide immediate results.
4. They want their achievements to bear the stamp of their unique ability and drive. The president stakes out his own "turf" and keeps others out.

Equally revealing are some of the chief executives' descriptions of successful business leaders:

Executive A: "The CEO almost by definition is the bulldog who exudes confidence and drive."

Executive B: "Successful business leaders have a peculiar ability to identify an opportunity, and the brains to figure out how to achieve the goals."

Executive C: "Single-mindedness is important. We do not get distracted by others."

Executive D: "Love of achievement. We are very concerned with achievement and fulfillment."

Executive E: "My greatest satisfaction is to create entirely new things."

Executive F: "I want a situation where it is not hard to show clearly what I did. I can *point* to the figures and say, '*I* did *that.*' And few of us want to be stopped by others. Right! Give us our turf and look out!"[2]

Away from his subordinates, the chief executive is frequently able to understand the problems caused by his leadership style. He readily admits that a successful leader is not likely to allow others in his organization to duplicate his style.

Thus he realizes that, by setting tight managerial controls (especially financial) and by making highly detailed plans (especially in marketing, sales, manufacturing, and engineering), he may unwittingly encourage dependency, submissiveness, and lack of initiative among subordinates.

Furthermore, the chief executive is very likely to trespass on his subordinates' "turf" when he believes a crisis exists. The vice president who really desires autonomy and the opportunity for personal achievement may find these denied him by his boss precisely when they are needed most—during a crisis.

When asked to describe the effect they have on their subordinates, the CEOs were frank:

Executive A: "I believe that a real business leader is incapable of generating a climate where people can grow."

Executive B: "Hell, none of us would work for people like ourselves!"

Executive C: "A real executive under any one of us would leave because he couldn't stand it."

Executive D: "We couldn't work for dominant characters such as ourselves. We are leaders."

Executive E: "Those who choose to work for us may need a security blanket. Maybe they need the feeling that 'I don't care if he tramples me or kicks me; I am drawn toward the success pattern.' "

Executive F: "I wonder if a successful leader has the ability to breed another in his image. I think it would be almost self-defeating."

When I asked these men if they had ever had frank discussions with their subordinates about the impact of their leadership styles, most admitted that they had not, for several reasons.

First, many of them were just beginning to realize that a problem existed. In a new setting, discussing the issue frankly with other company presidents, they were able to recognize more clearly their impact on their subordinates. Second, many believed that such forthright discussions would be threatening to vice presidents. Third, all agreed that it was not a part of the organizational ethic, "not the thing to do."

Negative Organizational Impact

The effect of a chief executive's leadership style on his subordinates varies with the individual and with the conditions under which the company is operating. During its early years, an organization is highly vulnerable. Like an infant, it demands constant attention and care.

Under these circumstances, subordinates are likely to feel that their single-minded, compulsive, hard-working chief executive is a critical factor in keeping the organization alive and growing. He fulfills their needs as well as the company's.

When a new company experiences a genuine crisis, many vice presidents like to know that their boss is "in there scrapping and battling with us." As times goes by, however, disillusionment sets in. Vice presidents begin to feel that when "natural" crises do not occur, the president creates his own, as a way of managing *them.* This causes confusion and resentment: "Why does he believe this is the way to motivate us? Dammit, we don't like it."

What vice presidents do not realize is that the president may create crises in order to quiet his own anxieties. In his loneliness at the top, the president wonders how to generate energy for the colossus he manages. By way of an answer, he does to the organization what he does to himself: creates challenges and then devotes his single-minded attention to meeting them.

PROGRAMS FOR CHANGE

What happens when co-workers see the skills of the chief executive as crucial to organizational success but, at the same time, chafe under his leadership style? How do they adapt?

Some subordinates are able to rationalize the president's negative impact on them: "He's overloaded." "He's under great stress." "What else can you expect from his type?" Or "You have to take the bad with the good."

(It is, of course, easier to accept the boss's behavior when he knows he has shortcomings in the area of human relations. One subordinate summarized his attitude toward his company's president in this way: "How can you get angry at a guy who realizes that at times he can be a bastard, doesn't want to be, but can't help it?")

A few vice presidents, whose styles are similar to the president's, never adapt. They are extremely unhappy in a tightly controlled environment and leave as soon as they find an opportunity to run their own shows, to do to others what their president has been doing to them.

The majority try to deal with the situation by building fires that will lead to organizational change. One strategy is to design programs which will involve every level of management in a confrontation with the issue of leadership style. In the next section, I shall describe four such programs, and their shortcomings:

1. *Management by objectives*—a system designed to involve executives in the definition of company and personal management objectives.
2. *Confrontation meetings*—a series of "encounters" designed to deal with the breakdown of communications within management ranks.
3. *Experiential learning*—a sensitivity or T-group session designed to develop participants' awareness of their own behavior and its effect on others.
4. *Organizational development*—a comprehensive strategy designed to promote individual and organizational change.

All four systems are received with enthusiasm when they are introduced. The chief executive may accept—even advocate—a new program, but his behavior invariably undermines its goals and eventually causes it to fail. From my experience with executives who have worked with all four systems, I have been able to identify some reasons for failure.

Management by Objectives

The idea of holding people accountable for meeting specific objectives usually pleases a chief executive: it fits in with his personal style. When it is time for the president and key vice presidents to implement the plan, however, MBO's supporters are inevitably disappointed. Top executives usually take a quick half-day course and respond with gusto that everybody else should take the *full* course to learn the required skills. Here is a typical example:

The CEO of an international corporation met in New York City with the presidents of 40 satellite companies from around the world. These men were divided into three groups in which they discussed the pros and cons of the MBO program to be instituted throughout the corporation. With the knowledge of the participants, these sessions were taped.

Analyses of the meetings revealed that the "styles" of the presidents in discussing human development inhibited their own development and the frank exchange of ideas. Even when talking about MBO, their behavior was inconsistent with its objectives.

When this inconsistency was pointed out to them, the typical response was: "Let those below me participate in the program; I don't need it." And when they were asked how a process that they did not find helpful could help others in their organizations, the CEOs gave many explanations.

Some of the presidents argued that the informality and congeniality which exist at their level of management would be harmed by the introduction of a formal set of procedures. Others felt that younger executives should experience a system of appraisal as part of an acculturation process. Still others emphasized that the MBO evaluation process would weed out executives who were unable to conform to the authoritarian management structure that must exist in business.

It is not difficult to predict the fate of the new program. The gap between theory and behavior will cause a breakdown of trust between superior and subordinate, and the program will soon lose its credibility.[3]

Confrontation Meetings

When a crisis in a company reveals that there has been a breakdown in communications, confrontation meetings may be planned to deal with the problem. Perhaps the crisis was losing a big order, not meeting a commitment to a valued customer, or discovering an instance of gross mismanagement.

To "get honest" and "level with each other," the top management group, including the president, may take part in a weekend session away from the company. If the executives are intent on finding constructive solutions to the crisis problem, they may be exceptionally candid in their discussions.

Consider this example: Executives from several levels of management met to diagnose the misuse of human resources within their company. During the meetings they described a number of company problems such as—

. . . communications from the top management level to other levels were, in their words, "too controlling";

. . . communications originating with other executive groups for the benefit of top management were "defensive" and "survival-oriented";

. . . marketing techniques "mirrored these defensive, survival-oriented reactions";

. . . risks were avoided because of the "win-lose dynamics within the company."

Top management was also severely criticized, with remarks such as—

. . . "they pit people against each other";

. . . "they want boat rockers, but no rocking boats";

. . . "they permit only enough middle-management involvement in decision making to pacify";

. . . "they think and talk big—act small."

When presidents are given the kind of feedback described in the foregoing example, they usually express "deep appreciation." But their private reactions are more ambivalent. They may feel disappointed, angry, or rejected. Sometimes a president realizes that many of his subordinates are dissatisfied because their own needs are so similar to his.

But he may also feel that people have ignored or forgotten his hard work in building the company. Or he may interpret the diagnosis of company ills as a rejection: "We don't need you any more." Or "The company would be better off without you." He may even be afraid that there really is little left for him to accomplish within the organization.

Whatever his initial reaction, the critical factor in determining whether or not confrontation meetings lead to organizational change is—again—the boss's behavior from day to day. If his leadership does not encompass the new spirit of tolerance and candor, the mood soon evaporates.

Experiential Learning

To focus on their own behavior within their organizations, many presidents attend T-group, or sensitivity, sessions. The overwhelming number of participants find the sessions "a wonderful opportunity for personal growth." They wonder how best to use their insights back at the office. Some ask their vice presidents to attend similar sessions, hoping eventu-

EXHIBIT I
Categories of CEO Experiential Learning Behavior

LEVEL I		LEVEL II
Individual	Interpersonal	Group norms
Willingness to experiment	Helping others to experiment	Trust
Openness	Helping others to be open	Concern for others
Owning up	Helping others to own up	Individuality
Zero line		
Not owning up	Not helping others to own up	Conformity
Not open	Not helping others to be open	Antagonism
Not willing to experiment	Not helping others to experiment	Distrust

ally to seed the organization with enough T-group participants to form an internal company program.

Recently, I had an opportunity to do a follow-up study on a group of company presidents, each of whom had attended at least one T-group session. (One president had participated in seven.) They sent me tape recordings of executive meetings held under their leadership after they had received sensitivity training. *Exhibit I* presents the categories of behavior used in analyzing these tapes.

As shown in this exhibit, the categories of behavior above the zero line ("willingness to experiment," "openness," and "owning up") facilitate interpersonal relationships. Their counterparts, categories below the zero line ("not owning up," "not open," and "not willing to experiment") inhibit interpersonal relationships. Behavior in categories closest to the zero line is the easiest to act out; behavior furthest away from the zero line is the most difficult.

For example, it is easier to "own up" to acceptable opinions or feelings than to experiment with ideas or feelings that, if not accepted by the group, will jeopardize one's self-acceptance. The behavior categories are grouped into two levels. Level I includes behavior which contributes to individual and interpersonal norms and Level II that which contributes to group norms.

My analysis of seven presidents' behavior during committee meetings shows that all scored high in "owning up." (See *Exhibit II.*) They expressed their ideas with confidence and candor. However, their behavior seems to fit into the "conformity" category rather than into "concern for others." Only 1% of the behavior seems to fit into "individuality," a category synonymous with "autonomy."

My analysis of the "openness" category (above the zero line in *Exhibit I*) shows that the chief executives were interested in learning from others; but my findings in the "not helping others to . . ." categories (below the line) indicate that the chief executives frequently would cut their subordinates short.

Several types of behavior were missing from these meetings. Each category had two components: an idea and a feeling. In my sample, no feelings were expressed. There was no behavior indicating a "willingness to experiment," no "risk taking," and no "trust." Nor were there instances of "helping others to own up," "helping others to be open," or "helping others to experiment" with ideas or feelings.

In other words, no chief executive's behavior in this sample was of the type to encourage human and organizational development. They did not invite others to share their responsibilities, did not develop cooperative relationships, and did not present opportunities for others to take the initiative and assume new responsibilities. In fact, the findings on

EXHIBIT II
The Behavior of Seven CEOs While Leading Executive Committees

	Percentage behavior scores						
Category of behavior	*CEO 1 (n= 135)*	*CEO 2 (n= 120)*	*CEO 3 (n= 70)*	*CEO 4 (n= 180)*	*CEO 5 (n= 100)*	*CEO 6 (n= 125)*	*CEO 7 (n= 125)*
Openness	19%	25%	17%	18%	20%	19%	17%
Owning up	71	73	83	73	78	63	71
Not helping others to own up	10	02	—	09	02	18	12
Concern for others	69	58	51	33	62	33	35
Individuality	—	—	01	—	—	—	—
Conformity	31	38	48	62	38	63	65
Antagonism	—	04	—	05	—	04	—

Note: n = number of units of behavior scored, on which percentages are based.

these seven presidents do not differ significantly from those on executives who have never participated in T-groups.

Why is it so difficult for these CEOs to use their sensitivity training in a normal company setting?

The primary reason is that most sensitivity laboratories last for only one week. In this short period, very few people can learn new behavior and internalize patterns that will not vanish under stress.

It is true that some of these executives had attended several T-group sessions. The difficulty is that few programs build on previously attended sessions. Moreover, to my knowledge, there are no programs which focus on the *process* of developing behavioral skills that are consistent with organizational development theories.

When a president returns from a sensitivity session feeling satisfied with his learning experience, but does not behave any differently from the way he did before, what do his subordinates do? Do they level with the president?

According to my studies, most choose not to. Those who do level report that their presidents welcome the feedback and are visibly disappointed with themselves for not behaving more effectively. A few vice presidents add that the feedback sessions have convinced them to attend a T-group to see if they can do any better.

In most of the cases I studied, the executives valued their president's commitment to personal development but were pessimistic about the likelihood of its permanence. In just a few cases, the chief executive was able to change significantly, and his new leadership style helped some of his vice presidents to "unfreeze." His insights started chain reactions that continued throughout the organization.

For example, President A invited his subordinates to confront him whenever his behavior inhibited them in decision-making activities. When the vice presidents realized that their chief executive really meant what he said, they became more candid. A few began to wonder how their behavior affected the president, and asked for feedback. The president gave his opinions, but was quick to caution that his was only one possible viewpoint and that perhaps they should ask their peers and subordinates for feedback as well. When the vice presidents acted on this suggestion, the process of inquiry began.

Generally, a vice president who rates his president as "incompetent" in interpersonal relationships usually receives the same rating from his own subordinates.

Organizational Development

Increasingly, the problems of leadership style are being seen in terms of the total management system. To meet the need for change, companies design strategies that will promote management reorganization. Sensitivity sessions and confrontation meetings become part of a larger, more comprehensive program for individual and company development. During these programs, it is common for the president and his vice presidents to work on team-building activities. The goal of each educational experience is to develop individual and group effectiveness.

Reports concerning behavioral change under this type of program are optimistic, but so far no directly observable data are available. Two instances of taped executive meetings show that the critical problem was again the inability of top executives to behave in accordance with their new values. They had not been effectively trained to put their theories to work in real-life situations. As a result, CEOs and their subordinates felt a sense of frustration and failure.

A Comparison of Two Views of Competence

Robert White defines competence as a concept that focuses on:

- Emphasizing novelty.
- Having few predetermined rules.
- Producing further difference-in-sameness.
- The subsiding of motivation when a situation has been explored and presents no new possibilities.
- Experimentation.
- Striving toward autonomy.
- Tending to vary behavior rather than to repeat it.

John J. Morse and Jay W. Lorsch accept the Akron manager's view of competence that focuses on:

- Emphasizing sameness and routine.
- Having many predetermined rules.
- Staying within the differences permitted.
- The continuing of motivation even when a situation presents no new possibilities.
- Minimal experimentation.
- Tending to repeat behavior.

I have encountered other CEOs who question the basic idea of providing more challenge and variety for their managers. They ask, why should they change things if their managers are satisfied?

These CEOs cite, for example, the research of John J. Morse and Jay W. Lorsch who found that, in an Akron manufacturing plant, the managers felt highly satisfied and committed; they expressed a sense of competence and high motivation to perform work that was routine, highly predetermined, and under leaders who made the decisions.[4]

But why did the employees feel a sense of satisfaction, commitment, and competence under these conditions? Morse and Lorsch say because they accepted the orders, performed their jobs well, and therefore felt a sense of success and effectiveness. The key word is "accepted."

How did the acceptance come about? One possibility is that they learned to adapt because, like Skinner's pigeons, this is how they obtained rewards.

But how do we know? Unfortunately, we cannot decide between the two explanations because the study used projective techniques whose results are easily influenced by the environment in which a person works.

Thus what Morse and Lorsch could be showing is that the men so internalized the work requirements that they lost the growth-oriented view of competence that Robert White described (the concept on which Morse and Lorsch base their work.)[5] (See [above] comparison of White's view of competence with the Akron manager's view, accepted by Morse and Lorsch.)

The answer to the question, why should things be changed and more challenge be provided if managers are satisfied, depends on how the CEO values human development and on whether he sees a relationship between personal and organizational development.

An instructive example of this kind of issue was provided about 15 years ago by a large, forward-looking electronics company. Top managers studied data on personnel in their manufacturing plants and found that very few bright young executives sought careers in manufacturing: there was more excitement and opportunity for personal growth in engineering and marketing. Indeed, the engineering plants sent their second-rate personnel to the manufacturing plants, where they performed very well.

The top managers set out to change the situation. They predicted that, if left to function as they were, the manufacturing plants would eventually be riddled with dry rot. After several years of systematic effort by top management, the company was able to attract to the manufacturing operations young executives who were innovative, experimental, and willing to take risks. The development of organizational potential was successfully linked to the development of management potential.

The strategy of trying to deal with the issue of leadership style through designed programs, such as the four we have just seen, will lead to organizational change only when it actually motivates people to modify their own behavior. The credibility of any management system depends on the extent to which the CEO and, subsequently, other top executives are willing to change. When their behavior is not affected by a management system, its failure is inevitable.

TOWARD IMPROVEMENT

Despite the disappointing results described in this article, I am not pessimistic about the possibilities for developing the human side of enterprise. These cases teach us that we are focusing on values and behavior that are extremely important. We are learning that, despite sincere intentions, executives who try to develop new interpersonal skills are, for the most part, unable to achieve frank and open interaction with their subordinates.

Nevertheless, many of these chief executives still hope to be able to develop more effective leadership styles. They believe that it is possible to improve the quality of life within their organizations, and that a more "human" work environment will improve company performance. They value both of these goals.

My recommendations for reducing the credibility gap between management theory and executive behavior are based on four assumptions:

1. Traditional management theories, even when effective, produce organizational atrophy—slow but steady deterioration. Under these systems, business operations may eventually grind to a halt.
2. Using traditional management theories, organizations tend to produce valid information for routine problems, but invalid information for unusual problems whose solutions involve risk taking.
3. Organizations which do not produce valid information for dealing with important problems are usually run by managers who "give themselves up" to the organization, rather than give of themselves. These managers look to the top for cues for change.
4. Real and lasting change requires the sustained involvement of top management.

To begin the process of organizational change, the chief executive should become aware of the extent to which his own leadership style is responsible for his organization's problems.

Next, the company should study the process by which it reaches important management decisions. Executives from within the organization can be assigned to analyze decisions which have already been made. (An example of this method was the Pentagon task force which produced "the Pentagon Papers" on Vietnam war decisions.) Some companies exchange executives to conduct these studies. In both cases, the men who conduct the studies gain a valuable learning experience.

Although this approach gets closer to actual behavior, it is nevertheless incomplete because it is usually based on interviews. Respondents may talk about their values and behavior, but without empirical data it is difficult to evaluate their observations.

The final phase of company development should include team-building sessions in which executives can examine their own behavior and its impact on others, the dynamics of problem solving, and the effectiveness of group activity. This training should not be expanded to other management levels until top executives are able to reinforce their new behavioral skills in their interactions with each other. When they have finally internalized new behavioral patterns, they will be better able to influence their subordinates.

As top executives' behavior becomes more consistent with their goals, the company should redesign organizational structures, management control systems, and pay systems to support the new values. If executives design the new systems themselves, they are likely to make an internal commitment to them.

In my experience, this commitment is usually accompanied by improved methods for monitoring executive behavior and for correcting behavior that is inconsistent with company goals. The company can then develop and increase opportunities for personal and organizational growth.

CONCLUDING NOTE

Because of the way most companies are organized, the chief executive officer is the focal point of power and responsibility for managing and renewing organizations. The CEO is therefore the key to the success of organizational development programs. All this is not new.

But what has not been spelled out clearly is the what and the why about the chief executive officer that makes him the key to the success of organizational development. The answer is: his behavior.

The way the CEO actually behaves is crucial for the survival of organizational renewal and change activities. It is his behavior (and subsequently that of other officers) that ultimately does or does not confirm the idea that organizational development is necessary, credible, and inexorably linked to his leadership style.

NOTES

1. See my articles, "Interpersonal Barriers to Decision Making," *Harvard Business Review,* March–April 1966, p. 84; and "The Incompleteness of Social Psychological Theory," *American Psychologist,* October 1969, p. 893.

2. See my article, "The Company President: Executive Leadership Today and Tomorrow," *Enterprise,* Fall 1972, p. 9.
3. See my book, *Management and Organizational Development* (New York, McGraw-Hill, 1971).
4. "Beyond Theory Y," *Harvard Business Review,* May–June 1970, p. 61.
5. Robert W. White, "Motivation Reconsidered: The Concept of Competence," *Psychological Review,* September 1959, p. 297.

UNDERSTANDING YOUR ORGANIZATION'S CHARACTER*

Roger Harrison

The failure to recognize the ideological issues that underlie organizational conflict is common among managers and administrators. Usually the issues are recognized only when they are blatant and the lines of struggle are drawn, as in labor-management relationships. But by then the conflict may well have developed to the point where a constructive resolution is virtually impossible.

While the term "organization ideologies" is perhaps unfortunately ambiguous, it is the best name I can apply to the systems of thought that are central determinants of the character of organizations. An organization's ideology affects the behavior of its people, its ability to effectively meet their needs and demands, and the way it copes with the external environment. Furthermore, much of the conflict that surrounds organization change is really ideological struggle (an idea that is certainly not new to political science but one about which behavioral scientists have, until recently, been curiously quiet).

For example, during the commissioning and start-up stages of a U.S. chemical plant in Europe, it became apparent that the Americans and local nationals involved had rather different ideas about decision making and commitment to decisions. Consider the approach of each group:

☐ The Americans tended to operate within what I shall later describe as a task-oriented ideology. In problem-solving meetings they believed that everyone who had relevant ideas or information should contribute to the debates, and that in reaching a decision the greatest weight should

---

* Roger Harrison, "Understanding Your Organization's Character," *Harvard Business Review,* Vol. 50, No. 3 (May–June 1972), pp. 119–128.

be given to the best-informed and most knowledgeable people. They strove, moreover, for a clear-cut decision; and once the decision was made, they usually were committed to it even if they did not completely agree with it.

☐ Some of the nationals, however, came to the project from very authoritarian organizations and tended to operate from a power-oriented ideological base (this will also be described later). Each individual seemed to be trying to exert as much control as possible and to accept as little influence from others as he could. If he was in a position of authority, he seemed to ignore the ideas of juniors and the advice of staff experts. If he was not in a position of authority, he kept rather quiet in meetings and seemed almost happy when there was an unclear decision or no decision at all. He would then proceed the way he had wanted to all along.

The task-oriented people regarded the foregoing behavior as uncooperative and, sometimes, as devious or dishonest. The power-oriented people, however, interpreted the task-oriented individuals' emphasis on communication and cooperation as evidence of softness and fear of taking responsibility.

Each group was engaging in what it regarded as normal and appropriate practice and tended to regard the other as difficult to work with or just plain wrong. The fact that the differences were ideological was dimly realized only by the more thoughtful participants. The remainder tended to react to each other as wrongheaded *individuals,* rather than as adherents of a self-consistent and internally logical way of thinking and explaining their organizational world.

In this article I shall present a theory that identifies four distinct, competing organization ideologies and their meaning for the businessman. But, first, let me attempt to further clarify the concept. Here are the most obvious functions that an organization ideology performs:

- Specifies the goals and values toward which the organization should be directed and by which its success and worth should be measured.
- Prescribes the appropriate relationships between individuals and the organization (i.e., the "social contract" that legislates what the organization should be able to expect from its people, and vice versa).
- Indicates how behavior should be controlled in the organization and what kinds of control are legitimate and illegitimate.
- Depicts which qualities and characteristics of organization members should be valued or vilified, as well as how these should be rewarded or punished.
- Shows members how they should treat one another—competitively or collaboratively, honestly or dishonestly, closely or distantly.

- Establishes appropriate methods of dealing with the external environment—aggressive exploitation, responsible negotiation, proactive exploration.

VALUES & IDEOLOGIES

An organization ideology, however, is more than a set of prescriptions and prohibitions. It also establishes a rationale for these "do"s and "don't"s. This rationale explains the behavior of an organization's members as well as the working of the external environment (in the latter case, by telling members how to expect other people and organization systems to behave).

The rationale of an organization ideology is similar to what behavioral scientists call "organization theory." The difference is that behavioral scientists try with varying degrees of success to keep their values from influencing their organization theories; people, for the most part, do not try to keep their values from influencing their organization ideologies. (This is one reason why education about organization behavior is likely to be so emotionally loaded; if you change a man's organization theory, he usually ends up questioning his values as well.)

Among people in organizations, ideas of "what is" and "what ought to be" merge into one another and are—or are made to appear—consistent. Here is an example:

The ideology of a large U.S. manufacturer of consumer products prescribed that work should be organized in the way that produced the most profit. If this meant that some organization members had boring jobs which offered little opportunity for satisfaction and pride in their work, then it was unfortunate but ideologically irrelevant. According to the rationale of this ideology, a majority of people did not have much aptitude or desire for responsibility and decision making, anyhow, and those who did would rise by natural selection to more responsible, satisfying jobs.

Some young managers, however, had rather more egalitarian personal values. They uneasily suspected that there were more boring jobs than there were apathetic people to fill them. They were very excited about a group of research studies which attempted to show that giving employees more responsibility and involvement in decision making actually led to improved performance. But in my discussions with the managers, I found that the studies' instrumental value in improving organization effectiveness was not the cause of their popularity; rather, they were welcomed because they helped the managers reconcile their personal values with the dictum of the prevailing ideology that work should, above all, be organized to produce the best economic result. (I have, in fact, found that behavioral research findings are usually accepted or rejected on such ideological grounds instead of on the probability of their being true.)

A CONCEPTUAL FRAMEWORK

There is a considerable body of thought in political science which holds that attempts to resolve ideological struggle are unwarranted interferences with the natural course of history and as such are doomed to be ineffectual.

I do not feel that this theory has been adequately tested, particularly in regard to organization change and development. The first step in testing it is to develop ways of discovering and understanding ideological conflicts when they arise in organizations.

In the remainder of this article I shall present a conceptual framework for doing this. It postulates four organization ideologies: (1) power orientation; (2) role orientation; (3) task orientation; and (4) person orientation. These ideologies are seldom found in organizations as pure types, but most organizations tend to center on one or another of them. I shall describe and contrast them in their pure form to emphasize their differences, and then indicate what I believe to be the strengths and weaknesses of each. After this I shall apply the conceptual model to some common conflicts in modern organization life.

Power Orientation

An organization that is power-oriented attempts to dominate its environment and vanquish all opposition. It is unwilling to be subject to any external law or power. And within the organization those who are powerful strive to maintain absolute control over subordinates.

The power-oriented organization is competitive and jealous of its territory (whether this be markets, land area, product lines, or access to resources). It seeks to expand its control at the expense of others, often exploiting weaker organizations. Even a weak power-oriented organization takes satisfaction in being able to dominate others that are still weaker. Such organizations always attempt to bargain to their own advantage and readily find justification for abrogating agreements which are no longer self-serving.

Some modern conglomerates project images of power ideology. They buy and sell organizations and people as commodities, in apparent disregard of human values and the general welfare. They seem to have voracious appetites for growth, which is valued for its own sake. Competition to acquire other companies and properties is ruthless and sometimes outside the law. Within the organization, the law of the jungle often seems to prevail among executives as they struggle for personal advantage against their peers.

There is, however, a softer form of the power orientation that is often found among old established firms, particularly those with a background of family ownership. Here the employees may be cared for rather than exploited, especially those that are old and loyal. Externally, the proprietors may hold to a code of honor, especially when dealing with others like themselves. This is the power orientation with a velvet glove. But when the benevolent authority is crossed or challenged, from either within or without, the iron fist is very likely to appear again. In such cases, the test of power orientation is how hard a person or organization will fight for power and position when these are at issue.

Role Orientation

An organization that is role-oriented aspires to be as rational and orderly as possible. In contrast to the willful autocracy of the power-oriented organization, there is a preoccupation with legality, legitimacy, and responsibility.

It is useful to see role orientation as having developed partly in reaction to power orientation. Competition and conflict, for example, are regulated or replaced by agreements, rules, and procedures. Rights and privileges are carefully defined and adhered to. While there is a strong emphasis on hierarchy and status, it is moderated by the commitment to legitimacy and legality. The different attitudes of the power and role orientations toward authority might be likened to the differences between a dictatorship and a constitutional monarchy.

Predictability of behavior is high in the role-oriented organization, and stability and respectability are often valued as much as competence. The correct response tends to be more highly valued than the effective one. Procedures for change tend to be cumbersome; therefore the system is slow to adapt to change.

Most commercial organizations are too constricted by market demands to afford the extreme rigidity of a pure role orientation or the worst excesses of its tendency to place procedural correctness before task effectiveness. Some businesses, however, which either control their markets or operate in areas that are highly regulated by law, exhibit a considerable degree of role orientation. The rationality, impersonality, and adherence to procedure of many banks, insurance companies, public utilities, and social work organizations are cases in point. Their role orientation leaves the customer, the public, or the client with little alternate choice in dealing with them.

Task Orientation

In the organization that is task-oriented, achievement of a superordinate goal is the highest value. The goal need not be economic; it could be winning a war, converting the heathen, reforming a government, or helping the poor. The important thing is that the organization's structure, functions, and activities are all evaluated in terms of their contribution to the superordinate goal.

Nothing is permitted to get in the way of accomplishing the task. If established authority impedes achievement, it is swept away. If outmoded roles, rules, and regulations hinder problem solving, they are changed. If individuals do not have the skills or technical knowledge to perform a task, they are retrained or replaced. And if personal needs and social considerations threaten to upset effective problem solving, they are suppressed in the interests of "getting on with the job."

There is no ideological commitment to authority, respectability, and order as such. Authority is considered legitimate only if it is based on appropriate knowledge and competence; it is not legitimate if it is based solely on power or position. And there is little hesitation to break rules and regulations if task accomplishment is furthered by doing so.

There is nothing inherently competitive about task orientation. The organization structure is shaped and changed to meet the requirements of the task or function to be performed. Emphasis is placed on rapid, flexible organization response to changed conditions. Collaboration is sought if it will advance the goal; allies are chosen on the basis of mutual goals and values; and there is little "advantage seeking" in relationships with other organizations.

The task orientation is most readily found in those small organizations whose members have come together because of some shared value, task, or goal. Examples are social service organizations, research teams, and high-risk businesses. Often, however, internal conflict and external stress drive these organizations toward power and role orientations.

Large organizations that operate in highly complex, shifting environments offer more durable examples. Companies involved with dynamic markets or fast-changing, complex technology frequently establish project teams or "task forces." These groups of specialists are selected to solve a particular problem and often operate in a very flexible and egalitarian manner until the problem is solved. The units are then disbanded, and the members join other teams to work on new problems.

Although the larger organization in which it operates may be basically role- or power-oriented, the project team or task force often exhibits a relatively pure task orientation. Moreover, these groups have been so successful that some organizations are trying to install a task-oriented ideology throughout their operations.

Some of the aerospace industries have probably gone the furthest in this direction, TRW Systems being a notable example. Although I do not know of any large organization that could be classed as "pure" in its task orientation, the success of such task-oriented programs as MBO is a sign of the growing interest among managers. Parenthetically, the most frequent reason for the failure of MBO is probably that task-oriented managers try to install it in power- or role-oriented organizations.

Person Orientation

Unlike the other three types, the person-oriented organization exists primarily to serve the needs of its members. The organization itself is a device through which the members can meet needs that they could not otherwise satisfy by themselves. Just as some organizations continually evaluate the worth of individual members as tools and accept or reject them accordingly, so the person-oriented organizations are evaluated as tools by their members. For this reason, some of these organizations may have a very short life; they are disposable when they cease to provide a system for members to "do their own thing."

Authority in the role- or power-oriented sense is discouraged. When it is absolutely necessary, authority may be assigned on the basis of task competence, but this practice is kept to the bare minimum. Instead, individuals are expected to influence each other through example, helpfulness, and caring.

Consensus methods of decision making are preferred; people are generally not expected to do things that are incongruent with their own goals and values. Thus roles are assigned on the basis of personal preference and the need for learning and growth. Moreover, the burden of unrewarding and unpleasant tasks is shared equally.

Illustrations of person orientation are small groups of professionals who have joined together for research and development. Some consulting companies, too, seem to be designed primarily as vehicles for members. It is typical of such organizations that growth, expansion, and maximization of income and profit are not primary considerations. Rather, the organizations, hopefully, are conducted to make enough money to survive and provide their members with a reasonable living as well as an opportunity to do meaningful and enjoyable work with congenial people.

There seem to be increasing pressures from the members of modern industrial organizations to move toward person orientation. Young professionals are pushing their companies for opportunities to work on interesting, worthwhile (congruent with their own values) projects. Engineers and scientists, for example, have refused to work on projects for the military and have been successful in getting transfers to nondefense-related activities. Job recruiters find that college graduates are often more interested in opportunities to learn and grow than they are in their chances for organization advancement. Such signs of social change illustrate why the person orientation must be considered an ideological force to be reckoned with, even though there are few contemporary organizations that operate in total congruence with its principles.

Strengths & Weaknesses

An organization ideology obviously has a profound effect on organization effectiveness. It determines how (a) decisions are made, (b) human resources are used, and (c) the external environment is approached. An organization ideology tends to be internally viable when the people within the system want and need the prescribed incentives and satisfactions that reward good performance. It tends to be externally viable when the organization it embodies is a microcosm of the external environment and rewards the same skills, values, and motivations.

External Viability

Usually, as an organization increases in size, its operational environment becomes more complex. Most arenas in which large companies operate change rapidly and/or have many features that require an integrated response. Worldwide markets and rapidly changing technology, for example, make heavy demands on the information-processing and decision-making capabilities of organizations.

The power-oriented organization is not well adapted to flexible response and effective information processing in such environments. Since decisions are made at the top, the information has to pass through many people who screen out the "irrelevant" data. Moreover, some may distort the message to their own advantage (aggressive competition is part of the ideology). And when conditions change rapidly, the time lag introduced by the filtering process may unduly delay organization response.

The role-oriented organization is also insufficiently flexible to easily adapt to rapid external changes. In order to achieve the security that is one of its highest values, it must perpetuate rather rigid roles and reporting relationships. This gives stability but means that even the most powerful individuals may be unable to produce needed changes quickly.

In times of change, established procedures often do not apply, and the information channels become overloaded with problems that require higher-level decisions. Consider what happened in the commissioning and start-up example referred to at the beginning of this article:

Because equipment was not working properly, many actions which ordinarily would have been dealt with by standard operating procedures required top-management decisions. But the ordinary channels would not carry the necessary volume of information, and the quality of decision making and problem solving suffered accordingly. However, when control was shifted to teams of experts clustered around each plant (a task-oriented system) the problems were handled much more smoothly.

Change-Oriented Structures. The task-oriented organization's greatest strength is dealing with complex and changing environments. Decentralized control shortens communication channels and reduces time lags, distortion, and attenuation of messages.

Both the power- and role-oriented organizations associate control with a *position* in the organization; neither provides for rapid and rational reassignment of appropriate *persons* to positions of influence. In contrast, the task oriented ideology clears the way for a very flexible system of control—one that can shift rapidly over time as differing resources are required by external problems.

Probably the best example of this system in operation is the project team or task force that is formed to identify, diagnose, and solve a particular problem. Even some rather bureaucratic organizations make use of these temporary systems for emergency problem solving. The task force leader is selected for his combination of technical expertise and ability to manage a small group in an egalitarian manner.

The temporary work system is a particularly characteristic response of the task-oriented organization to environmental change. These temporary systems can be activated quickly, provided with the necessary mix of skills and abilities, and disbanded again when the need is past. Their use provides what is, in effect, a continuously variable organization structure.

The person-oriented organization, too, is well adapted to dealing with complexity and change. It also features a fluid structure and short lines of communication and control.

Coping with Threat. In a highly competitive environment where organizations are frequently confronted with overt threats and hostility, the strengths and weaknesses of ideological types form a different pattern.

For example, while the power-oriented organization is not well suited to handle complexity and change, its structure and decision-making processes are admirably suited for swift decision making and rapid-action follow-through under high-risk conditions. It tends to promote tough, aggressive people who can lead the organization in a dangerous, competitive environment.

The task-oriented organization usually takes longer to respond, but the response is more likely to be based on adequate data and planning. In contrast to the power-oriented structure, which is aggressively directed from the top, it tends to enlist the full commitment of organization members at all levels.

The role-oriented organization does not deal successfully with sudden increases in threat because it relies heavily on established operational procedures. Consequently, its structure is too cumbersome to react quickly in cases of overt threat.

And the person-oriented organization has difficulty directing its members' activities in unison until the danger is so clear and present that it may be too late. The person-oriented structure, however, does offer some advantages—its members are committed and have a high concern for one another's welfare.

Probably the most viable organization in a hostile, threatening environment would have a combination of the power and task orientations. This is a difficult marriage, however, because the desire for personal power is often incompatible with the required willingness to relinquish control to those with the most knowledge and ability for the task at hand.

Internal Viability

The power-oriented organization is an excellent structure for attaching many eyes, ears, hands, and feet to one brain. It exercises tight internal control and integration. As mentioned earlier, the system works well when problems take the form of overt challenges that can be comprehended and solved by one or a few intelligent, courageous men at the top.

But when the power-oriented organization becomes large and complex, this control tends to break down. Under these conditions the role-oriented ideology is more effective. It provides rules and procedures that allow a high degree of internal integration with little active intervention from the top.

It is obviously more difficult to achieve internal cohesion under a task- or person-oriented ideology. For example, if the work is done by temporary project teams, how are their efforts to be coordinated to a common goal? When a problem-solving team comes up with a solution and then disbands, how is its work to be given impact and continuity in the rest of the organization? Some stable and central structure is needed to provide coordination, long-range planning, and continuity of effort. If it is too stable, however, it may become role-oriented (rigid and hard to change) or power-oriented (recentralizing control). The personal power and security needs of individual members may foster such developments.

These dilemmas of internal structure have led to various compromise solutions such as the "matrix organization." The term "matrix" is used because the actual working groups *cut horizontally across* the normal functional-pyramidal organization, bringing together selected individuals from different functions and different levels to work in a relatively autonomous, egalitarian group. Structural stability is provided by a fixed *role-oriented* framework organized on functional lines. Personnel are readily detachable from the functions for varying periods of time during which they join a *task-oriented* work unit or project team. They are directed by the work unit; but their pay, career prospects, and promotions emanate from the role-oriented part of the system.

Matrix forms of organization have been used with success in highly technical businesses operating in a fast-changing environment. Again, TRW Systems is perhaps the oldest and most comprehensive example. Considerable experimentation with matrix forms has also taken place in the chemical industry, both in the United States and abroad.

Although the matrix system can be effective, it often suffers from attempts of the role-oriented functions to overcontrol the task-oriented functions. The resulting conflict is usually won by the former, which has greater permanence and more resources. One reason for this difficulty is that organizations try to operate partially task-oriented structures without commitment to the ideology. Role-oriented people cannot be plugged into a task-oriented system without conflict.

Effective Motivation. While the power-oriented organization provides a chance for a few aggressive people to fight their way to the top, it offers little security to the ordinary person. It is most viable in situations where people are deprived and powerless and have to accept a bad bargain as better than none. For example, the power-oriented organization thrives in underdeveloped countries.

The power-oriented organization also has the problem of using too much of its energy to police people. Reliance on rewards and punishments tends to produce surface compliance and covert rebellion. Where the quantity and quality of work can be observed (as on an assembly line), inspection and discipline may keep the system working. But if the power does not command loyalty as well, the system usually breaks down. A simple example is the sabotage of hard-to-test aspects of car assembly by disgruntled workers.

The role-oriented ideology tries to deal with the difficulty of supervising complex decision-making and problem-solving tasks by rationalization and simplification. Each job is broken into smaller elements, rules are established, and performance is observed. When conditions change, however, the members are likely to continue carrying out the same (now ineffective) procedures.

The power- and role-oriented organizations simply do not provide for the development and utilization of internal commitment, initiative, and independent judgment on the part of members at other than the highest levels. Nevertheless, in societies where most people's aspirations are just to get by, or at most to achieve a measure of economic security, the power- and role-oriented organizations are able to function adequately.

In affluent societies, however, where security is more widely assured, people begin to look for deeper satisfactions in their work. They attempt to change tightly controlled work assignments and rigid internal structures. When trends toward task orientation ("useful," "meaningful" work) and person orientation (interesting work, self expression, and "doing one's own thing") begin to develop in the wider society, internal pressures for change develop within power- and role-oriented organizations.

Unfortunately, not all people can function productively in a flexible and egalitarian structure. Some people *are* dependent, apathetic, or insecure. They do need external incentives to work and directives or rules to guide their activities.

Furthermore, the task-oriented ideology has its own ways of exploiting the individual. When his knowledge and skills become obsolete for the task at hand, an individual is expected to step gracefully aside to make room for someone who is better qualified. Status and recognition depend almost entirely on task contribution; if the problems facing the organization change suddenly, this can produce cruel reversals of an individual's personal fortune and work satisfaction.

The person-oriented organization seems to be specially created to fit the work situation to the motives and needs of the independent, self-directed individual. It is flexible to his demands, whereas the power-oriented organization is controlling; it gives scope for his individual expression, whereas the role-oriented organization programs every move; it is concerned about his personal needs, whereas the task-oriented organization uses people as instruments for "higher" ends. Unfortunately, as discussed above, the person-oriented organization is less likely to be effective in the external environment than organizations based on the other ideologies.

TOWARD RESOLVING CONFLICT

One basic tension runs throughout the ideologies and organization types discussed thus far. It is the conflict between (a) the values and structural qualities which advance the interests of people and (b) the values and structural qualities which advance the interests of organizations.

I can identify six interests, all mentioned previously, which are currently the subject of ideological tension and struggle. Three of these are primarily interests of people, and three are primarily interests of organizations. The three interests of people are:

1. Security against economic, political, or psychological deprivation.
2. Opportunities to voluntarily commit one's efforts to goals that are personally meaningful.
3. The pursuit of one's own growth and development, even where this may conflict with the immediate needs of the organization.

The three interests of organizations are:

1. Effective response to threatening and dangerous complex environments.
2. Dealing rapidly and effectively with change and complex environments.
3. Internal integration and coordination of effort toward organization needs and goals, including the subordination of individual needs to the needs of the organization.

These are obviously not all the interests at issue, but in my opinion they are among the most salient.

Exhibit I shows the position of each ideology vis-à-vis each interest and indicates, as does the preceding analysis, that the four ideologies have quite dissimilar profiles. Each ideology thus "fits" the needs of a given organization and its members differently. For example, a small organization operating in a rapidly changing technical field and employing people who desire personal growth and autonomy might find its best fit with either the task or person orientation (this depends, of course, on how competitive its markets are and what financial shape it is in). A very large organization operating a slowly changing technology in a restricted market and employing people who desire stability and security might find that a role orientation would provide the best balance.

EXHIBIT I
Interests of People and the Organization Under Four Orientations

A. Interests of people

	Security against economic, political, and psychological deprivation	Opportunities for voluntary commitment to worthwhile goals	Opportunities to pursue one's own growth and development independent of organization goals
Power orientation	Low: At the pleasure of the autocrat	Low: Unless one is in a sufficiently high position to determine organization goals	Low: Unless one is in a sufficiently high position to determine organization goals
Role orientation	High: Secured by law, custom, and procedure	Low: Even if, at times, one is in a high position	Low: Organization goals are relatively rigid and activities are closely prescribed
Task orientation	Moderate: Psychological deprivation can occur when an individual's contributions are redundant	High: A major basis of the individual's relationship to the organization	Low: The individual should not be in the organization if he does not subscribe to some of its goals
Person orientation	High: The individual's welfare is the major concern	High: But only if the individual is capable of generating his own goals	High: Organization goals are determined by individual needs

B. Interests of the organization

	Effective response to dangerous, threatening environments	Dealing rapidly and effectively with environmental complexity and change	Internal integration and coordination of effort—if necessary, at the expense of individual needs
Power orientation	High: The organization tends to be perpetually ready for a fight	Moderate to low: Depends on size; pyramidal communication channels are easily overloaded	High: Effective control emanates from the top
Role orientation	Moderate to low: The organization is slow to mobilize to meet increases in threat	Low: Slow to change programmed procedures; communication channels are easily overloaded	High: Features a carefully planned rational system of work
Task orientation	Moderate to high: The organization may be slow to make decisions but produces highly competent responses	High: Flexible assignment of resources and short communication channels facilitate adaptation	Moderate: Integrated by common goal; but flexible, shifting structure may make coordination difficult
Person orientation	Low: The organization is slow to become aware of threat and slow to mobilize effort against it	High: But response is erratic; assignment of resources to problems depends greatly on individual needs and interests	Low: A common goal is difficult to achieve and activities may shift with individual interests

For most organizations, however, there is no perfect fit with any one of the four ideologies. The "ideal" ideology would possess some power orientation to deal smartly with the competition, a bit of role orientation for stability and internal integration, a charge of task orientation for good problem solving and rapid adaption to change, and enough person orientation to meet the questions of the new recruit who wants to know why he should be involved at all unless *his* needs are met.

But, unfortunately, this mixture of ideologies *and their consequences* for people and organizations will inevitably result in conflict, and its subsequent wear and tear on organizations and their members. Trying to mix ideologies may also prevent each type from producing the advantages that are unique to it.

On the other hand, I do not think that the most viable organizations and the maximum satisfaction of human needs will result from monolithic structures which are ideologically homogeneous. It seems to me that we must learn to create and maintain organizations that contain within them the same diversity of ideologies and structures as are found in the complex environments in which the organizations must live and grow. This means that organizations may have to be composed of separate *parts* that are ideologically homogeneous within themselves yet still quite different from each other.

Such organizations will be very effective in dealing with complex environments and maximizing satisfactions for different types of people, but they will be subject to more internal conflict and ideological struggle than most current organizations could tolerate. For example, instead of a "company spirit" there will be several "company spirits," all different and very likely antagonistic. In this environment of conflicting but mutually interdependent parts, the management—not the resolution—of conflict will be a task of the greatest importance. One can imagine, in fact, that the most important job of top managers will not be directing the business, but, instead, managing the integration of its parts.[1]

CONCLUDING NOTE

Whether men confront or avoid them, ideological issues will continue to sharpen of their own accord, both inside and outside the organization. As long as we continue to raise and educate our children permissively, the pressure from younger members of the organization for greater person orientation will increase. As operational environments become more turbulent and more technical, the attractions of task orientation will make themselves felt. Yet every change in organizations means some degree of power redistribution and with it some shift in rewards—such shifts will always be resisted by those with the most to lose, usually the older members of the organization who have a higher status. Thus I believe that ideological conflict will increase within organizations, whether that conflict is dealt with openly or not.

By dealing with such conflict openly, however, businessmen may find ways to manage it in the service of both the organization and its members and also to use tension creatively as well as competitively. Hidden conflict, on the other hand, tends to eat away at the strength of an organization and then to erupt when it is most dangerous to organization health.

In writing this article, I have attempted to render these inevitable ideological differences more conceptually clear. The next step is to develop a common language and set of norms that support both the open confrontation of such issues and the strategies for dealing with them in our organizations.

NOTE

1. See Paul R. Lawrence and Jay W. Lorsch, "New Management Job: The Integrator," *Harvard Business Review,* November–December 1967, p. 142.

THE DIFFUSION OF NEW WORK STRUCTURES*

Richard E. Walton

When organizations engage in experimental projects in work restructuring, an underlying assumption is that if the innovation is effective, it will be adapted and used by other units in the organization. Most of us would expect that an organizational pattern that is working better than the one it replaced will be recommended by superiors and emulated by peers. Experience, however, shows this to be not necessarily true: The assumed tendencies are sometimes nullified and offset by competing organizational dynamics.

---

* Reprinted with permission of author and publisher from ORGANIZATIONAL DYNAMICS, Vol. 3, No. 3 (Winter 1975), pp. 3–22, © 1975 by AMACOM, a division of American Management Associations.

I have studied a sample of organizations that made early efforts at the comprehensive redesign of work, asking: How much diffusion has occurred, particularly within the same firm? What are the vehicles for diffusion? What barriers are encountered? How does the character of the innovation affect the rate of its diffusion? Answers to questions such as these can help us formulate better diffusion strategies and tactics.

EIGHT EXPERIMENTS

The eight firms included in the study had the following characteristics: All started their research on work redesign in the 1960s; their early experiments involved relatively comprehensive work restructuring; these experiments were all judged initially successful; the firms had a number of physically separate facilities, usually geographically dispersed; the change efforts of all the firms received substantial publicity.

Of the eight firms, two are in the U.S., two in Canada, one in Great Britain, two in Norway, and one in Sweden. The firms in the U.S. are Corning Glass, which initiated a study in its Medfield, Mass., assembly plant in 1965, and the General Foods Corporation, which initiated an experiment in its pet food plant in Topeka, Kansas, in January 1971, although it had begun planning for change in 1968. The Canadian organizations are the Sales and Fabrication Division of Alcan and the Advanced Devices Center, a division of Northern Electric Company, subsequently renamed Microsystems International, Ltd. In 1964, a group of Alcan managers launched a project in one plant in the works at Kingston, Ontario; over time the innovations developed in the first effort at Kingston were extended to other existing Sales and Fabrication Division plants and eventually to a new cold rolling mill. The Northern Electric unit designed a radically different organization for a new semiconductor facility that was occupied in January 1966.

The European companies form the remainder of the sample. Shell U.K. introduced change in several locations in the mid-1960s, including a new refinery at Teesport, which came on stream in 1968. Several Norwegian projects were carried out in different industries under the Industrial Democracy Project, an action research program sponsored jointly by the Norwegian Federation of Employers and the Trades Union Council of Norway and guided by social scientists associated with the Work Research Institute in Oslo. The two projects included in this study were the fertilizer plants at Norsk Hydro in Porsgrunn and a department in the Hunsfos pulp and paper complex near Kristiansand. They were initiated in the mid-1960s.

A Swedish experiment in Volvo's truck assembly plant in Lundby, begun in 1969, has been followed by similar changes in a neighboring auto assembly plant, the design of a revolutionary car plant at Kalmar that went on stream in 1974, and a commitment to an advanced form of work structuring in a new Volvo plant in the U.S. planned for 1975.

An important similarity existed in the change strategies employed by seven of these eight firms. An early experiment in one unit of the firm was regarded as a pilot project from which the larger organization could learn. The positive results, if any, could demonstrate the value of work restructuring. Lessons gained from the experiment then could be made available to other units. The eighth, Shell U.K., by contrast followed a change strategy in which the demonstration projects were not the point of departure.

The extent of diffusion that has occurred within these eight firms has varied widely. In four companies (Corning, Northern Electric, Hunsfos, and Norsk Hydro) diffusion has been nonexistent or small. In three companies (General Foods, Shell U.K., and Alcan) somewhat more diffusion has occurred; however, the rate either has been slow or it has not been sustained. Only in one company in my sample, namely Volvo, was diffusion truly impressive. Managers involved in all the changes, including those at Volvo, clearly had expected more rapid and extensive change.

GENERAL MODEL

Before exploring the diffusion of "work restructuring," or the lack of diffusion, let us clarify what we mean by the term. The work restructuring approach pursued in the eight cases studied embraces many aspects of work, including the content of the job, compensation schemes, scope of worker responsibility for supervision and decision making, social structure, status hierarchy, and so on. The design of each element is intended to contribute to an internally consistent work culture—one that *appropriately* enlarges workers' scope for self-management, enhances their opportunity for learning new abilities, strengthens their sense of connectedness with co-workers, increases their identification with the product and manufacturing process, and promotes their sense of dignity and self-worth. The word "appropriately" is used in the preceding sentence to signify that the extent to which work structures can realistically depart from today's conventional work organization depends upon many situational factors, especially the type of technology involved, composition of the work force (Is it educated and skilled?), and economic forces

(Do they favor the expenditures of time and money involved in a comprehensive attempt at job restructuring?).

Each diffusion effort had its own unique characteristics, but they all also shared many points. A generalized model of the change efforts, containing seven aspects or steps, will highlight both the similarities and the differences. Although I have viewed the early experiments as the first of a number of steps in transforming work throughout the larger corporation, they were not necessarily so conceived at the time they were initiated, either by direct participants or by corporate officials.

Step 1: Initiation of the pilot experiment. Although perhaps similarly inspired, pilot experiments took a variety of forms. Some were in new plants—GF's Topeka, Corning's Medfield, Alcan's Center Plant at the Kingston Works, and Northern Electric's plant at Montreal. Others were in established plants—Hunsfos' pulp and paper mill and Volvo's Lundby truck plant. At Norsk Hydro, experiments were initiated simultaneously in an existing and a new fertilizer facility. The Shell U.K. demonstration projects occurred as a later step in the process of restructuring work, but they too embraced both existing and new facilities.

Some experiments involved relatively radical and comprehensive work restructuring at the outset—especially GF's pet food plant, Norsk Hydro's fertilizer plants, Hunsfos' chemical pulp department, and Shell U.K.'s new Teesport refinery. Significantly, each of these four facilities is relatively small, employing fewer than 100 workers, and involves a continuous-processing technology. Also, the way work was restructured in these continuous-processing plants is remarkably similar: Self-managing teams were formed to take responsibility for large segments of the process. Job rotation among team members was encouraged both to improve control of the technology and to provide intrinsically satisfying learning experiences for workers. Support activities, such as maintenance, quality control, and cleaning, were incorporated into operating team responsibilities. Because of the diverse abilities required to manage, operate, and maintain these technologies, team members received heavy doses of skills training. Pay was based on the relevant skills and knowledge a worker had acquired rather than on the particular job he was performing. New information and measurement systems were developed to enable teams to keep on top of their enlarged responsibilities.

Northern Electric's Advanced Devices Center, because it focused mostly on professional and managerial personnel, differed from the four continuous-processing facilities. The Advanced Devices Center featured a matrix organization, functional and business teams, elaborate communication schemes, open office layouts, and nontraditional titles and reporting relationships.

Other experiments—in the new plants at Alcan and Corning and the existing facilities at Volvo and Shell U.K.—involved more moderate change. Significantly, two of these, Corning and Volvo, are assembly plants where the nature of the tasks and technology provided relatively little opportunity for upgrading the abilities of the work teams. Thus in these plants emphasis was placed on freeing workers from the tedium of short repetitive work cycles and on steps that would improve communication. Within those constraints, both were bold efforts at work restructuring. The changes that evolved over several years were rotation among and/or enlargement of assembly tasks, the formation of teams, and mechanisms for worker participation or consultation.

An incremental approach to work restructuring in the initial projects in both the Alcan plants and Shell's existing refineries was necessary in part because of constraints related to collective bargaining.

The initial experiment in a majority of cases occurred at the urging of a middle-level line manager, typically a plant manager, or with his active participation. Staff people and outside consultants or researchers also played an active role in designing and implementing most of the initial experiments. In the Norwegian projects, the researchers actually sought out the companies and persuaded them to collaborate in undertaking the projects. Similarly, in the Corning experiment, a corporate consultant began by stimulating interest among supervisors to try their own mini-experiments, which, if successful, could lead to plantwide work restructuring. Interestingly, although the management and worker members of the Norwegian and the Corning experiments subsequently came to "own" the projects, dependency upon outside experts long remained a factor in these cases, each of which resulted in little intracompany diffusion.

Step 2: Pilot experiment declared early success. The study included only those experiments that were judged successful after a year or two, when participants had had significant experience with the new work structures and when operating results could be assessed.

Spokesmen for these projects claimed that they had produced improved performance, increased worker knowledge and skills, and resulted in a generally more responsible and motivating work culture. In no case were there wholly independent performance audits or measurements that would persuade the most ardent skeptics of work restructuring. While my own field visits led me to conclude that in most cases some discounting of claims seemed to be required, I accept the original judgments of early success.

Results claimed on both the hard and soft sides of the benefits ledger varied: Only about 25 percent of the Northern Electric workers said they experienced a relatively large gain in the quality of their working life; among General Foods workers it was 80 percent. The balance, at least during the initial periods, would fall somewhere between. Six cases reported quality improvement and more efficient production due to decreased scrap, less down-time, or more efficient methods. Also, most companies reported reduced turnover and absentee rates. A case in point: The pet food plant after 18 months reported an overhead rate that was 33 percent lower than in the old plant. The absentee rate was 9 percent below the industry norm, and turnover was far below average.

Step 3: Recognition and resources provided for further work restructuring. After becoming acquainted with the results of the pilot experiment, top management typically gave its blessing to the approach. In several cases, notably GF, Alcan, and Norsk Hydro, it became company or division policy to diffuse work restructuring throughout the various facilities. In Hunsfos, it became company policy to spread work restructing to other departments in the mill complex. In the case of Volvo, the recognition of work restructuring became very strong. The new president took a special interest in the subject and had made a dramatic commitment to the program in existing plants in the early 1970s. He personally had pressed for and contributed to a revolutionary approach to the designing of a new auto assembly plant in Kalmar that involved a 10 percent higher capital investment to accommodate the desired work structure. This action gave work restructuring a high priority in other plants. Exceptions should be noted in the cases of Corning and Northern Electric, where apparently no strong encouragement of diffusion came from the corporate level other than from organizational development groups.

In Northern Electric, in fact, the reverse was true. A new manager who took over in the third year of the experiment terminated it before it could have reached the diffusion stage. The new organization was regarded as a success at its home base, but corporate management took a different view.

In a few cases, recognition eventually took the form of a management philosophy hammered out by a group of line managers with the assistance of staff consultants more familiar with work restructuring. A General Foods statement, for example, emerged shortly after other corporate measures had been taken to promote diffusion.

Another diffusion measure was the assignment of specific responsibility for promoting work restructuring. For example, in General Foods, the line manager responsible for pet food operations at the divisional level was transferred to the corporate level and made an internal consultant to several dozen plants.

Step 4: More general interest in work restructuring aroused. In every case, these experiments have been the subject of widely circulated written reports in the news media, oral presentations to other groups, and visits by interested parties to the experimental site. Dissemination activities often helped the project leaders secure top-management recognition and approval, but they had other objectives as well. They were intended to interest and inform managers and union officials of sister units within the same firm and those outside the firm. The visibility and favorable acclaim, of course, were gratifying to the participants, who were proud of the work culture they had created and the performance results they had achieved.

Step 5: Change agents' interventions extend throughout the corporate system. We have already noted the tendency to designate some individuals or committees to help initiate projects and monitor their development. The change interventions led by the internal consultant at General Foods will help illustrate this aspect of a diffusion effort, although the activities are more elaborate than in other cases, except Shell U.K.

In late 1971, the newly appointed GF internal consultant, Lyman Ketchum, addressed a group of 150 top managers from operations, engineering, quality assurance, and personnel, together with several corporation group vice-presidents. Forms of work restructuring and their rationale were discussed. The chairman of GF and a key vice-president were present and sanctioned the role of the new change agent.

A steering committee comprised of the division operating managers was formed to guide the change activities. As a committee the managers assessed the progress of diffusion, and as individuals they were expected to collaborate with the change agent in his work in their divisions.

Change initiatives occurred at the plant level. Priority was given to new and recent plants over existing plants because more progress could be made with less effort. Further priority was given to larger plants because of their greater importance. Recognizing these priorities, the change agent began working with plant managers who manifested the most interest in change.

The change agent's initial work with plants involved a three-day meeting with the plant manager and his staff, who were encouraged to explore their own values and the connections between values and work structures.

These initial three-day meetings by themselves seldom produced much action. After a month or so had elapsed, the change agent usually scheduled another meeting with a group drawn from the next level below the plant manager's staff.

As a parallel activity, the corporate change agent organized three-day seminars on the techniques of work analysis and design; these were attended largely by staff personnel such as engineers.

Where a commitment to work restructuring developed, the change agent helped form a plant steering committee comprised of key line and staff managers, and union officials where appropriate. Subordinate action committees were formed to explore and recommend specific projects within a limited area of the plant. The change agent himself and other consulting resources were made available to the plant committees to assist them in the actual work restructuring.

Diffusion interventions at Norsk Hydro took a somewhat different form: The first major event was a policy clinic where managers and their union counterparts could discuss the ideas and techniques of achieving employee participation at the shop floor in the planning and introduction of change. These discussions were somewhat inhibited by managers who believed that the area manager was authoritarian and unsympathetic. The area manager discovered the content of these policy discussions and stopped them.

In 1971, a second effort was made with the responsibility for work restructuring initiatives assigned to the Joint Consultation Board. A supervisory training program was also introduced. Some new initiatives worked out; others did not.

By 1972 top management concluded that the diffusion policy still was not working. Middle managers were told to "get cracking," and a training program was devised to better equip them to play their role. In the meantime the area manager had been replaced, in part because he had not helped implement the work restructuring project. This development was offset by the departure of an influential union official who was interested in diffusing the work structures pioneered in the fertilizer plants.

A supplementary vehicle for diffusion was the conversion of the ten-man professional staff of the firm's industrial engineering methods group "from MTM engineers to socio-technical consultants." The head of this department understood the need for reshaping the role of the department and began in 1971 to reeducate the staff. Over time this development may greatly facilitate diffusion of the work restructuring ideas pioneered in the fertilizer plants.

Step 6: Facilitative networks develop. This is a step taken in only a few of the change programs studied. An interunit network of personnel involved in work restructuring is created to exchange ideas, to provide a supportive reference group for its members, and to build a constituency for change in corporate policies and procedures more favorable to work restructuring. In GF, networks of plant managers and their personnel managers are evolving to a point where many of their members can serve others generally as outside consultants.

Step 7: Personnel movement occurs. The transfer of experienced personnel from an innovative unit is a way of exporting the knowledge, values, and skills at the heart of work restructuring. The innovative unit then can educate the new managers who transfer into the unit.

A few favorable moves can be cited to illustrate the possibilities. In a strategic move at Norsk Hydro, the person who had been personnel manager in the Porsgrunn area was promoted to corporate headquarters.

He was intimately familiar with the fertilizer project and an articulate proponent of the underlying philosophy. He moved to a better position to advise top management on the diffusion of work restructuring. Not surprisingly, the advantage of this move to headquarters was partly offset by the loss felt in the local area.

The manager at Alcan's Kingston Works was promoted to a division-level position after the program was well under way at Kingston. Later, however, he reportedly lost touch with the innovations and became less supportive.

In Shell U.K., the transfer of key personnel was disruptive of the program under way in the U.K., but some moves seeded other parts of the Shell International organization—for example, the Australian unit—with managers who were committed to finding better ways of organizing work.

THE SHELL U.K. APPROACH

A major variation on the procedure in the other seven firms—that of starting small with a single experiment—is provided by Shell U.K. From the outset, the approach was conceived as companywide, comprehensive in its effect on the work situation, and planned to last from five to ten years.

The first step was not a demonstration project. Work redesign was undertaken only after large amounts of organizational time had been spent in sessions developing and affirming a supportive managerial philosophy.

Attitudes, in short, were changed before structure. Tavistock social scientists worked closely with an internal staff resource group to design the activities in this and subsequent phases, beginning in 1965 with the development of a philosophy to which senior managers could commit themselves.

The second phase was intended to ensure that the operating philosophy was freely accepted by all 6,000 members of the organization from senior managers to hourly workers. To accomplish this dissemination—involving active testing and consensus building—required 18 months, from fall 1965 to spring 1967—and a cascade of conferences.

The implementation phase was launched in March 1966 by a third top-management conference. The first strategic approach to implementation was to set up pilot projects that "could act as centers of organizational learning." These projects, set up in one refinery, did not go well. Moreover, the concentration of attention on a few groups at one site created resentment among many others who had been through the philosophy discussions, and who were emotionally and intellectually primed to implement the philosophy.

Next, the implementation strategy was altered, and responsibility for change was placed on the department-manager level across the company —an approach made possible by the massive dissemination process. To enable department managers to initiate their own change projects, short training courses were provided to teach them techniques of work analysis and principles of work restructuring.

A network of committees representing both management and unions helped to change work rules that otherwise would prevent many types of restructuring, such as flexible manning patterns and paying workers for multiple job skills.

Although pilot projects as centers for organization learning no longer formed the primary foundation for implementation, it was decided to apply the concepts to a new refinery at Teesport, where construction began in 1965 and which came on stream in April 1968.

Evaluation conferences were held in March 1967 on the previous two major sites covered, Stanlow and Shell Haven. Shortly thereafter, a number of changes took place that served to arrest the diffusion process and tended to demoralize the innovative systems already introduced.

PROBLEM AREAS IN DIFFUSION

My investigation attempted to find out why diffusion was not more rapid and extensive. The reasons ranged from defects in the design of the original experiment to unanticipated consequences of the success of the initial pilot project.

Regression in the Pilot Project

Because diffusion typically occurs over a significant period of time, the sustained success of early experiments can help build momentum for companywide change; conversely, emergent weaknesses in the pilot projects can erode initial support for change.

A clear correlation between the continued success of initial projects and the rate of diffusion is found in several extreme cases. Volvo's truck plant experiment has continued to be effective and has been followed by relatively high diffusion. The Northern Electric experiment was discontinued, and also produced no significant diffusion within the company. A similar consistency is found in the demoralization of Corning's Medfield experiment, after a period of effectiveness, and the lack of diffusion throughout the firm.

Both Shell U.K. and Alcan experienced moderate effectiveness in their early experiments and have shown moderate amounts of diffusion, although causal connections are not indicated. Shell U.K. achieved its diffusion soon after its change program was undertaken; the initial projects subsequently became somewhat demoralized and no further diffusion has occurred. Alcan has recently diffused the ideas of the earlier experiments into a new mill, although there has been a decline in management and worker involvement in the plants in which the earlier innovations were established.

There is not always a correlation between initial project success and diffusion. The strong success of the Topeka plant in GF is not matched so far by a high amount of diffusion, and in the cases of Norsk Hydro and Hunsfos, there is even less correlation. Continued success of initial change projects appears to be only one of many influences on diffusion.

What can cause a successful early experiment to deteriorate later on? I have noted several factors: (1) internal inconsistencies in the original design; (2) loss of support from levels of management above the experimental unit; (3) premature turnover of leaders, operators, or consultants directly associated with a project; (4) stress and crises that lead to more authoritarian management, which in turn demoralizes the innovative unit; (5) tension in the innovative unit's relations with other parties—peer units, staff groups, superiors, labor unions; (6) letdown in participant's involvement after initial success with its attendant publicity; (7) lack of diffusion to other parts of the organization, which isolates the original experiment and its leaders.

The seventh factor or principle, succinctly stated, is "diffuse or die"; it suggests that a circular relationship exists whereby lack of diffusion can *eventually* undermine the viability of the initial project, just as weaknesses that develop in the initial project can undermine the diffusion effort. The converse of this circular relationship is not strong; as I have noted above, continued success in the initial project does not necessarily lead to diffusion throughout the larger organization.

Poor Model for Change

Even if the pilot project remains viable over time, it may be an ineffective model for diffusion in the firm because its lacks either visibility or credibility. These deficiencies may reflect the behavior of leaders of the experiment, or they may relate to the way policy is formulated by higher officials. Also, many characteristics inherent in the site of the initial experiment affect its ability to stimulate further change. Consider the many conditions of the GF pet food plant that enhanced the success of that project: The Topeka plant was new, was located in a favorable labor market, required few workers, and was geographically separate from headquarters and other existing facilities of GF. Since it was a new plant with a new work force, no union agreement was required to establish the new work structure. Many of these conditions, of course, did not exist elsewhere in GF, and many managers asked, "Is work restructuring possible in other situations—for example, in a large, established, unionized plant?"

The credibility of the Corning and Northern Electric projects suffered not only for similar reasons but also from an additional site characteristic: The technology involved in the experimental plant was significantly different from that employed in other plants in the system.

In terms of site characteristics, Volvo, Alcan, and Shell U.K. appear to have presented relatively good prospects for further diffusion of a successful experiment. They were initiated in large, established, unionized facilities and involved technologies typical of the larger systems of which they were a part.

The prospects for diffusion of the work restructuring innovations at the Norsk Hydro fertilizer plants would have to be regarded as even more favorable. By 1973 a dozen different plants were adjacent to each other in the Porsgrunn area, each producing a different product—ammonia, nitric acid, urea, formic acid, magnesium, plastics, and so on. They were similar in ways that made the fertilizer work organization generally relevant: They employed continuous-process technologies, and large pieces of capital were manned by relatively small work forces. In addition, Norsk Hydro had operations in a number of other locations, and in fact was the largest industrial undertaking in Norway. Thus, one could project the spread of demonstrably successful ideas throughout the Porsgrunn works and other parts of the firm, and because of the firm's prominence in Norway, to other industrial firms in this small country. Obviously, for an explanation of why much diffusion did not occur, we will have to look elsewhere than to site characteristics.

The way the project leaders present the experiment to others in the firm will influence its visibility and credibility. One basic choice is whether to maintain a low profile or to seek visibility in the corporate environment.

A low profile reduces the career risks associated with failure, and less publicity also minimizes the risk of creating a "showcase" complex with longer-run adverse effects on the work climate. However, in the cases studied, the incentive to publicize the experiments increased substantially once they appeared to be successfully established. Visibility, it was felt, was essential if diffusion were to occur, and the natural pride in the innovation was accompanied by a desire for wider recognition—inside the company and beyond. Some favorable publicity often created an appetite for more. The project leaders sometimes lost control of publicity to other corporate officials and the media.

Except possibly for Corning's Medfield and Northern Electric's Advanced Devices Center, the initial experiments in my sample achieved sufficient visibility throughout their corporate organizations.

Confusion over What Is to Be Diffused

Even if the initial site is favorable for eventual diffusion and the project leaders manage the publicity effectively, higher management can botch up the process in the way they formulate and communicate the diffusion policy.

If the form of work structure indicated by company policy is stated too conceptually, the policy may be dismissed as abstract and platitudinous or action may be delayed because managers don't know how to translate the concepts.

On the other hand, if the ideas about the desired forms of work structure are stated too operationally, then they may be rejected as inappropriate by managers whose units have different types of work forces, different technologies, or different economic conditions.

Norsk Hydro presents an interesting case in point. Six years after the initiation of the fertilizer experiment and many years after it had become official company policy to diffuse this type of work innovation, managers still complained about the lack of clarity. Was the policy to diffuse "job enrichment," "autonomous groups," "organizational development," "socio-technical systems," or something more general that underlies all of these?

There was general agreement that diffusion would have proceeded more rapidly if it had been clear that the policy was for managers to pursue certain *aims* (such as making better use of the talents of employees and allowing for more day-to-day influence by employees over their work) rather than to employ particular *techniques.*

Inappropriateness of Concepts Employed

The long-run diffusion of work restructuring is affected by another issue: While the concepts should be inspiring, they must also be realistic.

"Autonomous groups" was the key concept employed in the Norwegian experiments to characterize the work restructuring innovations. The term, which many found inspiring, was later dropped because it was not feasible for many groups to become truly autonomous.

"Equal status" was a concept in the design of Shell U.K.'s Teesport work system. The term captured the imagination of the workers as well as the originators, but overstated what higher management was prepared to do. Differences persisted between blue- and white-collar workers, although all employees were placed on salary. The differences remaining were especially resented because of the expectations aroused by the "equal status" concept.

Deficient Implementation

The initial project may be viable in itself, but the follow-through may be inadequate, in terms of locating accountability for the change and providing "how-to" knowledge.

The first point has already been illustrated. Norsk Hydro unsuccessfully attempted to place the responsibility for diffusion with Joint Consultation Boards and then shifted it to middle management. Shell U.K. started implementation by selecting a few projects with heavy reliance upon a few staff people but then shifted to a policy in which all department heads become accountable for change in their units. Accountability for work restructuring in Volvo was clearest—it was an essential part of the plant managers' responsibility, period!

As is true with many types of change in organizations, "how-to" knowledge must be provided through training, consulting, or both. Resources for this seemed to have been a limiting factor at one time or another in GF, Corning, and Alcan.

Lack of Top Management Commitment

A period of sustained priority for work restructuring is important in achieving diffusion. The continuing interest and commitment of Volvo's president is a prime case in point. By contrast, the shifting priority given work restructuring in several other firms' studies hindered diffusion. An illustrative case is Norsk Hydro, where the work restructuring objective received lower priority during 1970–73 than it did in the period 1967–69.

Priority declined for several reasons. First, when the initial experiment was launched there was a high sense of urgency about improving industrial relations and productivity. But with a general improvement in industrial relations and the competitiveness of the business, the sense of urgency declined.

Second, according to the middle-level managers, they have come under increasing pressure to meet demanding volume and cost objectives, making it risky in the short run to start any major projects. One manager said, "I have the freedom to innovate but not the time."

Third, the company has been transformed by rapid expansion and revolutionary change in the raw materials and processes used in much of its business. The changes absorbed the attention of top management and the director-general became more formal and less accessible to members of the organization—at least to those who wanted to lobby for work restructuring.

The Shell U.K. managers perceived a similar set of changes as weakening their work restructuring program. In 1971, Hill reported that after mid-1967 there was a lack of continuing visible commitment at the top. In 1967, the U.K. company was reorganized to include North Sea exploration and production as well as U.K. refining activities, and a new chief executive was appointed. The refineries repeatedly requested assurances that the top management of the enlarged company endorsed and supported the philosophy behind the work restructuring program. When the new management team became absorbed in supply problems created by the 1967 Middle East War and failed to formally endorse an amended statement of philosophy tailored to the company's enlarged role, managers in the refineries became less willing to embark on change.

In many cases, including those just mentioned, inconsistencies in higher-management behavior weakened diffusion efforts. Even before they perceived that the program was down-graded, Shell U.K. managers were concerned that although they were asked to protect and develop their human resources, they were being assessed mainly on their handling of the technical system alone.

In the latter part of the 1960s, Alcan division management reportedly shifted toward a more directive, top-down type of leadership and away from a consultative, problem-oriented management pattern. This directly contradicted and undermined the innovative work structure that had been developed at the Kingston works and had an inhibiting effect on further diffusion of work restructuring in the division.

Union Opposition

Like sustained top-management commitment, union support or acceptance is a necessary condition for any significant diffusion of work restructuring. In some cases, union support has been, on balance, a positive factor. In other cases, perceived opposition by the union has been a reason for not trying to diffuse work restructuring into unionized plants. Mostly, unions have had more complicated effects—on the process of introducing change, the nature of the work structures introduced, and the work climate.

The Scandinavian union movement has been more positive toward work restructuring than trade unions in the U.K. and North America. Clearly, joint union-management sponsorship of the Norwegian experiments served to legitimize the program for workers. However, the actual effects of the union officials on diffusion within Norsk Hydro and Hunsfos were mixed, just as the effects on the management side were mixed.

In Norsk Hydro a particularly key union official had moved from the area and the loss of his support hurt the diffusion effort. In Hunsfos, where the chief shop steward and the company president were strongly committed to the diffusion program, local effort received no backing from the trade union movement. Although the trade union movement as a whole was not averse to the changes pioneered at Hunsfos, the chief shop steward reported criticism from other quarters. He said he took risks with his own constituency every time he "stuck his neck out" (for example, on a change that resulted in a crew reduction). Also, radical sociologists accused him of selling out to management, increasing company efficiency at the expense of workers.

At Volvo, the unions have played an active and positive role in the work restructuring program. Management had initiated the job redesign aspects of the program and the union the consultative aspects. Both parties, moreover, claim joint ownership of the total program.

In the case of the Shell U.K. program, the union deliberately slowed down the rate of diffusion of work restructuring during 1965–68 until productivity bargaining had progressed to the point where they had been able to establish the economic quid pro quo for certain changes.

The union had played its role in the recent demoralization of the Shell U.K. change program. Management negotiated wage increases in 1971 and 1972 that were below the national pattern, and then in 1973 the government constraints prevented the parties from making up the difference. The union has reflected and perhaps amplified worker resentment.

Another factor at Shell is tension around manning. Top management continues to put pressure on refinery managers to reduce the work force. When we recall that guarantees against dismissal and provisions for extra pay were a quid pro quo in the initial change program, we can see how reviving the issue has led to poorer union-management relations and inhibited the further diffusion of work restructuring.

Three projects started in nonunion plants of firms whose other plants were mostly unionized. Unions representing these other plants were expected to oppose or otherwise complicate work restructuring in them. The three firms were General Foods, Corning, and Northern Electric. In the case of GF, where work restructuring efforts have actually been undertaken in unionized plants, the collective bargaining relationship complicated change in the early steps but has not prevented it. With Corning and Northern Electric little or no attempt was made to diffuse change to union plants.

To summarize, unions' effect has taken many forms:

First, unions have influenced the basic climate for change. Sometimes the effect was positive, helping to legitimize work restructuring or entering into an informal problem-solving pattern consistent with the work culture sought by the work restructuring experiment. Sometimes the effect of unions was negative, inhibiting management from trying to diffuse change or formalizing and politicizing relations contradictory to the spirit of the work culture being diffused.

Second, unions have complicated the change process by requiring additional consensus-seeking efforts.

Third, unions have affected the preconditions for change or limited the nature of the change itself. Sometimes they have obtained assurances on job security and earnings maintenance and have bargained for workers to obtain a share of the increased productivity that resulted from more flexibility and reduced work crews. Sometimes they have prevented certain changes, e.g., modifications in job content that affect union jurisdictional boundaries or historical patterns.

Bureaucratic Barriers

The importance of this issue belies the simplicity with which it can be stated. Diffusion efforts are frustrated by vested interests and existing organizational routines that limit local autonomy.

Innovative plant managements have often felt harassed by staff groups, who for their part have often become irritated and impatient with many of the plants' demands for self-sufficiency and exemption from uniform company policies. These tensions may be present during the establishment of the initial experiment, and they are escalated when serious diffusion begins. "Experiments," by definition, minimize the scope and duration of the effects of the change involved. However, when the changes are declared enduring or an attempt is made to spread them, the stakes are raised for groups affected.

Bureaucratic barriers can be illustrated from the experience of one company, where managers themselves introduced the term. One problem relates to the level at which decisions are made in the line organization. In 1973, workers were operating informally without supervisors on two of the four shifts, but formalization of this arrangement and extension to a third and fourth shift was not within the authority of the manager of the innovative plant.

Another example involved the method for judging operator qualification for increased pay in the innovative plant. Central personnel insisted that the "theoretical" tests of knowledge appropriate for each job had to be mastered before "practical" knowledge could be compensated. Previously, theoretical knowledge could be learned and compensated *after* a person had shown he could perform the day-to-day operations associated with a particular job and had received an adjustment for that practical mastery. These events not only demoralized the participants of the project, but also discouraged other managers from initiating projects.

The experience of General Foods, Shell U.K., and other firms in which an ambitious diffusion effort has been undertaken are rich with similar illustrations, involving such issues as whether quality assurance procedures at plant level must be uniform throughout the corporation, whether a common job evaluation scheme should be applied to plants with radically different work structures, what should be the respective roles of central engineering and local staff in plant expansion programs, how much local autonomy should exist in creating and filling plant management positions, and whether reporting requirements must be applied uniformly throughout the system.

Threatened Obsolescence

A restructed work situation requires new roles and new skills and makes others obsolete. We have already mentioned the resistance of staff groups who may have to acquire new knowledge, develop new consultative patterns for imparting their expertise, and see some of their functions being performed by nonspecialists.

However, the greatest threat was to first-line supervision. The number of first-line supervisors was often decreased. Sometimes the position was even eliminated. Where the position was retained, the role was changed in the ways that required new attitudes and greater interpersonal and group skills.

Supervisors individually and as a group are weak compared with other groups potentially affected by new work structures. They themselves have not mounted much effective opposition to the diffusion or tried to shape the form of work restructuring, with one exception—Volvo, where within the past year the supervisor's union has taken an active role to protect its members' interest. In at least one case, Hunsfos, concern by workers about the effect of work restructuring on their supervisors created a major snag in the diffusion process. In many other cases, management's uncertainty about how to handle the potential obsolescence of existing foremen has been a factor inhibiting diffusion.

In some cases the resistance of supervisors and other salaried personnel was not due to a direct threat to their existing roles; rather, they felt neglected by comparision with blue-collar workers. They resented the fact that the blue-collar worker's job was enriched and his status and influence upgraded, while their lot had not improved.

Self-Limiting Dynamics

In companies that employed the most comprehensive diffusion strategy, there was a tendency for pilot projects to be self-limiting or "self-sealing." The tendency was strongest in instances like Norsk Hydro, Hunsfos, and General Foods, where a single small unit was involved in the orginal experiment and where serious efforts to introduce work restructuring into other units came only after widespread publicity on the success of the experimental unit.

One dynamic involved a "star-envy" phenomenon, which can be illustrated by Norsk Hydro. The original experiment in the fertilizer plants received an enormous amount of publicity within Norway and outside. The fertilizer plants became the object of innumerable visits by managers, trade union officials, social scientists, and schoolchildren. Top management looked approvingly on the project and made it company policy for others to follow the lead of the fertilizer project. Not surprisingly, the attention given the fertilizer groups engendered resentment and envy among the other persons who were asked to adopt the innovation in their own operations. The resentment was accompanied by resistance to the work restructuring program. The experience of the Topeka plant in General Foods was strikingly similar.

A second dynamic involved a shift in the reward structure. Payoffs for pioneers and those who followed them in the same organization differed in important respects, providing a much less favorable benefit-risk picture for the subsequent users of organizational innovations. Managers who adapted the innovation and succeeded received less credit than the pioneer received, and if they had failed, they probably would have lost more standing in management than the pioneer would have if he had failed. Managers who did not utilize the innovation often figured that while they might be prodded and goaded for not taking any organizational initiatives, ultimately they would be judged on the basis of production and profit performance. In short, they felt that they could afford to resist pressure.

A third dynamic involved the tendency for participants to feel special and to regard their experimental work system as superior. On the one hand, this feeling reinforced their commitment to the group and was a positive factor in helping to establish a new form of social organization. On the other hand, this tended to lead outsiders to conclude that the culture created was unique and to discount the general applicability of the experiment.

A fourth dynamic came into play at a later date. Rivalry sometimes developed among those engaged in work restructuring. They stressed minor differences in their approaches, while ignoring the similarity in underlying values and assumptions. One effect of this form of rivalry among change agents and among innovative units was to weaken their ability to form the collegial networks described as part of the general diffusion model.

A fifth dynamic also came into play at a later stage in those cases where diffusion did not occur fairly rapidly. It was a secondary consequence of two factors related above: the bureaucratic barriers and the special self-image developed by experimental units. The leaders of some innovative units had engaged in so many skirmishes with superiors and staff groups over corporate practices and were so aggressive in asserting the correctness of their positions that they hurt their careers. Observing this, some peers resolved not to get similarly burned.

OTHER INFLUENTIAL FACTORS

After having studied the diffusion process in eight companies and after having analyzed the situational factors that seemed to account for a generally slower-than-expected rate of diffusion, I became interested in assessing how inherently difficult or easy these new structures are to diffuse.

The early classic studies of diffusion traced the adoption of improved agricultural practices. More recent studies have covered other innovations, including farm practices, medical drugs, educational techniques, machinery, management control techniques, and so on. Should we expect diffusion of work restructuring to be relatively slower or faster than diffusion of innovations in these other fields?

Recent reviews of the literature on diffusion consistently concurred on a number of attributes of innovations that influenced their adoption rate. Most are plausible, at least on the surface.

1. *Relative advantage.* This is an obvious attribute that enhances the rate of diffusion. The cost-benefit analysis implied in this attribute includes not only financial but also perceived social costs and benefits. The problem with work restructuring is that there is a singular lack of agreement among its proponents over the benefits derived. Some stress tangible impacts on such factors as productivity and turnover; others choose to emphasize the psychic dividends paid to workers.

2. *Communicability.* Diffusion will be enhanced if the innovation can be explained easily and if its effects are easily separable from other influences in the environment. Work restructuring innovations rate low on this attribute compared with all other types of innovations cited. Volvo may be an exception. The changes were straightforward and readily grasped. Well-established production norms permitted an easy assessment of any loss of efficiency, and the desired decrease in turnover was

quickly measured (although not always persuasively explained). Thus communicability may help explain why Volvo's relatively simple changes on the existing assembly lines were diffused relatively rapidly.

3. *Compatability.* Diffusion is aided if the innovation is perceived as being congruent with existing norms, values, and structures. Again, work restructuring innovations must be rated low because by definition they call for important structural and normative changes in the existing industrial organizations. (Work restructuring threatens what many managers in the United States continue to regard as their prerogatives.) However, the same innovations would rate higher in compatability in Scandinavia than in the U.S.

4. *Pervasiveness.* This term refers to the number of aspects of the system affected by the innovation. Less pervasiveness permits more rapid diffusion. By definition, what we refer to as "work restructuring" strives to be comprehensive, embracing division of labor, rewards, supervision, status systems, and power relations. This factor, too, makes diffusing work restructuring inherently difficult.

5. *Reversibility.* Can an innovation be adopted on an experimental basis and reversed without serious consequences? If the status quo ante cannot be readily restored, diffusion will be inhibited. Many managers believe that work restructuring creates expectations that will become a liability if the innovation must be abandoned. My limited observations support that belief. This work restructuring may rate moderate to low on the reversibility factor.

6. *Number of gatekeepers.* Numerous approval channels that must be satisfied before an innovation can be adopted will tend to inhibit the rate of diffusion. In work restructuring, top management, departmental or plant managers, staff groups, supervisors, unions, and the workers themselves all have some gatekeeping role to perform. One could hardly imagine gatekeeping conditions less favorable for diffusion of new work structures.

Finally, a major difficulty in diffusing work restructuring is that frequently it's not literally a matter of "adoption." Because work forces, technologies, and economics affect the appropriate work structure, tailored application of the general principles of work restructuring is required rather than adoption of a predetermined model.

CONCLUSION

One important reason for the unimpressive rate of diffusion in the eight companies studied is that, especially in their more comprehensive form, these innovations have many attributes that make their diffusion inherently slow. Even if they offer relative advantages over existing work structures, their character and results are not highly communicable; they are not congruent with existing norms and values; their potential effect in a given work situation is pervasive rather than fractional; they are not readily reversed without incurring social costs; and too many affected parties serve as gatekeepers for the effective implementation of the innovations.

Another set of explanations for the actual diffusion observed in the eight companies relates to the barriers the diffusion efforts encountered and the efficacy of companies' strategies and tactics.

Many key areas are readily identifiable: Does the experiment continue to show good results? Is the experiment sufficiently visible and sufficiently convincing? Is organizational accountability for initiating change clear, and is know-how for implementation available? Is there sustained support for diffusion from powerful groups such as top management and union officials? Careful planning is required to ensure that the answers to these questions are positive.

Two problem areas deal with organizational dilemmas generated by the nature of the innovations. Work restructuring requires an increase in local autonomy, thereby threatening the power of central staff groups and some managers. It also threatens to make some roles obsolete or to eliminate the positions of some staff specialists and first-line supervisors. These problems are not easily resolved and require imaginative solutions —solutions not yet obvious to me.

Last, perhaps the most interesting type of barrier to diffusion is the self-limiting dynamics of pilot projects. Ironically, several of these are unexpected consequences of the success of the project: The greater the attention given pilot units, the more likely are managers of peer units to be "turned off" by the example. The more successful the pioneer, the less favorable are the payoffs and the greater the risks for those who follow. The more esprit de corps and sense of being special that develops in the unit, the less generalizable it appears to others.

Some of the implications of our analysis of these and other self-limiting tendencies are apparent once the dynamics are understood: There is an advantage in (1) introducing a number of projects at the same time in the same firm, (2) avoiding over-exposure and glorification of particular change efforts, and (3) having the innovative program identified with top management at the initial project stage.

As the examples of work restructuring in the larger society become more numerous, however, the self-limiting tendencies should pose less of a problem.

In conclusion, I expect relatively little diffusion of potentially significant restructuring in the work place—over the short run. Hopefully the long run may tell a different story.

Increasingly, what many employees expect from their jobs is different from what organizations are prepared to offer them. Work restructuring is the preeminent answer to closing the gap. I would expect the latent dissatisfactions of workers to be activated and pressure for work restructuring to increase as the issues receive more public attention and as more successful examples of comprehensive work restructuring raise the general level of worker expectations. I would also be surprised if future experiments did not profit from the pioneering efforts. Together, these factors should generate an increase in the number of diffusions and a hastening of the pace of diffusion. But how many diffusions and how fast the pace, I can't even begin to guess.

SELECTED BIBLIOGRAPHY

A useful volume of papers on the problems associated with work is *The Worker and the Job: Coping with Change,* edited by Jerome M. Rosow (Prentice-Hall, Inc., 1974).

Included in that volume is a paper of mine, "Innovative Restructuring of Work," which reports on other aspects of the study on which the present article is based. It describes the rationale for, nature of, and results achieved by a dozen pilot projects in work restructuring. It also analyzes the viability of these projects over time.

Two recent reviews of the factors influencing diffusion of innovations in a wide range of fields are Gerald Zaltman, Robert Duncan, and Jonny Holbek's *Innovations and Organizations* (John Wiley & Sons, 1973) and John Kimbeny's "Policies for Innovation in the Service Sector," prepared for the OECD Directorate for Scientific Affairs, October 1973.

The studies at the Work Research Institute in Oslo, Norway have also noted what Philip Herbst has called the "self-encapsulating" effects of experimental changes in work design. See Herbst's "Some Reflections on the Work Democratized Project—1974. I: The Process of Diffusion," Work Research Institutes, Oslo, Document 13/1974.

I wish to acknowledge the helpful comments of Chris Argyris on an earlier draft of this paper and the support for this research provided by the Ford Foundation and the Division of Research, Harvard Graduate School of Business Administration.

THE POLITICS OF IMPLEMENTING MBO*

George S. Odiorne

It is not likely today that many managers will object to management by objectives as a concept or philosophy. The question of available alternatives seems unanswerable in the face of such an eminently logical developmental system. Why, then, do people seem to have reservations about committing themselves to it? Why, indeed, do some find it impossible to make it work, while others report great success in its application and enthusiasm for its effects?

One of the major reasons for the failure of MBO in many organizations is that those in charge fail to recognize the political character of the implementation process. MBO is indeed logical and systematic, but it also must deal with a number of factors, including power and authority, the organization form, and the values and expectations of people. The MBO implementer, therefore, must recognize the reality of political constraints and manage them during the process of implementation.

If he fails to do so, MBO may start off with a flourish but gradually fade away; begin well, reach a certain level, and stall; or start well but produce a dramatic failure and be dropped, becoming a taboo subject thereafter. Success, on the other hand, results when MBO begins at a sound level of acceptance, gains from its own successes, continues to flourish and expand its influence and contributions, and is widely appreciated and supported.

Case studies of successful and unsuccessful implementation plans show that there are three major avenues currently used for implementation of MBO and that all three must be modified by political constraints characteristic of every organization. This article will briefly illustrate the three approaches, and then describe the political considerations that must guide them.

THREE APPROACHES

Methods of implementing MBO may rely on the use of raw power and direct orders, persuasion, or education. Case studies indicate that no one route is best; instead, analysis of the organizational climate and the situation will indicate the best approach—one alone or perhaps a

---

* Reprinted with permission of author and publisher from *Business Horizons,* Vol. 17, No. 3 (June 1974), pp. 13–21.

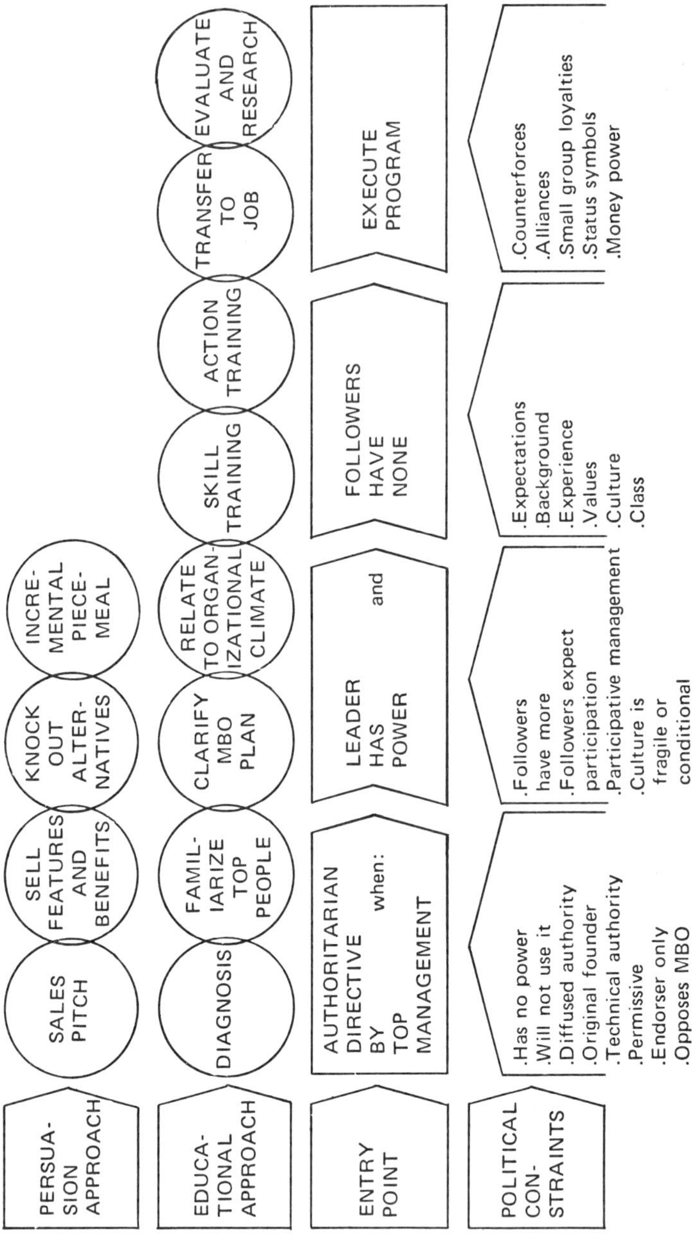

The Three Approaches and the Political Constraints

combination of all of them. A specific set of steps in linear form would be highly desirable, but such a method would probably miss the mark and lead to an implementation that fails in one or more respects.

Authoritarian Directives

It is an article of faith, supported by some research evidence, that the installation of MBO must start at the top. In part, such a beginning is justified. The purpose of the business flows down and the methods of getting there flow up. The strategies of the business are chosen by persons with high-level responsibility, whereas the operational objectives are the responsibility of lower levels. This might lead to the conclusion that the power of the higher ranks must be invoked to direct implementation. This approach, which Joseph Juran has labeled the "king's ear" approach, is founded upon the assumption that if the staff man can get the president's ear and cause him to issue the right directives everybody below him will obey. The concept is that of the self-executing order, a rare phenomenon.

Behavioral scientists deplore such autocratic methods but they are used in some organizations where tight technical organization and discipline are the mode of operation. Where the following conditions exist in the organization, such authoritarian methods will indeed work:

The leader has absolute power and is willing to use it.

The followers need the leader more than he needs them, because he has knowledge, skills, or resources which they need but that he can withhold.

The followers have lived under unexplained orders for some time, perhaps for their entire working lifetime, and have learned to expect them, even when the subject is MBO.

The situation requires autocratic orders. The leader is expected to state his orders quickly and clearly if he is in charge of a ship at sea in a storm, a plane in distress, or a temporary work force.

Under proper circumstances, autocratic implementation of MBO has been successful. That is not to say that all situations demand it; many are not suitable for autocracy—the college faculty or the volunteer group, for example. The major limitations of the use of force to implement MBO lie in the situation in which it is applied. Where the boss has no power or has power and will not use it, the followers expect to be consulted and have something important to withhold (and will do so). Under these circumstances, the authoritarian directive will produce counterresponses that block MBO.

Persuasion

One reason for the failure of MBO to achieve its full potential has been the misguided reliance upon persuasion as a means of implementation. The guru or inspirational speaker comes to a meeting of management and through hortatory lectures persuades everyone that MBO will be beneficial. Persuasion methods ordinarily can be distinguished by their content.

First, they appear to be balanced, that is, they explain all of the advantages of MBO, then turn and judiciously explain the disadvantages of not managing by objectives. This is clearly an advocacy approach designed to persuade. *Second,* features and benefits are grist for the persuader's mill. A description of the features and a discussion of the usefulness of each are persuasive tactics.

Third, in this debater's form of persuasion, all of the alternatives for solving some chronic problems are noted. Then each is knocked out in turn, excepting the MBO solution. The *fourth* form of persuasion, incrementalism, is probably the most risky. It consists of starting with a simple segment of the whole program and selling it. "You simply sit down once a year with all of your subordinates, and talk to them about their objectives" would be an incremental approach. Many instances of MBO failure have been caused by incrementalism in the introduction. The concept began as a change in the company performance appraisal system or as a salary review plan, but lost favor when the full implications of the time and effort demanded were realized.

Persuasion is the favorite method of hortatory speakers and consultants. It is detested and avoided by academics who would prefer an approach that relies almost wholly upon education, particularly in the underlying theory. As a complete method of installation, it obviously leads to disillusionment. Yet it has a useful part in implementation in the early stages, if only to get people to submit to education.

Educational Programs

One of the more successful patterns for installing an MBO program is a continuous educational effort which teaches the concepts, philosophy, and procedures of MBO in detail. As a training subject, MBO has many excellent features.

> Training should produce behavior change, and training in MBO is measurable. It can be readily determined if the training worked: Did the trainees set objectives or didn't they?
>
> The quality of the results can be noted clearly. The course may suggest, for example, that a manager should establish three classes of ob-

jectives. The effect on the manager can be checked by examining sample goals statements.

MBO comprises a sound basis for relating training to the job. Some training sessions require students to set objectives on their job as part of the course; they learn by doing what they are being taught.

MBO provides a vehicle for teaching more general management education. It can be the framework for teaching motivational methods, management functions (organizing, planning, and controlling), and such interpersonal skills as coaching, counseling, and listening.

MBO can teach interpersonal skills that can be applied on the job, rather than skills which the boss will not permit or endorse when the trainee returns to the desk or plant floor. This is especially true if the boss attends the session or is used as a trainer.

MBO can reinforce company objectives rather than become, as it does in many behavioral courses, an internal reform movement to overcome the organization's autocratic or bureaucratic tendencies or to produce some new kind of organizational form.

MBO is capable of maintaining a high level of trainee interest, since it deals with the real world of work and world problems, and with interpersonal and group relations problems.

Conceptually, it is easy to learn, for MBO training courses ask people to "talk shop"; they have a tendency to do this whether they are in training or not. Except for courses in which the trainers have worked hard at obscuring the obvious, the language is operational and practical.

The basic framework of MBO permits it to take a behavioral or logical systems direction without appearing contradictory or mutually exclusive. This means that it can appeal to the personnel and training men in the organization, as well as to the engineer, controllers, and dollar-centered managers.

Both insiders and outsiders can be used as trainers. The insiders have more knowledge of the business and can deal with real world problems, and the outsiders can be briefed sufficiently to relate to the world of the trainee.

THE POLITICS OF IMPLEMENTATION

The constraint of organizational politics is a formidable barrier to implementation. Unless it is taken into account, it will outweigh the logical and behavioral efforts that go into directing, persuading, or educating people to accept a new management system. Several political factors must be considered.

The Power Structure

An often overlcoked political factor affecting the implementation of MBO is the power structure of the organization. MBO is rightly seen as having the potential for shifting the locus of power inside the organization, and accordingly will meet political resistance from those who might be affected adversely.

The resistance of such persons as corporate attorneys or other executive staff members is frequently rooted in the probability of shifting power. A person who has developed a strong personal relationship with the top officers, in which they draw upon his counsel in all sorts of matters other than law or his specialty, is clearly threatened by systematic management. In one large firm, the corporate purchasing director had performed numerous personal favors for the president and his family, and had attained the status of a family favorite. When MBO was suggested, this family retainer saw immediately that his status could be threatened and he greeted the proposal with a flurry of cluckings and exceptions. He noted its flaws and limitations, insisted that it was nothing new, and adopted other delaying and obstructive tactics familiar to the MBO administrator.

In another firm it was the tax manager who headed up the political resistance movement against MBO. The manager had helped the family with the controlling interest to minimize their personal estate taxes over the years, and he hoped to retain his personal position of favor.

The Diffusion of Authority

In many modern corporations there has been a blurring of the decision-making power. Starting at the top, where the charismatic leader or dynamic chief has been supplanted by "the office of the president" generally occupied by two or three men, it is difficult to identify a single channel for decisions. This has some advantage in gaining acceptance for decisions, but it also generates political maneuvering in order to get objectives decided upon. In other organizations, the key committees of the board may produce some mutually exclusive objectives which they are pushing. These require some political tacking and hauling in order to make a particular position dominant.

In government, of course, the basic motivator of the system and its servants is political power, and the diffusion of power is well understood by most of the people who share in it. The cabinet member knows that bureau chiefs ostensibly under his control can lobby their congressman to protect a job or program. A letter from the congressman can always sway the bureaucrat. At the same time, the large departmental public relations departments in government can swing public opinion to press congressmen for increased space or increased military and welfare appropriations.

Such a political climate requires more patience, continuous effort, and persuasion to get a management style change such as MBO into effect. Even some trading of favors and arm twisting may be necessary.

The Fragility of Participation

Even in those organizations where participation of the lower levels has been designated as the mode of operation, it is possible that it can be withdrawn. Where the possibilities of power exist, there is a possibility that power once withheld will be reasserted.

Take the case of the governor of a state who was enthused about MBO and employed a participative style of management. He delegated extensively and pressed decisions down to the lowest possible level. This produced high morale at lower levels. But the governor left office and his successor immediately suspended all of the mechanics of participative management and centralized everything in his office. In the process, he declared his support of MBO, but in fact he killed it by locating total control in his office.

Similar experiences have been found where a humanistic president of a corporation installed a participative MBO program. Upon his retirement a four-star general assumed his office and promptly applied autocratic controls. He eliminated certain policy committees, scuttled meetings which had been the major vehicle for MBO, and ordered the appraisal form abandoned and training programs stopped. The reason he did so was plausible. The company had been in market trouble, and a lax style of MBO had made the corporation an easygoing but unprofitable place. After a turnaround, he retired. Major promotions were made from within, the earlier participative management style of MBO was restored, and the results were excellent.

It is a hard political fact about organizations, public and private, that MBO which is inextricably tied to participative management may be damaged if an autocratic boss gets on top. MBO which is top down and somewhat autocratic to begin with suffers no such setback. On the other hand, it never had the developmental and humanistic benefits of participative management in the first place.

The Problem of Countermoves

A strong move to produce an MBO program that would change the behavior of people or the arrangement of the organization and how it does its work can be counted on to produce an equal and opposite reaction somewhere. It may be expressed by scoffing; by wisecracks; by acronyms for MBO ("Massive Bowel Obstruction" or "Mr. Big's Obsession" to name two); or by overintellectualizing the obvious.

In other cases, the reaction produces some fairly stiff fights, scuffles, and corporate infighting. This is not peculiar to MBO, but is characteristic of political response to changes that will shuffle the power structure and power alignments in the organization. Changes in cost accounting or market research, a new salary system, or simply reassignment of parking places will trigger the counterresponse.

Predicting the reaction and pinpointing its source is one of the arts of the organization politician. He is then able to take corrective, remedial, or ameliorative action before the problem arises. In some instances, he finds these sources of reaction by testing his idea in tentative form, sending out position papers and holding discussions in order to elicit such responses. If the trouble spots surface after installation, they can be patched up through trading, arm twisting, or muscle, or by changing the program.

Even though most politically aware persons realize the advantages of option *b* over option *a,* it is often impossible to get complete support. Therefore, the need to modify and amend the MBO program after it is underway, for example in the second go-around, should be considered one of the political realities. Running roughshod over those who would resist a new idea not only stiffens the backbone of the resistors, but makes all changes less likely to be accepted.

Unit Loyalty

An often overlooked rule of allegiance is that people center their loyalties around the smallest unit of which they are a member rather than the overall organization. The basic unit for the soldier is his squad, not the armed forces or the free world. It is the engineering project for the engineer, rather than the entire firm. The personnel expert is often more centered in his staff department's goals than the corporation's.

This fact has great significance for implementing MBO. It means that the objectives must be related to this man, this job, in this unit, this year. Expecting people to be motivated by grand designs and overall global strategies is unrealistic and contrary to political realities.

In one large oil company, the MBO program met poor acceptance in the engineering and development departments, even though it was a smashing success in the refinery and the marketing department. The resistance in the two departments was not only embarrassing, but threatened to weaken the program in other areas as well. A wise MBO administrator suggested a conference in which the people in engineering designed their own MBO system, with special salmon-colored forms and a different kind of calendar of events. The program immediately began to operate smoothly.

Diversity in applications of the MBO program may be necessary for the political reasons of unit loyalty. Permitting variances in details, in application, in timing, and in sequencing of events may assist implementation.

The Individualists

One of the greatest potential sources of political opposition to an MBO program is the uniformity and conformity imposed by some systems. When the MBO program is seen as a set of forms to be filed—a cookbook set of procedures—it will run into individuals who resist.

The reasons lie in the value systems of technical, managerial, and professional people, who possess primarily middle-class values. They are most often the educated professionals, although a degree or college experience is not necessarily the sole criterion. People without degrees who have associated with such persons at work have often acquired their values. They cherish their own professional individuality, and while an objective observer might see this individuality as insignificant, it has an important bearing upon the behavior of the person. The desire to participate in decisions is strongly held by the middle-class employee, and denial of the wish will produce political effort contrary to the whole idea.

Sometimes the individualists will object to the name of a program. Some of the best MBO programs have found it necessary to adopt another label, calling it "goals management" or permitting major subunits to use their own names or acronyms. The fetish of maintaining a single unified program with a common label, often adhered to by corporate staffs, can work to the disadvantage of the program.

The image of being "unprofessional" or requiring unprofessional behavior can be the kiss of death to any kind of new procedure. The unexplained and seemingly pointless order or the cold memo not accompanied by a dialogue increase the likelihood that the program will be seen as an indignity or as unprofessional.

This perception can be extended to the specifics of the standards of performance which are produced from the goals-setting process installed. If it seems to be enforcing conformity and attacking present eccentricities, the whole program becomes suspect.

One of the major features of MBO which makes it politically palatable to professionals is that it is indifferent to activities but is deeply concerned about output. This assurance of the protection of individual idiosyncracies is important to professionals.

Status Symbols

Attention must be paid to the effect of the new system on the present structure of status in the organization. Status symbols are the subtle indicators of a person's standing in relation to others.

In some instances, these are the physical symbols of office, such as uniforms, desks, office fittings, parking places, and the like. In other instances, more probable in an MBO program, it will be the reduction in influence or authority for some, as the center of decision making moves to a lower level. In one bank where MBO was installed, the power to make certain equipment purchase decisions was delegated. Yet when the new equipment arrived the president was shocked. "My feelings were hurt that they hadn't consulted me," he reported later.

Social and status significance is attached also to certain prerequisites or roles. If an MBO system robs a person of such status symbols as authority to conduct the annual performance review or to award raises, resistance from the deprived can be expected. He is, in his own mind, forced to downgrade, depreciate, or even attack MBO. However, the true reasons for the opposition will not be revealed.

Such an attack is not conducted openly, of course, for the losses would appear to be a trivial, and perhaps even an immature, reason for attacking something as logical as MBO. Thus the attack will be couched in terms that are eminently logical and rational in language, even though the basis is far from being rational.

Organization Form

Among the more sophisticated approaches to political maneuvering to get an MBO system in operation is that of organizational planning. Decentralization, for example, is ostensibly an organizational structure change, but it also forces MBO into being. Decentralization is also a political action, for it represents a shifting of power within the organization. It is a blending of the bureaucratic form with centralized control, described by Max Weber, with the humanistic form in which lower level persons make more independent decisions, described by Joseph Litterer.

The dispersal of profit responsibility in many places simply makes it impossible for the top executive to control all the activities of all of the subordinate profit centers. Accordingly, the higher level of management must satisfy its domineering tendencies by defining results expected and measuring those results, meanwhile keeping its hands off the operations. This is far less a matter of being persuaded of the virtues of delegation and participative management than a simple inability to see everything.

When you run out of eyes, hours, and ability to see everything, you are naturally required to manage by objectives whether you like it or not.

Such exemplary managerial practices are likely to develop in organizations like conglomerates where the new units have been acquired in one bite. It is especially imperative when the acquired company was purchased on some kind of payout plan over the years, with strict contractual arrangements allowing the founding management to retain their positions as long as profits are satisfactory. Far better than a sophisticated training program is an installment method of acquiring new firms which promote MBO; the result is almost inescapably MBO. The idea, for example, that a corporate president can manage 100 divisions autocratically rather than by objectives is, on the face of it, impossible.

MBO also results in firms that are nationally dispersed (the Prudential Insurance Company, for example) with all but a few managerial functions distributed among the five or six large regional offices, each with a complete functional staff. The bank with 350 branches will probably manage them by objectives, even if it does not realize it is doing so. The alternative is an exorbitant computerized management information system (MIS) and communications system. It is far more economical and sensible to find good men, place them in jobs, get them committed to objectives, and control them by exceptions.

On the other hand, a centralized organization form with functional departments usually means that the MBO program is a form of artificial or arbitrary choice. Bosses who are in the same room or even the same building with all of their employees may declare that MBO is their official style. However, they often are playing house with the employees, and in fact do not manage by objectives at all, even when they talk a great MBO game.

The Effect of Alliances

Two or three divisions or departments, connected by a network of alliances, joint programs, mutual support, and interdependencies, can make or break an MBO program at will. The credit and sales departments, which share the task of keeping receivables under control, can make a shambles of capital management goals or they can make achievement seem effortless and natural. The industrial engineering department can team up with production to make MBO easy or difficult.

Alliances can be formed among groups that fear they would be weakened, and their joint resistance will benefit both. Hospitals are replete with examples of groups which might ordinarily find themselves in competition but are instead joined in coalitions in the face of threatening objectives. The surgeons and medical staffs competing for personnel and technician time will stand together against the administrator whose objective is to reduce technician costs.

Take the case of the controller who was committed to a computerized management information system. It was his intent to have an on-line, real-time, alpha-numeric tube in every manager's office. Thus, he would have daily—even hourly—control over every important input or resource to be employed in every part of the business. The personnel department at the same time was pushing MBO, suggesting delegation, freedom of action, and goals management rather than control of detailed activity.

In another office, the corporate attorney had built up a "Merlin the magician" relationship with the president. The counsel was in and out of the president's office, reporting little stories and advising on all sorts of things. He too recognized MBO as a threat to his position as high counselor. He teamed up with the controller to condemn MBO as a spurious and probably risky adventure that was probably not fully thought through and perhaps basically unsound—if not downright illegal. MBO never stood a chance. Power is not something voluntarily relinquished, and those who have it may see MBO as a shifting of power downward, and will accordingly employ alliances and political power to fend it off.

Money Is Power

Those who control money or produce it in large amounts have power and can sway all kinds of decisions. In one large electronics firm with ten divisions, one division produced 80 percent of the profit. The general manager of that division had far greater power over corporate policy than his rank would indicate. If he disagreed with or could not use a corporate policy, he would simply ignore it. Because he produced most of the profit, he was sometimes gently admonished but never severely crimped.

Such a power center is able to block new programs which do not suit its mode of operation. On the other hand, if the general manager of such a center can be persuaded or educated to adopt MBO it will probably become a corporate-wide system.

In other instances, it is a single function. Marketing is king in many firms where the "marketing concept" determines the basic strategic goals. In others, it is the technology center or the financial group. In highly unionized firms, the labor relations manager will have considerable influence, and often determines whether MBO will be given a hearing, to say nothing of its being implemented. Power is often rooted in the ability to affect revenues, expenses, or pricing.

Dealing with Conservatism

Kenneth Boulding has pointed out that change agents, liberals, and innovators are often characterized by high intensity behavior, while conservators and persons opposed to change are low intensity in behavior. The change-oriented person may have to be dramatic, shrill, strident, persuasive, and even flamboyant to get a full hearing. The best response for the conservative is to lower his voice and be rational, cautious, and meticulous.

It is the strategy of conservatism and calmness to propose that the change be examined in detail, that it be tried only in part, and that perhaps certain aspects have not been fully revealed. In the face of such a strategy of delay and obfuscation, the change agent must act with skill. He may upon occasion take the organization by storm. If he persuades the top man, gets his directive from on high, and proceeds with a vigorous combination of advocacy and education to build a plurality in the organization, he may get his way.

The true merits of education as a vehicle for change are seen here. The conservative critic can thus be isolated and quietly permitted to change his mind without engaging in high intensity tactics, for it should be realized that the strength of a countermovement is often related to the intensity of the attack on the status quo.

In some instances, the value of the outsider is that he can provide the decisive voice of change to break the deadlock of inertia created by the low intensity opponent. When the outsider is gone, then the less intense movements can begin. Once the silence has been broken, the insider MBO advocate can restore quiet, deplore the excesses which he himself introduced, and quietly proceed with his educational and persuasive efforts.

MBO has failed in many organizations because those in charge ignored the political considerations included in the implementation. MBO is logical, systematic, and so on, but it must deal with various problems and influences. This does not mean that politics is contrary to the management systems known as MBO, and that where politics enters changes and a new system cannot be expected to flourish.

Political behavior itself has purposes, and goals are the beginning point of politics as well as of business or administration. It does require, however, that the MBO implementer must not ignore political realities, and that his choice of methods of implementation must discriminate among alternative approaches, and that the political constraints are realities which must be managed.

PROGRESS AND PROBLEMS IN SYSTEMS ANALYSIS*

Edward S. Quade

It is not easy to tell someone how to carry out a systems analysis. We lack an adequate theory to guide us. This must be expected, for systems analysis, even more than operations research, is a new discipline. History teaches us that good theory usually comes late in the development of any field and after many false starts.

The attention of the practitioners, when it has turned to methods, has been focused mainly on the development of mathematical techniques for handling certain specialized problems, common in operations research, rather than on an attempt to build a basic theory for the treatment of broad context questions such as occur in defense planning. This attention to technique has met with great success. Models have become easier to manipulate, even with many more variables represented, and the computational obstacles in operations research now cause comparatively little difficulty. The more philosophical problems, however, such as occur in providing assurance that the model is meaningful, in devising schemes to compensate for uncertainty, or in choosing appropriate criteria, are most troublesome. Therefore, the many important and useful mathematical techniques of operations research are treated very cursorily in this book, although Chapter 13 tries to give some indication of their nature and limitations. Concepts and understanding—areas where the analyst as well as the user is more likely to err—are emphasized instead.

When the possibility of preparing a lecture on the procedures of analysis was first considered, the proper approach seemed obvious: Examine all available studies carried out to help military decision-making and extract the principles and methods common to the successful studies. In other words, isolate the ideas that make an analysis a good one. This effort did not turn out to be very productive. Either the sample was too small or we were not sufficiently perceptive, or (what now seems more likely) no universally accepted set of ideas existed. It was even difficult to decide which studies should be called good or successful.

One hope for guidance is to turn to science. In fact, it is frequently argued that operations research should be considered a science. But the goals are different. Science is concerned primarily with the pursuit of truth and a better understanding of the world we live in. Operations

---

* Reprinted with permission of author and publisher from *Analysis for Military Decisions* (Chicago: Rand McNally & Co., 1964), pp. 149–176.

research, almost without exception, is concerned with policy, that is, with more effective manipulation of the real world—even if this may have to be accomplished without full understanding of the underlying phenomena. Its purpose is seldom merely to understand or to predict.

There is little difference in method:

> . . . Both the exact scientist and the operations analyst tend to make use of what is sometimes called a mathematical model of the subject matter; in the case of the scientist such a model is apt to be part of the well-confirmed body of our scientific knowledge, whereas an operations research model is of a more tentative, *ad hoc,* character. In other words, even if the current status of science provides no well-established theory for the phenomena to be dealt with by the operations analyst, the latter must nevertheless construct a model as best he can, where both the structure of the model and its numerical inputs may be based merely on intuitive insight and limited practical experience by the analyst himself or by whatever expert advisers on the subject matter may be available to him. As further insights accrue and more experimental data become available, the operations analyst has to be ready to discard his first model and replace it with an improved one. This tentative procedure, dictated by pragmatic considerations, is thus essentially one of successive approximation. In this regard, operations research has a status similar to that of the so-called inexact sciences, of which medicine, engineering, and most of the social sciences are examples.
>
> Therefore, in comparing operations research with an exact science, it is with regard to exactness that operations research falls short, but not necessarily with regard to the scientific character of its methods. . . .[1]

Operations research attempts to use the methods of science. This means in essence that it strives for the same traditions. Scientific tradition holds that (1) results are obtained by processes that another scientist can duplicate to attain the same results; (2) all calculations, assumptions, data, and judgments are made explicit and thus subject to checking, criticism, and disagreement; (3) the scientific method is objective; its propositions do not depend on personalities, reputations, or vested interests; where possible it is quantitative and experimental. For operations research and systems analysis, however, these are still unachieved goals.

ENGINEERING AND SYSTEMS ANALYSIS

Operations research and, to an even greater degree, systems analysis seem to be more nearly engineering than science. For the purpose of making a distinction here, one might say that science finds things out, while engineering uses the results of science to do things cheaply and well.

While there are similarities between the typical engineering problem and the typical military systems analysis or operations research problem, there are important distinctions. Most of these are of a quantitative rather than of a qualitative nature. In military systems analyses

1. There are relatively many more factors that can only be estimated rather than measured or experimented with. Consider as an example the design of a "flyaway" kit, that is, a package of spare parts, tools, and equipment to be airlifted into the field to support a tactical bomber. Among a host of factors, the design depends upon the character of the war in which the bomber is to be used. But the pattern of future wars in which a tactical bomber might be used is a real uncertainty—not something that can be experimented with.

2. Even when measurements can be made, the results of field tests or of experiments made on the proving ground are likely to differ radically from results obtained under combat conditions.

Again refer to the flyaway kit problem; the peacetime demand for spare parts does not necessarily reflect the wartime demand the kit should be designed to meet.

3. The time period after which the answers become worthless is almost always extremely brief.

In these days weapons become obsolete rapidly. If we spend enough time in testing even to establish the peacetime demand for spares for our flyaway kit, we may have our answer too late to be of any help.

The time limit is important to the engineer also, but ordinarily not to the same extent. To the academic scientist, time may not be of particular consequence. He is after a high degree of confidence in his results, and whatever time it takes to get the degree of confidence he is after, he can usually take. The military analyst, on the other hand, must frequently reach his best possible conclusion in a limited time.

4. There is frequently no way to verify the conclusions of the study.

If we are lucky, before there is a war our flyaway kit will be replaced by another to complement a more modern aircraft, and we will never find out whether the original kit would have been satisfactory.

5. The value concepts are much more troublesome. Like engineering, the military analyses seek to help someone take action; unlike most engineering, however, the determination of objectives, costs, and criteria represents a difficult problem.

6. In military analysis, as opposed to its civilian counterparts, the interaction of the enemy's alternatives, objectives, and costs with our own is usually the major problem, and the interaction between our own

alternatives, objectives, and costs is relatively minor. While the need to treat *conflict* aspects of the problem does not necessarily make the analysis more difficult, it does introduce an additional set of uncertainties and complexities.

There are also some more subtle differences.

> For one thing, systems analysis is engineering at a high level in the sense suggested by the following example. A glass engineer successfully plans the production of certain kinds of optical glass on the basis of chemical knowledge; a lens-designing engineer designs camera lenses on the basis of a knowledge of optics, the techniques of lens manufacture, and the general capabilities of the glass engineer; a camera engineer designs a camera on the basis of his knowledge of many things, including what the lens designer can do; the aeronautical engineer designs a reconnaissance plane, using, among other things, his knowledge of what he can expect from the camera designer; the systems analyst designs a reconnaissance system knowing what he can expect from the plane designer. Of course, there is communication up and down the list.
>
> Military systems analysis may differ from ordinary engineering in its enormous responsibility, in its relatively poor data, and in the unusual difficulty of appraising the value system applicable to its problems, but these differences are not violent; they are quantitative, not qualitative. All the difficulties referred to occur in some measure in the humblest engineering problem such as designing a simple dog kennel.[2]

Perhaps no set of lectures has ever been directed toward those who employ civil, mechanical, or chemical engineers, and while it would not be impossible to imagine such a course being useful, it is significant that it is nonexistent or rare.

> If a city hires an engineer to design a bridge, it may perhaps have his work checked by another engineer, but the city fathers will not presume to study his report with a view to seeing for themselves whether the proposed bridge is likely to collapse. They believe, with more or less reason, that the field of civil engineering is sufficiently well developed and a licensed engineer so likely to be firm in his science that his judgment in this matter is overwhelmingly better than their own. Similarly, they will trust the authority of their engineer that the clearance, carrying capacity, safety, and durability of the proposed bridge cannot all be increased without an increase in cost. The trade-offs among these values might in principle concern the city fathers, and in special cases they will. But, by and large, there will be none among them capable of or feeling the responsibility for going deeply into these matters. Where, however, a defense system for the nation is concerned, tradition cannot be relied upon; for there is too little of it. The trade-offs between the various values involved are properly felt to be high concerns of the

nation and the immediate responsibility of high government officers. Of course, even in the case of the bridge, there are some trade-off considerations that the city fathers cannot dodge. They must make some decisions that depend on their estimates of the political temper of the city and of its probable future growth—decisions for which the civil engineer has no particular competence.[3]

THE PHILOSOPHICAL ASPECTS OF ANALYSIS

Systems analysis, particularly of the type required for military decisions, is still largely a form of art. An art can be taught in part, but not by means of fixed rules which need only be followed with exactness. Thus, in these analyses, we have to do some things that we think are right but that are not verifiable, that we cannot really justify, and that are never checked in the output of the work. Also we must accept as inputs many relatively intangible factors derived from human judgment, and we must present answers to be used as a basis for other judgments. Whenever possible, this judgment is supplemented by inductive and numerical reasoning, but it is only judgment nonetheless.

In fact, to a large extent, systems analysis and operations research are successful aids to policy determination in areas such as national security, where there is no accepted theoretical foundation, precisely because they are designed to make systematic and efficient rather than haphazard and unguided use of judgment by specialists or experts in the fields of interest. The essence of their method is to construct a "model" appropriate to the problem; such a model—which may be a game, a computer program, or a politico-military scenario—introduces a precise structure and terminology that serves primarily as an effective means of communication, and, through feedback—the countermoves in a war game, for instance—helps the experts to arrive at a clearer understanding of the subject matter and the problem.

There is a distinction here between operations research and what we term systems analysis. To be more explicit, consider what might be called a "typical" operations research problem by many of its practitioners. Although there may be several resource variables which are subject to choice, the problem usually can (by making enough assumptions) be put in a form where there is only one dependent variable—termed the criterion or measure of merit (frequently cost); this is to be optimized subject to some set of constraints. The relationship between this dependent variable and the resource variables is formulated mathematically. This allows trade-offs between resources to be investigated. On the other hand, the "typical" systems analysis problem is often first: What is the problem? It is frequently difficult to formulate a criterion because the objectives may be multiple and conflicting. Trade-off may have to be investigated between objectives as well as between resources. Moreover, it may be impossible to describe the relationship between objectives and resources in terms of known mathematical functions or even to describe it numerically or graphically. Without a means for expressing the relationships between these classes of variables, the only recourse for investigation of trade-offs lies in the judgments and intuitions of experts. Such judgments in systems analysis are, of course, in addition to those which are inherent in even the simplest operations research problem—for example, judgments about the scope of the problem.

To emphasize further this distinction between operations research and systems analysis, we quote (in essence) from one military report.

> The participants were asked to project their experience and thinking into an uncharted future where formal doctrine offered little or no guidance and where concepts of future war would not necessarily be limited by practical considerations of current organization, weapons, and budgets. *The work of the group, therefore, was not operations research.* Concepts and hypotheses were presented and discussed that could not be supported immediately by facts and figures or be analyzed in terms of experience or experimental data, simply because the necessary data did not exist.[4]

Again, from another source.

> The formulation of objectives and the action on the recommendations are not properly included in the activity of the operations analyst, being literally boundary conditions imposed on the freedom of his operation.[5]

While such activities may not be operations research, they are part and parcel of the activities which go on under the name of systems analysis.

This suggests that analysis in support of defense decisionmakers at the national policy level is different from operations research as traditionally viewed. As one participant puts it:

> . . . The traditional formulation of operations research problems in terms of ends and means—how can I maximize the achievement of an objective or a set of objectives for a given cost, or alternatively, how can I minimize the cost of achieving a certain set of objectives?—is proper, but limited. At the national policy level, the major part of systems analysis is the exploration of the interaction of ends and means. By that interaction is meant that what are objectives from one point of view are means from another; that what is worth trying to do de-

pends on what is possible to do, or on how effective the means for doing it are; and that any given objective is likely to be one of a number of alternative ways of achieving a still broader objective.[6]

Decisions pertaining to choices of alternative weapon systems or force structures and the strategies for their employment, made five to ten years in advance, are essentially matters of economic choice. Certain elements are common to such problems, although these elements may not always be explicitly identified by the analyst. . . .

1. *The objective* (or objectives). Systems analysis is undertaken primarily to suggest or, at the very least, to help choose a course of action. This action must have an aim or objective. Policies or strategies, forces or equipment are examined, compared, and preferred on the basis of how well and how cheaply they can accomplish the aim or objective.
2. *The alternatives.* The alternatives are the means by which it is hoped the objectives can be attained. They need not be obvious substitutes or perform the same specific function.
3. *The costs.* Each alternative means of accomplishing the objectives implies the use of specific resources which cannot then be used for other purposes.
4. *A model* (or models). The model is a representation of the situation under study designed to predict the cost and performance of each alternative. It abstracts the relevant features of the situation by means which may vary from a set of mathematical equations or a computer program to an idealized description of the situation in which judgment alone is used to assess the consequences of various choices.
5. *A criterion.* A criterion is a rule or test by which one alternative can be chosen in preference to another. It provides a means for using cost and effectiveness to order the alternatives.

It is easy to find statements in the literature of operations research which imply that analysis to aid any decisionmaker is really nothing more than the "scientific method" extended to problems outside the realm of pure science. Even though it is by no means clear that there is any unique method which might be termed the "scientific method," what is usually meant is that the analysis advances through something like the following stages:

Formulation —Defining the issues of concern, clarifying the objectives, and limiting the problem.

Search —Determining the relevant data, looking for alternative programs of action to resolve the issues.

Explanation —Building a model and using it to explore the consequences of the alternative programs, ordinarily by obtaining estimates of their cost and performance.

Interpretation—Deriving the conclusions and indicating a preferred alternative or course of action. This may be a combination of features from previously considered alternatives or their modification to reflect factors not taken into account earlier.

Verification —Testing the conclusion by experiment.

A systems analysis always involves the first four of these stages but frequently must omit the last. For military problems, experiment, other than a pseudo experiment by simulation, may simply not be available. . . .

Formulation

Formulation implies an attempt to isolate the questions or issues involved, to fix the context within which these issues are to be resolved, to define the meaning of the variables or factors that are operative, and to state relationships among these factors. The relationships may be extremely hypothetical because empirical knowledge may be in short supply, but they will help make the logical structure of the analysis clear. In a sense, this is the most important stage, for the time spent restating the problem in different ways, redefining it, or expressing its limits brings to light whether it is spurious or trivial and points the way to its solution. The tendency all too frequently is to accept the original statement of what is wanted exactly as proposed, and then to set about building a model and gathering information, scarcely giving a thought to how the answer will contribute to the decisions which it is trying to assist. In fact, because the concern is with the future, the major job may be to decide what the policymaker should want to do. Since systems studies have resulted in some rather important changes, not only in how the policymaker carries out his activity but in the objectives themselves, it would be self-defeating to accept without inquiry the customers' or sponsors' view of what the problem is.

An analogy with medical practice may be drawn. No doctor ignores a patient's description of his symptoms, but he cannot allow the patient's self-diagnosis to override his own professional judgment. The medical analogy is not entirely applicable, however; the businessman or military commander ordinarily knows more than anyone else about his actual operations and what, if anything, might be wrong with them.

How then is the analyst to know his formulation of the problem is superior? *His only possible advantage lies in analysis.* That is, the process of problem formulation itself has to be the subject of analysis. The system analyst always has some idea as to the possible solutions of the problem; otherwise, he probably should not be working on it, for his analysis will prove to be too formal and abstract. At this early stage the analyst essentially makes an attempt to solve the problem before the facts are known. It is this attempt which gives him a basis for better formulation.

Let us take an example of how an analyst might go about problem formulation. Take the choice of a criterion. It may be hopelessly impossible to think out a good one in advance. The practical way may be to take a rather crude value scale, see what solution its use leads to, and then, if the solution is not in accordance with common sense, revise it. For instance, consider the analyst who needed to lose weight and set out to use a linear programming model to evolve an optimal reducing diet. He decided that an ideal criterion would be to get the most volume within the constraints of the necessary nutrients and calories. Well, he put his model on the machine, ground away, and came up with watermelon. That showed him he had better consider dried weight to exclude water. When this was done he came up with bouillon cubes, which consist largely of salt. Since this would not be very palatable and might be injurious to health, he made still another choice, and continuing in this way, he finally evolved a satisfactory rule of choice.

The problem itself does not remain static. Interplay between a growing understanding of the problem and of possible developments will redefine the problem itself. Primarily, as the result of discussion, the original effort to state the problem should suggest one or more possible solutions or hypotheses. As the study progresses, these original ideas are enriched and elaborated upon. Each hypothesis serves as a guide to later results—it tells us what we are looking for while we are looking. The final statement of the conclusions and recommendations usually rests on a knowledge of facts about the problem which are not known to the analyst at the start. Frequently, a hypothesis must be discarded and an entirely new one considered. In the early stages it is not a mistake to hold an idea as to the solution; the pitfall is to refuse to abandon such an idea in the face of mounting evidence.

The process of analysis is thus an *iterative* one—a cycle of problem formulation, selection of objectives, design of alternative systems, data collection, model building, a weighing of costs against effectiveness, the questioning of assumptions and objectives, the opening of new alternatives, reformulation, etc. Figure 1 attempts to indicate the iterative

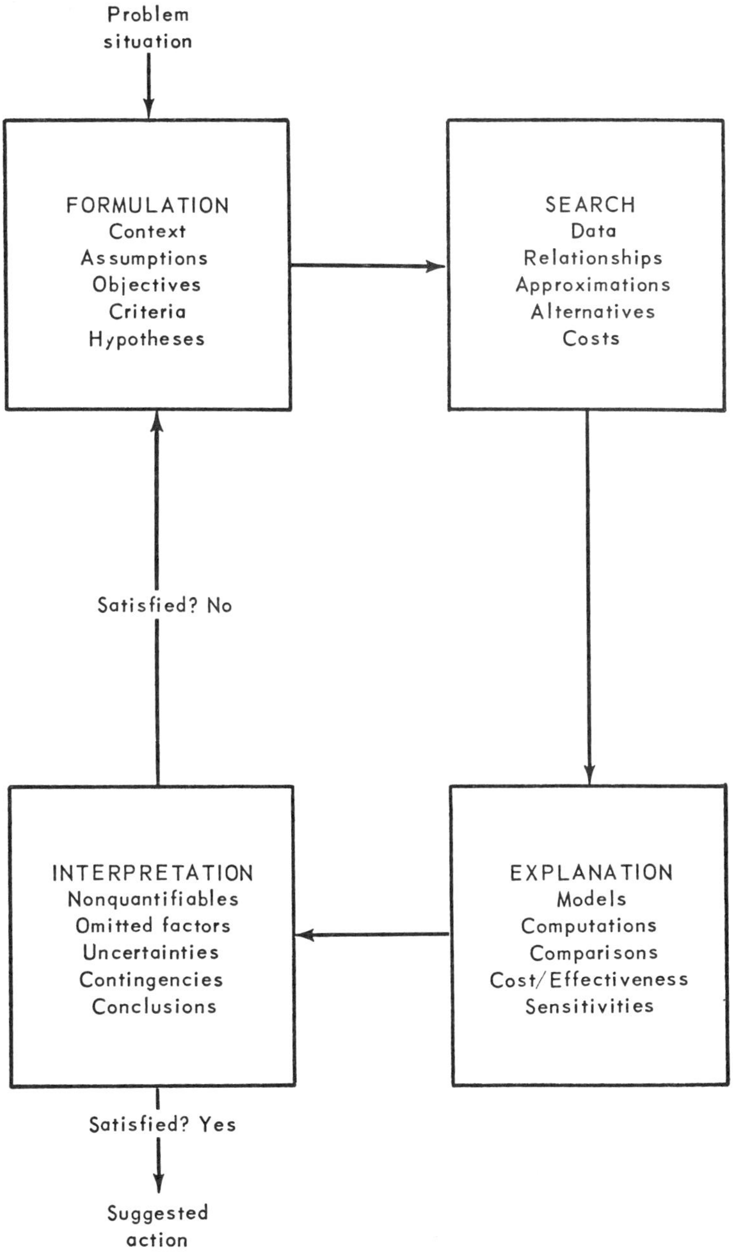

FIGURE 1
Activities in Analysis

character of systems analysis. The various stages are ordered only with respect to a single cycle; the approximate solution we obtain at the end of the first cycle helps us to better prepare a second formulation. Thus, in a sense, it is impossible to formulate a problem completely before it is solved, or, in other words, the final problem statement may have to be written simultaneously with the final answer.

In the problem of choosing objectives, the iterative character of systems analysis stands out. It is impossible to select satisfactory objectives without some idea of the cost and difficulty of attaining them. Such information can only come as part of the analysis itself.

It is a common error to believe that goals should, and can, be set independently of the plans to attain them. Yet there is overwhelming evidence that ultimate objectives are, more often than not, the result of opportunities that possible alternatives offer rather than a source of such alternatives. The point is that only part of the consequences of different goals can be anticipated without analysis.

Military analysis must frequently be undertaken with only partial information about the objectives, criteria, and preferences at higher levels. At the highest level, official statements of national objectives are likely to be either nonexistent or so vague that they are not very helpful. This is a situation that gives rise to "suboptimization"—that is, the selection of intermediate objectives and criteria for the problem that are consistent with and that approximate in some sense or other those at the higher level. Given limitations on time and manpower, a suboptimization may be the only feasible approach. For example, a recommendation to choose a particular defense weapon system may be made on the basis of its capability to intercept and destroy enemy missiles; this may be a substitute for the broader objective of minimizing the number of nuclear weapons detonating on our territory. Whether or not this is a good way to ensure that the analysis pursues the higher objective of limiting damage to population and property if war should come must itself be the subject of analysis.

Although many of the most valuable systems analyses have been suboptimizations, suboptimization may not be good enough and may not be the best that can be done. Analysis can sometimes eliminate, uncover, and reconcile objectives.

There is frequently more than one objective for a system; for example, "to make war unlikely and, in the event war does break out, to limit the damage to ourselves and to achieve a favorable military outcome and political settlement." To choose a system one needs to find some method of weighing competing objectives. How can we decide on a single objective? For one thing, we can examine each objective to see if it is important only as a means to another objective; if it is, then we can eliminate it. For another, we can examine each alternative to see if the attainment of any of the objectives would be unaffected by a choice among the alternatives. Again, if it is, we can eliminate it.

One technique to uncover objectives may be to confront the man who must act on the basis of the analysis with a list of alternatives and ask him if he would be willing to follow the course of action implied by each of the alternatives, were the analysis to indicate it as optimal.

If objectives compete, that is, if people disagree on objectives or if an individual cannot determine what his objectives are—one can try to find still higher objectives on which there is agreement. It then may be possible either to carry out the analysis with the higher level objectives or, by examination of the original objectives for consistency with the one agreed on, to make a choice. One thing we cannot do is construct from all the individual objectives some group objective by appropriately weighing all separate ones; this is a practical absurdity and it has been theoretically demonstrated that there is no unique and satisfying way to do it. If, in the end, all attempts to reduce objectives fail, it may be helpful to carry out the analysis for each objective.

A characteristic of systems analysis is that the solutions are often found in a set of compromises which seek to balance and, where possible, to reconcile conflicting objectives and questions of value. It is more important to choose the "right" objective than it is to make the "right" choice between alternatives. The wrong objective means that the wrong problem is being solved. The choice of the wrong alternative may merely mean that something less than the "best" system is being chosen. Frequently we must be satisfied with merely a demonstration that a suggested action is "in the right direction," anyway. This may be all that is possible.

To choose among alternatives, we must do more than determine which alternatives can attain a desired objective. Some criterion or test of preferredness must be employed; say, a rule to select for us the alternative (or alternatives) that yields the objectives for the least expenditure of costs or resources.[7]

Two rules for guidance in choosing a criterion, originally stated by C. J. Hitch,[8] are

1. A criterion used in a lower level problem should be consistent with that appropriate to the next higher level.
2. A criterion should not have to be repeatedly hedged by constraints to prevent it from giving absurd results.

As an example to illustrate the first rule, in determining a parking lot policy for an amusement park, the policy at the level of the people running the lot might be that of maximizing net revenues from parking. But this may well be different from the policy of the people running the park whose criterion might be to maximize the net revenues from the amusement park as a whole. In considering parking lot revenues, lack of parking for a few people, who then go elsewhere, might lead to considerable savings in land costs for parking and in salary for attendants, and thus in greater revenue for the lot, but the loss of good will might result in considerable loss of revenue for the park as a whole. A policy more consistent with the higher level, and thus a better policy for the lot, might simply be to provide parking for all who come—or even to provide this parking free of charge.

We cannot know a priori, however, that income from a parking lot should be small relative to income from the facility it serves. Whenever there is little opportunity of visiting the facility except by private car, the possibility of disguising a significant general admission charge as a parking charge may merit serious consideration.

As an example to illustrate the second rule, we can take any "ratio" criterion where a constraint must be imposed to keep the denominator away from zero.

Cost must be treated as a major element:

> Furthermore, there has long been a tendency in the Defense Department to state military requirements in absolute terms without reference to their costs. But the military effectiveness or military worth of any given weapon system cannot logically be considered in isolation. It must be considered in relation to its cost—and in a world in which resources are limited, to the alternative uses to which resources can be put. Military requirements are meaningful only in terms of benefits to be gained in relation to their cost. Thus, resource costs and military worth have to be scrutinized together.[9]

The costs to be considered in choosing among alternatives, moreover, should be the "new" costs, that is, the net additional resource drain or "incremental cost" that would be incurred because of the choice of a particular alternative. Because a certain system may inherit facilities, personnel, or equipment from previous systems, its incremental costs may be much lower than what it would cost if it were to exist "in isolation." Also, in a comparison of military capabilities, costs have sometimes been computed on the basis of what the various systems would cost independent of the existence of other systems or other capabilities. In this light consider, for example, a Navy supercarrier. In a paper comparison to estimate its value in a limited-war role, if no credit were assigned to its central war capabilities, then on a cost-effectiveness basis it would be handicapped unfairly in comparison with a weapon system that had only a single role.

Great attention must be paid to initial conditions; that is, to the assumptions that limit the problem and set the background against which the initial attempt at a solution is to be made. The situation is not like that of an empirical science, which starts with observed facts, but more like that of mathematics, where the results take any "validity" they might have in the real world from the initial assumptions. The difference is that for the systems analysis to give correct guidance, it is important that the assumptions be the "right" assumptions.

Even for small-scale problems, the number of factors under consideration at any one time must be reduced until what is left is manageable. In systems analysis, the complexity of the "full" problem frequently far outruns analytic competence. To consider in detail anything like the complete range of possible alternative solutions may be impossible. The vast majority will obviously be inferior, hence there is no harm in leaving them out. The danger is that some alternative better than that uncovered by the analysis will also have been left out. Constraints must be imposed on the number of alternatives to be examined, but by preliminary analysis, not by arbitrary decree. Such constraints must be regarded as flexible so that they may be weakened or removed if it appears in later cycles that their presence is a controlling factor.

Sometimes problems can be reduced by factoring out subproblems. This can be done when a group of variables having relatively little interdependence with the other variables can be treated separately.

Once the problem has been broken down into its components—which is what analyzing the problem means—some of the components can be further analyzed, using various techniques; but others may defy analytic techniques. In that case, because the problem has been broken into smaller pieces, the systems analyst may be able to find individuals who have direct, sound experience and on whose "considered" judgment he can rely.

Considered judgment differs from ordinary or intuitive judgment in that the logic behind the opinion is made explicit. Both are based on an individual's experience and background, but when the reasoning is explicit, an observer can form his own opinion from the information presented. Judgment permeates systems analysis—judgments as to which hypothesis is better than another, or which approach is more fruitful, or what facts are relevant. The ideal is to keep all judgments in plain view.

One methodological aspect of operations research, the reliance on expert judgment, has received little attention.[10] Only by replacing the surreptitious use of expertise by explicit and systematic application of it can objectivity be safeguarded.

Usually two or more experts are available. When they differ, there are several ways to try to bring them together. Using the consensus approach they can work individually and then seek methods for the best combined use of their findings; or they can work jointly in a group exercise—ranging from simple round-table discussions to reacting through a sophisticated simulation model—to obtain expert judgments from the group as a whole. Operational gaming, or simulation involving role-playing by the participating experts, is particularly promising when it is desirable to employ several experts with varying specialties in a context in which their forecasts cannot be independent but are likely to interact. Here the game structure or model furnishes the experts with an artificial, simulated environment within which they can jointly and simultaneously experiment, acquiring through feedback the insights necessary to make successful predictions within the model environment and thus indirectly about the real world.

Another method, falling somewhere between individual and group action, is the so-called Delphi technique. It needs further development and testing but is regarded by this author as very promising. It tries to improve the basis consensus method by subjecting the experts' views to each other's criticism without actual confrontation and all its psychological shortcomings (such as specious persuasion, an unwillingness to abandon publicly expressed opinions, and the bandwagon effect of the majority). The Delphi technique replaces direct debate by a carefully designed program of sequential individual interrogations (best conducted by questionnaires) interspersed with information and opinion feedback derived by computed consensus from the earlier parts of the program. Some of the questions directed to the respondents may, for instance, inquire into the "reasons" for previously expressed opinions, and a collection of such reasons may then be presented to each respondent, together with an invitation to reconsider and possibly revise his earlier estimates.

Systems analysis, as the name suggests, must be systems oriented. It is important to recognize that anything going on in one part of an activity, organization, or weapon system will likely affect what goes on in every other part. The natural inclination might be to factor out parts of the problem and analyze each separately, neglecting their interactions. However, the aim of analysis is to extend the boundaries of the system as far as required, determine which interdependences are significant, and then evaluate their combined impact.

For this reason, and because the context is naturally broad anyway, systems analysis usually calls for an interdisciplinary team consisting of persons with a variety of skills. This is not required merely because many factors and aspects are involved. Even more important is that a problem looks different to an economist, to a mathematician, and to an engineer, and different ways of looking at a problem are important in finding a solution.

Uncertainty in long-range military planning problems being as great as it is, it is well—particularly early in the study—not to attach much significance to small differences in cost and effectiveness of alternative systems. Specifically, it is important to look for differences that have a chance of surviving *any* likely resolution of the uncertainties. Rather than ask precisely how much better one alternative is than the others, the question to address is which alternatives have a clear advantage or even, initially, which will move us forward.

Search

This phase is concerned with finding the facts, or evidence, on which the analysis is based. It is necessary to look for ideas (and evidence to support them), including the invention of new alternatives, as well as to look for facts. Unless we have alternatives and ideas about them, there is nothing to analyze or to choose between. If in the end we are to designate a preferred course of action, we must have discovered earlier that such a course exists. In long-range problems, the total number of alternatives may be endless, and we must use judgment to eliminate those that are unreasonable.

Many facts are hard to come by. The actual operational performance of future weapons in combat cannot be predicted with any degree of certainty. Purely theoretical studies or operations research of weapon characteristics must be depended upon. In systems analysis, as contrasted with most other forms of engineering, a great many more inputs depend on judgment than on measurement or engineering analysis.

For many problems it is the availability of the facts which makes a solution possible. Consider, for example, the flyaway kit problem we mentioned earlier. The computation per se of the optimum kit according to some standard of performance, measured in terms of the expected loss in combat effectiveness attributable to kit shortages during the support period, is a relatively trivial problem. Surprisingly enough, the difficulty comes in getting the input data. This may involve such a seemingly easy item as getting a complete list of spare parts, as well as such an acknowledgedly difficult one as getting the data that tell how frequently particular spares are needed.

Indeed, even if the analysis is never completed, the collection of facts and their orderly presentation in tables and graphs can sometimes make the solution obvious.

It is sometimes said that when all the facts are known, the problem is solved. This may be true in a philosophical sense, but in a practical sense the real work may have only begun.

In practical problems for systems analysis, however, all the facts are never known. For example, to recommend a preferred interceptor combat radius, it is necessary to study interceptor and performance characteristics, radar coverage requirements, effectiveness, and cost as functions of combat radius. This involves a study of the possible target systems the enemy might select and the pattern of enemy attacks. Such things as radar, costs, proper deployment, interceptor armament, attrition, and the effect of other weapons must then be considered.

When should an inquiry stop? It is important to remember that in this sort of a problem, inquiry is rarely exhaustive. Inquiries are partial, and the decisionmaker must get along without the full advantage of all the potentiality of operations research and the scientific approach. Inquiries cost money and time; they cost in whatever values are concerned. They can cost lives; they can cost national security. It might be interesting to know what the Russians could do if we dropped an armed Atlas on Moscow. It might be an easy observation to make, but some of the costs seem to prohibit this type of investigation. One should never fall into the error of feeling that inquiry is free of cost. There are many contexts in which we can ignore the cost of inquiry; but paradoxes arise if we allow ourselves to forget that almost all inquiries must stop far, far short of completion either for lack of funds, of time, or of justification for spending further funds or time on them. It is out of the question to collect all the information that is required for exhaustive analysis, and it is out of the question to process it.

As an analogy, consider the example of a physician who uses a clinical laboratory to help him decide whether or not his patient has one of several ailments that have many similar symptoms. Even when all the reports are in, the doctor's inquiry may not be complete. He could probably do a lot more laboratory analysis or call in a specialist for consultation. If the problem is simply one of diagnosis, one of the best procedures might be to slaughter the patient and perform a thorough autopsy. The cost here is prohibitive, not only by the standards of modern society but simply by the fact that the physician's goal is to help the patient live a longer and fuller life. He would only frustrate himself if he bought knowledge at the price of the life he was trying to guard.[11]

Explanation

After obtaining some idea of what the facts and alternatives are, it is necessary to build up some way to explain them and to determine their implications.

In order to make much progress with real-world problems, we must ignore a great many of the actual features of a question under study and abstract from the real situation certain aspects—hopefully, the relevant ones—and their interaction, which together make up an idealized version of the real situation. This idealization we call a "model."

In the general process of formulating a problem and gathering data about it, the analyst will have developed some ideas of what the major influencing factors are, that is, the factors which provide discrimination with respect to the possible courses of action. To produce quantitative results, it is necessary to assign a scale of measurement to each factor and to show its dependence on certain parameters. Next, the interaction of the factors must be described. Then we have a model. In other words, isolating those factors pertinent to the problem or the decision at hand, abstracting them, assigning a scale of measurement, and then describing their interactions build the model.

The difficulty in model building is that we do not know at the start what is superfluous and what is relevant. We must proceed on the basis of experience and trial with preliminary models, conducting pencil and paper experiments to illuminate our preliminary judgments. Analysis, being iterative, is self-correcting; as the study goes on, the original model is refined and replaced so that behavior of the relationships being investigated is represented with greater accuracy.

For most phenomena, there are many possible representations; the appropriate model depends as much *on the question being asked* as on the phenomena about which it is asked. . . . A town can be modeled by a map if the question being asked is how to walk from A to B; but if the question is how to speed up the flow of traffic between the same two points, a much more elaborate model may be needed. There are thus no "universal" models—that is, say, no one model that can handle all questions about a given activity.

Sometimes representation by the model is mathematical, by means of a series of equations. At other times, particularly where detailed specification of the relationships between factors is extremely difficult—for example, in studying the behavior of human organizations—the representation may be by simulation or by a war game.

In operations research parlance, the term simulation is applied to the process of representing, without using formal analytic techniques, the essential features of a system or organization and analyzing its behavior by operating with the representation. Simulation is a broadly inclusive word used to describe various physical or analogue devices, such as a Link trainer, or a computer program which traces a strategic campaign through Monte Carlo operations, or a group of people or machines acting as if they were an air defense control center.

If working with the representation or model has some of the aspects of playing a game, particularly if human players are involved, the simulation is called a game. A gaming model cannot be expected to tell us what an optimal response to an uncertain state of affairs might be, but it can do much to make the players aware of such uncertainties and of the necessity of formulating their plans in such a way as to cope with all foreseeable contingencies. Indeed, an important asset to all systems analysis is the spirit of gaming. This consists in explicitly looking at possible moves and countermoves, in examining and designing a wide range of alternatives, and in looking for substitution possibilities —all against a hostile opponent.

Simulation, although relatively new in wide-scale applications, is an established operations research technique, which uses quasi-experimentation in an artificial environment for actual experiment in the real world. Its outstanding virtue is that it can be used to tackle seemingly unmanageable or previously untouched problems where a traditional analytic formulation appears infeasible. It is ordinarily an inefficient technique, however, to use in determining a sharp result, and it yields only a quasi-empirical form of knowledge, inferior to the functional relationships built up through the more traditional approach of using an analytic model. Simulation is a device appropriate to use before one has an adequate theory, for it provides a means to use the intuition and advice of experts in a systematic fashion and a way to go about building an analytic model by approximating the behavior of the random numbers, or physical counters, or human players with mathematical expressions.

The primary function of a model is "explanatory" rather than descriptive. Frequently it is not used to guide computation but solely to organize our thinking.

It should be emphasized that, in many important systems analyses, no need arises to build formal models, explicitly. When such cases occur, the analysis may be extraordinarily effective since it can be completely understood by the policymaker. The essence of systems analysis is not mathematical techniques or procedures. A computing machine or a technique such as linear programming may or may not be useful, depending on the problem and the extent of our information. The essential thing is a listing of the alternatives and an examination of their implications and costs so that they can be compared. What we say about models thus does not have much significance for analyses that require no more than a listing of alternatives and their implications, but is included because many difficult problems do require the use of well-defined models to guide computation.

The widely useful operations research techniques for optimization, when they are used at all in systems analysis, are used much more extensively in component studies than they are at the heart of the overall problem. Before any mathematical technique can be applied to a real-world problem, we must construct a quantitative model of the processes involved. This model expresses the effectiveness of the alternatives under examination as a function of a set of variables, some of which are under control. Once this is done, a solution can be determined mathematically, since formal statements of relationships between the variables exist. The solution obtained from such a model will be a usable solution to the real-world problem if and only if the model is a reasonably accurate representation of the real-world situation with respect to the question at issue. In situations of great complexity, such as those associated with major military decisions, only pieces of the problem can be represented with confidence. The submodels for these pieces or components can frequently be put into a form in which they can be handled by such techniques as dynamic programming or queuing theory. But even here, the new and more advanced techniques, while they are useful and promise to become more so, are seldom necessary since—except in relatively few instances—more elementary tools are usually adequate.

The design of models to assist in the decision process is in large measure an art. Wide experiences and the collaboration of many people are helpful, but it requires selection or composition, plus instinct and a sense of form, to achieve a desired effect.

Rules for model building are few in number and not very helpful. For example, it is sometimes suggested that the analyst should try to find models which explain more and more things within the same context. In operations research this leads to the construction of overly big models and attention to the model and not to the problem.

In building a model, assumptions are frequently made in order to handle something that is too difficult to investigate. For example, in the missile comparison of Appendix B, the model was built up step-by-step by a process of "simplification by assumption." Each target, for instance, was taken to be like every other target. This meant that in the model the targets (1) were of equal value to the offense, (2) required the same bomb yield to destroy, (3) were at the same range, (4) were protected by the same defense, and (5) were isolated so that destruction of one did not imply destruction of another. In essence, we made use of the assumption, fundamental to working with models but seldom stated, that by studying a simplified hypothetical situation we will get approximately the same answer we would get by studying the most realistic situation imaginable.

All of the assumptions of a model must be made explicit. If they are not, this is a defect. A mark of a good systems analyst (or any wise person communicating with others) is that he state the basis on which he operates. This does not imply necessarily that he makes better assumptions, but only that his errors will be more evident.

The contrast between the relative amount of time usually spent on designing a model and that spent in computing its consequences can give bias in judging what is important. The design of the model and the faithfulness with which it represents those aspects of the phenomena being modeled are significant for the question under consideration, not how far we push the computation.

The military analyst does not have, and cannot be expected to have, the precise and flexible means available to the physical scientist for testing his models experimentally. He cannot, for example, experiment with an actual war. The best he can do is to test his models by their workability. For example, he can try to determine answers to the following questions.

1. Can the model describe correctly and clearly the known facts and situations?
2. When the principal parameters involved are varied, do the results remain consistent and plausible?
3. Can it handle special cases in which there is some indication as to what the outcome should be?
4. Can it assign causes to known effects?

Whether or not one model is better than another does not depend on its complexity, realism, or computability but solely on whether it gives better predictions.

"Working" the model, trying out various strategies and concepts of operation, is the closest systems analysis comes to scientific experimentation. Deductions based on operating with the model frequently suggest new directions of effort. That is to say, starting with the relatively few parameters that characterize a system in terms of the model, it is sometimes possible to show that changes in these would improve the performance of the system as measured by the model, and then to suggest corresponding changes that could be made in the real system which would lead to improved performance in the real world. In this way, working the model contributes to system design.

It is also important to go outside the model: to contemplate changes that violate its assumptions and, in so doing, achieve a better model.

Two aspects of model building are particularly troublesome: quantification and the treatment of uncertainty.

Some variables are difficult to quantify, either because they are not calculable, like the probability of war, or because no scale of measurement has been set up like the effect on NATO solidarity of some unilateral

U.S. action. This leads either to their neglect, for they tend to be ignored, or to their recognition only through a qualitative modification of a solution reached by manipulation of quantified variables. Thus, when the problem of what action to recommend on the basis of the solution from the model arises, effect of the quantitative variables is built in, while the nonquantitative ones may be easily lost in the welter of qualitative considerations that must be weighed.

One argument for the omission of a particular variable is that the solution of the problem is virtually insensitive to it. The fact that many variables fall into this category makes analysis possible. If the results were *not* insensitive to all but a relatively small number of variables, analysis would have to yield completely to guesses and intuition. Insensitivity can occur either because a factor is irrelevant or trivial in its quantitative effects or because it has roughly the same effect on all the alternatives under consideration. *The point is that this insensitivity must be discovered.* Sometimes logical reconnoitering is sufficient, but usually analysis is required, possibly with arbitrary values assigned to factors we are unable to calculate.

If nonquantitative variables are not to be neglected without mention or dismissed with some spurious argument, such as the one that they act in opposite direction and hence cancel out,[12] then how are they to be treated? The usual method is to attempt to take them into account through modification of the solution rather than to incorporate them into the model. But this in itself represents a particular method of quantification, for, by altering the solution to take account of the previously omitted variables, the analyst is implicitly valuing them. Since we always have some insight into the range of values that a factor might take, we can, even in the worst cases, assign the factors an arbitrary value and observe the effect on the solution. It seems to be an empirical fact that actions taken on policy questions are based on the available numbers, no matter how relevant or sound they may be; consequently, every effort should be made to quantify.

Most aspects of problems of choice in national security require numbers; others do not. But the real issue is one of clarity of understanding and expression. Numbers are part of our language. When a quantitative matter is being discussed, the greatest clarity of thought is achieved by using numbers instead of by avoiding them, even when uncertainties are present. Only in rare cases is it possible to make a convincing comparison of alternatives without a quantitative analysis of the relevant numbers.

Systems analysis is concerned with problems in which the essence is uncertainty about the future; not only uncertainties about technical and operational parameters and the actions of the enemy, but also conceptual uncertainties. Such analysis, as well as any other attempt to answer the same questions, must necessarily face this uncertainty squarely, treat it as an important element in the problem, and take it into account in formulating recommendations. The treatment of uncertainty is not merely a difficulty in principle, but is a considerable practical problem. Somehow the number of cases made necessary by the presence of uncertainty must be limited and the total effort kept within reasonable bounds.

There are different degrees of uncertainty but for discussion here we will recognize two categories: We will call them, for want of better terms, statistical uncertainties and "real" uncertainties.

Statistical uncertainties—those having a more or less objective or calculable probability of occurrence—can be handled in the model by Monte Carlo or other methods. For instance, our knowledge of the situation may be complete and accurate, but a quantity may be stochastic or "noisy." An example might be the accuracy of a missile system. Alternatively, the quantity involved may have a unique value, but the determinate factors may not be measurable. Then again the quantity involved may be related to measurable factors in such a complex way that it is beyond our mathematical or engineering power to describe, and we must approximate the real situation by a simple description. For example, take the "lethal radius" concept of a nuclear bomb. Such uncertainties, like those in cost or missile accuracy, lead to risks that can be estimated and accepted. They can be annoying but not devastating, like, say, the uncertainties due to ignorance or to competition associated with the prediction of what the environment may turn out to be or the enemy may do during the lifetime of the systems under consideration.

Uncertainties about human factors, which have no necessarily logical construction, or about the future behavior of things, which is beyond the practical ability of analysts to predict, belong to the class of real uncertainties. Under real uncertainty, we consider events—like the probability of war—to which individuals may attach subjective probabilities, but which we cannot calculate. With regard to air defense, for example, real uncertainty involves such questions as "Will we have warning? If we get it, will we believe it? What surprises does the enemy have?" For such uncertainties, there is frequently widespread disagreement about the pertinent probabilities, and even confusion and vagueness within any one individual.

As a simple example, my son when he had just turned sixteen wanted to drive the car. Since he could not walk through a room without bumping into the furniture, the problem I faced was whether to let him drive or not. Here I had uncertainties as to how not driving would affect his personality and character during the next year or so, as well as those about his capability to survive in freeway traffic. This was uncertainty about empirical facts that were not and would not be available and that could not be made available to me by a realistic or thinkable course of inquiry. Therefore, my solution to this problem had to involve guesses and judgments which would never be confirmed, and even now I do not know whether I chose a good solution or not.

There is no foolproof recipe for handling uncertainty, but there are almost always measures that can be taken to make the consequences of possible mistaken prediction less devastating.

With regard to my son's driving, for instance, there were various ways in which I might have sought a good solution. For example, I might have (1) deferred granting the driving privilege for a while to see his reaction, or (2) set up a policy in which a near accident as well as an accident would result in revocation of his privileges, or (3) required him for a period to drive only in specified areas or at specified times. The last, incidentally, would have been not so much a way of getting data as a way of keeping him out of dangerous traffic while he acquired proficiency. I chose still a fourth way, requiring him to pass a course in a driving school reputed to have high standards (rather than teaching him myself and passing my own possibly bad driving practices on to him), and then taking the recommendation of the instructor that if he passed the test for a license, he be permitted to drive without restrictions.

In the analysis, as a prelude to finding ways to compensate for uncertainty, an effort can be made to *forecast* or map the many possible futures, rather than to *predict* a future environment in the sense of specifying a *single* sequence of events. Since the future is inherently unpredictable, it is too hazardous to proceed solely on the basis of a "best estimate" about the future military-technological-political environment. Instead, the analysis must reckon with the wide scope of possible developments and serious uncertainties that the future holds.

To do this, as far as the technical and operational parameters are concerned, one way is first to explore their limits and then make the calculations in terms of the range of uncertainty, using an upper and lower estimate in addition to a best guess. Although initially it is usually necessary to design the system or strategy primarily on the basis of best estimates, this type of investigation, through feedback, helps to modify them so that their performance will not be sensitive functions of parameters whose values are essentially unknown. And it must be kept in mind that alternatives are to be evaluated also by their flexibility to meet the unforseen, rather than solely by their optimality in meeting expectations. In cases of doubt, to overestimate one's opponent and to underestimate our own capabilities is not necessarily the safe thing to do. Overestimates do not necessarily lead to safety and insurance. They are just as likely to lead to despair and loss of morale, to the feeling that the attainment of certain policy objectives is hopeless, and thus to "strategies of desperation."

Of course, the best way to compensate for uncertainty would be to "invent" a better system or policy which would provide insurance against the whole range of possible catastrophes; the difficulty is to discover how to do this.

In view of the uncertainties present in any operations research model, how can one obtain useful information? This fundamental question confronts every scientist and requires *sensitivity* and *contingency* analysis. In addition to calculating initially with a range of values, it is necessary to find out how changes in the information put into the problem and the assumptions made affect the results.

In "sensitivity analysis" an attempt is made to determine how sensitive the results are to variations in key parameters and assumptions. The hope is to obtain a dominant solution in which the ranking of the preferred alternative is essentially insensitive to reasonable variations in values of the parameters or assumptions in question. "Contingency analysis" investigates how a system chosen with one assumption about the environment measures up to the performance of its alternatives when radical changes in the environment occur. Thus, sensitivity analysis might test the alternatives for a wide range of enemy capabilities or for the consequences of having planned for one level of capability when another is experienced. Contingency analysis might test the alternatives under a change in criteria or compare them in an environment in which France, say, had become part of the Communist Bloc.

Since a systems analysis is a study which attempts to influence policy, it must in the end present a convincing comparison of the relevant alternatives. Although it may be clear to the analyst that a certain course of action A is better than alternative possible courses of action B, C, D . . ., it may not be clear to someone who has not "lived" with the problem. One way to show that under any reasonable assumption the system or policy designed or selected by the analyst is indeed to be preferred is to use either an a fortiori or a "break-even" analysis.

To make an analysis a fortiori, we bend over backward in making the comparisons to "hurt" the system we think is best and to "help" the alternative systems. If it then turns out that after we have done this we can still say we prefer the handicapped system, we are in a strengthened position to make recommendations. Sometimes we cannot do this —say, if we concede the exaggerated performance claims for rival systems and the pessimistic estimates about the systems we like. In this case, and we might try a *break-even* analysis: We decide what assumptions must be made about important values in order to make the performance of the two systems essentially the same. Then we can simply ask people to judge whether these assumptions are optimistic or pessimistic. As Kahn and Mann put it:

> *More than any other single thing, the skilled use of a fortiori and break-even analyses separate the professionals* from the *amateurs.* Most analyses should (conceptually) be done in two stages: a first stage to find out what one wants to recommend, and a second stage that generates the kind of information that makes the recommendations convincing even to a hostile and disbelieving, but intelligent audience.[13]

Interpretation

After a solution has been obtained from a model, this solution must be interpreted in the light of considerations which may not have been adequately treated by the model, since the model was but a single representation of the real world chosen by the analyst. For example, the systems analyst (or for that matter the designers of the strategic offensive force) may have established the requirement that a force assure the destruction of, say 95 per cent of the targets at a minimum cost under a certain range of contingencies. But many questions occur. Perhaps the minimum cost is too high; maybe the tasks of deterrence and limiting damage could be better done by spending less on strategic forces and more on air defense. The 95 per cent may be too high, or too low. Someone must translate the percentage of target destruction into its implications in terms of more meaningful criteria, such as the balance of military forces, the will to continue fighting, and the effect on our diplomacy. The analyst may be able to help here, but the responsibility is someone else's.

The solution that has been simplified and possibly reduced to mathematical form by drastic idealization and aggregation is not necessarily a good solution of the original problem. A different model might be called for. At this stage, not only does the analyst attempt to interpret his work, but the sponsor or the real world gets into the iterative cycle again, to counteract the analyst's ignorance and thus produce better answers.

To form a basis for recommendations, any military systems analysis must at the very least give adequate consideration to

1. The objectives both of the nation as a whole and of the forces that are to implement these national objectives.
2. The military capabilities required to attain these objectives.

3. The enemy capabilities and objectives.
4. The technological possibilities.
5. The effectiveness of each posture, system, or plan considered.
6. The costs or resource implications of the choices.
7. The uncertainties in the above.

These things, of course, cannot be specified absolutely. They depend on each other, on the degree of security deemed adequate, and on the enemy's interpretation of our objectives and the actions we take to implement them; and they vary over time. Moreover, the entire structure is based on a set of assumptions, hopefully not arbitrary but objective. If action is to be taken on the basis of the analysis, it is important that the assumptions, as well as the goals, be the right ones.

There are special problems associated with military questions. Many factors used in the computations are not and cannot be measured. Sometimes this is because of time limitations; other times it is because factors such as the enemy defense strength, or degradation in combat of complicated man-machine combinations, are not accessible to measurement but have to be assessed on the basis of experience or pooled judgment. The results of computations must be examined to see if they depend critically upon estimations such as these.

In military problems, there are always considerations not subject to any sort of quantitative analysis. To achieve efficiency in a military context, factors other than cost-effectiveness are important—discipline, morale, esprit de corps, tradition, and organizational behavior. Such problems involve more than purely military questions. The size, composition, location, and state of readiness of forces influence our foreign policy and the freedom of action we have there. They also have a major impact on our domestic economy and public morale. The men who must somehow integrate these factors with the study are really doing systems analysis, but at a level so high it is hard to consider it as such.

It is important for the user of analysis to distinguish between what the study shows and the recommendations for action the analyst makes on the basis of what he thinks the study implies. Frequently, when new minds—management, for example—review the problem, they bring new information. Even though the solution obtained from the model is not changed, recommendations for action based on it may be. A model is only an indicator, not a final judge. . . .

There are numerous reasons why an interpretation is necessary. Mainly it is because major decisions, in the field of economic or military policy, are part of a political as well as part of an intellectual process. Consider, for instance, the following.

The relationship between "cost" and "effectiveness" of a weapon system for some given objective typically plots as in Fig. 2.

If a weapon system plots at A, then clearly the objective is too ambitious for the budget and someone must decide to look for a less ambitious objective or to abandon the system, or, as another possibility, to decide to spend a lot more money to get it to B. If at C and we still have money to spend, clearly we've put more money into the system than was economic and should look for another system and more ambitious objectives.

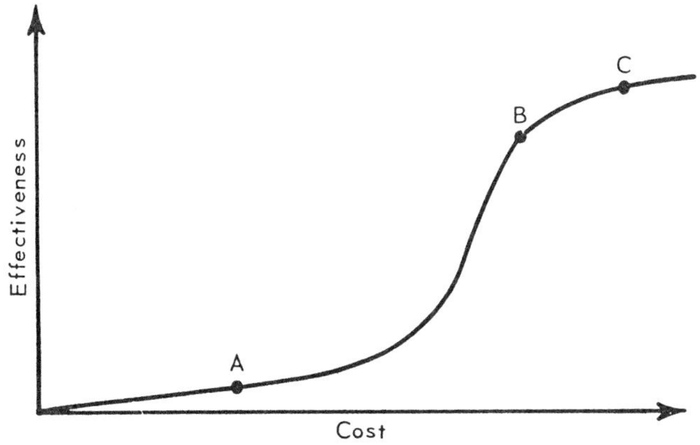

FIGURE 2
A Typical Cost-Effectiveness Curve

If, in the judgment of the analyst and those who use his analysis, the alternative ranked highest by the model is good enough, the process is over; if not, more and better alternatives must be designed or the objectives must be lowered. Analysis is sufficient to reach a policy conclusion only when the objectives are agreed upon by the policymakers. In defense policy in particular, and in many other cases as well, objectives are not, in fact, agreed upon. The choice, while ostensibly between alternatives, is really between objectives or ends, and nonanalytical methods must be used for a final reconciliation of views. Although the consequences computed from the model may provide guidance in deciding which objectives to compromise, such decisions are not easily made, and judgment must again be applied.

In the end, military decisionmaking, like systems analysis itself, is an art. After a certain stage, calculation may no longer be helpful. There are always considerations that cannot be measured—say, the importance of military gains against political losses, or public reaction to a temporary setback against the enhanced chances of a long term gain. Moreover, there are always considerations that have been measured or determined by judgment but not to the decisionmaker's satisfaction.

By definition, no judgment is known to be correct. Because systems analysis ordinarily goes beyond objective analysis, it relies heavily on considered judgment. No matter what may be the hopes of professional analysts, the judgment applied by the decisionmaker in the last phase of a study limits the influence of the previous analyses. At its best, analysis can only embrace a part of a broad-scope problem; it gets no foothold at all on many subjective elements, and before it organizes an understanding of all objective elements it becomes too complex to handle. Thus analysis can go so far and no further. But the restrictions on the use of analyses imposed by the refusal of policymakers to use it when they should can be pushed back by better analysis.

NOTES

1. Olaf Helmer, *The Systematic Use of Expert Judgment in Operations Research,* The RAND Corporation, P-2795, September 1963.
2. Unpublished communication from L. J. Savage commenting on an earlier version of this chapter.
3. *Ibid.*
4. Italics supplied.
5. Thomas L. Saaty, *Mathematical Methods of Operations Research,* McGraw-Hill Book Company, Inc., New York, 1959, p. 4.
6. Alain C. Enthoven, "Operations Research and the Design of the Defense Program," *Proceedings of the Third International Conference on Operational Research,* Dunod, Paris, 1964, pp. 531–538.
7. See, in addition to Chapter 5, C. J. Hitch and R. N. McKean, *The Economics of Defense in the Nuclear Age,* Harvard University Press, Cambridge, Mass., 1960; and Hitch, "Economics and Military Operations Research," *Review of Economics and Statistics,* vol. XL, no. 3, August 1958, pp. 199–209.
8. "Comments by C. J. Hitch," *Operations Research,* vol. 4, no. 4, August 1956, p. 427. His statement is paraphrased here.
9. Charles J. Hitch, Assistant Secretary of Defense (Comptroller). Testimony in *Systems Development and Management (Part 2),* Hearings before a Subcommittee of the Committee on Government Operations, House of Representatives, 87th Congress, 2nd Session, U.S. Government Printing Office, Washington, D.C., 1962, p. 515.
10. Except by Olaf Helmer. For additional information, see Helmer, *The Systematic Use of Expert Judgment in Operations Research,*

The RAND Corporation, P-2795, September 1963; Helmer and Nicholas Rescher, "On the Epistemology of the Inexact Sciences," *Management Science,* vol. 6, no. 1, October 1969, pp. 25–52; N. Dalkey and Helmer, "An Experimental Application of the Delphi Method to the Use of Experts," *Management Science,* vol. 9, no. 3, April 1963, pp. 458–467. (The discussion on the use of experts presented in this chapter is based on Helmer's paper.)

11. This is not to say he might not risk life in trying to guard it; he might order such tests as a spinal puncture or a liver puncture, or other inherently dangerous procedures. Many diagnostic procedures are dangerous and are used when the danger is justified, but a doctor will not make a complete sacrifice of what he is trying to protect.
12. It is not enough to know that two variables act in opposite directions; their quantitative impact must also be estimated.
13. H. Kahn and I. Mann, *Techniques of Systems Analysis,* The RAND Corporation, RM-1829 (DDC No. AD 123512), December 3, 1956.

Subject Index

Author Index

THE BOOK MANUFACTURE

Composition: SSPA Typesetting, Inc.
Carmel, Indiana
Printing and binding: George Banta Company
Menasha, Wisconsin
Cover design: Sandy Mead
Type: Times Roman